MOVERS AND SHAKERS

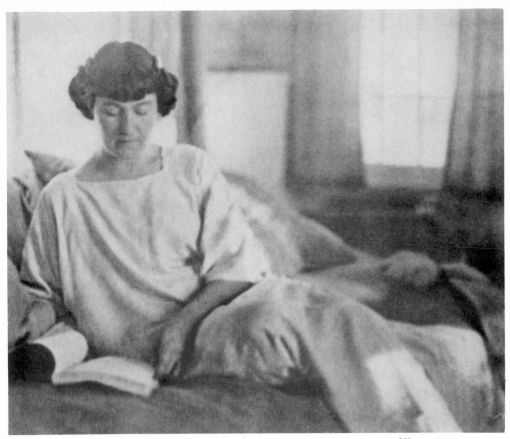

MABEL DODGE AT FINNEY FARM

MOVERS

· and ·

SHAKERS

◄●■●►

Mabel Dodge Luhan

University of New Mexico Press
Albuquerque, New Mexico

Library of Congress Cataloging in Publication Data

Luhan, Mabel Dodge, 1879–1962.
   Movers and shakers.

   Reprint. Originally published as v. 3 of Intimate memories. 1st
ed. New York: Harcourt Brace, 1936.
   Includes bibliographical references and index.
   1. Luhan, Mabel Dodge, 1879–1962.   2. United
States—Biography.   I. Title.
CT275.L938A34   1985   973.9'092'4 [B] 85-1169
ISBN 0-8263-0852-X (pbk.)

Contents

Illustrations following page 318

INTRODUCTION

by Lois Palken Rudnick

Introduction

Van Wyck Brooks opens his chapter on Greenwich Village in *The Confident Years* with the dramatic image of Mabel Dodge returning from several years residence in Europe "to dynamite" New York. She had arrived, he notes, at precisely the right moment, "at one of those 'heats and genial periods,' that Emerson described by which the high tides are caused in the human spirit."[1] Within a few weeks of her arrival, Mabel would be fully engaged in preparations for the Armory Show, the most important art exhibit ever held in this country, immersed in the anarchist politics of Emma Goldman, and on the verge of launching the most successful salon in American history.

Mabel's "coming out" in January 1913 was a rite of passage that contrasted sharply with those in her previous life. Born in 1879 to a wealthy Buffalo family, Mabel was schooled in charm and groomed to marry, like most Victorian women of her class. Stultified emotionally and intellectually at home and in school, she yearned for a life ennobled by Poetry and Beauty. After the accidental death of her first husband and the birth of her son (her only child), she was sent to Paris by her family. In 1905, she met and married Edwin Dodge. When they moved to Florence, Mabel was determined to make a new life that would express her aesthetic impulses. She devoted the next eight years to realizing her dream of the Renaissance. The Medicean villa she reconstructed, the clothes she wore, the *fin de siècle* consciousness she cultivated—all were materials for her living monument to the past. So too were the guests she collected to grace her salon and share her table: Gertrude and Leo Stein, Paul and Muriel Draper, Eleanor Duse, and Bernard Berenson. By 1912, Mabel found this Florentine world aesthetically and emotionally bankrupt. It seemed all form and no content.

During the years Mabel lived abroad, the industrial system that her financier grandfather had helped to build reached its apotheosis in America. In 1912, 2 percent of all Americans controlled 60 percent of the personal wealth of the nation: stocks, bank income, property, and business goods. One-third to one-half of the American people lived in poverty, or so close to it that they were pushed over the line any time they suffered illnesses or industrial accidents—in which the United States led the world. During these same years, ruthless exploitation of human and natural resources and the economic oppression of child and adult laborers created among some segments of the middle and upper classes what one historian has called "the Revolt of the American Conscience."[2] Progressive reformers took as their mandate the extension of the political rights to life, liberty, and the pursuit of happiness into the economic sphere.

During the 1912 elections, even establishment politicians were using the rhetoric of revolution. The Democrats under Woodrow Wilson proclaimed a "New Freedom," and the Progressives under Teddy Roosevelt, a "New Nationalism," both of which were dedicated to rectifying some of the worst environmental and human costs of America's industrial empire. The Socialists garnered the highest percentage of votes they ever received in a national election—6 percent of the presidential vote—as well as scores of state and local government offices. Certainly liberals had some justification for believing their programs might temper, and radicals some justification for believing their programs might transform, American social and economic life.

"Looking back on it now," Mabel writes in *Movers and Shakers*, "it seems as though everywhere, in that year of 1913, barriers went down and people reached each other who had never been in touch before; there were all sorts of new ways to communicate, as well as new communications. The new spirit was abroad and swept us all together." The "new spirit" of which she speaks found its leadership in Greenwich Village and its "spiritual home" at her 23 Fifth Avenue apartment. It permeated the theories of psychology, art, poetry, politics, and sexual relationships that made the men and women who lived in Greenwich Village imagine themselves capable of changing the political, aesthetic, and economic course of the United States. Free thinkers and lovers, disparate in their creeds, goals, and degrees of radicalism, they were united by their fight against those tendencies in American life that were driving their fellow citizens in the direction of increasing standardization, mechanization, and materialism. They have been called a lyrical left, whose cultural politics sought to undermine the property-oriented, regimented, guilt-ridden bourgeois civilization that had spawned most of them.[3]

Unlike the more serious and orthodox Marxist intellectuals of the day, and most working-class labor leaders, the rebels of Greenwich Village were as much devoted to "play" and "self-expression" as they were to unionization and the redistribution of wealth. Postimpressionism, anarchism, feminism, and Bergsonism all proclaimed the power of the individual to shape the self and the environment in terms of an inner vision. Their belief in spontaneity, liberation, and experimentation inspired the Pagan Routes, during which Villagers dressed up as nymphs and satyrs and thumbed their noses at uptown "Puritans." It informed the meetings of the Liberal Club held at Polly's Restaurant on Macdougal Street, where one was equally likely to find on any night an imagist poetry reading, a lecture by Alexander Berkman on the slaughter of coal miners in Colorado, or a discussion by Henrietta Rodman on working women's needs for cooperative housing and child care.[4]

Mabel's goal was to incorporate the chaos of the diverse social, artistic, and political movements supported by the "republicans" of Washington Square and direct them through her liberated life-force. In *Movers and Shakers* she tells us that she was an involuntary "instrument of the times." But while it is certainly true that she immersed herself in the vortex of radical activity swirling about her, she was not merely "Fate's chosen instrument." In fact, like Madame de Staël, she set out quite deliberately to make herself the mistress of the spirit of her age by meeting and learning from its most creative and committed men and women, many of whom are brought to life in this volume through Mabel's witty and incisive word portraits.

Of all the new friends that she was making, no one understood the impulses that drove her to embrace the spirit of revolution better than her confidante, Hutchins Hapgood. A columnist for the *New York Globe* who wrote about the sufferings of society's outcasts, he was a philosophical anarchist who supported revolutionary causes of every variety on principle. Like Mabel, he was a "Victorian in the modern world" (as he appropriately titled his autobiography), who shared with her Matthew Arnold's sense of living "between two worlds, one dead, the other powerless to be born." Both suffered the torment of feeling they were mere "spectators" of life who had known only the *forms* of religion, family, and community. Mabel and Hutch embraced the call of the younger generations of rebels in the hope that it would lead to a world in which they could feel "at home." Their open-ended commitment to change was paradoxically motivated by a profound yearning for emotional and spiritual certainty. They shared what William James had once described to Hutch as a "mad unbridled lust for the absolute," a nineteenth-century disease for which the twentieth century offered no cure.[5]

The intellectual confusion that attended Mabel's salon has caused some historians to view it as representative of the incoherence of prewar radicalism as a whole. But while critiques of its "radical chic" characteristics are certainly valid, the salon—and the movements represented there—must be viewed within the context of their times. The naïve faith shared by Mabel and her friends in the force of ideas to effect political and social change was not possible for the next generation of radicals. The word *innocent,* which is so often attached to them, speaks volumes about the world view that was possible before World War I. Men like Hutchins Hapgood, Walter Lippmann, and Lincoln Steffens believed that they could "deal Death" to injustice through words. They and their more activist colleagues who hoped to deal death to the economic system more directly were not always clear or programmatic about their means and ends. Their belief in a free play of ideas and activities that would lead to the emergence of healthier individuals and a more equal social and economic order allowed them to tolerate and promote a logically incompatible variety of points of view.

Mabel's salon revealed the full range of the strengths, weaknesses, and conflicts that marked the aesthetic and political avant-garde of the time. Most of the men and women who attended it were serious about their political and artistic ideals and commitments. Women like Henrietta Rodman risked their jobs (in her fight to have the City of New York allow married women to teach) and others, like Margaret Sanger, their freedom (in her fight to give birth-control information to working-class women). As Robert Crunden notes in his book *From Self to Society,* the "prize heads" that Mabel collected defined the issues that would be central to social and political analysis in the following decades.[6]

Ideas were more play than work for Mabel, in the sense that she was not committed to any one line of thought during her years in New York. But the people she most respected were those who risked "shattering themselves for the sake of their ideas," those most committed to discover "the truth" about political, social, and interpersonal relationships. Her openness to the ideas and issues that played out before her in her living room allowed her to taste rich and variegated slices of the intellectual life of her times. Indeed, as Frederick Hoffman says of her, she "all but established the pattern of the 'free-lance intellectual' of the early twentieth century."[7]

Mabel was, however, more than a spectator and catalyst; she also offered her purse and her person in support of the causes and the people affiliated with them whom she entertained. (Mention of her personal generosity is notably absent in her memoirs.) She was the first to help Gertrude Stein establish her reputation in America, through the distribution of Stein's notorious "Portrait of Mabel Dodge at the Villa Curonia"; she gave room and board to Robert Edmond Jones, an impoverished but brilliant stage designer; she posted bail for imprisoned radicals and wrote for radical journals like *The Masses* (anonymously); and she helped to popularize Freudian psychoanalysis (which many of her radical cohorts first discovered at her salon) in a weekly column she wrote for the Hearst papers. As a leading advocate of Modernism in all its forms Mabel represented, in the words of a newspaper reporter looking back at these times, "the most peculiar common denominator that society, literature, art and radical revolutionaries ever found in New York and Europe."[8]

Through her own writings and activities, as well as through the works of newspaper reporters, painters, poets, and fiction writers who "borrowed" her life and personality for their representative values, Mabel became a leading symbol of the "New Woman": sexually emancipated, self-determining, in control of her own destiny. To many she heralded Woman as World Builder.

It is that image—and the reality that belies it—which reveals one of the most interesting tensions in Mabel's life and memoirs. Her public, and many of her friends, believed that she was radical, emancipated, and a leading female influence in her time. Mabel, however, reveals in *Movers and Shakers* the rather large gap between her image as a liberated woman and the very confused Mrs. Dodge who "went alone, cut off from the ways of other people who all attributed to me far more participation in rich living than they themselves enjoyed." This confusion between image and reality was not hers alone. It was fundamental to the identity of the "New Woman" of the time.

Although Mabel never proclaimed herself a feminist, she shared with many of those in her circle the tension between their stated ideals of sexual freedom and the tug of traditional beliefs and the need for personal security. In Mabel's case this tension was increased by the fact that she had always believed that the only route to real power for women lay *through* men. Thus instead of listening to her own muse, as did the poet Whitman whom she aspired to emulate, she served as muse to men. Many forces in her life encouraged her, as well as other women of her generation, in this role. She had been trained from childhood in feminine passivity and learned well what Virginia Woolf called women's functions "as looking-glasses possessing the magic and delicious power of reflecting the figure of a man at twice its size."9 The male radicals of Greenwich Village further contributed to the confusion. Floyd Dell, Hutchins Hapgood, Max Eastman, and John Reed genuinely supported equal rights for women. But what each wanted in *his* woman was someone who would provide the best of all possible worlds. She would be the mother who gave them the security they had abandoned with their middle-class roots; the lover who was always available to fulfill their sexual needs; and the Muse who inspired them to great feats of creative endeavor. Although Village radicals worked to subvert the bourgeois morality and capitalist economics that kept Woman in her "place," the new sexuality still defined her primarily in terms of Man.

Mabel's tumultuous affair with John Reed provides a paradigm of what the modernization of women's ancient roles as mother/lover/muse meant for the New Woman. In Reed, she found a distillation of all the revolutionary ferment she had supported and promoted in her first few months in New York. Reed, in turn, was seeking the very kind of woman that Mabel thought she wanted to become, a female compounded of earth and heaven who would abandon herself to him in a relationship filled with beauty and joy, but no long-term commitments. At the time she met him, Reed had not yet found his direction in life; in fact, like Mabel, he was absorbed by all the Village revolutions. Mabel hoped that through Reed she could develop her full powers as an earth mother. She could help this ebullient but amorphous revolutionary to become a personage who would shape the direction of his times. The Paterson Strike Pageant brought art, politics, and love together for them in a supreme moment of ecstasy. But once she had succumbed to being Reed's lover, Mabel's equality as his partner in creative endeavor was lost and she became totally absorbed in him, dependent, and demanding (a scenario Mabel had experienced before and would experience again).

Their affair finally ended with the end of the era of radical innocence during World War I, a more than fortuitous coincidence in Mabel's account of the romance.

In 1915, Mabel retreated from the urban world of radical politics and art into the pastoral world of Croton-on-Hudson, insulating herself from the breakup of her affair with Reed and from the Great War. Here she met Maurice Sterne, a postimpressionist painter she soon determined to mold into a sculptor (in this she had little success, although she did help his career). One of Sterne's friends accurately and humorously described their relationship as "a five-year-long ring fight. No Queensbury rules. And many more than fifteen rounds. Both back in their respective corners, breathing messages of renewed affection and desire as they regain their wind."[10] Once again, she was faced with the dilemma created by her belief that as a woman she was capable only of "secondary" creativity. Thus she became Maurice's lover and later married him in the hope that this would give her greater control over his art and her own life. No sooner was she wed, than she realized her mistake and sent Maurice off on "their" honeymoon, to the Southwest. It was in Santa Fe, in 1917, that Maurice wrote Mabel the prophetic letter with which she ends *Movers and Shakers,* beckoning her to come to New Mexico and "save" the Indians.

Here, at last, among the Pueblo Indians of Taos, Mabel discovered a society that seemed to offer everything that she had lacked in childhood, failed to re-create in Florence, and could not find in Greenwich Village. The Pueblos were a model of permanence and stability, a 600-year-old community, where individual, social, artistic, and religious values were fully integrated. Primarily through the influence of Tony Luhan, first her lover and then her fourth and final husband, Mabel underwent a profound conversion (the subject of her last volume of published memoirs, *Edge of Taos Desert: An Escape to Reality*). Believing that she and Tony were fated to serve in a messianic role as "a bridge between cultures," she spent much of the rest of her life drawing artists and writers to Taos to help her celebrate and preserve what she believed to be "the beating heart of the universe."

In 1924, Mabel began writing her memoirs, four volumes of which were published in the 1930s. Her intention throughout was to offer her life as a metaphor for the decline of American civilization and its potential regeneration in the Indian Southwest. The writing of her

xv

memoirs epitomized her life's calling: the search for and creation of her identity. But here, for the first time, she was taking responsibility for that act.

At the time she wrote *Movers and Shakers,* Mabel was very much out of sympathy with the person and values she felt she had represented in the prewar world of Greenwich Village: her self-assertiveness, her need to manipulate and control others, her tenacious will-to-power, which D. H. Lawrence experienced in New Mexico even after her supposed conversion to the Indian way. Yet when Mabel wrote Lawrence about the writer's block she experienced with this volume, he reminded her that her passion for revolution had indeed been genuine and he suggested she read Upton Sinclair's tribute to her in his autobiography, *Money Writes!*.

In *Movers and Shakers,* Mabel creates her most absorbing and illuminating portrait of herself and her times. It is one of the best eyewitness accounts of Greenwich Village before the war as well as a fascinating account of the struggles faced by the "New Woman" of her day. At the time it was published, however, the reception by the left was hostile, to say the least. The Mabel Dodge who had been touted during her salon days as the harbinger of revolution was now viewed as the personification of the bourgeois degeneracy that brought on the Great Depression. Malcolm Cowley summed up her life story as "the case history of an art patroness under capitalism—a fable told round the fireside to edify and frighten little Russian children." Floyd Dell voiced a minority opinion, but one that is increasingly being heard as cultural historians re-examine this era. Yes, he admits, the bohemian rebels of Greenwich Village were eager, naïve, and sometimes silly. But Mabel's book is "quite a marvelous recapturing of the scent and flavor of that lost young world; it is because it is so true that it seems so fantastic."[11]

Lois Palken Rudnick

University of Massachusetts, Boston

Notes

1. Van Wyck Brooks, *The Confident Years, 1885–1915* (New York: E. P. Dutton & Co., 1952), p. 475.
2. See Frederick Lewis Allen, *The Big Change: America Transforms Itself, 1900–1950* (New York: Harper and Brothers, 1952), pp. 55–

56; also James Weinstein, *The Corporate Ideal in the Liberal State, 1900–1918* (Boston: Beacon Press, 1969) and Gabriel Kolko, *The Triumph of Conservatism: A Reinterpretation of American History* (Chicago: Quadrangle Books, 1967).

3. See John P. Diggins, *The American Left in the Twentieth Century* (New York: Harcourt, Brace, Jovanovich, 1973), Ch. 4.

4. See Allen Churchill, *The Improper Bohemians: The Re-Creation of Greenwich Village in Its Heyday* (New York: E. P. Dutton & Co., 1959).

5. See Hutchins Hapgood, *A Victorian in the Modern World* (New York: Harcourt, Brace, 1939).

6. See Robert M. Crunden, *From Self to Society, 1919–1941* (Englewood Cliffs: Prentice-Hall, 1972), pp. 1–4.

7. Frederick J. Hoffman, *Freudianism and the Literary Mind*, 2d ed. (Baton Rouge: Louisiana State University Press, 1967), pp. 56–57.

8. Quoted in an untitled newspaper article, n.d., in Volume 17 of the Luhan scrapbooks, Mabel Dodge Luhan Collection, Beinecke Library, Yale University.

9. Virginia Woolf, *A Room of One's Own* (New York: Harcourt, Brace and World, 1957), p. 35. On the "New Woman" in Greenwich Village, see also June Sochen, *The New Woman: Feminism in Greenwich Village, 1910–1920* (New York: Quadrangle Books, 1972).

10. Maurice Beebe, "Introduction," Maurice Sterne, *Shadow and Light: The Life, Friends, and Opinions of Maurice Sterne,* ed. Charles Mayerson (New York: Harcourt, Brace and World, 1965), p. xxiv.

11. Malcolm Cowley, "Fable for Russian Children," *New Republic,* November 25, 1936, p. 122; Floyd Dell, "The Scent and Flavor of a Lost Young World," *New York Herald Tribune,* November 22, 1936. Reviews of *Movers and Shakers* can be found in Volume 8 of the Luhan scrapbooks, Mabel Dodge Luhan Collection, Beinecke Library, Yale University.

glimmering white shawl, thickly embroidered with odd birds and reeds, hung faintly visible upon the white wall. Over the bed lay another with fringes to the floor. At the windows, yards and yards more of white silk. The room was dazzling with all this white on white, *"plusieurs nuances de blanc"* that Marie Bashkirtsev used to love. I loved it and I still love it, so I was hurt when Lorenzo said Mary told him it was in rather bad taste. I don't believe she did, anyway.

It seemed to me I couldn't get enough white into that apartment. I suppose it was a repudiation of grimy New York. I even sent to the Villa for the big, white bearskin rug and laid it in front of the white marble fireplace in the front room.

For furniture, there were mostly the delicate old gray French chairs and *chaises longues* upholstered in light colors, gray-blues and pale yellows. I had them also sent to me from Florence out of the little yellow salon. The most languid *chaise longue* in three pieces was there, all gray and butter-color, and there were many dim old carved and gilded frames with new mirrors in them and these made the room lively with glints and sparkles.

Almost as soon as I reached New York I began to collect old colored glass. So, little by little, there appeared more glints and twinkling points all over the room like sunshine in wine or in the sea, ruby red and emerald, and some very deep, bright sapphire blue, and these bottles and beads and goblets became dearer to me than the collection of dogs I gathered together in Italy had ever been. It was hard to find old glass in those days; the shops hadn't it yet, so only here and there, as one whizzed by in the motor, one noticed an occasional sparkle in some window. Then I would stop the car, rush in and buy it, breathlessly impatient, eager to get back to the seclusion of the limousine. I always hated shopping in America.

Perhaps the most lovable, delicate, and alien thing in the apartment was what used to be called a chandelier when I lived in Buffalo. There they were made of hideous factory metal and surmounted with "globes" to shade the gas. This Venetian one, however, was for candles and it was made of white porcelain. Its lovely curved arms were covered with birds and flowers in canary yellow, turquoise blue, green, all the lovely gay colors. Life-sized canaries perched among the gentians, blue birds among the roses. It hung from the ceiling in the living room, fresh as morning while the streets outside were dingy gray and sour with fog and gasoline. It overcame the world outside those walls. It made exquisite shadows on the white ceiling and altogether it acted as a charm with which to conquer cities. The first time I lighted candles in it I thought to myself:

"I have always known how to make rooms that had power in them. Whatever the need at any time I have been able to make for myself a refuge from the world, so I know that even if I had nothing I could somehow create an *ambiente* to creep into where I could breathe as I want to breathe, even though I would have to make it out of a nut and an apple and a stone from the brook. If I don't know anything else, and sometimes I am convinced I don't, I do know how to assemble things and make them do their work."

So when the apartment was all put together, it seemed, at first, to do the thing I meant to have it do. It diminished New York, it made New York stay outside in the street. But alas! I couldn't live by things alone. No matter whether I would or not I had to have human beings in order to be myself. But the setting I had made was never a suitable background for the life that presently surged into it, for no sooner was this peaceful fortress completed than I opened the door of it and let the town pour in! But why was it, I wondered, that, in my life, the actors and the settings never belonged together?

On the floor above me there lived a couple named Childs. I never knew them, never even saw them; a young lawyer and his wife, conservative and quiet, they seemed like gray shadows to me if ever I thought of them. One wonders how I seemed to them after I began having the anarchists and the others. Sometimes, later, I saw in the newspapers a certain Childs quoted in cases against agitators and revolutionists and I do believe it was he who lived above the porcelain chandelier, but I don't know.

On the top floor lived the Sulzers. Governor Sulzer! And what had *he* done to get himself such a black eye? I don't know that either, but only that he had been governor of the state and then impeached. I didn't even know what that word meant. One can go through life not knowing the meaning of an enormous number of words, yet knowing their effects. The effect of being impeached had made Governor Sulzer very dignified and mysterious even if he was not quite a gentleman in the Episcopalian sense of that word. "The Governor," as Mrs. Sulzer called him, was tall and thin and appeared to wear a high, white

6

collar and a stock, whether he did or not. He had long, gray, wavy hair, long, knotted fingers, and a wide, thin mouth. He also had wide-apart gray eyes, with a strange glitter in them, and he always screwed them up, glancing at people with an incredulous, doubting look. Mrs. Sulzer had been his housekeeper and he had married her. That was before he was the Tammany governor and lived in the "Governor's Mansion" in Albany and got impeached.

His life on the fourth floor of General Sickles's mansion was, apparently, as inactive as the general's, downstairs on the ground floor. One met Mrs. Sulzer on the stairs sometimes on her way to the Jefferson Street market where she went to buy her groceries. But the Governor one rarely met. He seemed to stay home all the time. I never saw their apartment and I can't imagine what it was like to stay in all day long. On the rare occasions when one met him in the hall, he looked very tall and thin and wrapped in a muffler. Really, he seemed like a character out of one of the less well written detective stories. Once I sent up a note and invited him to one of the Evenings. It was in accordance with the fixed determination I had acquired to be broadminded and without social taboos.

When he came in, dressed in slightly wrinkled evening clothes, he found himself surrounded with a lot of untidy young men with rumpled hair, and some elder ones, bald, with eyeglasses. Some of them had on dress suits and some of them had not. Some of the women were in *décolleté* dresses, while others wore shirt-waists and skirts. Anyway, it must have seemed to him like "a meeting" and it touched an old spring inside him and pretty soon he was making a speech! He looked over their heads, and spoke into the past. His phrases were made up of old political clichés that had lost their meaning, but that had still the power to galvanize their speaker. He was filled again with the old political juice by the mere utterance of certain sounds and syllables, so that one recognized him for an innocent character fooled by himself and quite carried away. These rather sweet, old-fashioned men are apt to get impeached, investigated, discredited, and put away by their more realistic opponents, because their own sound and fury hypnotize them and then they do things they shouldn't.

It was charming to see how patient everyone was with him. Even the I.W.W.'s only betrayed very, very faintly their excessive boredom.

7

After a while Mrs. Sulzer came down and took him home. Anyhow, he'd had an evening.

On our different floors we were all attended in our different ways. The general had a "secretary," an oldish woman who cooked for him and took care of him and who was said to be waiting for death. I had our Italian Vittorio, who looked, in New York, like a papal emissary, and an Irish cook named Mary Malone who was crazy, if anybody ever was, so baleful were her eyes when they rested upon Bobby Jones when he came to live in one of the rooms in the little Ninth Street house. The Childses had one neat, neutral-looking maid who glanced sideways if one met her on the stairs, but the Sulzers had only themselves.

Those were all of us under that solid roof, and our lives scarcely touched and never mingled.

John had been placed in a boarding school and Edwin and I were alone in these few rooms, after having had a large villa in the country to wander about in, usually filled with people staying, people lunching and dining, and with servants around all the corners.

The Carys were about the only friends I had in New York when I arrived from Europe. I had never lived there before, had never even stayed there for long at a time. My experience of it had been gathered in visits from Buffalo to my grandparents way up on Fifth Avenue at Seventy-Eighth Street in the early days when I thought everyone on the Street knew everyone else, as they did at home.

Now Grandpa and Grandma Cook were dead and the big, granite, vine-covered house had been bought by Mr. Duke, and he had pulled it down and built in its place a bare, square, white marble house like a lump of sugar; and Aunt Georgie had faded into a quiet life in Lenox with poor Uncle Carlos, who was very ill with something.

Of course, Mary Foote lived near-by at Number Three Washington Square, and I must have had a few other acquaintances, but I do not remember who they were. Edwin knew a few people, but not very many for most of his friends were in or around Boston.

When I was putting the new apartment together I was occupied and engrossed by it, but when it was finished, all fresh and sparkling, I grew melancholy.

More and more I began to hate the thought that I'd been forced back to America, to put John in school, and that Edwin was about to sally forth and rent an office and begin "to practice architecture," as it was so strangely called. It made it no better when he came in one day and laughed at the sight of me sitting there in one of my Renaissance Villa costumes, looking very cross.

"There was I all alone in a pink frock!" he giggled, quoting an old joke we used to have about one of Constances's stories.

He infuriated me. I grew quite ill and blamed him for it, for he was there.

I remember one week-end that John came to stay with us. He was still very Italian-looking, though later he outgrew it as the Italian influence faded out of him. Everything interested him, and Edwin and he used to go off together to football games up at the Polo Grounds, the two of them very cheerful and energetic together.

I hated to see them so cheerful. I hated to see them set off for that American Saturday afternoon, full of interest in that American sport. I didn't want to go, nothing would have induced me to go. I looked down from a great height at the American scene, visualizing in advance the crowd of dingy, dusty men and boys sitting in huge circles all chewing gum and wearing derby hats. I go into such a crowd? Never—not for one hour. I always did go on hating derby hats, though I capitulated so entirely in many other ways. Once, after an Evening, I found one of them left behind on the green velvet settee. It had K.K.K. in small gold letters inside the brim and I opened the window and threw it down into the street.

I bade my two Americans good-by in a very aloof fashion, trying to seem cold and contemptuous though my thoughts were hot and angry. I was persuaded that all these years I had been living abroad had been to give John the most *recherché* and lovely experience; of what use was it all, then, if he was to come back and have it all covered over with mediocrity and commonness? Common associations and companions until he too was of the dead low level of the average American boy?

I felt betrayed as I watched from the window, saw them hail a bus and climb to the top of it and go sailing away from me.

Unlike the Buffalo streets, New York was still crowded with strangers! The only ones I knew among the faces I looked down into from between my white curtains, were those of Edwin and John and they had gone off cheerfully to a football game and left me alone. Alone—

that was what I was, in that deathly still apartment. Alone at half past one on a Saturday afternoon with no place to go even if I had wanted to, and no one to talk to.

"Nothing to do" again! The same old recurrent dilemma! The mirrors on the white walls reflected each other's immobility. A dozen lovely Persian miniatures depicted life on oriental roof tops, their personages halted in attitudes of serene love-making, showing an existence where flutes and figs and bright, thick silk accoutered their moderated hours. The two turquoise-blue sea and sky pictures by Stephen Haweis hung still and unrevealing on either side of the wide opening that was between the living room and the reception room beyond. Under them two little painted Venetian commodes stood quietly bearing Venetian glass bowls of roses. Deep couches, covered with pale blue silk and velvet, had cushions of old damask and peach-colored brocade; there was a green glass bowl full of Curtis cigarettes on the low table nearest the largest couch—and there were books all about and the latest magazines. . . .

But how things die on one! There was no life in anything about me. A rumble-rumble-rumble on the streets outside, and inside a deathly stillness wherein one could hear oneself draw every breath.

It was from that day on that I began to fall quite definitely ill. Edwin was solicitous and sorry for me, as he always was, but I told him mournfully that it was he who was the cause of my ambiguous *malaise*. "I don't know . . ." I faltered, "but I think you must go away. Let us separate for a while and see if it won't help." Dear, kind, amusing Edwin! Why did I have to land my trouble upon him, blame him for it?

Letters from abroad would come to remind me of the lovely life I had left behind, and some of them like this one from Constance in Venice showed the perturbation of old friends over what I would do next.

Capello, Saturday.

Mabel, dearest, I have begun three letters to you—and torn them all up!— Things are desperate with me. I came away from the Villa because I was too unhappy inside, too hunted and haunted, to go on at the right (and decent) pitch. And if I couldn't manage it *there*—among all the soporifics and anodynes—amused by you, pleased by the beauty about me, drugged by the comfort and the talk—imagine if I can do it *here*.

So, of me, there is nothing to be said. "They are most helpless who had once most hope" . . . And what can I say of *you,* my dear, which matters to you one little jot? If only you will be wise—and kind, Mabel—! Don't, don't make mistakes now. If this be "quacking," let me quack! I do care so much about you. I wish I could shut you up in a high tower for a week, away from every brilliant conversation, and conversation-*list*—far away from all the *lists!*—and let you think. You have only got to know what you want to do. No one is more capable than you. No one gives herself less chance to be herself. *Quack.*

[picture of a duck quacking]

I hear that Robin came to see me off. Will you give him my love, and say how dear I think it of him to have thought of it?

Will you send me Lucy's address? I want to tell her about a wonderful man here who is in touch with every old picture—a man nobody knows of—Inédit and priceless—to whom I can introduce her.

How is Muriel, the rose-colored-Conder? I will send her a card when the sun comes out. We had one dazzling day and now a wild scirocco storm rages. Don't you know how, if your head aches, you can't remember when it didn't? I can't remember now if Venice was ever there.

I am still pining for my only purple cloak. St. Martin is nothing to me. At least he had half of his, but *I* am cloakless and most ashamed.

I wanted to write to Edwin but I forgot to ask him his steamer and he left Wednesday, didn't he? Or—hasn't he left? Do go into the corner and tell me things; you can't pretend you don't write letters after what I've seen you do!

Oh, and Mabel, I've sent Mrs. Thursby a note straight out of the Polite Letter-writer for Ladies and Idiots. It's posted, my dear!

I hear that all Pen's Asolo things were sold, "very badly," chiefly to Sullivans:—"hardly advertised at all" and sacrificed.

This was last week. If we had only known! And Mrs. Browning is trying to give away his statues: the ladies with legs, in the studio at the Torricello. "All legs are used."

Please post me another Portrait of M.D. I won't lend my own copy with the respects.

A toi

CONSTANCE.

It took time and increasing depths of melancholy and several nervous crises before our real separation came to pass. Edwin would go and return, go and return again; to Boston and back, to Buffalo and back. Although I was terribly lonely when he went, whenever I saw him again after an absence, when he would come rapidly into the apartment, ruddy and smiling and endlessly patient and hopeful, something would rise up from the bottom to repel him, a sort of nausea at the sight of his persistently debonair, hard-shelled, American aplomb.

This continued good cheer of his that came, I thought, from a refusal to look below the surface of life, from a constant outward gazing that never looked *within,* made me so furious at times that I wanted to hurt him. I suppose the truth was that I envied him his ease, though I fancy I need not have been particularly envious of one whose companion I was at that time.

If I had not been so self-centered and concentrated upon my own inner activities, I would have been aware that he was as preoccupied and troubled as I was, only that most of the time he tried not to heed it.

We gradually made connections with old friends and friends of friends and as time passed into autumn we were dining out and having people for dinner, and generally Edwin was the life of the party, taking all the responsibility for making it go, and he would seem to be in high spirits and full of fun and wit. Then sometimes in the middle of a conversation he would drop out, so to speak, his eyes would wander and grow blank so that only his body seemed to be present while his thoughts groped in the darks of his consciousness for the why's and wherefore's of our misery. These lapses enraged me unaccountably. Though I felt an habitual criticism of him for not analyzing anything, the instant he began to I felt affronted. I suppose I did not want him to find me as I was, there in the depths of himself. Anyway, that momentary blank abstraction that took no care of his face and left it looking empty and uncontrolled, sent a vivid anger flaming all through me.

I was always seeking for the causes and meaning of things under the surface, myself, feeling my way into the depths, and groping among the terrible and abhorrent shapes that live below the pretty aspects of ten o'clock in the morning, but Edwin had always seemed curiously unaware of the possibilities lurking in the soul. It did not occur to me that perhaps he had been wise enough to ignore them while he could. But here in New York they claimed him and drew him down, and I thought this widened the distance between us.

This made me wish him away. I persuaded myself that he stood between me and real life, and I decided that his way of thinking was commonplace, for I grew more and more intellectually snobbish, which is a kind of negativeness that always ruled me when I had no feeling for anything. Away, away, away, I pushed, further each week, and behind the compulsion to do this, there was always something crying deep down in me, something simple and faithful and affectionate that reached out after him, and his loving, loyal care that had come to me at a time in my life when I had needed it very much, and which had never wavered or failed me. But I could not go on holding him and driving him from me at the same time; the thing in me that had to adventure into new worlds was ruling me completely.

I don't suppose I defined to myself the fact that John was in school and would be taken care of by schoolmasters for the next few years so he no longer needed Edwin for a father, and that I had made two new friends whom I was anxious to explore, and that he was an insulator that stood between me and a new fire of life so that now I could not savor things unless he removed himself. At nearly all times we are mercifully saved from knowing the bare truth about ourselves so that it is only in retrospect that we can understand what has been going on. To have known that instinct and nature were determined at last to have their needs satisfied would have seemed too banal a motive for freedom, and doubtless I would have been too proud to try and be alone for such a cause. But the cunning of desire wears numerous masks, and this time it persuaded me that Edwin blocked my growth, and my need for new ideas and that the life of ideas could never flourish in his company.

If I wanted to go ahead and *live* mentally, I had to send Edwin away—that was all there was to it. If I were to escape from such afternoons as I had passed the day he and John went off so happily to the football game, then he must go away from me and stay away.

One of the places Edwin and I had dined together was at the Armstrongs'. There was a couple who struggled against the commonplace! He was a diminutive blond architect whom Edwin had known at the Beaux Arts, and he had a bothered, peevish expression, as indeed why shouldn't he, when everything in his existence annoyed him?

He was married to a tall, vague woman with waving hands, who had six or seven children, the eldest of whom was rather near his own age, and none of whom he liked. He was quite miscast in the rôle of father and breadwinner. He simply couldn't manage it.

13

He didn't know how to secure jobs and was constantly without any work. People didn't know how they managed to get along, but there they were in a battered old house somewhere in the east Fifties, and it was gauntly furnished with a few, large, dim threadbare tapestries on its cracked walls, some dissolute-looking but aristocratic Italian Chippendale chairs, and with candlelight flickering over it all.

Edith featured her vagueness. Her hair was misty about her pale face; her light blue eyes, half smiling, deprecated the confusion of her life. The dinners they gave were extremely sketchy: something carried in from the restaurant around the corner, while she hovered about and continued to toss her apologetic hands high in the air, laughing tenderly at herself for the situation she had created—the cold, scanty meal in the cold room.

While she deprecated and beamed, she managed at the same time to be forever rallying her little captured husband, who sat, hands in pockets, legs stretched out, with a wrinkled forehead. Children wandered in and out of the candlelight, looking picturesque and making indifferent remarks. A distinguished poverty was what Edith felt it to be—one knew that.

She seemed to grow vaguer and more confused hour by hour. By the end of an evening one had learned that she felt like a helpless beauty, that the tapestries were like a gallant shield provided for her delicate femininity, standing between her and the sordid world, and that she held Dicky inside the picture with a grip that would never break. And if one saw that had she redirected half the energy she used in holding her crazy composition together into some practical attempt to earn a little money, so that they all could have been comfortable instead of being merely artistic, one also saw that she would never, never alter in the least. The way she saw herself and her surroundings was final for it pleased her. Maybe it pleased Dicky, too. Some people like to pout and feel restive in bondage against a tapestried background. Certainly he, too, felt it was "distinguished" or "swell."

("That's really very swell!" Beaux Arts men were wont to exclaim.)

At dinner a funny-looking man sat opposite me. He was about thirty-five years old and his evening clothes looked a little queer to me, maybe because of his shirt, which was frilly, full of little tucks. He had nice brown eyes, full of twinkling, good-natured malice, and there was a squareness in his face, for his brow seemed square and his

14

jowls were square. He had finely textured, red skin, and though the lower part of his face was heavy and unmodeled, he had a very delicate, small nose. His mouth was his most difficult feature, because of the large teeth with slits showing between them that jutted out and made him look like a wild boar, though the rest of him looked quite domesticated.

His name was Carl Van Vechten and he came of Dutch parentage; this, perhaps, explained the porcine texture of his skin and the suggestion of the wild boar in him, for many Hollanders have that quality.

He seemed amused at everything; there wasn't a hint of boredom in him. "A young soul," I thought to myself in my superior way, as I smiled across at him.

After dinner he sought me out and made gay, affectionate fun of the Armstrongs in an undertone, standing there, his long body bent in two places, at the waist and at the neck. This threw his stomach and his jaw forward, while his knees wobbled. He was really queer-looking, I thought, his neck never seeming able to hold up his head, or his knees his body. When he laughed, little shrieks flew out between the slits in his big teeth.

"Really, those teeth," I thought. "They seem to have a life of their own apart from the rest of him. They are always trying to get on to the outside of his face. If they weren't there he'd be quite a different man, but his body has to struggle against them all the time!"

He amused me because he had such a sense of humor and was so full of life. When we were leaving he left with us and we took him along and dropped him at the Metropolitan Opera House, "Where," he said, "I have to meet some fellows in the lobby in the last act and see what we're going to say about it tomorrow." He was the musical reporter on the *Times* and took his sacred trust, apparently, rather casually.

"And if Mary fainted or anything," he went on, "or if the Opera House caught fire, or if the President was there," he embroidered; "after all, one takes one's job seriously, I hope," he concluded, looking at me sententiously, trying to screw his lips over his teeth, and shut them inside his smile.

I asked him to come and see me and soon he did and so began a

15

long, drawn-out friendship with ups and downs in it and a good deal of sympathy and anger alternating on my part.

He was the first person who animated my lifeless rooms. He entered the exquisitely ordered and prepared apartment and he enjoyed it so much that he seemed to give it a gently vibrating awareness of itself. He never realized that the lovely objects all gathered together in a perfect pattern had no life of their own nor even any borrowed life from me, and he gave them such an appreciation of the cozy living world they made, soft in firelight and sunshine, drenched with the smell of tea roses and heliotrope, and fine cigarette smoke, that there was an instant response from all those inanimate things and the place became alive for us and for all others who ever afterwards entered there. He set it going on its changing round of appearances.

But it is never enough to say somebody made a place live. One must somehow tell of the tone and quality of its life, for each one makes it differently. Carl's soft silk shirt had turned-back cuffs that were comfortably buttoned with gold links that had some dull, half-precious stones embedded sleepily there in the shining metal, and they surrounded his small wrists with a considerate look of well-laundered old texture, and the gentle, continuous friction of unperilous employment.

He wore a merry intaglio depicting Leda and the swan, set in a gold ring, an emblem of his attachment to *scabreux* subjects rather than to any ancient, half-forgotten truth, and his neckties came from Fifth Avenue shops.

That kind of life emanated from him to the rooms and set them instantly into a background for amusement.

With him "amusing" things were essential things; whimsicality was the note they must sound to have significance. Life was perceived to be a fastidious circus, and strange conjunctions were more prized than the ordinary relationships rooted in eternity. It was no more than fair then that life answered to this taste of his by fixing his unanticipated encounter with Fania into one of the few inalterable and permanent relationships in his set! That was a strange conjunction that was rooted in eternity, odd and everlasting.

After Carl's visit, Edwin seemed to belong there less than before it, so that my vital organs produced, accommodatingly, a rapid crescendo of obscure symptoms that sought to remove him instanter. Much of the time I lay listless on the pale French gray couch, dangling a languid arm, eyes closed before the recurrent death of the sweet antiquities about me that lapsed lifeless between-whiles.

It seemed to me I could no longer explore people with Edwin near at hand as it had been at the Villa, he working at his drawings in the hall while I sat in the little salon with Stephen, observing his strangeness, identifying myself with him temporarily so that I could add to my own essence a fraction of his.

In the Florentine days I had had to have Edwin near me, somewhere in the Villa, otherwise I felt exposed and unable to function delicately and distill the little bit of Stephen or whoever else it happened to be, whom I wanted to absorb. Of course then I never wanted all of any of them, only enough to color my life. But alone with anyone, I was alone with myself again and that was to be with nothing. Nothing happened, nothing could happen, and a strange nervousness would seize me. I would grow inanimate and dumb, with moist hands. I was lost in horror at the loneliness of being with another, only feeling the futility of everything, and there would be a sinking, ever sinking interest in that other or in anything he could say or do or that I could say or do. Yes, then I needed Edwin for my obscure security. His presence in that environment enabled me to get going. With him, not present but near by, I could be fascinating, warm, magnetic and mysterious to another. My power could rise in me and be under my control; I could fall in love and be unhappy or exalted; I could become inspired and make oracular announcements surprising even to myself; strangely penetrating intuitions rose to consciousness and I would feel a fire burning in me.

But somehow I had come to the end of that. Now everything was the reverse of what it had been. Now I could not act if he were there; he had become the obstacle between me and my continuing life. If I were to go on, although I had no idea where I wanted to go, I must rid myself of him. (Something went on crying way down in the depths of me, piteous, begging some way for mercy; but another side of my nature had the upper hand, and it was deaf and unheeding and quite relentless.)

Hutch Hapgood was the confidant of all my years in New York, beginning with my perplexity about my marriage to Edwin. I talked and talked to him, trying by the sound of words to understand what was happening in me. He wrote to me when I went away for a week-end to be quite alone and see if some counsel would arise in me:

Hotel Manhattan.
Monday.

DEAR MABEL—DEAR UNHAPPY ONE—

I think I understand now, and if I do, I go back absolutely on what I said at first, about E. I now feel sure that for your sake and his it ought to end. And I think it would be incredibly foolish of you—and weak—not to do what is necessary. I telephoned on Sunday morning, hoping to see you before you went away. John was well and good and happy—and the world is very beautiful and very, very sad.

H. H.

I want so much to see you—when you are rested.

There was a peculiar instability in me. The shock of uprooting my-self from Italy was as great, though in a different way, as had been the one I had passed through in leaving Buffalo. The need to make again an entirely new adjustment to life put a strain on me that re-sulted in a singular nervous sensibility that ended by making me feel I was extremely psychic. People in Europe had told me I was psychic, but only in America did I believe that I really was, or so it seemed to me.

It was as though the tissues of my brain as well as the corpuscles of my blood had been jarred apart, loosening their habitual hold upon each other, and allowing, in a new contiguity, the opportunity for other and different perceptions of reality. I will try to show what I mean by telling some of these trifling but strange experiences. The following, from a letter to an old friend in Buffalo, is descriptive of the gropings and uncertainties of my ignorance.

DEAR GEORGE:

I have been for some time past making a series of mental experiments—the results of which are interesting and worth recording. Having arrived at a point when I dare go no farther for fear of losing my mental balance, I shall stop, though somewhat reluctantly, for I shall have to acknowledge that though I could penetrate farther and farther into a psychic phase of experience, yet the brain, inimical to it, would be the cost to pay—and a mental disequilibrium would result—this intellect and its processes for which I have no great respect and yet which must be respected if one con-tinues to lead a practical existence!

I will try to tell you about this as clearly and simply as I can.

. . . every night before sleeping, with a great effort of the will, I drove my consciousness back, past the brain, back to that region where I felt therein waiting was that answering guest of the soul. This was very different from that *outpouring* of the spirit in prayer which is the usual experience and which usually results in a general refreshment and strengthening of being, through assimilation of strong *external* forces; and this latter experience does not seem to be antagonistic to the brain process as I found the former one to be, as I shall describe to you.

So, concentrating all my motive power upon that dim inner chamber, I invoked the silent consciousness, commanding it to speak, to answer my questions, to give a sign, to respond, and I signified that while I slept, while my brain was in repose, and my intellect unwatchful and away from its post, that it should draw for me the picture of the answers to my questions, that in dreams it should reveal itself, unseal itself and be known and obey.

The strong effort of concentration produced a sort of excitation in the brain and an insomnia followed which I utilized in deeper and deeper concentration. Finally, out of sheer fatigue I slept and sure enough I had evoked an answer. Like figures in a cinematograph I saw in a dream myself and others in action, working, acting, speaking, and clearer than any reasoning was revealed the hows and whys and all I had asked. Upon awakening I was unusually tired and nervous, but I kept this up for several nights with every time an added certainty and *power* over it. But in the daytime I suffered for it. I had almost continual dizziness, I could not concentrate even to read, my vitality grew lesser and every night the insomnia increased, though fatigue conquered and sleep came finally, bringing what I wished, the cinematograph pictures of life, fate, reason—wonderful flashes of light and truth.

However, on Sunday and Monday I gave out physically—quite done up—shaking with nerves and with really quite queer mental symptoms. I realize that this has been a torture to the brain; if continued I feel sure the brain would collapse from it. To the increased power of the psychic will comes, in proportion, a weakening of the mental grip. I do not attempt to analyze why this should be. I only know that I have it in my power to become more and more psychic and clairvoyant, but if I do, I shall certainly get more and more "daffy." This latter is awfully unpleasant and also makes one feel physically ill. I feel I understand now the way those have gone who have had their "brains turned" by occultism. It is literally a turning of the brain over into something *else*. I *know* now that one could get to "know" things, to clear away mists, to unravel the mysteries, but what is this *new* demonstration of life that shows one that one may learn, but that the knowledge must turn to ashes in one's hands—that one may know, but that some disposition which governs even the psychic realm has so arranged it that the knowing does not come into our material and practical existence, but that we must *leave* the planes of the mental and material, and go to a new strange place if one would have this further knowledge at all costs?

I fear I lack the courage. I feel that this new strange place might even turn out to be the asylum out near the park! I am just up today. My nerves are in bits. I have been making a new road and am back from a journey upon it. It is all wonderful, but it is not everyday life. I wanted to tell *some*one, so I write you.

As ever,

M.

Do you understand? It's all so vague and my terms not clear—and besides my head aches. Why should the brain be an enemy to this other side?

During the deep depression of those first months at 23 Fifth Avenue, when, although I was amused some of the time by Carl and others, I was really very let down and filled with hopelessness. I was so depleted in vitality that I was continually catching cold and finally contracted tonsillitis very badly. The doctors recommended having the tonsils removed, so I had an operation there in the apartment.

It was later on that Dr. Jelliffe told me his fascinating theories on disease and his belief that nearly all bodily illness is a failure of the spirit expressing itself at the physical level, just as disorders of the brain represent, at the symbolic level, the inabilities of the psyche.

Any illness of the respiratory organs, the throat, bronchial tubes, and lungs represented, according to Dr. Jelliffe's findings, a failure in aspiration—the breath of God gone wrong. Tumors, cancers and so on, appeared to him to be manifestations in the flesh of one's unsublimated hatreds for people or situations outside oneself whom one regarded as parasites and whom one was unable to successfully deal with. Most of the insanities that were not of organic origin were, he thought, due to one's own inability to cope with oneself.

Be it all as it may! Certainly my throat was testimony either to some lack of aspiration or of failure to achieve. I was poisoned by it and very ill after they removed the infected tissue.

As I lay in bed unable to swallow, I was hypersensitive to everything about me. The least sound seemed to jar through my whole being, a loud voice shook me from head to foot, and everything was magnified so that little things became of enormous importance. Light seemed cruel and shade seemed terrifying. No one was allowed in my room. I simply lay quivering like the needle of a compass during an electric storm.

But I was not only *disagreeably* affected. Lovely things were acutely lovely and significant as never before. The second morning after the operation, then, I lay in bed in the darkened room, outwardly as still as a butterfly in its chrysalis, but inwardly harboring a mechanism keyed up to vibrations finer than ever before in this life, when suddenly I perceived with all my senses, it seemed, a new and exquisite fragrance, a perfume, strong and delicate and never known before, which surrounded me. I could see the color of it, the pale apricot loveliness, and I could hear its sound, but I am unable to describe that. Oh! The lovely, lovely smell of it! It was so consoling and so unexpected.

Then I heard or felt far away in the bottom of the house the thud of the heavy front door closing with a muffled bang. A moment later our own door bell ringing, and then the door opening and closing. A pause and my bedroom door opening gently and Nina creeping in. I made out her shape in the shadow and recognized her. I hadn't known she was in New York.

She tiptoed to the side of the bed and laid a tiny nosegay of the strangest little rosebuds on the pillow beside my face. They were apricot-colored and very, very sweet. This perfume deepened about me, a smell never known till five minutes before, when I had smelt them on their way to me when they were still at some distance away outside the house.

There were two other unusual sensory experiences that I had in those months, one of sight and the other of hearing; and a third one that was, I think, a heightened perception of the invisible ether that surrounds us. This happened down at La Tourette, Mrs. Davidge's place on Staten Island, and I will tell about it in a later chapter. Just here I will recall the two minor and unrelated occurrences that I experienced, as evidence of the unstrung condition of my nerves, and the shifting, unstable state of what Frederic Myers called "the threshold."

Carl and I had formed the habit of telephoning each other every morning about nine o'clock before we dressed to talk over the day before or to make new plans.

One morning while I talked to him, as I sat up in bed with my breakfast tray beside me, my letters all scattered about on the quilt, in a pause between our two voices, I suddenly heard in the receiver a deep groan far away at the other end of the wire—a groan so fraught with pain and unhappiness that, though it was faint and far away, it made me shudder.

"*What?*" I heard Carl's voice exclaim. "Was that *you,* Mike?" (He always called me that, I don't remember why.)

"*No,* it wasn't! Did you hear it, too?"

"Heavens! I should say I did! Whatever *was* it?"

Then it came again in that instant. Far off and clear and unmistakable—a soul utterly sorrowful and without hope. We joked about it, but we were both scared of it. Later in the day we talked of it, each accusing the other of playing a trick, a ghastly one it would have been, too!

Several times after that we heard the dreary thing when we were talking to each other on the telephone. But after a while—later on in the year—it ceased and we never heard it again.

But I think the night I *saw* Evil was the most heartshaking of any of these.

I had had a pleasant enough day; I went to bed tired out and fell gently asleep almost at once. Sometime in the night I awoke and sat up in bed anticipating something, something that had seemed to call me awake into consciousness, and as I looked out into the complete darkness of the room, over beyond me suddenly rose a blue-black column of smoldering flame that flickered upwards through space, and when it reached a height of five or six feet, within it formed a huge, jeering grin. Faceless, mouthless, nevertheless in that roaring sulphuric fire appeared a mirthless, devastating grin.

"Evil!" I exclaimed out loud in my horrified amazement. "So that is Evil!" I knew then that, for me, that abhorrent, loathsome, utterly indecent and hellish laughter was the true aspect of Sin. Since that time I have been able to trace in myself filaments of a deep-rooted Satanism whose foundation is in the bottom of Hell and that flowers on the crusted surface of this life in the guise of a smile.

Edwin, so sorry for all this conflict in me, tried to find diversions to take me out of myself. He longed to find the elements that would mitigate his negative effect upon me and to bring them in to bolster up his claim to life in that place.

One day, he ran into Jo Davidson at the Brevoort Hotel, across the street. He often went in there to look about, for that was the locale where most anything from Europe might be picked up, and he hoped that something from the old-world environment introduced over here would perhaps be the right tonic once again. Jo brought others, like a child trailing strange bright rags of seaweed gathered on some shore whose waters spread to far neighborhoods. Hutch was one of the first of these (as maybe one of the last to be seen in this chronicle of falling sands) and he, in his turn, brought his affinities. In time there came Steffens and Emma Goldman and Berkman, that group of earnest naïve anarchists; Reed, Walter Lippmann, Bobby Jones, Bobby Rogers, and Lee Simonson, these but lately out of college; Max Eastman and Ida, Frances Perkins, Gertrude Light, Mary Heaton Vorse, and the Sangers; and all the labor leaders, poets, journalists, editors, and actors.

One led to another and they all seemed to have something in them that must be examined and understood, but they were formed into different constellations that rarely touched each other, yet each one was a fragment in the same large puzzle that must somehow be solved.

It was very confusing to me that though they were all part of one picture, they were so jumbled and scattered that they never made a discernible pattern; they were in groups that did not meet, yet in each of these groups would be found one or more who had had some contact with those in other groups. For instance, Jo had some slight affiliation with many of the particles in that hourglass, for he was extremely gregarious; when he brought James Gregg in to see me, Gregg turned out to have some knowledge of Hutch, and Mrs. Davidge, whom Gregg introduced along with Arthur Davies, she knew Hutch, too, and Neith, and Norman Hapgood. Everybody had a little knowledge or at least a fore-knowledge of all the others, and generally it was rather negative or *outré* or unsympathetic.

It was ironic that Edwin, in his effort to help me, launched the boat that sailed away and left him behind. With the most profound unconsciousness of my selfish ingenuity, I persuaded good Dr. Sachs, the psychiatrist who was attending me, that Edwin was the cause of my weakness and depression, so he procured that excellent Hebe, Miss Galvin, as a nurse-companion, to stay with me, counseled me to eat a great many beefsteaks and to take long walks, and explained to Edwin that it would be better for him to stay away until I was stronger.

CHAPTER II

Revolutions in Art

"HERE, Lady Mabel! Gregg wants to tell you about our Exhibition," cried Mrs. Davidge, bustling into my front room one day.

James Gregg was the principal publicity man for the big International Show. What he told me was that he and Arthur Davies, with others helping, were arranging a mammoth show of modern art from Europe, to be brought to the Sixty-Ninth Regiment Armory early in 1913. The public had never seen any really modern painting and sculpture and it was time they did, he said.

I knew that only one man in America had ever done anything for the young artists who were trying to break away from the academic conventions, and that was Alfred Stieglitz. At 291 Fifth Avenue, upstairs, he had a couple of rooms where he exhibited modern artists and it took courage in those days. He had plenty. He showed John Marin, Dasburg, Arthur Dove and others there and people came and gaped, or looked impressed, or wiped smiles off their faces. The American public was still strongly protected twenty-five years ago, and only a comparative few saw these rebel painters. Kenyon Cox and Royal Cortissoz were the outstanding art critics of the day, and they were poised at the Gate of Free Painting with flaming swords. Winslow Homer and George Innes had been the idols of the art columns and still were.

The most courageous man in the New York art-dealing world was Macbeth. He had an art shop and he sponsored Arthur Davies, and for this reason was considered too daring and eccentric for words. Davies painted very strange and poetic figures wandering in allegorical scenes. There was a great beauty in his pictures, half-domesticated and half beyond the pale. A good many people were attracted to his things and faithfully went to see each new group as Macbeth secured them. But the public, the great, blind, dumb New York Public, had never

25

seen anything, had never had any chance to see anything Modern, and so Gregg and Davies were determined to show them contemporary European Art.

Gregg found me listless—Ariadne with the tide low. "You know Gertrude Stein," he said, announcing it. This small journalist was a free lance becoming elderly. His eyes were brown and kindly and clever. He constantly stroked his curt mustache and always found it difficult to talk. The pen was his medium.

"Couldn't you try an article about her? It will fit in with the exhibition."

I soon found they talked about that exhibition with creepy feelings of terror and delight. It was an escapade, an adventure. I, grown familiar in Florence and Paris with Cézanne—whose apples and things were met with in a reassuring friendly way on Loeser's walls—and Picasso and Matisse, familiars at Leo Stein's apartment, perceived that here in this other world they were accounted dynamite. These gentle men like James Gregg and Arthur Davies proposed to dynamite America, so they evidently believed. Revolution—that was what they felt they were destined to provide for these States—and one saw them shuddering and giggling like high-spirited boys daring each other.

Edwin was away and I was alone in my apartment and I was glad to see a mood of any kind so that I might enter it and live. I liked to live. But I didn't feel much like doing anything about it. I couldn't turn on action even if I wanted to, for I was never a self-starter. Gregg must work harder. He did. He became more eager and more inarticulate, pressing me to try my hand. He would get it published in one of the art magazines that proposed to reproduce the pictures in the show and it would be sold there at the Armory during those days the exhibition lasted.

I felt a flicker of desire to have an article of mine sold in such a time and place, but no impulse to write one. I was too sick from Edwin's being commonplace, I thought. Yet I half promised Gregg to try and when he left the glimmering twilighted room, I noted the odor he left behind him, trailing in the gloaming and blending with hickory logs and freesia—a smell of Scotch tweed and very recondite Turkish tobacco that somehow told of an existence animated and zealous, accompanied by choice aids to the enjoyment of activity.

26

Gregg was a part of life, making it at first hand, not needing to borrow or steal it. Able, even, to share it.

Since he had been there with me, I was part of it then, the life he was making. I got up a little steam, took out the "Portrait of Mabel Dodge" by Gertrude Stein, and made a slow dive into it—presently emerging with a kind of article. Gregg, who had sat there with me, had certainly fathered it, so it was natural that it should have its being in surroundings of his—those pictures and statues coming over to the Armory. Although Stieglitz had published something of hers in his *Camera Work*, that was for the élite; and this was the first time the public over here had heard of Gertrude Stein, as well as the first time their eyes were shocked into a new way of seeing by those pictures painted in a new dimension.

That I helped her, not into the world she already inhabited with her zestful pleasure, but into this new world, is undoubtedly a fact. She, too, had a birthday in America. From that year, when her essence was poured into the public consciousness, she has crept through it like a slow, inevitable tincture coloring prose and verse. Langauge— the written English speech—has more than a little Gertrude Stein in it now. I would not write of her writing today, perhaps, so enthusiastically, but after all I am a good many years older. What I said then, was: God help me!

SPECULATIONS, OR POST-IMPRESSIONS IN PROSE

By Mabel Dodge

[*Arts and Decoration,* March, 1913]

Many roads are being broken today, and along these roads consciousness is pursuing truth to eternity. This is an age of communication, and the human being who is not a "communicant" is in the sad plight which the dogmatist defines as a condition of spiritual non-receptivity.

Some of these newly opened roads lie parallel and almost touch.

In a large studio in Paris, hung with paintings by Renoir, Matisse and Picasso, Gertrude Stein is doing with words what Picasso is doing with paint. She is impelling language to induce new states of consciousness, and in doing so language becomes with her a creative art rather than a mirror of history.

In her impressionistic writing she uses familiar words to create perceptions, conditions, and states of being, never before quite consciously experienced. She does this by using words that appeal to her as having the meaning that they *seem* to have. She has taken the English language and, according to many people, has mis-used it, or has used it roughly, uncouthly and brutally, or madly, stupidly and hideously, but by her method she is finding the hidden and inner nature of nature.

To present her impressions she chooses words for their inherent quality rather than for their accepted meaning.

Her habit of working is methodical and deliberate. She always works at night in the silence, and brings all her will power to bear upon the banishing of preconceived images. Concentrating upon the impression she has received and which she wishes to transmit, she suspends her selective faculty, waiting for the word or group of words that will perfectly interpret her meaning, to rise from her sub-consciousness to the surface of her mind.

Then and then only does she bring her reason to bear upon them, examining, weighing and gauging their ability to express her meaning. It is a working proof of the Bergson theory of intuition. She does not go after words—she waits and lets them come to her, and they do. . . .

It is impossible to define or to describe fully any new manifestation in aesthetics or in literature that is as recent, as near to us, as the work of Picasso or of Gertrude Stein; the most that we can do is to suggest a little, draw a comparison, point the way and then withdraw.

To know about them is a matter of personal experience; no one can help another through it. . . .

In Gertrude Stein's writing every word lives and, apart from concept, it is so exquisitely rhythmical and cadenced that if we read it aloud and receive it as pure sound, it is like a kind of sensuous music. Just as one may stop, for once, in a way, before a canvas of Picasso, and, letting one's reason sleep for an instant, may exclaim: "It *is* a fine pattern!" so, listening to Gertrude Stein's words and forgetting to try to understand what they mean, one submits to their gradual charm. Huntley Carter, of the *New Age,* says that her use of language has a curious hypnotic effect when read aloud. In one part of her writing she made use of repetition, and in listening one feels that from the combination of repeated sounds, varied ever so little, there emerges gradually a perception of some meaning quite other than that of the contents of the phrases. Many people have experienced this magical evocation, but have been unable to explain in what way it came to pass; but though they did not know what meaning the words were bearing, nor how they were affected by them, yet they had *begun* to know what it all meant, because they were not indifferent. . . .

Many roads are being broken—what a wonderful word—"broken"! And out of the shattering and petrification of today—up from the cleavage and the disintegration—we will see order emerging tomorrow. . . .

Anyway, once in circulation, she certainly stirred the sources of being so they revolved more nimbly. I like Gertrude's Revolution.

Over in Paris Gertrude was sitting waiting. Besides the article, we were trying to get Mitchell Kennerley to publish an earlier book of hers.

When I came back to America in the autumn she knew how I hated the idea of it and she sent several letters to friends to help me get going. She wrote me:

27 Rue de Fleurus.

MY DEAR MABEL,

. . . I have written to Hutch telling him about you and giving him your address. He can be reached at the Harvard Club in New York. I have also written to Mabel Weeks about you. Her address is Brooks Hall, Barnard College. She thinks I am departing from my best manner in your portrait, and she does not understand it. I don't know anyone else to recommend to you in New York. . . . Don't be surprised Mabel but I may be going over to England to see if I can find a publisher. I don't know very well what I am to do when I get there, but everybody tells me that I should go, that it is important to see the people oneself, and so I am almost thinking that I will. If you know anyone who knows a publisher and can tell me how to meet him, will you let me know. We have been busy very much as usual. I have a couple of new Picassos. We see a great deal of them. They live in this quarter and we are very chummy. The new Mme. is a very pleasant hostess and quite a cheerful person. The late lamented is gone forever. I don't know anything about her. Pablo is very happy. They are at Barcelona for Christmas, she is to be introduced to his parents as a légitime which I think she is although nothing is said.

There has recently been an American millionaire from Philadelphia who would have rejoiced Constance. He did literally wave his cheque book in the air. He came over to buy the Rouard collection, at least a piece of it and he was perfectly flabbergasted at the prices Europeans were prepared to pay and did pay for the pictures. He was the real thing in Constance's Americans. We have not seen much of the Dela Huneys lately. There is a feud on. He wanted to wean Apollinaire and me from liking Picassos and there was a great deal of amusing intrigue. Guillaume Apollinaire was wonderful. He was moving just then and it was convenient to stay with the Dela Huneys and he did and he paid just enough to cover his board.

He did an article on cubism and he spoke beautifully of Dela Huney as having "dans le silence cuie something or other of the couleur pure."

Now Dela Huney does conceive himself as a great solitaire and as a matter of fact he is an incessant talker and will tell all about himself and his value at any hour of the day or night to anybody, and so he was delighted and so were his friends. Apollinaire does that sort of thing wonderfully. He is so suave you can never tell what he is doing. He is going to do a portrait of me for the Mercure. I am not always entirely happy when I think of it. I have not seen Florence Bradley since you left. She is coming to dinner Saturday. There was an awful row about your portrait the other day at the café du Dôme. Someone had given a copy to Isadora and Isadora had given it to a man named Skeene and he had read it at the Dôme and there was an awful row. H. Gibb who was there gave a very amusing description of it. He said everybody remembered all their grievances against any member of the family and let loose. A few were earnest inquirers and a few were vigorous defenders. Mabel Weeks doesn't care about my last manner. You will have to convert her. Mildred Aldrich just read it and said she had no idea you were so energetic and comfortable. I guess that's all. If I go to London it will be toward the end of January.

Love to you and respects to Edwin, Yours,

GERTRUDE.

But there were delays. Maybe we were too busy to attend to her. She wrote these letters, one after the other:

27 *Rue de Fleurus.*

MY DEAR MABEL:

Are you all right. It's too soon to hear from you yet but I hope to when it's time. I got a wonderful letter from Constance so she is not dead yet. Apparently she did not know that you were not wintering in Paris. . . .

I got a very sweet letter from Acton thanking me for the M. and Picasso. And a very friendly and unconvinced one from Berenson. By the way, what is André Gide's address? Haweis writes that he is thinking of a lecture on Modern Art in Australia, but you probably know all about that. I have been laying off work for the last two weeks. I found I was very tired. I am much rested now. I have finished the Trio.

Let's hear from you soon. Respects to Edwin.

Always yours,

GERTRUDE.

27 Rue de Fleurus.

MY DEAR MABEL,

Nothing has come yet, not your article or clippings, but I guess they are on the way and if you have not sent a catalogue of the show will you send one. . . .

I wonder if Mitchell Kennerley is going to do anything with my ms. Will you ask him sometime? There is no use my writing to him as he does not answer. Perhaps you can find out. Miss Blood has just told me that Mary Berenson wrote to her that she has heard from New York that you are getting everybody to read the portrait and know my name. My big thing about the whole crowd over here is getting along nicely. I think you will like it. I guess that's all.

GERTRUDE.

27 Rue de Fleurus.

MY DEAR MABEL,

You must have had a good time at the opening. I guess I would not have minded being there with you. We have just gotten back from London. We did have an awfully good time. I will send you the photo of my portrait by this mail. It would take considerable time to get a larger one done as the only man who photographs Picasso's things well is extremely dilatory. He says that this one will enlarge very well. As to our summer plans, owing to stress of poverty, we will be staying in Paris surely through June. Then we will go somewhere for a month of high altitudes and then we will come to you which will be in August if that will suit you. The Picassos have taken a house in the South of France so they probably won't be able to get away as he has to go to Spain part of the time on account of his parents, who are alone and getting very old. . . . Miss Blood says that Berenson seems very feeble. He is very sweet, is polite and amiable to Mary, very kind to the Italians and intimate with Loeser. Everybody in Florence is afraid that he is going to die soon. She says that the Berensons and the Loesers visit and dine with each other and come to see her together. I am awfully glad you like Mabel Weeks, it would be nice if she came to the Villa this summer. She is a very pleasant companion, steadily so. Did I tell you that I heard Electra in London. I enjoyed it completely. It made a deeper impression on me than anything since Tristan in my youth. He has done what Wagner tried to do and couldn't, he has made real conversation and he does it by intervals and relations directly without machinery. After all we are all modern.

I guess that's all. I am waiting for your article.

Always yours,

GERTRUDE.

My dear Mabel,   *27 Rue de Fleurus.*

Your letter via Jo Davidson has just come, but not your article. Please send that, I want to see it, surely I will like it. Please send it quick.

There was a delay about the photo because Mike [Stein] had it done over as he said the other was no good for reproduction. He thought this one very satisfactory. I am sending you another copy in case you want it for anything. I am delighted about Mitchell Kennerley. I have not written to him about it because I knew you could do it for me so much better. I cannot tell you how happy I am about it all. Those Oxford men are going to print the two last pieces of the Constance Fletcher in the Oxford Fortnightly in April. I have sent her a copy of it, but have not heard from her since. I have just finished a rather amusing short thing about my London publishing experience. I am sending it on for you to read but I don't suppose it would do for American publication, so perhaps it will be best not to show it to anyone. I have gotten some clippings about the show that Stieglitz sent to a man named Hartley, they all seem afraid to say much, all except Hutch who enjoys himself. Send on anything that is amusing about the show. It sounds like an awfully good one.

Yours,
GERTRUDE.

My dear Mabel,

Your letter was a great comfort to me. I was kind of low in my mind about that publication end and even Wagner's letters were ceasing to be a comfort to me. I have been trying some English publishers with collections of the shorter and longer things, those you saw and the ones I did this summer and when I first came back, there is nothing doing. I am working on four books now. One is a long gay book and has lots and lots of everything in it and goes on. It will be quite long. I have written about 120 pages of it. Another is a study of two, a man and woman having the same means of expression and the same emotional and spiritual experiences with different quality of intellect. That is going very well and slowly. Then I am doing one that will be published in a couple of months that consists of many portraits of women. Then I am doing another which is a description of a family of five who are all peculiar and are in a peculiar relation each one to every other one of the five of them. This one is just fairly begun.

I am still sending the volumes of the short and longer things about but they come back, quite promptly and with very polite hand writing and sometimes regretful refusals. The long book is in America. I have not heard anything of it for a long time. You can understand how much I appreciate your letter. . . .

It has been wonderfully spring here for two weeks now. Also the futurists are in town. You know Marinetti and his crowd. He brought a bunch of painters who paint houses and people and streets and wagons and scaffoldings and bottles and fruits all moving and where they are not moving there are cubes to fill in. They have a catalogue that has a fiery introduction demolishing the old salons and they are exhibiting at Bernheims and everybody goes. Marinetti has given several conferences and at the last he attacked the art of the Greeks and Nadelman who was present called him a bad name and Marinetti hit Nadelman and they were separated. . . .

Much love to you always,

GERTRUDE.

The Knightsbridge Hotel,
Knightsbridge, London, S.W.

MY DEAR MABEL,

I am completely delighted with your performance and busting to see the article, send it as soon as it is printed. You must be having an awfully amusing time and there will be lots of stories to tell. It takes lots of showing to make them take me, but I guess you will do it. The portrait has been invaluable as you will see over here also. Mitchell Kennerley has a thing of mine, Many Many Women, which he has had about four months now. He said he wanted to see something of mine because Stieglitz had spoken of me to him and so I sent him that, but he has never written anything about it. I have not wired him because I supposed he was making up his mind. I will send you a little bunch of short things so that you will have something if you get a chance to place it, but make them pay for them because I don't want to get known as giving them away. Then we can have more money to travel with and I love traveling. We are having a very amusing time here and as yet nothing is decided but John Lane and the English Review are nibbling. John Lane is an awfully funny man. He waits round and he asks a question and you think he has got you and then you find he hasn't. Roger Fry is going to try to help him land me. Perhaps it will succeed. By the way someone told me that Davies was interested in my work. That might help Mitchell Kennerley. But the most unexpected interested person is Logan Pearsall Smith. He went quite off his head about your portrait and is reading it to everybody. Never goes anywhere without it and wants to do an article on it for the English Review.

Among other things he read it to Zangwill and Zangwill was moved. He said, "And I always thought she was such a healthy minded young woman, what a terrible blow it must be for her poor dear brother." And it seems he meant it. Then when Logan would persist in reading it and re-reading it, Zangwill got angry and said to Logan: "How can you waste your time reading and rereading a thing like that and all these years you have refused to read Kipling." And the wonderful part of it was that Zangwill was not fooling.

We have been seeing all kinds of people and last night we had an evening with Paul and Muriel [Draper]. We were there for dinner. Condamine and the younger Rothenstein were there and Condamine and I got along beautifully and were pleased with one another. Paul and Muriel have done it all right. But to begin at the beginning. We went to the Opera to see the first night of the Russian Ballet and there in a box was a woman who had we thought the most effective head dress in the house and it was a very gorgeous house too. We were interested and we found she had fire opals and a gorgeous fruit thing to go with them. We laughed and wondered if it was there that Paul had gotten the fire opal idea. Not at all, when we dined with them two nights afterward, behold it had been Muriel. They gave us a handsome dinner, the table a complete scheme in white only broken by the vivid color of food and wine. Their big room is very comfortable and very beautifully lighted with electricity and enormous candles. Paul, so he said, had just that day sworn off betting now that the house was complete and paid for. Muriel gathers the men and keeps it all going on steadily extraordinarily well. We had a very good time. Paul sings and on the whole better, but as sadly as ever. They know a considerable number of amusing people and the place is attractive.

For a while I saw quite a good deal of Grant Watson. He gets rather monotonous. It's good but it lacks variety. I don't know that he has seen Muriel. Paul owns all the things he gave us a list of and some more and he is awfully fond of the list.

Roger Fry is being awfully good about my work. It seems that he read Three Lives long ago and was much impressed with it and so he is doing his best to get me published. His being a Quaker gives him more penetration in his sweetness than is usual with his type, it does not make him more interesting but it makes him purer. Your portrait is being considered by the English Review at Logan Pearsall Smith's suggestion. You won't mind their publishing it if they decide to do so, will you? The things I am sending you are not at all selected, they are short things I happened to have with me here.

I am doing a good deal of work. The long gay book goes on very well. Another one of the five is finished, so is the one of the Two. I am doing a short thing of Scenes. Then I am doing two very short ones about the

34

English and about the Publishers, the British Museum and the Portrait Gallery, the long one about the whole Paris crowd goes on slowly.

I guess that's all for just now. Respects to Edwin.

Always yours,

GERTRUDE.

MY DEAR MABEL,

I have just gotten hold of your article and I am delighted with it. Really it is awfully well done and I am as proud as punch. Do send me half a dozen copies of it. I want to show it to everybody. Hurrah for gloire.

Yours,

GERTRUDE.

27 Rue de Fleurus.

MY DEAR MABEL,

I have just read your article over again quietly and I am startled to see how completely and fully you have told your story. It is admirable in its measure and amplitude.

Your sentences are full and simple. I am delighted and more than delighted.

I expected to be pleased and I am really stirred.

Always yours,

GERTRUDE.

MY DEAR MABEL,

I have just gotten through the clippings, golly there were a lot of them. I was delighted with the letters to you from the total strangers. Who did the type written parody about you and your entourage, it was thorough and intelligent and at times extremely good. Who did it. Do answer this question. And what book is Mitchell Kennerley doing and when is it coming out. He has an interesting handwriting and seems to have an extremely hopeful temperament. He sounds all right.

The other day I got a note from the representative of the New York Times who lives in Paris asking for an interview. He wants me to tell him about myself. I hope I will be satisfactory. He is coming here Saturday. There is no particular news here, I get awfully excited about the gloire but this last batch has quite filled me up. I have done a lot of work since I have been back from London. A good deal on long things and I have finished several short things. I am sorry that Georgianna [King] thing was not what Kennerley wanted, she was one of the very first to see the directions in Melanctha. When will the Stieglitz thing be done. Will it be a volume about the three things. They are selling copies of the magazine out in San Francisco and my old schoolmates are much taken with your article. I have given away all the copies you sent me. Miss Blood was some surprised. Oh, by the way, Loeser and Mrs. Loeser is going to have a baby. B. B. is getting much better. Their secretary got smashed up in Switzerland so Mary Berenson is secretary again. I guess that's all. I will send the things all back by next mail. Bully for us, we are doing fine.

GERTRUDE.

Regards to Edwin and Hutch.

After the International Show opened the noise began.

"Well, who is Mabel Dodge?" they exclaimed. And thousands of copies of *Arts and Decoration* were sold, for Gertrude Stein's Portrait of her, serving as an example of her style, was in it, and she had signed that article—and there was something new under the sun and everybody's blood ran quicker for it! A chance to laugh, to curse, to run cold from *words!* Oh! Look at the letters that poured in. People were struck by the thing and they tingled.

I suddenly found myself in a whirlpool of new, unfamiliar life and if Gertrude Stein was born at the Armory show, so was "Mabel Dodge." The way it happened was that as soon as I had written the article and given it to Gregg, he showed it to Arthur Davies and told people about it. Long before it was printed, they came after me and got me into the Exhibition part of it; asked me to help collect any examples of modern art bought in Europe, in New York, from people who would loan them; asked me to help with the money.

I had an automobile, with a smug chauffeur named Albert driving it in bearskins, and I had a small bank account with nothing much to buy except flowers and cigarettes. As soon as I collected a few pictures from here and there, feeling dignified in people's drawing rooms designating what I wanted, and had written a check for five hundred dollars and sent it to Davies, I felt as though the Exhibition were mine. I really did. It became, over night, my own little Revolution. *I* would upset America; I would, with fatal, irrevocable disaster to the old order of things. It was tragic—I was able to admit that—but the old ways must go and with them their priests. I felt a large, kindly compassion for the artists and writers who had held the fort heretofore, but I would be firm. My hand would not shake nor could I allow my personal feelings of pity to halt me. *I* was going to dynamite New York and nothing would stop me. Well, nothing did. I moved forward in my rôle of Fate's chosen instrument, and the show certainly did gain by my propulsion. The force was there in me—directed now.

36

I wrote a note to Davies and sent it along with my check. He and Mrs. Davidge amputated one phrase from it, had it printed on cards and autographed and handed to everyone who came to the show. This card said:

I'll be delighted to help in any way in the exhibition, because I think it the most important thing that ever happened in America, of its kind. Anything that will extend the unawakened consciousness here (or elsewhere) will have my support. Anything that will add to the racial consciousness and racial memory is worth while. The majority are content to browse upon past achievements. What is needed is more, more and always more consciousness, both in art and in life.   MABEL DODGE.

Davies's reply to that letter was full of something. It said:

DEAR MRS. DODGE:

It is a happy augury that you have, with my associates in the work of this great exhibition, put the true test of superabundance as an art valuation—a valuation of life; cowardice of inaction is poverty. And it is an orchard of bounties, I assure you, through which we go and make eternal as we make of our gifts fresh divisions, reflections of our deep gratitude. Also with simplicity we hope to overcome the parasitic disorder of those who rob life of beauty. That great art is a state of the soul and of positive benefit to all who can feel exaltation.

I am with regards,   Very faithfully yours,
                                                    ARTHUR B. DAVIES.
January 25th.

This seemed a highly fermented and boiling mixture of acknowledgment for money and a zeal directed towards other boundaries and it flattered me very much. Then they elected me vice-president of the organization, whose symbol was an uprooted pine tree. I instantly became an uprooted pine tree myself and it took years—positively *years*— to get rooted anywhere again!

Things, then, were flowing in and out of the apartment. Edwin had flowed out and stayed out. He shook his head and intimated I would go to the bad but when he read the article in *Arts and Decoration,* and then immediately afterwards kept seeing things in magazines and newspapers about Mabel Dodge, he had a "can-I-believe-my-eyes" sensation and wrote a nice letter in which he said that he was thrilled by

37

a certainty of my "approaching recognition" at last, and that he was sorry this had been so long delayed by his blundering interference. He told me I had been right all the past years—he had not understood me. It was a generous, appreciative letter and I was glad he wrote it.

Gertrude cooled towards me after a little though we still wrote back and forth for I had business to do for her, though I was the last who should have tried that—being so muddle-headed, forgetful, and self-centered. Once I asked Leo why she had changed towards me, and he laughed and said because there was a doubt in her mind about who was the bear and who was leading the bear!

CHAPTER III

Characters

LOOKING back upon it now, it seems as though everywhere, in that year of 1913, barriers went down and people reached each other who had never been in touch before; there were all sorts of new ways to communicate, as well as new communications. The new spirit was abroad and swept us all together. My own part in it was involuntary. The share I had in bringing people together was inspired not at all by any conscious realization in me, for I was at that time really more essentially an instrument of the times than ever before. Freed from Edwin's conservative habit, I thought, I was able to move as the spirit dictated. It was only afterwards that I rationalized the impulses that had urged me to act.

The International Exhibition of Modern Art was the opening indication of this new impetus. That is natural, for it is always the artists and poets who swoop ahead like heralds. One saw the same thing happening in Europe when the Russian dancers, actors, and artists cut an opening for the Orient to pass into Europe, which immediately afterwards became orientalized in clothes and in thinking. Women began to wear turbans and for the first time, then, trousers. For Russia was the last great closed gate between the East and the West. Men began to talk and write about the fourth dimension, interchangeability of the senses, telepathy, and many other occult phenomena without their former scoffing bashfulness, only they did it with what they were pleased to call a scientific spirit.

The essence of it all was communication. It was as if men said to other men: "Look, here is a new way to see things . . . and a new way of saying things. Also new things to say." As Hutchins Hapgood, always the ideal journalist, said: "This is news!" Gertrude Stein's writing had the same effect. It caused an inner upheaval.

And now I will try to tell of other factors that were working to

39

shake up and make over the fixed patterns of life. I had Miss Galvin
all this time. She whom Dr. Sachs had procured for me. "A great big
beautiful doll"—that is what she was—with glossy black hair waved
down over her ears and into a large coil behind, dewy black eyes with
long lashes, pink and white skin—a Hebe figure. She came as a nurse
but stayed to keep house. *She* always arranged the tea roses and freesias
and paid the bills and made it all in order, getting food I liked. *She*
always went up to the Fifth Avenue Bank the end of every month to
pacify them because I was overdrawn. Although our little Vittorio was
there, correct and willing, *she* opened the door if she heard the bell
ring, brought in anyone whom she knew I would want, brought them
in reassured by her large, natural personality, that overcame so well
the detrimental associations of revolutions.

I was at large, so to speak, for the first time in my life. Indeed,
"There was I all alone in a pink frock . . ." as Constance had said!
There was I on my own, unprotected—no Edwin being a husband
before or behind. I felt raw sometimes, exposed, but I held up my head
and looked aloof. I felt I must go through with it bravely and without
compassion either for myself or another. Myself I did feel sorry for
sometimes, but suppressed it. I felt I was a "strange, lonely little figure"
but awfully gallant. I was sorry no one but me knew how gallant I
was, but since they would have to know how scared I was while holding up my head and looking aloof, and I did not want them to know
that *ever,* they had to be content with my mystery. "A sphinx," the
newspapers called me in a little while, "with" (Oh Eternal!) "a Mona
Lisa smile!" I rapidly became an enigma to the public no less than to
myself.

So Miss Galvin reassured not only the watchfully prudent but allured
knockers at the front door—but she reassured me, too. I liked to fall
back upon her respectable and unknowing thoughts. Her realization
of Revolution was so absent that one may suspect she'd never even
heard the word. To her, life was just—you know—living, shopping,
eating, paying bills, and sometimes going to a restaurant to dinner
with Alfred, her beau, who worked in a bank downtown.

Now if I wanted to immerse myself in Revolution and so on, I did
need to know there was dry land at hand—and Miss Galvin was dry
land. Also I wanted other people to know I was, practically, surrounded by dry land even if I did venture into deep waters. I wanted

to be all kinds in succession and successfully—with the continuous possibility of being only one kind. That is to say, I wanted to be sheltered when I wanted to be—I was not yet the kind to burn my bridges altogether. Well, Miss Galvin made it all possible. Really, come to think of it, I doubt if I had had the courage to start revolutions if I hadn't had that placid, good-looking Miss Galvin.

Sometimes, then, the attitude would have to be earnest and subversive, calmly intent upon change, and sometimes with Carl there, it would be merely amused.

Carl was a vacation from the real business of life and art. He took me to hear the orchestra at the Metropolitan Opera House struggling in rehearsals, to grasp Moussorgsky's strange Russian composition, "Boris Godounov." This opera was, for me, that rarity one seldom is blessed with after the twenties, a new musical experience. Carl would come for me at eleven in the morning when the apartment was full of sunshine from the south windows and every light beauty showing cozy and warmed against the white walls, and he would be ruddy and washed—clean like a well-groomed young hog, his familiar clothes hanging nicely on his tall figure, bones embedded in small amounts of fine flesh. Then I, in long, flowing, soft things and a hat with drooping feathers, nicely veiled, would pin a flower into fur and move down the dim mahogany stairs past General Sickles's heavily bolted double doors out to the waiting Albert. The thin, metallic air of New York blew keen on moist skin, sensitive from bathing and firelight.

In the huge, dim Opera House, we could choose any mortal seat we wished. Now here, now there. Below on the aisle in any velvet seat among thousands all alike, or in the spacious boxes or even sometimes high up in the balcony, we sat alone in a dark crimson vacuum centered upon the orchestra pit where many little men in business suits sawed their way through the unnatural musical phrases, and, each time we heard it, coming nearer to a union with faraway Russia. I luxuriated in my privilege and felt important. I liked to be almost the only one there—save for a couple of men sitting near the musicians in overcoats with white silk mufflers gleaming in the dusky light, and perhaps some exciting creature like Nijinsky dashing up and down the aisle.

I had soaked in Bach, Beethoven, Schumann, Schubert, Wagner, Chopin, all the great ones, in the weekly symphony concert of my youth, and in Europe in the endless concerts in Paris, in Kursaals, in Austria, in Germany. When I was young, people were brought up on the classical European music; we had it constantly in our ears. It became so, and still is so, that comparisons between renderings by this conductor or that grew to be our main enjoyment for one cannot endlessly thrill with repeated aesthetic emotion. So we all became critics. We got the grand known music early and it became part of us and we were hungry for the new flavors of modern composers or unknown ones; when I heard "Boris" it was a wonderful event for my ears, and it became woven right into my tissues then, and every note lives somewhere in me yet. Above all I adored the great bells, nearly passing out of myself upon them.

"Don't let's miss the boom," I would cry, as, sometimes, we were delayed by this or that. The boom expressed everything for me! I was always hearing it when away from there and talking about it. A little later, in a play he started to write in Florence, Reed wrote my epitaph, remembering this:

EPITAPH FOR MABEL

> Deep in garden gloom
> Where sun never came,
> Kings sang long ago
> Her fascination strange:
> Warm as April snow,
> Ringed with icy flame,
> Doomed with season's doom—
> A living change—change—change—change. . . .
> Rippling windy laugh
> Shall her mirror seem;
> Keen, cold, amorous,
> The marble of her tomb—
> When she, glamorous,
> Shakes Hell's quiet dream:
> This her epitaph—
> "She loved the boom—boom—boom—boom—boom!"

Then the boom cracked! I felt myself going asunder—and suffered a delicious dread, for lurking behind me tiptoed a perpetual fear. I could not see its face, so I did not know what it was, but I supposed it was insanity. Anyway it was a dismal secret that I was bound to accept as part of everything else. The flowers and colored crystal, the white walls and silk embroideries—they formed the fair and orderly mask for some black and hideous disorder that was hidden from others and most of all from myself. But I guessed its implacable pursuit.

Miss Galvin's obvious unawareness of anything drear was mostly a comfort to me. But sometimes it made me tired. There is nothing so wearisome as obliviousness and she excelled in that. Her black head against the pale wall as she sat at lunch with Carl and me and Hutch, was a pure and beautiful triumph of the flesh, but her amiability accepted no more than the amiability of those with whom she ate, as though their pleasant laughter was all there was to them when it was, to tell the truth, the very least of them.

Our luncheons, though, would maybe have deceived a more subtle organism than hers, for they were so charmingly presented. The oval table caught the sunlight and it flickered over the gold and white glass and the Cantagalli plates, showing up the linen threads in Asolo linen —and it shone through the roses and yellow wine.

Cases of wine, Graves Supérieur, stood waiting in our storeroom— always white wine for lunch, red wine for dinner. My new friends liked good food and drink and so did I. Then Carl introduced me to little places where one could eat amazingly well and sometimes I would lunch out with him. Poligniani was one of these where the Italian cooking was better than in Italy (when eaten in New York!). Through the smoke of Italian tobacco, one saw Caruso and Prince Troubetskoy and others—gesticulating, imposing themselves with popping eyes empowered by the meek pastes and the mild Italian liquor.

Edwin Arlington Robinson and I used to lunch there sometimes, a little later. ("Surely you don't want to make me think you're happy," he said.)

One passes on the lessons one learns from others and it is curious how instinctively one chooses various resorts to eat in according to the nature of one's company. With Walter Lippmann I occasionally lunched at the Holland House; with Carl at Poligniani's; with Hutch at the Brevoort. But I don't know why one ever lunched away from home when it was so infinitely more attractive there. Coffee and cigarettes afterwards in the front room, where a beam of sunlight fell across the clear space like a band of gold, with blue smoke curling about the sad, doomed heads of mortal men, was altogether more agreeable than any place one had to go—yet perhaps it was the need to go—to move, to get out and come back, to change one's thoughts or to expend some energy, that sent one catapulting into the street and whizzing away in the motor.

From the moment I wakened and drank my coffee in the white bed, embraced by the silken curtains depicting reeds and roosters, the stirring within me began. I felt as though I had the works of clocks in my body instead of a heart and bowels. The dynamic whir and buzzing increased in rapidity and volume until it reached my head, and there it continued an accompaniment to the charivari between my ribs that was fit to burst my brain with its reverberating din—like ten thousand devils beating a tattoo against the walls of an impregnable hell. It was necessary to find an escape for these dynamos—so I would reach for the telephone, invite someone to go somewhere, call Miss Galvin and give her a dozen errands, call the automobile and hasten away full steam ahead.

If I stayed in the house to lunch, my life had mounted by that time to a pitch that overcharged the atmosphere about me with a crescendo of futile power. Everything seemed to go faster without going anywhere in particular. The sun grew more dazzling, the wine mellower and more potent. I felt these forces within me issue from the holes in my head where my eyes were, and when I looked at people they frowned a little and turned aside like embarrassed dogs.

Once as I left the lunch table for a moment to fetch something from my bedroom, I heard Carl say to Hutch in a low mockery of fright: "That woman will drive me crazy, Hutch. She accelerates the tempo so!" "Yes," Hutch agreed, "it's her vibration." While I couldn't rest for the crepitations within me, yet I was gratified at this evidence of my influence on others. That at least was, for me, a reward of virtue, for, I believed, this is my body holding within it all my power instead of spilling it in love.

I thought that power left my neglected womb and ascended to my brain, and from that questionable point of vantage it could challenge other brains. It seemed to me that had it stayed in its proper place men might have really loved me, but that at this particular time the pole was pulsating higher up. This caught men between the eyes, held them magnetized, fascinated, charmed, as men will be by the allure of a woman's lively calling essence, but left them entirely free below.

The attraction between Carl and me was, at its height, a mutual stimulation with none of the usual elements of sex. He sometimes grew playfully pleading, and let a doggy wistfulness spread over his nice animal countenance, but it was only in moments of *désœuvrement* when there was nothing to say and no place to go. I knew he did not really feel anything for me, and that he knew I knew it.

That side of him was quite occupied anyway with the young Russian actress, Fania Marinoff, whom he saw every day. I didn't know her at first, but I knew he was in love with some girl. He had been married to an early acquaintance from Cedar Rapids, but her similarity to him and her home association had been too heavy a handicap for a successful marriage. He had been divorced and now he found he could respond to the exotic small Russian because she was so different. Occasionally his Dutch warmth went out in warm friendships for other men, for he was full of dead sweet affectionateness that had to run over. Avery Hopwood, Pitts Sanborn, and others, I knew, he had been fond of, but Fania he loved then and ever after. That little young thing had been just the one for him.

"Do you know what love is?" asked Carl of me one day, with earnest eyes, allowing a mocking smile to twist his inadequate lips sideways over his unfriendly and unaccommodating teeth. "It is to feel the way a kitten feels when a man holds it high up in the air in the palm of his hand." I didn't know whether he meant the kitten didn't know enough to be scared of falling, or whether it knew with panic the man would let it down.

2

Jo Davidson first brought Hutchins Hapgood to see me. Everybody loved Hutch. He was the warmest, most sympathetic hound. God pursued him and he pursued God, looking into every dust bin for Him. He never thought he would find Him among the mighty, but always he was nuzzling among "the lowly, the lowliest, and the low."

He had deep, faithful-looking blue eyes whose lids drooped at the outer corners, and he had the massive arched nose of an eminent man. But he was not just an eminent man. He was an old bloodhound on a leash—with full, generous lips and melancholy jowls.

Neith let him think he was pursuing God, but she held the end of the leash in her enigmatic white hand and smiled a secret smile. For, like other women I have known, she didn't believe in his everlasting talk about his soul.

Hutch was so sympathetic! Always ready to have a tear in his eye! He dated back to William James and Royce at Harvard, and Wordsworth was his favorite poet.

" ' 'Tis the beauty, not the terror,' Mabel," he would often say, " 'that turns the traveler's heart to stone,' " telling about some dregs he had come upon where God was hidden. Hutch had warm, sympathetic, German blood. Somewhere he was German, I forget where; on his mother's side, I think. He would lean forward with clasped hands and let his whole face relax into sympathy, his bloodhound eyes suffused with the softest, deepest compassion. He had a philosophical attitude towards nearly everything. He told me how once in class at Harvard he declared to his professor, Santayana: "All women are beautiful," and he said Santayana stared at him for a moment in silence, and said, "That is the most philosophical remark ever made to me by an undergraduate!"

Whenever Hutch was touched enough by someone's pain, he got relief inside himself, and that made him feel God was there. He was a wonderful talker and his deep compassionate voice had a boom in it, and was like organ music. The book he wrote called *The Story of a Lover*, which told all about him and Neith, was just like organ music, too. It was suppressed (I mean by the censor!), because it was so essential it seemed strangely raw to the poor man. He had written other books when I met him: *An Anarchist Woman, The Autobiography of a Thief, The Spirit of the Ghetto, Paul Jones,* and several others. And some of these were about down-and-outs he'd met on park benches in his newspaper days, for he started as a reporter. When Lincoln Steffens was the editor of the *Commercial Advertiser,* Hutch was one of his reporters and Neith sat in the window at a desk in the office where the sun came in on her red hair. Hutch never loved any woman but Neith. He tried to, but he couldn't. He felt he ought to. He believed that if he could become successfully the lover of a woman, enjoying her body and giving her pleasure, that it would be the gesture of purest comradeship. But it was a gesture he could not make completely. He called himself an intellectual anarchist, but while he was intellectual, he was not anarchic in his essence. He had not even an anarchistic influence it seemed to me, but maybe I was mistaken.

He was one of the most attractive and lovable human beings I ever knew, and I soon became deeply attached to him and wanted to be with him all the time. I told him all about myself—everything—and oh! how he sympathized. Tears stood in his eyes and he passed his hand tenderly over my hair.

We spent hours and hours together in the white rooms, talking. And he brought all his friends to see me and took me to see them. It was through him I knew the anarchist group, the I.W.W.'s, the single taxers (of whom Lincoln Steffens was one, and also Fred Howe and Bolton Hall) and in fact, all the different kinds of radicals.

Hutch was sometimes a little drunk, and then he became more passionate and more eloquent. . . . "I consider it my first duty to undermine subtly the foundations of the community," he would boom, with a glass in his hand. When he'd had enough to drink, his pain would turn and he shook with robust laughter, but it always made the tears overflow and run down his cheeks.

Neith didn't come in town much. They had a large, red brick house with porches around it on a hill in Dobbs Ferry, up over the Hudson River, and as they didn't have very much money, Neith did nearly all the housework. They had no servants but Elina, a small, ugly Italian woman like an electric spark. With four children, Boyce and Charles, and the two girls, Miriam and Beatrix, there was a lot of sewing and other things to do.

Hutch worked less and less, apparently. He said the conditions of life, as it was organized, were against it. He couldn't, or wouldn't, adapt himself to them. He was in revolt, but his acts were never very dangerous. I only knew him to resist authority openly once.

Talking was his principal outlet—so he talked and talked, always advocating resistance to authority and exhorting people to subtly undermine the foundations of the community and so on. He used to talk on busses, on trains, on park benches, and wherever he found himself. He had a habit of bringing home anarchist friends of his, and they had to get off the train at Hastings and then take a bus over to Dobbs Ferry. Particularly spiteful he became when he got into the Hastings bus, because he didn't like his neighbors, whom he called Christians, and there they all were, sitting in silent disapproval of him, going home to their smug homes near him. Hutch would usher Hippolyte or some

47

other incongruous character into the bus, and the suburban ladies would all draw their skirts away.

Hippolyte Havel, for instance, was a Russian nihilist with a broad, low, intelligent brow, and long, black hair; he was very small, and very obscene in his talk. He lived with Polly and cooked for her down in Greenwich Village at the only restaurant of its kind. Later there were others: Black Cats and so on, but "Polly's" was the first.

Hutch grew so offensive, in his conversation, to the ladies of the bus that they complained of him—and the driver told him, one night, that he couldn't ride home in it. Hutch was in a booming uproar in a minute. The angrier he grew, the more he looked like a Lutheran preacher . . . the more anarchistic his language, the more respectable he became. He always looked respectable. That was his doom! He had such an eminent nose—and besides, his clothes were always so like a conventional business man's.

Hutch made an act of revolt. He climbed past the man at the door who was trying to prevent him, and he sat down and glared around at the ladies through his gold-rimmed spectacles.

"As a believer in Free Speech," he boomed, "I will continue to sit here in this bus and say what is in my mind. It is my inalienable right."

The ladies looked at each other. One got up and went out. The driver lost his temper and said he wouldn't start the bus till Hutch left it, if he had to wait all night. So it ended by the ladies all getting out and Hutch sitting doggedly. He and the driver tried to outsit each other. This went on for some hours and ended in a lawsuit.

Neith was really wonderful. She moved like a slow river and her hair was round and round her head in red braids. Her face was white and sweet and she had sleepy, green eyes that sometimes woke up. She seemed to feel that Hutch was at play in the city among the anarchists and radicals and that his ideas were no more important to real life than a bunch of red and blue balloons. She was as sweetly half-attentive, half-*distraite,* when he talked, as when one of the children told of his exploits. She always seemed partly absent, partly hidden from others, and when, after supper, the dishes cleared away, the work of the day done, she lay on the couch in the corner, her eyes closed, she seemed to be fully alive but sunk deep, deep into herself.

She was mysterious, though in a way very simple. She didn't care what Hutch said. I do not think his ideas were precious to her. But sometimes she would put her hands on his shoulders and look into his eyes with a vivid look, the life all of a sudden leaping in green sparks, incomparable life infusing her, demanding life in return. And Hutch's face would flush and flood with life, too, and his eyes grow a deeper blue. Then he would laugh like a boy and lose all his compassionate sympathies as he bent and kissed her—all of him, from his rudder-like nose to his full, curved lips drawn to focus towards her. He would flash an almost apologetic, smiling look at one as he did so—as though to make excuses for an interlude.

So I think Neith didn't really care very much what ideas he harbored. She wanted his love. Also she had to conceal her affectionate disregard for all this talk from him, and she could be seen making affectionate and patient allowances for him and for his friends and their opinions.

In the first part of *The Story of a Lover,* Hutch tells how he talked and talked to Neith in their early years. First and last, he said, he supposed those passionate attempts to reach her spirit and to communicate with it, would have constituted some real literature had they been recorded. But they were not only not recorded, they never reached her spirit. Never, he said, did he seem to be able to find her, the soul of her, and make himself known to her—the soul of him.

And not only that. She never seemed to *admit* his soul. This was, to him, a denial of his living essence. Unless he could find the ultimate core of that woman and touch it by talk, and awaken her from her sleep, he was a failure: so he wrote, over and over, in his book. And he went about the world with that everlasting feeling of failure in him. But he was not a failure. All the things he worked for have gradually come to pass, though today other problems are here now for the solving.

That beautiful book was a *tour de force.* He says in it: "I wonder if I have not been a mere spectator all my life!—A superheated observer? Have I ever been part of her real life? Is not my recurrent feeling of almost intolerable loneliness an index, a sign of her remoteness?"

Again he complains, "She has never accepted my form, my essential self as beautiful." And still another, "I hated and loved her perfect and never-failing egotism, the unconscious completeness with which she remained herself." His deep quarrel with her was that she never completed his intense need of being needed. Sometimes he quoted William James to me, laughing while tears stood in his eyes: " 'So long as one poor cockroach suffers from the pangs of unrequited love, this world is not a perfect world.' " Here is a picture he gives of her:

She had gone down almost to death, and when she emerged it was like the phoenix from the ashes. A new spirit, one of willful lovingness, breathed in all her being. There was a subtle change in her attitude toward the children. She had always loved them, but now her love was unimpeded. She accepted them at last! . . .

And now she had fully accepted me, but in the way in which she had accepted the children, the household, and her lot in life. But she remained herself! Always mysteriously remote from us, no matter how tender, not needing, though infinitely loving. How often when I have seen her slow, quiet, humorous smile have I thought of the Mona Lisa of Leonardo, of that unnervous strength, of the "depth and not the tumult of the soul."

And he says still further on:

I had loved her too much, or at any rate too actively; had not left to her enough to do in our relation, not enough initiative. This was a thought on which she constantly dwelt. Her deepest passion was to construct. She needed to build, to feel that of her own will she was bringing life to the relation.

He published the book anonymously and the critics never understood it. They said:

What the author of this book needs is a thorough psychic catharsis. He needs to be rid of a pernicious mechanism of sentimentalism and falsehood with which he is protecting himself. Not that he does not believe himself honest. He does; he believes he has searched into his inmost soul. And there, in his apparent honesty, lies the harmfulness of his confessions, both to himself, I think, and to such of his kind as his book may reach.

"Anonymous" is a constitutional neurotic. He is burdened by a persistent and harassing sexual tension which he is unable to relieve in his marriage relationship. . . . Likewise, whatever else "Anonymous" does represents an analogous effort to liberate this same sexual tension. His experiments in radicalism are merely sublimated attempts in this same direction. Finally, the writing of this book, from every page of which oozes forth a passionate intensity and over-emphasis, betrays his urgent, suppressed and frustrated need.

This was perhaps the first book, of which kind we have seen so many during these later years, wherein a person tries to tell really objectively of his life and its experiences. These accounts have ranged from the stories in *True Confessions* to the altitudes of our "best minds." Since Hutch's book, many people have been writing about real life in an urge to understand it and to make it understood. Characters like Bernard Shaw and other critics find this deplorable. But could they face themselves, seeing themselves in the "naked state," and merely as a part of a picture? One wonders.

When I knew him, Hutch was writing three or four small half-column things a week for the *Globe,* rather in the manner of the French *feuilletons.* The editor, an old friend of his, let him write about anything he liked—a spring day, a bottle of wine, a Labor leader—or whatever. Of course, he always wrote about himself, though he was too intelligent to betray this in any crass way. But he would take the train to town, go to the Harvard Club, and write five hundred words of sensitive, generally melancholy observations to add to the support of a red-haired woman who denied his soul, and four children who irritated him, not to speak of a mother-in-law whom he had upstairs and whom he did not love very much. He was really a puritanical rebel and people were growing increasingly angry at him, even afraid of him. More and more letters were sent to his editor, remonstrating about him and his opinions, until even the editor himself got nervous. I amused myself by contributing one of these to further confound him! I wrote:

To the Editor of the Globe—
Dear Sir:

A number of your readers are much puzzled concerning the attitude of Mr. Hutchins Hapgood as expressed in his article entitled "The Bottle" which appeared in your issue of Monday evening.

Just as we had really accepted Mr. Hapgood as an advocator of lawlessness, he neutralizes all his past statements. He says his boys listened to him with an air of doubt and of criticism of his wisdom which he loves to see in them. Why does he love to see this in them unless he is trying to foster in them the distrust of the conventional critic for that which is outlawed? And does he mean that note of discouragement to creep into his article at the possible effect his mother-in-law's austerity may have upon them? Surely if this has any truth in it, Mr. Hapgood's words about his father seem to us to be very applicable to himself—when he says: "My father in whose veins flows the purest New England blood and in whom the inherited spirit of Puritanism is very strong . . ."

The puritanical spirit can go no farther, it seems to us, than to assume the character of lawlessness that order may result from the disastrous example.

We hope our interpretation of Mr. Hapgood's article will not prove oppressive to him, because it pleases us very much.

And then finally one day Hutch burst into a really fine "apologia," in which he said:

> . . . I am accused of having an unreasoning and unreasonable interest in all things that are generally condemned by the community, such as cubist art, the I.W.W., the turkey trot, criminals, Mrs. Pankhurst, Mayor Gaynor, etc. Letters come in saying with varying degrees of passion, that I am a revolutionist, a skulking member of the Socialist party, an anarchist, an immoral person, an undesirable citizen.
>
> Let me take the simple statement which really covers all the rest, that I merely defend and exalt what is generally condemned; that I do this irrespective of the merits of the case, and simply in order to defend the extremely small minority, just because it is the minority, irrespective of whether the minority is right or wrong; that I attack the powerful and prevailing thing, in art, industry, in all fields, just because it is prevailing, irrespective of the merits of the case; that my formula is a simple and false one, which I apply and reapply with mechanical and monotonous precision.
>
> Perhaps the easiest way of replying is to admit that this criticism is in part true. I believe that the prevailing opinion is often wrong, that it gets in the way of true understanding, of the widest justice, and of the greatest beauty. I believe that the prevailing standards in art, politics, industry, literature, and morality are uninteresting and unvital, and that they stand in the way of true progress and of intenser and fuller life for all of us. I believe in what is sometimes called a revaluation of existing values, a fresh taking of moral stock, a strenuous accounting with ourselves and our institutions.

He went on to explain that he was a revolutionist because he believed that in any organized society there is a perpetual need to go back to first principles, "of showing that men are getting away in their actions and thoughts, from the deep moral ideals of the race." He explained that all the insurgents in politics, in art, in labor, are in that

sense revolutionary in that they want to change the present commer-
cialized, standardized, and crystallized system of society and put it
"back in line with the undying, old, deep ideals and lofty hopes of the
race when it has thought and felt most highly and most intensely."
And that, he explained, is really conservatism, not Revolution as it is
understood. He said that Jesus himself, though he attacked the institutions of his day, was really a conservative. He was trying to bring
men back to a realization of their own deepest wishes.

Hutch did admit, in this article, that the majority of the persons
representing this "insurgent-conservatism" were unworthy of the
cause; that the cause was far greater than they. And he admitted, too,
that often "they make a moral error of throwing over the fundamental
ideals themselves, in their eagerness to attack particular persons and
institutions which they think or pretend to think are wrong."

The reason I am telling so much about this "apologia" of Hutch's
is because I believe it expresses very clearly the opinion of many of
us today, over twenty years later. It formulates our own vague and
half-realized ideas.

He explained that he was and always had been a member of the
so-called "privileged class"; a part of the prevailing order. He said:

> I am helped by a whole set or system of circumstances which have noth-
> ing to do with my individual value. It is unjust that I should have so many
> privileges.
> But I am not content with my privileges. I want more, not only for
> myself but for my class—for the privileged class. I want the final luxury
> of assisting those forces in the community which I think are helping us to
> realize more fully our ideals. . . .
> I want to assist in my way all the forces in the community,—in art,
> education, politics, industry, which seem to me to be calculated, whatever
> they may consciously hold as a program, to increase the self-controlling,
> self-determining democracy of the community. . . .

His remarks about news were amusing. He said that *real* news was
connected, not with the weight of the interests of the day, but with
such appearances and events as were hopefully insisting on a reawak-
ening of our eternally conservative (though slumbering) ideals. A
newspaper should be engaged only with the *news*—with that in the
community which is *developing*. . . . In this way, he said, he criticized
in his articles the false and limited standards of penology, ideas about

criminality, our excessive respect for the respectable, our hatred of what interferes with our immediate interests.

Of course, he irritated and agitated people. He knew that; but agitation is the road to greater life—everyone tends to be lazy, to want to stay where he is. Routine saves effort. . . .

All the movements of that day that Hutch encouraged in his *feuilletons* (and his was sometimes the *only* good word they got) have been working themselves out to reality. The rebel artists he stood up for, the prison reforms, the eight-hour day, birth control and all the other controls, are here! The people he encouraged by a helping word have arrived or died along the way! Frank Tannenbaum is now an authority on prisons and has done a great deal to help reform conditions in them; but Hutch was the only one who had a sympathetic and interpretative line on him then. John Reed was accompanied on his first radical adventure by the deep, soft boom of Hutch speaking in his little *Globe* articles. The Labor leaders of that time—"Big Bill" Haywood, Carlo Tresca, Elizabeth Gurley Flynn—could always count on his sympathetic explanations. Today he would not have to fight so hard for free speech or the right to stand up for his opinions. Night after night on the radio we get our open forum. Our sedition! Government is assailed and the speakers are not gagged. The communists of today do not have to battle about for their "inalienable right" to free speech; they have it! America is all one big Hyde Park, with everybody up on a soap-box expressing himself. Well, Hutch started it, I do believe! (Oh, dear old Hutch! Writing of you brings back those days so clearly! How we talked and talked, and laughed withal! How eager we were, and how hopeful. . . . Can I, I wonder, interpret now the contacts I had with all of these people as broadly and with as much understanding as you did years ago when you were my guide through the labyrinths of character and endeavor? I will do my best.)

All that autumn Hutch and I were growing more and more attached to each other. Hutch, because I was such a perfect listener, so entirely understanding; I, because he was such a perfect listener and so entirely understanding. We told each other everything and we talked about our souls to our hearts' content. Each of us knew what the other meant. We sorrowed over each other and felt our mutual woe. We both felt like failures from the angle of worldly success, and we were proud of it, and we considered each other to be failures—and this drew us together into a luxurious, rich companionship. We thought we were the only ones in the world who longed for perfection; Hutch used to laugh and tell me James said to him once: "I cannot understand this mad unbridled lust for the absolute!"—but it seemed to us we would long for it till we left this life.

Once I wrote a poem for him and this is it:

MY BELOVÈD

I went from the house to seek out my belovèd.
All along in the street in the dusk I sought after him,
And soon I knew that he surely was near me
From the old immemorial thrill in my heart.

All along in the street dark shadows moved by me,
And among their dim shapes I eagerly sought him.
In my passing a blind old cripple caught at my heart,
And turning, I found in his eyes my belovèd.

Emma Goldman printed it in the mazagine called *Mother Earth*.

The reason we felt like failures was because we knew the world could not understand us—not our innermost selves. We could be superior and laugh at the world together in an ecstasy of companionship, and we knew we understood it, though we were beyond it.

It was not enough to meet in New York several times a week, we also frequently wrote long letters to each other. Hutch would write:

Hastings-on-Hudson.

DEAREST MABEL:

I was much moved by some of the things you said to me the other day. I hope you are right about yourself and believe you are. At any rate, you seem to be. You are a long way ahead of me. Sometimes I think I am not even on the road to that independence from the old self-conscious and social-and-sex-needing life. It is—the direction—more in my head, I fear, than in my nature. It is pathetic—that soul in me which jealously guards all that has been—will not let anything go!—Not a thing! I think Weiniger and Bergson (in that speech we heard) referred only to the self-conscious stage. My soul is the soul of that stage and has I fear little to do with the stage that is to come. I groan in my slavery and wish to have one unself-conscious moment—one moment of full cosmic sympathy. But I never have had even *one* moment. I see the thing you seem to have, but do not feel it. I want it only with my imagination, not with my temperament.

So you moved me deeply. I felt, not envy, but a kind of jealousy. I wanted to be with you, more than I ever have, but couldn't. You seemed farther away from me than ever—inaccessible. And I wanted to be near you more than I have ever wanted—far more! O, that terrible strenuousness that makes us strive for what we have not, even when our Natures recognize it as alien! I want the Beyond, but I want it to have the qualities of the Here! Impossible, maddening.

HUTCH.

When I first used to go out there to stay over night with the Hapgoods, it depressed me. It seemed so quiet, so lifeless. (Or was it I who was lifeless?) Anyway, I wrote Hutch a note—we were always writing our thoughts to each other at any odd moment—and I said I couldn't get *into* their atmosphere out there, that I felt insulated, like one looking in from the dark night through the glass windows; looking at it but not part of it or even able to be. This angered Hutch. He wrote back to me that there was something evil deep down in me.

Hutch's brother, Norman, had been with Steffens as dramatic critic. He was also a radical, but not quite so red a one as Hutch. He was the editor, now, of *Collier's Weekly,* a magazine that was considered very broadminded. He was thin where Hutch was solid and thick— and cold-minded where Hutch was warm. But he was a radical, just the same.

Then they had another brother living in the Middle West. This was Billy. He wasn't radical at all. He was a business man and he managed the family affairs. Now while Hutch and Norman were there in New York, living intellectual lives, being broadminded, advocating "public ownership," and other communistic principles, Billy ran the factory that gave them their incomes. They thought he was running it as people always had run factories, and so he was until one day he told them he had decided to turn it into a co-operative plant, giving all the employees their shares in the production.

Hutch and Norman were perfectly scandalized. "Why, Billy, you can't do that! You can't jeopardize the family's interests like that!"

"Sure I can!" answered he. "It's to the family's interest to do it. It's good business!" Now, all these years later, Norman advertises the very successful products on the radio!

56

Hutch was always talking about me to everyone in those days, telling them I was wonderful and making them want to know me, and
so Norman asked to be brought to see me. I invited him to dine, together with Hutch and Neith, and I think I did look nice in long
green and white things, with a silver net over my hair. In the salon
afterward, over coffee and liqueurs—more and more green chartreuse—
Norman grew more and more coldly warmed and his eyes glinted
kindly. He grew comfortably confidential and said he must leave his
magazine and take another tack, but he didn't know what to do.

I leaned forward and exclaimed in a soft voice: "Why not let *It*
decide?"

Hutch and I always talked about It. We knew what we meant:
that inner intuitive guidance that never fails one. Norman gave me
a sweet look, affectionately pouring me some more chartreuse. I felt
oracular myself, not to be treated indulgently. I felt I knew things. I
certainly felt I knew Norman would be better off for a little more faith
in the guiding spirit that Hutch and I called It.

But Norman was different. He was brittle and sure of his own
faculties. I asked Hutch the next day what he said. I knew he'd say
something. Hutch laughed and ran his hand over my hair:

"Oh, he's not *open,* you know. He *said,* as a matter of fact, well—
'Your little friend looks as though she'd be very sweet to go to bed
with, but as a counselor . . .' "

I broke in, very mad: "I suppose that's the way men talk when they
get together!"

3

When Hutch first took me to see Emma Goldman, I felt quite nervous as we climbed the flight of stairs to her apartment. I knew she
stood for killing people if necessary.

They called this Direct Action. And I knew, too, that she and her
group had been close to the act. Alexander Berkman had tried to kill
Henry Frick, and had been in jail for it for many years. Ben Reitman, Emma's present lover, was what was called a dangerous man.
These people were not intellectual anarchists like dear Hutch living
safely with Neith and the children. They lived under the constant
espionage of the police. I dreaded going into the apartment.

But what a warm, jolly atmosphere, with a homely supper on the table, and Emma herself like a homely, motherly sort of person giving everyone generous platefuls of beefsteak (they were great meat eaters) and fried potatoes! She didn't look wild or frightening. She looked to me, from the very first, rather like a severe but warm-hearted school teacher and I am sure that that was, essentially, what she was: a teacher, with a very prognathous jaw.

What will power! Sheer strength in that jaw and no sensitiveness. Berkman, or Sasha, as they called him, was a heavy-jawed man, too, bald in front, with veiled eyes and thick lips. Hutch always said there was something very sweet in him, but I never could see it, though I tried. After I got to know him well, Sasha tried to kiss me in a taxi once and this scared me more than murder would have done. I don't know why.

I felt, though, that first time, that I wanted these people to think well of me. They were the kind that *counted*. They had authority. Their judgment was somehow true. One did not want their scorn.

In the year 1913 the idea of taking a life was terrifying and abhorrent to everyone. Human life was infinitely precious; and to deprive another of it was the ultimate offense, as it was also needful of the greatest courage. No wonder, then, I approached the anarchists with a mixture of wonder, horror, and admiration. Perhaps, though, horror prevailed, since I couldn't face Berkman's kiss.

But it wasn't only the idea that he was a murderer that repelled me. No, it was another fear that remained always at the bottom of me. The need to be admired, even revered, and looked up to, threw me into a panic at the slightest sign of inconsiderate treatment. I knew men and their thoughts. I couldn't bear to have anyone think that my anomalous situation, that made me my own protector, was any augury of light behavior or undignified self-indulgence.

I was serious and I wanted everyone to know it. When Leo Stein said I was the most serious person he had ever known, it pleased me immensely. Berkman's kiss, his eyes half closed, his red mouth expressing nothing but an impersonal hunger, filled me with fear and indignation. The hackneyed but universal phrase, "I am not that kind of a girl," springs, perhaps, from every female heart wishing to appear sacred in the eye of man, man, whom we long to find godly!

Emma and Sasha and the rest of them accepted me because Hutch vouched for me. They all loved him, though he did a great deal to make their cause weaker, in a way, because, by writing sympathetically of them, he helped remove the terror of them from people's minds. He was always bringing different kinds of people together and neutralizing their power.

I saw quite soon, in my New York life, it was only the separations between different kinds of people that enabled them to have power over each other. I remember Lincoln Steffens and Hutch both said, later, that Bill Haywood never made another really convincing and impassioned speech against capitalism after he knew me and came to the Evenings. He hated capitalists until he knew them. When he knew us, he couldn't hate us very much.

But though Emma and her bunch (as they were always called in distinction from Bill Haywood and *his* bunch, or Carl and *his* bunch) had confidence in me and came easily to my house, still I always felt a reserve there that was never broken through. I felt they had Plans. I knew they had. I knew they continually plotted and planned and discussed times and places. Their obvious activity seemed to be publishing the anarchist magazine, *Mother Earth,* but beneath this there was a great busy humming complex of Planning; and many times they referred to the day when blood would flow in the streets of New York.

That day was to be, truly, their blissful and perfect consummation, to be lived for, to be worked for, and sacrificed for. Any one of them would have died to bring it quicker, for they were all sturdy, robust people, unafraid of death. There was blood in the air that year—there truly was. One was constantly reminded of it.

Emma was the mainspring of her group. The one who had the initiative, the judgment, and the strength. The others were her hands, though they, too, were strong thinkers. Berkman had a good brain and his book about his years in prison is pretty strong material.

I remember we had a correspondence over the thing he wrote in his book for me:

Dear Berkman,

You have asked me to write you an article for *Mother Earth*. I wonder what you want me to write about? Perhaps you want me to define my attitude towards anarchism. You wrote in your volume of Prison Memoirs:

59

To Mabel Dodge, for a deeper social consciousness and a more perfect crystallization of a definite goal to make the world a better place to live in for men and women.

Now any crystallization seems to me only an opportunity for further disintegration. A new spring board from which to leap forward towards new truth. It seems to me that no sooner has an idea become crystallized into an institution, a habit, or even a *party,* than it is ready for some spiritual dynamiting—the life that is in it released, and put once more in movement, for only in movement is there any liberty, and life can only develop under freedom.

I do not believe or disbelieve in marriage, but I do believe in love, which may exist either within the institution or outside of it, providing that it is free. Free love seems to me that love which has been released from any limitation of personality or self-seeking, and which finds its fullest expression in service.

I cannot imagine myself ever crystallizing into an anarchist or a socialist, any more than into a "society woman" or a Roman Catholic, because to become the member of a party signifies to me the exclusion of other parties. But I can conceive of being a woman of the world, taken in its broadest meaning—or a Humanitarian.

When I met Emma Goldman, my heart went out to her because she is a fine human being, not because she is an anarchist. Her genius lies, to my mind, in her rich capacious nature, and in the deep love of humanity that she has always given so abundantly to all who asked it, and to even those who have not asked it.

The party does not interest me, the individual does. His service is what counts. What difference does it make where he operates? The party and its "crystallized and definite goal"? Well, perhaps for some, but not for me. Some people are impelled to action by a definite goal, others, without any specific goal beyond love of progress in any of its aspects, are able day by day to illumine and enhance life for those with whom they come in contact, and this merely by the fact of their existence, and the love within them for all humanity, and in doing so they are making the world a better place for other men and women.

It seems to me that our friend Hutchins Hapgood is a good example of this. He is the true citizen of the universe, and he belongs to no party, rather he belongs to *all* individuals. I repeat what I said to you the other night: The true ideal with the largest reach would be to have *one* group of disorganized individuals if each carried in his heart just one essential— the love of *all*.

And so I am with you as one human being to another—and it is summed up better than I can say it in the words of Edward Carpenter—which you know.

Yours faithfully,

MABEL DODGE.

FRIEND MABEL:

I knew you did not like what I wrote in the volume, when you so unenthusiastically murmured, "Very good."

I did not write in your book what I wanted. What I wanted I did not know clearly. But I wanted—and I want—am wanting something. Your offer of friendship has gladdened my heart.

"A more perfect crystallization of a definite goal." I despair of clarifying myself to you on paper. I did not agree with Havel that all discussion is vain. It is only superficially true. Words indeed are poverty-stricken things, lacking blood and vitality. Yet personal contact and understanding does not depend entirely on words. Intuition and presence help where speech or expression fails. But the written word is almost hopeless.

I shall therefore not attempt to discuss all you said in your letter, except to make a few disconnected remarks.

"A more perfect crystallization of a definite goal" was badly put. Will you understand me if I explain my meaning to have been: "A more perfect individual crystallization of a definite purpose"?

If "only in movement is there any liberty and life can only go on developing under liberty" may be taken as the keynote of your life's music, then believe me, dear friend, we are by no means as far apart as I fear my unhappy remark in your book has caused you to assume. What you say of parties, dogmas, etc., I subscribe to, heartily.

Yet one thing—we are not monists but dualists. At least I am; if not a dualist, at any rate, a duality. And the Anarchist philosopher in me would agree with you entirely, but the Anarchist propagandist in me will not. The propagandist must, in a considerable degree, be a fanatic and even hate where the human in him yearns to love. This is perhaps the severest struggle in the inner life of such a one, and his deepest tragedy.

Your friend,

A. B.

4

At about the same time that year there was a Greek who came to my Evenings each week. His name was John Rompapas and he had a handsome head on a handsome body. Black hair and the darkest brown eyes far apart in his strong face. He was serious! My heavens, yes! He was heavy with it, and he was good. He wrote out all his ideas and sent them to me on blue-lined foolscap paper, calling it a "Book of His Life" that he was making for me.

Here is the letter that preceded them:

DEAR MABEL:

How I can see at the mirror of your thoughts! You say: "I love some-*one* better than anybody else." This statement in your letter clears everything. I am glad to hear a truth.

"Some day we may be good friends." But that does not mean that *friendship* might be established between us. (Yet, who knows?)

I believe that two of the same sex can be friends while their relation is passive. Also, two of different sex can be friends if their relation will be also passive. For similar state of existence we find also among inanimate beings—fixed stars, for instance—keeping the whole balance of their Society's existence.

But friendship is something *active* and can only exist in a relationship which is not passive.

In order to exist a very intimate friendship, they must have constituted formerly—whole or part—an existence of one body in another form—(I believe in science but not in reincarnation) and soon or late our sixth sense recognizes this.

Thus active friendship is established, and no extra qualities for friendship are required. Friendship is love is life— They like each other because they know each other.

I am a believer of "the absolute order of everything" and through constant study of natural phenomena (with no books) I have formed my own theories.

Little by little and week or month after month, you will receive (if you care) my book—my theory—my belief—at present I will say that I would love to see you—to know you better. But this desire *must be mutual*.

If a sixth or a seventh sense will ever be conceivable to us, we will see that we are not any better than anything else existing. For only through our feelings appears a difference in quality.

"Love is what holds in together the combination of atoms" and only as a combination we differ. And as we cannot recollect the reason of our first combination it is justifiable, this feeling of "preference for the best."

So as a Student of Life and seeker of the absolute "Perfect" I am like a *bee* collecting nectar and departing without injuring the flower.

Faithfully yours,

JOHN ROMPAPAS.

One of these "chapters" he called "Above Everything" and in it he tried to formulate his effort to individuate himself. These were the days when people in America were beginning to emerge from the collectivism of the past, were trying here and there to think for themselves and to be themselves.

John Rompapas was a good example of this. He had drawn himself up out of the life of an employee, where he had been only a cog in the machine, and he had, as he described it, gone on strike just by himself. As his life, he wrote, had been forced to grow under conditions, and as everyone lived all the time with "an adopted and enslaved ego" put upon them by the present system, the *feelings* he had he was obliged to consider as part of his life, and the experiences he had been through, under the system, as errand boy, clerk, and so on, were valuable to show him just how low an estimate he could place on himself while living in a so-called civilized society.

"It is very hard for me to express the feeling of going on strike alone, for it is strange, and, in a way, an unusual act. To go on strike as a member of an organization, on account of a general walkout, we feel certain strength, for our attempt at bettering our conditions is not as discouraging as it would seem if we went on strike alone. . . ."

"They wanted more wages," he wrote, "and they did not know that an increase of wages does not necessarily mean better existence." More abundant life was what John Rompapas was after! It appeared in his pages that he had a deeper understanding than most people of true communism.

He continued: "As I was also on strike, I said that either I was a fool, or the workers, all of them, did not know and feel why they worked and why they lived!"

He was free—he moved about, going from city to city. By constant effort he reduced his working hours to three a day "and even then I could not justify my work! I was doing nothing, really, for I was not producing things we absolutely need; and as I had felt over and over again, I realized that *every kind of work except farming is parasitical*, and it is immaterial whether we work, tramp, beg, or preach. . . ."

The thing we need, when once we realize we are above everything, that there is earth to walk on, and enough to eat on that earth, he said, is love. In those days the unemployment problem was a minor one. Really people could always ask for a meal and get it. But the great fundamental need of life, hard to fulfill without searching, was love between those of equal development. "Love just for the gratification of sex will never suffice. . . . When we meet an equal-to-us person we feel happy and content even if this person happens to be of the same sex."

So he met Anthony who was his *alter ego.* They moved about together, talking endlessly and trying to understand life more clearly. "In perfect understanding of feeling, one day arguing with Anthony on different conditions, we both simultaneously asked: 'Why names?' As the question was from the feeling to get out of this present system of ownership, we felt our reasoning was above the average, and our next question from another feeling was: 'Are we sane?' "

Rompapas, along with others near and far away from him, was thus struggling out towards a revulsion of the old values. *That same struggle is going on today.* It has advanced a good deal in twenty years. Many people now have individualized themselves up out of the collective mass and are in the transition state—being neither one thing nor the other, belonging nowhere. The world is full of lost souls, creatures who have lost their moorings, who have broken out of the pattern of established life and are whisked about with no sense of either past or future. They don't know whether they're going or coming, or what it is all about. It takes a good, strong person to go on strike all by himself, like John Rompapas, and not be destroyed. The worst feature of our highly individualized aggregation of disparate units is that we all dislike each other so! That was what made Lawrence's life so miserable. He wanted to like people but he couldn't. He was too individual in his reactions. He didn't throb in unison with the other numbered or unnumbered terrestrial souls!

John Rompapas didn't realize that he was breaking away from the tribe, the hive, the herd he belonged to, in order to develop some richer consciousness that he would employ perhaps in some future incarnation, or preferably expressed, that he would deposit into the racial reservoir, later on to be reassembled in some fine communal formation too far away and unknown to man for him to dream of, or for any of us even now to imagine in actuality, yet lived towards, assumed, accepted in advance and to be reached only when we have grown mature enough.

Communism is no empty dream. I mean it is no *empty* dream,

though it *is* a dream. It is the inevitable goal which our evolution intends us to reach. We are going there, no matter how many of us fall along the way. But it will not be as the communists of today picture it, I am sure. The communal life at a new level is something no man alive can prognosticate, nor any man prevent. All right! In the meantime, listen to how some of these broke the earlier molds and tried to make better ones, discarded though they have been.

The Evenings were established presently and John Rompapas was always there. He began to watch me with sincere and patient admiration that I accepted gravely, and he sent me cases of delicious, sweet, yellow, Greek wine.

But one time he came on an evening that was not an Evening, and, leaning towards me, his dark eyes swimming, he tried to kiss me. I put him gently away from me, and didn't show any anger or any other feeling. I just smiled mysteriously, the way one can do, but my heart was broken. I had become so sensitive, living exposed to the world without any husband, so jealous of anything that seemed to doubt my sexual seriousness, that I couldn't endure the idea that these men, whom I had allowed to come to my house freely, to find stimulation and refreshment in my hospitality, should assume that it extended to such liberties with me.

I told Hutch about it the next day, sobbing and dabbing my eyes. "Why *should* he do such a thing?" I wailed. "Why should they dare to think I am open to them just because I haven't an old husband spying around here!"

Hutch understood my feelings perfectly. With tears in his eyes—of sympathy, and weariness at the nature of man, and compassion for all women at their mercy. I felt better after I'd cried and he comforted me.

After this, Rompapas felt maybe I did not care for his book any more and he wrote me:

DEAR MABEL,
If this is no pleasure for you, nothing justifies an act which is not based on mutuality.

Am I not right? I am *not* writing *because* I *promised*—you must not receive because you promised.

For that will not be right. Is it not so?

JOHN ROMPAPAS.

John Rompapas turned away from me then, to Margaret Sanger, who was at the beginning of her Birth Control movement. He helped her a great deal. He was a good man and had solid qualities.

5

One of Hutch's best friends was Steff. Lincoln Steffens had been the city editor of the *Commercial Advertiser* in past years when Hutch was a reporter and Neith worked in his office, and later he had become managing editor of *McClure's*.

McClure's Magazine was perhaps the finest magazine this country has ever had. Of course, old McClure, Steff says, knew how to pick winners. He knew genius when he saw it and he gathered it up. First and last there were some wonderful people in that changing group: Ida Tarbell, Ray Stannard Baker, Witter Bynner, Willa Cather. McClure was enthusiastic about Willa Cather's quality before she wrote her first book, when she was there in the office. "Steff," he would say, "she's wonderful. She has genius. You'll see."

Lincoln Steffens had invented "muckraking" and had gone from city to city cleaning up politics, and these revelations appeared in *McClure's*. He was a delicately built little man, very flexible in his movements and with a rapier-keen mind. His brown hair came down on his forehead in a little bang, and he had sparkling steel-blue eyes shining through gold-rimmed spectacles, and a sudden, lovely smile.

Steff had a way of flashing up the corners of his mouth in that almost rigid sudden smile. He called himself the only Christian on earth and he wore a plain gold cross hanging on his solar plexus attached to his watch chain. There was a story about that. Steff loved his power over people and he had a professional sweetness in dealing with people that no one seemed able to resist—a forcing gentle tenderness. He had gone to Los Angeles to write up the story of the McNamara bomb when the gang blew up the big building, and he wormed his way, delicate like a thin blade, into the confidence of the prisoners who were being held for trial.

He told everyone that Christianity would work and he would prove it—so he determined to settle the whole affair before the men were ever tried. First he went to the "big business men" and got hold of them. He asked them whether they would promise not to proceed against the McNamaras if he could secure their admission of guilt. It was all a gamble because, as I recall it, there was no good evidence against them and several others escaped—in particular, one man called Schmitty. There was a $10,000 reward offered for *his* capture.

The "big business men" gave in to Steff's quiet power and promised. Then he went to the McNamaras and worked on them, telling them the bosses had agreed to the bargain. They wouldn't talk for a long time—they couldn't believe in Steffens's assurances. But finally he wore down their resistance and they told him everything. And the "big business men" went back on their word and got a life sentence for the Mc-Namaras, and Clarence Darrow, even then the biggest criminal lawyer in America, cried in court and Steff bought that gold cross and put it on as a kind of badge of failure—and what the McNamaras thought no one knew, for they decided silence was the better part after all and they never would say another word to people but set their jaws and went to rot in prison.

Steff couldn't get over it. He started to work for their pardon. So Steff was always interviewing governers. Sometimes he was almost successful. His friends got used to Steff's journeys off to interview governors. And what the McNamaras went through, never being able to accept their situation, but kept on tenterhooks of suspense, no one could judge. Steff was always reporting to them, his hopes, his failures. Finally, I believe one of them sent him word to give up, let it go. But Steff couldn't. By his personal influence he had put them there; by the same he must get them released. But he never succeeded.

In those days Steff—the little man—liked large equine women. One well-known woman had been a love of his. He had appeared on her horizon somewhere out west, and captivated her completely. But he seemed to like to dazzle their minds and then dance off. Undoubtedly what he loved was his power over people rather than the people themselves. After subjugating her, who thought she was subjugating him, he flickered away. But she was not the kind of woman that is easily abandoned. She pursued him to New York and camped upon his trail. She became another Nemesis. What is so relentless as conquest?

Steff's friends had to protect him from the determined women who went after him when he was through, claiming him, insisting upon his love, declaring they could not do their work unless he returned to them. One of these was not loath to talk about her dilemma. She told us all about it. What she needed, she said, was to have him come back to her and let *her* be the one to withdraw. It appeared to be not so much a wound to the heart as to her sense of power.

Well, power against power—Steff had more, the gentle, little, steel man. He was always free then because he did not know how to love. He learned later when Pete, his little boy, was born.

He was very kind and amused and patient, and he was without the tragic sense of life that Hutch had, so, one felt, tragedy would never really touch him. He would know how to dodge it and flit away. Well—he was safe all those years.

He always had an influence on young people and enjoyed having it, and there was always a small devil in him that liked to play with dynamite in human souls.

He always believed in the young. Twenty-five years ago when he was on *Everybody's Magazine,* he told his directors that they ought to be hunting out some new, young writers. They asked him where he thought he could find them and he replied: "I can find them. You wait and see," and he went to Harvard University and asked several of the professors there for lists of the likeliest boys they had in their senior classes.

One name that appeared on several of these lists was that of Walter Lippmann. So Steff sought him out and told him to report to him when he had graduated, and he returned to the magazine office and told the staff he had found a new writer. Of course they laughed at him—and they put the issue up to him in the form of a gamble. "You take him on, then, Steffens; call him your Secretary, if you like. Give him a chance to write—to prove himself, and at the end of six months if he has done anything worth while we will pay for it." Of course Walter did!

It happened that Walter Lippmann's class had a number of other brilliant boys in it. Several "movers and shakers of the world" were graduated with him. For instance, there were John Reed, Robert Edmond Jones, Robert Rogers (he shook the world a few years ago by telling his class at the Boston School of Technology to be snobs!), Lee Simonson, and others.

Steffens had been a friend of Reed's father in Portland, Oregon, and they were both members of the old Bohemian Club in San Francisco. This father went to Steffens and said: "I have a boy graduating at Harvard this year and going to New York afterwards. I think he's a poet; I don't know, though. I wish you'd keep your eye on him." Steff did. He was amused at the antics of the young, and he liked watching them. He put Reed on the *American Magazine* that he was editing at that time but he told Reed he didn't want him to really *work*. Reed didn't. Steff even went down to live with a group of boys of whom Reed was one, in that famous, ramshackle old house at 42 Washington Square South. It was kept by a couple of frowsy old landladies who cursed these young men when their rent was overdue and who nursed them when they were sick.

Reed wrote a long, gay poem called "A Day in Bohemia" while he was living there, and he dedicated it to Steff. In it he describes the place that was Steff's one-time New York home. He had had many homes. In his Father's House there have been, indeed, many mansions. This little, Machiavellian, itinerant preacher went up and down upon the earth shaking it in his own way. He said the same things over and over, gently, subtly, and unendingly. As one note, sounded on a violin string in just the right vibration and in sufficient volume, may shatter solid material and bring down a house in ruins, Steff's delicate music undoubtedly had its share in collapsing the civilization of the twentieth century.

6

Margaret Sanger was one of the radical group I came to know in the first months I was in New York. She was the Madonna type of woman, with soft brown hair parted over a quiet brow, and crystal-clear light brown eyes. Eyes that were of a one-toned brown, not fusing and mixing with other shades as in the case of more complex natures. She had a husband, Bill Sanger, who tried to paint, and two children.

It was she who introduced to us all the idea of Birth Control, and it, along with other related ideas about Sex, became her passion. It was as if she had been more or less arbitrarily chosen by the powers that be to voice a new gospel of not only sex knowledge in regard to conception, but sex knowledge about copulation and its intrinsic importance.

She was the first person I ever knew who was openly an ardent propagandist for the joys of the flesh. This, in those days, was radical indeed when the sense of sin was still so indubitably mixed with the sense of pleasure. Physical pleasure was, at its two extremes, made either into a sly, secret indulgence attributed to weak and regressing natures not only by the ones who sat in judgment but also by those who defiantly went their way in the pursuit of this little illicit delight, or else its pursuit was extolled by the so-called beyond good and evil philosophers like Nietzsche, who believed themselves supermen because, notwithstanding its sinful character, even because of its sinful character, they overcame its taboo in order to count themselves strong.

Either way it was certainly of questionable value. Margaret Sanger, then, was the first person that I, personally, knew, who set out to rehabilitate it, for never, not even in pagan times, so far as I know, was it accorded a scientific, wholly dignified and prophylactic part of right living—no, she was one of its first conscious promulgators.

Margaret Sanger was an advocate of the flesh. It was her belief that the attitude towards sex in the past of the race was infantile, archaic, and ignorant, and that mature manhood meant accepting the life in the cells, developing it, experiencing it, and enjoying it with a conscious attainment of its possibilities that would make previous relationships between men and women, with their associations of smirking shame and secretive lubricities, seem ignoble in their limitations and stupid beyond words in their awkward ignorance.

For Margaret Sanger to attempt what she did at that time seems to me now like another attempt to release the energy in the atom, and who knows but perhaps that best describes what she tried to do.

Her efforts to establish clinics where poor (as well as rich!) women could learn the prevention of conception, did not interest me so much as her ideas on sex life, though I was one of the first group to meet and discuss the possibilities of forming such clinics, and did my best to draw others in, others, Walter Lippmann, for instance, from whom I still have a letter telling his doubts of such dubious clinics and saying, "Besides, Margaret Sanger is not the person to do it."

But Margaret Sanger did do it.

No, it was in talking to her at home in my sitting room that I really got something from her, something new and releasing and basic. Nina and I, I remember, had a wonderful talk with her one evening—just the three of us at dinner—when she told us all about the possibilities in the body for "sex expression"; and as she sat there, serene and quiet, and unfolded the mysteries and mightinesses of physical love, it seemed to us we had never known it before as a sacred and at the same time a scientific reality.

Love I had known, and pleasures of the flesh, but usually there had been a certain hidden, forbidden something in my feeling about it and experience of it that made it seem stolen from life, instead of a means to that great end, the development of life, and the growth of the soul.

Margaret Sanger made it appear as the first duty of men and women. Not just anyhow, anywhere, not promiscuity, for that defeated its own end if pleasure were the goal; not any man and any woman, but the conscious careful selection of a lover that is the mate, if only for an hour—for a lifetime, maybe.

Then she taught us the way to a heightening of pleasure and of prolonging it, and the delimiting of it to the sexual zones, the spreading out and sexualizing of the whole body until it should become sensitive and alive throughout, and complete. She made love into a serious undertaking—with the body so illumined and conscious that it would be able to interpret and express in all its parts the language of the spirit's pleasure.

One day she gave me a paper of Professor Kirschman of Columbia, another of those who were bringing credit to sex and who also tried to bring some measure of reform into the old, dark, stupid attitudes about it. It was a paper he read in his courses in Social Science but it is still too esoteric a subject to permit a reprint of it here, although it is an attempt to give a degree of instruction in sexual intercourse for the promotion of health and the prevention of divorce.

These things are better understood today. Birth Control has many protagonists now, even in Congress and the Senate. When Margaret Sanger took up the fight she had to face prison for it, to have her house raided to remove pamphlets about it, and to be looked at askance by most "nice women." But she went through with it to success.

We are grateful to you, Margaret Sanger. You helped many women. And you helped me, in particular, to get rid of some old, old prohibitions, and to raise the curse a bit!

7

Hutch had first taken me to "291." This was a tiny gallery on the top floor of a building on Fifth Avenue, and Stieglitz, who stood talking there day after day, was the spirit of the place.

It was one of the few places where I went. It was always stimulating to go and listen to him analyzing life and pictures and people—telling of his strange experiences, greatly magnifying them with the strong lenses of his mental vision. His eyes, themselves, were like two powerful lenses surrounded by dark shades, and when he turned them upon one they burned through to the core.

He was always struck by the Wonder of Things, and after a visit to him, one's faith in the Splendid Plan was revived. I owe him an enormous debt I can never repay. He was another who helped me to See—both in art and in life. His belief was that he never gave in to anything except what he believed to be the best; that he never did anything for money or prestige or power, that he cared only for what he called the spirit of life, and that when he found it, he fostered it. If, like the rest of us he was in the dark regarding the masks of his colossal egotism, what of it? Only so could he get things done.

At "291" I met people who became the friends of a lifetime. There we gathered over and over again, drawn and held together by the apparent purity of Stieglitz's intention. He was afraid of nothing, and always trusted his eyes and his heart. Before the First International Exhibition he had already sponsored some of what were called the craziest painters in America—Marin and Walkowitz, Arthur Dove and Marsden Hartley, and he gave others like Andrew Dasburg the courage to paint things as they saw them. He provided an *ambiente* where the frightened artist dared to be himself.

I liked to go there with Hutch, for Hutch's sympathy drew him out and he was at his best when Hutch and I were with him. He was a delicate mechanism for registering life, and while his magazine, exquisitely composed and printed, was called *Camera Work,* he himself should have been called Camera Man, for he was that. When he took photographs, the camera and he were one. It was miraculous. No one will ever go beyond Stieglitz in photography.

I met Hartley there at "291"—that gnarled New England spinster-man who came to New York with his tragic paintings of New Hampshire and Maine landscape where the trees were fateful, and Hartley told me how Stieglitz kept him from starving. He sent Hartley to Germany soon after I met him and supported him through the leanest years, as he supported Marin. He showed us some curious black and white drawings by a schoolteacher out west. Presently he hung them on the walls. One in particular was very intriguing: a pair of curtains, one partly drawn to one side but not enough to reveal what they hid behind them. This was the first work we saw of Georgia O'Keeffe.

Andrew Dasburg was one of the most touching people I met at "291." Lame, but slender as an archangel and with a Blake-like rush of fair hair flying upward from off his round head. There were always attractive people at Stieglitz's place. And strange, alluring paintings on the walls that one gazed into while he talked, until, gazing, one entered them and knew them. The critics came there to listen and learn, and to argue among themselves, and Stieglitz educated many of them: Henry McBride, Gregg, Forbes Watson, Ralph Flint, and others.

In those early years he launched nearly all those painters who count today in America and without a particle of apprehension he hung up the work of artists whom the physicians diagnosed as paranoiacs and *dementia-praecox* cases.

The doctors couldn't see the difference between organization and disorganization. Because the patients in insane asylums made queer drawings and paintings, the doctors thought the artists who made pictures that looked queer to them were also insane. I asked Dr. Bernard Sachs for a card to Dr. Gregory at Bellevue so I could go and see for myself wherein they differed and wherein they resembled each other, but though he sent me the card, he disapproved completely of my wish to make such comparisons, and he said he thought it would be advisable for some of those artists themselves to apply for admission to the psychopathic ward: that the exhibition at the Armory was the best evidence of mental derangement flaunted in public he had ever seen and he advised me to keep out of it.

Stieglitz, however, never dashed, has lived long enough to see his psychopaths revered. What a dauntless spirit he had! Reviled by all the academic artists and critics, considered a freak, betrayed by some of the boys he had stood by and to whom he had given a chance to emerge from nowhere—Stieglitz was somehow tragic but never overcome.

CHAPTER IV

The Evenings

THROUGH these first contacts in New York it was not long before I had gathered a large collection of new acquaintances, for whenever I made a friend like Carl, or Hutch, or Steff, then they brought their friends to see me. Carl brought Donald Evans, and Jack and Helen Westley, Fania, and Justus Sheffield. The latter was also a friend of Hutch and Neith. And Carl brought Pitts Sanborn, another young musical critic, and Avery Hopwood, the dramatist.

The first of these, Donald Evans, was a strange genius. He was pale and thin, with that Welsh type of slabsided face that is as flat as a board. He had a long upper lip and narrow, dark, brooding eyes that seemed dead at times but that saw everything. He wrote strange Imagist poetry when he had the time and the energy for it, but his job, which was copy-reading on the *New York Times,* exhausted him. I showed some of his verse to Edwin Arlington Robinson, and he was interested in it and said: "If Evans ever outgrows that greensickness of his, he will make a real poet."

Donald was very much taken with Gertrude Stein's portraits of Matisse and Picasso and even the more esoteric one of "Mabel Dodge at the Villa Curonia," and he began a series of portraits of friends of his that were published in a "slender vol." called *Sonnets from the Patagonian* by the little Claire-Marie Press which he had instituted.

He hoped to do great things. He believed he would be a friend to youth and help them with his little venture. He wrote of it:

Monday.

MY DEAR MRS. DODGE:

Your interest in my book is very sweet to me and you opened up avenues of joy today for me. I cannot live and create without joy, and joy is so rare. To me you seem to be indifferent to "distinct and palpable" happiness, emancipated from humanness. It has struck me several times

74

before, but today I felt it acutely. You seemed very free and the vision of your freedom was intoxicating. But I, notwithstanding, clung to my joy in the bright bitter sunlight of your drawing room.

I feel certain I can arrange to be away from the *Times* Thursday, and shall probably be able to get Claire Burke. I am rather anxious to join in your "row," for I feel much on all sides of the question. That is why I believe Claire-Marie will be a success—its keystone is all sides of the question. I wish I could get you wildly excited about Claire-Marie. I mean the importance of having a publishing house which is fearless, intelligent, aesthetic, fresh and light-hearted, and, above all, commercially successful. An *endowed* house is useless and an invalid pale and chill. Claire-Marie, if it succeeds, means a refuge for the world's glittering ones—and flash and beauty and undulant youth need not go wandering. I think Claire-Marie can easily be made a success. I want your interest terribly, with your help I can make it succeed, then we can put it in other hands for safe keeping, for we cannot give up all our lives to a publishing venture.

Do write me a letter that will help—then your name will be blessed above the Virgin's, and the plan of God's predecessor will be carried out. God, you know, so marred the beautiful original plan that was handed down to him from the last bored Deity.

Donald Evans.

This *fin de siècle* attitude of his was rather boring and old-fashioned but there was something touching and wistfully hopeful in him, too, in the time I knew him, and it creeps out in his letters:

Sunday.

Dear Mabel Dodge:

On Friday I received packet of mss. from Gertrude Stein—new things apparently. Three symposia—with titles for each "Rooms," "Food," "Objects"—all rather delicious and new, beautifully broken up into wisps and flashes. I'm very much pleased. But I am in a quandary. No letter has come—nothing to tell me she accepts my offer—nothing to make me feel free to go ahead.

I shall phone you Monday to learn whether you have heard from her, and to get your advice about proceedings. You see I ought to go to press right away if it is to be out by May 1st, and it must be out by May 1st to get the best publicity before the summer silence sets in.

The mss. are the flashest I've yet seen of G. S. and I'm sanguine of a real success.

I shall phone you about luncheon time.

Faithfully,
Donald Evans.

DEAR MRS. DODGE: *Monday, 5 A.M.*

I kneel to accept the Cimabue trust—we must some day find out his name. I glanced hastily through the poems again and feel more certain I can do something with them. And I will as soon as I can find three clear hours for breathing space.

But all this is of small matter beside the golden voyage I have embarked on—a thousand and one sonnet portraits of you. Of course, I only hope to do ninety-nine, but that will be enough.

I have been up all night doing the first and enclose it. I think it the best sonnet I have ever done. It is flash; it is vervish. I shall feel hurt if you don't like it and my portrait-series idea. You yourself are ineffable; it is quite beyond belief that you exist; I even took pleasure in your quiet wisp of a laugh at me the other day, and so this early April morning I am magnificently glad to be alive, and turn away from my many Boulevards of Death.

DONALD EVANS.

THE LAST DANCE AT DAWN

And she was sad since she could not be sad,
 And every star flared amorous in the sky.
 Her pampered knees fell under her keen eye
And it came to her she would not go mad.
The gaucheries were turning the last screw,
 But there was still the island in the sea,
 The harridan chorus of eternity,
That let her smile because he saw she knew.

She even dared be impudent again,
 And bit his ear; the deaths were far away.
The Bibles orgied in the treasure vaults—
 She tried to rouge her heart, yet quite in vain.
The crucifix danced in, beribboned, gay,
 And lisped to her a wish for the next waltz.

CLAIRE-MARIE, *Publisher*
East Fourteenth Street, No. 3,
New York.

DEAR MRS. DODGE: *Wednesday.*

You may be interested to know that Claire-Marie will publish Gertrude Stein's *Objects: Food: Rooms* on May 1. I had a cable yesterday from her accepting the contract sent her and the ms. is now in the printer's

76

hands. As I wrote you before it is the loveliest piece of work I have yet seen of Miss Stein's.

You promised to write me an introduction, but I shan't have to hold you to it, as Miss Stein stipulated when giving Claire-Marie the ms. that there should be no dedication, introduction, etc.

I phoned you many times—but unsuccessfully—about a week, and then lost courage. I had wanted to get your views on make-up and so forth. However, I've decided on canary with a round green label for the board binding. Modish shades and effective!

If you'd care to send me a list of names of people who'd like to know about the book I'll have letters and catalogues sent them. Also if you'd like to read the book in proof I can arrange for it.

Faithfully,
DONALD EVANS.

The New York Times

Friday.

DEAR WONDERFUL PERSON:

Has Carlovingian Van Vechten ever told you of Allen Norton or his "Convolvulus," the most exquisite comedy ever written? If he has, I am sure you'll be mad with delight when I say that Norton and I are going to produce it early in the Fall. It will be the greatest theatrical sensation since "Cyrano."

Now, on my knees, I beg for your interest in the production. I want you to play one of the rôles, only you can play it. We are not getting professional actors, 'cause they'd spoil the thing. "The Convolvulus" demands artists. The company to produce it will be known as The Mummers. The theater either Maxine Elliott's or Berkeley, with a trip to Philadelphia to the Little Theatre. If it goes well, a series of matinees on Broadway. Allen Norton's wife is in it, and there will be one woman beside you needed. I'm asking Edna Kenton to join it.

The comedy is sheer madness, captivating and amazing. It leaves Gertrude Stein a very illuminating person.

Will you be in town at all this summer? I'll have the script in a few days and I'll send it to you, if you will promise to be interested. Or if you'd care to meet the Nortons I can bring them down anytime next week, literally any time you say, 'cause we're all full and mad over our idea. I'm sure Carl has told you how clever the Nortons are. Please say you will be an actress, remember I'm still on your knees.

Yours breathlessly,
DONALD EVANS.

That sounds odd, but I really meant *my knees.*

Life was too painful to Donald, and he ended it voluntarily a few years later than this period I am telling about. He had left a curiously strong impression upon the friends who were nearest to him and after he died Arthur Ficke wrote me:

Mrs. Maurice Stern,
Taos, N. M.
DEAR MRS. STERN:—

Donald Evans' death last spring has made a few of his friends feel that it would be a great pity if we neglected to preserve a record of his extraordinary personality. A number of us have consulted together with the result that a mad but rather entertaining project has been hit upon. It seemed to us that if twenty or twenty-five people who knew Donald would each one put down his or her own vivid personal picture of Donald, we would get a resulting portrait that would be perfectly delightful in its absurdities and contradictions.

I am writing to ask you whether you will not contribute such a sketch to the book which we have projected. Unless I am mistaken you knew sides of Donald that were not known to everyone, and I feel that your contribution to the book would be one of the very greatest importance.

The book is to be called *The Donald Evans Legend,* and to give you some idea of the character of the book, let me quote the beginning of what we had planned as a "foreword."—

"Probably no figure so mythical as that of Donald Evans has ever had even an imaginary existence. Faust, Til Eulenspiegel, The Wandering Jew, and Haroun al Raschid are all solid, demonstrable, and documented persons in comparison. Already the Evans-Legend has assumed large proportions; in fact, we must even today make a discrimination between the archaic—or as I shall call it, the Uhr-Legend—and the latter and doubtful forms, which I shall call the Neo-Legend. Doubtless exact discrimination between the two is not possible in the present state of our knowledge, and it is with no hope of finality that the present book is written. All that its authors can hope is that it will serve future and more learned students as a convenient compilation of the main legend-elements."

After such a foreword, each contributor can make his sketch as whimsical or as serious as he chooses. The sketches can be long or short. Only one thing will be requested of each contributor, and that is that he make his sketch the vivid personal picture of the Donald Evans he himself knew.

I am very hopeful that the project will interest you, and that you will be willing to contribute. Should any royalties result from the sale of the book they will be used for the benefit of Donald's daughter. It will be entirely a labor of love for everybody concerned, but I trust an amusing one both for the authors and the future readers.

Can you not let me have a contribution from you sometime during the next two months?

Sincerely yours,

ARTHUR DAVISON FICKE.

Nothing ever came of this good intention.

Helen Westley was married to a young actor. She seemed very strange and fascinating to me. Rather oddly like a good-natured lizard, she was dark and slim and quick, and very thin. There was something not unpleasantly reptilian about her, and this strangeness of hers allured the cold, intellectual Sheffield who constantly observed her, out of pale, frozen eyes. He had been at Harvard with Hutch and these two were often to be found in corners together, talking about William James and Royce.

The first Evening I can remember was engineered by Carl, who wanted to bring a pair of Negro entertainers he had seen somewhere who, he said, were marvelous. Carl's interest in Negroes began as far back as that, then. And it continued, taking him to Harlem, bringing Harlem to his apartment later on, so that others came to know that section of New York life, and it eventually grew to be very well known. Everything that took Carl farther away from Cedar Rapids was desirable to him at that time, though later he became conscious of his inexterminable love for it, and for old brick houses set in lawns, with rep-covered furniture and square pianos in them, and he capitulated and reproduced such a room in his apartment.

How Carl loved the grotesque! He loved to twist and squirm with laughter at the oddity of strong contrasts. When he told me he was bringing two Negro entertainers, he said I had to invite some people for the evening, since entertainers required someone to be entertained. I didn't know it would be as outlandish as it was, not yet knowing how desirable all that was different from his own early surroundings appeared to him.

I sat, that night, among a number of such disparate people as the Westleys, the Hapgoods, Philip Littell and his dear jenny-wren wife whom Hutch had introduced to me, Fania Marinoff, and others now forgotten, while an appalling Negress danced before us in white stockings and black buttoned boots. The man strummed a banjo and sang an embarrassing song while she cavorted. They both leered and rolled their suggestive eyes and made me feel first hot and then cold, for I never had been so near this kind of thing before, but Carl rocked with laughter and little shrieks escaped him as he clapped his pretty hands. His big teeth became wickedly prominent and his eyes rolled in his darkening face, until he grew to somewhat resemble the clattering Negroes before him.

I thought I didn't betray my feelings. I thought I sat there containing myself, but maybe I was mistaken, for I observed Hutch combining one of his sympathetic looks, that he flicked over to me, with an empurpled Teutonic zest that I knew he himself believed to be Gallic tolerance.

"I find this boring," I heard Jack Westley murmur to someone, as he turned away from the unrestrained Negress, whose skirt, now, was drawing higher and higher in a breakdown jig. "It's been done."

"One must just let life express itself in whatever form it will," I thought, to console myself. "If one has any value in oneself, nothing outside can harm it. One can let things happen around one and the world will instinctively know one's worth, if one has any. Nothing can change one's number if one has a number."

That was my only philosophy in those days. Let It happen. Let It decide. Let the great force behind the scenes direct the action. Have faith in life and do not hamper it or try to shape it. "I would rather be a leaf in the wind than the wind," I told Walter Lippmann in defiance of his own determination to decide everything himself, which I secretly admired a great deal since I knew he had extraordinarily good judgment for one so young.

So as readily as I let Carl bring Negroes (once), I let Steff suggest another pattern.

"You have a certain faculty," Steff told me one autumn afternoon as we drank tea together by the fire that glowed in the white marble chimney-place. "It's a centralizing, magnetic, social faculty. You attract, stimulate, and soothe people, and men like to sit with you and talk to themselves! You make them think more fluently, and they feel enhanced. If you had lived in Greece long ago, you would have been called a hetaira. Now why don't you see what you can do with this gift of yours? Why not organize all this accidental, unplanned activity around you, this coming and going of visitors, and see these people at certain hours. Have Evenings!"

"But I thought we don't believe in 'organization,'" I told him reproachfully, for had not he and Hutch said again and again that organizations and institutions are only the crystals of living ideas—and "as soon as an idea is crystallized, it is dead. As soon as one makes up one's mind it is time to change it!"

"Oh, I don't mean that you should *organize* the *Evenings*," he flashed at me with a white smile beneath his little brown bang. "I mean, get people here at certain times and let them feel absolutely free to be themselves, and see what happens. Let everybody come! All these different kinds of people that you know, together here, without being managed or herded in any way! Why, something wonderful might come of it! You might even revive General Conversation!"

So, really, the Evenings were, in the first place, Steffens's idea.

I never needed more than a hint of an idea, if it seemed a good one to me, to seize it and make it my own. Just a *little* push has always been enough for me if I liked the direction. Perhaps intuitive people like Steffens have sometimes seen the possibilities before I knew them myself—have noticed the bubbling before the artesian thrust and rise of energy—and by suggesting the activity already preparing to express itself, have helped to bring it to the surface. Certainly this is what skillful psychologists try to do.

Anyway, ideas so congenial as this one Steff offered seemed to me already mine as soon as he uttered them, and months later, when the Evenings had become a feature of New York life, I was able to take the entire credit for them in an interview by a Mrs. Pearson:

"THE PRINTED PAGE WILL SOON BE SUPERSEDED BY THE SPOKEN WORD," DECLARES MRS. MABEL DODGE, WHO HAS BEEN HOLDING A NEW YORK "SALON" FOR FREE SPEECH

All through the past winter at her apartment at 23 Fifth Avenue, Mrs. Mabel Dodge has been trying an experiment. A very puzzling experiment it was for those who were not "in the know." For two or three evenings every week Mrs. Dodge kept open house, and in her drawing rooms fore-gathered interesting and interested people of all types and persuasions.

Not all persuasions at once, however. At least not always. There were evenings when anyone could come, and others when "by invitation" was the rule, but always there was a subject or idea "before the meeting," and people spoke.

They didn't read speeches, mind you; they hadn't "got it up" before-hand; often they came not knowing what was to be talked of. The prin-cipal speaker was always someone whose chief work and interest the sub-ject was. He (or she) spoke "from the heart," and the others—writers, thinkers, artists, travelers, philosophers, politicians, and mere ordinary peo-ple—spoke in discussion, laid before the rest their views and experience and hammered the matter out.

It might have been stupid; discussions often are. Once or twice, indeed, it was stupid; accidents will happen, you know. That it varied, as a rule, from the mildly interesting or frankly amusing to the intensely absorbing and wildly exciting; that out of it all men and women and ideas and "movements" seemed to find expression and coherence, was due largely to the fact that Mrs. Dodge seemed to know everybody worth knowing, not in the society way, but in the real way, and to get the right people together.

A TALK CHANGE

One was sure of an interesting evening at No. 23 Fifth Avenue; but one wondered sometimes what was being aimed at. You might find, for in-stance, one evening, a learned and eminent professor from Columbia Uni-versity holding forth enthusiastically on Freud's theory of psycho-analysis to a roomful of absorbed "high-brows." Or it might be that Mr. Haywood of the I.W.W. would be expounding to the uninitiated what the I.W.W. really stood for. Or Lincoln Steffens, or Walter Lippmann, would be talk-ing about "Good Government"; a correspondent, just back from Mexico, would be telling about the war, or a scientist from England would make eugenics a topic; or it might be feminism, or primitive life, or perhaps anarchism would bring a queer but harmless-looking crowd.

Every live topic, movement, and interest of the day has been discussed at her house, but Mrs. Dodge herself takes no part. Plainly she is not attached to any of these things, but her level brows and intelligent eyes make one know she has an interest. Pressed for an explanation of her evenings—this is her own account of them:

"They were a kind of propaganda for free speech, but with my own views about *free* and about *speech*. I never discussed it with the grave

members of the Free Speech League, nor did they know I was in league
with them! I wanted to try and free more than speech—I wanted to try
and loosen up thought by means of speech, to get at the truth at the bottom
of people and let it out, so that there would be more understanding. Understanding! That's the one thing that men go on trying for through all the
changes of the world, quarrying it out of one material or another as time
passes. . . .

"When I came back from Europe last winter, it seemed to me there were
so many people with things to say, and so few places to say them in. There
seemed to be no centralization in New York, no meeting place for free
exchange of ideas and talk. So many interesting people only meeting each
other in print! So I thought I would try to get people together a little and
see if it wouldn't increase understanding, if they would all talk among
themselves and say what they thought.

"And I think I did. Some people even got to understanding themselves
better. And some who had been enemies for years in the hateful half-truth
newspaper columns, came more and more to understand one another as
they aired their views together in the open. The familiarity of people towards one another in the press is nearly always anti-social in its effects,
because there's no real contact in it!

"A collector of old manuscripts scolded me for my views. 'And do you
really imagine a time will ever come where the permanent record "will be
dispensed with"?' he asked. 'No,' I said, 'but I imagine that somehow
things will be recorded on the air with a kind of terrible permanence that
we do not even dream of.' He smiled and shook his head in the manner of
others who considered me decidedly unstable."

Imagine, then, a stream of human beings passing in and out of
those rooms; one stream where many currents mingled together for
a little while.

Socialists, Trade-Unionists, Anarchists, Suffragists, Poets, Relations,
Lawyers, Murderers, "Old Friends," Psychoanalysts, I.W.W.'s, Single
Taxers, Birth Controlists, Newspapermen, Artists, Modern-Artists,
Clubwomen, Woman's-place-is-in-the-home Women, Clergymen, and
just plain men all met there and, stammering in an unaccustomed
freedom a kind of speech called Free, exchanged a variousness in
vocabulary called, in euphemistic optimism, Opinions!

I kept meeting more and more people, because in the first place I
wanted to know everybody, and in the second place everybody wanted
to know me. I wanted, in particular, to know the Heads of things.

Heads of Movements, Heads of Newspapers, Heads of all kinds of groups of people. I became a Species of Head Hunter, in fact. It was not dogs or glass I collected now, it was people. Important People. I vaguely believed that anyone who reached eminence in the community, raised themselves above the level of the others, must have attained excellence, and excellence I always revered, and also individuality, difference, originality, any tendency that showed above the old tribal pattern. Each of these "leaders" brought his or her group along, for they had heard about the Evenings (by this time called a Salon) and they all wanted to come.

I had a little speech I made whenever I met a new, interesting person: "We're having an informal meeting of poets on Thursday at my house. If you or any of your friends are interested in Poetry, won't you come?" And they always did. Nearly always. Bergson didn't.

I sturdily maintained my attitude in letting It decide. I suppose I found this quite an easy way of solving the problem. And I would sit in the background and silently smile with a look of understanding printed on my face. I never uttered a word during my Evenings beyond the remote "How do you do?" or the low "Good-by."

I had a little formula for getting myself safely through the hours without any injury to my shy and suspicious sensibilities. As people flowed in, I stood apart, aloof and withdrawn, dressed in long, white dresses with maybe an emerald chiffon wrapped around me, and gave each one my hand—and a very small smile. It was the merest mask of cordiality—impersonal and remote. . . . "I hope you will come again if you enjoyed it."

Flushed and moist, with slightly disarranged hair (often gray locks), with foggy spectacles and quickened breath, those who, so they believed, said what they thought about things, wrung my unrevealing hands as they passed along. It was a wonderful new game, this Salon, and fired many people who had thought but hadn't the habit of saying what they thought, with a quite exciting sense of life.

Every Evening promised a problem. Did I long for other people's problems, or what? For instance, one Evening, when many artists were present, there had been a great deal of talk about the corrupting influence of money, of trying to please the public taste, for money, of the sacred freedom of the artist, and all that, and among them all Carl Hovey was there, listening with a smile on his intelligent lean face. Following that talk I wrote him a letter. He was co-editor, with Whigham, of the *Metropolitan Magazine*. This magazine was the most popular, and the most expensively printed and illustrated, ten-cent periodical of the day. Sonya Levien, a beautiful girl of Russian parentage, was Hovey's secretary and I always felt her judgment and her strength were a strong element in the office, as was the case with countless other anonymous women who were running things behind the scenes in New York. Sonya had that most enduring quality: worthy weight and substance, character in short. I adored it wherever I saw it.

So I asked Hovey to come for an Evening and to bring his art editor, Will Bradley, to meet the editors and artists of *The Masses,* a small radical affair that was the very antithesis of the plutocratic *Metropolitan*. In fact, the illustrators of *The Masses* often tried to get the *Metropolitan* to support them by buying illustrations so they could afford to contribute to *The Masses* for nothing, for Max Eastman and Floyd Dell couldn't pay them anything.

The art editor of the sumptuous *Metropolitan Magazine* was the one who chose and bought the illustrations for the stories, and who selected covers with pretty girls sufficiently alluring to attract tired business men on street-corner newsstands, where cherry lips and waving curls solicited cheerfully: "Take me home for ten cents!"

Now, Carl Hovey, nothing loath, replied to my invitation:

Metropolitan,
432 Fourth Avenue, New York.

My dear Mrs. Dodge:

I have not had a chance yet to see Will Bradley, but as soon as I do I will talk with him about your suggestions. I hope that he will like the idea, because I think it has the possibilities of a very interesting discussion.

Mr. Steffens was in here this morning and I talked with him about it and he told me that as he was going to see you he would explain the difficulty of doing anything about it in time for next Thursday evening. I will let you know what Mr. Bradley says in a day or so.

I enjoyed the Evening the other night enormously, and only regretted my inability to keep up with some of your gatling gun talkers. For sheer horsepower, the other side had so much the advantage, and lack of knowledge made them light for soaring.

Most sincerely yours,

Carl Hovey.

January 13th.

Well, it was a very amusing evening for everybody except Will Bradley, who was a very nice little man with the best intentions in the world of doing his job well, and according to the desires of his employers.

But some of the poor young men of *The Masses* had never seen the powerful editors of the *Metropolitan* to whom they had sold or tried to sell things, and now they confronted each other!

Perhaps the conversation was less general than on the evening the I.W.W.'s tried to tell what their philosophical views were to the moderate-minded Socialists. . . . On *that* Evening it grew, indeed, more and more general as the evening wore on. The Magazine Evening, however, was very much more particular and one-pointed in character, for all of a sudden the guests were telling each other what they thought of *each other,* and not merely their opinions of systems and policies.

Young Maurice Becker, hair on end, shook his trembling finger at the quaking Art Editor, Will Bradley, who really grew pale and cowered before the wild young man, who was intoxicated at his opportunity to let himself go, feeling as he did, protected by the four white walls of 23 Fifth Avenue and me in green and white who asked nothing better than the kind of reality he could provide.

"We give you every chance," Bradley murmured, when he had an opportunity.

"Chance? What chance? We never get a chance to *see* you and show you our stuff. We hardly know whether or not it reaches you, for often we can't even get it back. You sit safely protected from us. We can't get by the outside doors. If we do, we can't get by the telephone girl inside. *You* are far away inside somewhere behind your mahogany, surrounded with Spanish leather screens—and you send us your cold replies from there—if you reply at all. 'We are considering your drawings. If we find them acceptable you will receive $20 upon publication.' Have we any objection to your estimate of our work? Well, we can jolly well swallow it if we want to see it reproduced!"

"You must understand we publish a great many drawings and we cannot afford to be too generous to *one* and less to others. Many, we find, are satisfied with what we pay."

"How do you *know* they're satisfied? Has any single poor devil ever *told* you how generous he thought you? Do you know anything about what any of us think about you and your prostitute of a magazine? Have you any idea *at all* what *we* think of your 'pretty girl' and how we loathe ourselves for selling drawings to go inside your covers? My God!" he finished, with a gasp at his own surprising passion and eloquence.

I had lunch with Carl Hovey at the Ritz a week or so later, and he told me that Will Bradley went to bed after the Evening and wasn't up yet!

"It quite knocked him out," he told me, smiling. "He had no idea those young men felt like that. I think he means to try and have a more human relationship with them after this . . . if he ever gets up!" he added.

"Well, my idea is to get people together so they can tell each other what they Think," I answered. "These Evenings are making changes in a lot of different ways. Enmities fade away as soon as people talk. I have had people meet there who had been enemies for years in print, like Abe Cohen of the *Staats Zeitung* and some of the editors of our New York papers, and when they met face to face and talked, they found their bad feelings melted right away. They couldn't feel the same any more."

"I hear Bill Haywood doesn't hate the capitalists since he's come to know some of them," replied Hovey, smiling slyly. "You are going to pull the sting out of the old man if you're not careful."

"Oh, why, I'm not doing anything," I exclaimed. "I let them come, that's all. Life decides, not me. Maybe it's time he lost his sting."

There was a great deal written in the newspapers about the Salon; long accounts were printed every week and, of course, I liked some of the nice, dignified newspaper articles, but sometimes they were terrible. It all depended upon how one treated the newspapermen. There was the facetious type of reporting, which was quite trying, and which made me blush and grow prickly all over when I saw in the morning headlines: "THE SALON DODGE" and read what followed.

Though I never talked myself except to one or two people at a time, and preferably to *one,* yet I made a fetish of other people's conversations. Almost feverishly I wanted everyone to say what they thought to each other. Like Hyde Park, my drawing room became a place where anyone could air his views. Hutch thought it a vantage ground from which he could "subtly undermine the community," and others felt the same, each in his own way. I think they were all unconsciously freed by a feeling that it was under my protection because there I was, strong and calm and understanding, and it was my show after all, and my responsibility. They never knew how *I* quaked sometimes at the situations they plunged me into. I felt I was playing with dynamite and though I liked it dangerous, yet I was scared sometimes. And sometimes it was nearly so and sometimes actually and really so.

One night Bill Haywood, Emma Goldman, and English Walling, aided by their followers, arranged to tell each other what they thought. Now this meant that Emma and Bill and Alexander Berkman would try to convince the socialists that Direct Action was more effective than propaganda or legislation. They believed in killing, they advocated it when it was possible, and they had done it, some of them openly. Of course, the I.W.W.'s led by Bill Haywood, Carlo Tresca, Elizabeth Gurley Flynn, and Giovannitti advised sabotage for industrial machinery no matter what the risk might be to human life.

These "Dangerous Characters" were subject to arrest at any time they would forget themselves and say in public what they thought, so they were careful not to do it, for it was inconvenient and hampered the Movement to be locked up. But this Evening they were really going to say it.

There was a large gathering in the apartment, all kinds of people, some in evening dress and some not. Hutch and Steff, of course, intellectual anarchists *they* were. They believed in dealing Death by words and influence. They didn't actually care to shed blood, though they felt Emma Goldman and Bill had a right to their own methods.

Mary Austin sat with her lips thrust out and her eyelids heavy, her gray hair coiled high, portentous in prairie-colored satin. The Amos Pinchots, Helen Marot, Ida Rauh and Max, Gertrude Light, John Collier, Jo O'Brien—lots of people but all more or less especially invited that night, for I had switched the Evening from the usual Wednesday to a Monday so none but more or less radical sympathizers would be there. People who believed that others had the right to kill on principle, if they thought it Right: The Live and Let Live Kind of people.

Emma had a boy sitting next to her—a boy with a broad, white forehead, dark, waving hair and earnest eyes—a handsome, serious-looking boy of about seventeen or eighteen.

"A bright East Side Jew," she whispered to me as she murmured his name, "Frank Tannenbaum."

We were all ready for the Conversation to begin. Bill Haywood, like a large, soft, overripe Buddha with one eye, and the smile of an Eminent Man, reclined in the yellow *chaise longue* with two or three maidens reclining at his feet. They were young public schoolteachers who were circumspect and blameless from 9 to 4 every day but radical in the evening. The young admired Bill Haywood greatly. He was a Hero.

Amos Pinchot sat, with his usual kind look of unknowing, next his lovely pink satin wife who smoked a cigarette and smiled a tolerant smile. People continued to arrive belatedly in twos and threes, and then when everyone seemed to be present I told Vittorio to keep the front door closed and not to let anyone else in. There they were, safe, shut in with Mabel Dodge—all feeling secure except her.

However, on that occasion there was no need to quake, for those Dangerous People never did succeed in formulating the difference between Anarchism and the Philosophy of the Industrial Workers of the World, and Socialism.

Haywood, so impassioned a speaker out in the rain before a thousand strikers, talked as though he were wading blindfolded in sand. He couldn't get It into words. Walter Lippmann tried to draw him out. Walter was cast rather in the Buddhistic mold, too, only he was very firm and his face had a light upon it. He was remarkably certain in his judgments, sure of them, and very definite in his speech as well as his outline; and extraordinarily mature for his age, which was about twenty-five or -six at that time, I think.

Walter gave Big Bill several leads. In a kind but firm voice he asked him definite questions about the policies of the Industrial Workers of the World. Useless. Bill's lid drooped over his blind eye and his heavy cheeks sagged lower.

Emma Goldman, too, was not at all to the point. She was more than ever like a severe schoolteacher in a scolding mood. English Walling continued to be smiling and bland and with the usual socialistic manner. He, I think, felt Socialism triumphed that night, at least by default. There was a great deal of General Conversation, but no definition.

"They talk like goddam bourgeois," suddenly cried Hippolyte Havel in a high, peevish voice, glaring around through the thick lenses in his spectacles.

"My little sister!" he exclaimed to me later that evening, in his sweet whining voice. "My little goddam bourgeois capitalist sister!" And tears ran over his spectacles.

That Evening was not successful. There had been no form to it. Of course that was the risk one took when one let things be and did not try to shape events or direct the people there. Sometimes there would be a sudden quickening of the vibration in the place and men would surprise themselves by their own eloquence—things would happen of their own accord. And then again it would be quite flat as on this occasion.

I always decided more or less the *kind* of Evening we would have, and usually they were on the same evening each week so that people saved that time and did not make other engagements. I would ask some specialist, some Head of something, to come and tell his views to start the ball rolling—the Head of the Poetry Movement, or the Head of the Free Speech League, and so on—and then all the other Heads of movements and leagues and ideas would come, and they would question each other and tell their views as freely as they liked.

One night the artists were there listening to "Big Bill" Haywood tell them that he thought artists thought themselves too special and separate, and that some day there would be a Proletarian Art, and the State would see to it that everybody was an artist and that everybody would have time to be an artist.

Of course the Modernists who heard this—Andrew Dasburg, John Marin, Picabia, and Marsden Hartley among them—weren't so mad as Janet Scudder, who rose slowly to her feet, her eyes like pin-points beneath drooping lids, her lips drawn down at the corners, as she glared at the big man who grinned back at her. She said in her drawling voice, with an accent of scorn:

"Do you realize that it takes twenty years to make an artist?"

In a flash, I saw Janet's memories running through her mind. Her struggle to get enough money to leave Terre Haute, years of working for a scholarship. Her long journey to Paris, her years of drudgery there, drudgery and joy too, and great need for adjustment. Her hungers, her thirsts, her sacrifices for her work; her gradual, her so slow and so gradual success in her métier, the dull clay eternally resisting! Her years and years and years in a brown holland apron, in dusty studios; no money and poor light, no money and small amounts of food—years of it, until she saw her "Boy with Fish" or her "Boy with Flute" standing, cinquecento, in the Luxembourg, or in some American-Italian garden.

How could Bill Haywood know anything of all this? He couldn't, any more than Janet could see the pictures flashing in his brain at her indignant speech. Yet I saw his pictures as easily as I saw hers—and the impossibility. . . . Well, it wasn't for me to reconcile different points of view, I thought.

There was the beginning, in those days, then, of a new attitude towards the artist. His sacrosanct vocation was being slowly questioned, his divine right to all forgiveness by virtue of his calling was being disposed of, little by little. John Reed, coming under the influence of the more intellectual radical Labor leaders, heard it all discussed over and over again, and in "The Day in Bohemia" he reflected the healthy reaction of those hearty realists against the privileged beings who consider themselves more sensitive than others, an assumption imposed by themselves for so long upon Philistines and Pharisees.

On the Scudder-Haywood Evening, Bill was at his best, with Dasburg flashing and witty, and Arthur Lee, with terrific earnestness, trying to pound out his somewhat reluctant thoughts, and others cutting in, several talking at once, until in the end, we really had General Conversation and the air was vibrant with intellectual excitement, and electrical with the appearance of new ideas and dawning changes.

I remember once we had a Poets' Evening and there were all kinds of poets, some who wrote poetry and some who only intended to. At one time during the evening George Sylvester Viereck read some quite startling verses which caused Amy Lowell to rise and move out like a well-freighted frigate.

Edwin Arlington Robinson, the most eminent poet present, sat like a bump on a log and didn't express a thing; he never did tell me even afterwards what his impressions were.

By the end of February the Evenings were really getting out of hand. Walter told me I *must* organize them more, they were too confused and too crowded. I had left it to people I knew and believed in to come as freely as they liked and to feel they might tell their friends to come; but alas! this was a privilege and grew to be abused.

Too many hangers-on came only to eat the good supper displayed in the dining room when Vittorio flung open the doors at midnight. There would be quite a rush for the cold turkey and ham that waited, majestic, for the onslaught.

Over the whiskey and soda, or the beer and ale, the debates grew riotous and foolish. So Walter and Lee Simonson and Alfred Kuttner, young intellectuals, sure of themselves, believed more in ordering the universe than Hutch did; believed it could be done, that is.

Walter said: "You have a chance to do something really creative here, Mabel. Do try and *make* something of it instead of letting it run wild. Weed it out and *order* it."

I felt badly about changing things because I wanted to believe that It could take care of things better than I or anyone else could. "But," I argued with myself, "Walter is just as much an instrument of It as Hutch or Steff. I must do whatever is asked of me. I must decide nothing."

So I agreed to try *their* way—these young cocksure boys who knew it all. I wrote a paper to read to the crowd and went out, myself, on the following Evening. This is what I told them:

ADDRESS TO THE CROWD

1913

Someone will read this message to you all because I have gone over to Cooper Union for a little while to keep my promise to be present at the Protest Meeting of *The Masses* whenever it should occur.

No one in particular will speak tonight because I want to suggest a free discussion as to the value of these Thursday evenings—and to find out what you all think of them.

The discussion may be perfectly free and unrelated to me as a hostess because I have purposely taken an impersonal stand from the beginning, simply offering my house to you and considering myself just as one of those present, having no more authority than anyone else.

I suppose it has been a sort of experiment. When I came to New York to live last winter, it seemed to me that there were a great many interesting men and women, all thinking and doing different things, but there didn't seem to be any *centralization,* any place where all *sorts* of people could meet under one roof and talk together freely on all subjects.

And so I tried to bring some of them together. I wanted to see if it would prove *constructive* or *creative;* just humans meeting together with no attempt at organizing, directing, or controlling the energies present. And if it were merely entertaining, I thought, *that* would be creative enough, and it *has* been that, and sometimes it has been more than that.

And so, encouraged by those old fogies, Hutch Hapgood and Steffens, who believe in life, we've all met here together and let life take any shape it wanted to. And now I'd like to hear you all say what you think of it.

I know, for one, what I have gotten out of it—out of this accidental and casual method: and that is a number of new friends that I might not otherwise have had.

But now comes the younger counsel, saying: "You have tried this way— now try another way!"

And I am willing to try it so that when I come back in the autumn I shall know which way works the best (that is, which has the most vitality in it), and the most vital way of the two will be the eventual one.

And so I am saying to you now, reluctantly but hopefully, that this is the last Thursday evening of this kind, this spring. During March and April I will follow the advice of the younger generation. . . .

The Evenings will be on a different day in the week—they will have a more definite direction, there will be standards of ability, parliamentary rule, invitations!

I fancy, in advance, a groan goes up at this!

I myself have no preconceived conviction as to which sort of evening will be the most successful, but if I were not willing to try one as willingly as the other, I should prove myself to be narrow and illiberal.

I hope you'll all say what you really think about all this tonight, because when you come again you may not be allowed to!

—M. D.

By this time I definitely felt myself to be a Radical, and an article I had published in one of the current magazines tries to formulate my untrained thoughts:

January, 1913.

To the Conservatives:

The time has come to make an answer to your impatient complaints. A mysterious smile no longer seems to be a sufficient reply. Bergson is on his way over to us for a series of lectures at Columbia College; the vigorous pioneers for the renewed expression of life in art will soon show us what they have done at the great show at the Armory in February. It is time, indeed, that every one of us who has a conviction about life or a vestige of faith in it, should come out into the open and say so.

You accuse us of being a set of anarchists because we do not linger contentedly over the deposits of past achievement. This is as true of us as it is of any moderns who have ever concerned themselves with the hitherto "unknown." But we claim it is our special virtue that we *want* to know more and that our minds are open to new manifestations. . . .

The outline around many of the old forms must be admitted as too hard and too narrow. Its inelasticity constitutes its defeat. Recognized definitions no longer enclose the whole truth, and the first qualification of a definition is that there shall be nothing left over. There is so much left over, in many cases, that the important constituents are now mostly on the outside. And that is our area—the outside—that is where we have our being—it is our element and our native air, and the name that we give to it is the universal consciousness.

The need of every growing thing is for room for expansion, for self-expression. Have the limits of the academic in art proved wide enough for this process? "The great master is he who expresses himself perfectly within limits," you reply. Yes, but who shall fix the boundary? And in the technique of life, which is convention, who shall decide the ultimate horizon? In the institutions of today, is there room for unfolding? Does marriage foster the inherent nobility of the human animal? Does our prison system correct the mistakes of ignorance and give direction to rudderless souls? If not, then our institutions are crystals thrown off by civilization into the waste heap of the world, ready for the cosmic melting pot. These are questions that have somehow to be answered and because every question presupposes an answer, we know that we will find them—out in that open space where we are groping and where all the truth that we have already seized upon has been found, and given to you others for your comfort and security. In order that you may be conservative and skeptical (and cozy!) today, we are out in the untried—feeling our way towards the truth of tomorrow.

Mabel Dodge.

Well, the apartment became a kind of home for many people who came and sat there once a week and gave their souls a little fun. I remember complaining to Walter soon after I came to New York that people had no inner life in America. There was no opportunity for the *grande vie intérieure* that Violet and I had had together! Everywhere people seemed so *active* and in pursuit of the main chance in America. I think the Evenings gave to those who needed it an opportunity to be thoughtful and discursive and let ideas emerge quietly somewhat like the European life did. I had a good many grateful things said and written to me about this. As Hartley wrote after his first visit:

DEAR MABEL DODGE:

I want to tell you that I think we are going to have lots to say to each other and I want just to tell you of it. I felt as if I were in such a large place last night—a large place lighted with exceptionally good light. It had a sense of home to me. I walk always with my feet on the earth and yet I have of late the feeling of being a severed head despatched into unusual places—places so familiar and yet so alien. I was glad to be there with those fine people—they gave me so much to remember and I like remembrances of a finer kind. I liked so much the personal largeness of the one— and the delicacy of the other. Of the so-called "Russian" I have little to relate—since we are intimate for long. For yourself, well, we will, I think, have much to express, little perhaps to propound. All, perhaps, futilely from some points of view, and yet I think it will be lovely. I do hope you don't go away for long while I am in New York because I feel the need of unusual lights in dark places and there seems so much of this there around you.

Always yours,

MARSDEN HARTLEY.

Was it the climate, or what other imponderable force was it, that drove people so? There seemed no place to come to rest in New York, no time to dream and ponder. The only spot I knew of outside my own apartment where one could find a kind of peaceful activity was with Stieglitz, at "291." There one did have that sense of a spiritual home that a cultural environment and background always gives one.

CHAPTER V

The Case of Frank Tannenbaum

THE early months of 1914 were terribly cold, and while the papers tried to keep it dark, the question of what to do with the growing number of unemployed people was a serious one. The Missions did what they could. That unconventional man, John Haynes Holmes, fed a long bread line from his church every night, but there was no way to handle the bulk of the men.

Suddenly the boy Emma Goldman had brought to my house a month before was featured on every front page of the morning papers.

"Frank Tannenbaum Leads Men into Church," "Young Radical Attempts to Seize Church for Unemployed Men," "Tannenbaum Under Arrest for Illegal Assault upon Fifth Avenue Church."

Well, he had done it. Unable to go on listening to the endless discussions he encountered about the Problem of the Unemployed among the labor people, in their homes and in Headquarters, he had gathered up a couple of hundred of these homeless idle and on one of the stormiest nights of the winter he had gone around visiting different places of worship—a decided innovation.

The police were summoned and they drove the poor fellows down the aisles and out into the street again with clubs.

Tannenbaum was arrested and held in jail pending a trial, and his action had far-reaching results. To be brief, it brought the question of unemployment more immediately before people, especially church-going people who hadn't heard much about it, for the papers wouldn't publish anything up to that time.

Hutch took me to the trial. My life had been so housed and sheltered that I had never been in a court room before and I found myself impressed with the order and harmony around me. The dark mahogany in the large, dignified room, the modulated voices, the

96

light that fell from the high windows upon the well-shaped, hand-some head of Judge Wadhams and the finely modeled features of the boy, Frank Tannenbaum, were elements that created a solid comfort like that in a church, where one sometimes had a feeling of being surrounded, protected, and supported by the structural equilibrium that men know how to produce.

Because of the ups and downs of my own nature that were a constant source of puzzlement to me, I liked an atmosphere of lively balance but I did not often find it in churches; the balance would be there but not the life. Too sleepy and automatic the tempered ritual and the churchly voices. But here in this court room there seemed to be a gentle humming vibration that came, perhaps, from the composed attention and concentration of everyone in it, from the quiet business of law, the soft footsteps of alert men carrying papers and consulting each other in low tones. So as I sat there I felt my own balance restored to me by the surroundings and I did not have to do anything about it. I was enjoying "law and order." I sat beside Hutch in the front row—and Hutch took the opportunity to make some remarks to a reporter and as we went out on the street afterwards a paper announced "Mrs. Mabel Dodge gets a front seat! Among the crowd . . . was a sprinkling of professionals . . . Socialists and uplifters such as Mrs. Mabel Dodge and Hutchins Hapgood—who expressed the opinion that Free Speech was about to be upheld or strangled . . . !"

Of all the hundred and ninety men and boys who had been arrested with Tannenbaum, a few had been sent to Blackwell's Island and the rest discharged. Tannenbaum had been the only one who was indicted, for he seemed to be asking for it, and took all the responsibility for invading the church and demanding shelter.

Justus Sheffield had offered to defend Frank and he was extremely attractive in that somber room; his tall, controlled figure in dark blue serge imposed itself. He was so very blond and cold and almost cruel-looking that he seemed to shine against the blacks and browns of the background.

It took hours to select the jury and the lawyers both for the prosecution and the defense. They examined the veniremen chiefly about whether they were members of the I.W.W. or in sympathy with it, or whether they were members of any religious organization! There was a great deal of excitement growing in people's minds now the trial

97

had started, and someone came and whispered to Hutch that either the Mayor or the Police Commissioner had gotten in touch with the National Guard and the Sheriff of Greater New York and told them to be ready to co-operate in case of an outbreak.

When the trial started a policeman named Patrick Gilday was the first witness for the prosecution and he testified that at the meeting in Rutgers Square the night of the arrest a woman shouted out that the streets of Paris ran with blood when the church opposed the common people, and that Tannenbaum cried in answer to this: "And that is what will happen here!"

Tannenbaum went into the witness stand and made his own defense, which was what he had wished from the first. For a boy of his age he was unusually self-possessed. He admitted that he led "the boys" to St. Alphonsus's Church, and that while he was talking to the pastor, Father Schneider, in the rectory next door, they had gone into it. It was like this, he said:

"I asked for permission to go into the church with the boys and the priest would not give me that permission. I then asked for food which was refused, and then for money which was also refused.

"Then I said to the priest: 'So this is your Christian gospel?' And he said, 'Never mind about that. I will not allow you to talk to me in that way.'

"So I went out and told the boys the priest would not let us go inside the church. I went back to the rectory and saw him again, and I said, 'All right. No harm done.' I wanted to shake hands with him but he would not take my hand. When I went out again the boys had already gone into the church. I wanted to get them and lead them back to Rutgers Square and I went in after them, but when I wanted to take them away Lieutenant Gilday opened the church door and tapped me on the shoulder and said, 'Please wait. We are waiting for orders from Police Commissioner McKay.' Another policeman stood at the door and said no one was allowed to pass out. Gilday said he was sorry he couldn't let me out. He said, 'You are all right, Tannenbaum,' and I thanked him for his sympathy.

"I offered to take the boys out peacefully but he said they were acting under orders from the Commissioner. While we were waiting there some reporters came along and I told them if there was any trouble or anyone was killed, the responsibility would be on the police."

Then, shortly after that they arrested Frank and took him to the police station. When he was being cross-examined he told about the efforts of that evening. First the boys and he had gone to the old Bible House at Second Avenue and First Street where they received some food. Then they went to the Labor Temple at Second Avenue and Fourteenth Street where apparently they received nothing. After that they crossed over to the First Presbyterian Church on Fifth Avenue at Eleventh Street and here they received twenty-five dollars.

"Why did you go to St. Alphonsus's Church?" Mr. Press, the Assistant District Attorney, asked Frank. And he replied:

"Because we expected to receive Christian treatment there."

Then a strange bit of dialogue ensued: Frank said in answer to a question that yes, he took an interest in Christianity, and then Mr. Press asked:

"Who said, 'It is easier for a camel to pass through the eye of a needle than it is for a rich man to enter heaven'?"

"I think it is somewhere in the *New Testament.*"

"Did Christ say it?"

"He was supposed to have said it."

"Are you interested in his teachings?"

"I have read the teachings of Mohammed, Confucius, and Moses."

"But you do not believe in Christ?"

"Not as a God—not as a divinity."

"Why did you find it necessary to visit churches where his gospel is preached?"

"For the spirit they are supposed to represent—remember, supposed to represent."

"You are not a member of any Christian church?"

"I am not."

Many different witnesses were called for both sides, and a young reporter named George Kaufman testified how when Tannenbaum asked for food and shelter they were denied him, and he described that when Tannenbaum asked if they might sleep in the church, if they would do no harm and have it clean in the morning, Father Schneider replied:

"A Catholic Church is no place to sleep; the Blessed Sacrament is there."

Other witnesses described what happened, in such a way as to show that Frank had been victimized by the police. One fellow, Charles Plunkett, who had just finished fifteen days in the workhouse because of his participation at St. Alphonsus's Church, said that Frank had gone to the church after his visit to the rectory and called through the open door: "Come on out, boys. They don't want us." Then Detective Geogan called Tannenbaum into the church and told him to wait there! So that once he got in he couldn't get out!

It was quite a job to take care of all the witnesses for the defense who had waited for a long time. Especially the I.W.W. witnesses who knew what they wanted! "We want the State to feed us as it feeds its own witnesses!" they shouted in the corridor outside.

"Cut that out and move along," ordered the bailiffs.

"We insist that the State feed us!"

One of them said: "If we go, you can bet we won't come back!"

"Then you will be in contempt of Court," a bailiff cried.

"What do we care for contempt?" came back a thundering chorus. "What do we care for this court or any court? What do we care for your laws or any laws? We want the State to feed us!"

"Well, at least you'll get out of this corridor," and they formed a flying wedge and shoved them along out.

One of the defense witnesses told, through a German interpreter, that the crowd of Tannenbaum's followers had stumbled over his feet as he was kneeling in the church before an image of Christ.

". . . And after the crowd had been arrested," he said, "I found a number of knives and razors under the pews, which they had evidently dropped."

"But I contend," Justus broke in, "that there is nothing to show that that the parishioners didn't carry in these razors and drop them under the pews!"

Justus was very amusing, anyway, all through. When the District Attorney repeatedly called the boys "a mob" he interrupted him to insist that they be called just "men."

When we went out, after court was adjourned for the day, reporters flew at me with notebooks and flung questions in my face. I felt perfectly unequal to the moment, and yet I wanted to be fair to my own point of view, such as it was, vague and scarcely defined, and at the same time to all these other viewpoints as well. The evening papers reflected my lack of certainty.

. . . Mrs. Dodge said after the adjournment for the day that she wanted to correct the impression that she was a staunch supporter of the I.W.W.

"I am interested in the I.W.W.," she said, "as I am in other organizations. I am searching for the best way for labor to organize. The I.W.W. has consequently come in for a good deal of study on my part."

All the newspapers took this trial very seriously. Editorials, special articles, and interviews were printed day after day. Among the observations of many there were quite a few relevant ones. An editorial in the *Globe* began:

(*N. Y. Globe;* March 23, 1914)

TWO KINDS OF ANARCHISTS

There are two lawless elements in the community. One element is led by the reactionaries that are continually inciting the police to acts of illegal violence, demanding clubbings and arrests, in violation of the constitutional rights of freedom of speech and assemblage. The other is led by the small band of I.W.W. agitators who are continually inciting the unemployed to acts of violence against property.

A newspaper which clamorously calls on the police to break up parades and meetings, and a Tannenbaum who urges his followers to seize food and shelter, are brother and sister in the advocacy of anarchy. That one urges the ignoring of personal rights and the other the ignoring of property rights does not obscure the essential similarity of their points of view. Both are against the upholding of the part of the law of which they personally disapprove.

It is desirable at this time when these types of the anarchical disease are prevalent, to recall the words of a learned judge and a wise administrator—the late Mayor Gaynor. In a message to the Board of Aldermen, he said:

"I have particularly made the police authorities understand that those who entertain views of government, or of economic or social order, different from ours are not to be interfered with or denied the right of freedom of speech and assembly on that account. A propaganda by intellectual persuasion and peaceable means for changes in the form of government or in the economic or social order is not to be meddled with, much less suppressed."

This is the only possible attitude to be assumed by those interested in the preservation of law and order. Any other is lawless and anti-American. If illegality becomes the practice, as there is some danger, we have no right to escape immunity from the disturbances that have vexed the old world. Mayor Mitchel will do well to follow throughout his administration the principle that this is a government of laws, not of men, and that the right of the social reformer is as sacred as the right of any man to his property.

The *Times* went into the whole situation in a very fair and detailed manner which it is interesting to read after so many years:

SO-CALLED I.W.W. RAIDS REALLY HATCHED BY SCHOOL-BOYS. REAL HISTORY, TOLD FOR THE FIRST TIME, OF THE LATEST MOVEMENT AGAINST SOCIETY—PRODUCT, NOT OF THE I.W.W. NOR OF THE ANARCHISTS, BUT OF THE FERRER SCHOOL, WHERE THREE PUPILS ORIGI-NATED IT

It will be very much to the advantage of the conservative people of this town to learn more than they have yet taken the trouble to learn about the continuing and growing demonstrations which have been loosely lumped under the head of "I.W.W. raids." It is always to the advantage of a person who is attacked to know why he is attacked, who is attacking him, and where he may expect the next blow.

And this is an attack—an attack on the social system. Its aim is nothing less than revolution.

It has been taken lightly by this careless town, but it should not be taken lightly. It is the most serious demonstration that the revolutionary element has made in this country since the demonstration in Chicago in 1886, which ended in the conflict between the police and the revolutionists in Hay-market Square, the throwing of the famous bomb, and the hanging of the anarchist leaders.

The conflict was brought about when the police attempted to break up one of the revolutionary meetings. The leaders of the present movement openly say that a similar attempt today will bring about the same result. The blame, they say, will be on the shoulders of the police: as long as the police do not interfere with them there will be no bloodshed; if the police do, there will be. . . .

"I don't know whether it was consciously done or not," said Emma Gold-man to me the other day, and she smiled significantly as she said it, "but it was a very diplomatic move on the part of the authorities not to interfere last Saturday with the Union Square meeting and the parade on Fifth Avenue. I really congratulate the Mayor on that, congratulate him sincerely—if it was consciously done.

"Because you know that when hungry people are driven to desperation they can't reason. They ought not to be expected to, either."

Detective James J. Geogan is one of the policemen assigned to the following of the so-called raiders. He has been on the "cases" ever since Tannenbaum began his movement on the churches, and has watched it day by day. After the Fifth Avenue demonstration of which Miss Goldman thus spoke, he said:

"It is evident that the men down town (meaning his official superiors) do not recognize the seriousness of this movement. We who follow them from day to day see that they are gaining strength, and unless they are checked serious consequences may result."

REAL HISTORY OF MOVEMENT

The public appearance a week ago of Emma Goldman, Alexander Berkman, and the other anarchist leaders in this movement started by Frank Tannenbaum and heretofore called an I.W.W. movement, startled our careless town. The consternation it excited led to a lot of bewildered attempts to account for it, all of them entirely wrong. The favorite notion appeared to be that Big Bill Haywood and the I.W.W. had started the movement, using Tannenbaum as a tool, and that the anarchists had suddenly stepped in and wrested it away from them.

Believing that this movement is a matter of much importance to everybody, and particularly to the class that is menaced by it, I shall here set down the real history of this movement, which is printed now for the first time, and its aims. It will disturb some preconceptions, but it will be the truth.

This movement was not originated either in the councils of the I.W.W. nor those of the anarchists. It originated in a center of social disaffection which hitherto has not been mentioned in connection with it—the Ferrer School, at 63 West 107th Street.

Emma Goldman and Alexander Berkman did not suddenly swoop upon it after they saw its progress and the opportunities it afforded. They were privy to it from the beginning. The real originators of it told her their intentions before they made a move.

There were no leaders, either of the I.W.W. nor of the anarchists, sitting in darkness in the background and pulling the strings. The conception and the execution were those of young men, mostly hardly more than boys, never before prominent in any revolutionary camp. The I.W.W. and anarchist leaders alike—the Haywoods and the Goldmans—deliberately stayed out of it, out of both the direction and the execution of it, and left everything to these youngsters. They knew all that was going on, of course.

For nearly thirty years—ever since the outbreak of the Chicago anarchists—the revolutionary leaders have been hoping and cudgeling their brains for some move that would dramatize discontent as effectively as the strike that preceded the Haymarket collision had done. It finally came, not from them, but from the audacious brains of these boys, and was hatched in the Ferrer School, an institution less than four years old.

The soil, they exultantly say, is better prepared for the revolutionary seed than at any time in all these thirty years. The social discontent has grown and made itself felt to such an extent that now the authorities are more cautious in meeting it. In illustration of this growth they point to these two pictures:

First, of a little, blonde-haired, blue-eyed girl addressing a meeting of the unemployed in Union Square and quoting Cardinal Manning's maxim: "Necessity knows no law, and the starving man has a natural right to a share of his neighbor's bread." She added, "Ask for work. If they do not give you work, ask for bread. If they do not give you work or bread, then take bread." The community was thrown into a panic; the girl was arrested, tried, convicted, and sentenced to serve a year on Blackwell's Island. This was in 1893.

Second, of a little blonde-haired, blue-eyed woman addressing a meeting of the unemployed in Union Square and saying: "March down to the Mayor. March down to the police. March down to the other city officials. Make them tell you what they are going to do to give you food and shelter. Go to the churches, go to the hotels and restaurants, go to the bakeshops, and tell them they must give you something to keep you from starving." Her hearers formed in line and marched down Fifth Avenue, jeering the churches and the homes of the rich. No arrests were made. This was in 1914.

The girl at Union Square in 1893 was Emma Goldman. The woman at Union Square in 1914 was Emma Goldman. What has made the difference in 21 years?

"Times have changed," replied Emma Goldman when I asked her this question. "Even the courts would not send a person to jail for a year for such an utterance, if made today, as I served a year for making them.

"There is a great difference between the quality of the unemployed themselves then and now. Then it was just simply a blind groping, and now it is a consciousness that they are entitled to a share of the good things of life."

INTELLECTUAL PROLETARIAT

"Then it is remarkable, the change of the intellectual class toward the condition of labor. That is due to the fact that in the last ten years an intellectual proletariat has been developed in this country. There is a tremendous contingent of professional men and women everywhere who are proletarians."

"In sympathy with the proletariat, you mean?" I enquired.

"No, indeed—proletarians themselves. They have to walk around looking for jobs. The only difference between them and the men who work with their hands is the number of hours. The danger to present-day society is greater from these intellectual proletarians than from the unemployed, because they have tasted the good things of life and know what they are missing."

This movement, begun in the Ferrer School, is defined by Leonard D. Abbott, the President of that institution, as "a dramatic gesture of the unemployed." He explained the aim of it thus:

"The whole value of this church-raiding system lies in its advertising the issue of the unemployed in a way that is compelling and that makes everybody think. These tactics are an effort of the more adventurous spirits to dramatize the whole issue."

It originated with three or four "Ferrer School boys," one of whom was Tannenbaum. All of them attended the evening classes there, and the Ferrer School claims them as its product and is proud of them. Tannenbaum was not a representative in any authorized sense of either the I.W.W. or the Anarchists, though he was well known to the leaders of both. The whole idea was his own and that of his chums at the school, whose names are withheld by the school authorities for perfectly understandable reasons. . . .

These young men are not of the ignorant type that one would expect. The most prominent of them, with the exception of Tannenbaum, are men of education and culture. Some of them are writers, poets, artists. . . .

EMMA GOLDMAN'S DREAM

The leaders of the Anarchists and the I.W.W. kept ostentatiously out of the movement at first, but were delighted with it; not merely because it was in line with their ideas, but because it was a fulfillment of the hope they had always entertained that by the constant sowing of discontent the younger element would at last rise itself, without waiting for leaders. It had always been their dream to bring about social changes, as one of them expresses it, "through the workingmen themselves, as opposed to the socialistic conception, which does everything through the state."

Through all the twenty-one years since Emma Goldman was sentenced to jail for her vain effort to disturb the apathy of the unemployed, this has been her dream. She was delighted when she saw, as she believed, a beginning of an approximation toward reality, and she, like Haywood, of the I.W.W., stayed out and let them have full swing.

But she kept on aiding the movement by raising money, though she confined herself to that. "It has been a great joy to me," she told me, "to see the boys, some of them not much more than children, show so much organizing capacity and so much self-control, and I didn't want to step in. I knew that if Mr. Berkman or I did step in, the whole attention of the public would be fixed on us; besides, I was terribly busy. I had just finished the manuscript of a book on the social significance of the modern drama, which a Boston house is going to bring out, and I had pledged myself to have every line in by March 20th. I was busy with my lectures, too, and it was a physical impossibility to do anything for them."

On Saturday, a week ago, Miss Goldman and Berkman of the Anarchists, and Carlo Tresca of the I.W.W.'s, came to the front at the Union Square meeting, which so excited the crowd that it marched down Fifth Avenue.

Berkman says five hundred were in line. Of those who were at the Union Square meeting Miss Goldman estimates that fully half were "rebels," as she calls them, the others being unidentified unemployed.

This parade may have been made up in the same proportion of rebels and unemployed, but it was the rebels who led, inspired and guided it. Fifty of them were women, anarchist women—"our girls," as Miss Goldman always calls them.

"I was not in the Fifth Avenue demonstration," she said. "I left two hours before it began, and I didn't know it was to take place. When they got to the Ferrer Association headquarters they called me up. . . .

"Mr. Berkman told me all of this talk of our girls spitting in the faces of women was nonsense. Our girls wouldn't do such a thing. The demonstration was inspired, but orderly. They did make demonstrations before the churches and synagogues, but the quality of these boys is demonstrated in this wonderful fact—when they reached Mt. Sinai Hospital, they marched in absolute silence for two blocks so as not to disturb the sick people. Not a single paper mentioned that, because it would give these boys a little semblance of being human."

CONSTRUCTIVE ANARCHISM

. . . The Ferrer School, which thus produced this "dramatic gesture of the unemployed," was described to me by its president, Mr. Abbott, as a "laboratory in which new social theories are tested."

It is the first institution, he says, "devoted to the constructive side of anarchism." It is less than four years old, and it is turning out, and it is intended to turn out, graduates filled with a subtle discontent with the present social system and a determination to end it. . . .

Among them, then, were lectures by Elizabeth Gurley Flynn, the I.W.W. leader, on the Paterson strike, in which she was arrested; by Louis Levine and Andre Tridon on syndicalism; by Edwin Markham on poetry; by Guiterrez, the Mexican revolutionist, on Mexico; by Clarence Darrow, the McNamaras' lawyer, on Voltaire; by Emma Goldman, Berkman, and others. Robert Henri and George Bellows conduct the art class. Among those back of the enterprise are Lincoln Steffens, Hutchins Hapgood, Gilbert E. Roe, Theodore Schroeder, Bolton Hall, Alden Freeman, and others of the "intellectual class."

These were the classes which Tannenbaum and his colleagues attended; it was where they got their ideas, and it was in this building and after one of the lectures that they conceived and laid out their plans. From there they went to Emma Goldman's, twelve blocks away, and asked her aid in getting money.

As the movement gathered strength, the I.W.W. and the Anarchists joyfully fell in with it, and not they alone, but the apostles of discontent of whatever creed. Miss Goldman told me a surprising thing, which was that among those who aided in the raid on the churches were many who were neither anarchists nor I.W.W. men, but simply free-thinkers in religion.

"That," she said, "was the particular phase that appealed to them, not the industrial feature of the subject. They certainly succeeded in doing better anti-religious work than some of the secularists; they placed the church where Ingersoll couldn't have placed it."

The flames were assiduously fanned from two headquarters, those of the I.W.W. on West Street and those of the Anarchists at 313 Grand Street. They worked independently and were in all respects harmonious.

FOOD, NOT POLITICS, WANTED

"The break that is coming between the two elements," said one of them, "is largely over the question of organization. The conference of the unem-

ployed on Grand Street realizes the impossibility of organizing the unemployed, and simply stands for demonstrations that will picture the issue
vividly. The I.W.W. are trying to organize the movement. On that point
clashes have come.

"It has been the effect, too, of making sharper the divisions between the
Socialists and the I.W.W., for the I.W.W. very sensibly used the argument, 'What are your political methods going to do for the unemployed,
who are actually suffering? They want food, not politics.'"

On this matter of "dramatizing the issue" the leaders of the revolt believe that wherever they show their ragged regiments the picture is painted
on the mind of everyone who sees them. They are, these leaders say, a
forlorn and miserable-looking crowd, who will touch quickly the understanding of any spectator to whom unemployment has been merely a name.

"If you had seen the way they ate the sandwiches at the Ferrer School,
you would have had no doubt about their being hungry," said Leonard
Abbott.

"That crowd at Union Square," said Emma Goldman, "was the most
forlorn gathering of human beings I ever laid my eyes on. They were cold
and hungry; they shivered incessantly. One of these men is in the last
stages of tuberculosis; he has six children; the other day he was thrown
out of his miserable garret, where rags and junk were his furniture.

"We aim to call attention to the unemployed. Something must be done
for men like that one. If I owned a restaurant, or even a platform, and
the unemployed came there, I would let them use it as much as possible—
because," she added significantly, "the other way is a stupid way, it
doesn't pay.

"Will this lead to disorder? That will depend on the police. I don't believe the unemployed will submit silently to being clubbed.

"They do not want to cause a rumpus. But if the police beat them up,
I think the time is passed when people will submit to it. I think the editorial in the *Times* last Monday was more of an incitement to riot than
anything that I have said. It told the police to use violence. The editor
must know that the police need no such incitement.

"There are enough people of kindly instinct, of all classes, to assist the
unemployed, if they can be made to see what unemployment means. Then
the people would not be driven to desperation. But if they are to be arrested
by the police on one side, and resistance by the people on the other, who
can see the result?"

So little has been heard of the anarchists of late years that it struck the
town with astonishment to see their appearance in such menacing num-

bers. It has been so often said that they are dying out that their strength was amazing.

But if they are dying out, it does not manifest itself in their outward appearance. Five years ago Berkman and Emma Goldman got out their little magazine, *Mother Earth,* in a poor little tenement in East Twelfth Street. Later they were able to take an office on West 28th Street and present a much smarter appearance. Now they have a whole house, a brownstone one, at 74 West 119th Street, where they have several assistants.

Yearly Miss Goldman tours the country, delivering her lectures in the principal cities. When she began them she was frequently arrested; now she meets no interference and her audiences grow. There ar forty or fifty publishing houses in the country which get out revolutionary literature exclusively. A new one was recently started in this city, the Rabelais Press, run by a man named Rompapas. Anarchism may be dying out, but if one searches for signs of its moribund condition he is likely to find things that will disagreeably astonish him.

SHE NEVER RUNS AWAY

She is going on her usual tour on March 30th, and Dr. Ben Reitman, her manager, is in Chicago now arranging it. This accounts for the otherwise inexplicable fact that this picturesque and fiery rebel's name has not appeared in the reports of the Tannenbaum movement. "If he had been here you would not have heard him," said Miss Goldman, with a flash in her eyes unusual for her. In conversation, whatever she may be on the platform, she is the quietest and most impassive of talkers.

In the newspaper discussions of these things there are often references to the "Goldman-Berkman group of anarchists." The term is a misnomer; there is no such group, or rather the term implies divisions that do not exist. Emma Goldman and Alexander Berkman are leaders of all the anarchists, not only in this city but in the whole country.

Another favorite illusion is that these rebels, in times of stress, are in hiding somewhere, from which they emerge to create trouble and then disappear again. After the Union Square meeting and the Fifth Avenue march, it was reported that Emma Goldman had "fled from the city for the week-end." She was in fact delivering a lecture in Newark.

"As if anyone had ever heard of Emma Goldman running away," she said disdainfully. "Everyone knows where I live, and anyone who doesn't can ask the police—they know."

Emma Goldman, like many of her followers, was converted to anarchism by the hanging of the four Chicago anarchists after the Haymarket outbreak. That outbreak was the culmination of just such demonstrations as are being carried on now. These demonstrations continued until the Chicago police undertook to break up the meeting held at Haymarket Square to discuss the unemployment situation of that day; one of the crowd threw a bomb and seven policemen were killed. Seven of the anarchist leaders were convicted of incendiary utterances and four were hanged; one blew out his brains on the day appointed for his execution, and two were sentenced to life imprisonment, but were pardoned after the excitement of the time had died down.

That execution is always in the minds of the revolutionary leaders but it does not daunt them. It made an anarchist of Emma Goldman; after it Berkman assaulted Henry C. Frick and served sixteen years in prison for it. Haywood has since been on trial for his life. Elizabeth Gurley Flynn has served a prison term. Whatever is before them, it cannot frighten them or turn them aside. They are unafraid and indomitable. As Emma Goldman says, the police know where she lives, and no one ever heard of her running away.

This is the situation. This is the history and meaning of what we are now seeing. This is what confronts the social order. Is it, or is it not, worth serious thought?

I falteringly gave an interview to a nice woman on the *New York Evening World*, concealing as best I could my inner perturbation, and she wrote:

FAIR SOCIETY WOMAN DEFENDS I.W.W.; IS NEITHER ANAR-
CHIST NOR SOCIALIST, BUT THINKS UNEMPLOYED NOT
TO BLAME. "I THINK THAT THE UNEMPLOYED ARE JUS-
TIFIED IN DOING ANYTHING TO CALL PUBLIC ATTEN-
TION TO THEIR CONDITION," SAYS MRS. MABEL DODGE

"Anything that doesn't injure people," she qualified. "Of course, I don't believe in dynamite and that kind of thing," adds the Society Leader, but she would like to help in bringing about a proper organization of all labor.

Mrs. Dodge, who attends the Tannenbaum trial every day, says she is a student watching trend of events.

A sphinx is sitting in General Sessions Court, watching the trial of young Frank Tannenbaum, whom the police charge with "participation in an unlawful assembly" in St. Alphonsus's Church three weeks ago.

The name of the sphinx is Mrs. Mabel Dodge, and she lives at No. 23

Fifth Avenue. One of the reasons why she is a sphinx is because, living where she does live, she quietly orders her car every morning, bumps over the rough cobbles in the Centre Street district, and waits the day through in the crowded, not too well ventilated room on the second floor of the Criminal Courts Building, where the boy leader of the I.W.W. is fighting for his liberty.

Why is a society woman from Fifth Avenue interested in such a trial? Is she an Anarchist? Is she a Socialist? Does she belong to the Industrial Workers of the World? Or is she a Haroun-al-Raschid-ess, a descendant in spirit of the curious Caliph who would always desert his throne "for to admire and for to see, for to examine this world so wide"?

HER ANSWERS TO THE QUESTIONS ABOUT HER

These are some of the questions they are whispering in General Sessions: And this is what she told me:

"I am not an Anarchist. I do not belong to the Socialist Party. I am not a member of the Industrial Workers of the World. I am not a person who joins anything. I am a student and I am interested, keenly interested, in this trial and in all the circumstances of the recent I.W.W. conflict with the established order."

A few evenings ago Mrs. Dodge invited a number of I.W.W. leaders to her Fifth Avenue home. Among those present were gentlemen with the euphonious names of "Wild Joe" O'Carroll, "Chowder Joe" O'Brien, "Omaha Doc" Roth, and "Baldy" McSween. But again Mrs. Dodge blandly explained, "I invited these men merely to listen to their stories. I am a student and wished to get information at first hand. I did not invite them socially nor to feed them."

"What are your conclusions about them?" I asked. "Obviously they don't bore you. But are you pleased or disgusted? Do you agree with the people who sum up the I.W.W.'s as a 'bunch of bums'? Or do you consider them martyrs?"

Mrs. Dodge shot me an inscrutable glance. . . .

"If some of the unemployed," she hinted softly, "have qualities that are not altogether desirable, I think the blame should be placed on their environment rather than on the men. We all are acted upon by our surroundings, and respond to them. As for Tannenbaum himself, it seems to me that all the testimony goes to show that he is an earnest, sincere fellow, who tried to do the best he could for his people, those whom he pitied and wanted to help. . . ."

III

"But it is alleged that the men led by Tannenbaum pushed and knocked over men and women worshipers," I submitted.

"They didn't," replied Mrs. Dodge, more firmly than I had yet heard her speak. "And I don't believe the testimony of some of the police on this point."

Then she tacked sweetly in the opposite direction. "If you're going to write an interview with me," she observed, "I wish you'd say that I think Mr. Tannenbaum is receiving a splendidly fair trial. Judge Wadhams is a wonderful judge, scrupulously just, and insistent that the accused be given the benefit of the law, as much as the accusers. I think the radicals ought to feel very well satisfied with the conduct of this trial. . . ."

"Do you believe that the I.W.W. is sincere?"

"I believe that they want to work under the conditions which they have decided are just, including both the wages and the working day, and I think that they have a right to exact those conditions."

"And why, really and truly why, have you interested yourself in this whole affair?" I persisted.

But the sphinx of General Sessions only smiled and smiled.

(New York Evening World; March 27, 1914.)

Tannenbaum was convicted and given a year in prison, and the following is from an account in the *Sun* on March 28, reporting his speech before his sentence was passed. Judge Wadhams listened to him with attention and said he felt sorry Frank had not embraced the opportunities of this country. Frank said his home was a cell in the Tombs! He went on:

"There was once a person who said that society would forgive murder or arson, but that the one thing it would not forgive was the preaching of a new gospel," said Tannenbaum. "That is my crime.

"There is no instance in the world's history where the efforts of the slave class to free themselves have been considered legal. I belong to the slave class.

"I am accused of participating in an unlawful assembly. I don't know of any assembly on the part of working people that would be lawful.

"Why is there all this nonsense about bloodshed? The capitalistic class sheds more blood in one year than the workers do in five.

"Another thing I want to speak about is my attitude toward the priests. I am by nature polite even to my enemies. I tell you Dr. Schneider—that Dr. Schneider who was supposed to represent the gospel of Christ, the man who died on the cross—if He came to earth today Father Schneider would be the first to crucify him, in my estimation.

"I have only one thing more to say. Before I was arrested I never knew anything about the police or courts. I was ignorant of all such things. From what I have learned since, I have very little respect for courts or law.

"The day that I was brought into court, justice flew out of the window and never came back. Your jurymen never take the circumstances, the passions, the feelings of men into consideration.

"I didn't want this trial. I knew what I was going to get, but my friends insisted that I come to trial.

"It is my last trial. If I am ever arrested again there will be no more trials. These jurors are members of your class. They are capitalists in miniature. My crime was that of a starving man who tries to steal bread."

Judge Wadhams, in passing sentence, said:

"There is no place in the world where the workingman finds such opportunities as in the United States. Your father and mother realized that. They came here and brought their boy with them.

"You have failed to appreciate the spirit of American institutions. Most of those who come here from other countries come to work, to use every means to better their fellow men.

"True liberty can only exist through respect to the law, which all the people have adopted in order that all may have equal opportunity. Your offense was not in seeking to help your fellow men, but the way in which you did it."

When Judge Wadhams asked if he wished to be remanded to await sentence, he replied, "I do not. I want to be sentenced without further delay in this farce."

Although I was feeling flustered at having been drawn into the publicity, Walter had told me I could always get front-page space and I knew I should do what I could to help but I hated being called "an ardent Socialist" (who had ever heard of an ardent Socialist?) and a "society matron" and a "Red." Most of all I had hated being called a "sphinx"!

After the trial was over I agreed to write a short "statement" of my views if they would promise to print it as I gave it to them and they did, and this is what I wrote:

I have no unchanging convictions as to the divine rightness of any human institutions. The institution, *per se,* does not interest me; the indi-

vidual does. To me all people are just people—God is right to be no re-
spector of persons. The only difference I see in people is in degrees of
ignorance concerning themselves and other people.

I think most people are good. They are the interesting ones because
there is an infinite profundity in goodness, whereas evil is usually a
superficial thing. The badness of a so-called bad man isn't much more than
skin deep and with nothing underneath.

I think that most people love justice and truth more than they do injustice and dishonesty. Perhaps it is enough to say: most people love.

Afterwards I wrote a fuller account of my attitude or what I supposed it to be, and Viereck printed it in *The International*. It ended
thus:

. . . And everyone in that trial was doing the best he knew how, to
serve the system which he upholds. For each of them "the system" embodied "Justice," and each of them was loyal to it and each of them did
his "duty." From the police officers to the priests, the newspapermen, and
the attorneys, through the jury and back to the judge, there flowed one
stern purpose—the sincere and passionate desire to be loyal to that part
of the system to which each belonged. And one boy came up against this
organized loyalty asking for a little different justice than the one which
all the rest of them there had known and supported for so long. And
naturally he didn't get it.

And was there any place to lay blame when all of them were doing the
best they knew how to do?

All those who were present at the trial who were on the side of Labor
must have felt one thing, and that was that the way must be found to get
these honest men on that side.

How enlist this untiring energy, this devotion to a proven cause?

Just because these people serve an imperfect and narrow ideal so well
they would serve a better one still better.

How give it to them?

Because Frank Tannenbaum and others like him have asked for something else and will go on and on, asking and asking for something else
until they get it. But how?

Wage earners of America!

When will you so organize that by your collective action you will give
to these brothers of yours a deeper truth and a broader justice to uphold?

When it came out I received many letters and the following was
among them:

The Old First Church
Fifth Avenue, 11th and 12th Sts.
New York City
HOWARD DUFFIELD, D.D., *Pastor*

April 15.

MY DEAR MISS DODGE:

I have just received a copy of *The International* containing your interesting comment upon the Tannenbaum Case. I heartily agree with your view of the matter. In my opinion you went to the heart of the situation when you said, "The way must be found to get at these honest men on that side"; and you stated the exact problem which we are now facing, when you wrote, "How enlist this untiring energy, this devotion to a proven cause."

I felt perhaps specially interested in these statements of yours, for the reason that I had said the very same thing in almost the same words, from my pulpit on the evening following the visit of Tannenbaum to my Church, and elaborated those ideas in the morning sermon of Palm Sunday.

With sincere regards, I remain,

Cordially,

HOWARD DUFFIELD.

Miss Mabel Dodge,
The International Monthly,
715 Broadway, New York City.

It really became embarrassing to read in every paper one opened: "A Sphinx watched the trial of young Frank Tannenbaum. . . ." Not only our New York papers, but the Associated Press throughout the country fancied that phrase and hundreds of press clippings flowed in from bureaus until I was ready to go back to Florence and watch cypresses grow instead of trying to take an intelligent interest in movements!

So Frank Tannenbaum went to the island prison for a year. When he was released, I was living in the little Sharkey cottage in Croton— and Max Eastman and I talked over his future to see what could be done to help him.

Finally he came out to see me, graver, older, very pale. He had kept his eyes open and had learned all there was to be known about *that* prison. He wanted to stick to prisons, he said, wanted to learn more, to improve himself, and then to give his life to changing the conditions of prisons in America. He was crystallized in the prison complex.

115

Max helped him by giving him a job on *The Masses,* and his salary was paid by some friends who wanted to help him take the course at Columbia University that he wanted so much, and I didn't see him again for nearly twenty years, for I was passing out of the radical group into the artist group by that time.

CHAPTER VI

Unemployment

NOT long afterwards, while Tannenbaum himself was in jail, long articles appeared in the newspapers with such headings as: "Churches to Aid Jobless," and "Pastors Accept I.W.W. Gage: Will Aid Unemployment." And the church people woke up and began to take action. Emma Goldman and Berkman and the others decided to have a Parade—with demonstrations on Fifth Avenue. Even the Socialists got up a mild demonstration in Cooper Union, but that wasn't a brave one, for they had promised to let one of the I.W.W. leaders speak, then thought better of it; but he rushed forward onto the platform anyway so that let loose a riot, a real fight between the Socialists and the I.W.W.'s and the unemployed and the police who were there to keep peace.

After this outbreak and with other meetings scheduled, Steffens, with a leg on either side of the fence, feared trouble. So he went to some of his friends beforehand and the newspapers announced: "Police Will Be Lenient. Lincoln Steffens Promises the Meeting Will Be Orderly." However, this is the way it took place and was described and it certainly harrowed polite people: "Bearing Black Flag Mob Raids Fifth Avenue." "Following Incendiary Speech in Union Square by Emma Goldman, Alexander Berkman Leads 1,000 in Parade." "Anarchists Rout Fifth Avenue Throng!" "Emma Goldman Tells Mob to Storm Churches and Shops." "Reds Go up Fifth Avenue Cursing the Rich! Marchers Shake Fists at Churches and Clubs!" "I.W.W. Riot in 5th Ave.; Women Pushed Off Curb. Emma Goldman Urges Hearers to Invade Homes and Help Themselves. Cry 'Down with the Rich!' " "Marchers Drive All Well-Dressed Persons to Seek Refuge in Doorways."

The *New York American,* on March 22, reported:

From a human boiling pot in Union Square, presided over by Alexander Berkman and kept hot by the fiery words of Emma Goldman, a seething stream of excited men and women of the I.W.W. and anarchist organizations surged under the black banner up Broadway and Fifth Avenue to One Hundred and Seventh Street yesterday afternoon in one of the most riotous class demonstrations that New York had ever known. . . .

Lincoln Steffens, President of the Free Speech League, arrived at Union Square with the leaders of the unemployed. He asked a park policeman if the meeting could be held in the park without a permit. The policeman said, "No," and the speakers went into the street. Mr. Steffens left before the speaking began.

Miss Goldman directly urged the unprecedented demonstration. In her Union Square speech she was inflammatory.

"Fellow workers, friends, and detectives," she began, but her introduction caused such applause that she never finished the sentence. When she began to talk, her tight-fitting brown sweater was buttoned tight about her, but it was wide open as she gave her final message to the throng:

"I call upon you," she shouted wildly as she delivered this final message, "to organize and march on Fifth Avenue and help yourselves to the things you have created!"

There was so much excitement going on, it was natural to have an Evening devoted to a discussion of what the newspapers now began for the first time to call the "Unemployment Movement!"

While Frank Tannenbaum was in jail quietly reading an armload of books I sent him by Steff—Nietzsche, Karl Marx, Tolstoi, and so on—and Frank Strang Hamilton whom the papers now featured as "Tannenbaum's successor" was holding a mass meeting in Rutgers Square, we met to talk.

Bill and Emma and Berkman were there again, and Walter Lippmann and Steff and Hutch and all the other sympathizers. A great gathering. Before we settled down to the discussion, someone rushed up to me and whispered, "There are some newspapermen coming in!"

I glided importantly over to Walter Lippmann whom I was anxious to impress because he was so strong and young and opinionated and rational. I flattered by a feminine gesture. I laid the responsibility on him. My instinct assumed him to be more powerful than the anarchists, more manly, more succinctly male than any Killer or Talker at the Party, and I wanted to please him very much. So I gave him the initiative to act instead of giving it to dear Hutch or Steff or anyone else.

"There are some newspapermen coming in," I murmured to him, standing inert and submissive. It was a moment, really, for the most Direct Action! He was young enough to look a little flustered, though he continued to be Rational and grew stronger around the mouth. Walter was big and rather fat, but he had, I was fond of saying, intellectualized his fat so that it shone a little. He, too, looked like a Buddha, but undefaced like Bill Haywood who had lost an eye in a fight. Walter was never, never going to lose an eye in a fight. "He might," I thought, "lose his glow, but he will never lose an eye."

He moved quickly through the crowded rooms until he spotted the undesirables we had so carefully *not* invited. How he could tell them I couldn't see. They looked like everybody else there. Surely he didn't know everybody any better than I did. Was it not my contention that all people are just people and there is really only a relative difference between them? My Evenings were based upon that Idea. How, then, did Walter know the newspapermen from the anarchists? Some of them had on evening clothes and some of them didn't, just like the others all around. But Walter knew. He went up to a group of strangers and said:

"This is a private meeting. The Press is not invited."

One of them tried to hold him in an argument while the others peered around trying to spot Well-Known Characters. It was hard—almost impossible—to get them to leave.

"But," I thought anxiously, "surely we should not put them out. They are just *people,* too. They are part of Life trying to express Itself in a certain pattern. It chooses to include newspapermen tonight—why should I let Walter interfere?" I went up to him to stop him.

The newspapermen leaned eagerly towards me as though I were less a woman than a ten-dollar gold piece; little note-books were in their twitching fingers. I was quite scared and flustered, myself.

Walter somehow caught my intention and gave me a look that called me crazy. He was very incensed at the opposition the newspapermen gave him, stalling as they were, and his jaw kept looking more and more obstinate. It wasn't long, though; he had them out of the door and the door closed on them and their resentful faces. All of the morning papers, then, not only in New York but all over the country, were very mean. Here are some of the things they printed. I will not reprint all of them; only enough to show the type of things they said.

From the *Washington Herald,* March 11, 1914:

I.W.W. THRONG ARE GUESTS OF SOCIETY FOLK ON FIFTH AVENUE. WOMEN IN EVENING GOWNS ENTERTAIN BILL HAYWOOD, AGITATORS AND THE UNEMPLOYED IN HOME OF MRS. MABEL DODGE. A HORDE OF IDLE ALSO DESCEND ON THE UNIVERSITY SETTLEMENT, WHERE THEIR LEADERS CALL THEIR FORCES TO REVO-LUTION

Frank Strang Hamilton, the long-haired leader of the "army of unem-ployed," Big Bill Haywood, the I.W.W. leader, Rose Mahmer, the fiery young woman agitator, about a dozen of the unemployed and sundry anar-chists were entertained last night in the home of Mrs. Mabel Dodge, at No. 23 Fifth Avenue.

About 200 men and women, in evening dress, and nearly all, women included, smoking cigarettes, took part in the meeting. Between puffs of gold-tipped cigarettes men and women plied the visitors with questions about labor conditions and remedies for unemployment.

The meeting was supposed to be secret. Earlier in the evening Mrs. Dodge denied it was to take place but Hamilton named the meeting place. When he was asked what was the occasion for a clean collar, he replied:

"I have been invited by Mrs. Dodge to tell Fifth Avenue the condition of the unemployed."

The Dodge apartment is on the third floor of the Fifth Avenue resi-dence. It is under the apartment occupied by former Governor Sulzer and above that of General Daniel E. Sickles.

Just who attended the meeting could not be learned. There was commo-tion when the presence of newspaper men became known. Women in low-necked gowns hid behind escorts and tried to hide their cigarettes. The reporters left when it was announced it was a private meeting. . . .

From the *New York American,* March 12, 1914:

GUESTS DINE WITH MRS. MABEL DODGE AS BAND OF FIFTY
INVADE A SYNAGOGUE

The I.W.W. army of the unemployed had two new experiences to re-member today as the result of an active night.

Big Bill Haywood and Frank S. Hamilton had invaded the Fifth Avenue home of Mrs. Mabel Dodge, by invitation, and fifty of the army had been driven by the police from a synagogue. . . .

From the *Brooklyn Citizen;* March 12, 1914:

I.W.W. MEN STARVE AS LEADERS EAT. LATTER MAKE MERRY IN DODGE'S FIFTH AVE. HOME. DUPES FEED ON ELOQUENCE UNTIL AN "ANGEL" APPEARS. CROWD DESERTS FIERY ORATOR FOR FOOD.—HUSKY MEN, INVADING SYNAGOGUE, TOLD BY PRESIDENT FINKELSTEIN THEY ARE ABLE TO WORK. . . .

From the *New York Sun;* March 12, 1914:

LEADERS OF I.W.W. FIFTH AVE. GUESTS MINGLE WITH MEN AND WOMEN IN EVENING CLOTHES AT MRS. DODGE'S HOUSE. ARMY NOT SO WELL OFF. SLEEP ON UNIVERSITY'S SETTLEMENT BENCHES—PAY FOR THEIR OWN SCANTY SUPPER

The idle I.W.W. brethren slept on benches last night at the University Settlement after munching bread and drinking coffee that they had to buy themselves. These they speedily disposed of, to the accompaniment of the army's battle hymn:

> "O, why don't you work
> Like the other folks do?
> How the hell can I work
> When there's no work to do?"

At 23 Fifth Avenue the reporters were admitted by the colored factotum to Mrs. Dodge's rooms.

Several I.W.W. leaders who had left their marching friends in Rutgers Square were neatly and serviceably clad in gray sweaters and other habiliments that evoked no criticism. Most of the large number of women wore evening gowns. All were listening intently to the answers Big Bill Haywood was giving to a flock of questions about what was the remedy for the present social unrest.

There were present some men with long, black, flowing locks, who say they are anarchists, some of the Haywood type who say they are leaders of industrial organizations, some who belong to social uplift movements in

New York and have offices in skyscrapers down town, some women who didn't appear to have any occupations, but an overwhelming interest in the welfare of the downtrodden, and then, of course, the plain professional "unemployed."

"We will now listen to a speech from Mr. Haywood and others, but I wish to say that the movement of the I.W.W. into the religious institutions recently had better be left out of the discussion," said the leader.

RED BANNER THERE

Mr. Haywood and some others got up and moved to the center of the room, whereupon became visible one of the red I.W.W. banners used last year in the Paterson pageant in Madison Square Garden.

Just then one of the unemployed whispered to a woman in evening dress beside whom he was standing that reporters had entered the room.

A woman with a low gown removed her cigarette—several of the women were smoking and virtually all of the men—and said something that sounded like, "Oh, horrid!"

A heavy set young man came out and said that the gathering was for the purpose of discussing social problems and that all present were friends of Mrs. Dodge and that positively nothing should be published about it.

A man who said he lived in the house and was a friend of the General's asked a policeman outside if those people were going to be allowed to wake up his aged and ill friend. He was reassured and went back home. But the meeting lasted until late in the evening.

The directories give 23 Fifth Avenue as the residence of Edwin S. Dodge, an architect of 101 Park Avenue. An inquiry over Mr. Dodge's telephone last night brought the information that the meeting there was strictly private and that no information would be given about it.

CHAPTER VII

Psychic

MRS. DAVIDGE, Bishop Potter's daughter, lived down on Staten Island in a square old brick mansion that she had bought for a song from two old maiden ladies who were the last of their family who wanted to live there.

Clarissa Davidge was the unconventional one of her family. She was middle-aged and partially crippled so she walked with a limp, and she had a fringe like ruffled brown feathers and the brightest of brown eyes. Animated, eccentric, rattle-brained Clarissa! Always dressed like the doll of any little girl of ten who has had recourse to the family ragbag and secured bits of gay silk, fur, and lace, she was warmhearted, rather bad-tempered, and fond of expressing herself in a loud, high-pitched voice in a language rich with her own variations.

She collected. She collected old furniture and promising artists. Having transferred the family sense of excellence from worldliness and religion to poetry and paint and antiques, she furnished her house with spinning wheels, Cape Cod china, four-post bedsteads, a painter, and a poet.

She had a little shop on Madison Avenue that somehow combined old furniture, modern art, and promises of an introduction to Edwin Arlington Robinson, who, though not negotiable like Uncle Harry's pictures or the Windsor chairs, still represented solid value in the old red brick house on Staten Island because he was such a *real* poet and so unsociable. His shy withdrawal made him loom more and more significant there, so that he was actually more of a background and lent more to the atmosphere than the old hooked rugs, the lanterns, and the looms.

He and Uncle Harry had been "boon companions" once upon a time. They had been jolly, expansive, and immoderate together before

Aunt Clarissa got hold of them. They had been wont to sit up all night together in one or another of the warm, gilded saloons along Broadway and Uncle Harry had been the most wonderful talker. "A rare story teller," Robinson told me later.

I don't know how Aunt Clarissa Davidge accomplished it, but she sought to save them. Of course they were poor, for Uncle Harry never had been known to sell one of his queer pictures and Robinson had only had one job and that one he'd lost because he hadn't liked it. There was a tale I've half forgotten which Aunt Clarissa told—how Theodore Roosevelt had read one of the poems in a magazine and, hearing how hard up Robinson was, had sent for him and told him there was a job waiting for him down in the Customs House in New York.

The story ran that E. A. went down and sat in a chair at a desk in the dark, grimy official building. He sat and he sat and nothing happened. There didn't seem to be anything for him to do. Nobody gave him any work. He just sat in a silent place. Finally he wrote a resignation and sent it in to Roosevelt who ordered E. A. to his side. "What is this for?" he demanded, pointing to E. A.'s resignation.

"Well, sir, there's not enough for me to do there. There's not a *job*."

"Here, take it and go back," Roosevelt blustered, shoving the resignation at the bewildered E. A. "Your job's writing poetry, man! Go back down there and do it!"

Notwithstanding good intentions, special privilege, and what not, E. A. left the Customs House desk. Poetry wouldn't flow there. It was better to be at Aunt Clarissa's, first in an abandoned stable in the back yard of her house near Washington Square, and then on the tiptop floor of the old brick house out in the country.

Henry Taylor joined him, for they were linked together in Mrs. Davidge's intention. Paint and poetry went together in her mind. She was determined, however, to eliminate whiskey.

She started in, with great vivacity and concentration, to work first upon Henry Taylor. She never mentioned drink to him at all, but every night she sat and willed him to stop drinking. She was a reader of Judge Troward and others like him, Rudolf Steiner and so on, so she believed that we are surrounded by subjective Mind which is waiting for us to impress it with our wishes so that it may carry them out. Every wish, every thought consciously directed, is marked upon the sensitive surrounding ether, and is carried into form, materialized, brought to being, by Mind. This was called New Thought, and Aunt Clarissa certainly knew how to pull strings in that realm.

"Anything you want!" she would cry gaily. "A diamond necklace or *any*thing. Tell me your wish and I'll help you receive it."

So she silently and methodically begged Subjective Mind to deprive Uncle Harry of his faculty for drinking whiskey, and it did! In rather a short time he announced that he was *through*. He didn't want another drop. And from being a rather juicy, warm, roseate tippler, he turned into an old gray fellow. His hair turned white quite rapidly and his eyes lost their color and became blurred and rather crooked. His pictures, however, were more diaphanous than ever—and soon after his change he painted the King David all in cubes of light, opal and mother-of-pearl it was, with the wise, sad countenance of a prophet appearing through the pale tones.

It was about this time, I think, that I met them. Mrs. Davidge had asked me to motor over and lunch on Staten Island. I was to call for Glackens in Washington Square and bring him along. Betty Goodwin, who wanted to meet Robinson, was coming, too, I was told.

Glackens couldn't go, as it happened, so I motored over alone. The island was in some peculiar way cut off from the neighborhood of New York by more than the bay. It was forlorn, overlooked, unsuccessful, and forgotten. The ferry boat that carried us over bore this same stamp of failure and lifelessness. The current in which that portion of the bay and Staten Island hung, was simply unmagnetic—a dead pocket, so to speak. One felt outside of life in that belt, and very lonely.

I wasn't feeling magnetic myself, so I had nothing in reserve with which to combat the heavy, languid atmosphere on the island as we drove through the unsmiling landscape to where the lovely old pale brick house stood on a slight rise of land overlooking the dull scene, just a little way outside the village.

Aunt Clarissa Davidge knew about houses and chairs and chimney places, so that although the inside of the place was all, in a way, fictitious, yet it seemed real. It was furnished with "good, old pieces," and the house itself was "good." It was designed to impart a feeling of solid security, of unhurried cultured leisure, of comfort and ease and good living out in the country, and it did suggest these precious, recondite qualities.

Stepping, half hopping about, among the spinning wheels, stools, and old chairs and things, Aunt Clarissa masqueraded in a wonderful ancient brocade gown, with a contraption on her mottled hair that was made of bits of lace and ribbon.

She introduced me to a tall, slender woman with an eager face who seemed vivid and interested in life, Mrs. Goodwin, the Betty I had heard her talk about. Others were there and of course poor Uncle Harry, looking serious and sinister in a frock coat. I have forgotten who else, only remembering Edwin Arlington Robinson, who sat opposite me at lunch, and Betty Goodwin, who sat next him.

I had never seen anyone else, except Duse, with quite the depth of somber imprisoned heat in the eyes that this man had. He turned these infinitely dark eyes upon me, black burning deeps. No ocean has ever seemed so deep, no midnight so unendingly deep as those eyes. Was he conscious of the fire within? Did he know the singular discomfort he caused by the black flare of his glance?

The rest of his face did not know what the eyes disclosed. His nose was rather pointed and inquisitive, instead of all-knowing like the eyes, and his mouth had rather an inept Peter Newell look, awfully solemn, increasingly silent as the eager, animated woman beside him attempted to secure his attention with casual social ease. In fact her social ease aroused my envy and I thought:

"How obtuse that woman is! She doesn't know *beans!*" And I determined to succeed by some infinitesimal effort where she failed by all her massed endeavors. She pirouetted, flashed her teeth, beamed, became fond, maternal, encompassing, richer and richer in voice and bluer of eye. Mrs. Davidge chirped, responded to the advances Robinson neglected, hurriedly answered questions addressed to him that she feared he would not answer, laughed, gestured, and generally produced an impression of stimulated responsiveness that filled the air, and, possibly, deceived Mrs. Goodwin into believing it was Robinson's reward to her for her own expenditure.

There are frequent exchanges between persons in a tight social group that are in this fashion oblique and indirect, so much output, so much response—thrown out and soaked up by the cellular constellations present. However, both E. A. and I were very conscious and very aware. One small flash out of my silence and apathy in the midst of so much animation and attention caught him straight and won an instant answer—a flicker of understanding.

I think he was a stingy, inhibited man, always, but he gave me, that first time I lunched with him, one tiny, shy, burning, and directed glance that conveyed his complete realization of everything any one of us there could know, with something more than any of us knew and which I still don't know.

He flashed his nice perception of all the endeavors of women (poor creatures) and allowed me, or so I thought, a fraction of appreciation for my particular, more subtle manner of approach, as contrasted with the less specialized, unconscious, and possibly more biological method of the lady at his side.

Also he lost for one brief instant his solemn Peter Newell look (the look that somehow made one feel one could size him up in a limerick if one tried) and his face was ridden triumphantly by a sly, Yankee, twisted smile that spelled hardtack, axes, gnarled logs, and similar realities, and showed, resident within him, a humorous common sense, deeper than any present woe, and tougher than any repression that dominated his habitual manner.

At that first meeting, then, E. A. and I, in a reciprocal flicker of the utmost brevity, met, exchanged a certain essential knowledge of each other, realized each other, and for so long as we lasted, I knew, would be cronies, pals, comrades, friends, affinities, or whatever; too much *en rapport* to be lovers, too sympathetic, perhaps, to be lovers, if ever in this mortal universe he should take a lover, that man whose whole emotional drama had been carried on with the Bottle.

His friend Ridgely Torrence, whose skull is carven to represent an archangel's, just as Bayard's was, told me that at college E. A. was engaged to a Girl. But after a few months he came to her and told her he had been thinking it over and he knew he must decide between Love and Poetry—and he had decided to choose Poetry. So the engagement was broken.

This tale, filtered through the nature of another, may be colored, like all accounts, by the story-teller's essence. Yet it has a certain feeling of truth about it. E. A. didn't care for anything but Poetry, or rather for anything but that slow, tormentingly slow, drop by drop distillation of inner factuality which gains, for the prisoner of this function, the name of Poetry.

I saw Mrs. Davidge a few times after this, often enough to hear her opinion of E. A.'s opinion of Betty and of me—and also to hear her gay account of her "absent treatment" of E. A. I heard it from him, later, his side of it. At this time, her account was convincing enough:

"Uncle Harry and I made up our minds to help him." (Oh, yes, Uncle Harry was no longer convivial of nights!) "So every evening at 8 o'clock we just folded our hands and closed our eyes, and whether E. A. was there or not, we tried to take whiskey out of his consciousness. He found out we were doing it, so he always goes up to his room after supper now—but we go on working just the same. Well, the other night E. A. stopped in the doorway when he was going out, and he said, 'Well, Aunt Clarissa, you have stopped my whiskey. I can't drink whiskey any more, *but I can drink beer and I'm going to drink beer!*'"

Her eyes flashed with triumph! "Go on, E. A., turn yourself into a *tank,* if you *can,* but Uncle Harry and I are going to go on working on *beer!*"

("Why," said E. A., as we lunched together at Poligniani's one day, "I used to work my way down Broadway to the Ferry, stopping in every saloon, getting a drink in each one, free in conscience to drink, but after that I simply couldn't *taste* the stuff. Call it suggestion or anything you like, but there it is. Oh, she's a witch, you know.")

So when Neith and I went down to spend the night there, Aunt Clarissa was still Working on Beer. I was in rather a dilapidated mood when we went. I had had a depressing time with Edwin. Hutch, well, my sympathy with Hutch fluctuated, sometimes leaving me in the lurch. I felt down, depleted, gray, sad. And motoring along the dismal Staten Island roads was not exhilarating. Nor was Neith, so quiet, calm, and remote inside her white skin. She was never exciting to one outside herself, though I liked her very much always.

The compactly built old brick house was attractive, though. As soon as I came near it I loved it, but, as I said to Neith, I couldn't imagine living in it, not on Staten Island!

Tea in the old house was pleasant. No one there but Neith and Aunt Clarissa and I. I wondered where E. A. was. I hoped to see him again, for I was intensely curious about him, his way, his ideas, himself. The fire was glowing in the old-fashioned grate and Aunt Clarissa gave us lovely tea biscuits that she had made herself. We sat drowsy and comfortable and a little sad and lonesome by the fire in that room full of slightly tarnished but dignified colonial antiques.

"E. A. will be down to supper," Mrs. Davidge told us, "and then he'll leave us afterwards because he doesn't like our Work."

"What work?" Neith asked.

"You'll see," said Aunt Clarissa. "You know he *loves* red," she went on. "He always wears an old red hunting coat up in his room."

And instantly I saw him in it, working, writing, or just mooning, his long nose pointing out in front of him as he rocked slightly in a little mahogany rocker in the center of his rather bare room. I imagined him so vividly, sitting there lost in his thoughts, his red coat the only bright spot there, that I do not know whether I really saw him so later on, or whether the picture that returns to me now came to me in a purely imaginary fashion.

"How still it is here," I said, which is the inevitable comment everybody makes upon arriving at a country house, after having been in the city.

"Quiet and peaceful," agreed Aunt Clarissa in her high, strained voice, and with a manner that betrayed she'd give a good deal for something to happen! ("A quiet life may come to some who like it rather gay!")

The melancholy at the bottom of me oozed into my blood till I felt darkened all over by it. To add to the impression of drear though comfortable negativeness in the environment, it began to rain, so that we heard the patter of drops on the windows.

"I hope Uncle Harry won't get wet," exclaimed Mrs. Davidge. She expected him on a later boat than the one we had come on, and soon we heard the heavy mahogany front door open and close again with a bang.

I had meant to suggest sending our motor to meet him, but had felt too lazy to go through with the need to telephone to the village garage about it. So he came in his usual fashion—I think with the local motor company's taxi. It seems to me he ran the New York antique shop for Aunt Clarissa most of the time.

When the dinner bell pealed through the house, we heard a slow step on the stairs and E. A. came into the sitting room. He was without doubt the most inarticulate man I have ever known. He usually couldn't or anyway didn't say a word. And this time there was no flash between us, though he gave me a rather friendly smile, that was nevertheless distinctly stingy.

At dinner he sat there pleasantly. That is the very most that can be said of him. How I ever made friends with him, wrote him letters, got answers, consulted him about things, told him everything, in fact, and heard, in turn, his opinions of everyone and everything, is amazing to think of now, as I remember the hermetic exterior he presented, incapable, seemingly, of opening up, flowing out, or giving anything away, either for nothing or in exchange for similar currency.

"The man is a tomb," I thought to myself, disappointedly. "Sealed, too."

He sat with us for a little while, afterwards, in the warm sitting room, but not for long. At about half-past eight, he rose, walked to the door with a somewhat halting gait, his shoulders bowed a little, his tall figure stooping. He turned before he went out and said, "Well, good night!" And as he said it he flicked me a minute glance from the two dark funnels of his eyes; a little, wry, humorous farewell of comprehensive and friendly sympathy as though, in withdrawing his whole identity from the room, he would leave, anyway with me, his private approval; and I thought I knew, once more, that we were cronies.

We sat in silence for a minute, hearing him mount the stairs. Mr. Taylor appeared to be a silent man himself, gray and subdued and safe from drink; he, who E. A. told me afterwards was once the best of company, the grandest story-teller in the world, the life of any party.

Desultory chat went on between the three women. Aunt Clarissa was brisk and purposeful, though, biding her time which was soon to come. At nine o'clock she announced that the moment for their Work had arrived.

"You and Neith needn't stay if you'd rather go up," she said. But we were dying to stay. At least I was. So, sitting as we were, we observed her and her companion compose themselves as for prayer, with folded hands and closed eyes, and a hush, deep and close, fell over the room and over the house. They, those two, sat perfectly motionless, withdrawn, concentrated, impressing upon Subjective Mind the need to deprive Edwin Arlington Robinson of Beer.

Only a few minutes and they were out of it again, bustling Aunt

Clarissa and Uncle Harry, and not long after we all went upstairs to bed. Neith and I had two bedrooms that connected with each other, over the large sitting room where we had passed the evening. They were old-fashioned rooms, with oil lamps to light them, pleasant enough, I suppose. Above me I heard a slow creak, creak, which I gathered was E. A., red-coated in his rocker.

Neith and I giggled a little together in her room over the scene we had passed through downstairs, and then I returned and undressed and got into bed.

But I didn't feel sleepy. The rain came down dully outside in the garden, making a picture of rotted leaves, wet tree trunks and darkened red bricks, and far away a dog barked twice. My heart began to sag and then that old, familiar ache wrung it as so often before, and slowly a deep, a bottomless depression filled me, or rather emptied me, as though my being had a hidden leak somewhere through which my life would presently ebb away.

Heavier and heavier my limbs lay upon the bed, as that essence which alone lightens the clay seemed to leave the body that was powerless to retain it. This is the ultimate incontinence.

Soon I felt I was defenseless, and in my inability to cope with the darkness in me, I realized a return to childhood, a slipping back to immaturity, and all the strength gathered in the years was gone out of me.

And not alone in myself did I observe the change that I was powerless to control. The room itself, space, upon which we ordinarily exercise a certain influence by virtue of our essential power, gained now an ability to alter and assume other characteristics. It seemed to me that while the darkness within myself grew more and more empty, the darkness without that surrounded me grew full, inhabited and active. I felt that the place was alive—alive and terrifying, for Horror walked about me, Horror and Fear were presences in that room.

I had lost all ability to move. I lay completely passive and emptied of vitality—for how long I cannot guess—while the cold sweat that carried away every last vestige of my acquired endurance, the courage I had wrung out of living, poured off my inert body.

Now, while Horror and Fear are only general terms, and it was as large generalities I experienced them at first, after what seemed an endless time they began to assume characteristics, so that a *certain* horror,

131

an *individual* fear, were beginning to shape and reveal themselves to me. I could almost feel the meaning of it all, I could almost know what it was that surrounded me. I vaguely sensed a special occasion for a definite order of agony that the room contained and obliged me to share.

How many hours as we reckon time passed thus, I do not know. But when I was nearly worn down from the insistent vitality of the anguish about me, I heard the door open quietly and Neith stood by my bed. Bending over it, she said in a low, angry voice:

"Mabel! Mabel!"

"Yes," I breathed in abject thankfulness for her.

"Mabel, there's something queer in this house. I don't like it at all."

With an effort I put out a wet hand and drew her into my bed.

"It's *awful!*" I said.

Then she told me, still angry she was too, all she had been through in her room. She told me she had gone to bed and no sooner had she lain down than she had begun to feel, first uncomfortable, and then miserable. She felt, she said, someone else's misery. Agony. Like a live thing beating at her. She had felt obliged to participate in a dreadful terror that was not her own but that sought to enter her consciousness and take possession of her.

This she had fought off. She had tried to argue with herself, to sleep, to count sheep, to think of pleasant things and places. But the thing persisted.

Now I *was* scared! Neith of all people! Cool, skeptical, aloof! Neith who laughed at other people's talk of the Soul, who believed only in what she could see, smell, touch! I clung to her and told her that I *knew* an awful Thing was with us.

"What shall we *do?*" I begged.

"Let's get away out of here. I don't want to pass the night here. Let's dress and go!"

But how! The car was away down in the village. The last tram, someone had told us, left for the Ferry at one o'clock. What time was it? How long had we been lost in the spell of the house?

"I'd rather go home even if we have to walk!" she exclaimed, the usually so sensible Neith. "I'll stay with you while you dress, and then you come in my room with me while I do. We must keep together," she said with firm and angry determination. I myself was too far gone for anger. I was completely and solely scared to death.

She, more courageous, got out of bed and struck a match. Even with the lamp lighted, we knew there was Something besides ourselves in that room, dogging us, beating upon us, seeking to invade us. Always just behind me I felt the Thing. When I turned there was nothing to be seen, but to be felt, oh, *yes!*

Once in dressing I faltered. I thought I couldn't stand it. It would overcome me, the stark, awful, terrifying Something, but Neith encouraged me. Once we broke into insane, nervous laughter, as an objective picture of ourselves forced itself upon us. As I finished my dressing, knocking things over in my haste, and as I made ready to go with her to her room, a timid knocking sounded on the door into the hall.

Uncle Harry stood there, a lighted candle in his hand. In his bedraggled gray dressing gown he looked more like an old gray rat than ever; the candle threw queer lights and shades up onto his face.

"What is the matter?" he asked me in astonishment, seeing me fully dressed.

"There's something in this house," began Neith, bravely. "We *feel* something terrible here," I broke in. "We want to go—to go back to New York!"

"A ghost?" exclaimed Uncle Harry, joyously. "Oh, wait till I tell Aunt Clarissa, she'll be so *delighted!*" He scuttled down the hall, disappearing into the shadows.

"They can have their ghost! I'm *through* with it," announced Neith.

We went into her room and she began to hustle on her clothes, quite different she was in this haste from the self-contained, methodical woman I had known.

"I wish I dared go and tell Mr. Robinson, but I'm scared to."

"Oh, don't let's get him into this. Let's just get out of it quick," she rejoined.

Mrs. Davidge appeared now with Uncle Harry at her heels. She had on a complicated wrapper covered with bows and lace and her hair was obviously in curl papers beneath the silk cap.

"But you can't leave like this!" she expostulated. There was observable in her manner a mixture of elation and indignation. The Potter in her didn't like people leaving her house in the middle of the night for a caprice, but the individual in her was, as Uncle Harry had realized it would be, delighted.

To make a long story short, Neith and I departed in the dark and rain, caught the last train, reached the lighted, reassuring, commonplace ferry boat and collapsed on a bench.

We really didn't know what to do next. I had forgotten to bring the key of my house and we didn't care to go to the Brevoort for fear they wouldn't let us in without any bags, and we had left them behind so as not to carry them down the hill by ourselves. But my ordinary self was in possession again. I was so relieved I didn't care what we did for the rest of the night!

We finally reached the Grand Central Station in New York and made our way to the women's waiting room. There we slunk down on some seats and in the glare of electric lights, with the din of two cleaning women, with mops and tin pails in our ears, we spent the remainder of the night.

Aunt Clarissa and Uncle Harry arrived at 23 Fifth Avenue at ten o'clock the next morning with our bags. *She* limped into the drawing room somber, dignified, and rather cold in manner. The ribbons on her bonnet bobbed backwards, she held her head so high. Uncle Harry was subdued and, as usual, in her background. Sitting down, she spoke:

"We have decided to tell you about La Tourette," she began, for that was the name of the pale old brick mansion from which we had fled. "We haven't told anyone else this, but you evidently contacted the life of the past last night, so you have a right to hear about it." She settled herself more comfortably.

"The last of the family to own La Tourette were two old maid sisters and their bachelor brother. It had been in the family for several generations, and they were deeply rooted there. But the brother began to show signs of interest in a girl down in the village and this upset the two sisters.

"Then, as the tale out there goes, he began to grow sick. Doctors examining him said he was suffering from an obscure illness contracted years before in the Far East, a kind of jungle fever, and gradually he grew worse, for apparently nothing could be done for him. The sisters refused to have a nurse and took care of him themselves, and seemed to show him every attention; but finally, after some months, he died.

"The two women went on living at La Tourette just as they had always done, but they saw fewer and fewer people until one day they went to a real estate office in town, put the place in the hands of an agent for sale, said they would take anything they could get for it, and moved away out West somewhere. That's how I got the house so cheap.

"After we moved in, I heard a little whispering about the property from the village people. They hinted that everything wasn't as it should have been, that the brother had sickened and died too suddenly. . . . They spoke of poison."

"Well, it *was*," I broke in. "What room did he have?"

"Your room," she said, with a queer look on her face. *"And your bed.* We bought some of the furniture they left behind."

Later on I talked to E. A. about it. He said he knew the house was full of something strange, but it hadn't bothered him up there on the third floor.

"The living can fill a place with feelings," he told me, solemnly. "And they can fill it with thoughts. Lacking these they can fill a place with emanations." And he told me an experience he had had in Boston one time. He said he liked to take long walks, not noticing his surroundings particularly. He liked to walk in a long, uninterrupted rhythm while he worked things out.

"That's why I like to go uptown and walk round and round the reservoir," he continued. "When one walks on any of the avenues one is interrupted at every corner and one loses the rhythm. I liked to walk in Boston because there is less traffic there. Well, one day I started out among the red brick buildings of Boston and I walked and walked, not noticing much where I was going. After a while I came to myself. I was still among the red brick houses, but I noticed they were different. Different in quality from those I had come away from. Not different in shape or in color, but different in quality. I couldn't make out what that difference was at first. Finally I noticed a Negro, then another. I saw I was in the Negro quarter. The Negroes made the red brick houses different. They were coming through. . . ."

Ridgely Torrence, to whom I indiscreetly told the story of our night at La Tourette, backed up Neith and me. He, too, had passed a night out there. He, too, had had the room I had. And the way it had affected him was a perfectly sleepless night in that bed with dreadful pains in his body, so strong that he had felt impelled to arouse Aunt Clarissa. But he had stuck it out. When the sun rose the trouble had passed.

Hutch took occasion to write one of his little brochures for his newspaper about our experience. He called it "Two Women and a Ghost." He related it in detail, but, dismissing the ghost at the end, he finished by saying that one of the women (me!), he felt, had a spiritual pain deep down in her, and that, feeling at the time relaxed and tired, this pain had crowded to the surface of her consciousness and overflowed her being. That, having a strong personality, she impressed her friend (Neith!) by some power of suggestion, so that the other woman had been obliged to share this surging, escaping emotion. This interpretation, plainly, Hutch had drawn from his recent reading of Frederic Myers's *Phantasms of the Living*.

Whatever the solution, Neith and I would never face La Tourette again.

Nor did I, to my knowledge, ever haunt her any more, though we spent many nights near each other—unless, indeed, her reaction to the Villa Curonia, two years later, was of the same nature.

Often I used to see E. A. from that time on; we lunched out together, talking endlessly. He was also one of those who believe something was "going to happen"; he always felt things very sensitively. However, he had an idea that some kind of a natural catastrophe was drawing close and that it would particularly affect New York: an earthquake that would topple over all the skyscrapers, or perhaps a tidal wave that would wash the whole thing away. When he was in Boston shortly after, a soothsayer that someone took me to see prophesied the former event and I wrote to tell him so, to which he replied:

93 St. Botolph Street,
Boston, May 27th.

DEAR MRS. DODGE:

Thank you for your confirmation of the 'quake. Of course it is coming. I am sorry to disappoint you, but I don't believe the ghost had much to do with my bad attack. And yet, I can't swear that he didn't. I have heard nothing of Mrs. Taylor's illness, and hope that it was nothing serious. I shall be glad for any news of her, or of the ghost.

Yours sincerely,

E. A. ROBINSON.

He was always fun to lend books to, for he enjoyed talking them over after he read them and his judgment was sure, so he lighted up things for one. He was perhaps the most balancing influence in my life at that time in New York. I could talk over anything with him, books, people, and the daily surprises of my new days and he always, very delicately, pointed out the essential element in whatever we examined together. It was from him that I had the first setback in my enthusiasm for Gertrude's "Portrait." He never stopped joking about that, always bringing it up.

La Tourette,
Richmond, Staten Island,
10 August.

DEAR MRS. DODGE,

Many thanks for leaving the book, which I have found to be profitable and entertaining. I hope you won't be offended if I tell you that I find its picture infinitely more true to life than your portrait (Miss Stein's, I mean) seems to be.

How do you know that it is a portrait of you, after all?

Yours sincerely,

E. A. ROBINSON.

Sometimes I would take him to Stieglitz's where he would ponder upon the pictures hanging there, and then send me this kind of letter:

129 West 83 Street,
January 16.

DEAR MRS. DODGE,

Mr. Hartley's (I may have his name twisted) pictures started so many wheels going inside my skull that I left you to shut yourself into your car. Please forgive me for that, and for not coming around last evening. I meant to come, but something turned up that made it impossible for me to get there before ten, and I thought that would be rather late.

I don't yet know whether G. S. [Gertrude Stein] is your aesthetic evil genius, or whether I am a jackass to think that you take her seriously.

Anyhow I am sure that the world is better and more interesting for your being in it, and that, after all, is the only thing that really matters.

I'll return the Moore book before long.

Yours sincerely,

E. A. ROBINSON.

I wanted to share things with him, and I wanted to share him with my other friends, though of course that did not always work. Once I sent him some poems of Bayard Boyesen's. Bayard was the son of the Norwegian who taught at Columbia and who was the translator of Ibsen, and he was a young friend of Hutch's who sometimes wrote verse.

But E. A. found them unreal, not enough like "real life," as he told me afterwards. At the moment he wrote about them:

DEAR MRS. DODGE,

Please don't call me names—at least before your visitors. I have no theories in regard to poetic form, but will be glad to hear what the others have to say. I never read my own poems—even to myself.

I like the specimens of Mr. Boyeson but I have to confess to an old-fashioned liking for more tangible subject matter. You will come in time to realize that I am not so infernally modern after all and then you won't like me any more. Perhaps you don't anyhow.

I have enjoyed the books and will return them before long. I'm sending Mr. Boyeson's poems with this, trusting you may want them. Thank you for letting me see them.

Yours sincerely,

E. A. ROBINSON.

He seemed to like to talk over his things with me because I was not academic—and we often wrote notes back and forth about poems and plays:

DEAR MRS. DODGE,

By all means come along and have luncheon with us. The R. T.'s seem to be thriving, and I am in the process of finishing another book. I shall also have another play for you in September, but you are not to consider yourself under any kind of obligation to read it. I have a suspicion that you think me too far out of the world to write plays, and I don't say that you aren't right. Anyhow, there are no more plays in sight—which of course doesn't mean that I may not begin another next week.—It has been rain-ing here for the past forty days and today it is coming down a little harder than ever. If it keeps up, I shall send out a pigeon, like Noah. How are you?

Yours sincerely,

E. A. ROBINSON.

DEAR MRS. DODGE,

O, Lord, no. I'm not mad at you. I'm worse than that, for I'm puzzled. What you say of the Atlantic poem leads me to wonder whether you, like some others, think there are two people talking. Perhaps I should have put quotation marks before each stanza to make it clear that the wife is doing it all. The husband is there, of course, or she wouldn't repeat, as question, what little the poor devil finds to say. Probably he deserves all that he is getting.

This isn't just what you mean; I'm afraid it's the best that I can do. I am not conscious of any difference in the "wringing" process, and I fear that I'm never going to understand what it is that you don't find.

The poem was then so much in manuscript that I may have been fooled into liking it too much myself. Anyhow, I don't know what is the matter with it—though of course I am willing, on general principles, to admit the easy possibility of its not being good for anything.

I shall not be able to hear the talk next Thursday, but I hope to get around the week after. It is a little difficult for me to make appointments so far ahead, as one or two things are liable to come up to prevent. But I shall see you before long anyway—always with your permission.

Yours sincerely,

E. A. ROBINSON.

Our friendship, begun over at La Tourette, continued long after more emotional and disturbing experiences came and disappeared in my bewildered existence.

139

CHAPTER VIII

Tendencies

THAT I was leading an existence without any real direction occurred to me over and over again. I had been caught in the whirlpool of contemporary agitation and I seemed to be going helplessly around in circles, although perhaps my reserved expression made onlookers believe I was a leading influence who knew what she was about.

The fact is, I had rapidly become a mythological figure right in my own lifetime which, I am sure, is a rather rare experience. But the faculty I had for not saying much and yet for being there gave people's imaginations a chance to fabricate their own Mabel Dodge, which they did, attributing to her all kinds of faculties and powers.

The publicity I had been able to gain overnight for Gertrude had apparently been the starting point for the belief that I had only to be in some way associated with a movement of any kind for it to be launched. This belief spread in all directions and grew like a snowball, so that the success I was considered to be able to confer upon undertakings came to have a certain actuality. People attributed power to me and by their bestowal I had it, so I was able to secure a singular attention for anything any time and this made people eager to have my name on committees and prospectuses, or to have me associated with new movements.

I had the reputation for being radical, emancipated, wealthy, and daring but in reality I was none of these. My reputation had nothing to do with me. It never has had anything to do with me. At the same time I had a vague sense of responsibility about this automatic influence I seemed to have, and I wanted to do things with it. I had a sense of power but it didn't seem to have any savor in it; no real enjoyment. A feeling of power that translates itself merely into a sense of duty is no fun. I even missed the kind of sadness I had sometimes suffered at the Villa Curonia, for there was more real color in that than in my present life. There was no feeling of richness for me in this confusion of ideas and activities; it seemed like trying to live in one's head, to the neglect of the heart and the senses. But nothing touched my heart and there was not much to stir one's sight and hearing unless I made an effort to go to theaters or outside places, whereas before in Florence everything about one had been nourishing to the eyes and ears and we had rarely gone to places of entertainment, so I had not the habit of going out in the evening.

The most that happened to me, then, was an excitement somewhere in the region of the solar plexus and a growing restlessness.

I had the oddest experiences without ever having to do anything to bring them about, such as the dinner at the house one night with Schmitty, the associate of the McNamaras who got away and had a "price on his head," in company with a couple of lawyers, Gilbert Roe was one of them, I think, and Hutch and Neith; and we sat there in peaceful secrecy and security while Schmitty entertained us all with interesting talk, and was safe under a pseudonym.

Aleister Crowley was one of the strange creatures who turned up in New York that year. He was supposed to be a magician. It was said of him that he had celebrated the Messe Noire in London and for that reason had been asked to leave the British Isles.

The Hapgoods met him at dinner and found him to be a most conventional Englishman with good manners. Neith, sitting next to him, and remembering rumors, asked him if he was a Rosicrucian. He looked at her in apparent puzzlement and queried:

"Rosicrucian? Do you mean am I a member of the Red Cross? Oh, yes. . . ."

He gave lectures on esoteric aspects of Buddhism, and Hutch and I went to hear him one night in a house someone had lent him. The room he spoke in had a gold ceiling and was very stuffy. Mr. Crowley darted out onto a small platform dressed in the usual Nordic evening clothes, but in addition to these he had a broad red ribbon across his chest, and a sword that clanked buckled around his waist; and his rather thin hair was brushed straight up into a point that turned over towards his audience like the horn of a unicorn. Very odd. But his talk about Buddha was really excellent and there didn't seem to be anything *louche* about him.

Yet afterwards when he began telephoning and asking if he could

come to see me, he made me feel nervous. It was queer that sometimes at the telephone his voice sounded weak and thin and as though
he were scarcely in the flesh, and at others it was full-bodied and
robust, very hearty. I could never bring myself to receive him.

There was a funny original little man in New York, that year, who
had an idea for combating all the maladjusted people. He was called
Professor Blumenthal and he was the first vocational expert. He talked
to people and sized them up and told them what they should be doing.
He was quite ingenious and intuitive, and was one of those who
preceded the psychoanalysts.

Frank Harris and his beautiful wife Nelly came to see me several
times. Harris seemed to have a strange mixture in him of ferocious
sincerity, and a clever facile way of managing people. What I thought
was a dyed mustache gave his face a peculiarly intense look, black
against the white skin. He had a bitter intuition that made him know
himself and others in all their incongruous possibilities and he told me
he wanted to write a real autobiography some day; he said it with a
singular, almost fanatic expression on his temperamental face, and
smiled quizzically: "Frank Harris: the son of man!" Then he added,
"*And* the son of God."

Of course, Dr. Brill had begun his Freudian analysis before that
time, and it was thought to be just as queer as all the other attempts
people were making to achieve some kind of social adaptation. We
had him come down and talk to us one of the Evenings and several
guests got up and left, they were so incensed at his assertions about
unconscious behavior and its give-aways. Although I had invited Dr.
Sachs to come on the Psychoanalytic Evening, he repudiated my invitation with the tone of an admiral who has been invited to tea on an
enemy submarine. He said he was not at all in sympathy with the subject or with the manner of presenting it to the public, and, he added, he
considered the subject a dangerous one for me.

It was a very tentative period in many ways. For instance, we had
the idea of starting a club for men and women where they could meet
and talk together. The old Liberal Club down on McDougall Street
had been in existence for some time but there was nothing very attractive about it; no place to sit, no place to eat, and only useful, really,
for meetings or lectures. So I sent out this feeler:

May 24.

It is the intention of a number of people (most of whom you know) to organize a meeting place which will be in the nature of a club where both men and women can meet to eat and drink and talk together.

It is to be irrespective of any class distinctions; it is for people who are just people.

It is planned to secure and maintain a house with meals and other club accessories in the neighborhood of Washington Square.

The dues are to be small.

A meeting to discuss the project will be held at the home of Mrs. Dodge, 23 Fifth Avenue, on Wednesday, May 27th at 4:30 P.M.

If you cannot attend but are interested in the idea, will you please send a post card to the undersigned, 23 Fifth Avenue, prior to Wednesday next.

Very sincerely yours,

MABEL DODGE.

Our small club for men and women was a good idea but it never came to anything.

There was a club called Heterodoxy for unorthodox women, that is to say, women who did things and did them openly. Women who worked. New York was largely run by women; there was a woman behind every man in every publisher's office, in all the editorial circles, and in the Wall Street offices, and it was the judgment and intuition of these that determined many policies, but they were anonymous women. They didn't seem to mind being so, for the most part. They seemed to be content just to function without the credit. But the Heterodoxy was composed of women whose names were known: Charlotte Perkins Gilman, Mary Fels, Inez Haynes Irwin, Edna Kenton, Mary Shaw, Mary Heaton Vorse, Daisy Thompson, Fola La Follette, and others were already members when I was asked to join. Beloved Marie Jenny Howe was chairman of the club from the time it was created until the day of her death. She was a rare person who did a great deal for the liberation of women, and her loving wit helped her accept the sterility of her domestic life. She was married to a man who was deeply engrossed in humanitarian problems, who, while he was Commissioner of Immigration, made Ellis Island bearable for thousands where before his time it had been purgatorial. He really tried to make it hospitable and a temporary home, while in his own home he was one of those husbands who seem to be perpetually engrossed in thought and never on the spot. When he wrote his auto-biography and his wife read it, she exclaimed: "Why, Fred, were you never married?" He had neglected to mention this small fact.

All the Heterodoxy women were fine, daring, rather joyous and in-dependent women. I remember when the war was going on and La Follette was supposed to be "pro-German" how Fola was persecuted in many ways and many places for her father's attitude. People snubbed her, cut her, and behaved like idiot barbarians. She ceased to go about much but she generally came to Heterodoxy luncheons. That was a safe refuge. Everyone was glad to see her, no one there paid any at-tention to war hysterias, Fola was Fola, as she had always been. She would come in looking somewhat pale and pinched, but after an hour in that warm fellowship her face flushed and her muscles relaxed. It must have been a comfort to come there.

One of the bold new experiments that was initiated at this time was the first presidential or congressional survey and judgment upon the industrial system from the viewpoint of economic radicalism. I do not know whether the idea originated with John Collier or Frank Walsh, but Walsh was the chairman of what came to be called the Industrial Relations Commission, and many of my friends were very active in it. It has gone on functioning since that time and very usefully.

Collier wanted me to form a group of which I should be chairman, a group that would plan the programs and prepare the evidence to be submitted to the commission, and stay right with it.

Now Collier's leaping intelligence was impatient with the old pedes-trian frock-coated period of politics which seemed fated to extend in-terminably into the future.

He was ahead of his time. He belonged to a group that had not appeared yet where the business of Government would be informal, casual, daring, dangerous, and opportunistic; where the smile in the cigarette smoke pervades the confusion of insuperable problems.

This type, to which Collier was affiliated, feels that when old meth-ods and experienced executives fail, new untried ones may succeed—and leaping in the dark, takes a chance, and this unconventional atti-tude of mind was responsible for his surprising suggestion to me.

When he first talked of it, I disguised my inner recoil, and that night he wrote me the following open letter:

My dear Mrs. Dodge: *December 31st.*

To condense what we talked of today.

The object is to use the Industrial Relations Commission in a way to attract public opinion and possibly to formulate the industrial revolutionary idea in a somewhat new way.

I. The Industrial Commission

The commission exists because of the revolutionary movement. It was directly occasioned by the Paterson and Little Falls strikes and the Homestead war. Taft appointed conservatives on the commission and the Senate refused to confirm them. Wilson's appointees are three conservative Trade Union men, two conservative and one progressive manufacturer, and three members, representing the public at large, one of whom is a radical, the other a fundamental progressive, and the third is progressing. (They are Walsh, the Chairman, Commons, and Mrs. Harriman.)

The commission has employed Louis Levine to investigate unorganized labor.

George Creel is an important influence with Walsh, the Chairman.

Walsh has stated more than once and in a committal way, that the commission aims to get at the root of the industrial unrest, and will, in slang words, "go the limit." By this he means that the three members representing the general public will go the limit. But they cannot go it alone. They need radical guidance and radical support. The following are considerations which beset them:

  a. They are a minority of the commission.
  b. They must go to Congress in six months for a new appropriation. Already the business interests have sniffed a danger in Walsh and Commons. There must be a struggle for continued appropriations if radical work is to be done. A brilliant record must be made in order to get public opinion in back of adequate appropriations.
  c. The actual situation invites dramatic hearings and fundamental statement, and Walsh wants this kind of thing and wants help in getting it.

II. The Revolutionaries

Our emotions are away ahead of our facts. The facts which make each of us a revolutionist are largely unorganized, personal. If all of us run down to Washington in a miscellaneous way, testifying and advising, it will be more like Chinese fire-crackers than fourteen-inch projectiles.

Unless the revolutionary case is thought out and organized—unless the witnesses appear in the proper order and do team work, and are scheduled for dramatic effect, the hearings will fail of much possible effect.

Also, if the whole radical cause is left to Levine to formulate, we will simply get Levine's views, rewritten and improved, and at the most will have merely a minority of the commission endorsing Levine's views. We know Levine's views already. We don't want Levine's views or any other intellectual's views, but we want a body of testimony with dramatic carrying power which will bring out the fundamental conditions *and give a sense of reality to what is now so largely poetic and philosophic.*

III. The Plan

The suggestion then is that a group of the radicals be brought together and that they stay together to the extent of working out a program with reference to the commission—a program of results to be aimed at and also of ways and means. This group would be rather large; there would be a small steering or executive committee; my idea is that you be the executive of this committee. The group would frame up a program of hearings and would decide on the "leads" to be given the commission for investigation.

IV. The Time

The commission is already at work; hearings have begun. The matter is urgent. The commission will co-operate with such a group if it be formed, in the matter of hearings and of investigations. But if the commission should not co-operate, there is all the more reason to form the group and to create a situation which will force the commission to co-operate.

And let me say that it is Chairman Walsh himself who suggested the arrangement, and he has repeated the suggestion urgently.

Yours sincerely,

JOHN COLLIER.

My inexperience and ignorance of industrial problems was complete. Literally, I would not have known where to begin such a task as Collier wished me to assume.

Because I had energy and intuition, he probably thought I might do the job better than one of the more accustomed people already in the Labor Movement, but I hastily declined to be put to this test, possibly more because I was not really imaginatively interested in the industrial crisis than because I was afraid to tackle it. Certainly I felt I could have accomplished something if my feeling had been involved but it was not, and I should think Collier must have known that. Perhaps he counted upon the occasion and the immersion in it to focus my attention and call out any ability I had; certainly he was right in believing that any light one might possess should be flexible and able to be cast now here—now there—for we held the belief that ability should be usable wherever one wishes to use it.

But alas, these wishes! We cannot seem to control them! If Collier gradually became accused of lacking judgment about people and of trying to fit square pegs into round holes, it was because he did not take into sufficient consideration the basic fact that everyone is conditioned in his desires or absence of desire, and no one can wish as he pleases!

So I had to refuse and I sent this letter around:

January 3.

I am sending you a copy of a letter to me from John Collier of The People's Institute, together with a list of the other people to whom I am sending it. If the matter interests you and you are able to give some of your time to it—will you come to the first meeting on Tuesday evening, January the sixth, at my house at 23 Fifth Avenue, or if you are unable to come and yet are able to help, will you please send me word before that meeting?

As I fear I am not sufficiently educated, on the practical or technical side, to be the executive of such an undertaking—as Mr. Collier suggests—it will be necessary to name someone in my place or to make up an *executive group*.

Yours sincerely,

MABEL DODGE.

Suggested members of group to prepare case of Industrial Commission:

Mr. J. P. Warbasse	Timothy Walsh
William E. Walling	Helen Marot
William D. Haywood	Fred Howe
Jessie Ashley	Hutchins Hapgood
Louis Levine	Walter Lippmann
John Collier	John Haynes Holmes
Mabel Dodge	Frank E. Wolfe
Lincoln Steffens	Clarence Darrow
Gilbert E. Roe	Bolton Hall
Max Eastman	Emma Goldman
Ida Rauh	Frances Perkins
George Creel	Alexander Berkman
Harry Kelly	Joseph O'Brien
Marion Cothern	

Paul Kennaday was absent from this first meeting and wrote:

147

Paul Kennaday
780 Park Avenue
New York

March 14.

MY DEAR MRS. DODGE,

I can't be at the meeting this afternoon because I must go to Albany. Will you be good enough to present the following to the bunch?

1. We should first know just how much time the Commission is going to spend here and how much of this time we may have for our side.

2. Concentrate upon a few subjects.

3. Walsh has promised me to give the National Negro Association opportunity to present the Negro's industrial problem, the relation of the Negro worker to the white worker, etc. Dr. DuBois is to present this case and would no doubt welcome assistance in securing witnesses, etc.

4. Hours, pay, spy system, etc., on subways, L system and surface cars (and a selection from other topics discussed at our last meeting).

5. The enforcement of the labor law. There is a whole lot of stuff to be brought out here. The Factory Investigating Commission had a good deal of it but for problematic reasons did not press the point. The Civic Service Reform Asn., the Child Labor Com., and others can give a lot of information and any number of workers, men, women and children could be found to testify as to locked doors, unguarded machinery, etc., etc.

There are a lot of people "pointing with pride" these days to our N. Y. Labor laws as models and as evidence that labor is being properly looked after. But there is an undernourished inefficient gang holding down the jobs. This I have found, in talking in many parts of the state on labor legislation, is one of the first causes for that discontent the Commission is after.

Sincerely yours,

PAUL KENNADAY.

The minutes of the first meeting read:

MINUTES

March 19th.

We drew up our program today as follows:

Topics to present to Industrial Relations Commission:

I.

Discrimination by Unions   (In charge of Haywood
    Against Negroes   Dr. DuBois
        foreigners   Paul Kennaday)
        women

(Call as witnesses, Gompers, Mitchell, etc., Refugees Defense League, Liberal Immigration League.)

II.

Unemployment and Disemployed
(O'Brien, Sheffield, Haywood, etc.)

III.

(Lynch, Lovejoy)
Enforcement of Labor Law (George Creel)

IV.

Re-Interpret the Protocol (Ernest Walling—Hourwitz)

V.

Public Service Corporations (Kennaday, Lippmann)

Steffens and Fitch will work in these various depts.
Hearings will begin in N. Y. about April 20—and last about three weeks.

Obviously, what was planned was to express the views of labor, of the general public, and of government as the instrument of society, and to try to get its examination and findings outside of the concept of the profit system: to transvalue the profit system from the standpoint of labor, the consumer, and society.

The minutes of the second meeting read:

Minutes of Second Meeting

Meeting called to order by Mr. Lippmann.

Report of sub-committee read by Mr. Lippmann. Mr. Bolton Hall objects to Mr. Creel's epigram "not curb or reform special privilege, etc., but to inform the working class."

Discussion of Hr. Hall's motion to strike out this paragraph.

Amendment offered by Mr. Lippmann to cover this objection and passed by the meeting.

Further discussion of report as a whole.

Mr. Hall reads us his views on the function of the committee. Proposes to make a spectacular campaign on the price of *coal*.

Moved by Mr. Kennaday that the report of the committee be accepted with the amendment offered by Mr. Lippmann: seconded and passed.

Moved and passed by Mr. O'Brien that the present committee be left in power.

Moved and seconded that the committee get into communication with the Commission at Washington and report as occasion requires. Passed.

Moved that the committee be empowered to enlarge the membership of the larger committee—further that any member of the larger group may nominate members whose names are to be passed upon by the committee. Passed.

Meeting adjourned.

I did all I could to help this project along though I took no actual position in it. I thoroughly enjoyed the serious high tension of those meetings, which had something of the quiet busy hum of the General Sessions court!

Mrs. Borden Harriman was the only woman on the commission, an extremely good-looking and intelligent person whom I admired very much; young George West was Frank Walsh's secretary and was thought to be a promising boy.

The conference board went from city to city and always had good newspaper publicity, which was one of its chief aims; their material grew voluminous, and the Congressional appropriation for expenses enabled it to continue for quite a long period.

Frank Walsh never gave up his radical sympathies and from that time on has been an advocate of public ownership, and has had an important influence in that direction.

There were a good many courageous people to know in those days, people who risked shattering themselves for the sake of their ideas. Theodore Schroeder seemed to me to be one of these. He was a member of the Free Speech League and he was a Single Taxer. He was not very young but he was willing to die for his views had it been necessary.

So was Nancy Sankey Jones who lived openly with him for the sake of proving that love may be free. It hurt her and she was terribly conscious of her reckless situation, for she had been born and brought up among quiet decent people. She was not young, either. But she went through with it like a young martyr. She often gave one little blue sheets of sweetly printed love poems that were somehow of the suffering-hearted variety.

All kinds of people suffered and sacrificed and tried this and that. Life was ready to take a new form of some kind and many people felt a common urge to shape it. Everyone seemed to fumble and feel uncertain a good deal of the time, blind and unable to look ahead.

The most that anyone knew was that the old ways were about over, and the new ways all to create. The city was teeming with potentialities.

My correspondence grew voluminous, and it had tentacles stretching in all directions and through many layers of the New York world. It is surprising what a curious resemblance the letters of that epoch have to the letters of all other epochs! As I read them over I find they show the same eagerness, hope, despair, and envy that present themselves in some of the social patterns in decade after decade. The only changes seem to be in degrees of hours, and amounts, or in matters of title or neighborhood.

There were letters from unemployed and desperate people who did not know where to turn, letters from eager solutionists like Upton Sinclair:

Dear Comrade—Come to the Call office this afternoon or Rand School. Get others! In haste,
SINCLAIR.

Letters from publishers introducing young writers, angry letters from people who did not sign their names:

Mch 15.

Mrs. Dodge
DEAR MADAM,
Women that smoke are similar to the street-walking class, they are vulgar immoral people.
No refined Lady would lower herself.
Those women that smoke regret that they were not born males.
They are trying to ruin their health, cause their breath and fingers to smell, and learn their children the same habits providing that they have children instead of dogs.
Yours very truly,
M. A.

New York City,
Mar 27.
MRS. DODGE,
Pardon the Liberty I take in writing to you but I feel I must Compliment you on your success in getting your Picture in the Papers you must have been overjoyed to see it but let the Jews alone Rabbi Wise and Sheif the banker will look after them.
If you and any-more of your kind want to help the Poor of this City help the Germans and Irish who fought and gave they life for it the rich

Jews of the World look out for there own kind and that's how they get along there was no Irish man in that crowd with Seven hundred dollars in his Pocket who is the Poor of this City the spenders or spendthrifts the Irish and Germans only for them there would be no money exchanging hands you are making a Grand stand Play like all the rest of them you will have them looking for a Nights lodging some night and then you will take notice.

THE MAN FROM

AVE. A.

New York City,
March 15th.

Mrs. Dodge

DEAR MADAM,

A couple of lines   hope this will find you at home in time to receive it. I see in some of the Papers of this week where you said I'll be at home Wednesdays to my Friends do you call the Bums who you took in your home your friends if you call yourself a Lady, the Public don't   you can rest assured   a lot of Lazy Park Bums and loafers who would be walking away with vermin and Dirt before take a Job where they would have to work. The *Scum* of the Lower East side   a Pretended Lady as you make out to be taking a lot of Dirt In your house Annoying the rest of the Decent People who lives as they should in the house where you live in the Neighborhood   if you wanted to feed or do any charity take a Couple of Dozen homeless Innocent children from some home and give them a Treat not to a lot of the Dirty Lazy I.W.W.'s who are looking for food and a place to sleep and sit on the Benches all day.

AN OBSERVER.

Letters from lonely souls: ("I am yearning to meet somebody that I can unbosom myself confidently to. . . .")

Letters from playwrights introducing actresses and from actresses introducing actors.

There were invitations to various kinds of meetings:

I think this is amusing and significant, don't you?—M.

Why not? But is it a new way of getting patronesses to advertise? W. L.

New York, November 16.

Mrs. Mabel Dodge,

23 Fifth Avenue,

New York.

MY DEAR MRS. DODGE:

Can you come to a meeting this week, Friday at 3:30 at the McAlpin Hotel?

One of the large automobile companies is just embarking on a new policy of opening up its business to women. We are in a position to know that this is a sincere business undertaking, originating in the belief of the President of the Company and its Executive Committee that women will make successful automobile demonstrators and saleswomen.

We consider it extremely important that something should be done to encourage the Company in this policy, and to encourage the women who become pioneers in this field. Upon their success will perhaps depend the opening of an excellent open air occupation to thousands of women.

We are meeting on Friday to consider what our attitude should be in this particular instance, and also the possibility of forming a more or less permanent committee of thirty to encourage the opening of business opportunities to women. Will you come?

Very sincerely yours,

MARY BEARD
INEZ MILHOLLAND
MARION B. COTHREN
CRYSTAL EASTMAN BENEDICT
VERA WHITEHOUSE
GERTRUDE M. PINCHOT.

Friday, Nov. 20, 3:30 P.M.
Hotel McAlpin
34 St.

50 Cathedral Parkway, N. Y. C.
May 4th.

DEAR COMRADE:

I am very much disappointed that you have not turned up to help us. We need new people. You need only come for half an hour, and the reporters will print anything you say. *Please!*

Sincerely,

SINCLAIR.

Brevoort, Sunday.

DEAR MRS. DODGE:

Madame Yorska has written this letter and has charmingly asserted that I must have the privilege of knowing you. I am sure that I should like to, very much.

She has asked me to send you a copy of my play. I am afraid that it is rather like offering you my photograph, at once, but I do so,—only because I hope that it may amuse you.

Very sincerely,

ZOE AKINS.

The People's Institute,
70 Fifth Ave., N. Y. C.

DEAR FRIEND:

A Town Hall Meeting has been arranged under the auspices of The People's Institute, Friday evening, March 12th, at eight o'clock at the Cooper Union. We would be pleased to have you serve as a member of the Auxiliary Committee. The members of the Board of Estimate and Apportionment, the Mayor's Committee on Unemployment and the Brooklyn Unemployment Committee are being invited to be present and to occupy special platform seats in the spirit of the old New England town hall meetings.

It is hoped that such a meeting may offer a unique opportunity of discussing and reviewing the unemployment situation in our city by bringing out clearly what has been done to meet the emergency, and bring all forces into public conference to consider what still remains to be done.

Among those who have been selected to speak are Prof. Franklin Giddings of Columbia University, Max Eastman, Dr. Frederic C. Howe and Hon. Henry Bruere.

Conservation of human life is defeated by unemployment—unemployment itself must be defeated if life is to be conserved.

Sincerely yours,
MRS. JAMES P. WARBASSE
JOHN HAYNES HOLMES
FREDERIC C. HOWE.

P.S. It is requested that all acceptances be in by Thursday, March 4th.

Will you take over April or May number of *The Masses* magazine? Fill all space you can with plays, stories, editorials, verse, articles, suggest cartoons, anything you choose. Unconditioned freedom of expression. Will advertise you as editor of the issue. Probable circulation 2 or 3 hundred thousand from Atlantic to Pacific Coast. All profits yours.

MAX EASTMAN, *Editor.*

October 21.

Mrs. Mabel Dodge,
23 Fifth Avenue,
New York.

Dear Comrade: I think you may be able to help me with my Anthology by giving me some suggestions about revolutionary art. Have you any collections of this sort which you could lend me? Do you know Anatole Fischer? Ryan Walker told me to look into his work and that you knew him. Ryan says there is an agent at 56th Fifth Ave. who handles the work of Balfour Ker. I am very anxious to get in touch with Ker. The last address I can get was in France, from which my letter was returned. Doubtless Fischer would know. Give me as many suggestions as you can.

Sincerely,
U. SINCLAIR.

DEAR MABEL DODGE,　　　　　　*National Hotel, Washington, D. C.*

I doubt if I will be in New York to attend the Thursday evening discussion. But I thank you for including me among those who are especially privileged to express their opinion. However, if Hovey and Bradley are there, I will trust them to cover the whole ground and some more too.

Thanking you,
Yours sincerely,

Jan. 18th.　　　　　　　　　　　　ARTHUR YOUNG.

1202 Ashland Block
Chicago

March 31st.

MY DEAR MRS. DODGE,

I had intended writing you long ago about comnig to N. Y., but so many things have got in the way that I had no chance to go. It was nice of you to wish me to come, and I wanted to start at once for the lure of N. Y. is still in me. It is a dangerous place for me to visit.

I have an invitation to be there April 10th and am trying to arrange to go. Shall do it if I can, and will write and tell you in plenty of time if I can get away. I wish I lived there and I hope I can arrange to move, but there are so many things to think of after my long years here. Still, I could do it if I only did it. The Habit of procrastination is so strong and old with me that I am always intending to do things and never doing them. Anyway, when I come I shall come and see you.

Truly,
CLARENCE DARROW.

New York 3/13.

Mrs. M. Dodge.

DEAR MADAM:

I trust you will excuse me for writing this few lines to you, but as I happened to read in the paper that certain Leader from the I.W.W. was at your House having a conference about the unemployed I thought I would just tell you some true facts, do you realy think that this crowd running around the City looking for free Meals and Beds and refusing to do work if they could get it, do you think that they are the real unemployed of this City, *no* they are not, I am sure there are tousands of Family like myself, who has Wife and Children to support who are out of work and don't know where their next Rent or Meal will come from.

It is easy enought for a single Man to run around the street claiming he wants this and he want that, but he wont do this because he dont have to, any single Man can always find a living but what about a Man with a family, he can't, even he wants to, get on a farm, his Wife and Children are in the way—

I have only been out a couple of weeks, but every week you are out brings you back a Month. You cant continue to get on trust, the Landlord will not keep up doing without his rent, the Wife goes out to work trying to make a few dollars to get the Children something to eat, but if it keeps up, what will happen, well I dont think I will have to tell you, disposes— Family torn apart and God knows what, I dont say it will be as bad as that with me I hope not, but that is what happens every day in New York, that is the realy unemployed—that is the ones, that should be reached, not the ones that runs around claiming loud to the world what they want, but the quiet sufferer, the family. Trusting you will not feel offended for one writing this to you, I remain

Respectfully yours,

W. Buck,
981 Forest Ave.,
Bronx, N. Y.

FOR MABEL DODGE

One hour (or 500 words) of narrative or character study every morning after breakfast five days a week for the present.

When a subject fails you, analyze the character and problems of the first friend you think of.

Write these in note-books and preserve them.

Don't be afraid to hunt in your mind for the right word or expression. It may not be the natural word when you get it (or it may), but nature's words will be more ready to your mind the next time *because you have been looking round in your mind.*

Regard these things as an artist regards sketches. Don't take them too seriously, leave your hand free, but don't be afraid to make a good one when the impulse comes.

Dr. Max Eastman.

Prescription 831067543.
Date May 14th.

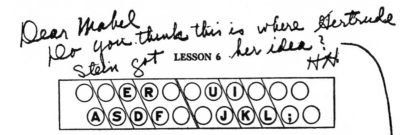

Dear Mabel Do you think this is where Gertrude Stein got her idea? HH

LESSON 6

R, left first finger   U, right first finger

afra afra ;ju; ;ju; arfa arfa ;uj; ;uj; afrf ;juj fraf ju;j;

aru; ;ura rural; rural; a rural lad; a rural lass; all rural

ar far afar all afar ar ark lark lard all lard a lark larks;

full dull lull lurk; as full as; as dull as; all full jars;

a rural lass adds a full jar; all rural lads ask a full jar;

Supplementary Practice

surf surf a full surf; all full surfs; all surfs full surfs

a fraud; all frauds; all rural frauds; skull skulls skulks;

LESSON 7

E, left second finger   I, right second finger

added added all added; all added a full jar; all jars added;

;kik; ;kik; alike all alike all like full jars; all like us;

eels sells dells led sled sleds fled flees feels reels keels

ills ails sills lids slide slides silk silk fills rills jill

see if all is alike see if all are alike; all are used alike

Supplementary Practice

all is all are all is like all alike all red jars are alike

a rural jade likes full red jars; all rural jades are alike

5

New York, April 1st.

Mrs. Mabel Dodge,
23 Fifth Avenue, N. Y. C.
DEAR MADAM,

The announcement that you receive various persons who class themselves as unemployed and I.W.W.s is most interesting, especially to one who has mingled with that class, as well as others, unknown and unnoticed. To have passed the stage of being drawn as a winning card and finely shuffled into the discard—a painful operation but nevertheless interesting.

It occurred to me that in the general scheme of life I may have developed sufficient excentricity to add a mite of information or diversion. I am of this class and a student of it. I am of little or no interest to anyone but myself. I am not even taken seriously, anytime by anyone. So that in asking your permission to call this evening at your home is asking a great deal, as the pleasure will doubtless be all mine. However, I will call you over the Phone at 7 this evening and you can tell me whether I shall call or not.

I will say for your information that my personal references are A1. I am not looking for charity, only a pauper seeking diversion.

Thanking you in advance for your consideration, I am

Most sincerely,
J. E. BENNETT.

The Commission on the Church and Social Service

New York City,
March 14.

Mrs. Mabel Dodge,
23 Fifth Avenue,
New York City.
DEAR MRS. DODGE:

This commission, representing the Federal Council, which has a membership of thirty denominations with about sixteen million church members, has a great opportunity to reach the churches.

At the present moment one of the more important things under way is the "one-day-in-seven" campaign for industrial workers. You would be interested in reading our other reports of industrial investigations. We are bringing the influence of the Church to bear in elevating child and woman labor and similar causes. An extensive social campaign is under way for the Panama Pacific Exposition.

Gifford Pinchot has consented to be the Chairman of a new Committee on Church and Country life, to bring the combined forces of the thirty denominations to bear upon this vital mission and opportunity.

Will you help us by enrolling as a sustaining member (for any sum you can afford), receive our literature as it is issued and keep in touch with our plans and progress? To all who send $5 or more, we are for a short time sending in addition a copy of a new book by the Secretary, *Spiritual Culture and Social Service* (which sells at $1.10) through a special arrangement with the publishers.

Sincerely yours,

ALFRED KIMBALL.

291 Fifth Ave.,
New York,
Feb. 13, 1913.

MY DEAR MRS. DODGE:

I have been trying to get Mr. DuBois on the phone but have failed. He is possibly busy helping hang the "Big Show." If you really feel that "The Portrait of Mabel Dodge" by Gertrude Stein will be out of place in Mr. DuBois' April Number, I would, in your place, merely write to him and tell him frankly what I thought. Personally I have very strong feelings on the subject of seeing good material misplaced under the pretense that the "people" will be interested in it. As an advertising dodge to increase the circulation of a magazine it might be good business, but I personally am not interested in business from any point of view. Too much has been already sacrificed to it in this country. I believe in giving people an opportunity, all people, a genuine opportunity, not a spasmodic one. A spasmodic opportunity is worse than no opportunity at all.

With kindest regards,

Yours sincerely,

ALFRED STIEGLITZ.

A group of Columbia students undertook to reorganize *The International* with Viereck acting as editor. They tried to enlist my interest without, I am afraid, success; I was too preoccupied with personal problems, I suppose. Viereck wrote:

The International
New York

February 2nd.

DEAR MRS. DODGE:

I am writing to find a way of reorganizing *The International* on a basis where it would be practically self-supporting and where it would be no burden to anyone.

Already Mrs. Guggenheimer has promised to let us have a little office free of charge. I expect Mrs. Wagstaff to take care of the salary of one of our employees and Mrs. Lewisohn to take care of the other. I also expect Mrs. Lewisohn to pay for one article every month, or a short story, according to her selection.

I expect Mrs. Wagstaff's brother to print the magazine at cost at his printery shop in Altoona.

May we count on a contribution from you? Would you, for instance, secure for us at your expense and your selection one article or short story every month by Hapgood or anyone else who is in sympathy with our spirit, and would you care to put up $15 every month for keeping the magazine on the elevated newsstands?

I myself will serve as Editor without compensation whatever. In this way we shall be able to bring out the magazine indefinitely free and independent, with almost as many pages as we have at present, without surrendering to the forces of Philistinism.

Will you let me know what you think of this matter and whether we may count on your help? Of course, it is possible that a large committee may take over the entire proposition but if this should fail then my plan would be the only one to save us from defeat.

With kind regards, I am, as ever,

Sincerely yours,

GEORGE SYLVESTER VIERECK.

The magazine did go ahead and do some excellent pioneering work; was, perhaps, the first periodical to have a really emancipating influence on young writers who heretofore had had no vehicle for their work.

San Francisco, Calif.,
June 4th.

Mrs. Mabel Dodge,
23 Fifth Ave.,
New York City.
MY DEAR MABEL DODGE:

The enclosed letter was forwarded to me from our office, and was received too late for my reply to reach the lady who signed it (and whose name, by the way, I cannot make out) in time for the date she wanted people to write. However, you may tell her for me that I would be very glad if such a proposition as outlined in her letter could be carried out in our City, especially if it will adhere to the formula of no distinction between class or people. That is one of the drawbacks in most civic centers and clubs. Also I should be opposed to any kind of a moral censor that might spring up in a place like that, for I do not think it can be successful unless it is really a free place for men and women to meet and discuss the pressing questions of our day. At any rate, I shall be very glad to assist in whatever way I can, provided, as I have said, the Puritanical whip is put away once for all.

I shall not be back in New York before the latter part of August, as I am having very successful meetings in California, and intend to remain here as long as I am wanted.

When I last saw you I understood you to say that you intended to return to Italy in April. It is evident that you have given up that plan. Do you intend to remain permanently with us, or how long? I hope you will be in New York when I go back there, as I want to know you more. I think I shall have more opportunity to meet people when I go back there than I did last winter.

Write me a long letter and tell me about our friends in New York and what you have been doing with yourself,—in fact, everything about which you care to write. Mail will reach me for the next three weeks at Mammoth Hall, 517 Broadway, Los Angeles, California.

If you see Hapgood, give him my love and tell him he is a bum friend. He has not written me a single line all these months, although he knew I was having a very hard time, laboring under all sorts of difficulties, not the least of them poor health.

With all good wishes,

Sincerely,

EMMA GOLDMAN.

And invitations to join all kinds of organizations such as the World Order of Socialism in England were interspersed in the morning mail with insulting anonymous outcries and comments from people who had been at an Evening and wanted to tell their afterthoughts.

There were all kinds of communications from people who had something to say and no place to say it and who sought for a chance in my house: ("I shall be delighted to receive notice of an audience with you for any evening and the chance to tell you more about Esperanto!") How long had poor Esperanto been seeking its outlet?

Then, often letters from old friends who still tried to guide my opinions!

New York Evening Journal
Office of A. Brisbane

December 1st.

MY DEAR MABEL:

I have only just now read your letter which apparently sent me some money for the Pankhurst dinner tickets. I hope the money got back to you. Of course I wouldn't take it.

I am only answering your letter now, because of the extreme cleverness of the last three or four lines. You have forgotten what they were, and I shall not repeat them. But they were extremely clever—and they were wrong.

Yours sincerely,

A. BRISBANE.

P.S. My impression is that Mrs. Pankhurst is about ten times as big as Joan of Arc—or a thousand times. Joan of Arc had no education, and therefore she knew nothing, therefore she could not do very much. I suspect that the uneducated people who are great in history, are great people because it has served the purpose of those better educated who came later to make them APPEAR great.

Joan of Arc, I suppose, was really "the mascot" of the French Army. The things that she did were probably as important as the things that are done by the mascot of a baseball team, or the goat kept on a battleship as a mascot. But then, as Galileo probably said when he declared that the earth was round, "I may be mistaken."

And letters from others who tried to prove things. That all religions have always been breeders of ignorance, for instance!

Generous offers of all kinds—about all kinds of things!

B. W. Huebsch, Publisher

April 14.

DEAR MRS. DODGE,

Steffens told me last night that Tannenbaum wishes to spend as much of this year's involuntary retirement in reading and study as possible, so I should like to send him a few books. Please tell me in whose care they are to go and suggest if possible the nature of the literature in which Tannenbaum may be interested.

Please accept for yourself with my compliments the new book by Bergson which I am publishing today, a copy of which accompanies this.

Yours sincerely,

B. W. HUEBSCH.

Demands for money for every sort of project, from Birth Control to new kinds of engines to supplant steam, gas and electrical ones!

Ingenious plans to bring all the labor class together, and pathetic notes from old servants in need who knew my father and mother in the past; many offers of positions on committees where periodicals were being instituted, like the *New Review,* etc.

February 5th.

Will you, if possible, attend a meeting at 4 P.M. Monday next at the home of Mrs. Mabel Dodge, 23 Fifth Avenue? Seven or eight people are being asked to this meeting and it is expected to decide whether the plan for acquiring the *International Magazine* and developing it as an independent radical organ is a practical plan.

Will you kindly let me know if you are coming?

Yours very truly,

JOHN COLLIER.

And then among these purposeful epistles there were sprinkled letters from the delightful dilettanti I had left in Florence that were full of a refreshing feeling of leisure:

. . . In France, considering how they show appreciation for the return of The Jaconde, someone suggests that France should return D'Annunzio to Italy.

Tante Salut

ARTHUR A.

And from my old friends in Buffalo telling me who had a new baby!

Invitations to meetings at the Town Hall on unemployment rubbed against notes from André de la Fouquière! Invitations from people like Alfred Knopf in the office of the publisher Mitchell Kennerley, to meet "promising young writers" like Joseph Hergesheimer! Frequent initialed letters from people who tried to take one down: (". . . Therefore dont think you are a wonderful person. you are just an ordinary human being, and must live according to your own conscience, whether right or wrong.—R. P.")

Or, like this one, from people like Baron de Meyer asking if he might borrow some glass! (". . . I have been persuaded to go to this big ball on Friday, and of all the simple and easy costumes, I am to be a gold Byzantine Mosaique from St. Mark, in the Suite of Theodora!—You have some blue beads hanging on your wall! Byzantine headdress in blue and yellow, and I want all imaginable blue and yellow stones and beads, I can find. I at once thought of those lovely stones, and wondered if you would lend me something toward my coiffure? It would be so very kind and anything you could suggest to loan in that line will be accepted with gratitude. I hope you are going to the entertainment, as I now really think it may be very wonderful, all the artists are helping and much is expected. Forgive my bothering

163

you, but it's such a problem to try and make oneself look like a mosaique!")

Letters constantly asking me to "speak"! Horrors!:

Mother Earth Publishing Association
New York

March 24th.

Mrs. Mabel Dodge,
23 Fifth Ave., City.

DEAR FRIEND:

I saw Hutch just now and he made what I think a very splendid suggestion—that I invite you to participate in the activities of the Anarchist Forum (circular enclosed). Would you care to introduce the discussion some Sunday next month? . . .

Cordially,

A. BERKMAN.

And Du-haut-en-bas notes like the following:

523 W. 122nd St.,
April 14.

DEAR MRS. DODGE:

I have your note of recent date. I do not mind putting off the revolution for one week. I should be very glad to hear John Reed on Mexico. His article in the *Metropolitan* is fine.

Sincerely yours,

LOUIS LEVINE.

And notes from illusionists, commenting on other people's illusions!

Nov. 20.

DEAR MABEL:

When does Stef go? Isn't he wonderful? Nothing can disillusionize him.

I spent last Monday night at Oyster Bay with Roosevelt, and loved him more than ever. You would have, too, I think. I'll tell you about it when I see you. How would Sunday at four suit you?

Yours,

W. L.

Was it any wonder my head was spinning with the contrast between these days and the Florentine dream life? I wondered what happened to these fabricated personae of society—such as I had become. What was to be the end of them?

This legendary Mabel Dodge lived alongside me for many years while I went alone, cut off from the ways of other people who all attributed to me far more participation in rich living than they themselves enjoyed. To be sure, at times I tried to identify myself with contemporary social changes, and to be guided by what Naomi Mitchison called "praxis," to persuade myself as she does, that I lived purposefully with a pre-determined social outlook. But truth to tell, this persuasion, which never lasted long, was usually the undying longing to share a group activity, the simple herding instinct. I had been brought up in an environment where altruistic attitudes were unknown, and afterwards the life in Italy had been all too concerned with aesthetics to be troubled about reforms. But I wanted a life in common with others. For instance, the idea we had for a small modern art gallery and art magazine in Paris!

With Jo Davidson and Yvonne, Maurice Aisen, Charles Fitzgerald, the Picabias, I practically agreed to leave the desert that New York seemed to us all and to go with them and start a really altruistic group life in Paris where we would be devoting all our vitality to an understanding of modern art, for the benefit of artists, giving them a vehicle of expression somewhat along the same lines as Stieglitz's *Camera Work,* and a little place as much like "291" as possible, where their work could be seen, and where our own "vie intérieure" would have a chance to deepen.

In Paris there was no one like Stieglitz who fostered the new art, and no way of educating the public so it would understand it. The only place in Paris where anyone could hear anything about modern art was at the Steins', in the rue Fleurus, and that place was something like Stieglitz's, only the latter reinforced his exhibits and his talk by his magazine where he magnificently photographed and printed almost all the pictures he showed in his rooms at 291, then called the Secessionist Gallery, and accompanied them by intelligent articles. True, there was Vollard, who was a real lover among the ordinary dealers— but only he among so many conventional commercial shopkeepers.

So, said Picabia, "My wife and I, Jo Davidson, Maurice Aisen— we could go to Paris and start a paper like *Camera Work.* . . ."

Maurice Aisen was a Rumanian chemist who told us all about the "Doina." How difficult he found it to explain this folk spirit of his country. It was the spirit of life, the force that is stronger than anything else in man, the element that overcomes materialism, the simple, irresistible, persistent soul of the people. He translated many of the folk songs into English, rather roughly but with much poetic feeling and I thought it should not be difficult to have them published by subscription. The group started to call me "Doina," but alas, I had not the simple continuity and persistence of that spirit. I could not keep things up. I would get started on an idea and then the impulse would die out of me. Aisen consulted Kreymborg about the Doina verses but he met with disillusionment there as well as with me; after a while he wrote me from Chicago in rather halting English:

413 St. James Place.

My dear Mrs. Dodge:

The "Doina" that Kreymborg possesses which he intends to publish in the *Glebe:* according to two of his letters recently received, not only he has my recent permission, in fact I gave them to him three years ago while in New York when he intended to publish them in *American Quarterly* which did not materialize then.—That he claims the Doina his work (according to your letter) why have me connected even in his discussion about it? I wrote the Doina then in a poorer English than I do now, yet what he did was to place the words in the grammatical relation, then we went over together and I told him if there was or was not the Spirit of Doina. The manuscript after came to me to Chicago, and I returned it to him after all the necessary correction has been done by me.—By his request recently, I promised him the greater part of Doina as well as all the poems of Cosbuc of which he has not seen them yet, to be published in one number of the *Glebe.*

Lately I have been too busy with my chemical works, so they are still in my possession.

Poetry here in Chicago has 12 pages of Doina and they will be published soon.

There is all about Doina. . . .

By the Spiritual-right, Doina no doubt belongs to you for there is Doina-spirit in you. Alas! We never came to a sound understanding, no doubt, due to your multiple activities that inclined me to believe you slightly and spasmodically interested; on the other hand my ferocious egotistic instinct, while seeking if not the immediate crystallization of Doina, at least a partial crystallization and not seeing it at the time I was in your surrounding in New York, I lost completely the belief of you being interested in it.

I finished Doina while in Chicago, and layed in my desk and it would have layed yet, would not Kreymborg have asked them, so Miss Monroe and Henderson of the *Poetry*—Voilà son passé et present,—quand au futur la vie est pleine de plus au moins grandes et petites consolations, et si un a gloire ce n'est point sur la terre de Doina, elle le sera sans faute de l'empire de son ciel. . . .

Have you a definite Idea about Doina? On one hand somebody is willing to publish them all, and since they are now ready to be published, what is your Idea how they should be done?

I gave you the full account of it—and I would be pleased to hear everything what's going on about, if there is anything at all. In case I have your permission I would write to Kreymborg and have him explain me, his attitude of his mal propre barardage. . . .

Too bad about Jo. Most of his worrying lies in his so numerous exitable preambules which led to his so pronounced Chanteclerism. This depresses both his financial personality as well as his real personality—the first manifests itself more often than required, while the most important of his individuality is depressed by the too much activity of the first, and so he is a spasmodic sculptor when he has the chance of being a sculptor.

I intended to be soon in New York, but it took me much more time than I expected to install my laboratory and at present my process takes up most of my time, so I can't tell when I shall be in New York. I might leave at a moments notice Chicago. But I shall sure be in New York between the 15-30 of April when I will sail for Europe.

Voilà tout

à bientot donc

MAURICE AISEN.

And Jo Davidson wrote too—trying to keep me to the Paris plan:

Henry Reinhardt

Modern and Ancient Paintings

Chicago

Thursday.

Dear Doina—Things are so far at a standstill. Nothing has as yet happened. But it will. It must. So I am not discouraged. You see I have faith. As to our Paris Scheme—I think that perhaps Fitz is a bit too cautious. The magazine will never cost $200 a month. Because it will be the simplest thing conceivable. Besides Maurice will get money from his father when he gets to Paris and it will be the easiest thing in the world to get contributions for it from People interested. The thing is we have enough to start with—and by the time that gives out there will be more coming—besides we are leaving out the possibility of sales which must come. Picabia will attend to that. I am sure, for he will bring people around who are interested enough and can buy.

Don't let us abandon the Idea. It's too good, and will make good. Be-

167

sides being of vital interest. Maurice will be going to New York soon. Talk it over with him. He has good ideas on the subject.

Chicago is very much worried about the International Show and is talking about nothing else. I have had some very good Press notices and if they help I ought to make a good deal of money—and the International ought to help me a good deal too. Because they speak of both Shows in the same breath and they all come to see it. So I trust to Doina that it will come out all right. Please thank Mrs. Muier for me, for her kind note with enclosure. She gave me no address or I should have done so myself.

I am feeling rather blue these days. The only use of Chicago is where there are things doing. But—not yet.

Well, Doina, I really wish I was in New York instead of this Doina-forsaken place. You see there is no Doina here and it's really very hard to get along without Doina.

So even letters make me feel a good deal better.

Be well and happy!

Jo.

Well, discussions, papers, signatures, and then nothing. I couldn't make up my mind to go. Then the others fell apart—and the thing fell through, like a good many other half-hearted hopes.

As for my emotional life, the early influence of my father and his prohibition about "kissing games," combined with his almost fussy sense of obligation about what he owed other people, continued to work upon me as it had in Italy. Edwin was gone and I was free and I felt it was about time for me to take advantage of this freedom I had wanted so much.

In the midst of all the talk that went on around me, I sat still and continued to think about love and how empty of love my life was. But one rarely heard that word spoken—though much was said about sex-expression. Finally I came to the conclusion that I was very old-fashioned and that what I needed and had never admitted to myself was this very sex-expression other people were so intent upon.

There was a young man in my immediate circle who shall be nameless (he is still a good friend of mine) whom I liked very much, for he was one of those earnest, intelligent people who are dignified, no matter what they think or do. His ideas were interesting and I was fond of him, so it occurred to me that perhaps he was one who could transform me into a completely independent woman and even make me happier.

So when within the curtains of my white bed one night I opened my arms to him, I fully expected to melt into the joys of the flesh and the lilies and languors of love. But not at all. I was completely cold to him, completely unresponsive, my blood and nerves not interested. I *was* disappointed! And not only I. My friend was making the most industrious efforts to be passionate and his embraces were conscientious and insistent; he put all his attention upon the matter but all in vain. His flesh and blood, too, were simply not interested.

We felt it was unfortunate and wondered why it was so unsuccessful, and he grew dogged about it. He insisted that we should not give up at once. So he took me to a hotel where, he said, we would feel more free and more at our ease, though why I could not see.

Alas! It only increased my feeling of detached observation, for it was gloomy and drear, a second rate place with shabby furniture and curious eyes upon one in the lobby. I tried to look aloof and *digne* as he led me upstairs after registering under a false name, but inside myself I felt perfectly disheartened.

However, at the same time I did feel rather more like an emancipated woman and I forced myself impassively to undress and get into the ugly bed with the grayish sheets, but I felt it was impossible to find any kind of expression in such a place. In fact, I felt far less congenial with my nice young friend than I did at home in my apartment. He suddenly seemed like a stranger to me. I felt he was a stranger, a commonplace, American stranger who had nothing whatever to do with me. He might have had on a derby hat, so little did he attract me! He had suddenly become a dose of medicine I must take, a kind of medicine that would usher me into the world of free souls. These unpropitious thoughts were passing in my mind while my companion was occupied in a solitary fashion trying to make the gesture of complete union.

I just let him struggle on, feeling discouraged myself, and foreseeing failure, and finally attaining a vague indifference, only wishing it would be over soon. It was. In the middle of the unseemly scene the bedroom door opened and a waiter stuck his head in, exclaiming, "You ring?" My friend took his chin out of my shoulder and shouted angrily, all his nice dignity gone: "Shut that damned door!" And the horrified face disappeared and we were alone again. But what I persistently called our love affair in my thought was all over. Never again did we try to find sex-expression; instead we talked and talked and talked about it.

The next day I felt the need to confess my sin. To get it out of me and onto another. I wrote the companion of my guilt and told him I felt I should tell Edwin all about it, since I wasn't really divorced from him. This annoyed my friend very much. He wrote me a wonderful letter. He made me see how it would hurt Edwin and what a selfish woman I was. So I have never told anyone about it till now. Not anyone but Hutch, of course. I told him everything always.

CHAPTER IX

The Day in Bohemia

THE first time I heard of John Reed was when someone brought me his gay verses bound in a little book:

THE

DAY IN BOHEMIA

OR

LIFE AMONG THE ARTISTS

Being a *jeu d'esprit* containing Much that is Original
and Diverting. In which the Reader will find the
Cognomens and Qualities of many Persons
destined one day to adorn the Annals
of Nations, in Letters, Music,
Painting, the Plastic Arts,
and even Business;

Together with

Their Foibles, Weaknesses, and Shortcomings.
And some Account of the Life led by
Geniuses in Manhattan's

QUARTIER LATIN

BY

JOHN REED, Esq.

NEW YORK

PRINTED FOR THE AUTHOR

MDCCCCXIII

DEDICATORY

TO

LINCOLN STEFFENS,

ONE OF US;

THE ONLY MAN

WHO UNDERSTANDS MY ARGUMENTS.

STEFFENS, I hope I am doing no wrong to you
By dedicating this doggerel song to you;
P'raps you'll resent
The implied compliment,
But light-hearted Liberty seems to belong to you.

Yes, my Bohemian picture's satirical,—
Method of drawing it wholly empirical,—
But there's anaemia
Ev'n in Bohemia,
That there's not more of it—*there* is the miracle!

Even in artists I notice a tendency
To let old Daily Bread gain the ascendancy,
Making that petty boss
Sort of a Setebos
'Stead of a useful but servile dependency.

How can an artist create his Utopia
With his best eye on the World's cornucopia?
See, for example;
There's recompense ample
In just writing this—let us call it—*epopaea.*

Not that we should be *too* earnest,—assumin' us
Free to pursue all the gods that illumine us,—
I don't mean to say
If I had my way
I'd make every man *heautontimorumenos!*

Yet without seeming too greatly didactical,
Would I could find the means moral and tactical
To put to rout,
With one hearty shout,
That bane of America, Art that is Practical!

Well, if these numbers recall a good year to you,
And, as to me, certain things that are dear to you,
Take them, you're welcome,
I'm with you till Hell come,
Friend STEFFENS, consider me quaffing a beer to you! . . .

THE DAY IN BOHEMIA

Muse, you have got a job before you,—
Come, buckle to it, I implore you.
I would embalm in deathless rhyme
The great souls of our little time:
Inglorious Miltons by the score,—
And Rodins, one to every floor.
In short, those unknown men of genius
Who dwell in third-floor-rears gangreneous,
Reft of their rightful heritage
By a commercial, soulless age.
Unwept, I might add,—and unsung,
Insolvent, but entirely young.

Twixt Broadway and Sixth Avenue,
And West perhaps a block or two,—
From Third Street up, and Ninth Street down,
Between Fifth Avenue and the town,—
Policemen walk as free as air,
With nothing on their minds but hair,
And life is very, very fair,
In Washington Square.

Bohemia! Where dwell the Sacred Nine,
Who landed, steerage, from the White Star Line. . . .

Say! unenlightened bards whom I deride,
Defend you Gramercy or Morningside,
As fitter spots for poets to reside?
Nay, you know not where Virtue doth abide!
Do GLACKENS, FRENCH, WILL IRWIN linger there?
Nay, they would scorn your boasted Uptown air!
Are marble bathtubs your excuse ingenious?
In God's Name, what are bathtubs to a genius!
What restaurant have you that to compare is
With the cool garden back of PAGLIERI's?

I challenge you to tell me where you've et
Viands more rare than at the LAFAYETTE!
Have you forgot the BENEDICK,—the JUDSON,
(Purest of hostelries this side the Hudson)
The OLD BREVOORT, for breakfast late on Sunday,
The CRULLERY, where poor men dine on Monday?
You don't remember THOMPSON STREET? For shame!
Nor WAVERLY PLACE, nor, (classic, classic name!)
MACDOUGAL ALLEY, all of stables built,
Blessed home of Art and MRS. VANDERBILT. . . .

Lives there a man with soul so dead, I ask,
Who in an attic would not rather bask
On the South Side, in lofty-thinking splendor,
Than on the North Side grow obese and tender?
The North Side, to the golden ladle born,
Philistine, suckled at a creed outworn!
Unnumbered Jasons in their motor-cars
Pass fleeceward, mornings, puffing black cigars—
We smoke Fatimas, but we ride the stars!

True to our Art, still there are variations,

Art cannot flourish on infrequent rations;
We condescend to work in humbler sort,
For Art is long and money very short.
Hence it is not so terribly surprising
That ANDREWS deigns to scribble advertising;
ROGERS, whose talent is of epic cast,
At Sunday-paper stuff is unsurpassed.
LEE teaches in an Art School he abhors,
And LEWIS tries to please the editors;
BOB EDWARDS, when he needs some other togs,
Draws pictures for the clothing catalogues.
And I, myself, when no one wants my rhymes,
Yes, even I relax a bit at times.

Yet we are free who live in Washington Square,
We dare to think as Uptown wouldn't dare,
Blazing our nights with arguments uproarious;
What care we for a dull old world censorious
When each is sure he'll fashion something glorious?

Blessed art thou, Anarchic Liberty
Who asketh nought but joy of such as we!

O Muse, inflate your pulmonary bellows
And sing ROG, ANDY, OZ, and all the other fellows.
Homage to FORTY-TWO, Parnassus Flats!
Hail to its Cock-roaches, its Dust, its Rats
Lout your Greek bonnet to the third-floor-back,
Hymn the two landladies, red-haired and black—
The amiable MARIE, the bland ADELE;
Our Spanish Jack-of-all-work, MANUEL.

FORTY-TWO WASHINGTON SQUARE

In winter the water is frigid,
In summer the water is hot;
And we're forming a club for controlling the tub
For there's only one bath to the lot.
You shave in unlathering Croton,
If there's water at all, which is rare,—
But the life isn't bad for a talented lad
At Forty-two Washington Square!

The dust it flies in at the window,
The smells they come in at the door,
Our trousers lie meek where we threw 'em last week
Bestrewing the maculate floor.
The gas isn't all that it should be,
It flickers,—and yet I declare
There's pleasure or near it for young men of spirit
At Forty-two Washington Square!

But nobody questions your morals,
And nobody asks for the rent,—
There's no one to pry if we're tight, you and I,
Or demand how our evenings are spent.
The furniture's ancient but plenty,
The linen is spotless and fair,
O life is a joy to a broth of a boy
At Forty-two Washington Square!

Third floor, Hall-room and Back, Elysian bower,
Where the IMMORTAL FOUR spent many a blissful hour!

175

The high sun-parlor, looking South and East,
Whence we discerned a million cats at least
Communing in the tenement back-yards,
And hove at them innumerable shards.
There spawn the overworked and underpaid
Mute thousands;—packed in buildings badly made,—
In stinking squalor penned,—and overflowing
On sagging fire-escapes. Such to-and-froing
From room to room we spied on! Such a thrill
Cursing between brass earinged women, still
Venomous, Italian! Love-making and hate;
Laughter, white rage, a passionate debate;
A drunken workman beating up his wife;
Mafia and Camorra,—yelling strife!
The wail of children,—dull, monotonous,
Unceasing,—and a liquid, tremulous
High tenor, singing, somewhere out of sight
"Santa Lucia!" in the troubled night.

Below's the barren, grassless, earthen ring
Where Madame, with a faith unwavering
Planted a wistful garden every spring,—
Forever hoped-for,—never blossoming.
Above, th' eternal washing droops in air,
From wall to window hanging, everywhere!
What poet would not yield to their allure
"The short and simple flannels of the poor!" . . .

LINES ON THE DUTCH TREAT

Souls of Scribblers dead and gone,
Where in Hades have ye known
Better wit or worser grub,
Than TOM MASSON's Dutch Treat Club?
Has the bonehead waiter brought
Chicken-pie, when chops you sought?
For a mess of asphodel
Do they charge so high in Hell?
Bloweth not a double rose
Fairer than the IRWIN BROS.
Nor by other name as sweet
Would be HUGHES or JULIAN STREET!

I have heard that on a day
J. M. FLAGG had stayed away;
If he did, I do declare
Dutch Treat would dissolve in air!
What blithe spirit could be found
To better make the world go round?
Without him how could we face
CHARLIE TOWNE or JOSEPH CHASE?
Who could hear without a sob
All the tales of IRVIN COBB?
Souls of scribblers dead and gone,
Where in Hades have ye known
Better food or worser grub
Than TOM MASSON's Dutch Treat Club?

So I arrive at work at half-past-ten,
Sneak to my desk, and madly seize my pen; . . .

So we go striding up the Avenue . . .

At KEEN'S CHOP HOUSE on Thirty-Something Street,
On Tuesday midday we were wont to˙ meet,—
Some for the talk, but most to simply eat,—
The pink of New York's chivalry, DUTCH TREAT!
FLAGG the unflagging, flaunting like a banner,
Carrying manly beauty with a manner!
A dozen masterpieces in each hand,—
(He turns out ten a day, you understand)
Reputed rich beyond the dreams of Art,
Yet democratic,—with a heart, a heart.
Each look a diamond, every word a pearl,—
Holds men enchanted like a clever girl.
STREET, with a romance on his eyebrow,—TOWNE,
Living the Poet's reputation down;
The ever-gay BILL DALY taking his,
Hellenic hair above an Irish phiz;
Two IRWINS (count 'em,—two); in conversation
Almost as clever as their reputation;
CHARLES DANA GIBSON, prisoned in a collar;
And OWEN JOHNSON (price, each word, one dollar);
WOODS-HUTCHINSON, with stories anatomic;
JONES, BURGESS JOHNSON, MASSON, of the Comic;

Old IRVIN COBB, father of mirth Homeric,
Boomer of tales—er,—wholly atmospheric;
As full of genial flavor as a ton
Of Rhenish grapes well-ripened in the sun.
Round him reels Laughter, with a face of gold,—
And from him flow all stories told or never told!
　Full many others. What things have I seen
Done at the DUTCH TREAT! heard words that have been
So nimble, and so full of subtle flame
As if that every one from whence they came
Had meant to put his whole wit in a jest,
And had resolved to filch from LIFE the best
Of even its dull numbers.
　　　　　　　　　Thus pleasure we
Then back to work again at half-past three. . . .

　Home through the dingy, white-lit, clangorous street,
Arms linked, the red wine dancing in our feet;
Past the Jew shoemen strewing in their caverns,
Past the fast-swinging doors of taverns;
Through shabby, work-free crowds adventuring,
Treading like rich men, heads up, arms a-swing,—
Dark sweat-shop girls, harsh-laughing as they go,—
Lovers, bound for the moving-picture show,—
Above, like hammers on the lid of hell,
The nervous, grating thunder of the El.
　Home, with our coats off and our weeds alight,
All windows open to the roaring night;
ANDY and OZZY at their checker game
Squabbling,—at Poker SAM and HERR the same;
ROG making observations quite satyric,—
Oblivious REED, at work upon a lyric,—
BOB HALLOWELL, growing dreamier and dreamier
To find himself in actual BOHEMIA!

"Is Mr. Reed in?" stand, boys! *Mecum dominus!*
It is the landlady,—her voice is ominous.
She enters; sits, swift falls the buoyant talk;
REED's limbs atremble,—ANDREWS' face of chalk;
OSGOOD alone his customary verve
Exhibits, and his customary nerve.
"Good evening, Madame!" cries, "Well, well, well, well!

"Indeed a pleasure,—more than I can tell—"
With a silk handkerchief dusts off his chair,
His eyes implore her to be seated there!
"I've come—" she says. "Our good-luck that is so"
And ozzy's bow is worthy of the Beau.
"My lodgers have complained—this afternoon—"
"Ah!" observes oz, "the weather's nice for June,—
"Why then complain?" The dame begins again:
"It is not of the weather they complain—"
Our champion agrees "Nor yet do we,—
"We're satisfied to let the weather be.
"And you, dear Madame? You are feeling tony?"
"To that your blooming looks bear testimony!"
She tries once more: "Well, in the room below
"A newly-married couple live, you know—"
"Twa-te-twa-twa," sings ozzy. "Who'd have thought it—"
"But then, that oughtn't to be talked of, ought it—?"
"And they complain—" "Oh, go no farther, please,—
"How sad are these unhappy marriages—"
"But—" "You've been married? Happily, I trust?
"Ah, well! Earth into earth, and dust to dust—"
"Then there's the man upstairs—" "What, married too?
"The sly dog! This will never, never do!
"We won't get married after this, eh, boys?—"
Cries Madame, "They complain of too much noise!"
"Ah," says defeated ozzy, quite resigned,
"Have you a certain culprit in your mind?"
   She sniffs, and straightway dons a mien of gloom,
While breathlessly we listen to our doom.
"I'm not one who would muzzle without ruth
"The harmless effervescences of Youth—
"I'm not one to lightly cry 'Heraus!'
"I want you all contented in my house;
"But I declare it seems a bit too bad
"For those as hadn't PAID to bother those as had!"
Silence; then cometh to our burning ears
Soft sound of sobs, and tink of trickling tears.
She weeps! Milady weeps! Blush, thoughtless boys!
Why in Beelzebub made you that noise?
   She's off again, "I do not like to say it
"But there's one rule here, and all must obey it;

179

"Those who have not PAID RENT for half a year
"Must keep the peace—they cannot rough-house here;
"My landlord duns—no cash,—you make a racket,—
"My lodgers leave,—I starve"—(ROGERS: *"Hic jacet"*)
Grief incoherent: with a furtive glance
REED searches through the pockets of his pants;
Nothing! He nudges HALLOWELL, who then
Slips him a surreptitious bill of ten.
"Madame," he cries. "Accept this little token
"And credit my arrears; in peace unbroken
"From this time on I promise you shall dwell
"The folks below, and he above, as well!"
Madame arises, smiles, and dries her tears,—
The episode is finished off with cheers.

    A knock. 'Tis HIRSCH! His devilish smile says, "Never
"Was anyone so altogether clever!"
Observe his air of "I-am-one-of-you"
Adopted for this babu *milieu;*
That laugh ironic, that superb *sang-froid*
Is like a character from Bernard Shaw;
His critic-analytic turn of mind
Dissects his friends, around, before, behind,—
Then, plumbs itself his intellect profound,
Till the *disjecta membra* strew the ground;
Indeed, so has he analyzed his soul,
That HIRSCH doth never seem entirely whole!
For all of that, a Voice Among the Dumb,
Who will speak great things in the days to come!
    And with him LIPPMANN,—calm, inscrutable,
Thinking and writing clearly, soundly, well;
All snarls of falseness swiftly piercing through,
His keen mind leaps like lightning to the True;
His face is almost placid,—but his eye,—
There is a vision born to prophecy!
He sits in silence, as one who has said:
"I waste not living words among the dead!"
Our all-unchallenged Chief! But were there one
Who builds a world, and leaves out all the fun,—
Who dreams a pageant, gorgeous, infinite,
And then leaves all the color out of it,—

Who wants to make the human race, and me,
March to a geometric Q.E.D.—
Who but must laugh, if such a man there be?
Who would not weep, if WALTER L. were he?
   A timid footstep,—enter then the eager
KEATS-SHELLEY-SWINBURNE-MEDIAEVAL-SEEGER;
Poe's raven bang above Byronic brow,
And Dante's beak,—you have his picture now;
In fact he is, though feigning not to know it,
The popular conception of a Poet.
Dreaming, his eyes are steadily alight
With splendors of a world beyond our sight;
He nothing knows of this material sphere,—
Unwilling seems, at times, to linger here;
Beauty is all his breath, his blood, he says,—
Beauty his shrine, and Love its priestesses.
Wildly he talks, with solemn, bell-like voice,
In words that might have been old Malory's choice,—
Proclaiming, in the manner of ascetics,
"For ethics we must substitute aesthetics!"
   Who's this, that like the West Wind, buoyant, free,
Blows in upon us? Sculptor ARTHUR LEE!
Soi-disant superman, and self-styled Lord
Of sculptors, preaching the inspired Word
Of Modern Art. You cannot hear him speak,—
Epic and dialectic, like a Greek,—
Without believing in his haughty claim
That the round earth will echo to his name.
   The unkempt HARRY KEMP now thumps our door;
He who has girdled all the world and more.
Free as a bird, no trammels him can bind,
He rides a box-car as a hawk the wind;
A rough thin face, a ruggled flow of words,—
A Man, who with ideals himself begirds;
Fresh from a fiery ordeal that has paved
The Pit anew—from terrors trebly braved
He rises, burning to avenge the wrong
By flooding all the stupid earth with song.
Here's to you HARRY, in whatever spot!
True Poet, whether writing it or not.

ON FIRST LOOKING INTO ROGET'S THESAURUS

Much have I traveled in the realms of gold,
And many goodly states and kingdoms seen;
Round Western towns and counties have I been
Where bosses fealty to Roosevelt hold.
Oft of one wide expanse I had been told,
That loud Walt Whitman ruled as his demesne:
Yet never did I breathe its pure serene
Till I heard Roget speak profuse and bold:

Then felt I like some lesser Hagedorn
When a new rhyme-tag swims into his ken;—
Or like stout Wheelock on the gladsome morn
When a new book is published,—and his pen
Scribbles another volume yet unborn—
Silent, upon a stool, in Hoboken!

Loud roars the conversation, as Olympus
Roars when the deities convene to gimp us;
KEMP thunders Anarchism, and is wrecked
On a sharp flint from LIPPMANN's intellect,—
Who Socialism in his turn expounds,
Which LEE declares is founded on false grounds;
ROGERS and HIRSCH with fury fight away
Upon what constitutes a perfect play;
SEEGER and KEMP twang each his lyric lute,
And Poetry disdainfully dispute;
ANDREWS, appealed to, climbs upon the fence,
And all combine, in scorn, to flog him thence.
Poor HALLOWELL's dilemma is immense;—
Too bold for that, too cautious to be bold,
He hesitates until the subject's cold;
While OSGOOD, WOLF, MC COY do stand aloof,—
Contemptuously watch us raise the roof.
Now with an easy caper of the mind
We rectify the Errors of Mankind;
Now with the sharpness of a keen-edged jest,
Plunge a hot thunder-bolt in Mammon's breast;
Impatient Youth, in fine creative rage,
With both hands wrests the quenchless torch from Age;
Not as the Dilettanti, who explain

Why they have failed,—excuse, lament, complain,
Condemn real artists to exalt themselves,
And credit their misfortunes to the elves;—
But to Gods of Strength make Offertory,
And put our young wits in the race for glory!
  Perhaps we flay our artists' lack of power,
Or damn with mirth the poets of the hour;
One in particular I call to mind
Who says he's left America behind:—

A GILBERTIAN ODE

O let us humb-ly bow the neck
To George Syl-ves-ter Vi-er-eck
Who trolled us a merry little Continental stave
Concerning the Belly and the Phallus and the Grave—

It would have almost raised the hair
Of Oscar Wilde or Bau-de-laire
To hear Mr. Vi-er-eck so frank-ly rave
Concerning the Belly, and the Phallus and the Grave—

And in the last an-al-y-sis
He says it nar-rows down to this:
A fig for the favors that the high gods gave!
Excepting the Belly and the Phallus and the Grave—

If you have drunk Life to the lees
You may console yourself with these;
For me, there are some things that I do not crave
Among them the Belly and the Phallus and the Grave—
What ho! for the Belly and the Phallus and the Grave
The Belly and the Phallus
And the ballad very gallus
              And the Grave!

  It borders midnight! Rattle all the doors
With the vehemence of the lodgers' snores.
Now one by one the geniuses do yawn,—
Rise up,—deliver parting shots,—are gone.
SEEGER remains. "The LAFAYETTE?" he cries;
"Aye!" (Fevered are our brains, and wide our eyes.)
ANDY alone declines to be seduced

But virtuously prepares him for the roost;
"You squander Youth," says he, "in dissipation!"
"For the Wise Man, all things in moderation;
"Efficiency—the Business Man—brain force"—
"Short sport!" we sneer. "Conservative,—and worse!"
Singing, the Four wend to the LAFAYETTE
Quite like a scene from Murger,—*sans grisette.*

A TRIOLET COMPOSED ON THE SPOT BY SEEGER

You are very well met
Reed and Osgood and Rogers;
At the old Lafayette
You are very well met—

Come, set 'em up! Set
'Em up, jolly codgers!
You are very well met
Reed and Osgood and Rogers!

Round a bare table in the bright cafe
We loll, while wild Italian minstreals play
"You Candy Kid." The flashing demi-monde
Carouses,—laughs,—grows fonder and more fond;
Frenchmen pursue th' eternal game of chess,—
Playwrights compose, and bards their woes confess
With a stub pencil on the table-top
(*Chef d'œuvres* perish with tomorrow's mop)
In a warm glow of Cointreau Triple Sec
REED has a million visions at his beck,
OZZY draws portraits on his unpaid check,
SEEGER draws rhymes from fountains never spent,
While ROGERS purrs, and grins and is content.

REED gapes, OZ gapes, and—SEEGER gapes,
Dark in the Square,—a few dull huddled shapes
Lie on the grass; a homeless, workless crew.
Chill is the air,—a distant clock strikes two;—
Sharp sounds the late home-comer's step, and deep
Breathes the wide-circled city in its sleep.
There is a slip of moon—Good Nights are said,
And arm-in-arm we stumble home to bed.

But at our door we hesitate, and grin,—
Someone talks on and on and on, within;
Now ANDREWS' voice, uplifted, tries in vain
To dam the flood,—as he for bed were fain.
'Tis REEVES the Philisoph, who can outpreach a
Young Baptist,—REEVES, the true Blond Beast of Nietzsche!
Our new Freethinker,—to whom all Emotion,
Enthusiasm, Faith, Love, Rage, Devotion,
Etcetera, is positively Boeotian!
Born to propound, unfold a tale, debate,
And charming, if he would not call so late.
  Poor ANDY sits in a hypnotic trance
Thralled by a psycho-medical romance
Dealing with Brokers, Cancers, Sexual Force—
In which REEVES is the Superman, of course.
We sneer, and sit, and fall beneath the spell,—
And Time stands still,—and we are thralled as well;
The charm is smashed; we hint "The hour is late"—
But REEVES continues boldly to narrate.
ROG suddenly remembers there is due
At nine A.M. an article or two.
And for his typewriter he makes a break;
For there's a spicy interview to fake,—
Dramatic dope, some fourteen thousand words,—
And verse, to fill a column and two thirds.
Slyly and quickly we become undressed—
Slyly and silently we seek the nest.
I doze; but hear, ere yet oblivion
Enfolds,—REEVES lecturing the rising sun,
And ROGERS, plangeant on his Remington. . . .

What fun, what fun they had!

CHAPTER X

Reed

AND now to go back to the earlier beginning of my meeting with some of the principal figures in this chronicle. One night Hutch and Neith came in town to spend the night with me and go to a party at B.'s, and I, who so very seldom went anywhere, particularly in the evening, went along too because I wanted to meet Bill Haywood. Hutch had told me so much about him and about the Paterson Silk Strike that he was leading, that I was curious to see him for myself. Hutch had written about him in the *Globe* a few days before, and what he said attracted me; he said:

The day after I saw Mayor Gaynor, I had a talk with William D. Haywood, one of the leaders of the Industrial Workers of the World, who had just reached New York from Paterson, where he had been arrested, convicted, and released by a higher court in a remarkably brief space. I was struck again by the real marriage there is between Haywood's feeling and his active life. His is not a complex or split-up personality, like that of the mayor. His nature is that of a straight line. It is quite consistent that he believes in "direct action" and is likely to be thrown out of the Socialist party. One feels that Haywood, right or wrong, is a strong, simple man with a unified personality. His thought and his action go together. You know where he is, at any rate; that you can depend upon him. He is not baffling and confusing because of a double or multiple nature, as our interesting mayor is.

Neith and Hutch and I dined in the white dining room where the pale, spring evening twilight from the street mingled with the candles on the table . . . and as we lingered there I asked some more about Haywood—and who this B. might be, where they were going to see him that night.

"B. is one of the young women whom our present system obliges to live what might be called a double life," explained Hutch with a wide, sly, loose grin, and warming eyes that moistened his spectacles so that he removed them to give them a polish with his big handkerchief. He loved the evidences of what he believed to be a distorted civilization, and he cultivated them. He seemed to be always looking for examples of suppressed individualism so that he could pour his affection and sympathy over them. He despised the mechanical and "crystallized" conventions of our system.

Neith fingered the stem of her wine glass and thought her own thoughts, smiling her secret smile.

"Well, who is she and what does she *do?*" I asked impatiently.

"In the morning she teaches in a public high school where she leads the youth of our country to respect the flag and honor our government, and at night she sleeps with Bill Haywood when he is in New York— which is seldom nowadays," explained Hutch.

"Many of our brave young American women are adapting themselves in this way to life," went on Hutch, "and thus doing their share towards a final disintegration of the community."

"It takes Hutch to see the profound significance of it," murmured Neith with an indulgent look out of her green eyes. "To themselves it's merely a job and after the job, relaxation. But Hutchie has to see rebellion and heroism wherever he looks! B. is quite a beautiful person, though," she added, seeming to wish to give her her due.

"I guess I'll go along tonight," I exclaimed as we left the table.

So we walked down to the Square and beyond it to one of the quiet streets, and there was a large bare room lighted with candles where a few men and women stood about chatting, or sat together on the floor, for there weren't many chairs. There was practically no furniture at all in the room except the people, and they weren't very decorative. B. was small and plump, with the blackest hair drawn down, Madonna fashion, against the whitest cheeks I had ever seen. She was as quiet and composed and unrevealing as an unlighted tomb.

Haywood sprawled in one of the few chairs, a great battered hulk of a man, with one eye gone and an eminent look to him: the regular "public man" look that is produced by a satisfied need to shine in a crowd no matter what ideas are the vehicle of this urgency. With the "conservative" and the "radical" extroverts, it doesn't matter what they think, so long as they succeed in standing up before a great many people and exchanging some vital force or other with them—they get a certain full, fulfilled, replete look that we have learned to call eminent.

Haywood's one eye had acquired a steady watchfulness. As Max Eastman had said, he looked like a sturdy old eagle. He was telling about the long, unremitting strike over in Paterson, New Jersey, at the silk mills; of the patience of the strikers over their fight for an *eight-hour day*.

"But there's no way to tell our comrades over here in New York about it," he growled. "The newspapers have determined to keep it from the workers in New York. Very few of them know what we've been through over there—the drama and the tragedy. The police have turned into organized gunmen. God! I wish I could show them a picture of the funeral of Modestino, who was shot by a cop. Every one of the silk mill hands followed his coffin to the grave and dropped a red flower on it. They cut their geraniums from the pot in the window—and those who hadn't any made a little flower of red tissue paper. . . . The grave looked like a mound of blood. As they marched they sang the 'International.' By God, if our people over here could have seen it, we could have raised a trunkful of money to help us go on. Our food is getting mighty scarce over there."

"Can't you get any reports of it into the papers by hook or crook?" someone asked.

"Not a damned word," answered Haywood.

"Why don't you bring the strike to New York and *show* it to the workers?" I asked in a small, shy voice.

Haywood, who hadn't noticed me before, turned his eye on me with an arrested look. I went on, feeling engulfed in blushes and embarrassment, but unable to be still, for this idea was speaking through me. I hadn't *thought* it consciously. It was another case of It!

"Why don't you hire a great hall and re-enact the strike over here? Show the whole thing: the closed mills, the gunmen, the murder of the striker, the funeral. And have the strike leaders make their speeches at the grave as you did in Paterson—you and Elizabeth Gurley Flynn and Tresca!"

"Well, by God! There's an idea!" exclaimed Bill Haywood. "But how? What hall?"

"Madison Square Garden! Why not?" I was excited now by my

own inspiration that, coming to me without any volition or expectation of mine, appeared simply wonderful to me. I sat there in an exalted, uplifted bubble of energy that had somehow arisen from some source within to delight me.

"I'll *do* it!" cried a voice—and a young man detached himself from the group and assumed a personality before my eyes.

"Well, if anyone can 'do' it, you can, Jack," someone laughed.

The young man came and sat by me. He was young, big, and full-chested. His clothes wrinkled over his deep breast. He wasn't startling-looking at all, but his olive green eyes glowed softly, and his high, round forehead was like a baby's with light brown curls rolling away from it and two spots of light shining on his temples, making him lovable. His chin was the best of his face, for it had a beautiful swinging curve forward—the real poet's jawbone, strong and delicate above his round throat. His eyebrows were always lifted and he was generally breathless!

"My name is Reed," he said. "That's a *great* idea. I'll go over to Paterson the first thing in the morning. . . . We'll make a Pageant of the Strike! The first in the World! Why, I see the whole thing!" he cried exultantly. "Why hasn't anyone ever thought of it before!" I thought in a flash of the cinquecento pageant in Florence when I had failed Gordon Craig, and it pricked with a small shame.

"Where do you live? I'll come and see you when I get back," he went on; his eyes were full of light now and he didn't see anyone around him. Already the strike pictures were forming in his mind and he saw them vivid and alive. I told him where I lived, and again he said: "The minute I get back I'll come and see you. I want to look over the ground in Paterson. Then we'll work this thing out."

He didn't *ask* me if I would—he assumed from the very first that I would work with him and carry the thing through. Had I not suggested it? He never realized how little I had to do with suggesting it—that it had just popped out of me.

When Neith and Hutch and I were back in that other world that my apartment was to me, I was glowing and enhanced. Neith said:

"You look like a big red rose tonight, Mabel, in that dress. Maybe you should always wear skirts of full crimson silk and sit on the floor and have Ideas! It's so becoming to you!" She was laughing at me with her gentle cynicism.

"You love ideas better than anything in the world, don't you, Mabel?" queried Hutch, smoothing my hair, as his eyes filled with his usual tears. His other arm, a glass of whiskey in his hand, rested on his knee as I had seen it so many times that it is photographed forever on my memory.

"Yes," I answered him slowly, "alternately with emotions."

"Whatever that means," added Neith.

I didn't see Reed again for over three weeks, for of course he got into trouble almost as soon as he reached Paterson. In his own words, this is what happened to him:

WAR IN PATERSON
[from *The Masses*]

There's war in Paterson! But it's a curious kind of war. All the violence is the work of one side—the Mill Owners. Their servants, the police, club unresisting men and women and ride down law-abiding crowds on horseback. Their paid mercenaries, the armed detectives, shoot and kill innocent people. Their newspapers, the Paterson *Press* and the Paterson *Call,* publish incendiary and crime-inciting appeals to mob-violence against the strike-leaders. Their tool, Recorder Carroll, deals out heavy sentences to peaceful pickets that the police-net gathers up. They control absolutely the Police, the Press, the Courts.

Opposing them are about twenty-five thousand striking silk-workers, of whom perhaps ten thousand are active, and their weapon is the picket-line. Let me tell you what I saw in Paterson and then you will say which side of this struggle is "anarchistic" and "contrary to American ideals."

At six o'clock in the morning a light rain was falling. Slate-gray and cold, the streets of Paterson were deserted. But soon came the Cops—twenty of them—strolling along with their night-sticks under their arms. We went ahead of them toward the mill district. Now we began to see workmen going in the same direction, coat collars turned up, hands in their pockets. We came into a long street, one side of which was lined with silk mills, the other side with the wooden tenement houses. In every doorway, at every window of the houses clustered foreign-faced men and women, laughing and chatting as if after breakfast on a holiday. There seemed to be no sense of expectancy, no strain or feeling of fear. The sidewalks were almost empty, only over in front of the mills a few couples—there couldn't have been more than fifty—marched slowly up and down, dropping with the rain. Some were men, with here and there a man and woman together, or two young boys. As the warmer light of full day came, the people drifted out of their houses and began to pace back and forth, gathering in little knots on the corners. They were quick with gesticulating hands, and low-voiced conversation. They looked often toward the corners of side streets.

Suddenly appeared a policeman, swinging his club. "Ah-hh-h!" said the crowd softly.

Six men had taken shelter from the rain under the canopy of a saloon. "Come on! Get out of that!" yelled the policeman, advancing. The men quietly obeyed. "Get off this street! Go on home, now! Don't be standing there!" They gave way before him in silence, drifting back again when he turned away. Other policemen materialized, hustling, cursing, brutal, ineffectual. No one answered back. Nervous, bleary-eyed, unshaven, these officers were worn out with nine weeks' incessant strike duty.

On the mill side of the street the picket-line had grown to about four hundred. Several policemen shouldered roughly among them, looking for trouble. A workman appeared, with a tin pail, escorted by two detectives. "Boo! Boo!" shouted a few scattered voices. Two Italian boys leaned against the mill fence and shouted a merry Irish threat: "Scab! Come outs here I knocks you' head off!" A policeman grabbed the boys roughly by the shoulder. "Get to hell out of here!" he cried, jerking and pushing them violently to the corner, where he kicked them. Not a voice, not a movement from the crowd.

A little further along the street we saw a young woman with an umbrella, who had been picketing, suddenly confronted by a big policeman.

"What the hell are *you* doing here?" he roared. "God damn you, you go home!" and he jammed his club against her mouth.

"I no go home!" she shrilled passionately, with blazing eyes. "You bigga stiff!"

Silently, steadfastly, solidly the picket-line grew. In groups or in couples the strikers patrolled the sidewalk. There was no more laughing. They looked on with eyes full of hate. These were fiery-blooded Italians, and the police were the same brutal thugs that had beaten them and insulted them for nine weeks. I wondered how long they could stand it.

It began to rain heavily. I asked a man's permission to stand on the porch of his house. There was a policeman standing in front of it. His name, I afterwards discovered, was McCormack. I had to walk around him to mount the steps.

Suddenly he turned round, and shot at the owner: "Do all them fellows live in that house?" The man indicated the three other strikers and himself, and shook his head at me.

"Then you get the hell out of here!" said the cop, pointing his club at me.

"I have the permission of this gentleman to stand here," I said. "He owns this house."

"Never mind! Do what I tell you! Come off of there, and come off damn quick!"

"I'll do nothing of the sort."

With that he leaped up the steps, seized my arm, and violently jerked me to the sidewalk. Another cop took my arm and they gave me a shove.

"Now you get to hell off this street!" said Officer McCormack.

"I won't get off this street or any other street. If I'm breaking any law, you arrest me!"

Officer McCormack, who is doubtless a good, stupid Irishman in time of peace, is almost helpless in a situation that requires thinking. He was dreadfully troubled by my request. He didn't want to arrest me, and said so with a great deal of profanity.

"I've *got* your number," said I sweetly. "Now will you tell me your name?"

"Yes," he bellowed, "an' I got *your* number! I'll arrest you." He took me by the arm and marched me up the street.

He was sorry he *had* arrested me. There was no charge he could lodge against me. I hadn't been doing anything. He felt he must make me say something that could be construed as a violation of the Law. To which he God damned me harshly, loading me with abuse and obscenity, and threatened me with his night-stick, saying, "You big — — — lug, I'd like to beat the hell out of you with this club."

I returned airy persiflage to his threats.

Other officers came to the rescue, two of them, and supplied fresh epithets. I soon found them repeating themselves, however, and told them so. "I had to come all the way to Paterson to put one over on a cop!" I cried. Eureka! They had at last found a crime! When I was arraigned in the Recorder's Court that remark of mine was the charge against me.

Ushered into the patrol-wagon, I was driven with much clanging of gongs along the picket-line. Our passage was greeted with "Boos" and ironical cheers, and enthusiastic waving. At Headquarters I was interrogated and lodged in the lockup. My cell was about four feet wide by seven feet long, at least a foot higher than a standing man's head, and it contained an iron bunk hung from the side-wall with chains, and an open toilet of disgusting dirtiness in the corner. A crowd of pickets had been jammed into the same lockup only three days before, *eight or nine in a cell,* and kept there without food or water for *twenty-two hours!* Among them a young girl of seventeen, who had led a procession right up to the Police Sergeant's nose and defied him to arrest them. In spite of the horrible discomfort, fatigue and thirst, these prisoners had *never let up cheering and singing* for a day and a night!

In about an hour the outside door clanged open, and in came about forty pickets in charge of the police, joking and laughing among themselves. They were hustled into the cells, two in each. Then pandemonium broke loose! With one accord the heavy iron beds were lifted and slammed thunderously against the metal walls. It was like a cannon battery in action.

"Hooray for I.W.W.!" screamed a voice. And unanimously answered all the voices at once, "Hooray!"

"Hooray for Chief Bums!" (Chief of Police Bimson.)

"Boo-o-o-o!" roared forty pairs of lungs—a great boom of echoing sound that had more of hate in it than anything I ever heard.

"To hell wit' Mayor McBride!"

"Boo-o-o-o!" It was an artful voice in that reverberant iron room, full of menace.

"Hooray for Haywood! One bigga da Union! Hooray for da Strike! To hell wit' da police! Boo-o-o-o! Boo-o-o-o! Hooray! Killa da A. F. of L.! A. F. of *Hell,* you mean! Boo-o-o-o!"

"Musica! Musica!" cried the Italians, like children. Whereupon one voice went "Plunk-plunk! Plunk-plunk!" like a guitar, and another, a rich tenor, burst into the first verse of the Italian English song, written and composed by one of the strikers to be sung at the strike meetings. He came to the chorus:

"Do you like Miss Flynn?"
(Chorus) "Yes! Yes! Yes! Yes!"
"Do you like Carlo Tresca?"
(Chorus) "Yes! Yes! Yes! Yes!"
"Do you like Mayor McBride?"
(Chorus) "No. No! *No! NO!"*
"Hooray! Hooray!! Hooray!!!"

"Bis! Bis!" shouted everybody, clapping hands, banging the beds up and down. An officer came in and attempted to quell the noise. He was met with "Boos" and jeers. Someone called for water. The policeman filled a tin cup and brought it to the cell door. A hand reached out and slapped it out of his fingers on the floor. "Scab! Thug!" they yelled. The policeman retreated. The noise continued.

The time approached for the opening of the Recorder's Court, but word had evidently been brought that there was no more room in the County Jail, for suddenly the police appeared and began to open the cell doors. And so the strikers passed out, cheering wildly. I could hear them outside, marching back to the picket-line with the mob who had waited for them at the jail gates.

And then I was taken before the Court of Recorder Carroll. Mr. Carroll has the intelligent, cruel, merciless face of the ordinary police court magistrate. But he is worse than most police court magistrates. He sentences beggars to *six months'* imprisonment in the County Jail without a chance to answer back. He also sends little children there, where they mingle with dope-fiends, and tramps, and men with running sores upon their bodies— to the County Jail, where the air is foul and insufficient to breathe, and the food is full of dead vermin, and grown men become insane.

Mr. Carroll read the charge against me. I was permitted to tell my story. Officer McCormack recited a clever mélange of lies that I am sure he himself could never have concocted. "John Reed," said the Recorder. "Twenty days!" That was all.

And so it was that I went up to the County Jail. In the outer office I was questioned again, searched for concealed weapons, and my money and valuables taken away. Then the great barred door swung open and I went down some steps into a vast room lined with three tiers of cells. About eighty prisoners strolled around, talked, smoked, and ate the food sent in to them by those outside. Of this eighty almost half were strikers. They were in their street clothes, held in prison under $500 bail to await the action of the Grand Jury. Surrounded by a dense crowd of short, dark-faced men, Big Bill Haywood towered in the center of the room. His big hand made simple gestures as he explained something to them. His massive, rugged face seemed scarred like a mountain, and as calm; it radiated strength. These slight, foreign-faced strikers, one of many desperate little armies in the vanguard of the battle-line of Labor, quickened and strengthened by Bill Haywood's face and voice, looked up at him lovingly, eloquently. Faces, deadened and dulled with grinding routine in the sunless mills, glowed with hope and understanding. Faces scarred and bruised from policemen's clubs grinned eagerly at the thought of going back on the picket-line. And there were other faces, too—lined and sunken with the slow starvation of a nine weeks' poverty—shadowed with the sight of so much suffering, or the hopeless brutality of the police—and there were those who had seen Modestino Valentino shot to death by a private detective. But not one showed discouragement; not one a sign of faltering or of fear. As one little Italian said to me, with blazing eyes: "We all one bigga da Union. I.W.W—dat word is pierced de heart of de people!"

"Yes! Yes! Dass righ'! I.W.W.! One bigga da Union—" they murmured with soft, eager voices, crowding around.

I shook hands with Haywood, who introduced me to Pat Quinlan, the thin-faced fiery Irishman now under indictment for speeches inciting to riot.

"Boys," said Haywood, indicating me, "this man wants to *know* things. You tell him everything—"

They crowded around me, shaking my hand, smiling, welcoming me. "Too bad you get in jail," they said, sympathetically. "We tell you ever't'ing. You ask. We tell you. Yes. Yes. You good feller."

And they did. Most of them were still weak and exhausted from their terrible night before in the lockup. Some of them had been lined up against a wall, as they marched to and fro in front of the mills, and herded to jail on the charge of "unlawful assemblage"! Others had been clubbed into the patrol-wagon on the charge of "rioting," as they stood at the track, on their way home from picketing, waiting for a train to pass! They were being held for the Grand Jury that indicted Haywood and Elizabeth Gurley Flynn. *Four of these jurymen were silk manufacturers, another the head of the local Edison company—which Haywood tried to organize for a strike—and not one workingman!*

"We not take bail," said another, shaking his head. "We stay here. Fill up de damn jail. Pretty soon no more room. Pretty soon can't arrest no more picket!"

It was visitors' day. I went to the door to speak with a friend. Outside the reception room was full of women and children carrying packages and pasteboard boxes, and pails full of dainties and little comforts lovingly prepared, which meant hungry and ragged wives and babies, so that the men might be comfortable in jail. The place was full of the sound of moaning; tears ran down their work-roughened faces; the children looked up at their fathers' unshaven faces through the bars and tried to reach them with their hands.

"What nationalities are all the people?" I asked. There were Dutchmen, Italians, Belgians, Jews, Slovaks, Germans, Poles—

"What nationalities stick together on the picket-line?"

A young Jew, pallid and sick-looking from insufficient food, spoke up proudly. "T'ree great nations stick togedder like dis." He made a fist. "T'ree great nations—Italians, Hebrews an' Germans. . . ."

"But how about the Americans?"

They all shrugged their shoulders and grinned with humorous scorn.

"English peoples not go on picket-line," said one softly. " 'Mericans no lika fight!" An Italian boy thought my feelings might be hurt, and broke in quickly: "Not all lika dat. Beeg Beel, *he* 'Merican. *You* 'Merican. Quinl', Miss Flynn, 'Merican. *Good!* 'Merican workman, he lika talk too much."

This sad fact appears to be true. It was the English-speaking group that held back during the Lawrence strike. It is the English-speaking contingent that remains passive at Paterson, while the "wops," the "kikes," the "hunkies"—the "degraded and ignorant races from Southern Europe"— go out and get clubbed on the picket-line and gaily take their medicine in Paterson jail.

But just as they were telling me these things the keeper ordered me to the "convicted room," where I was pushed into a bath and compelled to put on regulation prison clothes. I shan't attempt to describe the horrors I saw in that room. Suffice it to say that forty-odd men lounged about a long corridor lined on one side with cells; that the only ventilation and light came from one small skylight up a funnel-shaped airshaft; that one man had syphilitic sores on his legs and was treated by the prison doctor with sugar-pills for "nervousness"; that a seventeen-year-old boy *who had never been sentenced* had remained in that corridor without ever seeing the sun for over *nine months;* that a cocaine-fiend was getting his "dope" regularly from the inside, and that the background of this and much more was the monotonous and terrible shouting of a man who had lost his mind in that hell-hole and who walked among us.

There were about fourteen strikers in the "convicted" room—Italians, Lithuanians, Poles, Jews, one Frenchman and one "free-born" Englishman! That Englishman was a peach. He was the only Anglo-Saxon striker in prison except the leaders—and perhaps the only one who *had been* there for picketing. He had been sentenced for insulting a mill-owner who came out of his mill and ordered him off the sidewalk. "Wait till I get out!" he said to me. "If them damned English-speaking workers don't go on picket I'll put the curse o' Cromwell on 'em!"

Then there was a Pole—an aristocratic, sensitive chap, a member of the local Strike Committee, a born fighter. He was reading Bob Ingersoll's lectures, translating them to the others. Patting the book, he said with a slow smile: "Now I don' care if I stay in here one year." One thing I noticed was the utter and reasonable irreligion of the strikers—the Italians, the Frenchman—the strong Catholic races, in short—and the Jews, too.

"Priests, it is a profesh'. De priest, he gotta work same as any workin' man. If we ain't gotta no damn Church we been strikin' t'ree hund'd years ago. Priest, he ise all a time keepin' workingman down!"

And then, with laughter, they told me how the combined clergy of the city of Paterson had attempted from their pulpits to persuade them back to work—back to wage-slavery and the tender mercies of the mill-owners on grounds of religion! They told me of that disgraceful and ridiculous conference between the Clergy and the Strike Committee, with the Clergy in the part of Judas. It was hard to believe that until I saw in the paper the sermon delivered the previous day at the Presbyterian Church by the Reverend William A. Littell. He had the impudence to flay the strike leaders and advise workmen to be respectful and obedient to their employers—to tell them that the saloons were the cause of their unhappiness—to proclaim the horrible depravity of Sabbath-breaking workmen, and more rot of the same sort. And this while living men were fighting for their very existence and singing gloriously of the Brotherhood of Man!

The lone Frenchman was a lineal descendant of the Republican doctrinaires of the French Revolution. He had been a democrat for thirteen years, then suddenly had become converted to Socialism. Blazing with excitement, he went around bubbling with arguments. He had the same blind faith in Institutions that characterized his ancestors, the same intense fanaticism, the same willingness to die for an ideal. Most of the strikers were Socialists already—but the Frenchman was bound to convert every man in that prison. All day long his voice could be heard, words rushing forth in a torrent, tones rising to a shout, until the keeper would shut him up with a curse. When the fat Deputy-Sheriff from the outer office came into the room the Frenchman made a dive for him, too.

"You're not producing anything," he'd say, eyes snapping, finger waving violently up and down, long nose and dark, excited face within an inch of the Deputy's. "You're an unproductive worker—under Socialism we'll get what we're working for—we'll get all we make. Capital's not necessary. Of course it ain't. Look at the Post Office—is there any private corporation or private capital there? Look at the Panama Canal. That's Socialism. The American Revolution was a smugglers' war. Do you know what is the Economic Determinism?" This getting swifter and swifter, louder and louder, more and more fragmentary, while a close little circle of strikers massed round the Deputy, watching his face like hounds on a trail, waiting till he opened his mouth to riddle his bewildered arguments with a dozen swift retorts. Trained debaters, all these, in their Locals. For a few minutes the Deputy would try to answer them, and then, driven into a corner, he'd suddenly sweep his arm furiously around and bellow:

"Shut up, you damned dagos, or I'll clap you into the dungeon!" And the discussion would be closed.

Then there was the strike-breaker. He was a fat man, with sunken, flabby cheeks, jailed by some mistake of the Recorder. So completely did the strikers ostracize him—rising and moving away when he sat by them, refusing to speak to him, absolutely ignoring his presence—that he was in a pitiable condition of loneliness.

"I've learned my lesson," he moaned. "I ain't never goin' to scab on workingmen no more!"

One young Italian came up to me with a newspaper and pointed to three items in turn. One was "American Federation of Labor hopes to break the Strike next week"; another, "Victor Berger says, 'I am a member of the A. F. of L., and I have no love for the I.W.W. in Paterson,'" and the third, "Newark Socialists refuse to help the Paterson Strikers."

"I no un'erstand," he told me, looking up at me appealingly. "You tell me. I Socialist—I belong Union—I strike wit' I.W.W. Socialis', he say, 'Worke'men of de worl', Unite!' A. F. of L. he say, 'All worke'men join togedder.' But dese or-gan-i-zashe, he sayd, 'I am for de Working Class.' Awri', I say, I am de Working Class. I unite, I strike. Den he say, 'No! You *cannot* strike!' Why dat? I no un'erstan'. You explain me."

But I could not explain. All I could say was that a good share of the Socialist Party and the American Federation of Labor have forgotten all about the Class Struggle, and seem to be playing a little game with Capitalistic rules called "Button, button, who's got the Vote!"

When it came time for me to go out I said good-by to all those gentle, alert, brave men, ennobled by something greater than themselves. *They* were the strike—not Bill Haywood, not Elizabeth Gurley Flynn, not any other individual. And if they should lose all, their leaders, other leaders, would arise from the ranks, even as *they* rose, and the strike would go on! Think of it! Twelve years they have been losing strikes—twelve solid years of disappointments and incalculable suffering. They must not lose again! They cannot lose!

And as I passed out through the front room they crowded around me again, patting my sleeve and my hand, friendly, warm-hearted, trusting, eloquent. Haywood and Quinlan had gone out on bail.

"You go out," they said softly. "Thass nice. Glad you go out. Pretty soon we go out. Then we go back on picket-line—"

Of course I didn't think of Reed very much while he was away in jail in Paterson. My life was full of other people and things. For instance, I was seeing a good deal of Max Weber, who had flashes of genius but a stubborn, repressed nature. I liked his paintings and bought one. It was evidently strongly influenced by Picasso's blue period, and at first sight it looked like a pattern of rich crumpled textile—silk or wool, but upon penetrating further there were revealed to one three terrible witch-like crouching figures. Later he gave me several others. He was one of those who liked to think out loud with me near-by. All those artists whom I had met at Stieglitz's and with whom I felt a sympathy, were in and out of my apartment: Andrew Dasburg and Grace Johnson, his wife, Arthur and Freddie Lee, Lee Simonson, and others.

Buffalo people came and went: Mary Forman, married now to Conger Goodyear, Mildred married to Jim Crane, Charlotte still unmarried, Edwine Noye and Nina Wilcox, whose name was Bull now—they all flowed in and out of 23 Fifth Avenue. For I never gave up my old friends because I had new ones. I rather liked to show all these different ones to each other and discuss them with each other, not maliciously exactly, not maliciously at all, really, but maybe rather impersonally, as though they were specimens under a microscope.

At this time Mary Foote was round the corner in Washington Square and old Tante Rose was across the way from her in a studio apartment with a dark shiny floor, a few bits of blue china, and two or three scraps of brocade from Florence, for all the world like her old studio in Buffalo where she, too, taught me to See. She had a captive beauty named Frances Cavanaugh living with her. And many cats.

Meanwhile I had become interested in *The Masses,* a real, true radical magazine, fearless and young and laughing at everything solemn and conservative, with Max Eastman for editor. I liked him very much, and Ida Rauh, his wife—noble-looking, like a lioness. I became one of their advisory committee because I had such good "ideas" always surging up out of nowhere.

All sorts of people made use of me and of the free-flowing magnetic influence I seemed able to exert; also I seemed to them to have a lot of money. I was always getting letters like this:

13 West Eleventh Street,
April 13.

Dear Mabel:

I am appealing to you as the ablest committeeman of your sex.

Will you please call together the Finance Committee of the International Workers' Defense Conference at your house Wednesday afternoon, or if that is not convenient for you, the next available afternoon? You have somehow the magic of making people come to Committee meetings, which is a rare gift.

The members are Lincoln Steffens, Leonard Abbott, Berkeley Tobey, New Review; Viva Flaherty, Florence Greer, Helen Hill, Mrs. J. P. Warbasse, Jessie Ashley, Treasurer of the Conference, yourself and me. We must have a meeting this week and get some money in hand, in case all the tickets we have sold are not paid for by Sunday, so that we can pay the balance due to Carnegie Hall.

The prospects are for a big meeting.

Faithfully,

JOSEPH O'BRIEN.

Besides, I was still busy with all the correspondence about the Gertrude Stein articles, and boosting her work. I had many, many letters full of questions about it. It seemed people would never get through talking about her since reading about the portrait in *Arts and Decoration* during the International Show in February. And everyone was trying to write like her and making caricatures of her style and thus it seeped into our literature.

And Hutch always came to see me and usually stayed to lunch whenever he came in town, three or four times a week.

Then Carl was always there, too.

No, it was natural that I did not think very much about Jack Reed.

Reed blew in one day, pale and excited, and ready to start immediately upon the Pageant!

From that moment I was engrossed by it. I gave up everything to work on it. Reed was the executive. I kept having ideas about what to do and he carried them out.

We called a meeting at Margaret Sanger's house and got all the people interested who were good workers. He and I worked shoulder to shoulder and we were a perfect combination for work—untiring, full of fun, too, and perfectly thrilled by the handful we had taken up.

I was swept right away from Hutch and Carl. I had a kind of vision of them standing and looking after us with their jaws dropping open. Hutch continued to come and see me in the mornings—but soon he saw I was often out now or very occupied, and one dreadful morning when I had promised to be there and forgotten it, he sat down at my desk and wrote an article called: "Our Engagements." In the course of it he said:

I have been struck for a long time with the indifference of nearly everyone to the minor engagements of life. Very few people keep an appointment punctually. To keep a person waiting unless notice has been duly given or something extremely serious has prevented, is a distinct offense to a sensitive morality. It shows real contempt for the other person and implies that his time, convenience and purposes are entitled to less consideration than yours. It is an egotistic assumption of superiority, and by its commission tends to show that the assumption is false. It is not always a conscious offense. It is even more damnable when it is not, for then it shows an unthinking habitual selfishness.

And when we fail to keep our deepest engagements, such as those with big purposes which we have conceived, it means the death of the highest part of us, not only morally but mentally. The ugliest thing in the world seems to me to be to find an individual or a group or a community who has no direction, who has lost the direction, who has no underlying permanent convictions which carry him or them inevitably in the same general direction.

There is nothing without character—nothing in art, or literature or social movements, in conception of government—and what character is there in order to meet the immediate industrial and other exigencies of the moment, what character is there, for the sake of those minor things, in violating the deep principles which we have accepted, accepted because we must accept them, because they represent the true, the beautiful and the good?

No character, or weak and contemptible character!

And when we are indifferent to conduct on the part of our governing officers which indicates that they no longer are sensitive to our deeper ideals and our overwhelming purposes, to the general hope and direction of our lives, then we, too, are failing to keep our engagements, our deep and serious engagements, and we cannot do that without acknowledging that our character is weak and vacillating and that our high morality and our higher intelligence are conspicuous by their absence.

All of which, of course, was too bad, and everything, but I couldn't stop going, for I was off and away indeed. But though Hutch was hurt, yet he was very appreciative of Reed and deeply interested himself in the Strike. He wrote:

SEE NO SIGN OF STRIKE'S LOSS

When I saw at Haledon on Sunday at least twenty-five thousand Paterson strikers and sympathizers massed in the open air listening to some seven or eight speakers I perceived no visible signs of the weakening of the great strike. If nearly 30,000 people were willing to walk from Paterson, where they have been prevented from meeting and talking, to Haledon, willing to stand there for four hours listening attentively to their temporary leaders, following all their words with quiet attention, now and then broken by applause or by "boos" when the mayor, the judge, the police were mentioned, it would seem as though the reports of the last week that the strikers were on the point of losing, needed some modifying statements.

I never saw a more touching and beautiful sight. From an elevated position I could see the faces of men, women and children looking up to the speakers, who stood on the balcony of a house. They were thinking of things of the greatest importance to them, and indeed, to the whole of society, and their sensitive, expressive and tired faces responded to their emotions.

When Max Eastman, one of the speakers, told them of the importance of their strike, how this importance was shown in many ways, perhaps especially by the illegal and oppressive violence that had been used against them by the Paterson authorities, by their being jailed by the hundreds, their halls closed to them as well as the streets, and by the fact that their strike is first page news in the newspapers, all over the country,—I saw in many of their faces a solemn, timid, but deep pride. They are feeling their social importance, the dawn of a hope that they may be co-operators in their own destiny, that they may work out for themselves a larger life, may be vital factors in the creation of an industrial democracy.

And when other speakers dwelt on the fact that these strikers had in almost perfect measure conducted themselves peacefully, I could well believe them, even if I had not already been convinced that such was the case. When the speakers asserted that this army of workers had, in spite of their being near the bread line for months, in spite of the crude and brutally frank demonstration of the city authorities to break the strike— that these half-fed and desperately handled men, women and children had shown remarkable qualities of patience, perseverance and firm gentleness, I didn't need previous knowledge to be sure that they were right. The spectacle before me was enough.

When John Reed, the young poet, and energetic organizer of the pageant to be given by the strikers in Madison Square Garden, led them in the songs that they are to sing as they march to New York, and on the picket lines in Paterson, when his youthful, enthusiastic face looked out over the sea of humanity beneath him, and that mass of humanity responded in rhythm, with deep, unconscious felicity and grace and love of love and love of life, it was to me a spectacle that I have never seen rivaled on the stage.

And then there followed Reed other speakers, some of them I.W.W. agitators, but all of them intent mainly on the hope of the hope that was dawning and crystallizing in those thousands of human beings—the hope for self-control, for the higher initiative, for power over destiny, for true education, and for the realization of our much abused conception of democracy.

There was only one policeman present at this enormous gathering and he had nothing whatever to do. It was not even necessary for him to ask anybody to keep off the carefully taken care of bit of lawn that the lady who loaned her cottage to the strike leaders to speak from cared for. They all stepped carefully over this pathetically green place, as gently as if they were sparing her feelings, as indeed they were.

That was a symbol of the mood and spirit of these thousands of strikers. Consistently with fighting their industrial battle in which they have been firm and quietly unyielding, they have shown their patience, feeling for essential right and law, that breathing, deep-seated gentleness which is so marked in the mass of what is called the working class, and which marks them off sharply from the men who are sworn to maintain law and order, in this case of Paterson.

No matter what our ideas of industry and government may be, whether we believe as the big capitalists believe, whether we are Socialists, or merely desire to carry our traditional ideas of democracy as far as possible, I do not understand how we can fail to see that in these big mass movements of the workers there is an inspiring hope of a genuine extension of fundamental education leading to wider justice and more distributed welfare and intensification of real life for greater numbers of people.

I don't want to write here the narrative of the Pageant. I will quote from the press for that—but I remember so vividly some of the wonderful touches that the papers never got. No one realized the fun of having placed the letters I.W.W. ten feet high on each of the four sides of the Madison Square Tower in bright red electric lights, so that they could be seen from one end of town to the other. This brilliant idea was kept secret until the moment came to turn on the electricity, and then it was too late to get the heavy municipal machinery in motion to have the Seditious Blaze turned off. By the time the red tape was unwound, the show was over!

Everybody worked except me. But I was occupied, I thought, in inspiring Reed. Dolly Sloan accomplished prodigies of labor on this

Pageant, and I did a good deal of begging, for we begged, we borrowed, and we somehow raised the money to accomplish it. Girls went
to all the flower shops and asked for their red carnations for the night
of the Pageant. The generosity of people—especially the poor people,
was splendid. Reed worked night and day, half the time in Paterson,
half the time in New York. When he went to Paterson, he coached
the hundreds of people about the procedure of the pageant, and he
rehearsed their songs.

One of the gayest touches, I think, was teaching them to sing one of
their lawless songs to the tune of "Harvard, Old Harvard!"

In New York he was here, there and everywhere at once. Imagine
suddenly teaching 2,000 people of various nationalities how to present
their case in a huge, graphic, orderly art form! Imagine planning an
event to fill Madison Square Garden, a whole city block, where we
were used to going to see Barnum and Bailey's Circus, with three rings
and two bands going at once, and have it audible, visible, and composed enough to be convincing!

Reed dragged his classmates into it, of course. One of these whom
he called "the unspeakable Jones" was interested only in the theater.
This pale, nervous fish with the deicate chin, long-fringed, eager brown
eyes behind his spectacles, and a heavy thatch of hair falling over, was
ordered to produce scenery: "The mills alive—the workers dead"—
"The mills dead—the workers alive." He did.

At the back of the stage he calmly portrayed a life-sized mill with
lots of smaller mills at the side. The proportions may be guessed when
it is realized there were over 2,000 people on the stage at once.

"Our Bobby Jones," as Reed began to call him, insisted on making
it a Gordon Craig affair, and having a long street scene right through
the audience and up to the stage, and this was a most dramatic idea
because the actors entered at the far end of the hall, and the funeral
procession marched right through it, so that for a few electric moments
there was a terrible unity between all those people. They were one:
the workers who had come to show their comrades what was happening across the river, and the workers who had come to see it. I have
never felt such a high pulsing vibration in any gathering before or
since.

But the time was short in which to prepare it all, and Reed was
physically wearing out, we were caught into the magnetic, powerful

force that people can contact at such levels of the impossible—and we were both exalted spiritually, though very, very tired. That we loved each other seemed so necessary a part of working together, we never spoke of it once. There wasn't time, and that it was no time for love-making was accepted without words between us. We grew so sensitive to each other's will and thought that we were able to shorthand our communications and almost do without words. We got each other through our pores, and over the air.

I knew I was enabling Reed to do what he was doing. I knew he couldn't have done it without me. I felt that I was behind him, pouring all the power in the universe through myself to him.

He only faltered once—and that was the night before the Pageant—and so much still to be done. Everyone seemed to have failed. Nothing was ready.

I found Reed at his desk in an improvised office in the Tower at the Garden at 8:30 in the evening, sitting with his head in his hands, his light brown curls pushing up through his fingers.

"I can't *do* it," he groaned. "Mabel, I can't push it through!"

Instantly my heart was as hard as stone and I consciously drew all the force in me into a solid mass like a catapult, and directed it at him.

"Don't talk like a fool! You coward! Get up out of that chair and stop wasting your time *here!* What *you* have to do is get after some money *immediately*. Bruckow wants his payment on the building. . . ." Anything to get him moving again!

He got onto his feet and sort of staggered off. I felt a hilarious thrill go through me at the suspense and uncertainty of it all. In almost all such moments in life I have been aware of the strain without being strained—and terribly entertained by the agony of high endeavor.

And here is a description of how it appeared to the newspapermen:

Fifteen thousand spectators applauded with shouts and tears the great Paterson Strike Pageant at Madison Square Garden. The big mill aglow with light in the dark hours of early winter morning, the shrieking whistles, the din of machinery—dying away to give place to the "Marseillaise" sung by a surging crowd of 1,200 operatives, the fierce battle with the police, the somber funeral of the victim, the impassioned speech of the agitator, the sending away of the children, the great meeting of desperate hollow-eyed strikers—these scenes unrolled with a poignant realism that no man who saw them will ever forget.

That the Paterson pageant was a tremendous dramatic success no one can doubt. That it made money for the strikers can be readily believed. But its chief accomplishment is in having established a legitimate form of "demonstration" before which all others must pale. That such living drama offers superb opportunities for workingmen to get their grievances lawfully and effectively before the public must be plain to everyone. In future we may well find strikers spending their best efforts to get their cause "staged."

PATERSON PAGEANT PACKS THE GARDEN—MILL GIRLS PUT
   UP MOST OF THE $6,500 NEEDED TO MAKE IT GO—HALL
   BLAZES WITH RED AND SEETHES WITH ENTHUSIASM
   FOR THE "CAUSE"

Almost nothing happened at Madison Square Garden last night when about 2,000 silk mill strikers from Paterson, N. J., gave their Paterson Strike Pageant on a stage one-third again as wide as the Hippodrome stage—nothing except that everybody was on his feet all the time, men and women were humming—if they didn't know the words—the "Marseillaise" when they weren't humming or singing the "International," and the Garden was packed, jammed, and Sheriff Julius Harburger was exhorting the reporters, and folks who had come to the pageant in limousines were gazing raptly at nothing at all while the tears ran down their cheeks. It is customary to say that "the applause rattled around the hall like musketry firing." The applause last night didn't do any such thing. It was one chronic roar. When the pageant began exactly at nine o'clock, or half an hour later than the opening was scheduled for, there were few vacant seats on the main floor, the first tier seats were taken entirely, the balcony above was crowded, the balcony above that was also entirely occupied and the ten cent seats away up in the "heaven" were filled, while a line that reached back through Twenty-seventh Street to Fourth Avenue and up the avenue beyond the Twenty-eighth Street subway kiosks was clamoring to get in. . . .

I.W.W. STRIKE DRAWS 15,000 AUDIENCE—DEPICTS PATERSON
   INCIDENTS IN MADISON SQUARE GARDEN, INCLUDING
   FUNERAL OF MODESTINO

A most impressive strike demonstration occurred last night in Madison Square Garden, when 15,000 persons packed the immense building to see the Paterson, N. J., strikers enact the episodes of their labor battle.

206

More than one thousand silk workers took part. The scenery showed the mill scenes, depicted the progress of the strike, including a reproduction of the funeral of Modestino, the man supposed to have been accidentally killed by the police. Mrs. Modestino, in a box, became hysterical when the coffin was carried upon the stage.

Elizabeth Flynn, Haywood, Quinlan, Tresca and Lessig took part. Ten thousand dollars was taken in at the box office.

Paterson's protesting army of strikers came to New York yesterday with a smile that fifteen weeks of privation has not banished.

They came to "show themselves to New York" and to set at naught much of the adverse opinion that has existed.

One thousand and fifty of them—men, women and young girls—arrived in Hoboken in a fourteen-car special train which cost them 19 cents a head.

Once upon the New York side, by way of the ferries, they marched up Fifth Avenue to Madison Square Garden, where last night they produced their strike pageant.

The I.W.W. band—sweating with its prolonged and vigorous exertion—led the way, playing "La Marseillaise" and the "International Hymn."

Hannah Silverman, whose militantism has fixed upon her the romantic sobriquet of "Joan of the Mills," was a modest marcher with the rest of her sister strikers.

Mrs. Margaret Sanger, of No. 235 West 135th Street, and Harry Zettel, of Paterson, led the way under the guidance of Policemen Larkin, Morris, Kelly and Simmer.

Noticeably absent were the pyrotechnic I.W.W. leaders—Haywood, Tresca, Quinlan and Elizabeth Gurley Flynn. Order and circumspection of the quality to be looked for at a meeting of the Hague Tribunal prevailed throughout the march from Christopher Street to the Garden. . . .

MADISON SQUARE GARDEN THE SCENE OF MELODRAMATIC REPRODUCTION OF SILK STRIKE—1,029 ON GIGANTIC STAGE—BIGGEST CAST EVER SEEN IN A NEW YORK PRODUCTION STAGES ITS OWN SHOW

It is doubtful if Madison Square Garden, even at the close of the bitterest of political campaigns, ever held a larger audience than that which packed that great auditorium last night to witness the first production of "Big Bill Haywood's Paterson Strike Pageant," a spectacular production in which 1,029 Paterson strikers of many nationalities and ages played the leading as well as all of the minor parts.

The spectacle was in six scenes, and was intended to give a picture of the strike from the dawn of that morning, almost sixteen weeks ago, when the silk mill workers of the New Jersey city deserted their looms until the present moment, when practically every mill in the greatest silk manufacturing city in America is still idle, and when every other industry there is feeling the pinch of hard times due to the self-enforced idleness of more than 25,000 silk weavers and dyers.

It was said by the Industrial Workers of the World leaders, who managed last night's spectacle, that more than 12,000 persons had paid their way into the fair, and these, with the New Jersey strikers, who were admitted free, brought the total number of the audience to a figure that it was said closely approximated the 15,000 mark.

It was an audience every man, woman and child in which seemed to be enthusiastic for the Haywood organization and all that it stands for. . . .

John Reed, poet, magazine writer, and recent prisoner in the Paterson jail, has selected and outlined the scenes, all drawn from the events of the last three months in the great Paterson strike. His scenario is as follows:

Episode I

The Mills Alive—The People Dead. Going to Work in the gray dawn. Shambling along the street half asleep. Knots and groups forming. The beginning of the strike.

Episode II

The Mills Dead—The People Alive. The gathering of the people before the mills. The picket line. The Scab passes. Coming of the police. "Boo!" Clubbing and brutality. Arrest of forty pickets. "Boo!"

Episode III

The forty strikers brought before the judge. The policeman's story. Strikers attempt to answer. "Tell it to the next fellow! Held for the Grand Jury on the charge of Unlawful Assembly; five hundred dollars bail." Strikers: "Fill up de jail. We take no bail. To hell with the A. F. of L. Hooray for the I.W.W.!"

Episode IV

The armory meeting, A. F. of L. try to break strike. They refuse to let the I.W.W. leaders speak. "Let's go home." The police.

Episode V

A Sunday meeting at Haledon. Tresca just finishing a speech in Italian. "Musica! Musica!" The Italian singers. The German singers. The two bands. The strike song.

Episode VI

The funeral of Modestino Valentino. The coffin borne past, while each striker drops a red carnation into it. The burial.

Episode VII

The departure of the children. The mothers hold up their babies to Miss Flynn. May Day. The strike mothers receive them.

Episode VIII

A strike meeting at Helvetia Hall. Strikers with their backs to the audience addressed by Big Bill Haywood, who faces the audience. Also by Quinlan, Elizabeth Gurley Flynn, and Tresca. Pass the eight-hour law. They raise their right hands and swear they will not go back to the mills until the strike is won.

STRIKERS' PAGEANT A TRAGIC PICTURE; BIG CROWD SEES IT. JACK REED HERO OF BIG PAGEANT IN NEW YORK CITY . . . THOUSANDS AT I.W.W. STRIKE PAGEANT . . . FUNERAL SCENE IS FEATURE OF I.W.W. STRIKE TAB-LEAUX . . . FIFTEEN THOUSAND PERSONS IN MADISON SQUARE GARDEN SEE COFFIN BORNE AT HEAD OF LONG PROCESSION; WIDOW OF SLAIN PATERSON STRIKER AMONG THE SPECTATORS . . . PATERSON STRIKERS NOW BECOME ACTORS . . . NO MERE MIMIC FERVOR, THAT OF STRIKER-ACTORS . . .

etc., etc., from newspapers all over the country, as well as all the New York papers.

Immediately after the night of the Pageant—I believe the very next day—Miss Galvin, ever present help, John Reed, Bobby Jones, and I sailed for Europe.

We didn't see the avalanche of discrediting press notices that the newspapers followed up with after their first enthusiasm. We got away too soon. Fearful of the immediate sympathy that we had raised, orders had been given to the write-up men to take away the glory; but it was too late. Anyway, they wrote all kinds of rumors and sought to spread them as best they could.

They said, variously: "Claim Is Now Made That Pageant Lost Money . . . Fuss Over Pageant Finances . . . Strikers Look in Vain for Report from I.W.W. Leaders . . . Deficit of $1,996 from Strike Show . . . Instead of Making Rumored $6,000 Profit, Paterson I.W.W. Lost by Pageant at Garden . . . Many Loans Still Unpaid . . . Strike Pageant Was Money Loss . . . Backers of One Night Stand Are out $3,000 . . . Now It Is Explained That the Big Strike Pageant at Madison Square Garden Was Run at a Loss and 25,000 Local Strikers Who Hoped to Share the Profits Will Have to Whistle for Their Money . . ." etc.

But Jessie Ashley and others printed this statement showing the items of expense easily verifiable, and that was all of that:

PATERSON PAGEANT FINANCIAL STATEMENT

The Executive Committee of the I.W.W. Paterson strike pageant given in Madison Square Garden on June 7th, has published a financial statement of the show. The upshot is that there is a total deficit of $1,996.45, the statement showing total receipts of $7,645.40, and expenses of $7,632.30, with bills and loans unpaid to the amount of $2,009.65 and cash in hand of $13.10.

The first definite move to give the pageant was taken at the home of Margaret H. Sanger, a member of the I.W.W., and the date of June 7 was set three weeks before the show was staged. None of the people connected with the pageant had any experience of such work, and none knew what expense would be involved. They went at it blind.

Three days after the first meeting, a midnight meeting was held, at which were present Miss Jessie Ashley, William D. Haywood, Arturo Giovanitti and F. Sumner Boyd, when it was seriously debated whether or not to drop the whole thing on account of the many difficulties that had then become apparent, among them being the likelihood of a financial loss, and the too short time in which to stage the show. But for the fact that during the afternoon the check for the deposit on the Garden rent had been sent, together with the contract, it would at that time have been stopped.

Some eight days later the Executive Committee, which consisted of William D. Haywood, Margaret H. Sanger, Jessie Ashley, Mabel Dodge, John Reed and F. Sumner Boyd, called a meeting in the Liberal Club of all members of the various working committees to propose again that the pageant should be called off, in view of the enormous expense that they were quite unable to meet, and the fact that the floor tickets which were to carry the house could not be sold at the price decided upon, $1.50 each, in the time available. In other words, if the pageant could be produced at all, a financial loss seemed certain.

The meeting was attended by a number of New York silk strikers, who insisted that the pageant must be staged, that if those in charge could not do it, they, the silk strikers, would, and that they would also find the necessary money to finance it. For these reasons it was again decided to continue, and the strikers, from the bank accounts of some dozen of their members, raised the funds needed, appointing Rudolf Wyssmann assistant treasurer to Mrs. Florence Wise, of the Women's Trade Union League, who was acting for the committee.

On this basis the pageant plans went forward, and a great success was scored. Probably Madison Square Garden has never been filled before in three weeks. Certainly no such spectacle, presenting in dramatic form the class war raging in society, has ever been staged in America, and in its scope and the number of its actors and spectators, it is like most other American achievements—without parallel in the world.

Criticism charging misappropriation of money is, in view of the facts, obviously inspired by malice and a determined effort to slander and malign. Of all the people connected with the pageant, only three handled any of the receipts and expenditures, namely, Miss Ashley, Mrs. Wise, and Rudolf Wyssmann. Everybody connected with the pageant gave their services voluntarily, no one receiving remuneration in any form, and most of them paying their own expenses as well as lending money to make the thing a success.

Hopes of profit were naturally raised when the Garden was filled to its capacity. Such hopes were, however, based on incomplete information. Thus, hundreds of strikers were admitted to the Garden free on presenting their I.W.W. membership cards. Many of them had walked from Paterson, West Hoboken, Astoria, College Point, the Bronx and Brooklyn. The pageant was theirs more than anybody else's, and this feeling found practical expression as a matter of course. The floor seats, advertised at $1.50, had to be sold at the last moment for whatever they would fetch, most of them going for 50 cents each, because by eight o'clock, when the gallery, balcony and arena seats were crowded, there were but a few hundred people on the floor. It would have been a "floor frost" without hope of salvation had not the prices been cut at the box offices.

JESSIE ASHLEY,
F. SUMNER BOYD,
MABEL DODGE,
WILLIAM D. HAYWOOD,
JOHN REED,
MARGARET H. SANGER,
Executive Committee.

And then followed a detailed financial statement.

So Miss Galvin and John, and Reed and Bobby and Carl and I sailed away to spend the summer in Florence at the Villa Curonia.

Although scarcely a word of the personal kind had passed; we had taken for granted the inevitability of our love for each other, Reed and I. I had never experienced before such a passionate unity as there had been between us all through those days we worked together. He told me later that he had been constantly reminded of something George Meredith wrote about two lovers, of a perpetual flame that played back and forth between them. It had been like that with us. It had carried us on and on through those days, supporting us, and enabling us to do more than we could ordinarily perform.

We were free and ready to turn to each other. But, strangely, something in me resisted him strongly. I wanted a lover and I wanted to be loved, and Reed was entirely lovable, and admirable, too, I thought. Yet something in me held back from taking that step into love.

At first I felt this resistance for no reason, but almost at once it seemed to me I knew the reason. I told him I didn't want him to come to my cabin. I was afraid of that. I was afraid someone would see him and speak to me about it. I dreaded such a rebuff.

"You shouldn't care about that," Reed cried, bitterly. "If you cared for me nothing would matter."

"Oh, I do care, darling, but let's wait."

His fatigue translated itself into a desperate restlessness. The exaltation of our furious activity together began to turn into the intensest concentration of desire. He asked me the first night to let him come, and he asked me the second night. When I refused again on the third night, he sat down and wrote a poem and sent it to me at midnight. . . .

THE NEW AGE BEGINS

Wind smothers the snarling of the great ships,
And the serene gulls are stronger than turbines;
Mile upon mile the silent hiss of a stumbling wave breaks unbroken—
Yet stronger the power of your lips for my lips.

This cool beryl heavy death shall toss us living
Higher than high heaven and deeper than sighs,
But O, the abrupt stiff sloping resistless foam
Shall not forget our taking and our giving!

Life wrenched from its roots—what wretchedness!
What craving of tentacles like sea-things without eyes!
Even the black still slime is quick and bottomless;
I am less and more than I was, you are more and less.

I cried upon God last night, and God was not where I cried—
He was slipping and balancing on the thoughtless shifting miles of sea—
Impersonal he will unchain the appalling sea-gray engines,
But the speech of your body to my body will not be denied!

J. R.

So it went on through the voyage. Ah, "It's a heartbreak to the wise that things stay in the same place for a short time only!" Things don't stay in the same place—they go forward or they go backward. I didn't want to lose Reed, though I would have been glad if I had known how to preserve the intense life that we created together without (as I felt it would be) descending into the mortality of love. My blood longed for its share, too, of course, it longed for mortal life; but something in me adored the high clear excitement of continence, and the tension we had known together that came from our canalized vitality.

But this new and different tension did not satisfy either of us. It bred impatience in me and worse than that in him.

"Please, Mabel, please . . ."

"Oh, Reed, darling, we are just at the Threshold and nothing is ever so wonderful as the Threshold of things, don't you *know* that?"

But this meant nothing to him.

Bobby Jones hovered over us, drawing a vicarious delight from what he believed to be our splendid love. He had a great capacity for wonder, and Reed was his old classmate and his hero. Together with Walter Lippmann, Lee Simonson, Hiram Motherwell, Eddy Hunt, Bobby Rogers, and several others, he had been one in that brilliant group that were classmates at Cambridge. "Copey" had taken special pains with Bobby and said the world would hear of him later, and Bobby was on his way to Germany to study with Reinhardt, for we had formed what we called the "Robert E. Jones Development Company," and he had a modest budget in his pocket, and an encouraging letter from Germany:

March 7, 1914.

Prof. George Baker,
Harvard University, Cambridge.
MY DEAR PROF. BAKER:

I take the liberty of addressing these lines to you in the hope that they may be of assistance to Mr. Jones in carrying out his wishes. Mr. Jones, who had heard that I was a member of the advisory staff of Prof. Max Reinhardt's Deutsches Theatre in Berlin, visited me in Florence last summer. He showed me his work and expressed his wish to prepare himself as painter for theater decoration in costume and scene setting. I could give him no better advice than to come to Berlin, where the greatest costume library of the world stood at his service, where he could become thoroughly familiar with Prof. Reinhardt's methods of stage production, and where he could study the newest and best technical developments.

I am convinced that his talent for this work is most extraordinary, and that his industry is as great as his talent. . . .

DR. FREIHERR VON SCHLIPPENBACH.

One night on the steamer Bobby told me, shy and stammering, twisting his straw hat round and round:

"I feel there's something wonderful and immortal between you and Jack, Mabel. . . ."

"But I don't know how to keep it immortal," I told him ruefully.

Finally we reached Paris and there was a letter from Hutch already waiting:

Harvard Club, New York City.

DEAR MABEL,

Yes, I'm going with you—that part of me which is your part of me. Two true notes from you. The next time I shall write on your paper. This is only to tell you that what is between you and me can do no Wrong to anybody and is true, deep, and independent, and brings freedom instead of bondage.

Your apartment seemed haunted to me. I slept in the parlor, on the lounge, or rather didn't sleep. What memories! Shadowy but real qualities lurking all over the room!

Dear Mabel, five months ago we had only just met! There has been a world between us since, and yet, almost mysteriously, a world quite distinct and unrelated to any other that I have known—cut off, as I have said to you—dislocated—detached from the earth and its products both for good and evil, lacking the earth's ugliness and the earth's beauty. It is not a lily that grows from the mud. It is not a rose that comes from gnarled and rooted earth. It is a flower whose conditions, whose roots, whose origin is unknown to me—lacking in pungency and virulence and definite passion, but full of an unfolded, a comprehensive, serene bien être floating beneficently on invisible and insentient things.

That is rather mixed, dear, and I'll wait for a clearer hour. I am *very* tired.

Yours,

Hutch.

We went to the dear old Hotel des Saints Pères, and I sent Miss Galvin and John down to Florence on the train, for we planned to stay a few days and then rent a motor and drive through the south of France and along the coast to Italy.

And then . . . then Reed's room and mine were close to each other the first night in Paris. . . .

("Good-by, my lover, good-by!")

And now at last I learned what a honeymoon should be.

As soon as I gave myself up to Reed I was all for love and everything else well lost! Nothing else in the world had, any longer, any significance for me. I had built up an interest in life, a love for beautiful things, for noble ideas, and for interesting people; I had learned to be satisfied with flattery and adulation and influence. I had consoled myself with a belief that I was a maker of history, since people had told me I was doing that day by day; and because I remained silent and mysterious, while my life poured out of me and made itself felt without words, my own silence had finally convinced me, beyond the strength of any formulation, that I was indeed remarkable.

"The unclassified," Walter Lippmann had called me—"not belonging to any type, a sport," he said. Gifted, I believed, but fortified and amplified by containing within myself my own elixir of love. Power, I thought, *my* power, emerges at the source, that is, my sex, and rises, rises through my belly, through my solar plexus, through my heart and to my head—and all these I have dedicated to that Power that uses me for its own purposes.

And since I saw this happen over and over again, no wonder I had been full of its wonder, and often consoled for lack of love by its knowledge.

And in one night I threw it all away and nothing counted for me but Reed . . . to lie close to him and to empty myself over and over, flesh against flesh. And I was proud that I had saved so much to spill lavishly, without reckoning, passion unending.

So I came to Reed, then, like a Leyden jar, brimful to the edge, charged with a high, electrical force. And this seemed a marvel to him. He had not known any women like this. He had been living for some months with a lovely girl named Rose, a schoolteacher, fair and smooth and affectionate, and their life together had been of an intermittent nocturnal kind. After he and I started to work on the Pageant he went to her and said:

"I don't love you, Rose. I love Mabel Dodge and when the Pageant is finished I'm going to Europe with her."

He told me she buried her face in her hands and said,

"I'm very unhappy."

But after a few moments she looked up with a look of surprise and said, through tears:

"Why, no, I'm not, either!"

He whispered to me, that first night: "I thought your fire was crimson, but you burn blue in the dark."

So, overnight, a mania of love held me enthralled. I remember very little of those days except that they were interruptions in the labor of passion.

The second morning in Paris a prodigious knocking on Reed's door made him leap away from me to go to his room, and I heard a hearty voice accosting him:

"Hey, you scoundrel—don't you know the sun is overhead? Anne and I heard you were in Paris—get thee pants, old son, and come for

216

déjeuner with us." It was Waldo Pierce and Reed closed the door between our rooms and I heard the two male voices, insouciant and gay, chaffing each other. He dressed quickly and went out, and my heart began to break a little right then.

Bobby was prowling by himself all over Paris, happy.

When we motored away, somehow Carl was with us—and we rolled south through the June day—I in blankness—suspended—waiting for the night, the boys eager and interested in all they saw.

Everything interested Reed. His imagination was on fire in the old world. And Carl was maliciously charmed with Bobby and tormented him—teasing him playfully, frightening him dreadfully—the New England ascetic. It was a mad, happy, smoldering junket of a time. Reed always had to be carried away by people or things. Before the teachings of Steff prepared him for his excitement over strikes and pageants, he and Bobby Jones had been fully excited over a soprano; they had discovered her and they thought she was a miracle woman with an epoch-making voice. All the energy that went into launching Sally Mower! And apparently all forgotten now for other things, other ideas, other people. So he always went from thrill to thrill.

I hated to see him interested in Things. I wasn't, and didn't like to have him even *look* at churches and leave me out of his attention. When we reached Concarneau I thought I had lost him to the stones of that place, and when we found the Italians giving "Aïda" at night in the amphitheater of Verona, I was inclined to force him to go on, drive all night, anything rather than submit to the terror of seeing his eyes dilate with some other magic than my own. Everything seemed to take him away from me, and I had no single thing left in my life to rouse me save his touch.

But I could not hold him day and night. Only at night. Our journey, just the same, was happy and carefree and gay. Carl, glad to be away from his newspaper and his everlasting reports of music, was amusing in his florid, hilarious fashion. Every morning as we drove rapidly out through the quiet streets of some old town, Carl stood bowing right and left to the astonished citizens:

"*Au revoir et merci*," he called to them, raising his hat, his face twisted in his crooked smile.

"*Au revoir et merci. . . .*"

There stood the villa waiting! Was it possible only a year had passed since we left it for a new world? So much had happened!

And now Reed came to me down the silken ladder from Edwin's dressing-room upstairs and we were together in the low bed that had four gold lions at its corners, and for the first time that place was the cradle of happy love for which it had been created.

But was it?

What is the matter with life that nothing is ever right, I wondered. Now nothing came between me and my desire in the short summer night, but I was not happy.

("Love lies bleeding. . . .")

Reed was without words for all the beauty about him.

"But it's *old*, Mabel. It's beauty, but it's so *old*," he said over and over.

Until he went to Venice, though, he was not lost to me, in beauty. There the solid achievement of men seemed to strike him more strongly than anywhere else. He roamed silently about Venice unaware of me. "The things *Men* have done!" he murmured once or twice. "But I wish that I could have been here at the *doing* of it or that they were doing it *now*," he said.

Past or present, I did not care what they had done. I was jealous of the way he said *"Men."* I jumped into the automobile and returned to Florence, leaving him there to it.

When I got home I wrote him a long, passionate letter. I told him it was immature of him to be so overcome at what Men had done—the work of hands laying stone on stone, gilt on gilt, was nothing in my sight—nothing to compare with the odor of the jasmine in the window ("Men could not create that!") or the warmth of the sun. I tried to wrest him away from Things, especially man-made things.

He was sturdily loyal to his own wonder. He came back to Florence and we continued to argue. While our duet progressed, Bobby was going his way alone.

Longing to know Gordon Craig and possibly to work with him in his out-of-door theater, the little amphitheater with lichen-covered stone seats, he blithely went to see him. But Craig rebuffed him when he learned Bobby came from the Villa Curonia. He was still bitter with me. This was a real grief to Bobby, who couldn't understand anyone's having any *personal* feeling about anything when there was so much to do in the theater. He was always one or those for whom real life is unreal and only stage life true.

Arthur Acton liked him (perhaps a little to please me) and asked him to decorate some lunettes over doors in the Villa Incontri with frescoes. Then Muriel descended upon us with Paul Draper and Arthur Rubenstein. ("Another interruption," I thought.)

She came with a loud noise of ivory and gold one evening and rushed all over the villa till she found Bobby in Edwin's room in bed drawing pictures. He leaned against the old red damask wall behind him, startled; whereupon she pounced upon him, frightening him as much as Carl had done.

"Oh, what a darling!" she cried, and he, looking up at her, exclaimed reverently, "What a *marvelous* hat!"

"But humans are *terrible,* Mabel," he told me the next day. "I don't see how *anyone* can stand them!"

Now I had more than stones to make me jealous. Reed was terribly interested in *people.* I lost him every hour to "humans." Muriel and her satellites engrossed his attention. Then Stan Krayl padded up to the villa and told him about the Maremma—the long stretches of beach—the sea—and only the birds for company.

Mary Foote told me later that Stan ran off with Reed right under my eyes for a few days—but if this is so, it was so painful to me that I have completely forgotten it. That must have been an interlude, if it happened; for I remember how life went on at the villa, made terribly painful to me by his presence. Deeper and deeper I sank into my old depression. I could not smile, nor talk, nor join in anything with the others in the daytime. At night, however, I burned with blue fire for Reed; and every night I recovered him, reconquered him, triumphing over the day's loss. I missed Hutch and he missed me. He wrote:

August 6th.

Cafe Lafayette, New York.

DEAR MABEL,

I am staying at your apartment, and Lisa asks me frequently how you are and when you are to return. She says she doesn't like it without you. The place seems very familiar, and natural to me, and I sleep in your bed quite peacefully!

I am here trying to sell some of Neith's stories and two of my books, and think I'll be able to arrange to return to Provincetown in a few days for the rest of the summer. No more *Globe* work this summer, probably.

Not many of the bunch here now. An interesting Tom Mann meeting last Sunday. Haywood presided, looking very ill. I fear there's something serious the matter with him. Have seen much of Steffens. Went to a turkey trot with him last night! Dined the other night at Edna Kenton's with Mrs. Westley and Sheffield. These latter two seem great friends. Naturally much talk of you and Carl.

I am feeling very quiet these days—calm, my old nervousness, though there's much occasion to be nervous, is much less than ever before. I feel that I am stronger in health, and need less, than ever before. I find I am fighting away from intensity in all forms, and I am planning some real books! Excitement doesn't excite me any more and I want less and less of it.

I think of you constantly—of your kindness and insight and mental sympathy, your urge, your detachment, and your *desœuvrement*—and I wonder if you are happy and content—and I find myself hoping that you are, with something like intensity.

I shall be deeply glad to see you again—but I wonder if you really will return?

I don't know what I shall be doing next winter—probably more *Globe* work—the editor told me today that he wanted me for good—but I rather doubt if I shall continue.

I seem to be writing in a mist. I am drinking beer, the backgammon is rattling about me and New York streets are trembling with nervousness. But I am quiet, unreal and about to go to sleep.

Yours with old affection,

HUTCH.

Things were very gay at the villa. We all went for long drives to the neighboring towns, and sometimes we went over to an ancient swimming pool in a deserted garden a few miles away. Here Robert de la Condamine and Carl and Reed revealed themselves one day. I wrote about it later when I was doing articles for the newspaper, for Arthur Brisbane.

THREE YOUNG MEN IN A POOL

Three young men were walking in the country one sunshiny day. As they walked they opened their hearts and tried to show each other their different philosophies.

One said: "If you have genius it will take care of you. You need never hesitate before an undertaking, your genius will watch over you. You need never be afraid to plunge ahead, your genius will guard you always. Genius is the capacity for leaping without having to look."

The second one said: "I believe in experience. I don't want genius to protect me and guard me. No experience can harm the soul. The only thing that can wither or corrode the soul is lack of experience. I think we can go down into the depths and perhaps find a treasure. Certainly the soul is robust—it should not shrink before any depth or danger or darkness."

The third one said: "I don't know what you fellows are talking about, but here's a fine deep swimming hole someone has built and left to us— I say we have a swim."

So they all undressed in the warm sun and the cool wind. Then the first one, standing on the rim of the basin, said:

"I never learned to swim, but here goes!"

And he raised his hands over his head like a diver and plunged in.

The second one said:

"I never learned to swim, either, but I may learn something from this pool. Whatever goes down rises again, anyway—" So he, too, raised his hands over his head and plunged in.

The third one looked rather surprised at their hastiness, for he knew water.

There was no time left to him for wondering; in a moment the quiet pool was in the greatest agitation.

The first diver had sunk and risen again, gurgling and blowing the water from his mouth, and clutching the surface of the pond with wild pawing movements.

The second one had sunk and had risen to the surface long enough to throw up his hands and blubber: "Hel-l-pl-p!" as the water rushed into his mouth before he disappeared.

The third one made a neat dive into the pool and arrived with great precipitation under the water by the side of one of the submerged ones, and circling his waist raised him easily to the surface and held him there with one arm and then made rapidly for the other animated one, who was bobbing up and down and only held up by an occasionally correct pawing motion.

This one was also grasped firmly around the waist, and now the third one held them both up, while he went on treading water with his feet.

But how was he to get them out of the pool?

The stone brink of it was at least two and a half feet above the water. He could not lift either of them with one hand, and they seemed helpless in their muscles and overcome by shock.

The third one thought for a moment, and then he saw how to manage it.

"Look here, now," he said sharply. "You fellows make an effort to do as I tell you. I'm going down to the bottom and stand there. It's not so deep. I'll put my hands on my hips and, one at a time, you put your feet on my hip and then on my shoulders, and then you'll be able to reach the stone edge and pull yourselves out, see?"

They both nodded obediently. The third one drew a deep breath as they placed their feet on his hips, and then he sank himself slowly to the bottom of the pool and stood there, while the others clambered painfully up onto his shoulders and drew themselves out of the water.

Then the third one rose tranquilly and drew again a deep breath and made a fine resilient spring and landed with a flop like a seal on the warm stone of the parapet.

His companions looked at him mutely, their philosophy all gone.

The third one shook the water vigorously out of his ears.

"What you fellows need," he remarked, "is to learn how to *swim*."

In the evening we sat about and sometimes Reed wrote verses. One evening he got even with me by expressing some of his own jealousies of *my* interests. *He* was always jealous of God, for one thing, and my "everlasting It," as he called what Hutch and I had named "the inevitable." And he started a fantastic drama of which I have only a part left.

THE CHARACTERS

God Almighty, *an invisible, pervasive presence*
Inevitability, *a wind*
Paris, *a city*
New York, *not yet a city*
Florence, *once a city*
Gertrude Stein

The Three Drillers $\begin{cases} Big\ Bill \\ Facts \\ Memory \end{cases}$

Ten Pierrots $\begin{cases} Bobette \\ Twitter \\ Papapas \\ Poodle \\ Dock \end{cases}$ $\begin{matrix} Box\ Hedge \\ Paraffine \\ Goldoni \\ Sem \\ Fish \end{matrix}$

(Variously representing Bobby, Robin, Jo Davidson, Paul Draper, Rubenstein, Craig and Berkman, etc.)

THE VOICE OF HUTCH HAPGOOD
THE VOICE OF LEO STEIN

TEN PIERRETTES
{
Flamande (*Dutchy*)
Beata (*Bee Shostac*)
Dragon-fly (*Haweis*)
Quieta (*Stan*)
Moma Fredda (*Neith*)
Prinzessin (*Grace Johnson*)
Helenie (*Frances Perkins*)
Magpie (*Miss Galvin*)
Huzzy (*Edna Kenton*)
Kalsomine (*Maud Cruttwell*)
}

(It is also indicated that Muriel and Constance
Fletcher should be in this list, possibly.)

CHORUS OF PEDERASTS
CHORUS OF PATERSON STRIKERS
GRAND CHORUS OF CELESTIAL SWISS BELL-RINGERS
THREE FAIRY GODMOTHERS
THE FAIR VAMPIRA

(Other characters lost!)

PRELUDE

(*A Void.* GOD ALMIGHTY *discovered gazing with satisfaction upon Chaos, accompanied by the rhythmical humming of 1,000,000* SOPRANO ANGELS:

GOD:

In veiled and thund'rous majesty
And all that sort of thing
I throned my awful self on high—
The world's omnipotent king!
So organized was everything
For earth's felicity
That I for one—the truth I sing—
Was ennuyé thereby!
                    Thereby!
Was ennuyé thereby!
For an active little God am I!

223

CHORUS:

A pretty efficient—fairly omniscient—wholly sufficient little God is he!

GOD:

So I called my flaming army of Seraphim
And cried in a voice like the bursting of the sun:
"God's on the job—make the earth aware of HIM!"
And that's how it happened to be done!

CHORUS:

First he made the Morning—and then he made the Night;
Then Earth and Sea created he and was delighted by't!
And every living creature—the great to eat the small—
And Man to cap the climax, the greatest joke of all!
Hosanna! Hallelluia! To Him the highest praise
For what?
           For making Chaos in less than seven days!

GOD: *(Doing a pas seul*

Now that is off my chest, I feel I have some leisure
To hearken to my breast, and have a Delphic seizure;
By every Muse caressed,
I am so full of zest
My Genius will not rest
Until I've done my best on something that will please you:
I've time for my caprice, my art is superhuman;
I'll do a masterpiece, I've centuries to do 'em in,
Of Gertrude and of Allyce
And Helena of Greece
And Mademoiselle des Lys;
I have the recipes—I'll make the Perfect Woman!
       (GOD *produces his Recipe Book and turns over the pages, at the
       same time falling into prose:*

GOD:

Let me see. Here's the latest formula for the Femme Fatale: Figure
that will stand a Greenwich Village Uniform; thorough comprehen-
sion of Matisse; more than a touch of languor; a dash of economic
independence; dark hair, dark eyes, dark past.
       (*He rolls up his sleeves, takes down bottles from the shelf, and
       begins to stir the ingredients:*

VOICE OF LEO STEIN:

First define what you mean by Woman!

GOD: (*Startled, turning round, and letting the Recipe Book fall shut*

How?

VOICE OF LEO STEIN:

You evidently know nothing whatever about the elements of a Work of Art. Now my theory of Esthetics specifies that the perfect Creation shall combine the maximum of Resistance with the Maximum of Unity. . . .

GOD:

My dear Leo, what have either Unity or Resistance to do with a Femme Fatale?

VOICE OF LEO STEIN:

I've passed through that stage. . . .

GOD: *(Yawning*

Come again *soon!*

VOICE OF LEO STEIN: *(From a great distance*

The Universe is composed of words. . . .

GOD: *(Picking up the Recipe Book*

Damn! I've lost the place. Where was I? Let me see. *(Turning over the pages.)* I can't remember what recipe I was using. Was it this one? *(Reads.)* Peasant Queen. Frankness, a good deal of vitality, a soupçon of vulgarity. Health and solidity from working outdoors in the fields; calloused hands and weather-beaten skin. Heavy grace from carrying bundles on the head.

    (He takes down bottles as before and begins to stir the ingredients:

VOICE OF HUTCH HAPGOOD:

But what about her soul?

GOD: *(Turning as before, and again losing place in the Recipe Book*

What say?

VOICE OF HUTCH HAPGOOD:

Life is so complex! God is really Love, I think. I don't agree with you. Woman's Soul is only a conductor of the Universal. It is like a water-faucet. I happened to notice the faucet in my bath-tub the other day, and my eyes filled with tears. I consider it a symbol for Woman's Soul. So much comes out, and yet the pipe always supplies more. . . .

GOD:

What on earth are you talking about?

VOICE OF HUTCH HAPGOOD:

I don't know, but it's very radical—

GOD:

Hutch, you've been drinking!

VOICE OF HUTCH HAPGOOD:

You are very talented. Schiller would have made a hero of you. But you must learn to co-ordinate. . . .

GOD: *(Picking up the Recipe Book and turning the pages*
These interruptions disturb me frightfully. I don't know where I was at all. Perhaps it was this one. *(Reads.)* Femme du Monde. Slender, delicately blonde, intuitive, carefully nurtured, brilliant conversationalist, exquisite taste, the reigning beauty of her drawing room, spirituelle, many accomplishments, elegantly educated in art, music, literature and politics.

    (He adds these ingredients to the others:
    (Vaguely, in Chaos, a baby shape begins to take form:
    (Enter the FAIRY GODMOTHER, *out of breath.*

FAIRY GODMOTHER:
I'm absolutely worn out. The number of births this year is absolutely appalling. And I thought it was letting up a little, too. There seems to be a perfect epidemic of babies this year. And it falls hardest on me. How do you suppose I can get around to all of them? I haven't had any sleep for months. And here's another! I'm so tired I can't go a step further. So I'll just give this child all the gifts I have left in my sack, and then the other babies can do without.

    (She fumbles in her sack and takes out three shawls which she lays upon the child:
Here's Virtue; and here's Beauty; and here's Intelligence.

                      (Exit the FAIRY GODMOTHER.

GOD: *(Noticing the shawls*
What is all this truck and where did it come from? *(He irascibly sweeps away the gifts.)* But see! She breathes! She lives! The Perfect Woman! Let the Celestial Swiss Bell-Ringers approach. All right, professor.

CELESTIAL SWISS BELL-RINGERS:
Deep in garden-gloom
Where sun never came
Kings sang long ago
Her fascination strange:
Warm with burning snow,
Ringed with icy flame,
Doomed with seasons' doom,
A living change—change—change—change—change. . . .

Rippling windy laugh
Shall her mirror seem;
Keen, cold, amorous
The marbles of her tomb,
When she, glamorous,

Shakes hell's quiet dream,
This her epitaph:
"She loved the boom—boom—boom—boom—boom. . . ."

[End of the fragment.]

And when finally he capitulated to me and agreed that the past was past and the old age of Italian wonder was wearisome, he wrote this poem; and that day I knew I need not fear Italy any more.

FLORENCE

SUMMER OF 1913

Make way for him, Giotto, Dante, Bianca Capello,
And all the glories of an ancient anarchy,—
Make way, loud Byron, sinning by the rule of three,
For this becivilized, berouged, befinished fellow,—
Collector of green jade fruits, and amateur of yellow;
Even beside the Uffizzi and the Bargello
He looks incredibly mean!
Make way, dead giant Italy, for Robert de la Condamine!

O Heir of all the Ages! Why should they have an heir?
There is no legacy but ashes of old fiery Te Deums
Neatly arranged in libraries and museums,
So he can languidly sniff their immortal essence there!
Distill from their fury an oil to anoint his hair!
From their violence, strength for a minor poet's dare!
The Superman has mastered his own soul—
How less than these, who theirs could not control!

Here the air is choked with the crowding-up, struggling souls of the dead—
Here death is swifter than life, and the green sky spawns no bursting
     stars—
The peasants sing old songs, and sleep with their avatars,—
And the strong, heady tongue that was born of lawlessness, is talking law
     instead.
O Field of Dragons' Teeth, where turbulent armies bred,
Horrors and heroes the fruit of one monstrous marriage bed,
Miraculous Tuscan soil
That now breeds only the seasons, olive and vine, wine and oil!

Here where the olden poets came in beauty to die
I sit in a walled high garden, far from the sound of change,
Watching the great clouds boil up from the Vallombrosa range
And sunlight pour through the black cypresses, drenching the vineyards
    dry.
Here is the drunken peace of the sensuous sick,—and here am I,
Smelling the smoke from clanging cities, that hangs like a threat in the sky
Unknown to these clods
Who worship Bacchus and Pan, and the senile young gods!

Through the halls of the Medici, queenlier far than they,
Walks she I love, half peasant, half courtesan,—
In her right hand a man's death, in her left the life of a man,—
Beware which you choose, for she changes them day by day;
Sun and wind in the room of her soul, and all the beasts that prey!
O let us shake off this smothering silky death, let us go away,
My dearest old dear
Mabel! What are we living things doing here?

I had a resurgence of delight and some of my old feeling of power came back to me.

The next morning he was very ill with diphtheria.

Women of the type I was at that time like to have men sick in bed. Then a truce is declared. An illusion of complete possession takes the place of the feeling of strain that one has all the time that one is trying to hold the whole attention of a man. Temporarily he is ours without a chance to escape, without even the desire for escape. Delivered into one's hands, he is helpless as a baby—dependent upon us for everything, dependent upon our sympathy, our judgment, and our love. Ceasing to try and maintain his separate individuality by assertion of opinion or by independent action, a man sick in bed reverts to an undifferentiated infantilism.

"He's a perfect baby when he's sick!" How many women say that! "Something in us wants men to be strong, mature, and superior to us so that we may admire them, thus consoled in a measure for our enslavement to them," I thought. But something else in us wants them to be inferior, and less powerful than ourselves, so that obtaining the ascendancy over them we may gain possession, not only of them, but of our own souls, once more.

Yes, when they are sick, our watchfulness and our vigilance are relaxed. We cease trying to hold them in a certain mold, that shape that must conform to our ideal and whose slightest infringement threatens our security and peace of mind. We are no longer worried for fear they will drink too much (an indulgence that immediately releases them from their attitude of devotion to us), nor that they will look away from us to another woman. Depending upon them for our sense of identity, the feeling that after all one is real: to have them give us life by their glance and then to remove it by looking at another, is something we cannot endure and we seek forever to forestall these inattentions.

A lover sick in bed, one is safe for the moment! He can no longer plunge into work, and forget one's existence. The work is forgotten. The world, too, is forgotten. Ideas no longer defeat us by their maddening claims. A sick anarchist is no anarchist at all! And as for poetry—!

So I had Reed, I thought, for my own—but that was a pleasure soon over. No sooner do we get them where we think we want them, than we find we do not want them so. A man completely at a disadvantage, disempowered, and delivered up to us, we find to be no man at all. Is it possible, then, that one is more satisfied with the struggle than with the surrender?

Reed, sick in bed in the cool, brown and white, north bedroom, has left no impressions with me—nor even when we moved him up to Vallombrosa, where it was cool among the pine trees. I was bored then—and peaceful. Too peaceful to attempt anything beyond eating and sleeping and reading out loud. I made some effort to console him and cheer him, for he was very sad and impatient. Letters from Hutch reflected my own pale mood and were full of his familiar and congenial Weltschmerz:

DEAR MABEL,   *Provincetown.*

Neith spent several days in the hospital and is now resting at Dobbs Ferry. Expects to come here soon, if she is strong enough. She has had a hard time.

I came here with the kids and Elsie (leaving Elina with Neith) four days ago. I have done nothing while here except to look after the kids, feel numb generally—mentally and physically—and read *The Confession of a Fool* by Strindberg which I have just finished—a sincere thing which in spite of its sincerity does not convince one. The keener psychological analysis of a personality is, the more the personality seems to evaporate. The woman that Strindberg analyzes and pictures so searchingly and vividly means nothing in the end. The more sincere and keen he is, the more in doubt I am as to whether I came anywhere near the real woman. And he leaves me in doubt as to whether there is such a thing as a real woman, anyway, as to whether personality exists, as to whether it is not one of the last stands of the old metaphysical illusion.

That is the mood that Strindberg puts me in.

Not only Strindberg but just now all about me numbs me and makes me feel the unreality of everything. I feel keen about nothing just now. I don't want to read, or drink, or exercise, or think, and am good only to do what I must and not that very intensely. The children interest and irritate me. I love them and they vex me. I am good to them and inefficient with them. I take great pains, am very solicitous, but inefficient.

Several people up here—two or three brides and their grooms, have invited me to a couple of simple affairs. They seem unaccountably gay about nothing. The only thing any of them said that amused me was said by a man of 40 who has just married for the second time. I knew his first wife and know there were strenuous times between them. His bride asked me if I liked the sound of the sea at night. I replied that I did, that it was beautiful, but like all beautiful things, also melancholy. He then said, "I could not stand sleeping by the sea if she were not with me." I knew well what he meant, and I remarked lightly that all companionship was intended merely to dull the emotions which we would otherwise get too intensely from solitude and nature. His bride didn't like that! I don't think she cared to regard herself as a buffer between him and Life. . . .

After the children were in bed tonight, I went out on the beach, and heard a wild, true story that I must tell you when I see you—a woman, with whose little boy Boyce plays—I met her only tonight, after I began this letter to you—told me about how she went to an insane asylum— driven to it because she saw what was happening in the little village here. She saw so truthfully that her husband and the world thought she was insane. She saw what the community was doing to a little girl here—saw it in its ramifications and insisted on acting—hence the asylum. That was three years ago, and now she is a social rebellious philosopher, an anarchist without calling herself so.

I suppose you are having a gay and beautiful time in Villa Curonia! And that I seem very far away! But, I hope, still attractive? I think of you quietly and peacefully, and if I saw you walk into the room, it would seem as if you had never gone away. But the whole world is misty to me, at present. I think I never had quite the mood before—a distant, unreal, un-intense quality about everything. This letter seems that to me, too. It seems pale and vague and numb. Am I alive, I wonder? I don't seem to have any personality, any more than Strindberg's wife.

I wonder if I never drank again if I would always be like this?

Write me or Neith a few lines here, and tell us the news with you.

Affectionately,

HUTCH.

And often he would send me just some puritanical small observation, as:

Provincetown, Mass.

DEAREST MABEL,

I have just got round to your letter about the article on abstract art. I'll write a short article about it, if you write me that there is still time. I have delayed it so. I shall take the side of the abstract, which is still more important in life than in art. The nearer we get to the abstract in our human relations the more intense they are, the more emancipated, and the less connected with the weaknesses inherent in the "object."

It is fine to have John here. I wish he could stay longer. His voice is changing to that of a real man!

I wish you could have come and consoled me in New York! With all the old love,

HUTCH.

But the picture of that time is pale. I can more easily remember André Gide, who sat outside the hotel door clad in funny French knickerbockers, a black string hanging from his monocle, his eyes screwed up in an endeavor to find the *mot juste* for the story he was writing.

It was in the fall of 1913 when Reed and I returned to the apartment at 23 Fifth Avenue to live there together quite openly; though I was still accompanied by Miss Galvin, I felt courageous and high-minded about it. I hated the thought of clandestine nocturnal life, and I believed that I was strong enough to do openly whatever I did. Reed gave me that strength. And because I persuaded myself to feel thus, I persuaded others, too.

Bobby was in Berlin having a wonderful time, though he was rather delicate, and, I was sure, never had enough to eat. Letters like the following came occasionally from him:

Here beginneth a new volume. I'm not going to talk any more I hope about being sick, but I can't get away from the fact, I'm still a semi-invalid, and I'm continually used up, run down, all in, played out—no pep whatever, and it's hypochondriac, absurd, ridiculous. I eat enormous amounts four times a day and drink the nearest approach to cream I can find.

I've been depressed about it only once. That was when Sally Mower wrote me to come home and I felt too weak to make the effort—do still for that matter. What is life for but to do just such things for such people? She accomplishes at her best exactly the thing I'm trying to do, that is enough to give her any claim over me—well, she claimed and I didn't come across. I wonder—*so* strongly, whether you've been able to do anything for her. Of course if you can't and I can't somebody, something will help her; she is one of the ones who rides on the top: but why this waste of energy?

(Business of shrugging the shoulders as one who throws off a weight.)

Why not a performance—a pantomime, say—against a background of nothing but light—the performers paying a great deal of attention to decorative silhouette? The light changing in color but never in value.

To bad, I lost a very funny joke in the newspaper about the new Cubist Futurist Expressionism exhibition here which I haven't yet seen. It was about one of the pictures: Excrement of a Crazy Cow—*einer verrückten Kuhs*—and the puzzle was—what made her crazy? une cocotte—*eine kokotte*.

There's all France and all Germany.

R. E. J.

The Evenings, of course, had been in full swing before I met Reed and when we came back everyone expected them to continue, though I was faint-hearted about the semi-public character my life in New York had taken on (*faute de mieux!*), and I would have been content to settle down now to a quiet and cozy fireside with him. But no! Hutch and Neith, Steff, who knew Reed well and loved him dearly, Carl, and all the others simply insisted upon owning me, my house, my life itself, and they all just came along as usual.

Reed himself was ready for anything! Ready at any moment to pop off into some new enthusiasm. He always seemed to have his lungs too full, and he would draw in his round chin in an effort to quiet his excited heart. *Always* there seemed some pressure of excitement going on in him. His eyes glowed for nothing, his brown curls rushed back from his high, round forehead in a furious disorder, and the round highlights on his temples gleamed, his eyebrows went further up. . . .

I didn't want only to sleep in his arms. I wanted to *live* with him. It seemed to me, now, that to live quietly with him would be just as good as to work at high pressure with him had been before we went away for the summer. It seemed to me that I could live happily with him simply and quietly and slowly. But it did not seem so to him. Life—just everyday life—little things and gentle hours were not enough. He was too young and too full of urgency and excitement. From the break of day he was eager to be off and *doing*.

I took my breakfast in bed, and he ate his at a little table by my bedside because I wanted him to. But he might as well have been gone from there for all he was with *me*. He drank his coffee with the morning newspaper propped up before him, his honey-colored round eyes just popping over *"the news!"* Any kind of news as long as it had possibilities for thrill, for action, for excitement.

Now newspapers have never meant anything to me.

I have never read the news in all my life except when it was about myself or some friend or enemy of mine. But what the morning paper said was happening in Mexico, or in Russia, or at the Poles, seemed to make Reed's heart beat faster than I could, and I didn't like that. I felt doomed.

"Listen to *this*—" he would cry, and then he'd read the thing out loud, crackling the sheets of grayish paper, getting the still-damp print on his fingers, using me merely as a focus, to intensify the loss I felt of his attention that now the world had won him away from me again.

This was disheartening and it hurt me, and I was relieved when breakfast was over, the newspaper fallen to the floor, and he was on his feet eager for the street. Though I hated him to go out and leave me, I hated worse to have him there forgetful of our essential life together. It was hard and I did not know how to change it.

Each day as soon as he was gone out of the house I felt deserted and miserable and as though I had lost him forever. Yet no sooner was he away from me for an hour or two than he was eager to return, and he would come bounding up the dark, quiet stairs past General Sickles's rooms, until he was with me again. Yet out he'd go in a few moments, a perpetual unrest urging him back and forth—never satisfied to be where he was.

"We can't seem to live with the men who want to sit at home with us, and the men we want to live with can't sit at home with us, and there's no peace to be found either way," I thought to myself in these days, and I was wretched. He liked people and he liked importance and he grew more and more inflated by mine or his (it didn't seem to matter which, at first) so to please him I tried more than ever to cultivate those barren fields that before I knew him had constituted my only consolation.

I invited more and more people to the Evenings and I tried harder than ever to interest and attract them, making the ancient mistake of believing my victories would act upon Reed like an aphrodisiac and that when my value appeared greater to others, it would appear so to him and would make him want to be with me all the day.

On the contrary! My triumphs served to stimulate him to greater achievement in that world where men *do* things in order to prove themselves powerful to themselves. So a spirit of competition sprang up between us! If I had power, he, then, must have more power.

Desperate, I tried to hold him closer by laments. I grew pale and wept and I held him tighter and tighter.

When he came in one night and told me he had walked and talked with a strange, beautiful prostitute on the street, had felt her beauty and her mystery, and, through her, the beauty and the mystery of the world, I threw myself on the floor and tried to faint. Overcome by commiseration for an unhappiness he could not understand but which he knew he caused, he promised me he would be faithful to me forever—and that no one should ever separate us. Believing that since it was a *street walker* that had been the cause of my grief, if he cut out talking to them in order to learn their secrets and their mysteries, he would no longer hurt me, he had no hesitancy, one night, in telling me that the young wife of a friend of ours and he had stood talking at the front door while the early fall snowflakes came powdering down on their faces—and all the time they talked he felt her strange purity was whiter than the snow, and colder—and yet that she revealed without knowing it a peculiar impersonal attraction that was as hot as hell and spoke directly to him behind her shy, correct, Nordic demeanor.

I was perfectly stunned. He seemed to *have* to have these imaginary experiences with everything and everybody, and to *have* to come and tell me about them. I shut him up hard about this girl, whom I had only known for a short time.

She was a lovely maid with an oval-shaped head, chaste bands of

brown hair, and a body that was one of the most perfectly proportioned ones I had ever seen. I hated to think of Reed talking to her
on our front doorstep, and guessed how her soft, stupid fire called
through her obtuseness. She became a menace that I added to my
secret list of fears.

I showed a contempt that was stronger than I felt. If I had been
jealous of stones in Verona and doges in Venice, in New York I was
jealous of his ideas about women. I tried to hem him in, and I grew
more and more domestic except for the Evenings, when I sat tragic and
let It do what It wanted.

Hutch had to hear all about the peculiar struggle going on between
us and had things to say about Sex Antagonism. He was so eloquent
that Steff suggested an Evening given to the discussion of this subject.
Everybody thought Hutch and the others would probably be so brilliant that we'd better try to record the conversation, so Steff secured a
stenographer and put her, unbeknownst to Hutch, behind a screen
where she was instructed to take down the whole evening's talk in
shorthand!

Unfortunately, in the first place Hutch was a little drunk, and in the
second place the stenographer was unfamiliar with his kind of mentality and couldn't fill in mechanically what she missed in the detail
of his talk—as she was used to doing in the business office. Hutch's
talk was never composed of the old familiar phrases of business! I
suppose the poor woman couldn't make head or tail of it. There were
large empty places in her report which is transcribed below as I got it
from her late that night. This is what she secured and I reprint it
here because it just about describes how ideas muddled through!

Mr. Lincoln Steffens:

"Our hostess has asked me to call you to law and order. Now I will say
one word about her. She is an executive. She had an idea the other day
and she went to work and carried it out. The idea was to get Mr. Hutchins
Hapgood in a corner where we could really get at him on any subject he
might propose himself. He is going to talk on the subject of Sex Antagonism. As to Mr. Hapgood, he speaks with his mind and with his heart.
When he speaks with his heart, it is pretty hard to review him, but when
he speaks from his mind, it is easy.

"I take pleasure in introducing Mr. Hutchins Hapgood."

MR. HUTCHINS HAPGOOD:

"I think it is a contemptible thing to make a speech, because I have tried, and as my friend Mr. Collier said to me at one time when he was entrusting one of his poems to me, he said: . . .

"When I was asked here by your hostess, I did not realize that she really expected me to *talk*.

"I being a willful democrat have always been a . . . When the thing came up before me, I perceived, after all, that judging by the conditions of our society, if we have not yet turned into a democracy, we have realized we must begin from a society basis.

"Whenever we know a thing, we cannot communicate it. On the spur of the moment I selected a theme which is in itself an earnest of democracy.

"It is obvious that the establishment of a social center is a feminist impulse. It is the only cause which spreads a natural form of ways in which even the conservatives generally connect it, so that those people interested in the labor movement, if they also have common sense, must be.

"I see one great difficulty, the same difficulty which the Socialist movement undergoes, and that difficulty is judged by the words 'Sex Antagonism.' Formerly sex antagonism meant that a man found that, being more or less submerged by the idea of distinction, he felt that any women that interested him too much were successful encouragements. It is a personal feeling. We find that people regard to be able, rather, to take a woman, get possession of a woman, that he or she is submerged under the control or made a slave by other peoples. We find even today a man says he must not feel himself under the control of a woman; he must be free. Oscar Wilde talked about these things. They recognize sex antagonism because they have very small personalities. . . . Somebody, too, considered personality an important thing; inferred that by omissions or by modes of stretching the vision —— are able to co-operate. I must work against this diabolical . . . and make a philosophy of it, just because I have such an instinct. Philosophy determinated facts. . . . If anything interferes with me, when he is threatening my slavery with the development of a sensual impulse, and with the woman, of course —— . The fact is that a woman is a devil. I mean I know three or four people who think the same, that the woman that he was in love with was a devil, or the man that she was in love with was a devil, that they destroyed personality, the fine esthetic impulse of that human being. That was the devil incarnate; that was the individualistic plan of sex antagonism and social valuations in our day, he spread all over the universe, with all the mechanism, the innovations he tries to maintain, to concentrate his impulse and individualistic . . . But in the last few years it seems to me that sex antagonism has developed socially, rather than that of the individual, and therein I see its danger, and therein do I regard it as something connected with suffrage often.

"It is the only political party that has any significance, but it has significance enough to make it important. It has indulged in lies. (Socialist Party? Suffrage Party?) It is said that of course it is necessary, fundamental, that a certain capacity for realizing that democratic ideal. It is all social, moral, fervor; all idealistic lies. But what is, after all, morality of art, of everything that we hear about in reform? What has been inaugurated in order to maintain the condition of warlike advantage of any people? I think probably it is wise in doing that, because we are all weak. The Socialist wants to accomplish his aim. Therefore, probably being weakening, he must lie in order to gain publicity. The feminist movement is lying also. They are interested in accomplishing certain things. But, in order to get freedom for women, which is a part of the Socialist labor movement, they have to transmit the supposition that the man or the devil is either a devilish thing, or somehow or other they conspire against women, against the social spirit, against certain good people.

"*As a matter of fact, there has been no conspiracy either in the labor movement or in the feminist movement.* I do not know whether it is possible or not to be fair, to realize that the problem is: How get the heat without the lie? The question is, if you will, can we help it? Can we help these two movements to accomplish the social purpose that they are organized for, without accepting and embracing all the lies which they have embraced in order to give their movement power, force? I do not know whether it is possible or not, but for the moment I would ask you to consider that question of the absolute—that everybody is absolutely true and just—that there is no sex antagonism. My wife is always telling me that love is a misunderstanding between a man and a woman. I do not really believe it is. I think that love is an understanding between man and woman, and that all we are doing now is to remove all these obstacles in the way of understanding between man and woman.

"I notice now among the feminists that the women are getting a sex antagonism. They are organizing women's clubs. Men's clubs are bad enough, but why is it to be held up as a reform movement? There is nothing I loathe as much as a man's club. It is the dullest thing in the world, it is an isolated center, and to the women it is reactionary. There are women who say: 'We must have the same prerogatives, the same isolation, the same stupidness the men have. The men have it, and we will do just as the men. We will assert that the men have their clubs in order to make plain their power over the women.' They are going through the same policy the Socialist movement has gone through. Mrs. Pankhurst and all the rest of them, they say . . .

"I think that the feminist movement is a movement which is inspired by the very best things. There is in our attitude, I have no doubt, the feeling . . . You might say the slaves, the workers, are women. There is no idea of complexity. Man is spoiled by his sex and by his power. But time and the sex of man always dies for some certain . . . And the women, being slaves as workers, the women have certain kinds . . .

". . . of man hiding. That is true enough, but the women are making the mistake of trying to get more than they have, to make morality the force of their movement, and there is where they are probably to make a mistake before they get through. But once there is going to be a reaction. The men are in fields of their own in everything.

"Man has now a deep, primordial pain, which he never had before, because not only has he a pain, but he has a pain in connection with jealousy. That is the first time man ever felt jealousy. They also have a feeling of the injustice of it, because they know that the woman's propaganda is all wrong in morality. They know that the feminist propaganda is wrong. They know that they have a real sentiment, a genuine feeling about history. Their feeling about law and order is a genuine feeling. It is not because they want to keep the workers as slaves, or the women as slaves; it is a sincere feeling. They know they are right, and they also know that this feminist movement is barbaric, savage. They have a sentimental interest in history. They know that the women are . . . That they love immorality and all sorts of things primordial. They know that they have not any purpose at all, but they also know that the woman is fiendish. They know that the real truth, the vitality in the world . . . And the man who is intelligent knows that the vitality of women . . .

"He is also sensitive, consequently he is placed in a very unfortunate position. He has not a moment, so to speak, he has not the vitality that the working class has, that the women have. He is a dead one as far as his intelligence goes. He is a bad lover. There is not a single man today that is able to be a good lover, because they have taught them their own . . . Man, therefore, is dead to his own. Why should women, therefore, unnecessarily place upon men an immortality that is false, in fact, that is not true historically any more than any of them conspire against the labor class? People do not conspire—they act, they act through impulse. There is no conspiracy except by a select few, and then there is diabolical conspiracy going on the universe. I have great sympathy for the men. I realize that women are the things, women and laborers, that are the devil. Men are the victims. I would like the women to have enough real humanity, enough consideration, to realize, to see that, after all, they have got to do . . . That is not a difficult proposition. The next best step towards revolution, a step of knowledge to the labor movement and to our feminist movement, the completeness of . . .

"They agree in saying that the only way is by pouring into themselves all the fibers that come down into the social center of life. When we get that, it will bring a revolution. I am a man, and I have known . . .

"I would not have made this little talk tonight if it were not for the fact that I have seen several tragedies in the last few months. A man is a suffering animal. He is suffering because . . . theoretically, and before his theories, before anything else, man truly never suffered much, because they are living in the future and having strong impulses, stronger than the woman has. A man suffers anything, he suffers and knows that he is dying, and in all their principles of life, hate, and all their prejudices, and all their feelings are ornamental. It is the fruit of their over-organization."

MR. LINCOLN STEFFENS:
"I felt that Mr. Hapgood was talking from his heart. (*Laughter.*) But there is one point that occurred to me, and that is this, and that is the only hope of the world—if women are the workingmen, and the men are dead, in what sex shall we put the women?"

MR. HAPGOOD:
"That reminds me of a monkey story I heard the other day. I read it in the Sunday *World* three weeks ago, a story about a scientist's . . . about some wonderful . . . impulse, that one very important contribution to the Darwinian theory was that monkeys, when sitting in the trees, when they were all swinging in the trees,—there was no anarchist among them at all, no criminals, nor anything else like that—suddenly a monkey desired another's flesh. But he could not live in the trees among decent monkeys and eat flesh. They would ostracize him; he was driven out of society. Then when he had to go to the jungle, he descended from the tree and went to the jungle in his desire to drink blood and eat flesh, and satisfy his criminal tendencies. Man has a practical lesson of criminal instinct in the monkey, and I believe that is the same criminal instinct of today. I do not believe that the criminal instinct . . . but I am quite ready to believe that certain anarchists are the people who . . . not because they are better than anybody else, but because they are criminal, and because they have a desire to adapt themselves. Strenuousness, man weakening in protection, is democratic in your own sense, whether you do not see that democracy must be limited by protection. The sex distinctions are only a thing like time and space, something by which we go through our experiences. Time and space

do not exist for the time that we need them in order to straighten our lives. It is the same thing with sex. I do not know what the I.W.W. are going to do in regard to the biologic government of man. Any group of men that is trying to do something to the worship . . . these men, if they have enough intensity, govern purposes. I think among the several groups of Buddhists, some of them simply worship a shrine. We are moving backwards in life."

A VOICE:
"What is the difference between the sexes?"

MR. HAPGOOD:
"It seems to me that the angle of approach is important in one respect, that the only important thing in the world is the absolute. When you get blasé, just as in the so-called free America, you get blasé about the principles of free speech, etc. That is because we are too familiar with conception. Every approach is only intended to revivify, and revive, and accentuate, and we might almost say solidize, through an unfamiliar approach to it. I regard as one of the most unfamiliar approaches . . .

"The I.W.W. has the most remarkable philosophic and conventional principle that ought to be realized by everybody who claims to be interested in democracy, more so than we can possibly imagine. What is the I.W.W.? Simple to give a concrete example, and the need of self-control, self-education, self-revolution. We do not want masses; we do not want any kind . . . it does not make any difference what their ideas are. The fact that they are willfully determining independence is a most remarkable demonstration of what we philosophically . . .

"And yet these people are regarded as anarchists, as people that are against our ideas. They really have our ideas, the I.W.W. people, and much more honorably than anybody else. I look around here tonight and I find that all these people here are not nearly so law-abiding as they are. I see one newspaperman over there; I know perfectly well that he has not any conception of what the fundamental conceptions of democracy are. From his point of view . . . He is the man, really, that departs from the normal. Emma Goldman is one of the best-known outcasts of society that ever belonged to the United States! In my opinion, Emma represents an infinitely greater amount of law than the government does. She is much nearer right than the government is."

JOHN ROMPAPAS:
"You say that we all see the devil in the other sex. I do not agree. I think that he makes a fundamental mistake, a natural mistake. I think

that we have a second feeling of the angel in regard to sex, not of the devil. That has a sex antagonism, and still regards the other sex as angel, and not as devil. It seems very clear. I firmly believe that there is no person who has not got in himself the ideal him or her. All of us, no matter how low an intellect we have, we all dream of a certain ideal person, and when we are in love with a certain person, and we are not satisfied mentally, physically, equally satisfied, we leave that lover. When we meet that ideal person there is the attraction of the two persons. Because there is the unavoidable change because of the rule of change, we have an antagonism of the sexes against each other, and therefore antagonism comes in, as of sex."

MR. HAPGOOD:

"He wrote a book that has not been published. I enjoyed his book very much, but that does not mean to say I understood it at all. But I am morally certain that metaphysics has a better *a priori* rating than before he wrote it. He was suffering under a tremendous difficulty. He did not know the English language at all, and when he was writing of perception, conception, and institution, to be sure when he began he did not know the difference between perception, conception, and institution ——"

ROMPAPAS:

"I realize the change that—"

HAPGOOD:

"He had some very fundamental conceptions, had a very simple conception, which was the mutual attraction and revulsion of life. He worked that out in a very remarkable way. In this remarkable experience he really was able to set forth his metaphysical principles from the specific experience, that the woman failed in her metaphysical association with John. John was a real man, and said good-by. . . ."

And here the recorder broke down altogether!

"Quite Steinesque," said Steff, when he read it.

Hutch was very fond of his inventive paraphrase of "How to get the light without the heat!" He used often to revert to it, on account of the spiritual hard times he had with Neith. He would come and tell me about these complications and how difficult it was to tell the truth and yet how hard to deceive. At the end he would say, ruefully, "Our great problem: *How to get the heat without the lie!*"

This letter came to me almost as soon as we returned from Europe:

N. Y. C.
September 8, 1913.

My dear Mrs. Dodge:

Welcome back, for I hear rumors of your speedy home-coming! When you have time to spare for small matters, could you bring Jack Reed and me together? I have lots of news—or so I think—and it may fill up an hour of idleness.

Please give my love to Reed, and believe me
Sincerely yours,
F.

I didn't want Reed to see F.: a narrow-shouldered socialistic English bank clerk whom Jessie Ashley had become interested in and brought into one of the Pageant committees. I didn't like his snarling, carping way: a mean coward, I thought to myself. I showed Reed the note from him but quickly covered it with something more exciting so he would forget it. However, it was always enough for me to register a fear to make Reed register an unconscious wish to explore the object of it. It was very queer how this always happened.

He brought F. in one night and they talked all the evening while I sat forgotten. They talked wildly—over the possibles: the possible revolution, the possible New Art, the possible new relation between men and women. I felt defrauded and left out and also very mad to have such a common little thing spend an evening with me whether I wanted him or not. I went to bed long before he left—and heard him flattering Reed as I undressed with the door ajar.

I kept Reed awake for hours arguing with him about his new friend. About his mediocrity, his superficiality, his unworthiness. "Why don't you pick out someone *worth-while* for a friend? F. is craven. I heard him laughing at Jessie Ashley and saw him showing you that gold rabbit she gave him. I don't think that's very nice. . . ."

When I came in from the swimming pool where I often went, at eleven o'clock the next morning, I found a note from Reed.

Good-by, my darling. I cannot live with you. You smother me. You crush me. You want to kill my spirit. I love you better than life but I do not want to die in my spirit. I am going away to save myself. Forgive me. I love you—I love you.
Reed.

Just that. And all his things were there as though he would return for lunch—his brushes, his clothes, everything. Simply vanished.

I turned ice cold all over and rushed down to the motor where Albert still waited for the afternoon orders.

"To the Hapgoods'," I gasped. "Hurry—hurry!"

I cried all the way out. As the wind dried the tears on my cheeks, others fell. I felt completely defeated. I felt I could not live without Reed. I didn't know where to begin. My only conscious thought was to find Hutch. Hutch would understand and help me. Where *was* Reed? Where could he have gone? I looked out to the world where I had seen only him for months, and now I could not see anything. Houses, trees, streets—they were all meaningless to me without Reed against them. Truly he was all I had lived for of late.

I rushed into the big red brick Hapgood house calling Hutch, but he didn't answer. Only Neith's mother was there, leaning over the banisters and saying in a dead and buried voice:

"Hutchins is in New York. So is Neith."

I was stunned, because I had already pictured Hutch waiting to comfort me. I groped my way to the spare room I always slept in, and flung myself on the bed and sobbed loudly. But no one heard me but that mother-in-law of Hutch's, and so it was wasted. She came once and looked at me over her spectacles from the doorway—but she said nothing and went away again immediately. I lay there and continued my weeping. I put everything in me into it, into keeping it going good and strong and deep.

Hutch and Neith came back at dinner time and heard me from the hall below. I heard the mother-in-law telling them something in a low, cold voice and they came up to me.

"Well, what's the matter?" said Neith, sitting down beside me and pushing the hair out of my eyes. She spoke in her lovely, slow voice that was never loud or surprised. Hutch peered down at me through his shining spectacles, waiting.

"Reed has *gone,*" I wailed, and held out his letter to Hutch.

To my surprise he laughed boisterously while Neith looked sad and continued to stroke my face, saying nothing. I remember feeling surprised that it was Neith who gave out a real feeling of sympathy, while it was Hutch who seemed merely amused. I was accustomed to see their rôles reversed in everyday life. Generally it was Hutch who sympathized while Neith refrained from expressing anything more than a slightly cynical amusement.

243

The room was dark and cold, and I was dark and cold inside. They asked me to try to come to dinner but I refused, and Neith brought me something to eat on a plate.

All night I lay awake floundering in a black empty place. There seemed no place to come to rest. Reed had gone away, taking the universe with him.

And all next day I wept weakly and without hope. I had not cried like that since I had my heart broken in Buffalo. I felt my flesh dissolve in salt water—and my head grow lighter and more empty. Hutch recovered his usual tender manner and spent much of the day with me, talking and telling me stories of his own tragic disappointments.

"If you suffer enough, Mabel, you will know the Absolute," he said. I sobbed that I didn't *want* to know it, I just wanted Reed *back*. "Can't you find him?" I begged. "Send some telegrams!" But he demurred and begged me to wait. Neith and he left me to myself for a good part of the day—and I wept silently, sometimes angry, and sometimes just lonesome.

The third day I woke up in the morning and saw the sun was shining. I felt weak and cold as one does after a great illness—but I saw the sun was shining. I mean I saw this as a fact that lived in and of itself and because it was itself. It had nothing to do with me or any man. And I loved it and felt grateful to it. Next I felt I wanted to get up and see the world once more, so I dressed myself, staggering a little as I did so, and when I was ready I went down the stairs, clinging to the banisters.

The family were gathered about the breakfast table and Hutch got up as I came in and examined me over his spectacles.

"You are having a wonderful experience, Mabel," he began to boom, but I shut him up.

"I want to get Carl and all of us to go and lunch at Poligniani's!" Hutch laughed, and so did Neith.

"All right!" they both exclaimed, and Neith softly closed her eyes at me tenderly.

I enjoyed feeling frail and sensitive that day at lunch! Every sound was clear and magnified many times. Everyone stood out sharply like objects in a garden after a heavy rain. The world looked particularly bright and sparkling and I felt as though I had been drenched and was drying in the sun. Everything looked new to me, every street and every house, and terribly interesting and vital. The world had been given back to me once more.

Carl was more interested in me than usual, too. He was quick to feel a change in people he liked—and I smiled at him with a new tremulousness.

"What's the matter?" he asked.

"The world has just been born," I told him.

Of course when I went back to 23 Fifth Avenue after lunch and found it so empty and cold, my exaltation fell a little. What was I to do with myself? I scarcely knew what to do next. I groped like a baby learning to walk. But I made an effort and asked someone to dine with me—Walter Lippmann, it was—and I listened to him talk and although my mind was rusty because I hadn't used it much lately, I began to be interested again in impersonal things. I moved through the hours as though in a new world, and I saw myself undress and go to bed alone in the still room as though I watched a stranger.

The next morning I woke alone and just a faint beginning of gladness for aloneness itself was lifting in me when Reed burst into the house.

Pale, with black shadows under his eyes, his curls on end, he fell on his knees by me and buried his head against me.

"Oh, I couldn't *bear* it," he cried. "I can't live without you. I missed your love, your selfish, selfish love," he cried.

Composed, myself, I saw my hand smoothing his rough, round head.

"Your way, not mine," he murmured deeply into my side.

So it began again.

That night he told me it had been as terrible for him to leave me as for me to be left. He told me he wandered without knowing where he was going until he found himself stumbling up to Copey's door in Cambridge. Dear old Copey, who had told him he would never be a writer till he'd been a lover. He went up to Copey wild-eyed and disheveled.

"I've been a lover," he shouted, "but now I've lost my love! Tell me what to do! I can't *stand* it!"

"You go and tie your head up in a Turkish towel soaked in cold water," Copey told him, "and then come back and tell me about it."

Now I had, in a way, cried myself inside out when he left me. I could never weep like that for him again. Yet when, some weeks later, Carl Hovey asked him to go to Mexico and send back articles about Pancho Villa and the land, for the *Metropolitan Magazine,* I was devastated. I lost the sense of the world I had recovered as soon as Reed was sleeping with me once more, since, as usual, I had easily forgotten what had happened to me. I didn't realize that when he was gone I would have awakened to it again perhaps gladly.

I tried to make him give up the commission. I tried in every way but he would go.

"It won't be like leaving you the way I did last time," he said. "I will take you with me in my heart.—But we *must* be free to live our own lives—dearest!"

"But I don't want to go with you in your heart—I want you *here!*" I moaned. "I can't be free without you!"

The night before he left to go to Washington for letters of introduction, on his way south, was an Evening. We gave up the hours to talking about Mexico and the whole subject was covered. I don't remember a word of it. All I remember is seeing Reed, puffed up and excited, his curls tossed back, standing up and declaiming wildly, and Steff quietly twinkling at him from a corner. When most of the people had gone, I sat watching F. and Reed arguing over something, and I drank glass after glass of whiskey and water.

That night was a welter of tears and love. I wanted to drown him in myself so that he couldn't leave me—but he rose early, kissed me and left me sobbing with my face in the pillow.

Miss Galvin stood by the bed and looked sorry.

But no sooner had I drunk my coffee than I was galvanized by a sudden compulsion to run after him and go along with him to Mexico. In a moment my heart sang and I was off and upon my way. He was ahead of me by a few hours and had to stop in Washington, so I took the train to Buffalo and spent the night talking to Charlotte, who seemed to me, in the imagined urgency of my life, to be living on a sandhill deserted of all life. By comparison, my life appeared a many-colored changing kaleidoscope full of significance and reality. Yet when I confided to her that I was leaving to join Reed in Chicago and go to *Mexico* with him, she looked appalled, shocked, unenvious and rather disdainful. We were completely out of sympathy.

"Where *did* you get that orange sweater?" she asked me. "I never *heard* of anyone wearing such a color! It makes you look like a tuffy-wuff! Are you sure you can get *into* Mexico in such a thing?"

I had wired Reed I'd meet him in Chicago. When we met I was disappointed that he looked merely rather glad instead of overjoyed. The man in him was already on the job. The woman's place was in the home!

In the train he kept going away and talking to men in the smoking room and trying to pick up odds and ends about Mexico that would help him when we got there. Since I had had my way, and was, after all, with him, I made up my mind to be very good and not a bother, so I didn't interfere.

But as soon as we arrived in El Paso and had rooms in the large ugly hotel, I began to wonder why I had come. Reed rushed out, was all over the town, making arrangements, trying to see his way ahead. He wanted to get down into Mexico immediately.

I looked at the pale blue mountains on the horizon and somehow I couldn't see what I was going to do in El Paso while he was over there, for I saw soon enough, I couldn't go with him. He was going to be with Villa's army, riding on troop trains and God knows what. At first I thought I would try to make myself a little life in the strange town and wait for him there. I went out alone and wandered around, looking for atmosphere. I bought some queer-looking un-familiar Mexican fruits and some figs and brought them home and put them in a dish on the hideous oak table in my room. I tried to behave like a traveler in a new place, savoring new flavors. But I couldn't fool myself into enjoying this sort of thing all alone. I went out again and bought some Mexican opals and a piece of queer em-broidery and brought them to my room. Still it remained unfriendly and colorless and I wasn't in the picture at all.

I had written to Steff on the train and I wrote another long letter to him and Hutch and told them I had joined Reed and to go on and have the Evenings without me. Steff answered me, but I received his letter in New York quite a long while after I got back, for I left to return the day after I wrote him. I said good-by to Reed and journeyed home again, feeling very much out of sorts.

Steff had written encouragingly:

The Players,
16 Gramercy Park,
Dec. 24, 1913.

DEAR MABEL DODGE,

If Jack is as good a correspondent—as vivid, complete, and entertaining as you are, he will make a success. And he will make a success even if he isn't. I was away when your first opus came. I got all three together. I was delighted. I shall forward them to Hutch tonight: for they seem to have been aimed at his heart through mine.

It's all right. He may not see that, and so I'll have it all.

Now that Jack is gone and Hutch isn't here, we may talk, you and I, and I know you too want to know first about the Salon. The last one was good, of course; I spoke! There was a goodly crowd. Emma and her bunch were not all present, but Mr. and Mrs. Joseph Fels were there with George and Mrs. Lansbury, the co-labor member of parliament who was imprisoned for his part in leading the English Larkin demonstration, and both Lansbury and Fels spoke. My thesis was that it was wrong to have convictions, and since I included even my thesis in my address, I got away with it. I only talked about twenty minutes, and spent the rest of the hour drawing out the conversation. This was livelier and more general than before, but it still is not a Real Conversation. I can't make out just why, unless it still sticks in everybody's head that speeches are expected. We must do something about that. But not until you come back.

Neith and I and a few others decided during the last one that we'd hold no more till you returned. Our intention was not to hurry you back. Not at all. It was simply that we felt that we needed you to keep up the interest. We didn't care to risk it by ourselves.

Bill Haywood is back. I haven't seen him, but I was at Mary O'Brien's last night and she had seen Bill. She said he looked better but troubled in his step and as he wrung his hands. His doctor said he was not ill, but old; ten years older than his age. But Mary says he has imported from England some ideas; also that he left some there. He taught the British, for example, how to "boo" the police. That's something.

I've a mute little Christmas card from Jack's mother. I dread writing to her, but I must. Mothers don't like to have their boys war correspondents, till they get back. Then they like it very much. Mothers are very womanly, aren't they?

But I must quit this and get out of here. I'm at the Club. It's deserted, luckily, and there's the shadow of a Christmas tree over it and the white linen rich. I have no place to go, so I'll go there and—work. I can forget when I work. I think what I write shows it!

Give my love to Jack, if you communicate with him, and if he gets too deep in to hear from, come home. We'll all be glad to see you. And Jack is all right: Drunks and youths are watched over by both Gods and devils; each side has hopes of winning them yet. So you can leave him to his luck and his joy. He will love the adventure. And won't it be good to hear him tell about it!

Come home, therefore, and reopen the Salon. Hit the speechmakers and encourage the short questioners and the quick commentators.

A happy New Year to you,
Truly yours,
STEFFENS.

I stepped back into 23 Fifth Avenue and began to make a life for myself without Reed. He wrote me vivid, loving letters—but by the time they came I had drawn myself up out of the web. It was during the weeks he was in Mexico that I became interested in the Tannenbaum trial. And then I entangled myself deeply with Andrew Dasburg and the Lees.

At first, to pass the time, and because I did not like to be alone, with nothing to do, and then for their own sakes, I had Andrew Dasburg and the Lees with me quite often when Reed was in Mexico. I had seen a good deal of Andrew before that, but I hadn't thought much about him until I came back from El Paso, alone and disconsolate, to find that he had painted a remarkable picture that he called "The Absence of Mabel Dodge."

As soon as I saw this painting I knew what he felt, as indeed anyone might if they looked into it. Andrew, who before this had painted rather sensitively realistic things, had suddenly burst open on canvas. It was all a flare of thin flames with forked lightnings in them and across the bottom of this holocaust, three narrow black, black, black bars. I was inwardly pleased and flattered and my first thought was that I wished Reed was there to see it. I wanted to show it to him not only because I thought he would like it but because I did myself.

Later I asked Marsden Hartley to write him a letter and describe it. Marsden wrote rather well, I knew, and that would be the next best thing to Reed's seeing it himself.

He wrote:

My dear Reed:

Mabel D. has asked me to tell you something about a new picture of our mutual Dasburg's, which interests us so much, and in which we think he has brought up his particularly personal element. It came out of a vivid experience which he, Dasburg, passed through here in the house at a recent Thursday evening when Mabel was off in Texas. She was kind enough not to tell anyone so that the affair might go on of its own accord—but I was the first to get a sense of vacancy in the place and waited and waited for her appearance hopefully—and when I learned the real fact, tried to get used to the situation which naturally was difficult—but I could see Dasburg was quite troubled and asked me secretly where M. D. was. I replied "in Texas." Dasburg was evidently wholly amazed inside—evidently disappointed with her absence—so much so that he threatened to go home. I insisted that he remain and stick the evening out, which he consented to do—and did—but evidently it gave him one of those definite inner shocks which we all, as sensitives of one type or another, understand well. And he told me that it stayed with him well through the night so that he was somewhat sleepless—more than he has ever been accustomed to. Anyhow, as a sensitive, knowing and understanding such things, I know that Dasburg has really come up to his actual self in this thing.

To describe it is difficult. It is full of the lightning of disappointment. It is a pictured sensation of spiritual outrage—disappointment carried way beyond mediocre despair. It is a fiery lamentation of something lost in a moment—a moment of joy with the joy sucked out of it—leaving the flames of the sensation to consume themselves. I should not be wording it or trying to. We are glad because Dasburg has proved what he actually is—he has proved to be what I imagined him and I have quite some eyesight. He has pushed himself off into his own high place in the mind and I know he will stay there well. We are quite some together of late as a result of proving my own feelings about his particular personal essence. If we who think this have pushed or helped push him off into his own place then this is very, very well.

I listen with great interest always to the passages Mabel reads me of your intense Mexican days. I think of you often and like to.

Cordially yours,

Marsden Hartley.

Then I hung the picture up on my wall and there it burned in front of everyone. I began to see Andrew every day, and he showed me that he was suffering with a conflict of some kind.

He was so angelic-looking that it was hard to believe the flesh of him could feel what other people endured. His eyes were blue as sapphires, and they had a mystical red spark in them. His skin was very fair with a tremulous rose that came and went in his cheeks, and his fine blond hair rushed electrically back from his round brow and seemed full of white sparks of light.

He had a frosty glistening light over him, and at the same time a warmer fire ran in and out of his blood. He limped a little and always walked with a cane. His body was strong and light—broad at the shoulders with narrow hips; it had an upward spring that seemed like a tree growing visibly. His lameness was rather attractive, though it was always a gêne to him. He had fallen into an old quarry when he was three years old and never recovered properly.

As a flame darts out of itself and penetrates another element to destroy it or itself be quenched, so Andrew flickered out to me despite his own desire to be loyal to the absent Reed. And though I was at least chemically all avowed to Reed, I encouraged Andrew because I wanted to be warmed by him: it was comforting. Sometimes I felt sorry that I had become attached to Reed, for Andrew had more weight and significance than the boy that Reed would always be. I felt: here is one I shall always be fond of no matter what happens and I never felt this for that poetic youth. But there it was! I met Reed first and I must stick to him, my inner moral tyrant insisted.

Just to be alive and alone was not to live and feel, or experience life. It was only after a great shock of some kind that I could sense the life in the moment without the stimulation from someone else, for example that time I raised my head from the ground and looked about me after Reed ran away from me. Something in me had to be shattered by a blow that hurt enough to make a surcease of suffering appear an exquisite pleasure. I needed to be ground into the earth by an iron heel before I could see the sun shine.

Ordinarily, to be alone was to doubt my own being, so little did I live in the life about me.

And to live with Reed stimulated something in me so I felt a flowing appreciation of little things. Not his things, not his ideas. I really didn't care much for his ideas and neither did he in any ultimate way. He had successive bonfires in him and I wasn't burning in the same kind of fire he was at that moment. I wasn't dying to alter everything.

The outside of the world wasn't enough to hold me. No. What he did was to make me myself feel real and like other people. He was able to make me contented and reassured, and as I had had precious little of this I craved it; while he, the instrument of my re-established equilibrium, had nothing but contempt for contentment and believed it was only good enough for slaves. But I wanted rest. Like Kundry I cried desperately out of my nerve cells: *"Ich bin müde!"* I wanted to sink down by the fireside with him there to make me recognize and partake of its warmth.

But Reed! The poem he dedicated to Max Eastman tells how he felt and what he admired:

A DEDICATION
(*To* MAX EASTMAN)

There was a man who, loving quiet beauty best,
Yet could not rest.
Attuned to the majestic rhythm of whirling suns,
That chimes and runs
Through happy stillness—birth in the dawn, and stark
Love in the dark;
The unconquerable semen of the world, that mounts and sings
Through endless springs,
And the dumb death-like sleep of the winter-withered hill
That warms life still;
There was a man who, loving quiet beauty best,
Yet could not rest
For the harsh moaning of unhappy mankind,
Fettered and blind—
Too driven to know beauty and too hungry-tired
To be inspired.
From his high, windy-peaceful hill, he stumbled down
Into the town,
With a child's eyes, clear bitterness, and silver scorn
Of the outworn
And cruel mastery of life by senile death;
And with his breath
Fanned up the noble fires that smolder in the breast
Of the oppressed.
What guerdon, to foreswear for dust and smoke and this
The high-souled bliss

252

Of poets in walled gardens, finely growing old.
Serene and cold?
A vision of new splendor in the human scheme—
A god-like dream—
And a new lilt of happy trumpets in the strange
Clangor of Change!

In his absence, then, I didn't want to die down. Andrew's proximity
made me stay alive and love Reed still, for I did love him in spite of
a dissimilar thinking—and not only because we were mated and congenial in sex. He was lovable in himself. I loved him.

But love, like any other recognition in me, waned in the solitary life.
I was unable to keep body and soul together when left to myself;
utterly impoverished I became, and unable to pull myself up by my
own boot straps! I fed my fainting blood with tonics that came my
way. I kept up my interest by any means I could, until Reed should
come back.

Andrew flared out to me and nearly lost his identity. One night
when we were all passing an evening together, and Genevieve was
there, she and I became involved together over a fine gold chain
strung with fire opals. We each pulled at it, wrapping it around our
wrists. More was in it than appeared on the surface. We plunged into
each other's eyes and dragged at each other and finally the chain
snapped. . . . A trivial scene, full of potentiality and invisible forces.
The next day brought me this note from Andrew:

1:30 A.M.
It seemed as tho' it were I who were tearing the jeweled chain from
your wrist, or mine. I felt the tug and the pull and the pain when it freed
the hand. It ended here as I was without it—you held it and did not give
it as you were to do, that you were to seemed like certainty. This was my
delusion, the lie to myself as it seems.
                                    Good night.
                                                    DASBURG.

His personality became curiously interwoven with mine. I used to
look at him and feel him flow up to me and enter me: a kind of
hypnosis by which I drew him into me to feed myself. Anyway I was
stimulated by him, and I felt I must write Reed all about it.

Arthur and Freddie, too, seemed to love me, and Freddie, lovely
classic mädchen, a true Canova, came to enter into me too, and soon

began to stay the night with me in my white-hung bed, letting Arthur go morosely home by himself, he not knowing clearly how he felt, for he himself wanted attention and yet was jealous because Freddie clung to me. I never touched her as she came close to me in bed. It was not like that. I was only thrilled to touch the souls of all these people and have them come close to me.

Arthur told me I set a little dynamo going inside him. He said he knew how Freddie felt about me—and he modeled her on her knees, with her head bowed on the ground, and called it "Adoration of Mabel Dodge."

The place became full of a powerful electric, or whatever, force. Andrew wrote me a strange letter and then called me on the telephone and said he couldn't bear it: that he didn't know how to express it. I told him to say it with paint and he sent me this brief note:

If my note of yesterday is madness, it is because I was mad. You tumbled me to earth beautifully in the phone booth. I thank you.

Sincerely,
DASBURG.

But though he had felt momentarily repulsed, he started a "Portrait of Mabel Dodge" that eventually hung opposite the "Absence" on my wall. This one was a quiet blaze—compared to the first one—showing a red tulip in its center, and somewhere the emerald stone of the ring I always wore. After doing it he seemed appeased. Paint has always been his antidote.

About this time Nina Bull had come to New York to stay with me and she saw Hartley's paintings hanging at "291." She, too, must have her fling with modern art. So she arranged to exhibit Marsden and Andrew at the Albright Gallery in Buffalo, and a few others that Stieglitz let her take.

This, needless to say, was the first time *Buffalo* had ever seen any pictures of this kind. Neely Sage was now the curator of the Gallery, and Nina and I managed her easily. Andrew, Hartley and I went up for the event.

I had bought one of Hartley's paintings, a portrait of Berlin, all blue and white and red, made up of triangles, soldiers on horseback, shields and Buddhas; and Nina decided to buy one, too. She took the ineffable one in mother-of-pearl tones with the burgeoning sap-like movement that rises in exaltation to the great word "Extase" painted across the upper part of the canvas. An extraordinary painting of the organic palpitation, I suppose. This picture caused the Buffalo people to jeer in an unholy delight when they saw it in the Art Gallery and afterwards in Nina's drawing-room.

I felt like a traveler back from distant planets when I sat among the familiars in Buffalo. I felt incompatible with them and older than they. Though I often saw Buffalo faces in the rooms at 23 Fifth Avenue, yet there my own atmosphere was too strong to allow them to overcome me. Here in Buffalo I had to remember myself all the time, to remember my opinions, my convictions. I found myself wondering what "they" thought of me and whether they knew I lived openly with Reed without being married. The solidarity of the old tribe made itself felt and almost weakened me, but not quite.

However, I had to combat it consciously, that thick, soft, compelling security they all made together for each other's benefit. Safe and certain and unquestioning, the Buffalonians lived together in unreasoning conventionality and I had escaped and dwelt outside the walls.

My own situation suddenly seemed to me full of danger and drama. I felt, in Buffalo, both stronger and weaker than I felt in New York.

Marsden sat silently in the large living room—occasionally rolling his enormous diamond-shaped blue eyes and drawing down his thin lips. His bony aquiline nose arched more than ever in Buffalo, and he repeated more frequently his curious gesture of running his whole thin face through his large bony fingers, crumpling it together into folds as one gathers silk.

Freddie Lee and some of the others wrote me from New York, and I held on to them in thought to ballast myself. I loved to be missed, although I never missed anyone myself. I only missed a certain chemical in some people that deepened my own chemical flow—never their minds or their souls. I often wondered if we have not some organ in us whose function it is to deepen impressions like the wash that brings out negatives, for I myself felt like a negative until someone stirred something in me that washed through my being, enhancing and deepening my experience. I was all for Reed, but I needed the strange psychic stimulation I procured from the attention of others directed upon me.

To be back in Buffalo in Nina's lovely new house out near the Park was not to be really in Buffalo as I had known it in the past. It was not to be in Buffalo or in any place, really. I felt suspended in space, unable to alight and sink in anywhere. I could not dwell in the thought of Reed, for I was not the kind who can exist in any thought. So I turned more and more to Andrew, and I lived in the electric atmosphere that surrounded him. Sometimes he seemed to flame like a star and sparks ran off the breezy hair that aureoled his round head and made him look like a Blake drawing. His body, so slim and broad, was strong, as an organic thing full of terrible forces can be. I felt the wonder of life in him, tempestuous, rising like sap. There was a heady fascination in his vivid personality—eyes shining like sapphires turning suddenly black, and the quick rise and fall of color in his cheeks. His vitality swept him off his feet sometimes, until he seemed like a young tree bending in a great wind. Andrew always had powerful living currents running through him. I took refuge in his atmosphere and felt it was like a shelter from the lonely emptiness of Buffalo. There is no consolation in the world like the living energy in a human being, nothing so admirable and repaying. Whenever I think of him, I remember him always as someone particularly endowed in this life in spite of the blunders he, in common with us all, has been unable to avoid making. His significance has not been in what he has done or left undone. It has been with him since he was born and rises perpetually out of his essence.

I wrote Reed all about Andrew, and how very attractive he was to me. I sent Andrew to him like a blue ribbon, down there in Mexico where he rode with Villa and his army. He sent back a letter full of the intoxication of supremacy:

"I will write all our names across the sky in flame," he wrote. I wish I had his letters—so vivid and alive. But I burned all the packets of them one day in Croton to please Maurice, who in his turn loved human sacrifices.

When Reed came back from Mexico, he was, once more, The Hero. He had gone through a great deal of dangerous adventure successfully. Everyone was enthusiastic about his articles in the *Metropolitan Magazine,* which had had the effect of winning a great deal of sympathy for the Mexican peons in their battle for the land.

Reed published the articles in a book called *Insurgent Mexico,* and had two de luxe copies made bound in red morocco, for his mother and me. He dedicated the book, however, to his mother and this made me silently angry. I myself, obscurely, wanted to be his mother.

We had a "Reed in Mexico" Evening for him and he stood up in the crowded rooms, eyes shining and curls bobbing back, temples agleam, and told everybody all about it. I stood off in a corner and looked at him and wondered why he looked so puffed up, as though he had been inflated by a pump. His chest swelled up under his chin and he had to compress it to get the air into his lungs to speak with.

I, rather self-consciously, wanted to blend all the colors of my life together—and so I had asked the Headmaster of John's school in Morristown where Reed had been to come and hear him talk on Mexico, and he sent Reed the following note:

DEAR JACK: I planned to reach Mrs. Dodge's house last Tuesday night to meet you again and hear about your remarkable experiences in Mexico. School opened, however, on Monday, and the chance of giving myself this satisfaction faded away.

We, the boys and masters, hope you can get a chance to run out here some day and give us the benefit of your remarkable experiences during the past few weeks. May we hope for a talk from you some day at the opening or close of School, i.e., 8:30 A.M. or 2:00 P.M. or on a Saturday or Sunday evening, say at 8:15?
Yours as always,
F. C. WOODMAN.

Whereupon I took it upon myself to arrange to carry Reed and Steff over to the Morristown School to talk to the boys. Reed had gone there to school not so awfully long before John. It amused me to be able to take Reed back so that he could impart his experiences to John, for I always felt that one must be able to juggle with the world as one wished and never feel hampered no matter what one did.

I remember how mad I was one day with Walter. We were lunching at the Holland House and Walter was illumined and relaxed. I had been talking with him about living with Reed, and asking him, who was so wise and well balanced, if *he* thought it was all right, and no drawback.

"As you conduct it, yes," he said.

"But it has always been considered a *limiting* situation," I went on, eager to hear him say more flattering things.

"It all depends on the person," he answered. "There is practically no limiting of *your* movements, is there?"

"No," I assented.

"Of course you can't live at the *White House* with Reed," he continued, "but you don't *want* to, do you?"

"Yes," I cried, up in arms at once, "that's *just* what I want. I *want* to be able to live at the White House if I *want* to!"

"Well, you can't," laughed Walter, shortly. I was furious.

The evening at the Morristown School was extremely nice. Steff addressed the boys first, introducing Reed, just a few words. He told them that Reed had worked with him on his paper and he had always told him two things: "Write what you see. Learn to see, and then write what you see. And the other rule, always to remember to think straight and honestly. I always told him," said Steffens, with a lingering emphasis, "it doesn't so much matter what you *do* so long as you *think* right."

Reed gave the boys an exciting account of Villa and the battles, and John was very proud of it all, and especially at the end of the evening when Reed gave him the camera with which he had taken all the photographic illustrations for his articles. A very warm, pleasant evening all round, followed by this note from Dr. Woodman:

> Morristown School,
> Morristown, N. J.

My dear Mrs. Dodge:

I cannot thank you enough for managing the visit of Jack Reed and Mr. Steffens, and that interesting evening which seems to us more and more remarkable as we look back on it. We are really much impressed by what Reed said, and the manner in which he did it.

I am reminded about the Hutchins Hapgoods who came here with you one day. Is there anything for us to do to get them more interested in the School, as the boy seems to be quite old enough to come? I shall be glad to have any suggestions from you.

> Yours very sincerely,
> F. C. Woodman.

Reed was not home for long. Carl Hovey sent him to Colorado to write an article about the Coal Strike. There had been a good deal of bloodshed at Ludlow at the hands of the militia, and Trinidad was the center of trouble when he got there. He wrote a blazing thing called "The Colorado War," headed thus:

Herrington (Attorney for the Colorado Fuel and Iron Company): "Just what is meant by social freedom I do not know. Do you understand what the witness meant by 'Social Freedom,' Mr. Welborn?"

Mr. Welborn (President of the Colorado Fuel and Iron Company): "I do not."

While he was out there he sent me this letter (the only one I have left of many, many that were burned):

Dear Mabel, I have a little story to tell you. It's about a girl's getting a soul, and I was unconsciously and blunderingly the cause of it. Virginia Bean is about twenty-two years old, rather pretty and very unusual-looking. She plays the violin really beautifully and stirringly, in a strictly academic way. Her mother is a large, jolly woman who has roughed it somewhat in the old West, of great force of character, and has been "in society" for about eight years, long enough to talk about "culture" and "social technique." She is a very solid lady, with a religion and ideals. She is naïve: told me the other night that during the long years she had been married (we were talking about free love and free other things) she had often in a fit of pique wanted to leave her husband, and the only thing that had kept her from doing it was the knowledge that there had never been a divorce to stain the history of her family! That reason she thought was good. And so the human race needed traditions and laws to keep it from running awry. She was glad that thing had held her back.

Well, we kept on talking. I timidly said that we none of us knew what the human race was going to be, so it was criminal rather than useless to set up any moral standards for children. "Ah," she said, "we know anyway what it ought to be." I said that the world at the time of the Spanish Inquisition knew pretty well what it ought to be too, and taught its children that a universe without a Catholic hell on earth was pretty incomplete. But we all slowly got over that idea, although the ideas of the time set the race back.

Virginia asked me what I thought of her playing. I told her if she could get a soul, she would be a real artist. But, she said, I don't see how one can get a soul without letting go all the ideals and standards of life one has set before oneself to hold one to the right. There isn't any other way, I told her. There isn't any law you have to obey, nor any moral standard you have to accept, nor in fact anything outside of your own soul that you have to take any account of.

By this time the mother was intuiting danger, and she smashed at me with the remark that I was young and would get over it, and after I was married, etc. But Virginia had the bit in her teeth. When you get married, she said, if you believe these things, why do you have the marriage ceremony? I told her that I was not sure we would, but that if we did we would use it as a convenience, and when everybody used it as a convenience, it would breed a contempt for the marriage service that would abolish it as a binding superstition. Her mother cried out at that, and so did Virginia. And then the girl said, in a sort of whisper, "Where on earth did such terrifying ideas come from? Do you mean to say that everybody should do just exactly what they want to?" That was just what I did mean. "But I was awfully impulsive. Lots of times I've wanted to run away from my family, which I loved so dearly." Well, I said, what kept you from it? Was it fear of doing wrong? Was it belief in God? Was it any divine command? "Oh, no," said Virginia. "I didn't just because I knew I'd be sorry to have lost so much if I did. But if I had been doing what I wanted to—" You'd have done the same thing, says I. Virginia screamed right out loud. "Now I've got it," she said. "My soul—" Yes, your soul. "But I'm a cynic," she said seriously. Her mother echoed her, saying that she had the hardest time in the world with Virginia's cynical attitude. "Why, do you know," said Mrs. Bean, "my daughter actually says that all women are just ready to be captured by anyone that comes along! The idea! She has never been in love with anyone herself, and she doesn't know." Good for you, Virginia, I said. Being a cynic as you call it is the only thing that has made you play as well as you do. "I'm going to do it," cried the girl suddenly. "What, dear?" her mother got anxious. "From now on I am going to belong to myself!" Of course to that the mother just frowned, because she didn't understand at all. "I never felt such a strong wind!" cried Virginia irrelevantly, as we went away.

Last night she wrote me: "You have knocked the earth out from under me and I'm floating in the air. Don't think I'm in love with you, because I'm in love with life all of a sudden, and now it seems something to be lived instead of just something to be endured. I've been working. I'm going to play, now. I think that you mean that commonsense is all right in life. I've got too much of that for foolishness. Don't be afraid you've wrecked my family and me. I may and am sure to cause them some pain. But after I've been drinking a little heaven you shall hear my violin."

You dearest old thing in the world, I want to tell you that that is the most exciting thing that has happened to me since I have been in this part of the world. I wish it could have been you that told her, and could show her at the same time what a marvelous thing is the result of a soul. You are so beautiful to me for just that soul of yours, and so alive. You are my life.

I told Virginia last night that I would try to get some more Russian music for her, the Ballet (new music), Rimsky-Korsakoff, "Scheherazade," "Boris"; if any violin scores, but if not piano scores. She knows very little later than Brahms, and these things will complete the job of ruining a perfectly good music-teacher in the high-schools. Will you get them and send them here for me? Villa again put off his departure, so I am going tonight.

What you say about the Thursdays is more or less what I told you happened about our Tuesdays at the Lafayette. Lippmann is an organizer, and they all seem to want a gas-burner furnishing steady flame rather than an anvil shooting sparks. Steff is a little wrong. I hate the idea of the orderly restricted discussion but perhaps I'll like the thing itself. Please tell Steff that I'm terribly proud of his letter to me, and have no time to answer it now. You know how much I have always loved him, and I guess so does he.

Good-night and all the love in me.

R.

When Reed came back from Colorado it was evident to me that he was becoming more and more the Hero to everyone, especially to Women. There was a German girl named Babette—whom everyone called "Babs"—who was a friend of us all. She worked at the People's Institute with John Collier. Oh, how we were all intertwined!

She was very fresh and buxom and more emancipated than most of us others. I saw her looking with favor on Reed and I immediately wrote her a note and told her I wouldn't have it, and that my instinct and my nervous system had told me all about her intention and that she could stop right there. To which she wrote the following answer:

Friday afternoon.

Dearest Mabel, I just came home and found your letter—read, reread and reread it, till my heart is dizzy and my head aching.

No, *I don't understand.*

Of course I felt something in your voice when I called you Wednesday night. I knew something was wrong, but I didn't know what. Yes, Douchka, I positively deny the truth of what you say.—I like Reed, to me he is a dear boy— And I know him no more. I don't say this because I want to change your feelings. I know I can't. I don't intend to.

And there never has been any desire for him. If I showed it in my eyes it was not desire for Reed you found there, but just plain desire for the male—a male, if you want it, coming from abstinence—that is all. And that something you would have found whenever I talked to or was near any attractive man.

Yes, Mabel, you taught me a lot about myself when I told you about M. After what you said, I sat down and thought a good deal—and of course you were right—deep in my heart I knew and was not surprised. Since it has been even harder to pay the penalty.

I am absolutely frank, Mabel. As soon as I see a thing I will own up to it. I will be perfectly frank with you—I am now. I cannot write further than my sight goes—it might not be very far—perhaps your letter will clear my eyes entirely: if it does, I will write you so.

I am still at a loss and I am crushed. Not 1,000 Reeds could change places with you. I love you, Mabel—it just hurts dreadfully—but I cannot do but accept.

If I could pray now, I would pray for one thing, and that is that your primitive instinct and nervous system will want to see me again.

Thanks for your frankness and thanks for your absolute kindness in writing that letter.

BABS.

Dear old Babs. She was attractive and serious-minded. One of those who had "dignified sex expression."

About this time, Babs and another girl decided to conduct a purely philanthropic campaign against prostitution. They determined to remove the sting of it from the souls of young men—and to accomplish this they offered themselves freely to anyone who wanted or needed them—they made a *gift* of themselves, and went about with a sort of put-upon, martyred air, that was strangely colored with an early Christian maiden atmosphere exceedingly misleading, considering its source.

All this time Freddie and Arthur were growing more and more devoted to me. This strange love of theirs for me bound them securely together. Freddie wrote:

> Restons quand même et pour toujours les fous
> De cet amour presque implacable,
> Et les fervents, a deux genoux
> Du Dieu soudain qui regne en nous,
> Si violent et si ardemment doux
> Qu'il nous fait mal et nous accable. . . .

I am relating, in these volumes, my intimate memories, and in the life of any woman these are recollections of love or the devilishly ingenious substitutes for love procured more or less deftly by her unconscious being.

By love I do not mean only the ultimate sexual act, though this is perhaps the cornerstone of any life, and its chief reality; but I include that sweet, deep psychic relationship that enables one to live more fully than anything else, and for the sake of which all power, influence, success, achievement, discovery, ease, or wealth are thrown aside and known for what they are, the second choices of less fortunate people.

This is especially true of women. It is indeed the happy woman who has no history, for by happy we mean the loving and beloved, and by history we designate all those relatable occurrences on earth caused by the human energies seeking other outlets than the biological one. It seems we must include the mystic marriage of the essential spirit in human beings when we use the word biological, for unless the spirit is satisfied and fulfilled, the creature is not satisfied. Coition alone never released or satisfied anyone, lacking the needful intrinsic elements of what we call love.

That I have so many pages to write signifies, solely, that I was unlucky in love. Most of the pages are about what I did instead . . . many, many pages that I leave unwritten would be filled with accounts of how I passed the time—the innumerable activities of an energetic woman crossed in love. That I was crossed in love—"unlucky in men," as Mrs. Hopkins said—was due to my own selection, of course. But why I chose men too immature to satisfy me, or too lacking in essential qualities—ah! that question must be answered later on. Perhaps my unsatisfied maternity helped me choose these younger ones: since I had no maternal feeling for my own son, I must take it out on other women's sons. Certainly Reed was a child compared to myself. Well, since I wanted sons, certainly I got them. . . .

And now to go on with the story.

When Reed was away from me I seemed to be able gradually to accumulate an essence of myself that permeated me and made an atmosphere around me. Added to my own distillations were the opinions of people who had watched things happening, and as I have related, had come to believe that I had a peculiar faculty very valuable to any undertaking. Besides, the Salon idea had hit the New York people very hard. They were never tired of talking about it, and the stories were fabulous.

So I experienced in between times again that phenomenon of power conferred upon one by opinion. And maybe that is where all power comes from, that of witches and saviors alike, and of all leaders. But the peculiar thing about it was that when I was living with Reed at home my power seemed to leave me, for he seemed fundamentally hollow in activity and could give no rest to one. At least it seemed so to me. And he never satisfied me. The substitute for love called power thrilled me more than he, though I always preferred to have him there and to feel uncertain and unsure of him and of myself rather than to triumph, with him away, in what Donald Evans so wittily called "the tragic turnip field."

Finally I believed the lack to be in myself when I found myself perpetually unassuaged—and, I thought, only religion will fill me, some day I will find God.

CHAPTER XI

Peyote

DURING the Spring of 1914 in one of the intervals when Reed was away, I had a strange experience with my friends. Bobby Jones had returned from Germany and was staying in one of the rooms in the back end of the apartment on Ninth Street, Andrew was in and out all the time, and Genevieve Onslow was staying for a few days in the other end of the apartment, too. Genevieve had returned from China and was on her way home to Chicago. She was in a highly stimulated mood—full of a mystical elation, and scraps of Chinese philosophy fell from her occasionally.

"If you *want* to do a thing, Mabel, don't do it, but if you *feel* to do it, do it," she would exclaim. But I didn't know what she meant.

The Hapgoods had a cousin staying with them, Raymond Harrington. He had been living among the Indians in Oklahoma doing ethnological research. He looked rather strange and had sunken eyes and an intense expression. I had never seen any Indians, but I told the Hapgoods that I thought he looked like one and they agreed.

Now Raymond told us about a peculiar ceremony among the Indians he lived with that enabled them to pass beyond ordinary consciousness and see things as they are in Reality. He said they used an Indian medicine called *peyote* in the ceremony, and sang all night long. He told us that the Indians that belonged to the Peyote Cult were the most sober and industrious of all, that they made better beadwork and seemed to be able to recover old designs through their use of the stuff and to become imbued with a nobility and a religious fervor greater than those who didn't use it.

We were all most curious about it and begged him to tell us more. When I pressed him, I found he actually had some *peyote* with him; then of course I said we must all try it. But he was grave and said it was not a thing to play with, that if we would go through with it seriously he would try to reconstruct the ceremony for us and give us an opportunity of experiencing the magnificent enhancement and enlargement of consciousness possible only through its power. It was not like hashish or any other drug, he said. In fact, it was not a drug at all, but a marvelous vehicle of the Indian life enabling one to be more deeply and wholly and concisely what one inherently was when not inhibited and overlaid by the limitations of the senses we used every day.

We were all thrilled.

Certain things were necessary to the ceremony, Raymond said. We must have a green arrow, some eagle feathers, a fire, the Mountain of the Moon, and the Peyote Path. All these he must procure or simulate to compose the structure of the experience. Then there would have to be singing. The singing must never cease all through the ritual. One or another of us must always be singing, taking up the song as another left off. And we must enter the event after fasting, and continue all night until the morning star arose, when we could break our fast with fruit juice and then eat.

Raymond himself was very serious as he told us about it, almost somber, seeming wholly a convert to the practice. We grew serious, too, and tried to carry it all out as he desired. We decided to ask Max Eastman and Ida to come because Ida was a friend of Genevieve's; and we were to have Andrew, Bobby, the Hapgoods, and Terry.

Terry was a grand anarchist, possessing a beautiful skeleton, a splendid head with noble features, a great quantity of iron gray hair and Irish blue eyes. He was a literal I.W.W. and a true anarchist. When he was a young man he passed up the capitalistic system and swore he would never take a job or do a day's work under it, and he had carried out his vow. He was incredibly poor, thin to starvation, for he was nearly always hungry, but he never did an hour's work for anyone or "earned" a dollar. He was a splendid talker, a dreamer, a poet, a man. Wonderful Terry! Mukerji has written of him in *Caste and Outcast*. In that book he was Jerry, one of Mukerji's two companions in San Francisco; but Mukerji had not the depth to reach, himself, to Terry's deep levels.

Raymond went out and found a green branch to make the arrow, and he found the eagle feathers. For a "fire" he laid a lighted electric bulb on the floor with my Chinese red shawl over it, and for the Mountain of the Moon—I forget what he did about that—but the Peyote Path was a white sheet folded into a narrow strip, running towards the east along the floor.

The evening we were to engage ourselves to experiment with consciousness, none of us ate any dinner. We, at Raymond's order, had dressed in our best, and the room had been thoroughly cleaned beforehand. Everything had to be tuned up a little for this, evidently—all of the accessories and surroundings must be of the finest and cleanest, the most shining. Like Church, I thought to myself.

At nine o'clock we extinguished the lights and sat on the floor in a crescent shape with the Peyote Path running eastward out of our midst. Raymond, who constituted himself the Chief, sat at the foot of the path behind the fire, an arrow in one hand, and a few lovely eagle feathers in the other. The *peyote* lay in a little heap in the center of the space before him. It looked like small, dried-up buttons with shriveled edges, and it had a kind of fur on the upper side.

Raymond told us to just take it and chew it, as many as we liked—but, once we began the Ceremony, to beware of stopping before it was over, when the Morning Star should rise. He looked so somber sitting there cross-legged that I was filled to bursting with sudden laughter. I was thrilled and excited and amused.

Suddenly Raymond seized a piece of the *peyote* and popped it into his mouth and began to sing. At last he raised his chin and began to howl like a dog, as it seemed to me. I looked covertly at the others.

The mere presence of that *peyote* seemed already to have emphasized the real nature in us all. I was laughing, but Neith looked down at the fire, distantly grave and withdrawn, beautiful and strange. Hutch appeared rather boyish, like a boy in church who lowers his head and peeps over his prayer book at another boy. Bobby's face was simulating a respectful attention, while it hid his thoughts. Ida looked more like a superior lioness than ever, cynical and intolerant; Max grinned amiably, complacent and friendly to anything, and Terry seemed more remote than the others—as he contemplated the end of his cigarette (for cigarettes were *de rigueur* and, in fact, compulsory, I believe).

Genevieve Onslow's frog-like eyes were brilliant and intense. Her thin face looked like parchment. Andrew's brows twitched as he gave and yet did not give himself to the occasion; a half smile played over his sulky lips, but it was an irritated smile. Only I seemed to myself to be just exactly as usual, unaffected by anything and observant of it all.

Raymond chewed on his *peyote* and sang his song that was like the howl of a dog. He swung the tempo faster and motioned to us to begin.

Then we all, in our different fashions, reached out and took the *peyote* and put it into our mouths, and began to chew upon it. But it was bitter! Oh, how it was bitter! I chewed for a little while and watched the others. They all seemed to be chewing away, too. Everybody chewed.

But after a while, as I swallowed the bitter saliva, I felt a certain numbness coming over me in my mouth and limbs. But it was only over my body. My brain was clearly filled with laughter! Laughter, laughter, laughter at all the others there. Laughter, and at the same time a canny, almost smug discretion took possession of me.

When Raymond had chewed up his first *peyote,* and the others had all chewed theirs, he, still singing, handed his green arrow to the one who sat on his right hand, and motioned him to sing, and motioned to us all to take another *peyote* with him.

Raymond's unfortunate neighbor didn't know how to sing Indian songs. Raymond, with an urgently anxious look on his face, continued to sing himself, as he beckoned the other to sing. Evidently he *must* sing—it was frightfully important.

Raymond impressed this need so acutely that Hutch (it was Hutch!) actually lifted up his voice—and popping a *peyote* into his mouth, sat with the green arrow in a hieratical pose, and howled in a disjointed and unrhythmical way that, however, did not seem unpleasant to Raymond. It was evidently not so much the *way* you did a thing, it was that you *did* it, that counted.

Presently, I raised a *peyote* to my mouth, made a movement with my lips and, prudently, I secreted it deeper into the palm of my hand. Shaking with ghoulish laughter, I held it until my first move to take it was forgotten, and then I thrust it behind me on the floor. But the others chewed and chewed on their second *peyote,* and each of them had sunk just a little deeper into themselves—had become a trifle *more* themselves. . . .

Useless to describe the slow inward progress of the *peyote*. On the surface everything remained the same. Forgetting self-consciousness in a deepened being, each one sang in his turn. Some time after the second *peyote,* Max and Ida got up and left almost unnoticed. My one and only taste had started me laughing and the laughter endured. Everyone seemed ridiculous to me—utterly ridiculous and immeasurably far away from me. Far away from me, several little foolish human beings sat staring at a mock fire and made silly little gestures. Above them I leaned, filled with an unlimited contempt for the facile enthrallments of humanity, weak and petty in its activities, bound so easily by a dried herb, bound by its notions of everything—anarchy, poetry, systems, sex and society.

Bobby! Look at Bobby's beard! Like a Persian miniature of a late period, not well drawn, inexpressive, he rolled subjugated eyes, increasingly solemn as he viewed the changing colors unrolling before him. And Hutch! Good heavens! Hutch looked like a Lutheran Monk! Genevieve stared continually at a spot on the rug before her, her eyes enormous now, the whites showing all round them in an appalled revelation of something.

But Terry! Almost I stopped laughing when I looked at Terry, for he had increased in stature. His head was huge, and clear cut, every bone in his face, as he looked with a terrible intensity of Seeing at the lighted end of his cigarette. No, I could not laugh at Terry. He frightened me a little.

Another thing that was noticeable was the eerie effect upon everyone's expression from the dim light of the "fire," that electric globe smoldering under the red shawl. It reminded me of the ghastly results we used to procure as children by having two of us stare fixedly at each other, while another turned the gas jet up and then lowered it; continuing thus, we were able to induce the most devilish expressions, with deathly shades of color that fluctuated with the varying light. So now, although the light was fixed, though dim, it seemed that various and strange changes came over the faces before me.

The night wore on, and a more and more peculiar atmosphere enclosed us. The songs kept up—monotonous and outlandish, and gradually my laughter wore itself out and I grew weary and longed to leave. For me to long to leave was but a signal for my departure, for I was an impatient soul—undisciplined. I began to whisper and make signs, nodding my head towards my bedroom, and most of the others, I discovered, were as ready as I to go. As inconspicuously as possible, then, the Hapgoods, Bobby and Andrew and I rose—and stood—looking at the others.

But the others were oblivious. Harrington, Terry and Genevieve continued their fixedness of attention upon other worlds than ours. They were lost to us. They did not see us or take any notice of us at all. We crept off to bed, I to my white room at the far end of the suite, the Hapgoods, Andrew and Bobby out through the kitchen to the little bedrooms beyond in the Ninth Street part of the apartment.

After I was in bed I lay still and listened. The weird song from the front room came only in a faraway, muffled fashion through my closed door. I visualized the scene I had left, the darkened room, the "fire," the Peyote Path, and the Mountain of the Moon. I saw, in my mind's eye, the three people sitting there absorbed, unheeding, lost.

And my mind grew angry all of a sudden. Very angry! To think that that was going on there in my house and *I could not stop it* if I wanted to! Until this thought came to me, I had not particularly wanted to stop it, but as soon as I did think of it, it frightened me by its intensity. It was not so much that something was going on, but that something was going on *in my house* that I could not stop even if I wanted to. And instantly, because this was the case, I wanted terribly to stop it. I *must* stop it! But how?

Nothing could reach those entranced people. They were gone! Gone into the *peyote* world and I did not know how to follow them and bring them back. I grew more and more angry and more in a panic than ever before in my life, except, perhaps, that time at Aunt Clarissa's on Staten Island.

How could I stop that thing?

I began to throw all my attention into praying, with the fullest concentration and passion of which I was capable—praying to It—to that Force in which I believed and which I thought I knew how to contact.

"Oh, Great Force, hear me! Stop that thing in there! *Stop it!* STOP IT!" I breathed my whole being into my prayer.

And as I prayed I heard in the distance—further away than the muffled chant—a sound of steps, of hobbling, hasty steps, and the tap of a cane, coming nearer and nearer through the silent house. I held my breath. The hurried steps came nearer and nearer—they were coming from the other end of the house. I recognized them. Only Andrew sounded like that. I had summoned him. Let anyone, who doubts these possibilities, try once with power and passion to invoke the Force that lies about us.

I lay scarcely breathing now and waited for him to carry out my prayer, and I heard him stamp as though in a fury, past my door, through the dining room and the next room, to where I knew the three others sat cross-legged and oblivious on the floor, enwrapped in another consciousness than his.

I listened to him "stop" that thing. I heard him trampling heavily about, uttering short, angry words; I heard the windows thrown up, and I heard—what was that?—something like a dreadful cry of anguish. An instant's silence, and then a tapping at my door.

I turned on the electric light and I jumped out of bed and rushed to open it a crack. Genevieve stood there. Her face gleamed almost phosphorescent, her large eyes, showing the whites all round them, glared at me.

"Mabel!" she gasped. "Oh, Mabel! It is *terrible*," and she was gone.

I flung on a dressing gown and ran out. Andrew was lurching around the room with a furious face—looking like an avenging angel, striking his cane into the red shawl that lay in a heap, at the white sheet that had been the "path," and at the few *peyotes* that were scattered, now, about the floor.

Terry sat gazing fixedly at the end of his cigarette—but Harrington looked about him dazed and horrified.

"Stop, man! That is terribly dangerous!" he said over and over as I came in.

When Andrew saw me, he cried:

"After I got to bed I suddenly felt I couldn't stand having this thing going on any more! I *had* to break it up."

"Where is Genevieve?" I cried.

But she was gone.

While I went to call Hutch and Neith and tell them what had happened, Harrington sat like a haunted, helpless creature in a corner of a sofa and Terry, moved now to the little room off the drawing room, sat serene and attentive, always gazing at the end of his cigarette.

Genevieve was gone. There was no doubt about that. We hunted the rooms for her, but she had fled like a phantom out of the apartment, down the stairs and out—out—

Where?

And now we entered upon the second phase of that crazy night.

The thought of Genevieve out in the windy streets of the city was unthinkable, the condition she was in—unaccountable for herself—unable to explain anything—not even knowing where she was—it frightened us all. We didn't know where to look for her—where to go first should one of us start out after her.

I saw Hutch fumbling on his hands and knees behind a chair and went to look closer and ask what on earth he was doing. He gave me a queer look. He was gathering up bits of *peyote*—whole ones and the broken ones I had thrust behind me.

"If the *Police* should come in here and find this . . ."

Police! Heavens, I *was* scared!

Harrington, muttering to himself in a corner, seemed not to be with us at all—no more did Terry, sitting alone and smiling down at his cigarette. Hutch and Neith and I and Andrew—we were the only ones to deal with the situation and we hadn't the remotest idea where to begin.

A sharp ring at the telephone startled us all. I ran to answer it and it was Max.

"Genevieve is here," he said. "We heard her crying under the window."

"How *is* she?" I cried.

"Well, I don't know. We will put her to bed and see you in the morning."

The sickening light of dawn began to creep into the rooms and show up the strange disorder about us. Furniture displaced, the red shawl and the white sheet lying on the floor. And two men with white faces with us, but not of us.

The fear about Genevieve somewhat allayed, we turned back to the *peyote*—that most mysterious of all the growing things that I had ever encountered.

Hutch, lowering his voice, came up and spoke to me. I noticed he had altered. He appeared diminished and shrunken as though he had lost fifty pounds of flesh. He was pale and he looked awed.

272

"Mabel," he said, "I have learned tonight something wonderful. I cannot put it into words exactly, but I have found the short cut to the Soul."

"What is it?" I asked.

"The death of the flesh," he almost whispered, and I saw from his eyes that the *peyote* in him lent a far deeper significance to the words for him than for me.

"I *saw* it," he went on. "I saw the death of the flesh occur in my body and I saw the Soul emerge from that death."

"I saw no such thing," said Neith, smiling with a beautiful strangeness. "As I sat there, I saw the walls of this house fall away and I was following a lovely river for miles and miles through the most wonderful virginal forest I have ever known." She was elated and enhanced.

"I saw what Sex is," Andrew broke in. "And it is a square crystal cube, transparent and colorless; and at the same time I saw that I was looking at my Soul."

Then Harrington sprang up. In the early cold light of the morning his face was greenish and his eyes stared horrified.

"I can't breathe," he gasped. "My heart— Get me something. Some fruit . . ."

Scared, I ran into the kitchen looking for some oranges. When I came back Hutch was bending over him.

"It is like a palpitation," he said.

And Terry sat on—smiling, not hearing or seeing us—just gazing down at his cigarette.

"If only the *day* would come," I exclaimed. "And the cook and breakfast and everything!"

Finally we were seated at the table and we were drinking coffee. Harrington sat with his head in his hands and sometimes a violent shaking came over him.

"You don't know what you did," he said once to Andrew.

And all this time Terry stayed where he was, never coming near us; serene and immobile, he sat with one long leg crossed over the other and seemed to ponder on illimitable things. We carried some orange juice to him, but he did not see us.

Andrew continued to expostulate and explain his action—almost to himself, it seemed.

"I *had* to do it," he said wonderingly, over and over, and Hutch, not listening to him, repeated his own wonderment in rumpling tones, meditatively:

"Think of it—to learn the way to the Soul—the shortest way . . ."

Our cook looked at us curiously as she served our queer breakfast. I can't imagine what she thought and no one but myself noticed her. It was, as usual, my curse to be aware of all the elements at once.

Then Max and Ida came with Genevieve and left her, not saying much beyond the need to get a doctor for her. Max sort of slipped away quite quickly, but Ida stayed.

Genevieve was just gibbering. She was making curious rapid movements, her eyes rolled in her head, she ran with dreadful haste into her room, Neith and Ida and I after her. She began to pick up one thing and then another.

"I must go!" she cried, not looking at any of us. "I must see father. I have something to tell him." She clasped two little silk Chinese slippers to her breast. "Father always came and sat by me when I went to bed and was frightened," she said, and her words came tumbling with utmost haste from her white lips. "And now I must tell him something." There was a terribly touching quality about her that made one want to cry, but I swallowed this feeling and ran to ask Hutch what to do.

We thought it best to telegraph her father and then to get a doctor for her, so I wired Mr. Onslow:

GENEVIEVE ILL WITH A NERVOUS BREAKDOWN
MABEL DODGE.

To which he replied immediately to Genevieve, saying:

I AM COMING TO MY LITTLE GIRL AS FAST AS
POSSIBLE   KEEP UP YOUR COURAGE DEAR
FATHER.

Hutch said, "We must call Harry Lorber—he is discreet. He won't talk." And he rang him up.

This East Side Jewish doctor was the friend of all of us and of all the Radicals. He was used to dilemmas. He examined Genevieve carefully. While he was there she seemed not to see him, and kept staring off into a corner of the room. Harry led Hutch and me out of the room and said quizzically:

"Dope, hey?"

"We don't know," replied Hutch, earnestly, "what it is." And he told Harry all that had happened and produced one of the *peyotes* to show him.

"I never heard of it. I wonder if it is anything like *mescal*. That comes from old Mexico. This stuff has a powerful action on the heart and is evidently a hypnotic. A highly strung girl like this might easily be injured by it. I'd like to study this queer-looking little button," he went on, smiling at the thing in his hand. "Evidently Dasburg gave her a terrific shock by breaking in so brusquely upon the dream state it produces."

He was pacing up and down the room, now.

"She must have a nurse," he said. "I know a good girl." And he telephoned her. Then he gave Genevieve some medicine. "Don't let her out of your sight," Harry cautioned the nurse, "and watch her pulse. I'll come back in a couple of hours."

Then he went up to Terry, whom he knew, and spoke to him. Terry looked up for the first time in all that long night and smiled the most illumined smile I have ever seen. His eyes were blue like gentians.

"Harry," he said, "I have seen the Universe, and Man! It is wonderful!" Then he got his hat and just walked out and I don't think I have ever seen him to talk to again.

Genevieve seemed to give up, then. She let us do as we would with her and we established her on a *chaise longue* in the front room. She seemed to give up like a child and did not try to go on gathering her things to pack them. She lay there staring and staring out of the window, quiet now, not speaking, nor seeming to see us, and the tears streamed down her face.

"Genevieve," I whispered, "what do you see?"

"God," she replied, never moving her eyes.

"And is it . . . ?"

"It is very, very sad," she said from the depths of her soul.

I left her to the nurse and went to my room, but I hadn't been away more than a few moments when the girl came running in, exclaiming,

"Is she *here?*"

"No! Did you leave her?"

"Only to get her a glass of water. When I came back, she was gone—!"

Heavens! It was too much. With the uncanny, unhesitating certainty of a lunatic, Genevieve had seized her first chance. She was out in the street again. We had lost her, maybe this time for good.

Really, I didn't know where to turn now. For I called Ida and Max and they had seen nothing of her. Besides, instinctively I knew she would not go to them a second time when they had delivered her into our hands and we had held her against her will. Hutch was awfully upset, too.

"We *must* not let this get into the papers," he said, with the journalist's realization of their possibilities. "Yet we may need to notify the police," he went on. "I think I'll call John Collier."

Collier was over at the People's Institute. He was one of the really emancipated people I knew and he had an extraordinarily youthful face that sometimes looked like that of a good child and sometimes was consumed with hate.

It was Hutch who had first told me he was a genius, and I believed that he was. His work was sometimes mixed up with poor people, generally foreigners, whose European cultures he tried to preserve. He was constantly organizing pageants wherein Syrians, Slavs, or Italians could parade dressed in their native costumes and occasionally he pulled off a brilliant innovation such as turning the Public Schools into Recreation Centers and having Play Streets in the heart of the city. He was a reformer—and his friends were reformers. There was something drear about some of them but not about Collier. He had a deep flame in him.

Luther Gulick, who invented the Camp Fire Girls, and Fred Howe, who tried to make Ellis Island human, were his friends, and he knew all the city officials—so I suppose Hutch thought of him on that account, in the dilemma we were in.

We telephoned and he came right over, for the People's Institute was only a short way up the Avenue. He came into the apartment with his green eyes slightly malicious, but always amused, and his untidy hair falling over his brow—a small, *chétif* boyish figure with a great many strings in his hands that we knew he could pull if he wanted to.

Hutch told the strange story over again as briefly as he could. We were in a hurry to get something done. Genevieve was lost and her father had probably started for New York. What should we say to him if he came before we found her?

Collier drew down his thin lips and raised his eyebrows.

"Undoubtedly you could all be indicted under the illicit drug act," he began, in a low voice that could strike terror into his listeners. His method was the kind that first alarms and then allays. He described the worst possibility, then proceeded to remedy it.

"But we didn't know it was a Drug!" exclaimed Hutch, impatiently.

"That doesn't *matter*. It evidently *was* one. A very interesting one, too. I'd like to experiment with it sometime," he continued, pedantically.

"Well, you can't *now*. What do you think we'd better *do?*" queried Hutch. "You know the resources of the town better than I do. Shall we send out a general alarm—or something more discreet?"

"Well, of course I can call up Sheriff Harburger and put him on to it, or I can go to a private Agency and get a couple of good men, but I'm inclined to think the least publicity we give it the better, considering how well-known Mrs. Dodge and this house are. Some cub of a reporter would get hold of the story the minute it goes outside these doors. Someone may have *already* got it!" he went on, brightly, almost hopefully, I thought.

The time was rolling by and it was getting later and later in the day. My feelings were very mixed. I didn't think anything would happen because I didn't feel that certainty I always had inside me before disaster, a kind of realization before the event, of what was to come, that, if I examined it and trusted to it, never deceived me. And yet the talk of these two men was alarming. What bothered me most was that I should be personally implicated in the eyes of my acquaintances with a situation that was ambiguous enough to deserve, even at any angle, the name of a "Dope Party." Horrors!

I had heard of such gatherings and they were the antithesis of all I wished to stand for. The level of my life, at least in my own eyes, was infinitely raised above such sordid sensationalism. The very word "dope" annoyed me, and seemed to cling to me like pitch. I longed to be well out of its circuit—yet there I was, hemmed in, unable to run away and forget the whole disagreeable scrape, obliged to cope with a situation brought upon me by the others, who should have had the thing at *their* house, not mine, I thought. Why should *I* be the one who would have to bear the brunt of all that might result from their crazy cousin's peculiarities?

Well, it wasn't the first time, nor the last, that my shoulders would support an unexpected and undeserved opprobrium, I went on thinking. I felt more and more aloof, disgusted, bored, and disconnected from the whole thing. Why, I had apparently been the only one who had known enough not to seize the stuff and swallow handfuls of it! And yet there I was probably with a "dope party" staring at me from the pages of all the evening papers.

I felt pretty helpless with the stormy petrel that Collier had turned into and the inefficient and unresourceful Hutch who had no ideas at all when they were really needed.

I don't remember what they finally did, how we found Genevieve, what happened next, or anything about it. I know that every one of the others who had been at the apartment that night talked about it *for years,* and even still continue to do so, that I kept forever hearing echoes of every description about it, some of them of the worst kind. Undoubtedly that legend has encircled the world.

I know I never saw Genevieve again and that she didn't want to see me, and that her family have never had anything but a horror of me, filled with blame and the darkest suspicions, but that I have some strange communications that she sent me after a while from Chicago, composed of symbols and hieroglyphs with a phrase or two interspersed, and that these symbols are among the most ancient known and are found, faintly recognizable, carved on old rocks in the Indian country, though their meaning remains unknown to scholars.

I know, indeed, that that night was another-world night when, undoubtedly, the white apartment with its colored glass was the scene of something more esoteric and indecipherable than it ever housed before or since. But why it should have been brought to pass in *my* rooms, bringing in its train unmerited and hateful "allegations"—that was perhaps the greatest mystery of all, at least to me!

Terry I never saw at close hand, only in the distance at Eugene O'Neill's in Provincetown; Genevieve I never saw, though I had those strange papers from her that she sent while she was still under the influence of the *peyote;* Raymond Harrington, I never saw either, though I have heard of him at the Heye Museum in New York, where the Indian collection of ceremonial regalia connected with *peyote* in the Southwest is the finest to be found anywhere in the world.

CHAPTER XII

Approaching End

EVERYWHERE hope—everywhere expectancy.

Reed was at his most expressive moment in the spring of 1914. The poet is destined to give words to life, and he, feeling the pressure of forces in and about him, tried to tell of it. He never completed these breathless, groping phrases. They are only snatches of happy and hopeful words that noted what so many were already calling the New Day, and they are the last happy and innocent words he ever wrote:

Only the mass . . . the multitude . . .
Only the majestic sweep of people:
The seeping stream blends everyone.
The brain that thinks, the body that is capable of action, the space animate
    with form unseen, the object tangible . . . all the expansive breath of
    life . . .
A stretch, unending, of expression . . .
The plain, smooth, merging crush of birth and death.
Nothing separate, nor lost, nor helpless, nor oppressed . . .
But greeted, welcomed, challenged. . . .
Nothing dead:
But life made up of dying.

Vivify with this your squalor and your dust!
Make to faith your cringing mistrust, and your careful lying . . .
Rickety, uneven stairs;
Rooms that press and rub the dirtiness within . . .
Broken window-panes;
Thresholds worn and splintered . . .
Crumpledness of long-worn clothes. . . .
Flat and lifeless thread:
The shiftless placing here and there;
The pasty, flat, uneagerness . . .
The inbred selfishness . . .

The sapped, dry, tiredness of over-lived creation,
Of passion given no clear understanding. . . .
The skins beneath (the life beneath the flesh),
Pulled, drained, shrunken . . .
Aching emptily.
The airless cells called bodies:
And the fear . . .
The crouching fear of hate . . . and no weapon.

In your close-veiled silentness,
Dark in the whispering hope of life,
(Watching eagerly: hidden faces turned, expectant,
Slowly, passionately, grows a grayness.
Creeping . . . softly spread . . . expanding. . . .
Dawn . . . the LIGHT!)
Life in a daring Mothering of Man
Unveils . . .
Flings wide the covering of a white full breast . . .
Pours in a mighty gushing stream
Radiance; and tempting, wind-blown Life. . . .

The great, new day; with white winds washing it,
And wide-spread distances lying open in it:
Walls that hold themselves in readiness to move;
Poles that stalwart stand . . . erect . . .
That stiff in swelling passion stand
And walk, over moist, welcoming, close-molding earth.
Movement upflung! . . .
Daring as the dawn . . .
Surging unrestraint . . .
Things shining, clear, demanding, giving:
Living eagerly with lust for living . . .
Journeying through deaths that bear to new lives . . .
Youth . . . and the song of passing, given, youth.

This your Faith . . . your hope . . . your journeying:
This your aching muscles . . . this your strength withheld.
This in your hearts! . . .
And a bursting freedom in your living!

Revolt? . . .
A cheapened thought!

Faith!
The dim faith of no knowledge;
The faith that glows with a dark, crude, glowing.
Acceptance of the barriers;
Welcoming of wall and narrowness:
Happiness that swells and sings; that lurks in ooze; that penetrates brick
    and stern demand; that hides; that has its exultations in the secret
    heart of you: . . .
Happiness that laughs in silence . . .
The happiness of faith.

Let go the cramped, engulfing, round of hate,—
The sterile unbelief of things: . . . and lost hope.
(Dawn! . . . the Light! . . .
The radiance that is no light. . . .)

Faith that accepts:
Finding poverty a store of life to give . . .
Narrowness, confinement . . . as a new-found intimacy, of objects unex-
    plored:
To find the space that's life! . . .
The poles, the tracks, the cobble-stones, the gutters,
The same, stuffed, broken, window-pane . . .
As the great glad joy of nothing new . . . !
The unexploredness of things close . . . and forgot.

Hear the daring chant of space!
Step with a firm full stride of Faith!
Upset the force of things that are your menace,
By calmly passing through them,
To laws living in your heart.

When it grew warm in New York, Reed and I went to Provincetown. It was just a double line of small, white clapboarded cottages
along a silent village street, between the bay and the open sea. A few
people we knew took these cottages in the summer. The Hapgoods,
the Jig Cooks, Mary Heaton Vorse, and others. Once I saw slim Helen
Westley sitting flat on her bottom outside John Francis's general store
with wide gold rings in her ears and she looked exactly like a dark
gypsy.
    We all used to go there in the summer time and half camp in those

cottages, and there was the cleanest smell of decaying fish and elm trees in the air, for the Portuguese sailors went out in fishing boats every day, and all the native life was concerned with fish. The beach wasn't very clean, though, at low tide, but the wind blew through the cottages and rid us of towns. The streets were quiet and empty and everyone there knew everyone else.

People amused themselves with private theatricals. It was there that the Theatre Guild was born. The "Provincetown Players" put on plays by Neith and George Cram Cook and 'Gene O'Neill—that wide-mouthed, anguished, sunburned boy, in an old barn on the shore, and Helen Westley found she could act. In fact they all found they could act as well as write the plays!

So I went there for a while before going abroad with Neith, and Reed and I had a cottage. I wore Peter Thompson sailor suits with bloused tops and long skirts. I liked their coarse, dark blue flannel feeling. I didn't wear a lot of things under them as other women did— just a chemise seemed enough.

Reed always kept asking people to stay with us and one was that unspeakable F. I hated so. He seemed to me just a cad, but he flattered Reed and loved him, too. He professed to be a socialist. He lived on women. First on his wife and secondly on A. Z. It was the second that seemed so hurtful and outrageous. A. Z. was a lawyer with a broad forehead, blue eyes, and white-parted hair. She looked like Emily Dickinson or Mary Wollstonecraft and she was utterly irreproachable. That terrible F. somehow seduced her and turned her into an eager, avid, desperate female. She suddenly seemed to be all tentacles where before she had been a comfortable, folded-up octopus. It was dreadful. Dreadful, too, to hear F. *laugh* about her to Reed! Oh, dear, it was horrible to think of the extent of her dislocation.

I had to have *him* there in that cottage. Then I met Bobby Rogers who was another of Reed's classmates, and came along with Bobby Jones, and Lee Simonson and Hi Motherwell and the others, when they got a few days' holiday.

Bobby Rogers was fat and wore spectacles and was Bostonian. He was very facetious and breathless. It was difficult for him to strike just the right tone with me because he was so conventional and so was I at heart, but after he'd been there a while he struck it. But in hitting it correctly, he wandered up and down a scale that was suitable to almost all the disreputable and questionable characters in literature, because he was "literary"—and had never lived in any real places. I think I finally made him like me for myself, which must have helped him a good deal and he acted grateful. I have some lovely letters from him. I asked Walter to come down. I told him I'd made a friend of Bobby Rogers whom I knew he liked very much, and he was glad.

One day Reed wanted me to go out in an old dory with him, so I went. He rowed cheerfully out until we were quite far from the shore before we noticed it was filling with water; I couldn't swim, but he could, and I saw him begin to unlace his shoes.

"What *are* you doing?" I asked irritably.

"It's sinking," he answered. "We've got to get out."

"Out *where?*" I inquired, angrily. By that time we were really sitting in water and the boat began to turn sideways.

"Slide out!" commanded Reed, "and kick your slippers off." I *hated* that, but it was necessary. I found myself in the OCEAN clinging to a sinking dory. Reed was hallooing loudly towards the shore and had attracted the notice of some people on the beach who began to launch a boat far away in the distance, and row towards us. My blue flannel dress weighed me down terribly, and I could feel it drag the boat farther under the water. Reed was swimming actively and giving me directions that I couldn't understand and meanwhile the rescuers were approaching. I knew I was almost drowning and didn't really know what to do about it.

"Undo your skirt," shouted Reed as I came up to the surface. I felt his hand under my chin.

"I c-c-can't!" I choked.

"Well, *I* can," he replied and fumbled at my belt. I began to fight him, then. I didn't want him to take my skirt off.

"I'm not *going* to be rescued with my skirt off," I spluttered. An unattractive picture of myself being hauled into the rescuers' boat dressed in the upper part of a Peter Thompson sailor suit and practically *nothing* else, had appeared before me. Truly I preferred to drown than to be in such a foolish position.

Reed cursed and dragged at the skirt which came off and sank, leaving the lower part of me scantily draped in a shift and a pair of white stockings. The rescuers were upon us by that time and nothing was to be seen of our dory. All that the enthusiastic rowers in the rapidly approaching boat saw was a girl in a sailor blouse with two large blobs of hair wound in eights over her ears, tears running down her cheeks, and an angry swimmer accompanying her.

"Here, give us your hands—we'll haul you up," exclaimed some nice young men. "Up with you!" they encouraged.

Reed swam round and round with his teeth clenched.

"I don't *want* to be hauled up," I wailed, clutching at the side of their boat.

"She's lost her skirt," ground out Reed in as low a voice as he could —though the water and the wind and the men were making a great noise. Somehow they understood. I pretended I didn't even *see* them as I clung to their boat and they rowed swiftly ashore—with Reed sitting in with them. I just ignored the whole thing. I looked away into the distance and the tears ran down my face. Good-naturedly they, too, pretended not to see me. They pretended I was not even there.

They trawled me along behind them for ages it seemed to me; but after a while I felt the sand under my stocking feet and let go. I let go and stood on the ground and the boat darted away from me; I walked a little way in and then sat down in water with my back to the whole thing—and let them beach the boat. They left it there and left me there in my indignity—and they walked off down the shore. Even Reed walked off down the shore. When there wasn't a soul in sight, I crept farther out of the water—and hiding the lower part of myself in its charitable waves, I waded down the long stretch of pebbly sand till I came to the rear part of our cottage. Reed came out with a blanket or something. Memory covers my humiliation—somehow I got into the house and clothed myself.

Two weeks later I was walking in the evening on the sand with Reed and I saw lying before me a greenish-black, high-heeled slipper— hateful—discomfiting reminder! I pretended I did not see it. Maybe so did he. Anyway neither of us seemed to notice it. . . .

Reed's other friends came and went but F. mostly stayed. I wanted Walter to come and offset his uncongenial presence and wrote begging him to try to get away. But he could not come.

Neith and I had planned to go to Florence for the summer, and I think I left Reed in the cottage in Provincetown when we went. Either that or he was off reporting something for Hovey. I can't remember. I only recall Neith, Miss Galvin, John, and Boyce, the oldest

Hapgood boy and John's best friend, Beatrix, aged three, and I, all together on a dreadful Italian steamer bound for Naples.

Reed was to join us later at the villa—and Carl, too, was to come down from Paris and stay with us.

There was a queer atmosphere on that boat. Neith and I wondered about it. It is hard to name what it was, but the days seemed dreamlike and unreal. The summer ocean was oily-smooth, there was a glare in the light that came off the water, and there was, too, a peculiar calmness over the aspect of things, so that we lost the sense of time. We just slid along silently suspended in a void, emotionless and unaccented.

I, myself, had sunk into the unrelated blankness from which I suffered when I found myself unattached to someone, and no longer borne up and supported by the male contiguity through which alone I seemed to become real to myself. When I was out of tangible connection with someone outside, everything seemed to run down in me, and I did not respond to anyone or anything. I experienced nothing but the fatal inner immobility from which I had suffered as a child, feeling nothing but an emptiness that became a positive pain in its agonizing negativeness and I carried about with me the awful vacuity that was like hunger and thirst.

Why couldn't I continue to live in the thought of the one I loved? No, it seemed I must hear, see and touch in order to feel. If the actual moment held no living creature beside me, it was as though he did not exist. Only the proximity counted. If he were not with me, it was as though he were not.

Again I resumed the masking smile that was no more than a willful muscular contraction, as I sat on the small deck with Neith and the boys. Her own harmony apparently depended on nothing outside of herself. She moved sweetly and slowly through life, enjoying it with mild appreciation, feeding herself on herself—uninfluenced. Did she guess my aching indifference to all things? No matter how well we knew each other, yet we never fathomed each other's secret mode of being.

It seemed to me that the dreadful suspension of life that I was experiencing was a reflection of the outside world. Everything was abated within and without. But whereas Neith continued to function, agreeably enjoying herself, and observing, with detached interest, the changed look of sky and sea and the light upon them, and was able to comment with a smile: "The world looks queer. It's as though it were dying or dead, somehow," I partook of that death—dying with it.

We reached Florence where the villa awaited us as usual—smoothly in order, servants assembled. And here I revived a little in the interest that Neith took in it all. How beautiful, after New York, the Villa Curonia appeared, serene upon its hill, with the roses and jasmine about it. The little yellow salon was as ever full of my collection of *"le chien à travers les âges."* They sat there in china, *papier mâché* and ivory, with cheerful grins or ghastly contortions upon their countenances, while the dim pastel portraits of the Austrian grand duke and duchess looked down haughtily from over the yellow damask couch. The grave light in the long north salon was over the white-vaulted ceiling and falling quietly upon the golden rug. In the Gran' Salone the late afternoon sun came in the French windows from the south and the west and filled the vast room with a blessed beauty that was always like a promise of peace and security, and it bathed us in its warmth as it reflected upon us from the deep crimson and gold of the walls.

Nothing could have been more peaceful and decorous than our meal that first evening in the candle-lighted dining room. Neith fitted so well into those fine surroundings, her smooth red-gold head against the crimson damask of the high-backed chair. The boys—I cannot see them. . . .

We lay smoking upon long chairs on the loggia all the evening and watched the moonlight change the forms of things as the hours passed —and when it came time to sleep, and we went up to the two bedrooms with our Florentine oil lamps throwing great shadows over halls and corridors, Neith exclaimed: "How peaceful this place is! Made for rest!"

I had given her Edwin's room and I was in the brown and white room alongside it. As we kissed good-night and closed the door between us, the heavy shadow of emptiness came down upon me again.

I lay awake for some time and my eyes were turned inward to examine, as always when it lay within me, the monstrous shape coiled there that I could only call by negative names when I tried to define it, but that never could be wholly named or known. Finally I slept— a lifeless sleep.

In the morning, after we had breakfasted in our separate rooms with the familiar gardenias upon our trays, I went in to Neith to see how she was. She sat up in the low bed where, when Edwin was away, I had seen a succession of disparate faces confront me on past mornings: Gertrude Stein, Stan Krayl, Yvonne Davidson, Bobby—and she smoked her perpetual cigarette. Upon her serious face I saw an expression I remembered, in a flash, I had seen before at Staten Island.

"How did you sleep?" I asked her brightly, above the weight I carried over my heart.

"I didn't sleep. I couldn't," she answered.

"Oh, Neith!"

"How strange this house is," she went on. "It seems to have a life of its own, a conscious life of its own," she repeated.

"What do you mean? How?"

"Well, at first I read awhile and then, after the lamp was out and the house grew quieter and quieter, I felt it take on a change of some kind. It drew itself together, it watched. *The house actually seemed to be waiting for something.*"

"Oh, Neith!"

"Yes. And I felt horribly afraid of something—something that it was waiting for. It seemed to me, too, to be waiting for me to go to sleep, to get out of the way, before the other thing that it waited for could come, or could happen, or *whatever* it was. And it seemed to me I must defeat it, that I mustn't sleep, that I must watch, too. So I did. All night the house and I *watched* and what it waited for could not come because I stayed awake! But it's quite different here in the daytime! It sounds foolish to say such things with the sun shining like this. Maybe I was just too tired and excited to sleep."

I said nothing. But there we were—haunted again! With my slackened spirit, I felt no particular interest—only a boredom that anything more should turn up to cope with. I had no energy to give to anything.

We passed the day somehow—no impression remains of what we did. I suppose we motored down to Doney's at noon, and saw the same faces and drank a sherry or two, and passed the hours as always before in pleasant untiring ways. But I remember that at twilight Neith's face grew serious—not alarmed, but grave. Miss Galvin must have been there and the two boys and little Beatrix, but no recollection of them comes back until we were up at the Albergo in Vallombrosa where we were obliged to go the next day. Yes, we were driven out of the villa—at least Neith was, and I went too, not wishing to stay there alone with my own obsessed soul. For the second morning, when, after a night of heavy suffering sleep, I went in to see Neith, she was pale and weary-looking and she said:

"I can't endure this, Mabel. I didn't go to sleep at all last night. I had to keep the lamp burning until daylight."

"Oh, heavens! What a nuisance! What can it be?" I cried, at a loss. My limbs were as though loaded with lead—and every nerve in my body ached and dragged. I carried a demon of energy within me that could not get out. Around and around in the cage of my strong body, seeking an exit, unable to pass. I felt like an engine, the demoniac turning and twisting of the imprisoned, leashed, ever-accelerating, gathering volume, consuming the fuel of life forces, creating its inapplicable power. Bent upon creating but without the clue to direction, cornered and turned into destruction by the absence of the transforming medium, I was like a child with a dynamo that required the most cautious and careful operation. How tragic it can be to harbor such energies without the ability to use them!

"There is a life here that the house knows and in some way shares," Neith said, slowly. "Last night it was more apparent, even, than the first. Soon after midnight I felt it draw together with a kind of fierce concentration—and while it watched and waited, it pushed against me as though it wanted to eliminate me—to drive me back and away from it.

"I know it seems perfectly idiotic and unreasonable, but I don't believe I can stand it! I think I'll have to go. There's no use in fighting it. It's a good deal stronger than I am."

"But here we are all settled!" I cried. "What can we do? I don't want to stay here without you—and yet it does seem too bad with everything in order for us—and it *is* comfortable."

"It's beautiful," she answered, "but if I am not allowed to sleep and have to fight against some malign influence that wants me gone, it isn't going to be especially beautiful or comfortable." She ended, with a bit of asperity, for evidently her lovely quiet nerves were worn and irritable—so rare a thing with her!

"Well, let's go up to Vallombrosa for a few days and then try it again here. We can leave Galvin here to look after the servants, and wire Carl to come up there." For he was to join us from Paris the following day.

We went that morning to the white-roomed Albergo, high up on the mountains among pine trees, and Neith slept for twelve hours that night, and I continued to bear my darkness and depression, for it was the same for me wherever I was.

Carl came the day after and was disappointed when he heard that we intended to stay up there. The Villa Curonia with the gardenias and the moonlighted loggia was much more what he wanted than pine trees. And of that time up there with them, I have no more memory than if it hadn't happened.

Cut off as I was from everyone, when I did notice them it was with criticism. The negative things, the disagreeable things about others, stirred me to a furious hidden tribulation and I exclaimed to myself about them while wearing on my face no more than a mask of quiescent boredom.

Carl drank glass after glass of wine from the robust dark bottle with its label of "Beaune. Jules Senard" done in eighteenth-century script, and I looked across the table at him and called him names in my heart, and thought him insensitive and unknowing of the delicacies of living. I wished that people like Walter were there, believing I would have been buoyed up by more stimulating society. I wrote him so but he only replied on a card:

Well, I can't help it if you will crawl off to inaccessible places.

Jack's *Metropolitan* wonderful—Mexican stuff as good as the rest. Colorado penetrating, satisfying and maddening.

Best to all of you.

WALTER.

I see myself dragging my feet among the pine needles. Great calm pine trees covered the mountain and worn paths ran between them. The suffering in me grew more intense and I could not bear it. I did not miss Reed, although apparently it was his absence or the withdrawal of his essence from my organism that caused my distress. I did not long for him consciously, though I was not *living* with him away. I knew he was coming pretty soon, but it did not seem to matter. I was in the empty present, forgetting how it had ever been to feel differently or that I would ever know felicity again.

Then, suddenly, in the melancholy inanition of the days, a crash came that threw us all into activity.

War was declared.

What a scramble! Down into Florence again—into the bank and to the consular office for Carl and Neith, for all they thought of was to get home while they could. Everyone in confusion—difficulty in getting money—moratorium declared—voices raised—all the usual vibrations of life upset.

As for me, it didn't mean a thing. It didn't interest or excite me, or even reach me. I dwelt alone in a deep contempt for wars, for anxieties, for humanities. My isolation at that time was doubtless at its zenith.

Then by some chance, at whose instigation I do not know, I sat in the small, dark salon of a Christian Science Healer in a narrow street in Florence, a woman whose name and face made no impression, but whose presence raised me. Presence? Being? Vibration? Whatever the alchemy, I left her after half an hour restored to life, to the world about me, happy, elated to come back, a trifle ashamed of my recent darkness, but adjusted once more to the pattern of which I was a part and able to function in it naturally. I didn't need to force myself to smile, to think, to be. I was.

Now my faculties were heightened. It seemed to me a freshened perception of all things had resulted from the damming up of the flow. I sat alone in the yellow salon and closed my eyes and had a vision of the nations changing form like the bits of colored glass in a kaleidoscope. The world was undergoing a mighty shift, and the hard foundations of all things moved under them. All forms altered and fell into new groupings. The world was a fluid again—everything would be different from what we had known.

It seemed that there was a total change to realize and accept without hindrance or demur. Of what avail to go against the evolutionary Will? In New York we had sensed the approach of a vast overthrow and had worked for one. That it had occurred in a manner unexpected to us and in Europe, instead of locally, was none of one's business. We had had the intuition of an imminent revolution—and a revolution was upon us. The revolving of the wheels would perhaps crush our conveniently systematized lives—but possibly, I thought, a new world is being born today—a new cycle, a new beauty. Had I not written of Gertrude's work: "Life at birth is always painful and rarely lovely"?

A few days after the declaration of War, Pius X died. We are all in the crowd outside St. Peter's watching for the Cardinals' smoke to rise. The Roman mob! The space is so crammed that we are like an ocean moving and we seethe back and forth. Pale nuns press against us on one side—soldiers on the other. Priests and prostitutes, clerks and countesses and Roman matrons, are fused into one living organism. Beatrix disappears beneath the mass and Carl recovers her to lift her shoulder-high. The men take any liberty they like—we are pushed, pinched, and buffeted. There is a fierce, low vibration running through this solid humanity. What is a human being? What is this turbulent, animated, rich, dark animal thing called human nature?

Among the cables from Hutch, my family, and Fania, calling us all to come home, one came to me from Reed telling me to wait and meet him in Naples. He would sail at once and we would go up to Paris together. I caught his excitement and enthusiasm—his eagerness to be on hand to "report" this war. I was quite surprised at the extreme self-centeredness of my companions. No one was thinking of anyone but himself. I was a little appalled at the idea of being left all alone in Naples—I who had never been alone in my life anywhere—and though Miss Galvin wanted to stay with me and see things, I did not want her on my hands when Reed and I should be going to the war together, and I told her she would have to go home. There was some altercation about her ticket and I believe I could not get the money out of the bank for her so that she had to use her salary. Anyway, whatever it was, I recall her for the first time in a towering rage that made her go into the street in Naples and smash a plate glass window where a portrait of the Kaiser gazed at the agitated passersby. This of course added to the complications, for we were forced to adjust it.

Carl and Neith thought only of one thing: to get back to New York on the first boat they could. If I didn't want to go with them, that was my affair, they said. It had never occurred to me that anyone would treat me so. I had been so accompanied all my life! I told them I would stay behind and wait for Reed, but I didn't speak to Carl for years afterwards!

So they sailed, taking John with them, and I remained in the hotel high above the Bay of Naples feeling strangely denuded and as though unscreened.

But the new unnatural feeling of naturalness remained with me throughout all the bustle and confusion. I had seen solitary women in hotels in America and Europe and had always wondered what it felt like to be alone in such places. It must have made them feel so unreal—so *not there*—I thought; and now here I was, "all alone in a pink frock" in a hotel in Europe, in Naples, that ambiguous city, and I scarcely knew how to acquit myself. So a visitor from another planet might have felt, I thought, if suddenly thrown down there.

But the peace and lightness lasted while I worked out how to live and be alone. I did what I imagined other women would do in my place. I bought some embroidery things and I sat in my window overlooking the bay and sewed! I walked sedately back and forth to my meals in the large dining room, composing my features into an expression of calm aloofness. In the afternoons I drove about the town in the rattly-bang *fiacres,* taking a mild, polite interest in the place, and the days passed in a peculiar serenity and loveliness. As though the lower region within me had been sealed up like a wound that had healed, I forgot the depths. I lived above them in the sunlight where birds and flowers and little cakes were the truer realities. We forget! How easily we forget.

There was scarcely any war excitement that I could see, in Naples. Blue skies, blue sea, and peaceful hours for me. Perhaps the only week of perfect serenity in my whole life up to that time, recalling somewhat the easeful living of pregnancy, yet more living and keen than that. For I tasted every slightest variation of pleasure in things outside myself—whether of light or shade, of perfume or of sound. I lived in things outside myself, little unemotional things that yet constituted life. At last I knew what life meant to others and how others were able to live. I was like Edwin at last.

This went on for perhaps ten days and then Reed reached Naples. Without hurry, without either dread or longing, but with the pleasure that lay in any movement, I dressed myself carefully in a long white ruffled dress and a flowery hat and with my white lace parasol over me, I waited on the dock.

Reed burst in upon my even days like Miss Galvin crashing through the plate glass window. He was untidy, curls damply disordered, breathless, and evidently containing more excitement than he could conveniently hold. My calm seemed to amaze him. He had never seen me so self-contained—neither happy nor unhappy, he said. But I thought I was happy and I smiled a complacent small smile like the one I had seen on many people without understanding it. The smile of un-knowing, the secure smile of obliviousness!

He was eager to be away to Paris immediately, yet he had never been to Naples and he said he *had* to see Pompeii, and Vaia of Dante's time.

We drove out there in the sunshine and I felt so composed seated beside him in my French embroidered muslin dress with flounces from my feet to my waist! We reached that place where sulphur fumes escape out of the ground here and there near the entrance to the cavern —and at the sight of the wavering, thin, white smoke arising from the bare ground, I had a faint return of my own familiar and subterranean malaise; a stirring of the depths that I repressed at once.

At the cavern's mouth there was a tall, dark Neapolitan with legs bared to the thighs. He made Reed roll his trousers up as high as they would go, so he could wade through the separating water between the outer and the inner entrance.

"Abandon hope all ye who enter here!" There were the familiar words above the cave's opening and the dark-skinned Charon waited to carry me across but not in the boat. He lifted me high in his arms, so the white flounces billowed and my knees pressed his belly, and motioning Reed to follow, he waded into the black water, forward into darkness. Reed didn't like to see me in these arms, but making a grimace, he accepted it and splashed along behind. A poor little show it was, this Inferno. Since Dante's day we had learned more grandiose ideas of hell, yet in the dimness of that place under the earth my indefinable anxiety returned. My equilibrium still remained undisturbed so that I was balanced between the world of white muslin, that simple world of pleasant small realities, and an inner world of vast, dark and terrible pain. In Charon's arms I was upheld, observing and experiencing, both at the same time. . . .

How recount the gradual fall from bliss? Did the return to earthly love bring it about? Did I forfeit my wholeness when I lay in Reed's arms again, tearing open the entrance to the nether world until I was like a wound that gaped between heaven and hell?

The darkness and depression were down upon me again like a heavy world shutting me away from those who stayed outside in the sun.

Reed stayed outside. Even though his had been the hand that thrust me below once more, he himself remained above in the light. The alternations of influence that people have upon each other are hard to understand. Once Reed had given me life and a feeling of reality—and losing it in his absence, an unknown woman in Florence had restored it to me. And now Reed was the one to take it away again. How can one ever call one's soul one's own while one is so at the mercy of others?

In Paris we established ourselves in a somewhat dreary apartment on the Rive Gauche. Or was it I who was dreary? I stayed in bed a good deal of the time. Lifeless. Reed was out all day. Panting with pleasurable activity, his eyes shining, the two high lights on his round forehead gleaming below his nodding curls, he rushed with his friends into the affair of the war. It was always activity he adored, almost any exciting activity. He was not essentially radical or revolutionary; he loved it when things happened and always wanted to be in the center of Events. Any great events. All the other American journalists were already in Paris and everybody was excited, pleased, happy. Everybody but me, I thought. Afterwards I wrote an article for Max Eastman to publish in *The Masses* called "The Secret of War," describing the happiness of those men in Paris. The cafés surged with officers in brand-new uniforms and shining eyes. The male population in Paris was as lustful as the Roman mob.

I made one feeble attempt to connect in some way with the Red Cross Society. But either I was too half-hearted or they were too organized. I answered questions and left my name and address, but never heard from them. Sometimes I dragged myself along the quays or sat upon a bench; I had scarcely enough vitality to reach home. Most of the time I was alone all the time in the lifeless apartment. Reed was in his element of course. But what was my element?

He was sorry for me, but he had no idea how to help me when he saw me like that. At night a fierce and melancholy love rose in me and, as we joined our bodies, tears flooded my face and dried against his cheeks; but this was only an eruption from just below the surface—it did not come from the real depths and assuage me. The deeps were not tapped. Sealed, they labored at their peculiar destiny.

One day before we left for London where Reed wanted to go, he came in and told me he had seen R. T. in the Luxembourg Gardens.

N. and he were living near by in a studio. I begged him not to force me to see them. I had no energy to pretend either pleasure in them or that mutual interest that people feel for each other. I was jealous, too, or envious, of the easy give and take of flowing intercourse. I was a weak, unstrung creature—at war with myself and lost to life. At such a disadvantage that I felt like shunning everyone, yet dreadfully lonely when I was alone. I really wanted Reed to be with me every moment and he was never there.

In London it was worse—and I decided to go back to New York and be miserable at home where at least I could be comfortable, for to sit solitary in a hotel room was growing to be more than I could endure. I think Reed was relieved when I told him, though in a way he liked to have me there waiting for him, longing for him to come back. Men do not really mind a woman's agony and loneliness; it gives them a sense of their own independence and security; and they like women's jealousy, too.

I had always tried to hold Reed to me so firmly that he could not pass the barrier of my will and take another woman, and though one part of him declared independence, and he always argued with me about "freedom" and the right to live one's own life, yet another part did not want to be free—that element of his soul that escaped both him and my own grasp, did not want to be loosed. So for the most part he was firmly welded to me. In all these months he had never even touched any other—and no matter how weak I grew in my split, disintegrated substance, at least I held him close. Sometimes he felt rebellious and cheated of some part of life, but he was caught nevertheless and tightly held.

The only thing I remember in London was lunching at Muriel's. Her house was lovely and full of beautiful things, but we had only boiled rice and coffee, though she was not perturbed at her poverty. She and the others lunching there were hilarious, finding the whole thing very "interesting."

"Interesting!" That was always Muriel's word! *Everything* was *interesting!* "Well, that is a way as good as another," I supposed, and again I was full of envy at the capacity for living they had and that I only had in spurts, or in alternation with the deathly lapse.

Reed was to return to Paris and to try to get to the front as soon as I sailed. I tried to wring promises from him. He would not forget me, nor spoil our love, or go to another? No—he would never forget me or do anything to hurt our deep and inevitable love. He would love me forever. He could never love another. This was till death. I wanted these words before I heard them, but though they were true they did me no good when they filled my ears.

The journey back on the steamer was ghastly. I shared a cabin with a stranger—quite a nice woman to whom I could not speak a word—nor show a smile.

A new life began at home in New York. That fall I moved from the apartment on the third floor to the one that had been below me—and this change seemed to be the beginning of a different existence. It was not as attractive in some ways. The ceilings were higher and the rooms seemed more formal, though they were disposed in the same way as the ones above.

The depression gradually wore off. Hutch and Neith were there, and Walter and Andrew, and others whom I liked. The sun came into my bedroom in the morning, and as I drank coffee and opened my letters and waited for the telephone to ring, life seemed lively.

I had had a letter from Reed from Paris. A brutal, reckless letter written in a café on blue-lined paper. It told me desperately, wildly, that the night I left London, he had got drunk in a sailor's dive and slept with a prostitute. It seemed written in a spirit of dismal levity. I did not feel badly. Somehow I understood it and felt sorry for him. I guessed the utter relief that he had felt to have me gone and his regret that he should feel relief—the reaction after restraint when the pressure was lifted. And anyway I did not love him any more. How it passed or why, I did not know at all. There was no reason, no cause. It seemed that with the lifting of the black mood I had been under, the whole of the old life had lifted itself out of me with it. I was someone else. I scarcely knew Reed, my lover. But I knew well and affectionately Hutch and Neith and those whom I had not loved in that way. My sense of significance returned and I wanted something else again.

One morning a cable was brought in to me from the Brevoort Hotel. It said:

N. T. AND I HAVE FALLEN IN LOVE WITH EACH OTHER

MY HEART IS BROKEN

REED.

I laughed.

I called Walter on the telephone to tell him about it and I sounded more rueful than I felt. After I read him the telegram, I cried: "Isn't it childish! I am tired of being the mother of men!"

"I should think you would be," he answered, sympathetically. "But take a long view of it and presently it won't seem so bad." I acquiesced with a sigh.

Walter was a little amused. He wrote me a card from the Harvard Club saying he had told me so! told me so!

The truth is that Walter had upset Reed's feelings in the spring by going into the *New Republic* magazine that was just being organized, for Walter had been one of the young radicals along with Reed. He, too, had talked of changing the world and Reed said he was a renegade to affiliate himself with a periodical subsidized by a "capitalist" like Mrs. Willard Straight, and he wrote Walter this. Walter, very effectual with his pen, replied with a scathing answer, the substance of which was that when Reed had burned himself out in the radical movement, he would still be active and useful in it in his own way. Reed and he split then and Reed had the letter framed and hung it on his wall in Washington Square for all to see—rather a showy revenge. But they had patched it up. Walter had written me:

DEAR MABEL:

Next week is to be my last trip to Washington for a month—at least I think it is. Then I'll come out. You know I want to come, but I never get a full day free.

I wrote Jack the other day that I thought it was nonsense for us to quarrel and that I was sorry I'd hurt him. He replied at once, reciprocating.

Write me things.

Yours always,

WALTER.

Hutch got a cable too! Reed apparently consigned me to his thoughtful care! He immediately came to town and found me quiet. This surprised him and he wrote me the next day:

2022 *N. Pennsylvania St.,*
Indianapolis.

DEAREST MABEL,

I was deeply relieved to get the cablegrams exchanged between you and Reed, as on receiving Reed's cablegram to me I felt worried about you. But I see that you are taking it beautifully, and although you will probably suffer a reaction and be much depressed, yet it will not be as bad as I thought. I was not sure but what it might mean the same to you as it did last year, when he went away for a time. I believe your readiness for the Cosmic Sense accounts for the fine way in which you are able to take what would ordinarily be a very severe blow. And I congratulate you with all my heart and love you deeply—more than ever. You have become deeper and far stronger than you were when I first met you. I believe you are really winning out in the big game of life—becoming Mistress of your soul, perhaps because the larger life is entering into you, invited by the hospitable way in which you have opened yourself up to life's forces.

I'll write again soon. Wish I could see you, but I don't think you need me, or anybody.

With great affection,

Hutch.

Soon an incoherent letter in halting English came from N. in Paris. I had made a magnanimous gesture and written to her when Reed's cable came. I forgot what I said, only I had tried to assume a magnanimous attitude. It had not been difficult because I felt so very little concern.

Paris, Nov. 6, 1914.

Dearest Mabel,

Your word to me yesterday has been the deepest revelation to me of you. Do you grasp what has happened and you can still send us so much sweetness, so much understanding. You are better than a sister, perhaps because you are a sister in love.

When I think of the many tranquil hours of our spirits' intimacy, when I think of R. of whom I was so fond in spite of my being always misunderstood and sniffed at—O Mabel, I do not know myself that I could actually do what I have done. But I sent you the word that comes nearest to the truth: "force vitale" delivered me and there is only Reed who responds to it and who is thrown by the same force towards me. It is the nearest I have ever been to the inward force of existence of earth.

My body and my mind have wrangled and fought against doing to you and R. so much harm, and I still suffer horribly at the thought of you and him. I do not know what will happen to R. It can still result in dreadful things happening to Reed and me from him. Because he can only see adultery on my part and intruding on Reed's. O how easy it would be if it were that.

Mabel, I wish I could tell you everything from the first moment and have you tell me your pain. Your word gives me hope that deep in us you and I could find the bridge to each other. Do you remember the last night before I left New York? We sat in the back of the car and I leaned my head back and begged you to tell how happiness between a man and woman was possible. And all the time my heart cried with the bitterness of it and your words, for they too secured to me only sadness and the feeling that a complete union was impossible.

To emerge out of our own dependencies towards the deepest desire in us, to find ourselves answered, desired, thrown together in the profoundest roundness with a man's being, that, Mabel, I do realize I need. That Reed gives me, will give me altogether when also our bodies complete each other.

Mabel, do you hear me, do you listen to me? It is so serious and that is why I must hold all my strength together now for it. O if R. were honest and saw the inevitableness and the necessity of my demand for a divorce.

Such a dearness in the way you address the cable: Chez John Reed, 76 rue d'Assas. Only you are big enough to see that nothing lies in my staying here. What happened happened before. But the earthquake in me shook me so that I had to be taken care of, had to have a real bed, air and food. Before that I had been through with the diphtheria already, even been in the street and restaurant and park. R. and I stayed here a couple of days together until something terrible and so humiliating for me happened. I was very sick, wanted to go away alone to Alice's room (the little *couturière* who made your clothes). She was the only one I knew. But when she came my heart failed, the doctor came and I could not move for days. Alice has been staying with me ever since and is good to me. And Reed has prevented me from the worst.

I intend to go to Hanni in Germany to get my strength back to tell my family nothing can stop me to get the divorce. And I will marry Reed. We both must.

Mabel, now I feel myself a spirit and a woman on the warm earth and, what I never did before, the substance and cause for a child. When you get this letter, my friend Mabel, think of me simply. I feel so humble, so released of the obscurity of human relations and if you can, send a word to me, if you can still understand and love what life brings. Address me N. T. Rheinland. But you need not for my sake if you do not feel yourself.
Mabel,
do we understand one another?

N.

Reed's friends who had grown to believe in our relationship felt much as Bobby Rogers felt. As he said in the following letter:

Three Spruce,
November 12.

DEAR MABEL:

I've kept postponing writing you all the week since Walter told me about the muddle; I'm rather a coward about things that hurt me. I'm not sure that I had best say anything, only I can't see what good friends are if they are not to say what they feel.

If I blunder and stumble where perhaps I ought not to walk at all, forgive me.

I've known Jack for nearly eight years and been very fond of him. I have often been vexed with him; this is the first time I have ever had to feel sorry for him. I am very sorry now.

To be frank—perhaps you may have known of it—about a year ago I rather resented your influence with Jack. I was afraid it might take too much of him. This summer I realized it was the best thing that ever came to him. You gave him more than anyone else I knew possibly could—I began to think you might make him what it was in him to be, and I was very glad. I never doubted but what he would go on growing stronger and happier and more able with you. That is why I am sorry now for him above all.

It is hard for me to be angry with him; it means simply that he hasn't got something I always hoped he had—call it loyalty—to ideas, to people. He will always be true to "himself"—till some day he finds how that empties the world of happiness for him. He thinks he is freeing himself from weakness; he is only cutting himself off from strength.

I am fond of him as always, I am sorry for him—but in this I want you to know that my loyalty is to you. You have been more than kind to me merely as one of his friends; now I want to be your friend, too, for my own sake. And I think that those who care most for Jack will feel as I do. The others do not matter. I won't say anything more about it now; only don't forget that I am at your service.

Thanks awfully for sending me the *Masses* article, even if it did arrive addressed to Robert Jones. It's got lots of life in it and more understanding. I thought you said to me last summer that you couldn't write or something? Nonsense! Your ability to get behind and find a synthesis makes me despair.

And it cheers me to find someone else preaching my own little pet theory: that the veneer of civilization is very thin indeed and only efficacious when the mind of man is at rest. But at times of crisis, of urgency and danger, the lava boils and bubbles up over the thin crust, the essential nature of the beast not so dormant after all.

301

That is what makes me skeptical of all Walter's faith in humanity that you insist on, that man can raise himself to incredible heights. He seemed to think that all our good is only undeveloped and all our bad simply the result of bad education and environment. Again, nonsense! This crisis and all others like it when the thin crust of civilization bursts under pressure, make me sure of it. Walter, with his ideas of bad education, was beginning to shake me in my very firm belief in *original sin*—this war has restored it triumphantly. It's not education, it's the thing that can never be educated—not in the next few aeons anyway.

It's not merely love of fighting, though. I think you're wrong there. It's fear and hatred. Fear for those things peculiarly yours, your home and your language, your country's integrity—all that dumb, misunderstood thing called patriotism—and hatred for the stranger, the man across the border, the man who has different manners, and tongue and ideals. They blend together, this fear and hatred, into one thing we call patriotism and which finds expression in joyous fighting. They don't want to fight individuals—of course. The Englishman doesn't hate a German, but he hates Germans—and he is absolutely right in hating them. Simply because they are what he is not and doesn't want to be.

I forgive your fling at Gilbert K.—There is one Allah and I am his prophet—but he and I are right in this.

How is Walter going to quench this fundamental and illogical passion in us all? He says somewhere in his book—and the figure shows the weakness of the idea—that "man must raise himself by his own boot-straps," the *one* thing he can't do. Walter refuses it but negates it. He throws away all authority—which resolves itself into the fact that man shall have still one more terrible authority—himself. For the authority which is oneself is at once tyrannical and very weak.

So don't call it mere love of fighting. There's something immeasurably stronger beneath that. Modernism deplores it and tries to shut its eyes to it—but it's there. And will be there to all eternity, the earthpart of man.

I like Mrs. Bull's paragraphs too. She expresses exactly what you feel on reading the Kaiser's prayers and the Archbishop of Canterbury's prayers and our own prayers for peace—that we have unconsciously gone back to the limited tribal gods in the hope that one's own may be more efficacious than the other fellow's.

And how about the women who are banding themselves together all over England to keep the enlistment rolls full? As long as it seems unnecessary that her own man go, women will hate war, but when it is a question of that which they love no less than the men, their feelings are no different, I believe. Would you want to make peace with the Japanese at your gates?

I think the *New Republic* people are to be congratulated on their first number. There is certainly nothing like it in America. I hope they do not over-estimate the number of people who really want ideas, presented without dilution or trimmings or pictures, etc. But I am naturally a pessimist about the human race and what it wants and what it can do. And I hope they are not going to take themselves too seriously, as if they were the first ever to bring thought to the adjustment of current problems, nor forget that they are only current problems. In short, they mustn't get too Olympian. Jove nods sometimes.

It occurs to me that I have been writing an awful lot of drool, giving my pet hobby-horses a fine airing in spite of their limping gait. If so, just take me down a peg for my soul's good.

We had a fine visit from Walter. He certainly is in fine fettle these days; whether it is the book or a regular job or the responsibility of finishing up the incomplete work of the Creator, I don't know. But I have never seen him happier or nicer.

Just to make sure I don't spill over on another page, I'll say good-night.

Yours,

BOBBY.

Well, I thought, as I faced forward into the year 1915, that is the end of *that*. I had said good-by forever to Reed in my heart. To the gay, bombastic, and lovable boy with his shining brow; to the Labor Movement, to Revolution, and to anarchy. To the hope of subtly undermining the community with Hutch; and to all the illusions of being a power in the environment. My young lover was gone, and, it seemed, gone with him were the younger hopes of change. With a world at war, one somehow ceased to war with systems and circumstances. Instinctively I turned once more to Nature and Art and tried to live in them.

PART TWO

For Maurice Sterne the Sculptor

. . . This is what I wish my book to be. My own sense of this universe is my warrant for it. It lives in me and I feel my life through it. If any part of it becomes obscured, in so far I feel maimed and limited; with its growth I grow and with its weakness I fail. I refer to no authorities for though I have gotten what I could where I could, it is real for me because it is mine. It is autobiography, not theory, life, not speculation.

—Leo Stein.

CHAPTER I

Little Elizabeth

STILL like a bird within a glass-walled room, the spirit was desperately beating its wings against the impediments between it and freedom.

This had become a time when many people frantically tried to find salvation outside themselves. They consulted psychics and they went to all kinds of Healers and Doctors and Psychiatrists. Although Europe was at war our northern continent seemed to stand firm, yet invisibly it was sinking. Psychologically, what has been told happened to Atlantis was taking place once more and people felt it even though they did not know it. Something was breaking up and passing slowly away out of the world—a civilization was going to pieces, and this is a story of how that happened to one person; it is no more than that, and it is not a history of outward events except where they affect her life.

Within myself I felt an ever-increasing need for help of some kind and I looked for it where I could. At least I was not worried about money as were so many of my friends. But there is a peculiar sense of insecurity that finally comes to people who have money they have inherited. I had never done any work of any kind, for nothing had obliged me to and so there never seemed to be an incentive. When Reed had tried to tell me about work: "Any job has something more important in it than the job itself," he said; but whatever he was trying to tell me was incommunicable. I had no idea what he meant.

I remember he had come in one day and found me idle and unhappy and terribly bored with everything. He had just been talking with an old professor of his—George Baker. When Reed had asked him how he was, he had answered, "Oh, busy and interested."

"Busy and interested," repeated Reed, looking at me meaningly. "It seemed to me so significant. I thought of you. Why *don't* you *get busy,* Mabel?"

307

"I'm not going to *fool* myself into anything," I had replied, angrily. "Why should I *make up* a job? If there's a job for me, it will come after me. If there isn't, I'll live on my income the best way I can. Why should I *make up* work just for its own sake?"

I felt too proud to work at anything less than an *inevitable* job, though I suffered from an emptiness of living that ate into me, except when I was caught up by some vital experience.

It is my impression that this empty feeling is really the most insecure sensation known to human beings. When one is not wholly occupied by some absorbing and congenial work, or all caught up and unified by a vivid love affair, there is a dreadful frightening burden of time and space and energy deep down in one that seems to threaten one's safety. Oh! the alarming danger of a regular income, that means for many people time to think and nothing to think about!

After Miss Galvin smashed the shop window in her attack upon the Kaiser in Naples, I never saw her again. Reed had disappeared somewhere into the war zone in Europe with his new love. I was alone in my apartment for a while, until Bobby came back from Germany.

I began to wish for a baby very much. At last, it seemed, instinct needed a chance to express itself. When John was born, I had been too occupied with another kind of emotion to have any feeling left over to give to him, and all through his first years of babyhood, it was as though I had been away from him, though he was always right there. I never knew John as a baby. This thought comes back over and over and tightens upon my heart like a hand.

Now he was in Morristown School and I rarely saw him except for an occasional week-end he passed with me in New York.

I didn't feel in the mood for Evenings any more. I didn't feel like seeing anarchists or socialists or single taxers or members of the Free Speech League. Besides, they had all strangely disappeared from my life when the war broke out.

In the new, more formal, high-ceilinged apartment, although it was all in white like the one before it, and had the same glinting colored glass and French painted furniture, there was a different atmosphere about me. Perhaps I felt tired of trying to be emancipated. I don't know. I only know that I wanted my life to be very comfortable and orderly, and I longed for intimate, domestic pleasures more than ever. I wanted to feel something I had never felt and that I needed to feel:

308

the solidarity between a woman and a baby. Something I had noticed in rooms, on trains, under spreading trees, anywhere, it could happen; the relaxed, unthinking unity between a mother and a child when they are loosely clasped together—the similarity of their vibration, of their bloodstream. I began to long for this nourishing and reassuring congress. I was lonely: a lonely single unit. I had to combine, to circulate with another, so I would feel like a river again and not like a block of ice.

Not only had whole groups of people disappeared from 23 Fifth Avenue, but many individuals who had been intimate there were gone. I did not *care*. I did not miss any of them: Andrew, undergoing some mental stress out in the country, making and burning an effigy of me, as someone told me, the Lees, Reed, Steff, and others who were absent, they were blotted out of my memory.

No, the time had come to make a new pattern. The old form was broken.

I began to visit different orphan asylums and places of that kind to look for a baby to adopt, and I learned something that had not occurred to me before: there are very few healthy babies without parents. I had imagined there would be hundreds. No luck. I had almost given up. Over and over the matrons of places told me they had no good, healthy babies both of whose parents were dead. I had stipulated that because I did not want to be bothered or embarrassed later on.

Then one afternoon Albert drove me to the great dour building that housed all the different layers of Charity, and I went again to the children's floor.

"No, no babies. But there's a nice little girl. Why don't you take her?" I looked to where she pointed to a blond child seated on the floor and playing with a doll.

"I don't want a grown-up child of eight or nine years!" I exclaimed indignantly.

"But she's such a nice little thing and the people she has been with have returned her to us after keeping her a year because she isn't very good at her books." This somehow appealed to me.

"Take her home for over Sunday and see if you don't like her," the woman urged.

She was a jolly little thing with fine curly fair hair, like feathers, round, pink cheeks, very pretty blue eyes, and a turned up nose that suggested the Irish very strongly. Something in the low forehead and the way her brows hung over her eyes was a warning perhaps, but the vitality of the child, the gaiety and the sweet pink and blue and blond colors of her covered it up.

It was fun to take her to Wanamaker's and buy her some pretty clothes. A white muslin with blue ribbons, another one with pink, and socks to match, and all sorts of little drawers and petticoats; and fun to take her home to the apartment and give her a warm bath, and then to powder her, and curl her hair in ringlets.

How she danced and laughed, like a little dog scampering about after one has bathed him! I almost expected her to rub her head on the rugs and bark, for I had only given dog baths up to this time and she acted the same as they did.

It was fate for Elizabeth that Walter should be the one to whom I telephoned that afternoon.

"Come down to tea, Walter. I have something to show you."

When he stood before the fire in the white room, the little girl flung herself against him and clasped him about the knees and laughed up into his face. And Walter, with a strong predilection for Nordic blonds, laughed across her to me and nodded his head approvingly.

I don't think Walter ever knew how strongly he figured in my fantasies. Certainly he never realized what a factor he was in Elizabeth's life. The fact is, like most real women, all my life I had needed and longed for the strong man who would take the responsibility for me and my decisions. I wanted to lie back and float on the dominating decisive current of an all-knowing, all-understanding man. I had never known any such man. There had been someone in Buffalo who appeared to be that kind and in many ways he had been decisive and protective. But in the large issues he had not kept his promises or acted with real manliness; at last, I had had to discover that in crises it was he who let the women decide. So that need in me for a man who would act like a man had remained as strong as ever it had been in my childhood, and Walter seemed to be about the only person I knew that I could really look up to, which I did in my imagination. It was a small private image and it helped me along.

I did not adopt Elizabeth legally. I told them at the Charity Organization that I would take care of her and educate her. As I look back on it now, I think all I wanted was to make a picture of her. The raw human blood instinct for a baby had been defeated, for I still had nothing in my arms. I was still without the·warm lump to hold and to relax with. Elizabeth was too big. But it was fun to dress her in her white muslins and her pink and blue ribbons.

I was not happy in these days. The heaviness and the darkness were never far away. I read a great many mystical books, those by Evelyn Fitzgerald, the writings of the Saints, and Plotinus, Rudolf Steiner, Troward, and works on Rosicrucianism. Anything to help me through "the dark night" that always fell upon me when I was not either happy or unhappy over a man; for at these times I contained a vacuum and I had to struggle up through it by any means I could find. My life alternated between these extremes, and I never knew which was the more real. Certainly love made me responsive and more like the other human beings about me, yet the dissatisfactions of love, or perhaps my way of loving, always plunged me down sooner or later into the dark abyss.

There was a Christian Science Healer whose name I have forgotten, who came to me now and gave me Treatments. She was a smiling, rouged, blue-eyed woman with gray hair, and with very ornate clothes and jewels. She drove down in her car from somewhere on the upper West side of town near the great Christian Science Church.

We had no conversations at all. She arrived, smiled; I smiled, perfunctorily; she sat down, we closed our eyes and she treated me silently for perhaps twenty minutes. At the end of that time she left, after a cheerful handshake. Each time she left me lightened, the weight gone, the more usual aspects of life appearing to me in place of the gloomy and forbidding ones that haunted me before her coming.

But it did not last. Christian Science Treatments did not seem to change one. They colored one differently for a while, then the color wore off.

Of course I saw the Hapgoods all the time. They had become the most permanent friends I had. I was angry at Carl, so I did not think about him any more. I had almost forgotten Edwin, to whom, however, I was still married, and Buffalo was dim at the moment.

I think I must have been very lonely for a time, for I had lost the world again. The way we lose the world is that we open our hands, either from indifference, or because we are holding on to somebody and cannot keep everything at once, or because our vitality sinks so far down we haven't the strength to retain it. The world never gives one

311

up. It is something in oneself that gives it up. The instant one relaxes one's fingers, everything slips away: people, power, influence, or any worldly thing. There is no cohesion apart from one's own coherence. So it is that when one's virtue has gone out of one, one loses the world, and it makes one desolate and scared.

I suppose at times I was near to losing my mind altogether, since it is only in mind that objects or things have any real existence, and my hands had opened to let things slip away and my mind was empty of them. It was as though everything lost its specific gravity and sank away through me. My heart was a deep pit.

I thought of Collier who understood everything. One could talk to him of anything in the world and he would understand; he seemed to have a boundless grasp of human possibility. He was in the Smoky Mountains in Carolina and I wrote him, telling him about my strange unbalancings, my ignorance of my own nature and what happened to me, and how I felt like a foreigner among human beings. I recounted the odd sensory experiences I had had in the past, with voices, odors and sights like the evil grin I had seen in my room. I wished I could be near him to talk, for I needed help so very much, and asked if I might go to see him in the mountains, and bring Hutch, too. Alas! He wrote:

Andrews, N. C.

DEAR MABEL DODGE:

I should like very much to see the racontes of your experiences. . . . You mention Prince. He seems to me a good clinical man and a good observer, but an incompetent philosopher. Am just reading his new book *The Unconscious,* which is disappointing. He thinks in the style of a poor woodcut, not of a steel engraving (for precision) or a photogravure (for atmosphere).

Now here's something personal. I rather hope you won't come to the mountains here—not in the near future, that is. This wish, and its reasons, have just become conscious in the last three days. This is probably a correct account of it: I have been over-stimulated—cumulatively—for seven years past. Over-stimulated mentally, emotionally, and especially in psychic ways. As yet, no corresponding exhaustion has shown itself, but another effect which is good and bad at the same time—namely, a condition like that which appears in true *dipsomania,* of a susceptibility to stimulation which is out of all mathematical relation to the cause. I seem to have an original tendency, plus a deeply-impressed habit, of hypersusceptibility to stimulation. Two years ago when I came to this country, the influences—

various and sundry—so worked on me that I became entirely sleepless, and a pint of whiskey at four in the morning would only result in a lively feeling, so then I went back to New York in a hurry. The same effects, though attenuated, have appeared again. . . . Last night I rode a witch's broom over the universe, figuratively speaking, for a million years. The inrush of pleasurable feelings in the ten days past has gradually worked up into the thought-centers, and that mediocre Morton Prince book (mentioned above) has gotten a month's work (and a month's results) out of me in two days.

Well, I came here to get above or below all these whirling streams—because they can never reach a large part of Being, and because I suspect they are actually impeding a final stage of organic growth and brain-growth which is yet in store for me; and for other reasons. . . . You, Mabel Dodge, are one of the two most mentally stimulating people I know—in your case I don't fully understand the reasons as yet. . . . You see, I thought I had overcome the diathesis I have described, or that the conditions of life here would fully keep it in check, and since a kind of up-rush three or four days ago, which is increasing, I have learned that I was mistaken. . . . This is no fancy or momentary reaction, but very sure and decisive, though I can't tell how long it will hold good.

I very much want you to understand this. . . . You will, for you virtually stated the case in your letter which came yesterday. It is more complicated—has more elements—than I have stated here, but they all fall within the boundary traced above. . . .

Eh bien, this condition is a real nuisance, for it not only means (if it continues) that I can't do all the things humanly that I had hoped (this summer) but that I must curtail immensely the study I had planned to do. Of course I have known all along, in that heart-of-hearts that has to pound violently to be heeded, that I couldn't "eat the cake and have it too!"

. . . How the season rushes on! The ground is nearly as white as snow with apple-blossoms now, the nearby knoll is a fountain of green, the lilac hangs heavy, the blooming sourwood has stormed the mountains to their crest. And a thousand puffs of white are shot skyward along the foothills —the dogwood in full blossom. And the bees—their moaning is louder than Junaluska's.

April 27.   Every good wish from   JOHN COLLIER.

P.S. I have kept this a day, to see whether it held good. So far, it appears to. I am clearly in an unstable condition—and just at the rim of insomnia.

J. C.

And at the same time he wrote to Hutch:

April 26, Andrews, N. C.

DEAR HAPGOOD:

I have written to Mabel Dodge, a letter of which she will probably tell you, saying that I hope she will *not* come down here, not in the near future at least. This is to say that the reasons, though they might have been even more forcibly stated, do not apply to you. In brief, I have been increasingly over-stimulated for years past, and have come away in the hope of getting into a new sort of mental and psychic life, and had been careless enough to believe that the conditions of life here would overcome the tendency to be over-stimulated—the hyper-sensitiveness to stimulation—which underlies the mere fact of overstimulation in the past years. But I find the same susceptibility continuing, and shall have to curtail the study I had planned to do, etc. Well, Mrs. Dodge draws the mind out of one, in ways that you know, and challenges the psychic centers, and would in general counteract the placidity, dreaminess and life of the brown plowed earth which is the thing I need—perhaps critically need—now.

The above would apply to you in greatly diminished measure, if we sat around in the front yard talking, but if you came we wouldn't do that, but would go straight into the big woods, up above the mile line, where the earth-tug gets you like a whirlpool and where it is all hard work of a new kind beside. Even such surroundings wouldn't neutralize Mabel Dodge, I fear—therefore I hope she won't come. Of course I don't know that there was any real likelihood she *would* come, and I am beginning to fear there's little likelihood you *will* come, but please consider that you are more wished-for now, by both Mrs. Collier and me, than you were when we urged you in New York. I do hope Mrs. Dodge will understand —and not be puzzled or hurt.

Good wishes,

JOHN COLLIER.

So I was left battling with myself and my emptiness.

Bobby Jones came home some time in 1915. He had been studying with Reinhardt in Germany. He had hoped to be with Gordon Craig in Florence, but Craig heard he was staying with me there and wouldn't even meet him.

Bobby looked incredibly thin and ill. He had spent nearly all the funds from the Robert Edmond Jones Improvement Society on photographs and so on, instead of eating. He went into the small connecting apartment on Ninth Street and I was not so lonely, for he was amusing and full of gaiety and wonder. Whenever my mind was a

314

little bit entertained, I felt life lighten, for I suppose I suffered from what has been called boredom. I called it the sense of futility, for it seemed as though I could see through things and know that in themselves they were not worth while.

Bobby made me forget this sometimes. He was so young-minded, so full of fantasy, and so in love with the theater. (How *could* he be in love with the *theater,* I asked myself.) He loved colors and materials and liked to handle them. He had long hair now, and perhaps to balance his square, solid brow, he had quite a long beard such as one sees on Jesus Christ in a certain type of painting. He posed a good deal— to himself as well as to others; he did not have any individuality of his own yet so he borrowed one, but his vitality bubbled up in ecstasy and enthusiasm. I had little of this at the moment so I borrowed his. In this way we are all vampires sometimes. I really dipped into Bobby's pool of life and drank.

He attached himself to me and I became his mother. We used to go out to the Hapgoods' sometimes to spend the night, for they still had that rather dreary but ample environment at Dobbs Ferry where Neith drifted slowly in and out of the large rooms. She set the table and helped the small, Italian cook with the dinner. We had red wine and were half conscious of the draft at our backs and around our legs, for there was so little furniture to consume the space.

Hutch sat at the end of the table forever conscious of Neith. He boomed his philosophical *bon mots* and looked to her for applause, but she was always meager in her responses, scarcely lifting her eyes from her plate. A kind of spiritual shyness or self-defense prevented her from exposing herself to Hutch. She would steal sly glances at Bobby or at me, though, and close both green eyes in a slow, jocular wink. There was something very inimical and cold to her husband in this aside, or to something in him that she needed to be aware of. She seemed to be always on the defensive. He continued to assault her. All through their married life it has been so. And still is so.

At the table—that island under the hanging light in the center of the large, empty dining room—there sat the four children, slowly taking on the characteristics, or their opposites, of their queerly assorted parents. The children listened to Hutch delivering philosophical paradoxes to Neith across the table—half veiled innuendoes that were trying to lay her out and failing, sliding off her guarded front, unable to find an opening. Charles looked sympathetically at his father, though not understanding why he felt this sympathy. His gold-rimmed spectacles reflected the light but not the heat of his father. Boyce looked faintly disgusted sometimes and went up to his room as soon as dinner was over where his Wild West things from Sears Roebuck fed him his delight.

The two little girls, Miriam and Beatrix, were very dissimilar. Miriam was a pale, blond child, weedy and delicate. There was some dissatisfaction in her that sometimes turned her face querulous and gave her a whine. Exquisitely made, fine throughout, a pastel in quality —it only needed some kind of spiritual therapy to bring her into tune and harmonize her. Only!

Beatrix, on the other hand, was without a dark tone or a psychic blemish. She was sunny all the time: an imp with honey-colored curls and eyes and very delicately repeating the somewhat prognathous jaw of her father. Slim as a willow wand and dancing on tiptoe. This child, however, had a physical handicap, a tubercular gland in her neck that had to be endlessly cared for. Sunbaths, rest, milk.

I think Miriam was her father's favorite girl. It always seemed to me that he felt an affinity with her indefinable discontent, and he constantly yearned over her. But Neith loved Trixie best. She seemed to have no soul to bother about!

And so they dwelt together, producing for each other what Hutch called "the savage joys of family life!" and Bobby and I used to go out and stay with this thing called a family at Dobbs Ferry quite often. After supper Neith would lie on the couch in the corner of the living room with her eyes closed as though she had earned her recess. She continually separated herself completely in this way from her surroundings. After giving them something they needed, she would go quite away and leave them by closing her eyes. On some evenings she would sink away from them until bedtime. This used to make Hutch wild, for he wanted a continuity in his predicament and one of his favorite phrases was Pater's about "burning forever with a hard, gem-like flame." But he had to let her go. He knew if he persisted too far she would frown suddenly and her green eyes would glare quite fiercely at him. She evidently had to go away into her depths and preserve herself.

One night out there I was awakened by the tall specter of Bobby at my bedside.

"Mabel," he murmured in a low voice, not to disturb the others sleeping all around us in the large, square upper story, "I've got an awful pain, an awful stomach-ache!"

"Well, go and tie a wet towel around it!" is what Bobby *says* I answered him, when he tells the story now. But I think it was not quite so inadequate as that, though I forget. Anyway, in the morning we are motoring back to New York in the open touring car and Albert is, of course, driving us, and Bobby is hanging over the side of it, vomiting with terrible nausea.

As soon as we reached 23 Fifth Avenue, I sent for Dr. Harry Lorber, and he rushed Bobby to the hospital in an ambulance. Appendicitis—and perhaps it is too late. Perhaps it has ruptured.

I felt terribly. I felt all the responsibility for it. I should have done something for him the night before, but I hadn't known what to do. What if he should die?

They were to operate the moment he reached the hospital—at that very instant, as I sat in the white room by the fire, perhaps they were even then cutting him open. I closed my eyes and with all my power I sent my life to Bobby to save him. All my unused, waiting power I directed over to him where he lay in the hospital—and with complete concentration I lodged myself, my force, my living spark, in him to reinforce him.

I felt myself sitting on the chair in my room with my energy streaming out of me. Like ribbons of fire it rushed from me with terrific velocity—a flow unchained and undiminished by flowing. I felt it going directly to Bobby and entering him for about fifteen minutes. Then it ceased and I knew it was all right with him. This was a strange new experience and very real.

I drove to the hospital, but he was still under the anesthetic. Dr. Lorber said: "At first I thought we had lost him, but he rallied."

I waited until he was conscious and they let me go in to see him, and when I came up to him, he opened his eyes and smiled and made a movement of his hand to me to bend down to him.

"I thought I was dying," he said, "and I didn't want to. Then I felt you coming to me. I felt you streaming into me like strong ribbons of energy, helping me. And that saved me."

317

I nodded. I knew it was true. Afterwards, when he came back to convalesce in the apartment, we talked it all over many times and we were filled with wonder. He said I had created him, that I was his real mother; and there seemed to be, truly, a psychic bond between us.

GERTRUDE STEIN AND ALICE TOKLAS

Goldberg

HUTCH

Goldberg

LINCOLN STEFFENS

WALTER LIPPMANN

Goldberg

Goldberg

JOHN REED

Goldberg

ANDREW DASBURG

MAURICE STERNE

Genthe 1915

ISADORA DUNCAN

ELIZABETH DUNCAN

MAX EASTMAN

DR. BRILL

JOHN AT PROVINCETOWN

Goldberg

LEO STEIN

Goldberg

BAYARD BOYESEN

Goldberg

BOBBY JONES

CHAPTER II

Isadora Duncan

BEFORE Bobby came back from Germany I was living almost alone, then, in the early winter of 1915, for one could not count little Elizabeth, my new acquisition, as a companion.

After some weeks of suffering I had reached a balance of some kind, and apparently to belong to myself was good for me. It seemed to me now I could feel my roots reaching down to the center of the earth where they fed richly. When Ducie Haweis wrote me from Florence after she went to live with the tempestuous Marinetti: "I feel uprooted and as though I were lost," I answered her: "You cannot be uprooted for your roots are in the universe"; and this was something I had lately learned.

So I felt, and forgot I had ever felt otherwise. The moment has always been everything with me—with no past and no future. If it is a good moment, all is well forever. If it is a bad one, everything is lost and there is no hope.

This, then, was a good moment. I felt strong, serene, and self-possessed. I could close my eyes at night and get in contact with a vast responsive force that seemed to wait there for me at the center of being, of my being. I called this Nature. Nature rose in me, filling and enhancing me.

This was a very fine moment in life. I was not aware that, loosed from Reed, my powers ebbed back into my own reservoir and fed me where before they had been feeding him, and perhaps, too strong for him, had been poisoning him so he had needed to save himself from me. Anyway I was agreeing with myself! I felt wonderful—adequate. . . .

I went to see Isadora dance with her young girls and the mass of little children she had brought from Russia. It seemed to me I recognized what she did in the dance, and that it was like my own daily, nightly return to the Source. Power rose in her from her Center and flowed vividly along her limbs before our eyes in living beauty and delight. We saw a miracle happen before us when Isadora stood there, passive, and Pure Being incarnated itself in her.

This was not something special to her and a solitary flowering. It was based upon a principle, not upon a personality. It was a way of life that she said could be learned. She said that, from the stage. She said she wanted to teach all the children of America how to be, how to move, how to walk and run. She said she called it dancing, but it was *being* that she wanted to teach. She asked for a Place to teach in, a large Place—and then for children.

She seemed to be hungry for children—many children—since her own two had drowned in the Seine. I saw her arms reach out with an expression of hunger in them when she talked to the great audience in Carnegie Hall, and asked for a thousand little poor children to teach, and I wondered what fatal mistake she had made in her life that had swept that automobile out of control, to go plunging into dark waters. Somewhere the hand had faltered . . . her hand, her beautiful hand dripping essence of life, had lost its magic and turned deathly, dealing herself her own death-blow.

And now she went hungry until she could be filled again with other children—other limbs and bodies—hundreds—thousands—she needed to fill her and satisfy that implacable craving. . . . So there she stood on the bleak Carnegie stage asking for a Place to teach in, and children to teach.

There was a candor on her brow, a purity one seldom sees. The fire she knew how to release in her blood, traveling along her body, burned her clean and clear. No one could look so chaste and new as Isadora, washed in her own fine energy. This, then, I thought, is what genius is . . . it is knowing how to release the energy in one's atoms and then the flesh is born again.

And anyone can do this—it may be taught—and Isadora wanted to teach it. One idea we had was to try to arrange to have Isadora dance in the Harvard Stadium at Cambridge and perhaps in the Yale Bowl, with a crowd of little children, and Walter was going to help with this. Bobby Rogers tried to discourage us and he sent me this poem which I relayed to Walter:

Dear Mabel, while you're able
I beg you to retreat,
'Twill put you out without a doubt
To carry out this feat;
For just to rent the Stadium
Would be like buying radium,
And the old Yale Bowl is an awful hole
For dancing children's feet,

I think 'twould be much jollier
To pass it on to Collier,
Or maybe Hutch would like so much
To do what you require;
If Mr. Luther Gulix
Can't muster the spondulix,
Just put your bets
On Herman Metz
Or Mrs. Untermeyer.

There's one more thing I'd mention
And call to your attention,
Mayor Curley is a terror
Whom nothing classic suits;
He doesn't care for artists—well,
Who prance around *au naturel,*
They must be dressed, from coat and vest
To overshoes and boots!

He'd think it quite deplorable,
However Isadorable,
To see a thousand kiddies
Cutting up like ancient Greeks,
And all of Boston's Hoi Polloi
Would make the welkin ring with joy,
To see him go
And pinch the show
Despite the Duncan's shrieks.

I do not want to be grotesque,
But sane and calm and Lippmannesque,
And so this verse
Breathes—not a curse,

But my most earnest prayers:
For (though I won't make any row)
What *is* a Dora anyhow
That she should keep
You from your sleep
To manage her affairs?

R. E. R.

I want this back by return mail.

M. D.

Let's go on in spite of him. Curley is not Mayor of Cambridge and could not interfere.

W. L.

But it fell through, somehow, and we tried to think of something else for her.

Several of us conferred together. John Collier was the one who knew how to "organize" things, how to get things done in cities, and it was decided that the Mayor, young Mitchel, must be brought to see Isadora in the "Ark," and she must ask him for an Armory to teach in.

She had taken, in a business building, a sort of loft that she hung with her vast blue curtains the color of robins' eggs, and there, with her young girls, and all the little Russian children she had brought with her from Europe, she made a life for herself. I had never been there, but many of my friends had, and told me about it, Max Eastman, Percy MacKaye, Mitchell Kennerley, and Arnold Genthe among them. She called this refuge of hers the Ark!

Isadora came to my apartment to talk over the matter of an Armory. She lay on the French *chaise longue* and the room grew different. There was something frightening about her actual presence in a place; the vibrations became loosened up, broader, more incalculable. She made one nervous. Anything might happen. Percy MacKaye, gaunt, with long, unruly hair, leaned over her and his eye was like a cock's, swiveling in the side of his head beside his long, beaky nose. He was always excited, not, one realized, in his blood, but in his brain. Enthusiasm galvanized him. He continually saw things were *wonderful, marvelous!* Dear Marion, his gray-haired wife, saw to it that he ate and slept, otherwise there was no telling how he would have fared. He had the poet's frenzy and he often brought out a "slender vol."

Percy leaned over Isadora and she looked amused, though languid,

322

and slightly contemptuous. She had not enough mentality to estimate correctly the value of anyone's poetry, but the instinct of her blood could always report to her the degree of a man's virility. She seemed vigorous and alive alongside Percy and made him appear febrile, and I was not comfortable with her. She made me feel disorganized.

I do not remember that much was said that day about Isadora's need for an Armory, but we had promised her she should have one and we went about the business of securing it for her, or rather of giving her the opportunity of getting it for herself.

How carefully we planned it! I got Walter interested in it because I knew he would give "cachet" to the event and we invited several "eminent" men to come to make it appear more significant to the Mayor. Collier was to bring him at four o'clock, and Isadora was to do the rest.

John Collier still worked at the People's Institute a little way above me on Fifth Avenue and 13th Street. Have I told how he looked then? He was a small, blond Southerner, intense, preoccupied, and always looking wind-blown on the quietest day. Because he could not seem to love his own kind of people, and as he was full of a reformer's enthusiasm for humanity, he turned to other races and worked for them.

He still had that job of trying to preserve the flavors of other nationalities when they came to New York. Singly, he tried to stem the ponderous tide of Americanization. He worked indefatigably; with committees and sub-committees he strove by means of pageants, parades and prizes, to persuade Italians, Russians, Germans and all the others, to keep their national dress, their customs, their diets, their religions, and all their folk ways. Breathless, his green eyes burning, he dashed about looking like a Blake drawing drawn by Peter Newell.

One of the things he did, too, was to organize a kind of Exchange among the poor, whereby an old piano might be traded for a hand-cart, and so on, according to people's varying needs. His drawback was that he seemed to be all in the air, wind-blown, as I have said, and not down on the solid ground. Yet he was very useful helping to get things done, for he had close contact with the political city machinery. I have told how we first turned to him to help us find Genevieve Onslow when she rushed out of my apartment the night we made the experiment with *peyote*.

Walter and I, and Walter's inseparable companion, Alfred Kuttner, arrived at the Ark a little before four o'clock. The place was large and dim and romantic-looking, with a few shaded lamps burning. It was a contrast to the hard, bright city streets we had left, and Isadora in a flowing Greek dress, ample and at ease, made us look and feel dingy and utilitarian. Particularly the men, as they stood beside her, appeared stupid, inexpressive and as though cut out of wood, there was such a radiance about her compared with other mortals.

I felt myself to be inferior, gauche, and graceless, but forcing a bright, self-possessed smile, I introduced the men I had brought with me. I could see Isadora appraising them as she glanced over them. Others came forward: Augustin Duncan, with his round, candid forehead and tip-tilted Irish nose, Marguerite Duncan, his wife, a tall, adequately Grecian type with pale gold hair and flowing draperies, and some of her young girls: Anna, Liza, Teresa, Irma. . . . There were six of them and Isadora had given them all the name of Duncan. They called her brother "Uncle Gus." They were lovely, with bodies like cream and roses, and faces unreal with beauty whose eyes were blind like statues, as though they had never looked upon anything in any way sordid or ordinary.

The glamorous way Isadora herself saw life was immediately apparent all about her. She was able to project her vision upon the ether, and others, then, saw as she did. These girls, one realized, shared her conception of life and the dingy loft, hung with tall blue curtains and lighted softly with pale lamps, was for them all a temple of Beauty and Art and they were Priestesses. Whatever they did was sanctified in their own eyes by the way they saw it, and awkwardness and ugliness were their only taboos.

There were several extremely large, low couches with great piles of pale cushions, grouped about a couch larger than the others, and there was a great black piano with candles burning on it. The plan that had been arranged was that Isadora's young girls and some of the little children, whom we presently saw in groups in distant corners all in pale blue melting into the folds of curtains, should dance for Mayor Mitchel and show him what she had taught the little Russian proletariat, and then ask him for an Armory in which to teach our own young proletarians from the East Side. She had promised to teach them for nothing in exchange for having the Armory to do her other work in.

We stood, in our own darkness, waiting, and speaking in subdued voices. It was difficult to feel oneself either good, or beautiful, or even true in these surroundings. I saw Alfred Kuttner's pale eyes darting, behind his unaesthetic eyeglasses, unable to come to rest. The Buddha-like curves of Walter's face had the heightened lights they took on when he was exhilarated and amused. His slightly exophthalmic eyes bulged and shone. He generally managed to wear his dark serges with a certain distinction and he did on this day. His clothes looked elegant and clear cut, but having the significance of another world than this one he was in.

I felt myself to be shorter and more square than I had ever been in my life before, and my gloves suddenly ceased to fit my hands. As we realized, in those first few moments of our arrival, that the "Ark" was really not meant to perpetuate *our* species, so, I imagine, was the feeling that swept over our young Catholic Mayor as Collier ushered him into the place.

He stood for an instant, hat in hand, near the door, quite a large space between him and Isadora's group and us. He was tall and thin and he had a nervous Irish face that looked deprecating, as Collier, with his singular way of reaching across space with his whole body, seemed to span the gulf between them and Isadora with his announcement:

"*This* is Mayor Mitchel. . . ."

Isadora started. She gazed. . . . All of her, with almost terrible expressiveness, revealed her classic disdain for everything physically meager or insufficient. She was disappointed. One saw distinctly that, to her vision, the play was improperly cast. The beautiful girls behind her reflected her aloof and arrogant rejection; secure in beauty themselves, they gazed coldly at the spindling young man. He looked plain and miserable.

However, Isadora, recovering in a flash, made a noble gesture of resignation, large, magnanimous, and charitable. She swept forward, her dress fluttering out behind her, with shining, candid brow and outstretched hands.

"Why," she exclaimed, "I thought you would be an old, old man with a long, white beard!"

325

Venerable, so she had imagined this ruler would be, something like Jove, perhaps. Mayor Mitchel bowed jerkily; with one hand he gave a pull to his mouth and chin, and held his hat against his stomach with the other.

Isadora reached out and seized his free hand in both hers and pressed a piece of paper into it. The Mayor looked horrified and gazed down at it in acute bewilderment. Who can tell what went through his mind? Collier secured the scrap after they got outside, to find that she had written on it Plato's remark about when philosophers would be Kings and Kings philosophers, this world would be better off. . . . Just a hint, perhaps, that she had intended to convey!

Still grasping his hand and holding it in both her own pressed against her warm body, while her arm covered his black, official sleeve, she led him to the large, central couch, which, really, suddenly appeared throne-like with its massed orange cushions banked high, and flanked on either side with lesser ones, where the girls and the other Duncans drifted and disposed themselves in exquisite groups—Greek vase and frieze profanely living.

I suppose the Mayor, confused as he was, realized Isadora's intention to enthrone him beside her on the orange dais and saved himself just in time, for, before she could draw him down beside her, goddess-like, and compel him to some god-like attitude, he broke away from her gentle hold, as a little boy will twitch himself out of the grasp of his mother, and, looking somewhat wildly about him, made a dash for the piano stool. That appeared to him, apparently, the only austerely congenial seat in the place. The stool gave a swift turn as he struck it, nearly upsetting him, but he laid hold of the piano and steadied himself, still holding his derby hat protectingly against his solar plexus.

We got ourselves seated somehow on those divans. Collier was the least self-conscious of us all and leaned back almost reclining, feet crossed, shoes muddy, ashes dropping from his cigarette onto the silken covers. He searched the corner of the ceiling with meditative eyes, seeking solutions to things, oblivious of himself and everyone else.

I was unpleasantly able, as usual, to feel the various incongruities and I saw at once that Walter did not look well on that couch. Had he seated himself crosslegged and wrapped a shawl about him, one of the many soft, careless-lying shawls about the place, he would perhaps have looked like a young Buddha. But our life, our bringing up, our kind of self-consciousness prevented him from such ease and adaptability. No, he must sit there on that low seat, bolt upright, his clothes creased in the wrong places, looking ungainly and uncomfortable, losing in authority, though apparently not in humor, as I noticed, for his eyes kept on twinkling.

Isadora left the Mayor to the piano stool for the moment. She would not *force* him to lie beside her on the couch, she said with her speaking shoulders and brows, as she sank, with movements like falling water, down to the cushions. The little children came running out of the corners of the room and sat all about the couch on the floor at her feet.

I wished that she would get to the real reason quickly now that we were there; that she would lose no more time; that she would do her stuff so that we would be justified. We were all waiting now, for something to happen. Well, it did.

Isadora suddenly drew herself up on one elbow and looked intently and accusingly at the young man on the piano stool.

"Mayor!" she cried in a ringing voice, "why don't you release that poor woman you have in prison for murdering her children?"

Oh, Medes and Persians! Could anything more unfortunate have been conceived? Mrs. Snippen had been convicted of the deaths of her several children; she was locked in the Tombs. It had been a singularly horrible crime and any mayor would have felt it a blot upon his term of office. She had been tried, convicted, imprisoned. What a subject at what a moment! The Mayor stiffened and stared. These matters were not to be discussed with ladies at afternoon teas (for so, no doubt, he considered the situation he found himself in). He stared, helpless, unable to deal with her, but Isadora went on:

"How do you suppose she feels shut up there? How can *anyone* be certain she did it? How can anyone believe a mother would or could kill her children? That poor creature! I have wanted to go to her and sit beside her. . . ." She covered her eyes with one hand. She became Niobe.

The Mayor coughed nervously and looked annoyed. This was too much, he was thinking. He glanced sideways, appealingly, at Lippmann, at Collier. Collier came back to us.

"That matter is not within the province of Mayor Mitchel," he explained, kindly. "Now, I have told the Mayor something of your methods of teaching. He would be interested, I think, if you could show him some of them."

"Oh, my methods of teaching are probably very different from anything *he* has ever known!" Isadora exclaimed rather truculently, throwing a disparaging look at the Mayor's spare form. She gave a sweep of her hand towards the girls who lay like nymphs on either side of her and towards the children who sat on the floor at her feet, their flower faces turned up towards her as to the sun.

"*These* children have always had a *beautiful* life," she cried. "Look at them! *They* don't have to get up in the morning and go down to breakfast with their cross fathers and mothers! *They* don't have to go to school with horrid dirty school books in satchels! *They* don't have to go to church on Sunday and listen to stuffy old men in ugly buildings!"

A wave of consternation swept right through our party uniting us, and Isadora's protégées glowed all together in their accord with her. On Gus Duncan's face I caught a glimpse of distress from his mingled thoughts. He agreed with his sister's ideas, yet he could see and understand how these men felt at her words. Marguerite Duncan was looking quite worried and came and sat beside Isadora, who was off on her great theme. Nothing on earth could have stopped her now.

"*They* live in beauty," she went on. "Music and art and poetry. Great poets come and read their verses to them. For as long as they last, that is, in this terrible American life! The last time I was here I had three poets. I went away and now when I come back they are all gone. . . . Gone! One is dead, one has gone crazy, and one is married. . . . But others appear . . .

"The greatest musicians come and play for these children, and the children dance for them and inspire them. Painters, sculptors, come and get life from them and teach them in return what they know. *That* is education. Living education." She was certainly living herself as she flung these words at our young Catholic Mayor. She glowed and burned, her dark hair flowing off in crisp waves from her righteous white brow. Her dress slipped from her shoulder and showed her breast.

The poor young man was all at a loss. Anything to bring this terrible thing to an end so he could get away and never come back—get away to join his wife, as he had promised, at five o'clock to dance at the Plaza Hotel.

"I hoped we would see something of your work," he suggested, timidly. That was what had been promised him. She would show her pupils' "work" and then she would ask for the use of an Armory and he would tell her he would see what he could do, and it would be over—a short half-hour on his way uptown.

But this!

Isadora had either forgotten what the Mayor was there for, had forgotten the Armory and the thousand little poor children she wanted to teach in it and that she must ask him for it, or else she had revolted too far away from him and all he represented. Perhaps he did not seem real at all to her. Anyway, she threw away her chance.

"Oh," she answered, coldly, "I do not think the children feel like dancing this afternoon!"

In no time at all he was up and gone from there, Collier shepherding him out, and Isadora was stretching herself with a lazy long reach and laughing softly.

"Come, let us rest and drink wine and forget that young man. How could New York be other than it is with a ruler like that?—Marguerite, can you fetch us some white wine? And we will go into the inner room, for the children must practice here now."

She took my hand with a loving look and reached out to the others —to Percy and Lippmann and Kuttner, and swept us all to an anteroom, smaller, more intimate, where there were other couches, a dressing table draped in a glittering Egyptian scarf, and here again we tried to dispose ourselves as best we might.

Marguerite Duncan brought a decanter of white wine and some biscuits and Isadora lay back and seemed perfectly happy. She went on, almost in a monologue, for we were all dumb and had nothing to say.

"But this is a terrible city! Do you know what happened here the other night? Why, it seems your people have no feeling for beauty at *all!* We had been having some wonderful hours . . . music, dancing. . . . The others had all gone except Count von Dernburg, the German emissary, you know." (She explained as though probably no one there had ever heard of him.) "He was lying beside me on this couch drinking this same yellow wine, and a beautiful blond woman was lying on his other side," she said, looking roguishly at Marguerite, who maintained a face like a mask.

"Suddenly we heard a loud knocking on this door which leads out to the hall-way. I jumped up and ran to open it. I was frightened and thought maybe it was fire. . . . But what do you think? Two police-men stood there. They looked very disagreeable and tried to poke their heads in and look around, but I stood before them and asked them what they wanted.

" 'We want to know what kind of a place this is, anyway,' one of them said.

" 'Place?' I answered. 'Why, what business is that of yours?'

" 'Well, what goes on here?'

" 'Goes on? How do you mean?' I asked.

" 'Well, what do you *do* here? What kind of business do you carry on?' He sounded worse and more rough all the time. Dernburg just lay there and blinked! He never tried to help me with those bar-barians!

" 'Why, we dance here,' I told him. 'We dance—and sing and read poetry and try to bring some Beauty into life.' Then the other police-man, who hadn't said anything, nudged the first one.

" 'Summons her,' I heard him say. Suddenly I had an idea. No wonder they were cross. What a life! Having to go around all night looking into people's lives. Hateful. Probably they were hungry and thirsty. I took some money from my table and pressed some bills into their hands.

" 'There, go and get a nice supper somewhere and some good Ger-man beer. I know how you must hate what you're doing.' They looked at the money and one of them said:

" 'Well, see you don't make too much noise,' and they went off down the stairs. Wasn't that quaint? Noise!"

At this point Walter, who had drunk the wine, got up and put down his glass and took his watch out of his pocket. The classic protection of modern men!

"I'm afraid I'll have to go on," he murmured with a decided look appearing around his jaw. We all went out together through the door where the policemen had thumped, and as we went down the stairs, Walter exclaimed:

"She ought to be repressed! If she had told that story before certain

330

other people, with Dernburg over here on the mission he is on, it would ruin him!"

The traffic seemed to belong to a different world than the one we had left. Everything was different. How was it possible that such different lives could exist one within the other?

"It is evidently impossible to do anything either for or with Isadora," said Collier, pedantically, when I talked to him about it afterwards. "I'm afraid Mitchel won't forget that afternoon for some time."

Neither would any of us, I thought. What was there about her that was so upsetting and disturbing? She herself was serene enough, but she set curious forces loose about her, flowing up and out through her flesh. She was a channel for great powers—she had opened a passage for them by her indefatigable exercises and unending work, for she had always been a great worker. But one couldn't do anything with her or for her, or fit her in. *Intransigeante!*

Afterwards, Walter wrote:

Harvard Club,
Jan. 26.

DEAR MABEL,

I'm utterly disgusted. If this is Greece and Joy and the Aegean Isles and the Influence of Music, I don't want anything to do with it. It's a nasty, absurd mess, and she is obviously the last person who ought to be running a school. I want you to let me off the committee; you can tell the others I'm too busy.

I went into this because like a damn fool I deluded myself into thinking that we could have one spot of freedom and beauty. I should have known better. Those spots exist only in the imagination we weave about performers like Miss Duncan. I should have known better than to be dazzled into a short cut to perfection—there are none, and Isadora is not the person to show the way.

Please don't show this letter to anyone. Just let me slip out as quickly as I can. And some day soon take me again to see the children dance.

Yours,
W. L.

CHAPTER III

Elizabeth Duncan

A DIFFERENT story, and yet much the same! All the Duncans lived in imaginary worlds, each one different from the others, only resembling each other in a common fantasy: their idea of the Greek life. They had been "set" in this form by their mother in their earliest days back in San Francisco and every one of them held to it. It was far more real to them than everyday life.

Elizabeth has talked to me by the hour, telling about their evenings when they were children in their home where they had so little comfort. After working all day, the mother playing a piano for Elizabeth who was giving the dancing lessons that her mother had taught her, Gus selling newspapers, little brother Raymond delivering parcels for one of the shops . . . and Isadora . . . I cannot remember that she did anything then to help—unless she was helping Elizabeth to give dancing lessons, too. They gathered around the oil lamp after supper and their mother used to read out loud to them from the *Iliad* and the *Odyssey*. The gods were more familiar to them than the San Franciscans. Their daily life was barren, dreary, and without any of the fun that ordinary children have.

"Pa" Duncan was either not there at all, or was so useless as not to count. I cannot remember what I was told about him. But of "Ma" Duncan I have a very close picture. That tall, strong, Irish woman made her children. She fed their imaginations with the lives and stories of gods and goddesses, and in contrast with what they saw around them, these lives were definitely more attractive than the lives people lived in San Francisco, so Greece became a Mecca to them.

I think Isadora was fifteen or sixteen and Elizabeth a little older when they were finally able to start upon the memorable pilgrimage that none of them ever forgot. They set off and sailed for Greece and the gods; and since those days, only Gus Duncan, of all four of them,

332

has capitulated to modern dress. Gus wears a frock coat and trousers. (Perhaps his blindness has come upon him so that he need not see them!) But "Little Brother Raymond" has always gone on wearing toga and sandals and weaving silks and wools! Elizabeth is comfortable in soft draperies and glove-like shoes; Isadora was always dressed like an antique statue.

After my disappointment over her when I found one couldn't do anything with her, I had not gone near Isadora again. I went to see her dance whenever she appeared because she seemed to me, when she was on the stage, to be the most truly living being I had ever seen. There she made one live too, made one know more deeply and vividly the splendid and terrible potentialities one bore within oneself. There on the stage she seemed to be disposed to control and direct her essence, submitting it to form and limitation, so that it became a movingly living art; she did not shatter one as she seemed to do when one was with her in a room. She was creative instead of disintegrating.

I have seen her do a maenad's dance in *Eurydice* when her hair seemed to turn into coiling serpents, and her eyes turned inwards and her fingers changed into long, cactus-like projections, and the cataclysmic violence of the demon struck up through her, appearing to rend her cell from cell. And this life she let loose up through her body was not good or bad but merely undifferentiated and voluminous.

Yet the spectacle of this marvel, the participation in it that one experienced as a spectator, was never disintegrating: it was a strong catharsis, a release to one's own burden of buried life. I have wondered since if it was not because when she was on the stage she was wholly conscious of herself and what she was doing, while in real life, in a room, she seemed to be unconscious, undirected, her being at large. Perhaps there is nothing in the world so dangerous as wandering human energies.

Elizabeth Duncan marched into my sitting room one early spring day, sent to me by the ubiquitous Collier. She was a vivid spark of life with her little body erect and prim in a long, burnt-orange velvet cloak trimmed with red fox fur, and a bristling red fox turban on her head. Her bright brown eyes were sparkling and witty, her nose uptilted like Gus's; her lips were thin and stretched rather tight over teeth. She had ever so slightly the projecting jawbone of a goat, and sometimes when she was meditative, she would chew a blade of grass or a rose petal with a rotary movement. This kind of mouth I have come to recognize as Irish.

Behind Elizabeth was the eager face of Max Merz! Oh, how much we suffered from that pale-eyed Austrian and his stubbornness. He was delicate and graceful and clad in a morning coat and striped trousers—quite chic. He was the manager of "The Elizabeth Duncan School" lately escaped from Darmstadt.

How she ever managed it, we never knew. Her tales were fabulous. No Duncan could tell the truth if it was truth to tell about ways and means. Somehow, she, seeing the European world totter, had gathered her brood and carried them across a world of enemies. Six little German children and their Austrian director, across France, into England, and over to New York without any very great difficulty, just by faith and a certain childlike directness.

"It had to be done." That is all she said. She had no money, no place to live, nothing to eat. They had been given passage across the water, but they had no funds to go on with. What did Elizabeth want? She wanted to teach—just as Isadora did. All the Duncans wanted to teach. They had a vision and they wanted to tell it.

Elizabeth was a great teacher. She had taught Isadora from the time she was a child. Hour after hour she sat and coached her in the long past days, while their Ma played accompaniments on the piano. Then, when she thought Isadora was able to dance and to bring to life the movements on the Greek vases and the sculptures they studied so diligently, she went out and got engagements for her to dance in San Francisco in some of the great houses. When they made a little money, they came to New York together and got a few engagements to dance at parties in private houses. The first time Isadora danced publicly out-of-doors was at a garden party at Wheatleigh in Lenox that Aunt Georgia gave.

When Isadora began to dance professionally on public stages, she used to say she could do nothing unless Elizabeth sat close to her in the wings of the theater. It seemed that Elizabeth drew her dancing power up out of her. She danced, then, to Elizabeth in the early days of her career. Later, she learned how to summon it at her own will and she drew away from Elizabeth and her more austere life. Still later, she lost this power to evoke the genius in herself, after she learned to drink champagne too freely. Calling it Dionysian to quaff great

334

goblets of wine did not lessen its evil influence upon her. The day came when sometimes all her calling and willing could not rouse the drugged spirit in her, and her audiences booed her from the stage . . . and she staggered off, foolishly lost. It was heart-breaking. No one could stop her or control her, ever, after she tore herself away from her sister's influence. No, one just couldn't do anything for Isadora.

After her children were drowned, she seemed to go rapidly further and further away from reality—or what most people call reality. In her book, she calls it fate—a dark fate, but fate or not, her hold on consciousness was broken. What an agony it must have been to be her lover as Paris Singer was for so long. They had some happy times when the children, his and Gordon Craig's, were alive, for Isadora always had a curious domestic side that liked to picture them all living like a family in a Golden Age—the golden-bearded father, the long-limbed, dancing mother, and the little god and goddess making lovely pictures all together. And he loved them all tenderly and wanted to make them happy. He took them on a journey to Greece on his yacht—Elizabeth went, too—he entered into the Duncan dream of antique beauty and tried to realize it for them. But something broke it all in pieces—real life was too much for Isadora.

Elizabeth told me how he threw himself on the bier in Isadora's house when the children lay there together. "I loved them both the same," he sobbed.

Well, that really was the end of Isadora. It was mostly torment after that, and slipping, and sliding, with her best hours only during hard work and her dancing, though she tried in every way to be happy. Lovers—lovers—and wine—with nothing allaying that hunger and thirst in her, and no way of understanding it, no realization. Every year less consciousness—and with a vitality and a vigor that remained undrained. Like all tragedies, Isadora's came from not knowing.

Elizabeth, now, for all the Duncan fantasy, was very shrewd. She was cool, humorous, unprincipled, and calculating. But she was adorable. She had a marvelous quality. She, too, could transport one to another world where everything was blithe and lovely—a young world of childlike gaiety and whimsey.

What she wanted to teach was a happy thing. "I don't teach *dancing,*" she also told me. "My teaching is a way of living."

I recognized then that Isadora had been quoting Elizabeth in her speeches to audiences, but she had not understood what she meant. Her body had been a mouthpiece for Elizabeth, but her mind had never known, quite, what her body said.

Of course now I turned to give Elizabeth the attention I had wanted to give Isadora.

Elizabeth came frequently to the apartment. She became for me one of the few great women friends I have had at intervals during my life. I have had many companions and acquaintances among women, but only four or five wonderful combinations entirely amusing and congenial and worth all men put together. Three of these were Irish women, and they all had an instantaneous perception of the life going on around them, and a humorous and zestful bite upon trifling things, extracting the utmost flavor and fun and fancy out of nothings.

Women like these put the value and significance into the passing moment for people like myself, who, when alone, sink into the immobile trance. We can, in their company, appreciate and estimate the taste of wine which, if we drank it alone, would be merely a possible stimulant and not always even that.

As I write these words, I have a memory of Elizabeth sitting crosslegged with her soft, white handwoven wool dress of Greek draperies all heaped about her, sipping a minute glass of schnapps, and smacking her thin lips. She had a long upper lip, sagacious like a nanny goat, and the bright, haughty eye of that creature. She held herself very erect, her head back so that her small chin ran right along the line of her throat. She must have always been conscious of the tendons that held up her little round, smooth head, with its delicate band of white gauze pinning her brown hair close.

Elizabeth sat and smacked her lips at each taste of liquor, and whoever was with her was made to realize the savor of it in their own mouths, and so went deeper into flavor and savor and experienced for themselves somewhat of her enjoyment. Isadora drank thirstily to still a craving, but Elizabeth tasted. Everyone, I suppose, falls into one or other of these two kinds of drinkers, just as, with food, people are divided into those who like to chew and those who like better to swallow. For myself, I love to swallow. I want it slipping down my throat.

Isadora heard Elizabeth and I had become friends, and she resented it. The Duncans were a clan who were indivisible in the spirit, but

336

who, upon the stage of the world, strove to wangle the prizes away from each other. Though all four of them were loyal to the early Greek imprint, and though they were all single-mindedly sacrificing everything that, no matter how alluring, did not conform to their need to restore, by fair means or foul, that pure, uncompromising Beauty known once to this world and lost—yet no one of them hesitated to grab at what one of the others had secured.

But no Duncan ever fished in the perilous world-stream for personal pleasure or gain, nor did they strive to outmaneuver each other and seize each other's counters for any need of comfort or ease. No, that faraway and ever-impelling vision, reborn every morning in each Duncan breast, cried for exit, must be expressed, and funds were always needed for this purpose. Seen by each of them a little differently according to four separate natures, Beauty, then, had to come to being one way through Isadora, in another quite different way through Elizabeth.

Isadora had something large and amply pagan in her lines, "nobly antique," in a spacious abandon. Elizabeth was a little Tanagra figure, restrained and perfect in her classic decorum. She loved order and the pure design. Her hair was never disarranged, each turn of her head on the long throat clear-cut, and the line running succinctly down over the shoulder to the fine hand with its long, supple fingers. Poise, authority, awareness—the complete Teacher even when she had her thimbleful of schnapps! That was Elizabeth.

She walked upright into the sunny white room at 23 Fifth Avenue one afternoon. Laughing made fine lines branch from her bright brown eyes.

"I met Isadora above here on the corner," she cried, gleefully, "and she asked me where I was going. When I said, 'To see Mabel Dodge,' she turned white—and what do you think she called you? A double-faced Chinese cat!"

I wish I could remember in Elizabeth's own words the long saga about the struggle between her and Isadora to show the world the Beauty. How they tried to work together and could not. How Elizabeth secured a "patron" in the Grand Duke and a beautiful school building in Darmstadt. How Max Merz, seeing Isadora dance for the first time, was infected by the magical vision and forthwith was sucked into the Duncan constellation first by Isadora, then by Elizabeth, who seized him when her sister ignored him, and made him manager of the School.

Elizabeth took a handful of German children and worked over them for years in the School; years of disciplined living, of exercises (the everlasting Bein-Schwingen!), of careful diet. She made a perfect small world for children—she made it lyrical and lovely with the music of Schumann and Schubert, and with the great poetry of all the ages.

The little girls grew up without any knowledge of the sordid elements in other lives. For picture books they had volumes of antique sculptures. Their bodies unfolded gradually in the rhythm of the years and no fashions in dress preoccupied them with anguished queries about becomingness, for they always wore the same little blue tunics and they were always becoming. The only change they knew in dress was to slip into a slightly larger tunic from time to time. On the street they made a lovely picture in their small blue caps and long blue capes.

Merz directed. From him came a few ideas of hygiene, little lectures upon the stars, and some of the more mystical aspects of science. His favorite aesthetic period was the Biedermeier which I believe he secretly preferred even to early Greek. His favorite author was Nietzsche, though the children heard a good deal about Goethe.

Great men went to visit them in their seclusion and seemed to get refreshment there. The living poets and philosophers of Germany and Austria were the friends of the School, and artists and musicians from many countries sought out the small and magical enclosure. From the East Rabindranath Tagore came and talked with them and they danced for him. Under the trees in the garden, men could forego the effort to think and concentrate and plan. Being sufficed.

Into this little heaven in Darmstadt, Isadora descended from time to time. As Merz said, Isadora went in and out of many worlds. When she came, usually bringing her accompanist or a poet or something, they made a festival of her visit. The children, as well as Elizabeth and Merz, loved any ritual. They would crown her their beautiful Queen, and, seated upon a dais, she would watch them dance before her, or she would step down and dance with them, teaching them and correcting them.

Finally, when the girls were about sixteen years old, Isadora, as though she had been waiting until they were ripe for her purpose, came to the school and asked Elizabeth for them. To take away with her about the world. She wanted a chorus, she said. Well, Elizabeth hadn't been training them with any particular practical purpose in mind. She had been living, herself, in her work, and teaching them a way of living. Just putting that thing in the world in that place.

But Merz was dumbfounded. He had had a more expedient outlook than Elizabeth. Perhaps he had been training them to be teachers, to divide themselves like cells into a number of small Elizabeths and go out in the world and make other little heavens. Just what the Grand Duke had expected to come of it all, is uncertain. It was, to him, perhaps, like an exquisite picture growing before his eyes for which he was indirectly responsible.

Elizabeth worshiped Isadora's genius. She knew, better than anyone else, the way Isadora saw life. She understood her paradoxical and capricious nature and it did not seem untoward to her. She had drawn Isadora's essence up from its depths and she knew it too well to gauge it by the standards of this world. If Isadora wanted the girls, she should have them. If she could express herself more completely with them supporting her, let them support her. Let her take them. She did. Anna, Irma, Lizel, Isabel, and Teresa; and to all of them the name of Duncan. Gertrude stayed with Elizabeth and Merz. Perhaps she had already given her little tenacious heart to Merz; perhaps she had not enough beauty for Isadora to want her.

Merz was overcome by this wholesale, swooping grab of Isadora's! All those careful years of training, the endless, patient, happy hours to end in this—the stage, the world, the supper parties! Merz had not the early Greek visualization of life that all the Duncans lived by. They were completely unhindered by the conventional gauges of profit and loss. Youth, beauty, virginity, Isadora, Dionysius! Men, passion, tragedy, life the Bacchanalia with Isadora its priestess. To Elizabeth I fancy these girls figured like tracings on a Greek vase whose probable destiny is to be shattered, a vase holding a precious liquor for a little while to comfort and amaze mortals, and then to be gone. Nothing was too good for Isadora, dancing Beauty, and evoking with her body the pristine life on this earth again. When she told me about it, she laughed her undaunted, impudent, Irish laugh. Nothing, Elizabeth thought, was too good for Isadora.

The younger group that was left to her took the place the others had

left. Erna, Dora, Josephine, Hallie, Senta, and Anita—and to all of
them, too, the name of Duncan! They were the children that Elizabeth brought to America in 1915.

They were lovely, clear-skinned, wide-eyed little girls from eight to
eleven or twelve years, with beautifully tended bodies and well-brushed,
shining hair. What had happened to their parents, no one seemed to
know. Least of all, I think, Elizabeth. She gave an entertainment and
everyone who saw them dance their little compositions to the music of
Schumann, Chopin, and Schubert fell in love with it all, and straightway believed that life was not so awful as it had seemed before that
hour.

CHAPTER IV

The Elizabeth Duncan School

HERE was something to work for, I thought. If people can be developed like these children, then we must have a school in America where Elizabeth can make American children beautiful like these little nymphs. It was Collier's idea and he began to plan. In the meanwhile money must be found to rent a suitable house for them and to furnish it somehow.

Now I had saved a thousand dollars that I had meant to spend buying an abandoned life-saving station on the dangerous coast across the dunes from the village of Provincetown on the bay. It was a lovely weathered building half covered with sand with an old boat-house near it. It was the only building over there except the new station about a mile below. There it was, lonely and aloof on the high sand bank above the beach where the fierce waves pounded in all day—a wild enough spot to suit anyone.

I had meant to dig it out and do it over, painting it inside like a ship and furnishing it like one. But when Elizabeth came along with those children, I knew it would be more fun to do something with them than with paint and sand and sea, so I told Collier I would give that money to start them off and we would try to get some other people interested in them, too.

It wasn't hard to start it. What was difficult was trying to work with them afterwards. With Merz especially. Elizabeth didn't do a thing but teach, or sit with a tiny glass of schnapps in her long, fine fingers. But Merz was terrible! The school had to be founded, incorporated, and directed. There had to be patrons, directors, and committees. The exasperated correspondence that took place between Collier and Merz and all the others is a wonderful record in itself. How people *act!*

It was strange that some of the people I was associated with now

341

were the affluent German-American owners of the silk mills in Paterson, whom Reed and I had tried to defeat with our pageant! Now we joined in sympathy, working together to help Beauty into the world.

Merz, in an obscure mixture of emotion and practicality, began to have an idealistic enthusiasm about me and in a wish to tell me the story of his life, started a series of "epistles" to me in German, with careful translations accompanying them. They were very interesting but I do not wish to weight this book with them or with the painful struggles that arose first to prevent the school from being a German institution run by Germans in a country that was on the verge of war with Germany, and secondly from attempting to direct Merz. But we certainly did have a time!

The perfect house was found for them on a high hill over the Hudson River at Croton. It was a large, airy, brown house with a view of the country for miles and miles on all sides; that lovely rolling New York state country, crossed by the stone walls that separated the rich fields, country where the deer wandered and rabbits flickered in and out, and where the wild pheasants passed to and fro with mincing steps, dragging their long tails.

Near this high dwelling and a little below it, there was another house of the same character, where the children and teachers could sleep. We took them both.

Meanwhile, Collier told Sam Lewisohn about my decision to interest myself in a school instead of in an abandoned life-saving station. Sam, the son of the copper king, liked this. Those very wealthy people are often scrupulously generous, thoughtfully so. He told Collier to tell me he would buy the station himself, and if I would do it up for him exactly as I had intended doing, and for the same money I would myself have spent on it, and we would share the place, turn and turn about. Also, he added a kindly check of five hundred dollars for the Duncan School.

That was nice.

I was always proud of the way I did that job at a distance. I thought out the whole thing, every detail of it, ordered it, and got it executed by letter. I am so glad I saved the fascinating correspondence with John Francis, who kept the principal store in Provincetown and who carried out my orders! They form part of the long volumes of letters

I have saved to while away the hours when I am too old to do more than remember!

The building was entirely of weathered wood inside and out and built very tight and ship-like. I had its walls painted white all through the inside, shiny white, and the hardwood floors cleaned and waxed. All the dishes were of Italian ware from Capone's in Boston, and were rudely decorated with fishes. I had a great brick fireplace built at the end of the living room, and many low couches, with cushions covered in blue and white printed stuff, placed against the sides. Two of these great couches were from Isadora's Ark, sold after she left! Several huge majolica platters, displaying fabulous fish, hung here and there on the walls. In a shelf for books, volumes about the sea and the life of the sea.

There was a small, perfect kitchen. I made it as complete as could be, though everything was very simple—almost austere. The beds were narrow, white ones, with perfect mattresses, and white spreads, and everywhere the white and blue paint glistened and shone. The place was an excellent one when it was completed, trig and shipshape and to the point.

It cost about a thousand dollars, and Sam was delighted with it when he saw it. He was very proud of it, too, and I believe it was a relief from the grandeur of the Fifth Avenue house with its tapestries and marbles and picture gallery. When Sam took it over, I got him to give John Francis a gold watch with an inscription inside the cover. He had been very diligent and faithful in carrying out orders and had suffered, as much as any three men would have, from the awful responsibility combined with his usual melancholia and anxiety. I think it took at least ten years off his life!

For all Sam's delight in the place, he used it very little, and I only used it once, which was the following summer of 1915, with Maurice. Sam finally sold it to Eugene O'Neill, who loved the sea, and for whom it seemed, really, to have been designed. Later it slid into the hungry ocean and people wrote articles about its having been 'Gene's home, and described it all very accurately, and no one remembered who made it. Ah, me!

Of course, one of the first things I did was to turn little Elizabeth over to the School. Elizabeth Duncan was rather dubious about the child. She judged illy of her from the shape of her fingers and fingernails and by her brow. Sweepingly, she declared no "fine energy" could flow out of such unintelligently shaped bones. However, the exquisite, delicately spun hair was a good sign. We would see. Elizabeth sized up intelligence and character by the qualities and shapes of the body. In the body she believed she could read the destiny of any mortal. Of course, there was a margin of hope even for clumsy and dull children if taken young enough. The human spirit could be drawn up through the coarsest material, the most intractable forms.

The little girl loved the School, as indeed all children did, though oftentimes there was not very much beyond porridge and milk on the table. But in that bright entourage there was a full reassurance of quick and golden life, the golden age we all so wistfully search for among the gray shades that surround us.

I myself could scarcely heed any more now the continuous flood of letters that kept coming as usual about Birth Control, Industrial Relations, Free Speech, and all the other forms of social maladjustment. Little by little I ceased to attend meetings that required my presence as an influence for Change. I just lost interest in that fabricated puppet, Mabel Dodge, as a Creature of Importance in her Time, and I longed only for peace and more peace, for innocent fun with Elizabeth and to share the Irish glee that flooded her.

When they moved into the house on Mt. Airy, high above Croton village, at Elizabeth's suggestion I rented the Sharkey Cottage, just below them on the winding country road. It was a little, old, white house of four rooms, with a tiny attic. In the front, there were a dining room and a sitting room, and behind these, a kitchen and a bedroom. It was small, old, simple, and supposed to be haunted. Bobby, who had a shack on the place for a bedroom studio, saw the ghost once or twice: a nice old lady.

Of course, I kept the apartment at 23 Fifth Avenue and left the dignified Irish cook, Hannah, who had supplanted the crazy Irish cook who hated Bobby, to take care of it with Domenico, that faithful Florentine who had been with me for two years.

My life was thus divided for a while between New York and the country. In New York the hastening, frantic stream of traffic flowed through the streets, sometimes overflowed them into the apartment, fighting, struggling, grasping at shadows that seemed essential could they once be caught, it was all flowing away from me and I was glad to let it go. The lovely, quaint countryside seemed to have the truer living in its deep pulse. Once I tried to persuade Hannah to come out and stay a few days and cook for us and take care of the little house. But she had been born in New York and had never been out of it in her life. She was horrified at what *country* was and longed for the pavements.

"I never knew you had to walk on the *dirt* in the country," she said, and she begged to go back to "civilization"—an hour away on the train.

Of course I had had to do up the cottage, papering its walls white, and painting the old woodwork white, too. It had a very beautiful old wooden mantelpiece with panels and cupboards in the sitting room—perfect proportions.

Elizabeth came walking down to see me, her full white woolen tunic and pleated skirt swaying about her. She walked briskly with a cane, and planted her sandals very firmly. We would climb the hill till we came to the fields where we could sit and gaze all around us, and watch the big white clouds go sailing along in the clean blue sky. We sat together in the new grass and felt we were being taken somewhere. I said:

"Don't you feel we are riding along on the world? I feel there is so much more *riding* up here on the hill than when I am tearing along in the automobile." Always after that we used to say we were going for a ride when we walked up to the top of Mt. Airy and sat in the grass.

Bobby was happy in his shack which might have been a castle for all he knew. He was making a little model for Granville-Barker's production called "The Man Who Married A Dumb Wife." This was Bobby's first opportunity, secured for him by Neith through Emilie Hapgood, Norman's divorced wife, after various attempts on Neith's part!

DEAR MABEL,

Emilie tells me that she can't find that play, Bataille's "Enfant de L'Amour," anywhere, and she's afraid they can't get it from France in time. They wanted to produce it in December. Can you think of *anybody* who might have it? Would you ring up Jenkins' bookstore on 6th Ave. and ask him? Are there any French bookstores in N. Y.? I *wish* I could get hold of it. E. rang me up at ten o'clock the other night to ask *what*

Jones taught at Harvard! She asked if you didn't think he was a genius. She seems to think so but to have cold feet about getting him to produce a play. She wants to give him a job. Can you supply any information as to his abilities? *Has* he ever produced a play? Justus is out here! Sorry not to see you today. Do come out Wednesday? That *pigeon* has not returned. Do you suppose it went back to the shop?

Love,

N.

Bobby made a great success with it. Walter said that Bobby was that rare thing—a success overnight! It was his first and only *hand-made show*. He made every single thing for it himself, the settings, the costumes, the hats, the shoes. Out there in his studio hut he snipped and sewed on bright pieces of cloth all day, and when evening came he wrapped himself in a square of red broadcloth and strolled around the peaceful countryside, free to brood on his work, to evolve it in contemplation. He fitted perfectly into the Duncan School. The children and Elizabeth and he were all of one vibration and shared a similar fantasy. Oh, yes! It was a snatch of the Golden Age for us all.

Max Eastman had a cottage a little further down the hill. He used to come to see me sometimes until Ida learned of it and was hurt. He tried to make me write poetry, of course, because he did, and so sometimes I would.

My life was gathering and accumulating in me. Now I felt full of abundant life. I learned a way to sink back far into myself and there I found more and more strength—as though I contained a deep pool of refreshment and delight. This I called upon often, always naming it Nature. I felt the rich stream of life that rose out of the earth and I loved to lie upon it, under some strong tree. I had attained a perfect and unfailing contact with the country where I lived. Max, who was sensitive to women, felt, I suppose, the mediumistic part I had come to play and seemed to feel the earth life that was using me to pass through to whomever could take it. Anyone who becomes a nature medium, a channel for the earth-forces, has a peculiar strength and charm. Max stared at me as we sat by the fireside in the evening.

"You have something strange, something mysterious about you," he said. "What is it? There is a queer light in your eyes, behind your eyes—witch-like. . . . What is in you?"

"Nature," I answered him, feeling Nature like a living being dwelling in me. Max felt attracted—not to me, but to that life in me.

346

I was not interested any more in a personal relation because I was satisfied. Little happenings were beautiful in this new life. It was a life without colored glass, or French furniture, or hanging white silk. To see the evening sun come in the door from the porch and fall on the supper table, shining through a tumbler of red wine, falling on the orange-colored cheese and the fresh brown loaf while we sat—two or three of us—idly, at rest, after the purposeless day. How good it was! While in New York the women hurried to check the population, or to raise wages, or to "swing" some urgent affair, we sat in Sharkey Cottage and sipped our wine and watched the beautiful plumes of the asparagus bed move as though a hand had passed over them. Of course, the asparagus bed shouldn't have had plumes at all. But I didn't know that. I didn't know anything practical about the country. I only knew how good it felt to be there.

Now I drew John from the atmosphere of the stuffy boarding school and I gave him, too, to Elizabeth Duncan. Among the little girls he was the only one of his kind until, in a little while, other small boys arrived.

Of course Elizabeth put short, blue drawers and a short, blue-belted tunic on John. Barefooted, with the bow and arrow raised in the archery class, he was beautiful. There he was, transported to Mt. Olympus on Mt. Airy. The earth has no age. The children lived in its early Greek expression, that is all.

Elizabeth held her classes in a room where, through the windows, one could see the distant hills falling away behind each other.

"Touch the hills!" she would cry. "Reach out your fingers until you can touch the hills." The sensitive young flesh quivered and stretched out towards the skyline. The slender arms grew longer, the fingers tapered out beyond their own limited boundaries. When children try to reach the skyline every day, they end by coming really a little nearer to it than if their reach is only so far as the arithmetic book or their plate at the table. Elizabeth Duncan developed beautiful bodies. Her "long line" became famous when the children danced and seemed to be playing with sunbeams they plucked from the sky.

"Up! *Up!*" Elizabeth would cry in her lesson. "Don't stay down on the *ground* when you can go so high! *UP!*"

Merz rushed to town nearly every day for consultations and meetings.

347

"We *must* be grounded and founded," Elizabeth said, and Merz had to attend to it. She avoided all the business she could, though sometimes she would accompany him if her presence, her "atmosphere," was a needed persuasion. Then, sitting still, looking lofty, the long upper lip firm and sagacious, trying not to be impudent and spoil everything, but bright brown eyes shrewd and twinkling, she attended a gruesome meeting of business men, dusty, smoky, rich, and powerful. Coming back to quiet Mt. Airy was heavenly afterwards, to her white robes, her little glass of schnapps.

On her dressing table were bright, innocent baubles that she and the children loved: many bead necklaces hanging over her mirror, and silken scarves floating over the edges. To her they were the crown jewels of her school, made by the little girls for Tante, as they all called her. They loved and feared her. She made life thrilling and uplifted, but oh! she had a sharp tongue and she never spared it. With a dry giggle she pronounced sarcastic judgments on awkward poses or heavy treads. No one *dared* be clumsy anywhere near Elizabeth. It was a crime. Ugliness in a body could be forgiven, but stupidity never. No one ever laid so much stress upon the intelligence of the flesh as Elizabeth. To be near her was to awaken cellularly and I seemed to feel my ignored blood cells stretch and begin to live. Even Merz's flattery had to have a form to gaze on, some actuality, and there really came a new shining to the tissues as soon as attention reached them.

"Look at her shine!" cried Merz to Elizabeth one evening. "She is become like a little Buddha!"

I sat on the couch conscious of peace and plenty. The full blue tussore silk billowed comfortably about me. Did I shine? Well, probably I did. To shine was the order of the day in my new surroundings with that sibyl, Elizabeth, drawing light up out of everyone.

I know Bobby shone. It was easier for him than for anyone except the children. He had a pointed beard and a red square of cloth and a pair of scissors and he shone like the morning.

CHAPTER V

Maurice Sterne

IT was sometime in the spring and Elizabeth and Merz thought it wise to give another entertainment in New York to show the children's work. Several little American girls had been added to the group that had come from Germany, and already they showed progress in the "long line," and the beautiful life of fantasy had begun to clothe them with a delicate poetic glamor that softened their native quality.

I sat with some friends in the ballroom of one of the big hotels and in front of me I was happy to see dear little Alice Sprague and Mr. Sprague. Alice Sprague was one of my earliest memories, dating back to twilights in Buffalo when, as a little girl, I had seen her pass down Delaware Avenue in the dusk, more like a creature from one of my favorite books than a flesh-and-blood go-to-market-and-dance-at-the-Charity-Ball woman, like all the others there.

She had a great deal of black hair parted in front and drawn back into a broad, low coil at the nape of her neck, and over it a low, flat hat with a curling feather that drooped over her ear to her shoulder. With hands meeting in a small fur muff, eyes downcast in reverie, she floated along down the avenue without anything accented in her pace. An upturned Da Vinci smile hovered over her face. She reminded me of Emily Brontë, William Blake, and the Virgin of the Rocks. She was another who preferred her own fantasies to the usual realities, and she embodied naturally without need of teaching the doctrines of Emma Curtis Hopkins, whom Bobby, Eve, Nina, and even Maurice, later spent hours and dollars trying to learn and live by.

Alice Sprague saw only beauty wherever she looked. It came easy to her. She has never known another truth than beauty. How wise! What people call *facts* escaped her. Well, after all, how much more true are others' facts than her fantasies? It will take a hundred hundred years to know!

349

Between her and her husband sat a black-haired man with red cheek-bones and a white brow. One noticed him at once in a crowd, for there was something vivid and colorful about him that marked him out among the other more neutral personalities. He seemed sensitive to attention, for he moved as I sat examining him and turned, with a slow, almost secretive caution, his large brown eyes in my direction.

"Well," I thought, "who might *that* be? He really has a face!" His straight, fine, black hair, fine, almost, as feathers, fell back in long locks in the manner of Liszt, and his broad forehead had a pale, innocent look, especially at the temples where people show for good or bad. His long-lashed brown eyes were nothing more or less than *orbs,* there was such a splendor in their liquid regard. The nose, of a Biblical dignity, had a good bone ridge; but below it, oh, dear! his mouth, when he forgot to arrange it, was not so good—more or less a thin, straight line, without curve or meaning. When he did arrange it (for it was his instinctive preoccupation to do so) he could at best only shape it into a self-conscious kind of smirk or tighten it into a stingy, pursy bunch of lines.

What I liked about him was his handsome look of suffering. A dark torture ennobled him and added a great deal of dignity to that countenance that would in later years become decidedly patriarchal. He was positively enveloped in a cloud of secrecy and caution. The man might have been in a jungle, so watchful he was, so studied every glance and motion. That interested me. I wondered what it was all about.

The little girls danced their blithe spring dances to the music of Mozart that Merz was drawing with excellent and tender execution from the big, black piano. The dark stranger in front of me became an excellent foil, in my view of them past his somewhat sinister and world-marked presence, for their reassuring freshness and charm. He was like a threatening cloud and they its silver lining.

But no one in that gathering responded more deeply than he to their innocent appeal. After the first numbers, tears brimmed his shining eyes as he clapped two large, white hands. Turning his profile to little Alice Sprague, a deep dimple appeared in his rosy cheek and a double row of white teeth flashed as he exclaimed in a low voice,

"Ah! They are ador-r-rable!"

"What an Oriental charm the creature has," I thought. But when he turned his full face around with the smile still upon it, and I saw not only one dimple, but two, and the stretched lips expressing something inhuman, almost canine, he seemed to me lessened.

"No! The man needs his suffering," I decided.

As our eyes met and we regarded each other, he let the unbecoming grimace fade, and quickly drew his lips into the line that expressed self-control, determination and poise. He held my glance with the most practiced and impelling stare, not quite rude, very stealthy and exceedingly magnetic. He managed to keep it under cover and unseen by others.

"Well, *really*," I thought, "such technique!" I was becoming very curious about him, for he had a certain force, a conquering air despite his lips. I always loved the slightest appearance of masterfulness in a man, because it hinted at an opportunity for me to exercise my strength. In the intermission, Alice Sprague turned and introduced us:

"Mr. Maurice Sterne," she said.

I had heard of *him,* of course: the Russian painter who was having an exhibition at Birnbaum's Gallery. He had spent a year on the island of Bali—practically the first white man other than traders ever to go there—and he had brought back a big collection of drawings and paintings of native life.

As we talked together for those few minutes, several well-defined phases of his make-up showed themselves; the man had form and everything he expressed was clear-cut and had a certain massive quality to it. When he changed from the studied and cautious hunter of dames to an aspect of naïveté and bubbling delight, then he had something juvenile about him. His lines grew younger. He looked like a little boy. His body looked square and as though he would be taller when he grew up. What an anomaly he was! He was a mixture of old and complex racial turmoil, a darkness shot through with lightning; something dangerous in him threw out the warning to beware of him, yet how easily he was moved by goodness, how appreciative of little Alice Sprague, of the Duncan children, of Elizabeth herself. He loved goodness. I thought him very romantic. He represented the unknown, the undisclosed soul of Russia.

The man went armed in society. He defended himself by attack. His eyes were loaded weapons, projecting across the space between him and women, who seemed to him "to matter" as he called it later, a volume of magnetism that entered them and worked in them and joined them to him. He had fascination that he knew how to exert even while he himself remained unmoved and uninfluenced; he had exercised this function for so long that it had become second nature to him.

He just looked his look, now here, now there, and everywhere. Thus he imposed himself upon his milieu, and lost a feeling of anxiety that haunted him. Before men should remind him of the shortcomings in his nature that he wished to forget, he hastily engaged the attention of women and tried to keep himself comfortable by the consciousness of his power. Out in the world people were never a source of pleasure or benefit to him. It was combat between him and others. Overcoming, impressing, convincing! What a struggle! Only at the small, crowded flat up on West End Avenue, where Mama lived and cooked the food of his childhood and wore the hot black wig of Yiddish widowhood, could he relax and be natural. Yet not even there! Something compelled the man to flee that familiar ease and shirt-sleeved relaxation. Everything irritated him at home, and everything away from home frightened him.

Well, he had caught my attention that night. The next day I went to see his work. The first thing I told Birnbaum was that he was a sculptor, not a painter, for that impressed me immediately. His forms were so plastic, so tactile. He was a magnificent draughtsman but his color seemed unrevealing and uncertain.

His vision of things was strange. The Bali people seemed to be a distinguished, reptilian race, elegant and haughty in their frenzied dances, and in their dark magical rites; a dark and livid race made somewhat gruesome by the artist's predilection for yellow-greens. His conceptions were always statuesque, and his need to portray the three dimensions in form had developed an ability in him to make paint do the work of clay so that there was a stereopticon illusion in his pictures.

Birnbaum, professionally enthusiastic at all times, seemed quite overcome by the genius of Sterne, and exclaimed that no one for years and years had arrived in New York with work of such magnitude and individuality.

"What an original!"

352

"He would be more original if he had not seen Gauguin," I answered, rather pertly I fear. "But he has none of Gauguin's sweet, sad, amiable laziness." These Balinese natives were galvanized by Sterne. Even in repose, the single praying figures sitting cross-legged and construed into the inevitable pyramidal form so fashionable in art at that time, had an intensity not usual, I am sure, on the indolent southern island.

I bought one of the smaller drawings, a pyramidal priest in brown chalk, and took it home with me. It was the effect of Sterne's magnetic *look*. Like his paintings, he interested and repelled one. I thought it would be amusing to see him again sometime.

CHAPTER VI

Reed Again

YES, he came back as he had done before. Always, as soon as I had regained my independence and the physical and emotional life that he aroused in me had subsided in his absence, he returned. But this time I was determined to go on possessing myself and not to lose my balance. I had my deep exchange with Nature, now, and this satisfied me more than any man had ever done. I would not be fool enough to lose all I had gained, for I had arrived at this security after a great deal of searching and unhappiness.

Reed had left N. After going through the drama of reaving her away from R. and taking her to her family in Germany, announcing to them his intention to marry her, all the usual conventional difficulties a man will undertake for a passionate indulgence that is masking all the world for him, he had come out of it and remembered me. Well! Well! Well! Yes, there was no one like me. Once a man loved me, he said, he could never get over it. . . . He could not live without me. So he had come back to me!

Reed's boyish face, all curves and glowing with eagerness, the adorable high lights shining on his temples, his light hazel eyes, his humor, not quite vanished but peeping through here and there, seemed, over the gulf I had crossed, very dear and lovable. His untidy curly hair waved off from his round brow with its usual energy. He was like a little boy come home to his mother after an escapade, disarmingly anxious to tell her all about it. Here he was home again, the hunter home from the hills.

I did not feel like his mother or his lover any more. I had escaped all that and crossed a wide gulf where I found my own mother and needed no human relationship except friendship, the easy, entertaining intercourse with Elizabeth and her school, that I had now.

He was indifferent to the mess he had left behind him: tearful N.

creeping back to R. and R. defiantly possessed of a young Russian girl about to have a baby. Yes, Reed ignored all that.

Carl Hovey, still his editor on the *Metropolitan Magazine,* wanted him to start off immediately on a new adventure: the Balkan States and Russia, with young Boardman Robinson along to do pictures to illustrate his stories. Stories—that was what Hovey wanted him to go after. Reed had a romantic mind, he said, the boy saw things dramatically. He was not political-minded at all and he was to keep to the story of things as they crashed to pieces. He was to leave in a week. He begged Hovey for ten days and got them.

(Ten days for love—and I didn't want any love!)

Another new idea had him in its grip. As soon as he had finished this thing in Russia for Hovey, he would rush back and we would be married! See—he had already bought a ring, two gold circles that were linked into one: that could be divided but not separated. When they were together they made the usual rounded wedding ring— slipped apart they formed two links in a chain.

(Heavens! I did not *want* it!)

And we would have a real place of our own. Up in the Ramapo Hills across the Hudson, he was going to buy a big piece of land, and build our house. He had it all in his mind already—that house. He wanted to have a permanent, stable place of his own, now. He was through with other kinds of love, he only wanted me.

I do not know how I broke it to him that it was too late for all this. Somehow I managed to tell him, but he couldn't accept it because he couldn't understand. At first he thought I was revenging myself on him and he waited for that to pass, confident that I would merely get over my wounded pride and be as before. He actually betrayed the patience he was counseling himself and I could see he had a lover's tolerance for what he fancied was the natural defense I had built up between us in his absence. A little while and it would pass.

But I was worse than cold or hard with pride. I was indifferent. Insulated from him and from the hot and harmful fevers of the world, I hugged myself close to nature deep below all this surface excitement. As he talked to me, I contrasted his offer of life with the cool, perpetual replenishment to which I retired every day, many times a day, and every night before sleeping, and his outlook seemed thin and meager.

355

"No, Reed, I can't. It's all finished for us," I repeated over and over. He just couldn't believe it.

"But *why*? What's *happened*? What has come between us?" he kept hammering at me; and when I answered, "Nature," he was completely baffled.

He came out to the Sharkey Cottage in Croton, and he saw Elizabeth Duncan and the little girls. Of course he felt the beauty up there in the school, and the cottage on the roadside of Mt. Airy seemed made for love. I was gentle with him. Mrs. Kruger, who came to cook for me, made a nice country supper. Ham and salad and cottage cheese, red wine and a great chocolate cake. The evening light came through the doorway and fell on the red table cloth until presently the stars came out and the evening was cool. I could see that it must have seemed peaceful after N. and Europe.

I forgot whether Bobby was with us that evening for supper or not, but certainly he was not there afterwards when the time came for Reed to go if he would catch his train back to New York and I had to tell him to leave. Up to the last minute he had believed it would end happily, the quiet evening in the country, and he seemed unable to accept the fact that the end would not be happy. That was the moment when at last he realized I had not been pretending—that actually love did not bind us any more.

I closed the door on him, blew out the candles and, forgetting him entirely, I went to my appointment. Nature awaited me in the lone dark and I sank with relief into those depths.

Afterwards, I heard from Steff what happened to Reed. Outside in the rough country road, he seemed to lose his reason and his memory. More by chance than design, he turned down the hill towards the station. He stumbled along, seeing nothing, unable to think of anything. He fell down many times, and automatically picked himself up again. The road finally reached the Highway and he saw the feeble lights of the dingy depot.

Then Steff took a hand. Reed had appeared to be on the edge of a breakdown: brain fever or prostration. Steff told me how he found him in his room in Washington Square. He appealed to me in every way he could for Reed's sake, just to help him over the few remaining days, to send him on his job happy; the break could be deferred. It didn't seem right, somehow. It went against the grain with me, for I

356

had an honest habit. I didn't pretend. But Steff made honesty seem petty, and compromise more large and generous and human than sincerity in human relations.

I agreed, reluctantly, to take Reed back for the few hours before his departure, to content him, to fool him, and to quiet him. I took Steff's way rather than my own natural one, and by so doing brought, I fear, greater disaster upon Reed in the end than had I stuck to the truth.

Yes, he was happy. The reaction from despair inflated him with an enormous confidence and triumph. Yes, I let him put that ring on my finger and I slept with him in the white bedroom in the apartment. Without emotion, yet with an agreeable flow between us of a physical kind, we passed a couple of pleasant nights together.

He never reached the core of me again as he once had. My spirit was safely anchored deep in the natural universe and did not participate in the surface life of the flesh and I remember I felt sorry for him for this in an impersonal way. But he was not sorry for himself. He wanted new photographs of me to take with him and I had little Goldburg, an acquaintance of Ida's and Jo Davidson's, just starting in business, come to the apartment. He was struck with a certain expression he saw in me and posed me, eyes closed, head tilted back, a candle burning on each side. I relapsed back into my central home. . . .

"Take *that!*" I said to myself, exultantly. "That is *I*." Curiously enough, the developed picture looked unusually sensual, triumphantly exposing a secret lasciviousness. It seems that we have not a wide range of expression! One serves often for another.

Reed tried to clinch us together in every possible way. He told everyone we were to be married upon his return and he told Hovey to regard me as his wife, to refer all questions to me that needed decision, and to communicate to me every cable or message he sent the magazine from Europe.

I let this pass over me like wind. It did not seem to concern me at all. Steff, I thought, had persuaded me to do what I was doing and it seemed more his affair than mine. I liked Reed. I really liked to see him happy. When he left, after a long, passionate, more loving farewell than he had ever expressed when I had really cared for him, I forgot him before the day was over; nothing had happened so far as

I was concerned. From the tender, he sent me the first verses of a poem he had begun about us:

Pygmalion, Pygmalion, Pygmalion
A hillside meadow loved Pygmalion.
Where a great shining rock like a fallen shield
Lay heavily in tall grass, he rested once.
Long, long it tenderly held his body's warmth
And the apple-tree that shaded him remembered him.
Grass that was just born broke gladly beneath his feet;
Grass that was old felt green beneath his feet.
And the wide view that sank like a heart after pain,
Miles over toppling hills to the wide still river
Robed itself in opal, golden and haze for him.

All the meadow loved young Pygmalion.
And when he went away—though never, never
Had anyone save Pygmalion rested there,
And though the sun's shadow stood still between light and light
While he was come and gone—he left loveliness there;
Longing of the starved heart for a lover gone
When all is as before and yet how empty!
White moved his body, crushing the ferns in the valley
And the rock and the grass and the trees yearned after him. . . .

Pilot going! Must stop.

Love,

REED.

I returned to Croton and the mild, sweet country enveloped me. I participated in the moods of the day and the nights and grew more serene and more secure than ever. Whether it rained or the sun shone did not matter. There was strength in either way.

I remember sitting up in bed one dark, stormy morning and I could hear the rain beat against the house. Looking through my bedroom door, across the sitting room, I saw the panes of the front window streaked with rain. How good the cool water felt to the earth. An immense satisfaction flooded me as I realized in myself the fast flow of nature and its excellent enjoyments. At that moment the figure of Max Eastman passed the window. Head down, contracted against the wind and wet, he pressed up the road, the picture of misery and unrest. He seemed an outcast of the earth—one of those who are her fair-weather lovers, whose spirits depend upon sunshine and slump into dismay when the storms come. I felt superior, somehow, and glad I knew what I knew. I sent him some verses I wrote after he had passed ". . . mortal, lift thy longing to the drifting stars. . . ."

CHAPTER VII

Sterne

IT was with a feeling of aversion that I noticed his dark brown look fastened on me from across the hall. He leaned against a column and smoked a large cigar in that light airy place where the children danced with bare feet. I can't remember how he got there. I suppose one of the German-American friends of the school must have brought him— Dr. Genthe, Mr. Stallfort, the Stoehrs, or one of those.

I knew that there was a sequence in his appearance in Croton following upon my purchase of one of his pictures. Nothing stimulates an artist's interest in one quite so much as having one buy something of his. There is a sane pitiful reason for this and it is not so mercenary an interest as people think. Their insatiable hankering for appreciation has been satisfied, their uncertainty about their work and what they are doing has been quieted for a moment. Painters are often unsure of themselves, secretly wondering just what use it all is, and usually unable to *see* the good or bad qualities in their canvases. A sense of guilt pursues them, for a painter who just paints and does nothing else has not satisfied his masculine pride and his muscles are unappeased. Yet the convention among them is to save their best energy for their "work." They try to exercise in paint all the functions of men, and indeed it must be work just to bring about this substitution! I imagine that the famous "moods" of the artistic temperament, in particular the painter's divine discontent, come very largely from lack of exercise, for sculptors are far more cheerful, and their products less embarrassing. Sculpture is much less excremental in character than painting, even modern sculpture, and also less erotic.

Sterne, more than any artist I ever knew, craved reassurance. He had a large-boned frame, he was broad and strong; in a flannel shirt, given an ax, he would have had the appearance of a Russian woodsman. On his canvases the Bali people writhed and jerked and twisted in elegant paroxysms, or, in yogi postures deeply meditated, yet his own body was not satisfied by this vicarious activity. One can follow the complex and unconscious inner reasoning by which he, like his fellow artists, persuaded his defrauded tissues that the purchase of his "work" signified real expenditure on his part, energy spent, laid down there in paint, exchanged for money, the symbol of power. He was *worth* something in spite of his secret doubts of himself.

Oh! The poor things! Why must they be driven into these devious alleys, transforming their energy into one faculty after another, saving it from one outlet so that it shall come out somewhere else, and spoiling themselves as men in the process?

Sterne would have been much nicer if he had chopped a cord of wood every day and painted the rest of the time. But no! He was an *artist!* When he was a boy of ten, he tramped the New York streets and sold newspapers to help his mother. Certain incidents occurred, the usual ones that bright, good-looking boys attract, and he went to the Art School, then to Europe. No more exercise, of course! When I knew him, he was under forty and his large joints were so stiff that often they creaked. He was an *artist.* Nearly all painters have stiff joints, ulcerated stomachs, or lumbago.

Sterne never walked. He rode in the street car rather than walk. When I met him, he was resting on his laurels and enthusiastic press clippings came to him daily through the mail and he lay reading them on a *chaise longue* in the apartment Nazimova had lent him, with a decanter of whiskey, a siphon, and a box of cigars by his side.

Nazimova and he had been young together. Before either of them had become fixed in the habit of substituting acting and painting for living, they had had a passionate love affair.

I do not know how soon it was that I felt impelled to turn Sterne into a sculptor, but very soon, I think. I simply longed to have him work in clay and execute in the round his insistent need to express bodily life and the action of muscles and bone. I do not mean that I realized about him then what I do as I write this in later years. I did not think it out. I simply saw that his painting was sculpturesque, plastic, three-dimensional, and ugly in color. I thought:

"The man is meant for a sculptor—what fun it would be to make him into one."

But he was alien, standing there in the Duncan School smoking his black cigar and fixing that heavy, concentrated look upon me across the room over the glossy heads of the Duncan children. Trying to catch one's eyes and hold them, to pour the stream of magnetism from him into one's being through these small loopholes, to get and hold one so.

That evening Elizabeth and Bobby and I walked up Mt. Airy road together. There was a heavy mist in the air. Elizabeth was wrapped in a soft white woolen shawl thrown over one shoulder, and Bobby had his red thing around him. We carried a flashlight and we turned the streaming ray up to the wide space about us. The shadows of our bodies made vast dark magnified figures in the fog over our heads and we hugged ourselves and encouraged our frightened wonder and laughed with terror and glee at the spectral shapes of ourselves in the night. We liked the eerie feeling of mystery that came from the huge, thin reflection of ourselves. We cultivated our innocent fear and ignored the more real and actual dangers of life.

I saw Maurice frequently after that. He came to the apartment in town and talked by the hour and told me all his problems. He was a good talker and though he was not an intellectual man, he had a lot of fanciful ideas and intuitions about everything. He was quite clogged with art theories, with theories about "significant form" and all that.

The odor of his perpetual cigar was distasteful to me, for I hated them from childhood, since my father had always smoked them; but I tried to ignore what I didn't like about him and the cigar was part of it.

He told me one day he had been to see Stieglitz. They had talked of me, and Stieglitz had said:

"You'd better watch out with her. She's a live wire." Maurice laughed when he repeated this. He laughed with a choking, nervous gasp that rose like air escaping involuntarily from his lungs whenever he was apprehensive. He was full of nervous fears mixed with humor. Fears about everything: about money, work, women. Sometimes he was nervous about making a break of some kind, and often this fear would cause him to overstep the line and say something he shouldn't, with a burst of ruddy laughter.

He was what is called a self-made man and he had had practically no schooling, no training in the customary human behavior, and had had to pick it up as best he could; in Europe he had amassed a great deal of the kind of culture that comes from loving nice women and talking with their more or less cultivated husbands, sitting in cafés or strolling through art galleries.

He had always been alone with himself, though, hiding from the world as best he could his incomplete development. He had done very well. Sitting there, in his heather-colored Scotch homespun clothes with a sweet wholesome smell coming from them, his *digne* black locks falling back from his white forehead, a look of weary fortitude gave him character. What matter what it came from? I don't suppose it matters what the exercise is, so long as an endeavor is made, for quality will come from almost any effort persisted in long enough and people who make no effort are always second-rate.

Sterne had a certain fineness when he was serious. When he relaxed, grew gay, or, dressed in white summer clothes with a panama hat encircled with a black band, he sallied out in search of "material," he just soared away from the American scene: stood out too much. When he was cheerful, he was a little vulgar. People like him do not know how to be happy and it does not become them. No one of his kind should laugh.

He had swallowed the culture of the ages too rapidly and perhaps it poisoned him a little. The slow growth that should have taken three or four generations to produce him, had been crowded into twenty years. When a man or a race has to make a new adaptation it is sometimes unsuccessfully hurried, like an apple that is rotted before it is ripe, as are many of the Negroes in Harlem.

My life was woven of different colored threads in the spring of 1915. I still lived much of my life in town and from my desk I carried on the correspondence with John Francis in Provincetown that instructed him in every detail about the life-saving station. I thought about it until I saw it exactly and brought it into being, all gleaming and redeemed by the lovely white and blue paint, the shining walls and floors.

I longed to see it and I rented a cottage in Provincetown for the summer, against the days when Croton would be hot and humid from the sun on the river.

Frank Tannenbaum came out of his year's imprisonment that spring, too. For a long year now he had been shut up just on account of one winter's night in a church. It had given him a chance to think and to read the books we sent him. It had given him a chance to study prison life, too. When he came to see me in Croton, his young mind was made up about his future. He wanted to get some education and then to devote himself to prison reform. Max and I talked it over and arranged for him to work part time for the *Masses* magazine that the former was editing, and planned it so he would have time for classes at Columbia.

Elizabeth was inclined to be cool when I took Frank up to the school. She saw his awkward clothes and shoes and his rather stiff body. She did not notice his fine, clean-cut features, the broad white brow, and the dark eyes with their quick thoughtfulness. She had heard from Merz, I suppose, that he was a "radical." She knew I had known anarchists before she arrived in America and to her all of that kind of thing meant sensation and lawlessness. I never succeeded in my life in having the people I knew mix comfortably; they were all specialists and separated from each other by the exclusiveness of their varying tastes. I didn't care much. I just switched on one viewpoint and switched off another; I have often thought that hardly anyone I knew would recognize me if I were overheard talking to any of the others!

Bobby was in the little back room in the apartment when I was in town. He was well on his way now, since his success. Young men came to see him, boys in their early twenties, carrying portfolios, eager to show him their own designs. Rollo Peters was one of these, a fresh-cheeked child with eager, shy ways, and Kenneth MacGowan was another. Lee Simonson, the thoughtful Persian-looking boy with enormous, melancholy eyes, visited Bobby out there and together they talked and talked for hours with the enchanting fervor of their youth. What a lovely time it was!

It was not long before Maurice began to make tentative efforts towards me. He would assume his rigid look of concentration and with lips firm in a straight line, he timidly advanced his large, white hand to lay it on my knee or on my hair. He acted a good deal like a man unaccustomed to horses who attempts to ingratiate himself by a cautious caress while remaining well on the lookout for a kick. But I did not kick him. I realized that he had a small range of behavior with women, that his experience of them hadn't given him a very good opinion of them, and that while he felt no real impulse to make love

364

to me, was in reality quite indifferent to me in that way, he really believed that all any woman could want of a man was caresses. He was grateful to me for buying his drawing, perhaps I expected him to repay me with love, he thought. Very well, he would carry on the same old game he had always played. Perhaps I would buy another!

I drew away from him and laughed at him. "No, Maurice, it's your work I'm interested in, not you!" I was immune, I thought, what need had I for men, I who had so far outrun them, and their limited understanding, and capacity for life? I was inflated and I felt very superior. This inflation is self-sustaining. I had no one to tell me or show me I was selfish and anti-social or that I was headed for a fall, as are all who try to preserve a separated pleasure.

Maurice looked half hurt and half unbelieving. He withdrew his capable hand and lighted a cigarette, and turned his head away from me with the corners of his mouth drawn down and his eyebrows raised. But he watched me carefully with cautious glances like a dog who imagines he is unnoticed. So we played a game of hide and seek with each other.

One night I motored him out to Croton for supper in the Sharkey Cottage. We took a lunch basket with us and a lovely bottle of Graves. Maurice loved to drive in automobiles. He lay back on the leather seat luxuriating in the ease of it. He was always very conscious of his surroundings, observing and estimating them.

"At least he is a *man*," I thought. He had acquired a poise in the course of his years. He was dignified and massive—villainous, perhaps, in spots, but something to grapple with. There was nothing flighty about him as about the lovable, immature Reed. He was a "Serious Artist." At first I felt completed and protected by his presence near me in the large car as we sped through the twilighted streets of the city, and adequately companioned for once. But as we left the crowded streets and talk lapsed between us, I began to realize a peculiar loneliness that he made me feel, and a great desolation fell upon me.

I felt terribly alone in the world and it was he who made me feel it. I looked at the people whom we passed and whether they were with others or alone they all seemed more at home on earth than I. I was single, destitute and disgusted. In vain I tried to retire into my secret self and to commune with the reassuring presence there that never failed me in those days. It was no use. A dry and dreary malaise filled me instead of the up-rushing joy.

I stole a glance at the stranger beside me, but not too cautiously to deceive him. He was watchfully aware of every move I made and I caught his observant eye upon me. He misinterpreted my notice of him and with a practiced stealth, he slid his large, white hand under the light summer carriage robe and pressed my knee. There was a cold, speculative look on his face that accentuated our separateness. He was gauging the situation, estimating again. Calculation was his habit; it was a part of his seriousness. I felt him to be a deadly enemy. The evening light faded out of the sky.

No matter what we think and feel, we carry on. We reached the cottage on Mt. Airy and I dismissed the car and bidding Albert return for us at ten, we made our way into the peaceful little place and lighted the candles and the lamp. I even lighted the small fire laid in readiness in the chimney-place.

When I came back from the bedroom where I had left my hat and smoothed my hair, I found Sterne lighting the cigar. Never mind. Here we were—we must make the best of it.

The supper and the wine were good and it was a pleasure to eat and drink with him because he had a grave, pleasurable way of appreciating such things, and he gave a proper value to them, so that they were enhanced for one, and made more important by his consciousness of them. He had sense of food, as many Europeans have, and it too was a part of his seriousness.

After the meal was over and the sweet evening air was filling the room from the hillside beyond the open door, both of us eased by the wine of the apprehension of life, we talked together of many things. He seemed to want to come closer and be confidential, tell me his secrets, and he told me about the love of his life.

She was a married woman in Germany. She was the only woman he had ever really loved. And though she loved him, she loved her husband, too, and she would not deceive him. She was beautiful. Tall and slim and with great, dark eyes. He had loved her for years; he had lived near her in Rome; his studio was across the way from her house. He had tried in every way to recover himself; but no other woman had reached him so deeply as she, though he had had many loves.

366

One night in desperation he had persuaded her friend Olga to let him come to her. B. and her husband, he knew, were out at a ball. He lay beside Olga, and as he tried to forget the other woman a frightful crash of thunder shook the house and frightened them both. Soon after, he heard B.'s carriage drive up to her house. He heard the horses' hooves on the cobbled street outside the window and he pressed his lips once more and more desperately against Olga's breast. But she, too, heard and recognized the carriage sounds and she slyly slipped her hand over his heart to measure its beat. When she felt it racing, she rose from the bed and left him alone.

Finally his old friend, Madame Du Bois Reymond, seeing he was unable to save himself, unable to work, decided to rescue him. She helped him go to Bali for a year. There in Bali as he lay on his couch in the hot evenings, he heard the drums in the village. He thought about B. constantly. In the daytime he worked. The Bali people were enchanting, naïve and unafraid and love meant nothing to them. A beautiful Bali girl attached herself to him and she used to come and see him in the early morning and dance before him. He was fond of her, but he couldn't love her—no one but B. reached his heart. . . .

He had a graphic way of telling a story and made one see how it all looked. He had brought a small stereoscope out to the cottage and he had hundreds of photographs of Bali and the natives. I was amazed at the purity and childishness of these people after seeing his sinister studies in paint. They were exquisitely proportioned and radiant with a fresh youthfulness; they in no way resembled his pictures save for their costumes—the long trailing batiks! Who says nothing exists save in the eye of the beholder? Yet undoubtedly he had labored to reproduce that young old race in all its excellence, for I realized he had used his little stereopticon contrivance for the purpose of reproducing exactly, in his studio, those rounded limbs, that seemed to be bathed in an effulgent light we are not accustomed to in our countries.

Listening to Maurice, I grew more sympathetic to his nature if less convinced of his art. He was the victim of one of those so-called fatal attachments, whose intensity and apparent inevitability make them appear admirable in a world of easy love. Hutch had always extolled the *inevitable* in any relationship; he admired the fated and helpless victims of the heart and the nervous system, for he was not, himself, one to challenge destiny and overcome the stars, and one perforce grows to find significant values in one's own limitations. Hutch had taught me too to admire the inevitable wherever I found it—so now I read more significance and weight into Maurice than I had before and by the end of the evening I was about to respect him and look up to him.

When I went to my room to get my hat, for the motor would soon be there, he followed me. He came up behind me and flattened his body against me until I felt all of him. I tried to get away—and only dragged him along with me. I fought and wrestled in that ludicrous backward embrace and took to kicking him. Well, he had expected that. I got free of him for a moment and stood panting, with my back against the foot of the bed. I held on to the footboard with both hands and tried to get my breath—and in an instant he had lunged again and clamped himself on to me!

"Darling!" he breathed hotly into my ear. "Darling! I *love* you!" How many times had he practiced *that* in his life? *Darling.* How I hated the word!

Heat burned in me now. I got really angry. Maybe he had meant it so: meant to somehow arouse some feeling in me, something to work upon. The man had method. He leaned over against me and I was bent back upon the hard metal until it hurt me, but I kept my face beyond his reach. He himself enjoyed the struggle, for his body had a chance at last to wrestle and constrain its material, and his muscles, pent up for too long in paint, expanded and contracted in a great burst of rude delight. But muscle for muscle, my own were adequate! I managed finally to throw him off.

The drive home was far more pleasant than on the way out to the country. We were more intimate, more cognizant of each other's flesh, more realistically aware of each other's hair, skin, limbs, and lips and all their odors than we had been before. We were as cold, as strange, as distant in heart, as ever, but we existed, each for the blood cells of the other. Besides, Sterne was solaced by his struggle and I was pleased by my success in overcoming him. We were as lonely as ever, but more comfortable. Exercise, no matter what kind, will overcome horror.

When he reached his home that night, he sat down and wrote me a note that he despatched to me in the morning:

Monday.

What was it, this strange beauty of today? It's still over me, its strange beauty still around me.

The bygone ages?

Crocodiles—swift motion—water-lilies—lilies of the valley—Iphigenia—the wind, Sun?

All this—more: mystery of the present bathed in the mystery of the past—effecting the mystery of the future?

Who the spirit whose closed eyes and lingering kiss awakened me this morning?

> "Pallas, thy bidding we obey:
> And bless thee, for mine ears have heard
> The joy and wonder of a word
> Beyond my dream—beyond my dream. . . ."

M. S.

May 31st.

Well, it did seem a portentous description to cover and condone his little athletic outburst!

The sentimentality of it only made me realize more strongly that he was playing some game. I could not feel he was sincere, and I felt a weariness at the thought that actually I had undertaken a task with that man that would be horribly difficult if I had to put up with his boring flights of fancy all through it. I would certainly stop any more pseudo-classic love letters, however! I would harry and taunt and enrage and injure him. I would light a real fire in him before I was through: when I had him malleable I would make him throw away his yellow green paint and take to clay. I would do this no matter what obstacle came between me and my intention. Had I not seen he could sculpt. from that head of his in the Brooklyn Museum?

I knew that something had got started that no matter how weary I grew, no matter how bored or disgusted, I would see through to the end. I was grappling now with the essence of the man hidden deep below his insincerities, and his incongruities. His essence was strong and pure, though overlaid with so much of the world's harm. I turned to it and went forward.

CHAPTER VIII

Finney Farm

ONE day Elizabeth asked me to walk over and see Finney Farm. This was an old place she had already visited herself because one of her American pupils lived there. She said it was beautiful—a picture of real life.

We went through a grove of trees on the north side of her houses, climbed over the hill, and descended into a low valley where there were two or three rather dismal farms with mournful machinery decaying in the fields of small, grayish white cottages dwarfed beside large, desolate barns. It was quite a long walk, with many stiles set in stone walls, and the ups and downs of New York State.

"We are on Hessian Hill now," said Elizabeth when we started to climb a wide slope.

"Why *Hessian?* Because *you* are here?" I asked maliciously. She giggled and raised her eyebrows.

"That *ought* to be the reason but it's not! No. On account of the Germans who were paid to win a battle here in the war. They were paid to win it and they won it. They were called mercenaries and they were Hessians and now this is Hessian Hill and Finney Farm is on the eastern slope of it."

We plodded on through tangled hedges filled with all kinds of glossy green shrubs and vines. Sumach, lots of it, and beautiful dogwood with rich, white flowers; ferns uncurled from the black earth, and there were many wild flowers.

We came to a lane running westward toward the river that was shining like a gray ribbon far below us, and down that lane we went, with a high hill running steeply up on one side, and on the other, rich hay fields crisscrossed with low stone walls and dotted here and there with enormous old maple and oak trees. Elizabeth padded by my side in her sandals, chewing a long, green blade of grass. She wore a wide-brimmed farmer's straw hat and her tunic was looped up. She told me about the Finney family as we descended the shady path.

"There's old Mrs. Finney, that's Katherine's grandmother. And there's her two daughters, Katherine's mother, and Charity, a spinster. They're old-fashioned people. They live right off the farm. Cows, chickens, an old horse named Charley, and a hired man to do the outside hard work. They do all the real work, though. Take care of the houses, make butter, and raise their vegetables."

Pretty soon we saw the gaunt, stone peaks of an old roofless structure looming up through the tops of trees below us.

"That's the old barn," Elizabeth said. "It was burned out ages ago. It would make a beautiful place to dance in!"

Then presently we saw the roofs of the farmhouse flat below us, the stable, the tool house, and a green painted cottage, all grouped behind it. How peaceful it looked! A complete human habitation. The large farmhouse had the somewhat dingy color of old white paint and the windows were shuttered with turquoise blue blinds.

"I am going to come and live here," I announced, suddenly. Life was shaping itself for me. I saw, dimly, the form of the future crystallizing in a new pattern. Elizabeth laughed, outright.

"That's like you," she giggled. "I dream and dream, but you act. How will you take this away from those people who've lived here so long?"

"I don't know, but I will," I told her. In fact, I already lived there. Before I ever saw the front of the house or its owners, I saw myself living in that dignified and settled environment, supported by its deeply rooted walls, backed up by its respectability and its permanence. My life was going to need its peace, its strength and its protection. So something unthinking but wise in people always plans their campaigns, I think.

"It's a good place to Work in," I found myself saying. What did I know about Work?

"That's what *I* thought," she answered, ruefully. "Well, good-by Finney Farm!"

I felt a trifle remorseful, but more than a little ruthless. My unformulated intuition needed Finney Farm more than she did. She had her two houses.

By this time we had passed the farm buildings, the bright patches

371

of flowers, and the huge gray skeleton of the barn, half covered with thick ivy, through whose wide, empty window-spaces long strands of Virginia creeper hung in rich festoons. The luxuriance of it all, the country opulence and wholesomeness were full of reassurance to me. How had I put up with my New York apartment for so long? I contrasted it with this shining, cleanly spaciousness and remembered with distaste the flakes of black soot that lay each morning on the tarnished ivory window sills left open overnight, and then out here the little Sharkey Cottage was only a tiny playhouse.

The farmhouse was planted on a level spot on the hill with two big plane trees in front of it, and an apple orchard on the southern slope that ran down steeply so that from the bedroom windows on the second floor one could look in between the gnarled trees and watch whatever was taking place there. Later that same year I sat in bed and saw the deer moving by, for their runway across the state passed through those trees, and wild pheasants strutted along and quail hid in the dry grass.

We went up the steps onto the porch that was on two sides of the house, the front and the north side. The French doors of the library and the dining room were outlined with the turquoise-colored shutters. As we went into the hall, we smelled rose geranium and orange flowers from the damp, sunny conservatory.

The first impression of that house was of wide rooms, shining white woodwork and waxed, oak floors. So sweet and clean it all seemed! Nice Finney Farm!

Elizabeth knew where to find Mrs. Finney. I followed her down into the dairy in the cool cellar where the stout old lady was surrounded with shelves of immaculate milk pans.

"We've come to buy some honey," announced Elizabeth.

I don't know how, but in another week I had leased it for two years—Charley and the cows and Jerry the hired man and all—and the Finneys were able to go to Florida or California or somewhere as, they said, they had longed to do for ages.

My long struggle with Maurice was already under way. I unhesitatingly did all I could to strengthen my influence over him, and to bind him to me. I invited him to Provincetown for the summer and told him he could have the life-saving station to work in. The name appealed to him, with his undercurrent of apprehension! He said he would come if I would let him do a portrait of me and I shuddered inwardly at the thought of the color it would be, but I agreed. I realized that part of his reason for doing the portrait was for the advertisement it would give him, for artists often think in these values, but I was not averse myself to the advertisement a portrait by him in the New York gallery would give me. I determined, however, to help along as much as I could with this production so it would do justice to us both!

Maurice really did like and need something I had in me. My certainty and assurance about life at that time gave him a great feeling of security. He liked to feel I was taking the responsibility of him, he who had fended for himself for so long. He was curious about my apparent strength, and questioned me.

"What is it, Mabel? What makes you so fearless about life?"

"Nature," I answered him as I had answered Reed. But he could not understand that. Whatever it was, he loved it. He told me he had always loved the most gentle, feminine women until now—helpless and delicate ones. But now, he thought, he was beginning to love other qualities. Decision and courage and that honesty he felt in me.

"And that walk of yours!" he exclaimed, with a burst of nervous laughter. "You walk like a Prussian officer!" Himself, he walked with a rather conscious swagger, a swing of the broad shoulders. Rather graceful, really.

He tried to be circumspect with me, observing precisely how much and how little I wanted of his caresses. He was all prepared to be good and he reminded me of a little boy from the underworld all dressed up for a Sunday-school picnic.

I could appreciate his relief at the plan for the summer; no need to worry over what to do or where to go—the next few months were settled. He who was incapable of a decision, who could never make up his own mind about anything—well, he was in firm hands now. His long, black hair fell back over his coat collar. He smoothed it down until he looked like a horse with his ears laid back.

"But, darling! I don't know if I can *stand* it if you keep me away from you! I didn't mean to fall in love with you—but there's something *compelling* in you! I feel you will help me smoothen out my life."

How often I was to hear *that* phrase! Poor Maurice. There was

373

something naïve and lovable in him that was penetrating me with an insidious sweetness. I realized I must always be hard and firm with him—always from that time on. I could never allow myself the luxury of weakness, of giving up or of letting things slide between us, for I hated to think where they would slide to. I thought unless I held him up he would sink by his own weight and I would sink with him.

Sometimes I would fasten my eyes on his when he was trying to hypnotize me—and I, in my turn, then, would by a certain power that one may use, lift him: lift him higher, holding him up in a bright, cold, empyrean place where unearthly vibrations flickered like frosty crystals, and where the warm, slow magnetism of his familiar plane hardened and lost its glow. Only a moment or two of actual time, but ages through space; and when the break came and we returned to *here* and *now,* he would gasp and laugh like one who had been ducked into a cold, salty sea; and he would cry: "What is it you do to one! Where do you take one *up* to?"

He referred to this once in a letter, too, from Provincetown: "It is the feeling of perfect equilibrium when near you which makes co-existence with you so splendid. With others I have scarcely felt it even in supreme moments of unity—but with you, Mabel, it is different; your mere presence creates a magic sense of adjustment and harmony in me which gives me poise. A poise not down below, but somewhere in the higher regions where the air is purer, the atmosphere clearer and where I can breathe more freely."

He liked to feel me holding him up there where one doesn't really belong. It wasn't as hard for him as it might have been, for not by his effort but by mine was he suspended in a more rarefied atmosphere than that to which he was accustomed. Poor, poor Maurice! His destiny was always to be where he didn't belong, for some obscure striving and ambition in him lured him near to alien heights and then his own magnetism, meeting elements in others, persuaded them to perform the chemical miracle that supported him above his natural zone. I do not mean I held aloof from physical intimacy with him only to keep him in his place. It was that I felt the need to be cool and spiritually hard with him, remote and untouched at the core of myself where I lived my essential life and from where I drew the strength for such difficult undertakings as his artistic metamorphosis. But I believe he sensed the store of energy I hid from him, and something in him had

374

to find it and tap it. The best way, in his opinion, was the usual way.

I felt very weary and emancipated. When he argued that it would interfere with his Work if I didn't let him make love to me, that old persuasion convinced me that I might as well be hospitable to him without stint and not be narrow-minded. Since I had told him it was his Work that counted with me, and this was true, and I had taken on myself to mold and change it, then I had no right to withhold anything that prevented him from being free to function as I intended he should. I was as cool and logical as possible about this. He was not—yet—physically attractive to me, though his Scotch tweed coat had begun to have an endearing influence with its whiffs of wholesome scent. I stifled all tendencies to soften and melt and be at rest, though I was already tired of the attitude I had assumed. I put my attention on to Work.

"Why wouldn't it be a good idea for you to make a lot of life-sized studies before you begin on the portrait? Quick drawings with the brush in sepia, or in cobalt blue?"

"What a good idea! Yes—in different poses. It will free my mind and my hand, and I will grow used to you before I start the real portrait."

He bustled around and bought pounds of different-colored papers in huge rolls, and tubes of new paint. I was determined not to let him have more than one tube at a time, for when he mixed them, no matter what colors they were, they seemed to me to lose their value.

Is it surprising that I should have really seized upon this man, determined to change his whole scheme of work? To pull him about and alter his make-up? No, countless women have done that to men, are doing it, and will go on trying to do it. The surprising thing is that one tells about it and gives the show away! But that is the way I was thinking and planning then and that is the way many women do, and will go on doing until they learn better. (Forgive me, all you women!)

CHAPTER IX

Provincetown

MOTORING to Provincetown with Maurice, we had to spend a night somewhere on the way. After riding for miles in the long, summer twilight, I remember standing, dazzled by the light at the hotel desk, in a large, mahogany lobby, hearing Maurice ask for a double room and bath, and feeling perfectly limp and miserable. I had accepted what I called to myself the minor inconvenience of a physical relationship with him to further my scheme, thinking that by so doing I would remove our two bodies from the foreground, since they had become obstacles to the work I planned, and stood in the way of a complete influence over him.

So it only meant (at least that is what I thought at the time) that I must be extremely vigilant and, separating my body from my soul, offer the one to him and withhold the other, reserving the spirit, keeping it intact and uninvolved. As Hutch would perhaps have said, giving the heat without the light! But in spite of this logical thinking, when it came to acting out my beliefs, a large and inviolable part of me hung back and revolted against any congress whatsoever with this vivid-looking man who was nothing more to me than an unknown person with whose career I wished to experiment.

Homesick and aloof, I stood by the polished wood counter and the clerk swung a large, open Register Book around to Maurice to sign, sweeping me at the same time with a look that affronted me by its depreciating appraisal, though I very well knew that half a glance at Sterne would make it fairly impossible to rate any woman with him a wife, and that to be considered at all respectable, in his company, would have needed the habit of a Mother Superior and bone-rimmed spectacles. Yet it seemed to me my rôle was precisely that of a superior and spiritual mother who was trying to shape unwieldy material into an image that would be more pleasing. Why, then, such a sinking feeling?

However, as my spirits went down, Maurice's, in the same measure, went up. He was positively flamboyant when we were finally shut into the lonesome hotel bedroom together, and he began exclaiming "Darling!" and showing his teeth before the bell-boy had the door closed.

Really, I never felt less emancipated in my life than I did that night! I knew the man considered me an experienced woman of the world and that actually he was rather nervous, in spite of his feeling of increased importance at being alone with so sophisticated, so dangerous, a person as myself; and I knew that, to preserve and add to my power over him, I must never let him know my childish and bourgeois Buffalonian trepidations. In spite of everything, however, I held fast to my aim, and so did he to his—but they were different in character, our ambitions, and separated us more than they drew us together. The flesh, then, among these complex motivations, had no sanctity, and scarcely any authority.

In his white pajamas with large bedroom slippers on his feet, he recovered a hint of the innocent patriarchal atmosphere I had noticed about him, and the potential Hebrew Prophet reappeared once he shed his tweed overcoat and his soft brown felt hat, and drew from his tie the sinister black opal pin that gleamed intermittently with a dark and baleful blue light. He laughed with the gasp that sent the air in a rush from his lungs as he climbed into bed and I obediently received him. And this for ART!

We labored in the dark, he with his eyes closed, trying to imagine he had B., his early love, there with him. He had unfortunately told me that this was his habit when making love to other women; I, with a certain common-sense thrift, endeavored to get as much enjoyment out of the exigent situation as I could. His strong, rather bland hands traveled over me, sizing up shapes, as sculptors hands are made to do. His finger-tips were more interested in form than in sense. They were always studying. No sooner was the spasmodic embrace completed, than it was forgotten in the thoughts about Art that surged up in his mind. He began to talk about his work.

"I have a great gift of visualizing," he said. "If I can first visualize a thing, I can draw it. To me, it seems, I grasp Essential Form more completely if I visualize it to myself than if I *look* at it. Now these

377

curves, darling, these volumes and masses, I can see them in my mind;
I could get up now and draw them without *looking at* them; I have
taken them into my psyche by touch, that is really 'knowing' a woman
as it speaks of it in the Bible. . . ."

"I think you were meant to be a sculptor," I murmured drowsily into
his shoulder. I fell asleep, worn out by the dreary vicissitudes of evolution, while his voice went on and on in the night, delivering a little
lecture upon Form.

We arrived conspicuously in Provincetown. I had engaged one of
the beautiful little white clapboarded Portuguese fishermen's houses
that lined two sides of the long main street and the salty smell of the
bay permeated its small, tidy rooms. It was a curious setting for the
dark, ornate stranger I had in tow. But I soon had him settled in the
building adjacent to the life-saving station across the dunes, busily preparing his materials for his work. I do not know how many months
of his life he has passed doing that, but if all the hours were bulked
together, it might add up to years.

"I must prepare my materials!" In this way the moment to start work
may be deferred without too great a feeling of guilt. To *start* to work,
at least to paint, was as excruciating for Sterne as it is for most artists.
Once he had decided what he was going to do, had evolved his scheme,
had taken the plunge, drawn, even, the first line, he could go on without anything more than nervous irascibility, and spend his energy on
that intense endeavor of his to make paint do more than it was possible for it to do, but each new start was like dying, for him.

I organized my life. It had different parts to it that must be brought
somehow into a whole. I had two houses to live in. Across the sand
dunes the Peaked Bar life-saving station on the coast, and a fisherman's cottage on the bay! I had John coming soon from school for
his holidays, Bobby Jones coming from New York, and I had asked
several friends to visit me: Hazel Albertson, Bobby Rogers, and others.
I wished to consider Sterne simply as one of a number of the elements
of the summer; I did not intend to have him fill up my foreground,
for he had not that importance for me. In the first place, I wanted
always to feel the lovely, new, free, unattached ownership of myself
that enabled me to retire alone to my depths, forgetting the whole
world, and I didn't want people to begin to assume that we were
having a love affair, because I didn't want them talking about it all

around us, for that kind of attention on one vitiates the air, sucks the life from it, steals one's freedom and spontaneity and energy. Besides that, I was afraid of criticism.

The Hapgoods were already there and I made an arrangement with Neith to form a joint household for meals—thus taking care of John and the others, and I hired a Portuguese girl for a cook over at the Peaked Bar House.

Maurice plodded obediently over across the dunes every morning— after those nights when the salts of the sea and the salts of the flesh had shifted and blended together on the coarse sheets of the fisherman's bed. He left me to myself. I needed to return to myself after each night, to gather myself up and to remember what was what. He was magnetic and the peasant blood in him was like a strong essence. This quality of his chemical make-up was perhaps the source of his vivid appearance, but it was not, like that, open to criticism, could not be rated as good or bad taste, had nothing to do with his opinions on art or his ability to talk about them, nor did it make him dependable, courageous, and manly. It was just a strong, magnetic essence that emanated from him and I had underestimated the attraction it might have for my own undifferentiated essence. My blood cells soon responded to his, quite of their own accord, without waiting for orders from my guiding will. I had divorced my body from my soul. Well, flesh and blood set up their own autonomy quite soon. Together, had we been chemically visible, our combination would have caused the angels to open their eyes.

In the morning I sat in the small parlor before the fireless brick chimney place that I had had built before I arrived, for I was constantly building fireplaces in those days, though I never lighted the one in that cottage, never needed it. I sat alone in the room, and it had the curtains drawn to shade the light. I wanted to sit in a peaceful place and sew, and so I hemmed several dozen small linen table napkins. Hutch came in and talked to me.

"I never saw you more self-possessed than you are this summer, Mabel," he told me. "You seem to belong to yourself at last. Do you hear from Jack?"

"Hutch, I do. And I wish he'd leave me alone. I don't care for him any more. It's *over*. Steff made me pretend it wasn't, but it is! Hutch, won't you write and tell him this for me and send him this ring? *I* don't know what to tell him. You'll know what to say. Will you? Look at these letters from Hovey. Jack will be all right."

DEAR CARL HOVEY: *Bucarest, May 24.*

Here is article number three, "The Serbian Front." If everything goes right, you will have already received article number one, "Serbia Between Battles," and article number two, "Salonika, the Eastern Gate to War." Robinson's sketches for the first two went forward at the same time as the manuscript and his stuff for this one accompanies it.

I am sending two copies of this article by different routes, as I have done with the others. And I am also sending two copies of these photographs which I herewith enclose and which were taken by a young fellow here for a book he wrote and which he swears have not appeared elsewhere. Better copyright them.

I am much better, having stayed in my room for four days and lived on a diet of milk and slops generally. Tomorrow morning the doctor will come to say whether or not I can leave for Russia immediately. If I cannot, that means an X-Ray examination and a consultation to find out what I've got. But I will have wired my plans before you get this. Nothing serious, I think.

Let me say, in conclusion, that this is a damn fine article, one of the best I have ever written, and all new stuff. We are the first to make that trip and the first to see Goutchevo, etc.

We've both worked like hell here and done nothing else. Hope you'll be satisfied.

Hope to send article number four, "Shot at Sunrise," before I leave.

As ever,
REED.

P.S. Photographs too expensive. Will get them in about a week, and send them.

Had X-Ray and am afflicted with gravel in kidneys. Much better. Off for Russia.

Couldn't finish "Shot at Sunrise"—too tired.

R.

Metropolitan
The Livest Magazine in America

June 2nd.

DEAR MRS. DODGE:

I have just had a cable from Jack saying that he has sent three articles from Bucarest. That was all there was in the cable, excepting that he told me to let you know.

Most sincerely,

CARL HOVEY.

Metropolitan
The Livest Magazine in America
432 Fourth Avenue
New York

June 23rd.

DEAR MRS. DODGE:

We have had two articles from Reed and about thirty drawings from Robinson. One is called "Serbia Between Battles," and the other, "The Eastern Gate of War." Both drawings and articles are immense. The first lot will be in the August number, and we are giving it plenty of space.

Reed and Robinson are at present prisoners at Kholm in Galicia. A few days ago I heard from the Secretary of State that they had been made prisoners by the Russians and were suspected of being engaged in Anti-Russian propaganda. It appears that they had passports from the Embassy at Bucarest and also letters to a member of a notorious Anti-Russian Society in Galicia. Their Bucarest passports would not be good credentials under the circumstances. Whether they have lost or for some reason could not use their American credentials, I do not know. Anyhow, Secretary Lansing has received from us full information as to their status as correspondents and has communicated with the Ambassador at Petrograd on account of Robinson's British citizenship. We are looking for their release at any moment, as all that is necessary is to establish their status as correspondents of the *Metropolitan*. The American Ambassador at Petrograd cabled that if their status was established, they would then be expelled from Russia, but if not, they would be court-martialed. In other words, they would be sent out of Russia anyhow. This is too bad, and whether their imprisonment has been a very uncomfortable thing or not, we cannot tell. They may have managed to turn it into a big lark. The Russians are always arresting somebody. I will let you know as soon as I hear from Lansing that they are released. Also I will send you proofs of the first article just as soon as we get them from the printer; this will be within the next few days.

Please give my love to Hutch and Neith. I would like nothing better than to come up and see you during the summer, and will surely do so.

I think it is hardly possible to place the travel article. I have sent it to *Scribner's* and *Century* and they turned it down. I do not know of any other market for an article of that sort. If you would like to have me do so, I will send it back to the author if you will give me his address.

As ever,

Yours sincerely,

CARL HOVEY.

Metropolitan
The Livest Magazine in America

DEAR MRS. DODGE:

I meant to have written you that Jack and Robinson were safe and well
and out of prison. They were prisoners for about a week before Secretary
Lansing and the Ambassador at Petrograd secured their release. Apparently they were taken from Kholm in Galicia to Petrograd. I have
received a cable from Jack saying that they had been released and were on
their way to Bucarest, but they must have changed their minds as I got
another cable asking for money, saying that they would stick around
Petrograd for a few days. I judge from this they are getting along well
with the Russians. They must have seen a great deal in Russia. I do not
think Jack has been particularly well to judge from his letters, but he seems
to get about and is working hard; the third article called "The Serbian
Front" came through and is strong and richer than the first two. Our
August issue with Jack's article and Robinson's drawings and a triple
blast from the Colonel makes very strong stuff. I will send you an advance
copy within a few days.

I think I shall have to go to Kennebunkport on an editorial errand about
the 17th. Would it be all right for me to stop over at Provincetown, say
about the 19th or 20th? I do not care at all where I sleep and don't know
whether you and the Hapgoods could take me in or not, but if there is
any place near by, that will be all right.

As ever,

Yours sincerely,

CARL HOVEY.

Hutch read the letters and took the gold ring.

"Poor Jack," he said, but he did not look exactly displeased. He got
up with an energetic and purposeful expression. "I'll try. I don't want
to *hurt* him. I think I can tell him what you mean. . . . You'll always
be his friend. But I can see what you mean. You are quieter now.
Your interests are changing. I think this Platonic, protective interest
you have in Sterne is very good for you. I believe you'll do him a lot
of good, too." (Ah, it hurt, this first attempt to be reserved with
Hutch, and not tell him all about it!)

"What do you think of him, anyway?" I asked.

"Maurice? Well, there's a warmth about him. Of course, he's not
our kind at all. Your interest in him is in his work and what you can
do in that way. It will be interesting to watch. . . ."

"It's queer. But I don't trust him," I said.

382

"Well, I suppose he can't trust himself," answered Hutch. "Leo says women have spoiled him."

"Well, why should I want to trust him?" I asked disingenuously.

Hutch soon brought me the following letter he had written to Reed. I gave him the wedding ring and he enclosed it in the envelope and sent it:

I fear that Mabel is worrying about your coming to Provincetown. She has had no impulse to write you since you left—she says she couldn't help talking to you to a certain extent when you were here, as you seemed to need it. But she knows the old feeling is dead and she deeply desires that you shall not be hurt and disappointed. She is well satisfied, I know, with her general state of calm and unemotionality, and she would hate to have you come to Provincetown and demand what she cannot give or otherwise make the summer more of an upheaval for her than she feels she can easily bear. She wants to be quiet, impersonal, and the thought that you may come and break it up is distressing to her, on her account as well as yours.

She would deeply welcome you as a friend, a very near friend—but she feels you cannot become that, on account of your nature.

As for me, Jack, I feel sure of one thing. Mabel will never again be to you what she was. If I know her at all, I know she cannot repeat an experience, a feeling, that is gone. She felt for me once, I think, and I would just as soon try any impossible thing as to try to get it back. The feeling she had for me has now changed into a deep and I think permanent friendship. It's just what she and I want. I wish something of the same kind might be between you and her. But she thinks you cannot do it. I don't know.

But don't come to Provincetown with the thought that Mabel is to be as she was. She will have other friends come, in whom she has cool and refreshing interest. You can only be one of them—perhaps the best friend of all, if you want it so—but that old feeling, that eternal illusion, will never return.

You will suffer if you return with that idea—and that is partly why I am writing. Partly, too, it is because Mabel wants me to.

I have felt much nearer to you this last year. I think I understand your feelings, and they reveal attitudes which would be like my own in similar situations.

Affectionately,

HUTCH.

I had been receiving many letters and postcards from Reed ever since he left, and the end of *Pygmalion* where he tried to voice my vague feelings for what I had called "nature."

383

White moved his body, crushing the ferns in the valley,
And his happy singing died along far roads;
But love followed after him—flickered across his sleep,
Breathed pride into his walk, power into his hand,
Sweet restlessness into his quiet thought—
Till he who had needed life now needed more;
And so at last he came to the hills again.

Pygmalion, Pygmalion, Pygmalion—
He said in his pride, "Thou art wild, and without life!"
Never feeling the warm dispersed quiet of earth,
Or the slow stupendous heart-beat that hills have.

Pygmalion, Pygmalion, Pygmalion—
He wrenched the shining rock from the meadow's breast,
And out of it shaped the lovely, almost-breathing
Form of his dream of his life of the world's women.
Slim and white was she, whimsical, full of caprice;
Bright sharp in sunlight, languid in shadow of cloud,
Pale in the dawn, and flushed at the end of day.
Staring, he felt of a sudden the quick, fierce urge
Of the will of the grass, and the rock, and the flowering tree;
Knew himself weak and unfulfilled without her—
Knew that he bore his own doom in his breast—
Slave of a stone, unmoving, cold to his touch,
Loving in a stone's way, loving but thrilling never.

In smothering summer silence, pricked with crickets,
Still fell the smiting hammer; happy and loud
Swelled the full-throated song of the adult grass. . . .
Full-breasted drooped the tree, heavy with apples. . . .
A wind worn lean from leap-frog over the mountains
Spurted the stiff faun-like hair of him—whipped desire,
And a bird sang "Faint-faint-faint with love-love-love!"

Blind he stood, while the great sun blundered down
Through planets strung like beads on careless orbits;
Blind to the view that sank like sleep after love,
Miles over blazoned hills to the brazen river,
Ceaselessly changing, color and form and line,
Pomp, blaze, pageantry new to the world's delight. . . .

Hot moist hands on the glittering flanks, and eager
Hands following the chill hips, the icy breasts—
Lithe, radiant belly to swelling stone—
"Galatea!"—blast of whispering flame his throat—
"Galatea! Galatea!"—his entrails molten fire—
"Galatea! Galatea! Galatea!"—mouth to mouth. . . .

Pygmalion, Pygmalion, Pygmalion—
Rock is she still, and her heart is the hill's heart,
Full of all things beside him—full of wind and bees
And the long falling miles and miles of air.
Despair and gnawing are on him, and he knows her
Unattainable who is born of will and hill—
Far-bright as a plunging full-sailed ship that seems
Hull-down to be set immutable in sea. . . .

Reed wrote joyously, his thoughts centered on his new house across
the Hudson River in the Ramapo Hills. And Carl Hovey kept on sending me copies of his letters and cables to the *Metropolitan Magazine*
office. They did not seem to be for me. It was someone else, who had
taken the place of Reed's Mabel, who read his letters in Provincetown.

He was overflowing with happiness; even when he got sick in
Bucarest, it did not seem to affect him. I have his Russian passport;
out of sheer exuberance, he wrote on the outside of it for all to read
who could read English:

I am a German and Austrian spy. I do it for money.
REED.

He felt, he told me afterwards, immune from sin, sickness and death,
as though nothing could ever hurt him again.

CHAPTER X

Peaked Hill Bar House

SO Sterne quickly grew into less of a stranger and Reed more of one, and imperceptibly, they exchanged places in the unseen world. I was devoted to a collection of oriental books that I took about with me, and it seemed that Maurice must find them congenial too, for he looked like one of the personages in the Upanishads. Sometimes in the morning after breakfast before he left for the dunes, I would persuade him to come out on the beach for a little while, and I would take a book along and read passages out loud to him. The lovely fresh mornings with gentle air and uncomplicated, natural things all about one! Maurice's black head against the clear blue sky was like the painting in a Persian miniature. Sitting together on the pale sand with the grasses bending mildly about us in the breeze, I bent over my big book:

". . . The pinkâra is the earth, the prastâva the sky, the udgîtha heaven, the pratihâra the regions, the nidhana the sea. These are the Sakvari Sâmans as interwoven in the worlds.

"He who thus knows the Sakvaris as interwoven in the worlds, becomes possessed of the worlds, he reaches the full life, he lives long, becomes great with children and cattle, great by fame. His rule is, "Never complain of the worlds."

Peaceful and holy moment! And then as likely as not there would come fluttering along the light, soft summer skirts of someone and the atmosphere would change, grow tight and anguished for an interval and pass again, and I would resume to my stranger:

"The altar is man, O Gautama: its fuel
speech itself, the smoke the breath, the
light the tongue, the coals the eye, the sparks
the ear.

386

On that altar the Devas offer food.
From that oblation rises seed.

The altar is woman, O Gautama.
On that altar the Devas offer seed.
From that oblation rises the germ. . . ."

As soon as John came, I had Hazel come to stay with me; probably to dilute the atmosphere. Maurice had everything prepared for work by this time, so there was no longer any excuse to put off the sittings, and Hazel and I moved over to the Peaked Hill Bar House and slept in the large, airy upper room where, from the dormer windows, we heard the great breakers pound all night on the beach below us and I had John, with Bobby, staying now in the cottage on the Bay. Such planning and moving—to keep things both together and apart! Our household arrangements were very complicated, for some of our meals we took with the Hapgoods!

Maurice was a studio man and he had been staying in it most of the time until Hazel came, but I noticed that when we moved over to the Station, the first morning at breakfast he lingered and lingered at the table, leaning back in his chair, and smoking his cigar with a meditative and calculating expression on his face.

Hazel was blond and rosy. She always wore white jumpers and bloomers and her legs were well muscled and rounded from farm work, for she and her family lived at the Chestnut Hill farm near Newburyport—that farm where Walter and Bobby and Carl Binger and all the others had spent so many happy week-ends when they were at Harvard. Hazel was, though on a high level indeed, a superior flirt. She liked to have them all interested in her at once, though she never seemed to have out-and-out affairs with them. Some inhibition of her own prevented that, perhaps, for she was free enough to do as she liked, her husband having left her; and her own intelligent understanding of life would not have stood in her way. She was more truly "emancipated" than I ever was!

When men focused their attention upon her, she laughed and the pupils of her eyes grew black and shone like stars between her screwed-up lids. That was what I saw at her first breakfast with Maurice. The shining black excitement in her eyes, the laughing, rallying voice of her! Maurice was as quiet and watchful as a hunter.

The only movement he made was when he slowly raised his cigar to his lips. He had his concentrated expression on his face, the slight frown between his brows, the mouth drawn taut, and his eyes were shooting streams of magnetism across the table at her.

Good heavens! It is impossible to describe what a shock it was to me when I realized that this must be a *habit* of his; that it had not been my own particular charm or any special need of his for me and only me that had set him hunting me down in precisely that way. Though I had recognized he had a practiced technique, it had been impossible for me to realize that he *habitually* paid such attention to women. A woman, unless she is extremely conscious, cannot help believing that she is really the only one to awaken the deepest interest of a man. When I saw Maurice gazing at Hazel across the breakfast table with exactly the same fascinated and fearsome expression that he had turned upon me to attract and hold me, that look compounded of defense and attack at one and the same time, I suffered a complete realization of the worthlessness of our relation and its banality.

At that moment, too, I grasped another fact. He was free and I was ensnared. I was implicated, entangled, and bound up with him by the unprincipled and undiscriminating tides of the blood that ebb and flow with no standard save natural attraction, and once released are harder to turn back than the waters of earthly rivers.

How foolish I had been to think I could direct these elemental forces and hold them subject to my will! The blood has its own will, and the soul is indubitably compelled to follow in its track. My will, I perceived, was not my own at all. In less time than it takes to tell, it was concerned solely with the conservation of the fleshly joy. Maurice and I had hunted each other down—well, I had no intention of letting him escape. With an awakened sense of his diminished value, I was ready, just the same, to sacrifice all other and greater values to hold him: my friendship for Hazel, who was, I believed, essentially more worthwhile in every way than he, my independence, my pride, and even, if necessary, my ambitious wish to turn him into a sculptor.

I broke impetuously through the magic that was weaving itself back and forth between them, and hastened Maurice out to his studio and drew Hazel to the beach. I tried to draw her out about him, but she was reserved.

"I can't tell *yet* what I think of him. Wait a few days." I determined she should be gone before many days had passed! I went to the studio and took hold of the slipping, sliding, unanchored spirit of that man. He was busy with some studio task.

"You must start your work now," I said. "You've let *days* go by and nothing done! I can pose easily now we are staying over here—let's begin today—this morning!"

He looked at me and laughed out a nervous gasp that left his mouth open and showed his tongue lolling like a parrot's tongue between his teeth.

"But, darling, I'm not *ready*. My materials . . ."

"You're as ready as you'll ever be," I broke in, in a rage, and seated myself on the couch. "How shall I pose? What do you want?"

"Well, really, darling . . ."

"Go on. You've got to work or else I'll break this thing all up. . . ." Work had now become a weapon of defense to save my pleasure for me! Ah, and what hifalutin aims had been the start of this!

Maurice sulked, turned into a little boy. He hastily seized a drawing board and a stick of brown chalk. Work had become for him the means of preserving his comfortable summer arrangement. I took the pose he suggested and he took the plunge he had been nervously postponing—and the series called "Portraits of Mabel Dodge," exhibited that winter in New York with so much success and with so much talk of masterly draughtmanship, was thus begun that morning!

And this is Art! It is time that some of the tomfoolery and awesomeness be removed from the subject. When we learn what some of its true incentives are we will stop talking of its sacredness and about its inspiration. Art is often an evasion and a subterfuge: a coward's defense. The world is cluttered up by artists and their "productions." So I thought as I lay on the couch with my back turned to Sterne, and he diligently drew it with the heavy strokes that constituted his "line." My two braids hung loosely over my shoulders. I seethed within, though I lay ever so motionless. The waves pounded below in the sunshine and a few lazy flies floated around the room with slow jerks, singing their entranced song.

"There is a strange relationship of forms all through nature," declaimed Maurice, suddenly.

I turned my head and looked at him over my shoulder. He sat with his little stick of chalk poised in the air, and stared at my hip through his half-closed eyes. There was an intensely serious and concentrated expression on his face—and his mouth was drawn into the taut straight line it took when his attention was fixed. But no stream of magnetism poured incontinently from his eyes. It was, rather, as though he drew into himself from the object before him, by some magical optic power, its significance and true inwardness.

"The human form is like a mountain range—it has its peaks and valleys, the same relationships. . . . I don't see you as a woman now, but as a conglomeration of related forms. . . ."

"Oh! Stop talking and work!" I cried to myself as I turned my face back to the wall with a grimace on it he could not see. I hated him. As a man, he was impossible, and to tell the truth, I didn't care anything about him as an artist, now. Something had switched around inside of me. But just the same, I intended to see the project through. It was necessary to dignify what existed between us, unless I then and there broke with him and dismissed him from my life. I suspected I should do this very thing, yet could not, somehow. He was so complete an object there, so massive, considerable and definite, and that blood sympathy was established between us that was almost impossible to withdraw from.

"Well," I argued to myself, as I lay there with my back to him, "at least he is real of his kind. He is not shadowy and attenuated like so many of the men I am used to. There is a dignity about him in spite of his flashiness, a vague worthiness in spite of his unethical behavior. He is undomesticated. He hasn't a notion of how to act. He will always bother and embarrass me by his lack of instinct, and he doesn't care a scrap about me, really! Yet there is something irresistible about him. I will hang on—and see how it all comes out."

I think it was then in that first hour of overt antagonism that the idea of marrying him came to me, presenting itself as a means of controlling and holding him. I do not know if it occurred to him at the same time, but it must have been very shortly after, if not then, for he broached the idea to me after an explosion of mine about Hazel.

He had continued his optical assault upon her at lunch—at dinner. He forgot I was there, and slid off into that habit of staring at her that caused her eyes to darken and made the nervous giggles ripple over her lips. I left the table the third time it began, and that made him notice me. He followed me out to the sand bar beside the house and sat down patiently, taking my hand in his.

"What is the matter, darling?" he queried.

"You know very well what the matter is. I won't have it. You ought to be ashamed after what there is between us. *Have* you any shame?"

"Why, Mabel, darling! Do you mean Hazel? Why, she means nothing to me! She seems to be a very nice girl, but no one seems to *amount* to anything beside you."

"Well, what are you trying to do, then? Why this portentous attention? Is that simply your idea of being *polite* or what? You don't seem to have the slightest conception of how to behave! I think, really, we'd better separate—now—before we get in any deeper. I'm *bored*. I didn't suppose I'd have to undertake your education!"

Maurice looked pained and at the same time stimulated. I was struggling with a desire to weep and lay my head on his shoulder and be comforted, but that, I knew, I could never do. I must be hard, firm and uncompromising. If I kept him, I must make him fit into my surroundings and I could not do that if I allowed myself the slightest weakening.

Maurice craved molding. He *wanted* his character shaped and to have someone take the responsibility of doing it. It never occurred to him to do it himself. No, his solid, Jewish puritanism wanted him to be orderly, disciplined by the human law of society, and patterned like other men, but as for working on *himself,* regarding *himself* as material more worthy of an artist than paper and paint, oh, no! His strong sense of form that struggled for an outlet, that would have been capable, once directed, of making a real man of him, that feeling for form, he saved for his *Art* and sweated it out in paint.

"Mabel, you are right. I suppose it was very wrong of me to look at Hazel like that. I can't seem to help it when I see an attractive woman. I can feel my magnetism pour out through my eyes and fasten her for me. Afterwards I am exhausted. I don't know why I do it. . . . I've always done it. . . . It's gotten me into lots of trouble, too."

"Do you mean to say you know you oughtn't to do it and you do it anyway?"

"Why, yes. Everybody is weak. We aren't all like *you,* darling," he said, admiringly. "I know *you* wouldn't be weak!"

(Oh, wouldn't I, if I could!)

"Well, Maurice, if you want to stay here near me, you've got to stop it—that's all. It's disgusting—vicious. I *hate* that kind of looseness."

"Oh, I feel you will make me different, Mabel! I really want to shed those old ways. No one has ever helped me. I feel we could have a beautiful life together. My Work would gain if I could break up that thing. It's like hunting, with me. It means *nothing*, really. A waste of power. . . . If only we could get married, darling! What do you think?"

"Oh, I don't know, Maurice. It might simplify things. But I don't think we *really* care for each other, do you?"

"I don't know. I admire you. I respect you. I love our beautiful relationship. . . ."

"How about B.?"

"Oh, that was different. I was young and romantic when I fell in love with B. Now I am much more serious. I have my best Work ahead of me to do. I have never been satisfied with what I have accomplished—no matter how hard I try."

"Well, Maurice, you are a natural *sculptor*. You shouldn't be trying to paint."

"Why do you say that, darling? My painting has been admired very much. I want to improve it of course. I want to work very hard this year. I must smoothen out my life, settle down. . . . Perhaps we should talk it over with our friends before we decide, but I feel that if we married it would settle something."

We talked of this again and again. I think we were both of us repelled and attracted at the same time by the idea. One day he wrote to me:

It worries me, dearest, that you are not feeling well. I had to think of it all day when preparing my canvases, when reading, at lunch, tea, dinner. I only forgot for half an hour when I sat on the dunes and watched the setting sun.

How glorious it was today again. The sky the most glorious opal I have ever seen. But what fascinated me most was a fish the sea had cast upon the beach—it struggled frantically on the wet bank. Now and then a wave would almost reach it—then lightly some waves would wash over it—but not with enough force to bring it back to the sea. Then a wave at last carried it back but a stronger one cast it out again. When its violent struggle and flapping almost ceased, and it looked as if it would perish, a huge wave came near, washed far over it and carried it back to the sea. It is happy now—don't you think so?

MAURICE.

392

CHAPTER XI

Oh, Maurice!

THE imperceptible shift I made, from the source of power in myself to the power in Maurice, took place so unconsciously that I did not realize what was happening. All my attention was on him and so all my satisfaction or discontent had to come from him. In the last analysis, what one wants in oneself or another is their energy, their power. This makes virtues and vices lose their values; and Maurice's value for me, his irresistible and all but priceless possession, was the power in him. Neither of us defined this to each other, but he was aware of something in himself. He said:

"I have a streak of pure gold running through me, Mabel, even if all the rest is worthless."

The life at the inner center of people may be buried ever so deep, it may be of all degrees of fineness or grossness, but whatever its quality, it constitutes the reality of each human being, and without always knowing we are doing so, we judge people by it alone. When people's spiritual energy has ceased to well up in them, we say they are dead, although they may still be walking about. Anyway, we have no use for them. But when we see a man or a woman whose power rises in him like the water in a spring, we are immediately attracted to it. We cannot resist trying to tap it, somehow, to get it for ourselves. Maurice had this power in him and so I could not give him up.

But my old uneasiness and depression returned to me, fluctuating with happy moments, or hours of intense and willful bossiness when I felt compelled to manage him and everyone else with a rod of iron.

Since Maurice simply couldn't control himself and cut off the stream he had started flowing out of his eyes onto Hazel, he was obliged to try to hide it behind my back, and although he showed an almost ludicrous indifference towards her when I was watching, yet I felt the unseen and unheard vibration of his being in the stillness of his body when they were near each other. There was an undercurrent of it going on.

When I happened to be absent from them, I *knew* he turned it directly on her, for I caught tag-ends of it if I came back unexpectedly, and this aroused a perfect fury in me. It caused all my own energy to mount in waves of passionate resentment, a flood of instinctive rage that came from a sense of loss, for since I drew upon him now for life, I felt defrauded if anyone else got any portion of it. Poor man! He was my bank. Let no one try to rob me!

Of course this was the true, involuntary, and undefined life that went on below the surface of our days. Our obvious existence took place more or less peacefully between the sand dunes of the Peaked Hill Bar over on the lonely coast, and the cheerful little village across the two miles of fine white sand.

I continued to pose for Maurice every morning, and to limit him to the single tubes of blue, or to the sanguine. He made a large number of drawings, some of them very fine, all of them of Mabel Dodge, that now are scattered about the world so widely that while one of them hangs in Mrs. Gusdorf's dining room, there is one in Peiping and another in Nova Scotia!

I contrived to separate my life into different parts that did not touch. Of course I had expected to blend these into one whole and perfect pattern, but I had found, as soon as John came, and as soon as Hazel came, I must keep them all apart—and hop from one to the other, insulating myself from each in turn, for John had his strange antipathy for Maurice, and they just couldn't be mixed.

Maurice and I continued to play with the idea of marriage in much the same way that one pokes at a snake with a stick. The idea was dangerous and revolting; yet we couldn't leave it alone. When, as I soon contrived, Hazel left for Newburyport, I told her Maurice and I were thinking of getting married and asked her what she thought of it. I was half anxious to show her he was *mine,* and half wishful for her real opinion of him. But alas! How can one ever get a *real* opinion from a human being when we are all under the influence of the wishes planted in our blood? Hazel, too, could appreciate and crave the secret energy in Maurice. I could not help thinking she was loath to have me possess him out and out, when she sent me this letter from the Boston boat, for it was far more critical of him than her darkling eyes and excited laugh had shown her to be. Or was it only another case of the cool estimation of her mind in direct antagonism with the involuntary and uncritical blood? She wrote:

Boat. 3:30.

MABEL DEAREST—

My very first impression—quick and uncerebrated—is that it would be a mad thing to do. Perfectly mad.

I can stop and reason—find perfectly good ones on both sides, but you didn't ask for that.

And this in spite of the fact that I like him very much—the combination just feels like an illegitimate one.

You're more like me than I thought, even. Please let time clarify things—it always helps. The relationship wouldn't be constructive. It would be like subjecting a sweet, true, human thing to the glaring, merciless, temperatureless sunlight of the North Pole. Believing diametrically the opposite isn't so important—but that there's no unison of spirit which is the breath of life to you. The very feeling that there is no "trust" is proof. Your rhythms are totally different.

Oh, look out on the far horizon and bring your centers home.

HAZEL.

It troubles me—I've been sitting here looking out to the far horizon almost with a prayer on my lips—and it doesn't seem any other way.

Whichever way you choose, finally, must only make it possible for you to find beauty and truth, somehow. You're a strong, brave soul—and I've infinite faith in you, but that isn't the question, is it?

To me life is so much in the individual (so much a thing that cannot be wrecked) that, except for John—I should think that it made little difference. Only I'd never make it legal. It's the only way I'd feel sure of him—S., I mean.

Oh, there are so many things I want to say to you.

I wish I were down by the sea with you.

S. would never be held by anything human. The reason you feel that you can't trust him is that he is responsible to nothing except the truth that he sees; he is not either good or bad. He is perfectly beyond human judgment; he is not pagan nor altogether Eastern, he is dissociated from life. He sees things only as shimmering light. You would never feel as if you had "gotten" him—he's not tangible spiritually. It's strange that he should want to marry, I think. It almost seems as if he doesn't understand himself.

I'm sending you this as it is.

The last of it wrote itself.

395

Hazel gone, I took up my abode once more in the Provincetown cottage and slept there with John, leaving Maurice to sleep at the life-saving station. Every morning I traipsed over through the sand to the Studio with a basket of lunch for us.

The white dunes billowed like the waves of the sea and often changed their shapes when the wind blew in from the coast, but all the way in and out between the scraggly bushes that persisted in their deep-rooted existence, I could see the low buildings on the Peaked Hill Bar ahead of me on the high ridge of sand that marked the coast line. Up and down, in and out, I picked my course, leaving footprints behind me that would be gone by evening.

One morning as I plodded along, and my mind was as usual seething with the problem of Maurice, and the conflict between my revolt about him and the fixation I had upon him, I rehearsed as one does what I should say to him when I reached him. I saw him before me in my mind's eye, earnest and serious and convincing, at his best, suffering from his own conflicts, dignified by agony.

("We must separate, Maurice. We are too dissimilar. I want to be alone again. . . ."

"But, Mabel, you help me so much. You are helping me to smoothen out my life. You are showing me something so much finer than I knew before. If you send me away, I will only drift as before. . . . I need someone to hold me up as you do. . . . You are so strong, darling.")

I knew how it would go. It had become a routine for us, and I would be unable to withdraw my essence from the sticky blend it made with his. We had pooled our energies—how could we ever separate them again?

While my inner vision was upon us as we talked, my eyes were fixed upon the tiny studio far off ahead of me against the summer sky; and suddenly I saw the minute form of Maurice, like a tiny insect, appear at the door and hesitate there for an instant. I saw him dart around the corner of the building. He circled it and then he reappeared at the other side. He did not seem to be looking for me across the wide rolling dunes in front of him, but only all around his neighborhood. I saw him hasten over to the main house and enter it for a moment, and then return to his studio. He passed his hands over his head, like a thoughtful fly, as he paused at the door before going in. All this I saw as plainly in the clear air as one may see the purposeful life of the insect world at one's feet.

I wondered and kept on walking. In twenty minutes or so I had covered the distance between us and, just before reaching the studio door, I whistled as usual—and looked to see him come to meet me as he always did. But there was no sign of him, so I went in and found him sitting before his drawing board, looking like an aggrieved prophet.

"Why do you play tricks on me, darling, making me leave my work while you whistle me and then hide like a child?" He drew in his mouth and raised his eyebrows.

"What do you mean, Maurice?"

"Oh, I know you were hiding—but where?"

"What *are* you talking about?"

"Where did you go when you first came? You must have amused yourself, darling, at my expense! I didn't realize we had any *hiding* places on this barren ridge!" His fundamental dislike of the austere spot revealing itself!

"Maurice, I don't know what you mean. I just came—*now*. I saw you, though, when I was walking over, go out and look all around. I wondered what you were doing."

"R-r-really, Mabel?" When he was excited, many r's rolled in his speech! "Why, darling! What can it mean? I heard you whistle outside and then I saw you pass by the window in your pink dress! When you didn't come in, I ran to look for you. I went all over, but I couldn't find you. But you were *here,* dearest! I would swear it. You know how sure my *eyes* are—they are never mistaken."

"I was thinking hard about you, Maurice. I was seeing you and me in the studio talking—"

"Well, you were *here*—your spirit came on ahead of you, in your pink dress and carrying the little basket! *Darling!*" He seized me and gave me a great hug. "I think our beautiful relationship is ver-r-y spir-r-itual, darling—that is why!"

What could one do with such a man! He was so disarming sometimes. Anything that seemed to prove his spirituality and goodness made him happy and removed his sense of blood guilt. How could I abandon him to his secret sins, sins as secret to his own understanding as to mine? He was a victim to some strong, dark, hidden influence that guided him. I would stay by him and fight it.

But no sooner was Hazel out of the way than, almost it seemed without his realizing it, Maurice's glances fell upon Neith Hapgood! Grave and green-eyed Neith, who was so quiet and deep.

I don't remember when I noticed it. Of course we had that rather complicated arrangement by which we took some meals at the Peaked Hill Bar House and some at the Hapgoods. I think we all met for the evening meal at their house—but this is very vague in my memory. Anyway, the connection between Neith and Maurice became apparent to me, the same silent stream pouring out from Maurice to her and binding them together. I caught the steady, concentrated stare of them upon each other—the one corroborating the other . . . and the vision of Neith returns to me as, fresh and smiling, she appeared unexpectedly at the door of the studio one afternoon.

She was dressed in a pale green mull dress and she wore a wide-brimmed hat on her red head. She came without explanation or invitation, at a time when we held inviolate those working hours when the light was "good."

Neith was ordinarily so quiet, so lacking in initiative, that Hutch was sometimes irritated by her habit of living in the restricted silence that differed so much from his hail-fellow-well-met sociability. Neith really didn't like people much and she never attempted to disguise it. However, she liked Maurice's rich, simple quality and she opened up like a closed flower and, with quiet directness and deliberation, dressed herself in her green mull and floated over the dunes.

I was unable to disguise the antagonism that I felt for Neith from that moment. Our old friendship, and the friendship between our sons, the real love between Hutch and me, counted for little beside the overwhelming need in me to protect my relationship with Maurice which every little thing seemed to me to threaten. By the coldness I showed her, I managed to isolate him and keep him to myself. When she sent me a letter asking for an explanation of the change, I threw the onus of my annoyance upon household matters. I blamed her for details concerning the meals, and for a carelessness in the Portuguese cook! And to keep my group separate from their group I said I didn't want John to play with the rough Provincetown boys!

We had quite a long correspondence about all this, into which

Hutch entered, writing in moralistic, rolling phrases, and quite laying me out:

DEAR MABEL,

I ought not to be surprised at the haste shown by you in coming to conclusions on insufficient knowledge, as I have always known that to be a part of your character. But I am yet surprised that you take Julia's word for everything. We know Pauline to be especially clean. Her kitchen is always a model in that respect. John is a good boy, but that is no reason why you should jump to conclusions about other boys or allow your nervous impatience or sense of discomfort to betray you into hasty judgment. It is not judicial, and what ought to appeal to you, it is neither Christian nor religious.

Affectionately,

HUTCH.

P.S. I know what you have in mind about the boys here, and I feel it too. But I also feel something else. I don't think it does John any good—or Boyce—to feel any baseless sense of superiority—to run away from a social situation does not solve it—and these are more than one set of social faults.

Manners acquired easily are not very deep—and what is called manners are often worse than roughness. You know nothing about the boys you are criticizing. You are unwilling to put yourself in a position to know—and yet you are very free in your judgment.

I didn't care. I now had Maurice completely to myself, I thought.

However, I found this did not suit me. In fact, it was an atrocious situation in which I found myself with Bobby and John and Maurice all thrown together in a narrow, uncongenial group with Bobby and John unconsciously banding themselves against Maurice and me. Maurice was too absent-minded and indifferent to notice their distaste for him. He went on with his drawing and pervaded the place with his cigar, his dark, flowing Orientalism, and his little dissertations upon Art.

Since I held my household more or less continuously together now over at the Peaked Hill Bar Station and away from Provincetown, they couldn't go in bathing as they previously had done in the Bay, and they clamored for their swim. It had always been considered a dangerous shore where the Station stood and people rarely went into the ocean there, though it was very tempting with the great waves breaking on the fine white sand.

"Please let us go in swimming over here, Mother. . . . We'll be careful."

"The sand shelves off too suddenly, they say," I replied.

"We could go in a way up the shore by the new Station," Maurice broke in. "There where they run the life-boat down into the water."

"Well, you can try it once—but be careful." I gave in and saw them go off in their bathing suits down the beach.

I thought I would like the moment to myself, but no sooner was I alone than I felt desolated by the bright, dehumanized aspect of the place. The shining sun, the blue and white water on the sand, and the house half buried on one side where the wind had blown the sand banks higher than ever, though I had had it dug out earlier that year.

I felt a peculiar unrelatedness to those very elements that only a short time before would have sufficed to cheer and fill me. Nature now seemed to turn her attention from me, though she smiled and shone in clear beatitude. The earth and sun and water had separated themselves from me and I could no longer participate in their life, for, abandoning these elements for the man, I seemed to have passed into his focused and separated nature that was unable to touch and share the life of the earth. I felt excluded and uncomfortable. I had evidently become alien to nature too as I had often felt him to be.

I hastily put on my broad-brimmed hat with the chiffon scarf floating from it, and snatched up my parasol with its chiffon ruffles. Descending the sandy cliff, I began to make my way up the north shore towards the new life-saving station.

Walking was difficult, more difficult than across the dunes to the village. I had on high-heeled slippers and openwork stockings. My long, full, lace and muslin skirts tangled themselves about my ankles, the morning wind blew the chiffon across my eyes and the floppy brim of my hat down against my nose, but I bent my head and waded on.

Octave Feuillet starts his novel, *Les Liaisons Dangereuses* with the words, *"L'homme est un animal imprévu sur la terre!"* Myself, that day, I felt irritated and out of sympathy with this earth upon which I had been cast and I condemned it with all my heart.

Suddenly a peculiar sound broke in upon my solitary anger and made me raise my head and brush the chiffon scarf from my mouth. From the distance, hoarse, hollow, bellowing cries came over the water. I stopped and gazed ahead along the shore. There, a quarter of a mile away, I saw a sight that made my heart stop beating!

Three dark heads bobbed up alternately in the dark blue water and then sank into it again. As each one reached the surface, it gave off a raucous, uncontained yell and disappeared. These heads were bobbing like apples touched in turn by a playful finger. My three loved ones! The three nearest to me in the world!

At first I couldn't move. I was stricken. I stood planted firmly where I was, like one of those strange flowers that sometimes appear in the sand, growing large and lustrous, apparently without roots and the need of nourishment. As I stared, fascinated and breathless, at the merry action of those three heads, there were only two. One had ceased bobbing. Which one? It was too far to see.

I had to move. I started forward. Every step seemed slower and heavier than the last. Hurry—in the sand that grew more difficult every instant. I kept my eyes on those two peas so lively there among the waves. The cries grew fainter. Would I never reach them?

As in a little scene gazed upon through the large end of an opera glass, now the life-saving boat appeared running down to the water pushed by a number of men. Quickly they thrust it into the sea and were in it rowing like mad. But now there was only one little ball bobbing up and down in the waves. . . .

What a value we are constrained to attach to those atoms that, bobbing in a blue ocean, appear so insignificant and lacking in dignity!

I pressed on through the sand, grinding my foolish French heels into it. When I reached home that morning, my feet had worn through the sheer stockings as though the flesh had burnt them.

The men in the life-boat fumbled about in the water as I fought my way toward them. I couldn't see what they were doing. Anyway, they fumbled, and then started to row back. It was all a tangle. When they reached the shore, I could only decipher one person in a bathing suit and he started down the beach toward me.

Slowly his form and his familiarity emerged. John. He reached me. His face was blue, his teeth chattering. Neither of us paused, but pressed on past each other.

"They are working on Mr. Sterne," he stuttered from purple lips. His face seemed to have had its humanity washed from it, so little expression was in the features and the swollen red eyes.

I struggled on. It didn't matter greatly to me who was who. They had, all of them, the power to galvanize me and send me pounding down the beach. I held my chiffon parasol over my head and my thin skirt in one hand and I had no feeling of any kind except apprehension and breathlessness. Emotion was almost drowned in the blood that rose in my ears and throat and haste had taken charge of all my parts. Haste was driving me beyond myself.

Another figure loomed, approached me—another human engine dripping and disguised. Bobby reached my side, but as we passed he uttered no word. He just opened his blue mouth and his red eyes in a look of monstrous astonishment at my appearance. In that ultimate moment of drowning and resuscitation, in his horrible physical distress, in spite of shock and exhaustion, Bobby was a theater man. The vestiges of his consciousness noted with appreciation the combination of my costume and my expression. He was able to tell about it afterwards with the intense delectation of a producer to whom dramatic effects are dearer than life.

"You should have seen her! She came pounding down the beach in a lace dress, a lace hat with long scarves of chiffon floating behind, holding a ruffled white parasol over her head—and under it the most *horrible* face I ever saw in my life!"

I reached the life-saving station after an eternity. It had been the longest mile I ever experienced. Some men, two of them sketchily clad in rather queer-looking underwear, were rolling Maurice over a barrel. I saw his purple tongue.

"Can you save him?"

"Wal, I don't know, Ma'am," one said.

As my breath was returning now that I had stopped rushing, I felt more at ease. With this greater ease, thoughts, or rather inclinations, began to arise in me.

I felt, at last, completely severed from Maurice. I found myself hoping that he wouldn't recover and continue to complicate my life with his alien presence. This was not as inhuman as it seems in words and these unuttered wishes are not uncommon, I am sure, but are merely the practical realizations of our essential selves to whom, really, life and death are not momentous. To the unconscious there is no death. Since we are here, we want to remain ourselves it seems, but unimpeded and not inconvenienced by our mistakes.

The body of Maurice, as it lay swollen and shapeless over a barrel with its discolored face and swinging arms, had lost its charm, for, when a human being loses his form and color, he becomes just a lump of earth. Where once he thrilled and mesmerized by his fire or his beauty, he only repels. Thus we are all intrinsic artists and maybe love is largely an aesthetic response!

Feeling, then, coldly embarrassed and detached from that scene of resuscitation, I turned and walked away home.

That I was not the only one to take this life and death affair lightly was shown to me when I reached the Peaked Bar House and found John and Bobby wrapped in blankets sipping hot lemonade. They were laughing somewhat too hilariously in their relief.

"I just hope you'll never see yourself as *I* saw you," Bobby exclaimed, rolling his eyes, his damp hair on end. *"Never* have I seen such a face!"

"And do you know what?" said John. "Two of those lifesavers had on only their underclothes, and when they saw you coming they yelled, 'Gosh, here's a lady coming!' and started to jump out of the boat into the water and swim away."

"But the head one made 'em stop and save us," finished Bobby.

"They'd rather have let us drown than have you see them like that," said John.

"I know how that feels," I told them, sympathetic with the poor lifesavers. "I told Reed here two summers ago—or, good heavens, was it last summer?—well, anyway, I was ready to *drown* rather than be saved with only the top of my sailor suit on."

"Well, anyway, *we're* saved," said Bobby brightly. "How's Maurice?"

"Oh, I guess he's saved," I answered. I felt a slight guilt and remorse for my recent heartlessness. It didn't seem possible he *wasn't* saved, too. I began to feel sorry for him.

"Well, it was *his* bright idea we should all be tied on the same rope like pearls on a string. I think he was trying to look after John and me! Of course, when the undertow pulled one of us under, it pulled the others, too—so nobody could help anybody."

We felt quite cozy alone there sipping our drinks, but it didn't last long. Soon there was a commotion outside the door. The lightness in the air fled and a heaviness came down on my spirit for Maurice arrived dramatically supported on each side by a station man, adequately clothed this time.

So different from my other two, I thought, he had to make a *thing* of it! He had to extract all the significance there was in the event and then overexpress it!

With a wild look in my direction that was supposed to reveal he was helpless from exhaustion and shock, and to wring some adequate attention from me, he stood there, with his lips open, leaning heavily on the two husky, smiling seamen. There was a couch at hand, but he wouldn't take to it without my help. My other two sat and grinned and sipped their hot lemonade with the usual Anglo-Saxon refusal to co-operate in a drama. I rose with rage in my heart and smiled.

"Come, Maurice, lie down here. Do relax, for Heaven's sake!— Thanks a lot for helping him over," I said to the awkward lifesavers.

"Oh, wal, that's our job, Ma'am," one of them said, and they turned to leave.

Maurice reclined on the couch and pressed his black hair back from his white brow. He turned a look of dislike and reproach upon Bobby and John, who refused even to look in his direction. They *hated* having him come so near drowning.

"A terrible experience, darling," said he with a very strong accent, excluding them from his presence. "I felt the water going deeper, deeper into my lungs—it was like becoming another element. I tried to catch hold of the others but I only went down with them. Then I felt Death approach like a visible entity. It was so str-r-range! I seemed to See Her. It is very curious," said he, "how I *visualize* everything!"

He looked quite ruddy now and rather sumptuous with his hair tossed back and a bright rug over him. "You must r-r-really send those men something, darling," said Maurice. "If they hadn't come quickly, how differently this would have turned out! And how they worked over me! Pumping—pumping—massaging."

"I'll send them a box of cigars," I said.

" 'Not too much, God knows, for such a faithful friend,' as Queen Victoria said when she presented John Brown with a pair of oxidized silver cuff-links on his birthday," cut in Bobby.

"I hope this isn't going to interfere with my Work," said Maurice. I turned a look on him. "I'll see that it doesn't," I told him.

"Oh, gee! I guess I'll go over and have dinner with Boyce," said John.

"Well, you won't," said I. "You'll stay here, all of you, and rest."

John and Bobby looked at each other. It was as bad as drowning—all tied on the same string.

CHAPTER XII

Leo Stein

LEO STEIN had left his villa, his Cézannes and Renoirs and come to America. He was in Provincetown, probably staying with us. I don't remember.

Leo meant a great deal more to me in America than he had in Europe. More and more nowadays I needed people of solid worth, people with ideas and character instead of those who were "intriguing." Oddities of nature had ceased to appeal; reality drew closer.

Leo had a genius for thinking. There were some pages he sent me once when I was first back in New York, pages so alive with the enthusiasm for reality, and rational thought and behavior that they had a strong influence upon my own changing nature. After twenty-five years they are living in me still.

He and Maurice had long, lone conversations about Art, and about Psychoanalysis, in which he was losing (or finding) himself at that time. Leo perched on a rock in Provincetown, and with eyes turned inward, spun a web of thought and wrapped it round and round him so that very little outside life could touch him. Or was he driven to incessant thinking because his other responses were so few?

When Maurice worked, Leo had to look for another listener, and often it was I, if I wasn't posing. He was at present analyzing himself and the strange validity of his relationship with Nina, whom he had left behind in Paris, for Leo and Nina made one of those odd combinations that baffle the onlooker, but whose essential reality is indisputable.

So Leo perched on a rock on his haunches overlooking the sea, his knees drawn up to his chin. His face was long and ram-like, his spectacles caught the sun and reflected it when he turned them on me.

"It's perfectly immaterial to me what Nina does," he told me, "as long as she doesn't lie. I dislike the implications in a lie. It is what she is herself that constitutes her value for me."

I stared at him moodily, unable to rise to such a height of love as his appeared to be.

"There is an amplitude in her nature—generosity you might call it. Other people seem thin and small beside her. Her nature has a massive quality. . . ."

As soon as he said the word "massive" I felt a pang, for that was the word I used to comfort myself about Maurice.

Leo faded from my view and I saw Maurice, his bony substantiality, his fine black hair brushed back from his white brow, his spotless linen shirt open at the throat. His cleanliness was always nice. But his mouth was not so fine as his eyes were. As I recognized this lesser feature he faded away. I was empty, deaf, and blind as I sat motionless beside Leo.

Where does one go when one is neither here nor there? After some moments I slid back into my waiting body and heard Leo say, "I have never seen anyone who could so completely absent herself by the withdrawal of her attention. The Absence of Mabel Dodge is a total departure."

In these days I felt again the sinking of my energy. It dropped like a stone into a bottomless lake and left me lifeless on the earth. I had just enough strength left to push Maurice away, and this I did, making him go to New York on the pretext of engaging a studio for the autumn. I was faint—famished for life after subsisting on the slim fare his company afforded me. Always single-minded, eggs all in one basket, attention focused on him like a searchlight, I had been unable to draw from him alone—massive as I had called him, substantial and male—sufficient nourishment.

My spirit waned. I pushed him away just in time and, even while I missed his colorful presence and everyone else seemed like Leo had said when speaking of Nina—thin and small—I hoped that he wouldn't come back. Even as I hoped this, my heart seemed to die within me and to reach out after him. I had to have him whether I wanted to have him or not.

I ordered the car, and taking Leo with me, I motored down the Cape. The first few miles were silent anguish, Leo staring at his thoughts and his fabricated systems. But I began to accumulate power back again from its mistaken deposit outside myself in Maurice. Soon I began to feel strong and serene and full once more.

When we drove through Orleans, I saw in the distance a beautiful ruined house among the trees. I directed the car to it and found it to be one of those two-balconied, wooden houses with columns so common in New Orleans. We surmised that the family who first settled this Cape Cod village had come from the South and named the place after the familiar home town, and, with the wistful need to perpetuate a known environment, had built the Southern dwelling place there on the north Atlantic coast.

I was ready for a house to love. Houses have always been my antidote for love! The great wistaria vine with a trunk a foot thick and with purple blossoms that covered the whole pale yellow façade of the old building, caught me and filled me with joy and excitement. I could not wait a moment to think it over. I must have it immediately so I could begin to plan and brood over colors and materials, the way the light would enter this room and that, the morning look, the evening look; already I was living in it, complete and assuaged.

Leo followed me around looking puzzled at such impulses. He tried to hold me back. But why should I let him hold me back? The house was a sure cure. It seemed to me that I was lucky to know what I needed and then wise enough to go after it.

We drove to business offices in the town and I somehow got the place then and there by means of such juggling as I have since forgotten, involving papers and promises. At last I'd wiped out the dark-eyed artist and gotten a house in his place.

Leo commented upon my calm serenity as I sat beside him with a brown chiffon veil wrapped around my white hat and felt its soft folds against my cheek. Well, I felt wonderful. That's all there is to it.

Maurice had been glad enough to leave the Peaked Bar House on that unfriendly, barren coast. He was tired of being held up in a taut, strained attitude, and tired of my criticism and contempt whenever he relaxed and let himself go where his inclinations led him. I think he went off quite joyously with secret thoughts of peculiar indulgences.

I had told him to go to my apartment and stay, for Domenico was there taking care of it, and it was a thoroughly attractive, cool place to be with all the furniture covered with green linen slips and dark awnings at the windows. He was honest with me. He wrote rather ruefully that he was surprised to find he could not stay away—that he wanted to return. But I answered we were better off away from each other for a while. We must find out the truth about ourselves. He replied:

September 11th.

DEAREST MABEL,

I got your letter a while ago, the second urging me not to come back to Provincetown. I had already made up my mind to leave this evening and now I don't know what to do. I found New York impossible, not only the heat, but my friends, my family—it all irritates me.

I miss you, Mabel—more than you suspect, more than I had expected. A while ago I had a burning desire to be with you—speak to you, and was furious with myself for having gone away from Provincetown. You know what happened? I was forcibly carried up to your apartment—this way I had the illusion of being near you and it helped. I opened the windows of your drawing room, took possession for the afternoon and I am writing this at your desk. It is strange: usually I feel uncomfortable to be at a friend's house when the friend is absent, but I don't feel any of this discomfort here. Is it because most people are physically related to their furniture and rooms, whereas with you the relationship is abstract, spiritual? You are really here, dearest. I speak to you, smile to you. Do you hear me? But I don't want to go off in that strain—I want to tell you of my liberty— the liberty I lauded so much the other day when I spoke about my aversion to renounce it. This liberty—well, I've discovered how really little it means to me. My tendency to idealize what has been, and my childish, naïve illusions of what might be—take the glow out of that which is.—Liberty in the abstract—that's what I want, not the crude liberty of action. To be free—yes—to be free to reveal your soul with all its stains and blotches to another—that is freedom. You, Mabel, are the first woman to awaken in me a passionate love for truth. I have devoted my life to the realization and expression of visual truth—so you grasp what it must mean to me to be able to express this inner truth also. Then you will understand the depth of my feeling for you. Obstacle No. 1 is swept aside. The liberty I valued so last week has ceased to be part of my vital needs. Leo, I suppose, would say it is a sublimation of an inhibition.—Apropos, the other night Leo and I were together from 5 P.M. until 2:45 A.M. Part of the time with Gans celebrating all sorts of things; Gans at the end of *his* "liberty" (he was to join his family the next day). Leo the fourth anniversary of his return to America, and I my death and resurrection. But after the celebration, Leo and I were left together and we discussed the great question for several hours. "Sheer madness," he said to me also, and I had to agree

409

with him. You know Leo has *such* a way of convincing you whilst he is talking. But what he said left an impression. He spoke very sympathetically and intelligently of your essential traits, your character. He painted a very precise portrait of you. I would call it an impression in quick-silver. He spoke of your passionate interests of no durability—of your incapacity for sustained emotion, of your restlessness, your craving for excitement and need of outside stimulus. I agreed with all he said and even added that your manifold variety of experience was due mainly to your impatience for definite results. You lose interest if the results are slow or inadequate. He thought it would be madness to do anything more or less irrevocable before we have smoothened ourselves out. All this did not help me much to come to a definite conclusion—for heretofore I had reckoned with my share of the obstacles only. Now, dearest, it really seems to me that we have not reached the stage where we can or ought to decide. We must, rather, try to find out more about ourselves, our strength and weakness. Surely with any experience we ought to be able to understand whether a union between us would be wise, or mad, whether the friction which is bound to arise between us would be cohesive, or disintegrative and destructive. To come to a definite conclusion beforehand would be like painting a picture before one has come to a clear realization of the subject —a practice responsible for much rotten art.

Dearest, you have no idea what a deep impression my experience last Sunday has made on me. Impression is the wrong definition, for I am conscious of a pronounced change, and would you believe it—to the better. All that was heavy, dull, all that I despised in myself seems to have left me when I drowned. I know Leo would merely call it reaction, but I know that it is more than that, for it is increasing all the time and if it were merely reactionary, the effects would have the tendency to decrease.

Darling, darling, I love you. Don't talk to me of breaking it all up. I won't have it.

I don't think anybody but myself can pack my things, so I'll have to go back to Provincetown against your will.

With all love to you—and a great deal to the others—

MAURICE.

I wrote of my indecision to Leo and he replied at once:

401 West End Ave.
Friday.

MABEL DEAR:

I received your letter a moment ago and shall answer it before going out, which I must do a moment hence. Maurice dropped in last night a little before six looking very brilliant and told me the story of the drowning. Afterwards he mentioned the fact that you had spoken to him of our talk concerning the marriage project and my disapproval. He asked me why. I started to tell him. Then Howard came back and we went to dinner at the Manhattan Club. We had a good dinner and a good time talking till after twelve when Howard had to go and Maurice and I walked uptown together and resumed the interrupted talk. I told him all that I thought. Then he told me at length what he thought. It seems to me that we are agreed, he and I, about everything in the matter except his own bottom. He believes that he stands on the rock and I believe he stands on shifting sands. He believes that the B. experience has given him stability; I believe that this is true as long as the relation lasts, but if it is really severed, then again the unknown.

Now, my dear Mabel, I really like you far too much to have any patience with your making an ass of yourself. Sterne doesn't want a mother except temporarily and unless you succeeded in dominating him more or less completely—in which case he'd be of not much more use to you than a pussy cat—you'd find after a while that mother was out of a job, though there might be one for a house-keeper.

As for a receipt for a friendly marriage, that's easy. Somebody when asked how to live to a great old age, answered "pick parents of notable longevity." For that kind of marriage all that you need is that kind of people. They should, I think, either have an interest in a common object or else they should be separately interested and find in their common life the elements of comfort and relaxation. You're both too seriously critical and exigent for that and Sterne is far too irritable. He is easygoing till he reaches the kicking point and then—he kicks. If he could be cured of wanting to kick, all right; if he is merely prevented from kicking, it's all to the bad.

Now I don't believe that you're seriously interested in what Sterne is doing and what's more I don't believe that in any vital sense you understand the problems (artistic) that agitate him. Art is something vital to you, I believe, as an experience; I don't believe it's vital to you as a problem—at least not, and that is what I refer to, an esthetic problem. It will always be so to Sterne, unless he changes very greatly and I think that after a while you would be bored by his successive discoveries of the truth, the whole truth, and everything but the truth.

For the relation of the second type that I spoke of, the material does not seem to me present either. It demands either profound sympathy and that I don't believe there is here, or else a sufficiently routine way of life so that the people are mutually dependable. Sterne would certainly be so for a while, but "man wants but little here below" but often wants it different, and you can't tell what solitudes or lack of it he may want all of a sudden when ginger is no longer hot in the mouth and inspiration fails. You, too—imagination doesn't boggle at the suggestion—may suddenly become violently taken of an enterprise that Sterne finds foolish and disturbing and if you surrender it will give you to chew the cud of resentment and if you don't it will produce tensions, etc. There seems to be no evidence that you love each other enough to make sacrifices cheerfully except of the things you don't care about and the smartest master of twelfth century science couldn't predict just what will be your next enthusiasm. You can't effectively bury your past selves unless they're dead and I think that in both your cases you'd discover a little after the funeral that you had to do with lively corpses.

Well, this letter could not fairly bear Browning's caption "Any man to any woman" and I don't think it would be good policy to show it to Sterne. As I told him yesterday, when you asked me my opinion I gave it chiefly with respect to your well-being. Of course, as you know, I know very few women, especially of the kind that radiate, as one might say, both tentacles and influence, and your dynamic breed may have more representatives than I suspect. Nonetheless I cherish you as my only specimen, and don't want to see you clipped either as to tentacles or wings. (You'll see if you put all these features together that you're rather a remarkable beastie.)

Sterne tells me that you are to be in N. Y. about the twentieth. I am leaving N. Y. about then to spend a week in Baltimore. This is sad, but if I don't see you before, I'll see you on my return, for I don't sail till the ninth.

My most affectionate greetings,

LEO.

I ought to have said something of Hazel's letters. I think she fails to recognize Maurice's notable streak of conventional morality—the recognition of formal obligation. He is not so much lawless as unformed.* His intelligence also is notable—disconcertingly surprising at times but that also is unformed and consequently it is all very undependable. When his soul was crystallized out, the process was not completed. There are numerous points of crystallization but much remains shapeless fluid and unless he gets himself straightened out no center of crystallization will dominate to utilize the mass of the substance in solution. I think that Hazel makes Sterne much more terrific than he is. He might perhaps have been terrific, but he ain't. A house divided against itself may fall and crash. It can be appalling but hardly terrific. Sterne is a house that doesn't know for certain

* Without formation—"informe."

which is its proper front. . . . Oh, the devil, I've got started on another sheet. And another figure of speech. What Hazel says about life being individual and "its not making any difference" is all right, perhaps, for Hazel. There are people to whom Brother, the body, and Sister, the "material soul," are so remote that whether these be cudgeled like an ass or flayed like a Mohican at the stake, makes little difference indeed. You have perhaps, even probably, affiliations with this saintly race, but you're no saint yet and I should try if I were you to get into training without assuming—(Here I was interrupted and went to Stamford. I came back for lunch with Lippmann and am now going out to Stamford again but the interval will suffice to finish this, I hope.)—any unnecessary difficulties.

I find your last letter on my table. It's not necessary to add to what I've already said because whatever else it lacks it's, I think, clear. As for your formulation—well . . . Only there's an absurd fallacy in it which makes it nonsense as a generalization. Either you're one of the objects and then it's only your egocentric impertinence that causes you to place in opposition everything else and you, or else it isn't true, because there are thousands of people in the world who can say "cigarettes are not good for me; I shall not smoke any more" and then don't. Thus, either your formulation is not true because it does not include the facts, or else it's untrue because it's contrary to the facts. Which horn of the dilemma you prefer depends on whether you believe that "you" means something besides the sum of your individual reactions or whether you don't. If you *don't* understand this, doubtless Walter Lippmann can elaborate.

I enjoyed meeting him and regret that a blunder on the part of the attendant made us waste time waiting for each other. I'm afraid I talked too much and heard in consequence too little from him. He has fine eyes and gives generally an impression of excellence of quality, but I did not get the impression (I refer merely to appearance) of great affirmation. I shall like very much to continue the acquaintance and if 'twere possible, I should come up to the Cape again even without waiting for an invitation.

Once more, *don't* be an idjut. LEO.

And my God! Hardly had I recovered from Maurice's troubling love when there he was back again!

Then Reed's letters continued to come to me all the while Hutch's letter was on its way, following him from place to place. They were wistful letters, full of a humility that I had never known in him. Boardman Robinson and he were imprisoned, while Reed spent his time drawing plans of the house we would live in up in the Ramapo Hills.

Reed seemed so familiar to me, his American essence was so plain and unequivocal, natural as bread and butter compared to the rich, exotic, dubious unfamiliarity of Maurice who was darkness shot through with golden gleams. To ponder upon Maurice's nature was like gazing at night onto the oily black surface of a restless ocean where phosphorescence, bunched here and there within it, breaks up the glassy opaqueness. Maurice's large, dark, secretive eyes, gleaming with pain and struggle or tender with pleasure at some aspect of beauty, then suddenly glazed and fixed with sensuality when his per-fervid imagination took hold of form and converted it into a vehicle of sex—all his aestheticism so sexed, his sex so mixed up with sight and mind—those eyes of his, constantly conveying to one how his cen-ters shifted and borrowed each other's functions so that in his own being there remained no form and no integrity, gave me no peace or security.

One never knew where one was with him. Yet the strange part of it was that the man fascinated me by his form. His expressiveness in gestures and looks had a certain round completeness, his body had mass. There was a dignity in his European decay that impressed me more than Reed's, or any other American's, budding culture. If Mau-rice was over-ripe, Reed was too green—or so it seemed to me when I compared them.

However, I needed something certain and familiar and real near me, and I wondered whether I couldn't persuade Reed to come and join us at Finney Farm, where we could be real friends. When I thought of him he seemed like a young green tree, strong and imma-ture, with potential fruit concealed in promise, while Maurice was indeed like the uprooted pine tree the Independent Society of Artists had chosen for their symbol! Torn out of the earth, unattached, cov-ered with the eager vines that reach out to spread over the fallen, hol-lowed out by parasitical alien life, and with his own life astray in him, though evergreen in a sense he yet offered no refuge for one, no sup-port and no protection. Yet there I was held by that nobility in the mass, in the broken Jewish entity.

CHAPTER XIII

The End of Reed

FINNEY FARM! The warm autumn colors were around us, apples on the ground, and the living room torn up while village masons sought to reproduce on a larger scale the beautiful little Colonial fireplace from the Sharkey Cottage, and painters laid white paint over the woodwork.

In the Green House at the rear of the farmhouse, Bayard Boyesen sat all day sipping whiskey and soda and occasionally jotting down a line of poetry. Bayard, another one engaged upon the titanic enterprise of disentangling himself from the handicaps of heredity and environment. He always loved the country best and when I retreated to Croton I remembered that we had agreed, the year before, when I was at 23 Fifth Avenue, that people would be driven more and more away from city streets. When I was discouraged and wrote one day to seek his sympathy, he had replied:

Agder Farm,
Royalston, Mass.

DEAR MRS. DODGE:

Is it the war or is it just living in America that makes all of my few friends write in a strain of spiritual discouragement? Not able to wish that you were in Italy? The thought is almost incredible! It isn't only the art there: nowhere else have I ever been so conscious of the beauty of things, and, above all, of the beauty of flesh. Just to walk in the streets at Naples is like being constantly caressed—and by such hands, such lips! But enough, or I shall throw my work away and take the next ship.

No, those words you quote are not true for me. Even intellectual despair cannot prevent my reveling. . . .

No, I should not like to be in New York just now, though I may spend a small part of the winter there. I dislike that city with a cordiality that rips me apart when I am in it. Here I have at least isolation in work and the forest trees, which, next to the sea, appeal to me more than anything I know—except . . . I leave that sentence as it is. No, I won't. The exception refers to human flesh and blood, sinew, tegument, bone.

That, by the way, is where one finds the mystic in life—not in the saints. The mysticism that has been drenched in the flesh has the color and richness that make beauty. It is by diving into the flesh that one comes to the limits of the material. But one goes back for another dive!

You ask what my novel is about; but to tell you of it adequately, I should have to write a letter as long as the novel itself. Suffice it to say that it will disappoint those few friends who fancy that I have literary ability. Damn it! Everyone seems to be crying for realism. One friend (whose opinion I value, too) wrote me that he looked forward to a scathing indictment of New England. Fancy! Fancy fiddling away one's time indicting anything.

If I had any comforts to offer you, I should strongly urge you to come here. Unfortunately, the longest drought that Massachusetts has ever known has dried the springs and shut off the running water in my house. One has to take only a sponge bath or jump, as I still do, into a very cold brook. Furthermore, I have ceased bothering about how I live, with the result that, since I returned last summer, I have done nothing towards refixing a somewhat dismantled house. And then, there is absolutely nothing to do here except drive. If in the face of all this, you dare to come, I should be more than glad to have you. A plan enters my head if you should decide to come. Why not motor up? If your car is in commission, we could motor from New York (I would meet you there) and have a very jolly trip through the autumn country. I could put your chauffeur up, and the car would be kept in a barn a quarter of a mile away. Take this plan for what it is worth; but take seriously what I say about discomforts: it is much like camping out here, except that one need not be cold.

Do you see anything of Hutch and the rest? I feel singularly out of touch with everyone.

Faithfully,

B. B.

Since I had quarreled with the Hapgoods I had not heard from my dear Hutch at all. I missed him terribly and wrote him a letter, seeking to make up. He replied, still holding off a little:

Provincetown, Oct. 29th.

DEAREST MABEL:

I too have lost whatever bitterness or resentment I felt. It seems to me I have never felt resentment towards you, even when I thought I saw real evil in you. Your letter to Neith, that part about my alleged statement "one of the most beautiful experiences"—did not cause resentment in me—though it was of a nature which looked as if it was intended to make trouble between her and me.

I saw—or thought I saw—you forming a mob-attitude towards Mary O'Brien. I saw or thought I saw you forming an atmosphere in which I was a weakened and demoralized being. I know that these mob attitudes always have *some* destructive effects on the object of them. I have seen you often as a destructive agent, but I have also realized that you were only one influence among millions, and that it is morbid to take such things too seriously.

I could find no possible theoretical excuse for some of your conduct and some of your attitudes—and yet I could not respond with bitterness and resentment at all equal in degree to the evil I thought I saw. I *suppose* that means that I love you. It may be that your love for me and mine for you has an unworthy Christian sentimentality in it—or it may be something much nobler; some genuine insight into real qualities of our natures that our intellects cannot get at.

Although we shall not designedly meet again, I have no doubt there is still something—whatever it is—between us that will endure.

Sincerely,

Hutch.

I needed other elements in my environment and I invited Bayard to join us. He agreed to come to us for a few months and there was comfort for me in his presence there at first, for the effort he made to save himself surrounded him with an atmosphere of high endeavor. Even in his repeated falls and failures there was always the stubborn certainty of final success, for he had a gallant indomitable power of will that held him together. His Greek profile and his beautifully chiseled lips were held in a careful mold as long as he was with people. But sometimes I saw him before he turned the corner of the veranda to come in to his meals with us, and his face was like that of a fallen archangel.

We moved into the farmhouse before it was ready for us and Bayard and Maurice sat in the library together in the evening, dissimilar but adapting themselves to each other for the sake of social comfort. Restless, I left them and went to the piano in the dismantled, cold living room that was not yet set in order, and played, hopefully, old ballads to hearten myself. The puzzle of my life lacked parts that would bring us together and make sense.

Reed returned to New York and I saw him. "When Hutch's letter reached me one evening I was beside a canal. I dropped that ring into it," he said.

"Well, I can't help it, Reed. You have always said we must be free and lead our own lives. I don't see why we can't be friends. I want you to come out to Finney Farm and stay, and do your writing."

He looked rueful. "I will try," he said.

It was not long before Hutch and I had fully made up and come back to our old affectionate standing. When he heard I was trying to combine such differing elements together, he wrote:

Provincetown.

Dearest Mabel,

I got a letter from you a couple of days ago, but didn't answer it as I wrote you several days ago and have been hoping to hear from you in answer to that. I take it for granted that you find it difficult to get away.

I am very glad that Reed is back and would love to see him. I hope he will be able to be at the farm comfortably, but I fear it would be very hard. I could not do it in a similar situation.

You know probably about Joe O'Brien's death. It is a real loss to me. Mary returns here today and I suppose I shall see much of her, as soon as I recover from a severe attack of rheumatism which makes it impossible for me to walk at present. I am writing in bed and Hippolyte and Emilina are taking care of me. I think I'll be up tomorrow.

I hope you will see Neith and be good to her. She is very tired, tired of everything, I fear. I hope she will rest, and work and play and come back with more buoyancy and hope.

I telegraphed Elina as you directed. Did you hear from her? Tell Bayard I'll look for his laundry as soon as I can get about.

I feel sad and old today—as if I haven't much to say, even to you, dearest Mabel—

Hutch.

Reed came and I gave him the third floor of the farmhouse. I liked to think of him up there with his typewriter in the window, working and occasionally looking out over the still orchard. I went in to town every day to fix a studio for Maurice on Tenth Street, for he was incapable of doing it for himself.

I painted the doors and woodwork of the large room black, and made the walls white. On a large couch I spread a cover of silk and velvet brocatelle that had a huge Renaissance design in black on a cream ground, and I sewed a deep border of black velvet around it.

418

A few black chairs and a black table completed this somewhat sinister background for Maurice's florid cheeks and silky black hair. He became a handsome Persian in this setting. I had not converted him to clay yet. His easel and paints were at hand. What would he paint here?

Reed tried to live in the attic room for three days. Then one morning he came to me and said, "I can't do it, Mabel. It's not natural. You and Sterne here and everything. . . ."

I felt very unsympathetic. He seemed unreasonable to me. Sterne wasn't even living in the same house with me for I had put him also in the Green House with Bayard. There these two creatures slept, as separate as the blond Nordic can be from the Oriental. They each used the same notepaper I had had engraved for them, which emphasized their independence of me living alone in the big house—Green House, Finney Farm, Croton-on-Hudson—which sufficiently answered, I thought, any queries about our intimate arrangements. Why couldn't Reed ignore the question of Maurice and me as all my other friends did?

"Why can't you people *live* your theories, anyway?" I cried. "You always said one should be emancipated and true to oneself."

He looked at me.

"I love you," he said.

I rolled my eyes. "Well, what difference does one house make from another? Here it's convenient for you, you have your work to do, I like to have you here. If you go somewhere else, how does that alter things?"

"I don't have to see and hear," he said.

"Where are you going, then?"

"I'm going to see if I can buy the Sharkey Cottage."

"And you'll come over often and everything?"

"Perhaps," he said, and left that day.

But the change was effected only by breaking something. He had to stiffen inside himself and feel coldly toward me so as not to mind too much. Soon I heard that he had bought the little Sharkey house, where I had hurt him so badly, but he had taken a room in Washington Square and he had met a girl down there and taken her to live with him. I was curious about her, and one late afternoon I knocked at his door. It was opened by a very pretty, tall, young woman with soft, black hair and very blue eyes, who held a lighted candle in her hand.

"Is Jack Reed here?" I asked.

He appeared suddenly behind her with rumpled hair and hurt eyes, and his temples shining as of old.

"This is Louise Bryant," he told me gravely.

"How do you do?" I asked her, but she didn't tell me. "Reed, I came to ask you for your old typewriter, if you're not using it."

"Louise is using it," he said.

"Oh, all right. I only thought . . ."

Actually, I only talked to him once again, though he was often near me in Croton and I heard pregnantly of the two of them living in the Sharkey Cottage. Later, on a rainy day in the fall I stood with him outside the Holland House. The avenue was greasy and shining with the wet, and street lamps, lighted early, were reflected on the pavement. Reed was looking at me with hurt and angry eyes.

"I have written the end of 'Pygmalion' over. I have written 'The Awakening of Galatea.' I will send it to you."

He had inserted a stanza following the line "Galatea! Galatea! Galatea!"—mouth to mouth. . . ."

> Light shadows of driven clouds on a summer lake—
> Ripples on still ponds, winds that ruffle and pass—
> Happy young grass rising to drink the rain—
> So Galatea under his kisses stirred;
> Like a white moth alighted breath on her lips,
> Like a blue rent in a storm-sky opened her eyes,
> Sweetly the new blood leaped and sang in her veins,
> Dumbly, blindly her hands, breast, mouth sought his. . . .

The winter passed without our meeting and then the next summer Hutch wrote:

Saturday morning.

DEAR MABEL,

This may reach you before my letter of yesterday, as on that I did not put the quickest address.

The cook is worried about the piano. She says she doesn't know the firm she ought to send it back to.

Since writing you yesterday, Neith has been worse. She spent a very painful afternoon and night. The doctor is coming today, and I shall urge the hospital. I think it will be a week before she can go to Provincetown. I have engaged staterooms for next Saturday, June 28th.

We have spent two sleepless, and Neith two painful, nights and I am draggled to the point where I am expressionless. Worry is the predominant feeling in me. Can a man be human when he is worrying? It is only rarely that anybody is really human. It is only the fine moments when the best of us can really attain to the quality of a human being.

Steffens came to see Neith yesterday, as also Sheffield. Steffens says Reed told him he loves you and will love you forevermore. . . .

Shall I tell here how the story ended? Louise had been married to a dentist in a small town in the West, but the girl was clever with a certain Irish quickness, and very eager to get on. I think Reed was a stepping stone, and through him she met a lot of people she never would have known otherwise. It had not seemed to me that she cared very much for him. When he was away on one of the writing commissions he always had for the *Metropolitan Magazine* and others, she had a brief passage of passion with a friend of Reed's and mine. I remember his telling me that after they spent a couple of days in the little Sharkey Cottage, when she went back to her rooms in New York, her canary was dead, lying on its back, frozen, in the cage. He told me how she cried. The following summer Reed took a cottage in Provincetown with her and we used to pass each other on the street but never stopped and spoke.

Reed had never been quite well, I think, since his illness in Galicia, and finally it was decided that he must have a kidney removed. He married Louise, before he went to the hospital, for convenience's sake. Rumors of their quarrels came to me from friends of both of us—from Jerry Blum and his wife, Lucille; from Max Eastman, and others. "Oh, *you're* not so much," Louise cried to him bitterly. There was the old competition in importance again!

Finally they went to Russia, like so many others looking for an escape. For Louise it was an opportunity to be on her way, and she wrote quite a good book; for Reed it was adventure again and perhaps a chance to lose himself in a great upheaval. He threw himself into action close to Trotsky and Lenin and when he died of typhus the Russians gave him a splendid public funeral and set a stone with a tablet to his memory over his grave, and Louise, draped in crêpe, the wife of a hero, threw herself on his bier long enough to be photographed for the New York papers.

Andrew saw her when she came back to New York, married then to William Bullitt, and she told him that as Reed died, he whispered:

"Listen. . . . I am singing a little song for you. . . . The whole world came between us. . . ."

CHAPTER XIV

Life at Finney Farm

FINNEY FARM was bright with sunlight and wood fires, and ruffled white muslin curtains so sheer that the movements of the leaves and branches on the trees outside made a lively dancing pattern at all the windows. In the big, homely kitchen, there was always a smell of baking and roasting, of cinnamon and apples and hot coffee. I loved the beautiful sense of home in the country. Maurice, when he was not in New York, wore high boots and his Scotch tweed clothes, and carved a turkey as we all sat at the wide, long, dining-room table. Bobby was often there, and Elizabeth with some of the little girls, Merz and Miss Gertrud. Bayard was a real decoration, always charming in rough, red-brown clothes, or fuzzy blues, and with a late, pinched flower in his button-hole—sweet william or nasturtium. There was the old horse named Charley in the stable, two cows for the man of all work, Jerry, to take care of, and pigs who took care of the garbage. In the house there were canary birds singing in the conservatory, and two cats, the black one Scuro, and a white one, Chiara, named by Maurice.

John came over from Morristown School for week-ends, and Boyce Hapgood used to come up from Dobbs Ferry to stay with him.

It was a perfect setting for an American country gentleman and his wife, but though the environment was perfect and I myself, I thought, could have settled down into a bounteous peace, Maurice was so Russian here that he seemed to complicate the dream. Somehow the very innocence and sweetness of the place showed up his difference from us and made him stand out instead of blending innocuously like a piece in a picture puzzle!

I imagine that what I really wanted was someone more like what Dr. Harding has called "the phantom lover," one who would exist mainly in my imagination, a projection instead of a reality; or perhaps, after all, I was conditioned to prefer the kind of American husband who is unobtrusive when he is at home, and that rarely. But Maurice was no phantom. He was more definite and real than anyone I had ever lived with. He had a strong presence, and the qualities that had made me capitulate to him were more emphatic than ever, here at Finney Farm. He was darker and more ruddy against the white muslin curtains, his cigar permeated the house and blotted out the mild conservatory perfumes. Sitting in the room beside the fire he diminished my other friends, Bayard, Bobby or Leo Stein, or whoever was there. He diminished me, too, and made me seem more of a brown wren than ever! When women came to the house, and I contrived for it to be seldom, Maurice sat and pondered them, silently smoking his cigar, wreaths of smoke about his strong, black head. I had to watch them grow conscious of him, start to make fluttering movements, and finally pretend they were interested in me. One of these, a casual guest to begin with, wanted to prolong the stimulation of Maurice's attention. She begged me to let her come out and stay in the stone hut down below in the copse where Washington Irving lived for a time. She said she wanted to be a hermit and to paint in illumined letters on vellum the story of my life! So now instead of using people I was being used by them! I did not like it much.

My poor Maurice! I had dragged him into this New York country life and wanted him to be no more than a table or a chair or a canary in the conservatory, just a part of the setting, but the man was a man after all! He was very much of one, in fact! He walked around with heavy steps upon the hardwood floors and without even trying he became master of the house. It was natural to him to overlook and forget women and often he forgot I was there. Sometimes if I saw him concentrating on some visitor, looking right past me, I would go up to him and murmur gently but with all the force I could inject: "Stop that, Maurice!" and he would flash a bright black and white smile up at me and exclaim, loud and disingenuous, "Stop what, darling?" Really, I couldn't do a thing with him!

A letter from Leo, comparing Reed and Maurice, came one day:

DEAR MABEL: *401 West End Ave., Sunday Morn.*

. . . I read Jack Reed's *Mexico*. His inwardness is without but he does seem to penetrate that. In thinking over the impression that I got of him last week, it seemed to me that he could never give up the search of adventure. He does not give me the impression of having much within and in order that he should play at the nozzle he must keep on filling up the tank and I doubt whether he can do that long without Excitement at the throttle. (That metaphor is *not* mixed though it grew and it grew.) The same to some extent appears to be true of Sterne, though in his case it is I believe largely a matter of neurosis. He, I believe, really has reserves, if he could tap them.

I met Belle Greene the other day. She seems to be alive. Also I went to the Harvard-Princeton football game and I didn't give a whoop in hell who won, though the whole was interesting. I find that I am not nationally or locally patriotic, but I still remain

Crotonically yours,

Leo.

How, how to get at those deeps in Maurice?

I had decided to give up my apartment in New York. 23 Fifth Avenue ceased to exist for me, and the anarchists and other radicals had disappeared out of my life along with Leagues, Movements, Committees, and Causes. The War raged in Europe but I was hardly aware of it out at Finney Farm. In fact, no recollection of it comes back to me, except a scene that took place months before this time at Sharkey Cottage. Elizabeth and I were sitting under a big tree in the yard peacefully enough, when Merz hurried up the road towards us with a newspaper in his hand.

"Ach, this is, for us, the worst yet!" he cried, thrusting it in front of Elizabeth's face. We read in great headlines of the sinking of the *Lusitania.*

"Now America comes in and we will be victimized," he went on. It seemed unreal to me. I never did really experience the War but I had some observations to write about it. I sent the following lines to Arthur Brisbane and asked him to print them in his paper:

To the Government of the United States:
We women want the war to stop. We want it more than anything else in the world.

We are not satisfied with the outlet the Red Cross is giving us. In fact, with the moderation of a certain wise man that we know, we "doubt the propriety of so much Red Cross," noble social effort though it is.

But we don't want to go on knitting and nursing and binding. We want to live and help others to live. We want peace.

425

But we are afraid that the big business men and corporations think they will suffer if the war comes to an end—too soon!

Won't you make them realize that they need not lose by a speedy peace?

Won't you tell them we will use the ships we have ordered for commerce . . . the munitions for reserve . . . our standing army to back us when we enter the League of Nations to insure Peace?

You have turned us, partially, into an agricultural nation. We *know* now the advantage of the home-grown vegetable.

We believe that were the War to end this autumn, we would have gained in some ways through our entry into it. But you must satisfy the business man with the peace proposal. You can only do that in one way. You must state in your contracts with him that *he will not lose* by an early settlement. You will help to shorten the War if you will assure him of this. And you will not lose by this generosity to him. You will gain more by covering his loss through an early peace, by saving yourself the extended expenditure of a prolonged War.

Take a large, generous attitude toward the business man. Promise him that he will be reimbursed for the extra machinery he has had to install to fill our war orders; promise him that he will be treated justly. Promise him that he will be repaid for everything he has laid out in meeting our demands, *except the energy* he has spent. He need not be repaid by us for his energy. God will repay that.

Don't be afraid of the big contracts the business men are bringing for war necessities. Accept them generously and shorten this War.

We want peace.

MABEL DODGE.

Read this! Arthur! Will you *please* print this in your paper *soon?*

But it was never printed until now when it is still true.

I scarcely went into town at all, for the people I really cared for came out to the Farm, not seeming to be perturbed by any relationship I might have with Maurice because they did not have to be sure it existed, since I had Bayard staying there, too, and Bobby often, and John at the week-ends. I managed to spread attention on all of these and did not have any special emphasis on one of them. But how dreary it was to have lost all interest in the outside world, and to have made a small universe for myself out there in the country, built around the unstable and shifting personality of that Russian! The core of my life was rotten. Often, after he left in the morning to go to his studio in New York, I felt terribly lonely and empty in that large, quiet house where all the life was going on in the kitchen, a place I seldom entered.

Bayard always stayed out in the Green House alone all day, except at lunch time when the gong would rouse him, and I, sitting with empty hands, saw him swing around the corner of the house, his facial muscles holding things together. He wanted to believe and to have us believe he was writing poetry. Sometimes he brought a few lines in for me to read, and they were always real.

I was often worried about what Maurice was doing in town. What did he do in his studio? I didn't trust him out of my sight, or in it. Sometimes he would come back in the evening, hurrying up the hill along the damp avenue where the sodden leaves were gathering in the ditches, and I, watching for him through the glass of the front door, would see the porch light fall upon his dark face, convulsed with some inward agony, unconscious of anyone, thinking himself alone in the wet night; at the noise of the opening door and my voice of housewifely welcome ("Hello, Maurice, I was watching for you"), a shadow of annoyance would pass over his eyes and a look of endurance would follow until he learned to remember that someone was probably watching and waiting for him at the top of the hill, and then, he, too, like Bayard, had his face ready for the light when it fell upon it.

Our evenings were set for pleasure and ease. Why couldn't we enjoy them? The hickory logs burned in the large fireplace, the lamps in their white shades illumined the white walls and the white muslin curtains; there were books and magazines all about, and bunches of late yellow chrysanthemums making a bitter sweet autumn smell and blending with the wood smoke.

I sat back in the depths of a deep-winged chair with my feet under me and watched Maurice moodily. I was always trying to read him. Bayard stared for hours into the fire, a half-smile on his face. He frequently seemed wrapped in dreams, but his presence seemed clear to me beside Maurice's singular emanations.

I will never forget the feeling that went through me one evening when I caught sight of Maurice stroking Scuro. The black cat arched his back with pleasure and half closed his peculiar eyes. Maurice's large hand rubbed him over and over rhythmically and Scuro turned about backwards and forwards, leaning his sleek head against Maurice's hip, brushing his long black tail close to the rough tweed. He

427

purred loudly like a little palpitating engine and closed his eyes ec-
statically. Now I could almost see the exchange between those two,
Maurice pouring his hot magnetism into the cat, the cat passing his
electricity up to Maurice. It seemed terribly dark and evil. Perhaps this
is "bestiality," I thought.

Maurice suddenly caught sight of my horror and laughed slyly and
silently. "Scuro is a nice cat," he said, persisting in his ministrations.
Scuro throbbed. At the continued revolt in my face, perhaps, Maurice
giggled with that sudden, breathless gasp that sometimes caught him.
His expression was rather foolish and mixed with fear, more innocent
than his laugh, more innocent than his hand. It was as though he
were doing something he was almost, though not quite, aware of. A
force moved in him for which his consciousness had no name, hardly
awareness even, until I brought it home to him. His nervous laughter
faded out and his lips tightened. He ceased fondling Scuro and looked
angrily at me. How I irked him! I had but added to his sense of sin
without the understanding that gives sin its value and meaning. Just
a feeling without thought. I saw how he hated me. Whenever his life
moved in him, I checked it because I could not let him be himself; I
could not stand him as he was; I must raise him and make him
different.

Well, if I hampered him, how he limited me, too! It is a terrible
thing to get all one's attention fixed on any human being, but when
one has been caught by one like Maurice, it is as if so little of one
can be poured out that most of one's energy is dammed up and sent
coursing backwards, poisoning one throughout and driving one mad.
He did not require my attention or accept it.

Only at night, after Bayard had gone off home with his mended face
and debonair manner, and Maurice and I put out the lights in the
house, and mounted the stairs to my bed near the window, then we
wordlessly, sightless in the dark, gripped each other's body and emptied
the sadness and venom of the day. Then for that fraction of time
we were together, without worry and without thought.

But that is not enough. No matter what anyone says to the contrary,
it is not enough to have the most perfect physical combination unless
there is an emotional consolation at the base of it. Hearts must open
and speak to each other else there is only a deepening sadness and a
sense of waste with every outpouring of love.

"Darling," Maurice whispered in the dark, "you are so wonderful. Why do I always feel that I have died after we have been together?"

Always, after that night when I watched him caressing Scuro and stopped him with the expression on my face, he identified himself with the black cat, without knowing it of course. He saved little bits from the table to feed it, and watched it by the hour through the winter evenings.

"Isn't he a da-a-arling?" he would exclaim. *"Look* at that nose!" And he himself, with his expression of a little boy, would seem then like a darling, too.

Chiara became Bayard's alter ego in Maurice's imagination. Maurice was always made a little uncomfortable by Bayard's fastidious manner and his cool, aloof way of life. Norwegian ice in Bayard's eyes chilled Maurice's hot, thick blood. The white cat was delicate and remotely beautiful, less savage than Scuro, languid and indifferent. Her blue eyes were like jewels. Everyone preferred her to the slinking, black, shadowy Scuro who sat on the roof by the hour watching for birds and killing them off one by one.

John hated Scuro. "I'm going to get that cat some day," he threatened at the dinner table as Maurice slyly tucked a shred of beef into the pink mouth. Scuro marched out of the room licking his chops, tail swinging high. Maurice looked furiously at John. "How can you think of killing anything as beautiful as Scuro!" he exclaimed, and threw a look of appeal at me.

"He's no good," he said.

At school that year John took prizes in everything. Over and over his name was called and he marched up to the platform to receive sets of books, and Maurice was the cause of this.

Reed had stood fairly well with John. Though his private self-esteem was hurt by what seemed to him an immoral relationship between Reed and me, still Reed was as easy for him to accept as anyone could be, for he had been a hero in Morristown School in his day, only eight or ten years back, and the masters there all knew him. John had felt a mixture of pride and shame when Steffens and I took Reed down there to Morristown to talk to the boys about Mexico. These strange complex feelings made him feel older, but it was easy to like Reed, who gave him the fine kodak he had used when he traveled around with Villa.

"Mr. Sterne" was different. John didn't like him, he couldn't bear seeing him around. For him he was always the stranger with the guilty secret and never anything else. And Maurice acted like a small boy in his jealousy of John; he felt a competition between John and himself. But John did not feel jealous of Maurice; he felt reduced by him. He felt Maurice was detrimental to him, lowering his self-respect. To make up for "Mr. Sterne and mother," John had to take all the school prizes. This helped him somewhat. I hope.

Poor Maurice! He made us all feel disgusted with ourselves. We had to work to keep on feeling ourselves above him and we thought we had to keep the atmosphere light and clear and free from evil and to counteract his powerful magnetism, for Nordic and Oriental blood can never understand each other. This conflict between differing blood streams and sexualities is as relentless and savage as the conflict between various cultures, in fact, one springs out of the other, and there seems to be no way to settle either of them.

It was not settling anything to try to make Maurice feel it incumbent upon him to live as I lived, to ape my kind of consciousness, to repress his incontinent warmth without understanding the reason for its incontinence, to be expressive, cool, and American, when in reality he felt sometimes like letting his sexuality ooze out all over him, like laughing boisterously and nudging with his knee, or sitting in a dark basement smoking cigars and blowing the froth off a stein of beer.

There were odors and perfumes in his mother's house as familiar to him as light, odors that stirred him, fusty, acrid or spicy. But he did not like them or want to like them. He wanted to like the clean smell of Colgate soap that he found upon me. "You smell like a new loaf of bread, Mabel," he told me one night. "Wholesome."

But did he really like my kind of wholesomeness? I hardly think so. I do not think he was *moved* by such unambiguous sensuousness. His nature could not have been satisfied, no matter how he tried!

Sometimes he tried to leave me. He would say he couldn't stand it and he would dress himself in a silk shirt and leave the house with a long cigar between his teeth. At the split between us my whole nature would stretch out after him; the unseen antennae in every cell that reach out all around us would strain, moving to find him in the empty space he had left, every nerve on end and crying for him. Why? Why?

Why did I have to want him there? At any rate, I had to have him back no matter how he hurt or repelled me. There was one time he left when all day and night I tried to reach him and failed and nothing made me forget him. When I walked up over the hill to Elizabeth's because I couldn't stand it alone in the house, everything went against me. Thorns caught me and scratched, roots of trees tripped me up, Nature was my enemy. My self-esteem and dignity were gone. My evening was formless and my white silk dress crumpled and untidy. The hours were so different from the clear-cut, seemly times when Maurice was there and we all obliged each other to maintain a pattern and a decorum of living. Did I need Maurice to create a form of life through this tension, and did I need to feel him strain up to me? And he? What did he feel away from Finney Farm? I could not follow him in my imagination, I couldn't conceive what he was doing. All I knew was that he, who fitted so uneasily into that cheerful American home, left it empty and lifeless when he went away. Bayard was no more than a conch shell for the fireplace, empty and polished. He provided no warm life.

And then a letter came from him and I could bear his absence no longer. I motored into town determined to ask his mother if she knew where he was. I sent the chauffeur up to ring the doorbell of the apartment and I sat in the windy street somewhere far up on the West Side where noisy children swarmed around the car—many little olive-skinned children with the sliding, dark eyes rabbity in the ivory and oil.

I had to have him. Revolted through and through I had to sit there and wait for him.

And then he was beside me, leaning into the car, his mouth turned up in a crescent-shaped smile, beaming, ruddy-cheeked and absolutely shining with a renewed Oriental *bien-être* that had returned on him with a rush in his short absence from Finney Farm. He looked more himself than ever, I thought.

He had acquired a new hat, pale gray with a black band, and this strong contrast simply leapt at one. I had kept his things subdued, but the moment he got away from me he bounded into the most extreme colors, heavy accents and exuberant effects.

"Why, darling!" he exclaimed, and his smile, I thought, must flash from Grant's Tomb to the Battery. "How lov-**v**-vely! I missed you ter-r-ribly, darling. How have you been!"

"Oh, Maurice . . . get in here!" I answered him half irritably, wholly relieved.

"But I can't, darling. I have promised to lunch with someone." And then added, "Can't we meet after lunch?"

"Where have you been, Maurice?"

"Oh, I had such an interesting time. I went to Coney Island!"

"Alone?"

"Yes, of course alone. I wanted to see it. Darling, what do you think! I won a tea set!"

"*What?*"

"Yes. Throwing balls. And I have something to tell you later."

As I drove away exasperated, yet relaxed by him, I knew I would not be easy in my mind until I had heard his confession. What had he done now?

I went and called up Walter Lippmann and asked him to lunch. I needed an antidote. Walter was thoroughly free intellectually. He was "Harvardized," well-bred, and in possession of himself. There was no incontinence there, no flowing sensuality. Rather, a fine poise, a cool understanding, and with all the high humor in the world shining in his intelligent eyes.

"How hard it is to find anything you can *love*," I complained. "What do you love, Walter?"

"The living world," he answered. Well, so did Maurice!

That night in the dark, my head on his arm, Maurice narrated his story.

"Darling, sometimes I feel that I *must* get away. The other day I just ran from Finney Farm and I thought I would go and see some of those simple people having a good time. I couldn't resist those balls, darling! I knew I could win and I got that lovely tea set. You wouldn't care for it. I gave it to my mother.

"Then that old *hunting* instinct awoke in me! I began to look at the girls. They are beautiful, those girls of the common people. But as soon as I looked at them and began to desire them, my feeling for them changed into the *artist's!* I began to see in planes and masses and my sexual desire turned into a terrific wish to *draw*—to repro-

432

duce those forms. That is always the way, darling! I wish my Art would let me enjoy myself!"

"Oh, Maurice! Surely there is another way still! If you really loved me you would be faithful in spite of yourself. You wouldn't have that hunting thing always leading you astray. You wouldn't have all those sexual cravings and you would be free to work."

"I don't know why it is, but I am contrary. Nothing satisfies me."

"Well, I *know* paint doesn't satisfy you, Maurice. I don't know about myself. . . ."

"Oh, darling, I do love you! Perhaps I have lost the capacity for that young thrill I had over B. but I know I love you, and need you, seriously."

"Maurice. Let me order some clay for you. Try modeling. It seems to me your hands just long to handle some solid substance."

"Later on, dear. I want to work out some problems first. I *know* I can make form as plastic with paint as a sculptor does with clay. . . . I *must* work more *seriously*. I have been spending too much time getting *ready* to paint. I think I'll get one of those young shop girls for a model," he mused.

I felt his flickering, unstable wishes, interchangeable in his bloodstream with the gray matter of his brain. It maddened me and left me feeling hopeless to know I had no solid foundation beneath me when I longed to rest upon him. A woman comes to feel she must be supported—must unfailingly be able to depend upon her man.

"I don't *want* you to have models down there in that studio! I know just what *that* means. When you can't paint, you'll make love instead. . . ."

"Really, Mabel, you are impossible. I *must* be free. I don't see how we can go on like this."

Sometimes I received letters from friends abroad who were in the midst of a variety of excitements. Stan Harding Krayl, for one, was having an adventurous time. She wrote me:

China Navigation Company's
S.S. Kinling.

DEAREST MABEL:

I wish you would write—perhaps you have and the letter has not reached me yet. My brother has been again transferred. Foochow this time. Decidedly preferable to Newchwang, Manchuria.

Since my last have had far and away the best fortnight of my life. This was a 16 days' boating expedition into Soochuan through the Yangtse Gorges. For me China has resolved itself into the Yangtse and the Yangtse when it is very green in the shadow of the Gorges. Was wrecked on the fifth day out and lost all my belongings, including all the sketches I have done since in China, my journal, etc.—and was stranded with nothing but my life. Providentially was overtaken at the critical moment by the only white man to go upstream that month, a consul traveling with two life boats. He left me one of these, also clothes and provisions so was able to go on. I will send you an account of the River. On the way down passed Gian Fan's—the great yellow junks towed upstream by their 60 to 100 trackers climbing along the rock path hewn in the rock. Yellow flags with their purple dragons sprawling after the sun—lemon yellow banners with huge cinnibar characters on them—copper-colored men rowing for their lives. Owing to the unrest, was unable to look about for old things. Have only a Chinese-speaking crew and servant with me so had to sketch all orders.

Arrived back at Ichang I found that my brother had been transferred to Manchuria. I stayed on at the dismantled consulate for fortnight and then had to leave just as the trouble began. Arrived at Hankow, found the city in a haze of smoke and firing going on. We were told that a battle was in progress. Incited a couple of young fellows on board to go out to the scene of action. We kept about fifty yards behind the firing line. The rebels were steadily driving the loyalists back. We were met with extreme courtesy everywhere and we felt that the rebels regretted that they were unable to offer us tea under the circumstances. It seemed difficult to imagine that this was war but for the dead and wounded.

It is so difficult to see things in perspective. Most people out here seem to think that the great war between Chinese and Manchus has come at last. Others, that it will all fizzle out, the loyalists gain the upper hand, the towns in the hands of the rebels be recaptured and put to fire and sword.

Went into the native city on the chance of getting good things looted from the Yamens but found the shops shut. The Revolutionists were busy recruiting and shooting any poor Manchu they could lay hands on. The people seemed a good deal upset and one breathed more freely when one was again within the strongly guarded foreign concession. The ladies and children have been sent away, but the men stayed to look after their property. I got three little pieces of China but they are worth more as souvenirs—one is for you if you like it.

One dies for news—do write c/o H.B.M. Consulate,

Foochow, S. China.

Please excuse untidy letter but it is difficult to concentrate. Wuchang, just across the River, is again burning.

Am well and happy.

With much love, always, dearest Mabel,

Your friend,

STAN.

But out in Croton life grew more and more narrowed down for Maurice and me. Because Max had sometimes tried to persuade me to write, to beguile an hour once I sat down and wrote about Maurice's day when he was absent from me, and my so different one. Max liked it very much. He said:

DEAR MABEL:

Thank you a thousand times. It is going in the next number.

You owed it to me, anyway, for didn't I tell you to do it?

You have a gift and energy of creation that ought to be more sacred to you than any personal thing. You ought to enlarge your knowledge, continually, so that you will have at the command of your talent every intellectual distinction, every subtle verbal power that analytic thinking has developed. (You have been enlarging your *experience* for a long time!)

This is an intense and compelling work of art, and I hope you know it.

MAX.

I saw Elizabeth less often now because I had no attention left over to give her, and also, not only was I retrospectively jealous of B. and the other women Maurice told me about, but so was he jealous of my "past," as he called it. When we had no present fear to harrow us, we both relapsed into moody brooding over each other's experiences.

He questioned me about Reed, about all that happened between us; and I, in an agony of need to confess and to wipe out everything that had ever happened with anyone who was not he, recounted all the phases of my love for Reed. I brought great packages of his letters as we sat before the blazing logs after Bayard had gone to his cottage. Maurice read them over, and together we threw them into the fire when he finished them. Anything to strengthen and cement our life together. . . .

Maurice came to the long letters I had written Reed when he was in Mexico, and that Reed had sent back to me to keep for him, be-

435

cause some day he meant to write a great love story about us. ("I will write our names in fire upon the sky," as he had written from Mexico.) Maurice read the story of my trip to Buffalo with Andrew and Hartley when we stayed with Nina and had the first modern art show there in the Albright Gallery. When he came to the expression of my admiration for and interest in Andrew, Maurice leapt up and crushed the pages into his pocket. "I can't read this here with you. I will read it when I am in town."

The fire cheerfully burned all the packets of letters. Letters from Mexico, from Paris, and London, and Rome, and from Czechoslovakia. All the gay, adventurous accounts of Reed's exploits out in the world. This wholesale sacrifice seemed to give Maurice a certain satisfaction. I was glad, if it united us any more fully.

He went to New York the next morning early, and I waited in anxiety for his return. I was afraid of the effect my letter would have on him, of the reproaches, and the renewal of his fears about my own fidelity—for he often used the past inconstancies I had confessed to him as an excuse for his incomplete confidence in me, saying that was the reason he did not feel he could give himself wholly to me. He was afraid of me, afraid I would let him down. Poor Reed had never once been afraid of that!

I waited all day for Maurice to call me on the phone, but he never did. Bayard and I lunched and dined together. Bayard grew a little more aware of me in Maurice's absences. I was acquiring some influence over him, and I was trying to get him to stop drinking. He always told me that anything that would soften the harsh, ugly outlines of life the way alcohol did, had too great a power ever to relinquish.

Maurice didn't come in until I was in bed lying awake listening for his footsteps, and when I heard him come up the stairs with his heavy, masculine tread, I turned on the light and flew to meet him.

His face was flushed and beaming. He showed all the signs of what is called "a good time," which means one thing for one person, something different for another, but is always some kind of outpouring and the relief of tension.

"Darling . . . I had a wonderful day!" he cried happily, smoothing back his long locks and looking somewhat like a broad, laughing Mephistopheles with his horns laid back. "I was having tea in a little place on Fifty-ninth Street. I had gone in there to read your papers where I knew no one to interrupt me. There was such a beautiful woman sitting at the table next to me! I don't know how it happened, really, but we spoke to each other. Then I asked her to have tea with me!"

My heart was sinking lower and lower as I listened in silence to this Russian anecdote.

"She opened her heart to me—this stranger! She was very lovely. Such delicate forms. And then I got very mad! What do you think? The woman who ran the place told me we couldn't stay there! Can you imagine that?"

"But why? What were you *doing?*"

"Nothing. She just came over to us and told us to go."

"Oh, Maurice! And that letter? Haven't you read it?"

His face looked blank. Then aghast. He began to run his large, flat hands through his pockets.

"Let me see. I had laid it on the table. . . . I was going to take it up and read it. . . . Then I began to talk and I must have forgotten it. Why, I believe I must have left it on the table when we went out!"

"Maurice!" I cried. "That terribly private thing! All those names in it! I *trusted* you to take care of it!"

"That awful woman must have found it. Isn't that *terrible!* What can I do? I'll go back in the morning and ask her for it."

"You *can't* do that. You'll have to let it go. How *could* you forget it and not think of it again? What did you *do* all evening? Where did you *go?*"

"Well, I felt so sorry for that scene, I took her out to dinner and we spent the evening together. . . . A charming, well-bred woman . . . very unhappy." He looked reminiscent.

I sat down on a chest and burst into tears, my hands over my face. It was all so horrible. I was trapped and unable to find a way out. I felt I must have help or go mad.

I sobbed for hours and Maurice did everything he could think of to comfort me. But he couldn't help me. Finally he gave up trying, for he was evidently very tired and sleepy. I saw him creep out and heard him quietly undressing in his own room, which a short while before he had moved into from the Green House. As I sobbed in impotent anger and misery, I heard him get into bed. Then I rushed in and flung myself on my knees beside him.

"Maurice, you are killing me! I can't *stand* it!"

I longed to lose consciousness, but I could not. Instead, he persuaded me into the warmth of his bed and tried, as usual, to comfort me with love. The wakeful night beside his peaceful sleep was the zero point between us.

CHAPTER XV

Dr. Jelliffe

IN the morning I decided I must have help from outside and I thought of Dr. Jelliffe, whom I had been to see when Genevieve Onslow frightened us so that night we experimented with *peyote*.

I drove into New York and called upon him, and we sat in his office. He was a tall, portly, clean-shaven man dressed in black, and his plump face was enlivened by a pair of small, intelligent green eyes.

"Jung has taught us," he said, "that when one reaches an impasse, it is because he is unable to function in the way his own particular nature wishes. When we try to force ourselves to go in directions contrary to the psyche, she rebels. You do not like your present life. Why?"

I launched into a description of my situation with Maurice. It was a great relief to talk, to tell it all . . . to tell how I hated things about him even while I loved him and was unable to live without him.

I enjoyed my visits three times a week to Jelliffe's office. He had a speculative mind with an amusing intuition. As he turned my attention more and more upon the inner workings of my own nature, curious spiritual events began to occur, and my starved perceptions, that had been centered for months upon Maurice, reveled in the new direction of interest. It became an absorbing game to play with oneself, reading one's motives, and trying to understand the symbols by which the soul expressed itself.

Psychoanalysis was apparently a kind of tattletaleing. I was able to tell, not only everything about myself, but all about Maurice. I grew calm and self-sufficient, and felt superior to him in the evening when, returning from New York, I found him still in the grip of his nervous fears and worries.

I tried to tell him about the system and how it worked, but he

439

hated it and said it all revolted him. When I told Jelliffe this, he exclaimed:

"Ah, naturally! He has a resistance. Whenever people particularly need psychoanalysis, they have a great resistance to it."

When I went to his office I always noticed a grave, sweet-looking woman sitting in an alcove at the end of the hall working upon papers, and I asked him who she was. He told me she was an old patient of his and of particular interest. "She has cured herself of manic-depression," he said, regarding me with an intent gaze. "I have written up her case for the *Review*. You must read it. You know that she is my proof that by understanding and hard work these manic-depressives may free themselves."

I longed to draw others into the new world where I found myself: a world where things fitted into a set of definitions and terms that I had never even dreamt of. It simplified all problems to name them. There was the Electra complex, and the Oedipus complex and there was the Libido with its manifold activities, seeking every chance for outlet, and then all that thing about Power and Money!

One of the most interesting speculations Jelliffe went in for was apparently a new field never worked much before—the set of symbols that compose all the parts of the body. The respiratory organs, he said, stood for human aspiration, the breath was no less than the Breath of God. Failure in aspiration resulted in a breaking down of the lungs, the bronchial tubes, or the larynx. The creation, birth, and development of the soul could be reckoned in these parts, and they corresponded with the lower organs of sex where creation on another plane was effected. "As below, so above." The creative word issued from the throat of man when he reached the true Power of manhood, and this was the birth of the mystic Rose on the Cross of the medieval Rosicrucians.

The appearance of a cancer in a person signified hatred. It was the parasite eating away the vitality of man. The bowels were the vehicle of the money power, excrement was gold, hoarded or distributed in circulation. . . . Ah, there were many fascinating explanations of the mystery of the body. Jelliffe had written a great volume that showed the body and its ills at three levels: the somatic, the psychic, and the symbolic.

Since I couldn't persuade Maurice to go and be psychoanalyzed, I made Bayard go to try to get over his drinking. He became as fascinated as I was, and this banded us together against Maurice, who felt decidedly out of things.

Maurice was always trying his best to be nice. Trying to be nicer than he was, really, so he did not allow himself to show his feelings about Jelliffe and psychoanalysts when he could help it, and so they emerged at unexpected times.

One Sunday there were a lot of us sitting at the long table in the dining room with the sun streaming in the south windows over the heads of eminent men. Jelliffe sat at my right hand, and Maurice carved a generous roast opposite me. Along the sides were Bobby and Leo Stein, Bayard, and John, and Jelliffe's son, Ely. Marsden Hartley was there, with his anxious, pale blue eyes flashing from left to right on everyone in turn. Stephan Bourgeois was there. He was Maurice's new dealer, a large, smiling German stuffed into a cutaway coat that he removed on Sunday mornings while he played Beethoven with a furious energy on the helpless piano in the white living room.

Jelliffe had been curious about the Finney Farm constellation and I had asked him for a week-end. In the morning he had visited the Green House and talked to Bayard. He had seen the two large, green macaws that stayed out there, and had observed them with a small, knowing, psychoanalytical smile. He had studied in diplomatic silence the picture Marsden Hartley was painting on the floor of the living room while Bourgeois hammered up and down the piano. Hartley told Jelliffe his picture was called "Handsome Drinks," and the doctor made out a glass of milk, a glass of champagne, and the Communion Cup. Before dinner he had found Bobby making sketches for a play, out on the dining-room table. These drawings decided him that Bobby, too, needed psychoanalysis, and before long I led him unresisting to Jelliffe's office. Palpably, Maurice had evaded Jelliffe's attempts to talk to him by always being in the room where the doctor was not.

We talked of many things at the table that day, and Ernestine filled our glasses frequently with the good Italian wine. I noticed Maurice, as usual, unable to resist pressing against the girl's breast as she held the plates to him to be replenished. I hoped Jelliffe was observing this, but apparently he was not. He was talking to Leo Stein about the theory of tension in the nervous system and comparing it to its appearance in works of art. "Its value depends upon the relative resilience of the parts," he said. "The importance of strain . . ."

I suddenly heard Maurice's voice, addressed to Ralph Roeder, with that nervous giggling in it, the breathless gasp, that showed his little-boy dimples. I looked at him and saw a hateful expression on his face; something spiteful and malicious flickered in his nervousness.

"I always think," he was saying, "that cats are more a man's pet, don't you, Ralph? It seems as though women take to little dogs and men to cats. I think every spinster should have a little dog, don't you?"

I felt a wave of hot blood suffuse me from my toes to my cheeks. It seemed to me that Maurice's implications were frightful. I glanced at Jelliffe to see if he had heard for I wanted to talk it over with him the next day. He was looking at Maurice with interest, but with no expression of disgust. Everyone had heard, for Maurice had raised his voice, and heads were turned toward him, but no one looked as if anything out of the way had been said. Bobby was answering him.

"I adore cats. Some people hate them, though."

"Oh, that's because they don't understand them," persisted Maurice. My anger rose in me. I would not have him dragging the tone of my dinner table down to the level of perversity.

"If you . . ." he went on.

"That's enough, Maurice," I exclaimed in a low, impassioned voice.

In an instant the laughing malice on his face was wiped away by a look of complete bewilderment. He hadn't the slightest notion why I had stopped him. He closed his lips tightly and bent his eyes on his plate. My interruption had been like the snap of a whip. All the heads turned toward me, now, in surprise; in Bayard's face a look of secret satisfaction, though quite without understanding. In fact, not one of them knew why I had shut Maurice up. Least of all, himself. But he had been hurt by my tone to him. He wrote a note next day and sent it to me:

Dear Mabel,

I've tried it—it won't do. There is too much antagonism in the air here, too much friction. I felt it yesterday when the crowd came, I felt it last night when they were gone, and this morning. . . .

Heaven knows there is enough hatred in the world, now—so I've decided to go before this antagonism develops into hatred.

There will be more harmony here when I am gone.

M. S.

I talked him out of leaving but I went in town to see Dr. Jelliffe, and asked him if he had noticed how Maurice had started to pollute the table, to throw mud on us all by his suggestiveness and his allusions.

"Why, no," Jelliffe said, "I didn't notice anything like that. I thought he seemed a little embarrassed, that is all."

"Oh, he is too devious for any of you," I cried. "Devious and unfrank! When I accused him of it last night, do you know what he said? 'Mabel, I was just trying to do my part.'"

"Maybe he was," said Jelliffe. "Certainly if he intended anything else, it was unconscious. Possibly your interpretation of it is colored by your own unconsciousness," he continued, looking at me searchingly. "You know we are always projecting ourselves. Often what we think we find in others is nothing but our own hidden life. What we need is the power to see in ourselves the traits and motives we imagine we detect in others! So long as we are merely subjective all our criticism is but self-criticism."

Heavens! I thought. I must track down *the Maurice* in me now! Was the real Maurice quite other than I had pictured him to myself? Heavens!! Was I attached to *myself* instead of to him as I had supposed? Was this the trap? But on the other hand, were the qualities I had admired in Walter also my own potentialities?

These were interesting, fascinating, new ideas. Unfortunately, they remained in the realm of ideas only and produced no change in my nature.

Maurice's letter later on shows he was quite innocent of anything *louche.* He said in a P.S.:

Something occurred to me last night. When on that Sunday night I spoke to Roeder about the animals, is it true that Jelliffe also, and not alone Bobby, looked at you "significantly"?

Be honest and tell me.   M.

The first time I had seen Dr. Jelliffe I remember him coming towards me, then, in his office: tall, in a black suit of smooth cloth, a little paunchy, his small, green eyes set rather close together, were speculative upon one. "A Roman Catholic priest," I had thought at once, for there was something all over him that was like that: in his glance, in the smooth, fine texture of his pale skin, and in his bearing. He was commanding, quizzical, sure of himself, and not to be moved. His features were small and fine, and there was a kind of impudence playing over them. His face looked as though he had put on a lot of thick make-up and wiped it off so frequently that its contours were modeled by this massage. Actors' faces often have this modeled surface.

Next, I remember him sitting beside me on the pale blue Louis Seize couch at 23 Fifth Avenue, probing me with his inquisitive eyes, asking me questions; and then it was I confided to him my curious hankering to cut off my hair. This interested him very much. No women cut off their hair in those days, and I had lovely brown coils in figure eights over my ears. Nice hair. But, oh! I longed to cut it with a physical yearning. I was dying to feel short locks against my ears—the *shorn* feeling that must follow the fatal clip-clip. I knew in advance the light and airy sensation that would come from a Dutch cut. I had seen illustrations in Howard Pyle's books, done by Maxfield Parrish that showed me how I would look! Yes, for a long time, now, I had wanted to cut my hair off, and I knew I'd be doing it one of those days, only I never arrived at the right and courageous moment of *doing* it! Jelliffe considered me gravely.

"And who do you know that has long hair like raus? *Who* is it that you want to shear?"

"What do you mean? *I* don't know. Who?"

"Phoebus Apollo!" he answered me with fearful solemnity, his little jowls quivering slightly. "The Sun!"

These unfamiliar quirks of his mind entertained me immensely. *"What* an amusing man!" I thought. But I disbelieved him. I loved the sun, I thought. It was the moon I did not like.

Soon after this, Edwin Arlington Robinson and I were lunching together in the Italian restaurant, and, as usual, talking of divers things.

"Do you know they have doctors now to cure the *soul?"* he said.

"Yes, and I'm going to be *done* some day," I laughed. "Just to find out about it."

"Dangerous business, perhaps. Maybe the cure is worse than the disease."

"Well, I'll let you know. . . ."

444

I was not finding it at all dangerous. It was interesting to watch my soul provide exciting subjects to discuss with Jelliffe. Whenever things got dull, something would turn up from down below to keep the ball rolling—and he and I chased it about. We talked for hours. He told me more strange and fascinating oddities and now I have forgotten them nearly all! Sometimes I argued with him by letter and he would reply.

My dear Mrs. Dodge:

I am sorry you feel I dogmatize: I myself am dogmatic that I have no right to do so. As a thorough-going sophist and pragmatist my own philosophy cannot and must not be imposed on another of different experience. With Protagoras, I hold, since we do not any of us act quite alike, so therefore we cannot perceive quite alike and that the only necessity for conformity in thinking is concerned with those things which are "necessary to live" as I have quoted it so often to you! We vary concerning those things which are not needed for a bare existence and may conduce to a life that is "beautiful and good." I feel sure you cannot find therein a dogmatic philosophy.

I think my dogmatism is concerned with the evidences of your unconscious solely. If your unconscious indubitably says, "This I wish to do—but I, my conscious, knows, it will lead to death, and not to a life that is beautiful and good," then I must confess I am dogmatic. If your unconscious says, "I am a man and I can procreate with my male organ," then I am dogmatic. "You can't and you need not try." This is not forcing a philosophy upon you. This is only telling you you are trying to do the impossible. Perhaps I fail to get this distinction over; if so, then surely I am at fault.

I am not one whit involved in forcing people to do anything. I am only trying to be a mirror in which one may read why one cannot do certain things in certain ways. If my reading and experience and knowledge of evolution has taught it to me from another side, I should not use that overmuch, else it might seem I was putting myself in front of the mirror.

Those things which are most strongly felt as resistances are the direct results of the patient's and analyst's blind spots. One must be very careful regarding the great tendency to displace the affect, born of the resistance, to something quite foreign to the situation.

I hope I can help you to see this on Monday. I am glad you can formulate my dogmatism, as you have; it is one of my difficulties, more born of the desire to hurry people along than to make them conform. I am after

445

all a wretched conformist myself and to be held up as a single pattern, machine maker of souls—although perhaps an hyperbolic way of taking your phrase—is a shock.

Very cordially,

SMITH ELY JELLIFFE.

How about Bayard? I hope he will write me.

It was customary during an analysis, Dr. Jelliffe told me, for the patient to be separated temporarily from the family, or from those nearest one, who were in some way involved with the compulsions and complexes of the case. I did not doubt now but that Maurice was the complete picture of whatever was the matter with me; that, could I but read it aright, would explain to me the difficult, incomprehensible make-up that hid the real self somewhere deep down in me. But I found I just couldn't define my impulses, no matter how strong or how real they were. They made me do things, they made me resent certain qualities in others, they *seemed* all right to me—rather fine, really—but name them I could not. Why, why did I have to wrestle so with this man, compel him to an exact fidelity, determine him to be a sculptor, lift him up and chasten him? Really, was it only myself I was working on?

At Jelliffe's request, then, I got him off to Pottsville to paint landscapes of snow, and the strain immediately lessened, and I resumed a way of life less concentrated and bent upon changing him. I found everything much pleasanter. But he was upset by the change:

Feb 2.
224 North 2nd St.

DEAREST MABEL:

Well, here I am in Pottsville, tired, sad and disgusted. But I'll stick it out even if it kills me. Yesterday I hunted for rooms and today we had a heavy snow storm. But nevertheless I sketched out of doors until I got chilled to the marrow. I wish I were in Croton. But that will come. What happened to me Monday? All day I was so anxious to see you. I felt only the deepest love—and then when I saw you there at Jelliffe's, a bitter feeling of resentment overcame me. Something would have happened to me had it not come out of me.

This, Mabel, is my strength and my weakness too: I never let poison secret in me—I let it out. I sometimes think that Bayard would be much freer if he could do it—a person like he is can't help feeling irritated sometimes—it must react on him. I was so happy to get your letter today. If I could have you, Mabel, and my work, too! Or am I one of those who can't

446

have more than one interest at a time? If my work got along there I would be quite happy—just happy in my work. Life here does not exist for me. It would be wearing a hair shirt. I'd gladly do it for my soul or what is the same thing to me—my work.

I was wise not to go out to Croton on Monday night. Oh, Mabel, I'll never forget my 5 hours' trip in the train.

With love and affection and everything beautiful.

MAURICE.

Love to Bayard.

DEAR MABEL:

We parted—you to find out what it's like to be away from me—I to learn what it is to be with you.

Yesterday was strange, terrible. For a few moments you took me where there is no horizon, no forms, no color, only pure, thin, colorless ether. My flesh revolted—demanded the familiar. Is it because we came forth from the earth that we feel this deep relationship with her? But why? Are we not Earth's Spirit which has burst its bonds in the birth of the flesh?

I used to believe that the birth of man is the death of the earth's body and birth of her spirit—just as man's spirit is born in his death. Spiritually we are children of the Earth—and Death is her grandchild. . . .

But yesterday you made me see and feel as I have never felt before that we are not only Earth's Spirit but carry within us *our own* soul. Past, present, future is one. It terrified me as all nakedness terrifies me, when I see it for the first time.

It is wonderful to see something new. It does not destroy, it creates the old.

But what you said about my work is only partially true. All this talk about the naïve vision, the forgetting of all one has learned! We are spirits within spirit—the eye's spirit, that which can reveal a new truth, new nakedness of Nature, is acquired in continuous sight. In order to give a true reflection of this sight, the greatest mastery is essential. The spirit of vision comes from the fingertips and leaves its impression on the paper—the stone.

But perhaps we agree, after all. We misunderstand each other's words only.

Salute.

MAURICE.

For me it was exactly like a holiday, as though Maurice had been a tremendous job from which I was granted a vacation—and what was left of the strange grind that constituted our love affair, was the love

without the strangeness or the strain. It seems to me I never loved
him with any ease except when we were separated, and then tenderness and a kind of compassion entered into me. I felt relieved of him
and wished I could give him the same relief that bathed me—that
let my nerves spread out in the warm free atmosphere of Finney
Farm when he was not there!

Alas, poor Maurice! How sorry I am when I remember it all! With
that same pity I used to think of him alone in Pottsville in his boarding house, so earnestly trying to be good and to love me as I insisted
he should, in the particular, dignified, worth-while fashion I required.
I was always so afraid he was not *noble* enough for me! Heavens!

He wrote me every day and his letters betray his lovable nature.

> *Thursday morning.*
> *Feb. 10.*
> *Pottsville, Pa.*

DEAREST MABEL:

Your Tuesday letters arrived last night. Thanks, darling, for writing so
often. I have already developed a devouring appetite for them—the only
one I have here that I can gratify. Whenever I hear the bell ring, I quit
my work to see if it's the postman. Just when would you want the article
for *Camera Work?* It all depends on that. If I'd have enough time, I'd be
glad to write something. Among other things I want to say in it that perhaps the chief reason so many of the younger men try to express themselves in abstract art is due to an overdeveloped critical understanding of
what is important in a work of art, without the necessary accomplishment
of a trained vision, a vision which grasps the abstract in Nature and knowledge and ability to express it. They have learned that what gives value to a
work of art is just this abstraction and failing to see it in objective nature
they revert to their subjective emotions and try to realize that visually.

Are you writing something for it or have you decided to be only the
power behind the stage?

You must have received my Tuesday letter by this time. I wonder if it
hurt you. I suppose you will think because I calmly can speak of taking a
studio in New York, etc., that my love for you, Mabel, is not very deep.
No, Mabel, it is perfectly wonderful to me how my love for you has grown
from day to day. Even the "storms" which every time they came I expected
would uproot it, only made the roots take deeper root in me. It is only my
work which I consider when I speak that way. Last night I dreamt that I
went back to Croton to get my things. I was packing, you were reclining
on the couch and watching me with an expression of indifference in your

eyes, whilst your *husband,* a man with a blond *mustache,* was conversing with you. I was so sad to go, every moment I wanted to go and tell you: it's no *use,* I can't go—but your stony look held me back. She doesn't care, it is better that I break with it all! At last I couldn't control myself longer, I went up to you and said: "it's no use, Mabel, I can't leave you." Then your expression changed, the indifferent look gave place to one full of tenderness and love. "That's right, darling, stay," you said. I awoke with tears in my eyes. Every night lately I dream of you. The other night I was also at Croton. I came unexpectedly and imagine my disappointment when I was told that you had only that morning gone to Pottsville to me. . . . I didn't know what to do, to go back or wait, when suddenly you came in and we greeted one another *cordially,* for we were not alone. Mary Foote was in the same room. You complained that you felt tired and lay down in your bed when we were left alone. I went up to you, we embraced and my head became all *dizzy* in your embrace. My brain felt just like a wave when it has reached its utmost force upward and is about to collapse. I awoke bewildered and with a feeling of dizziness. You must think I am getting interested in psychoanalysis to be writing down my dreams. No, I still have my old apathy for it, but I thank you nevertheless for offering to present me with a Dr. Jelliffe curse (pardon me, I meant course). If I should find out that I need it, I'd be glad to accept, but at present I feel that I don't need it, and never shall need it.

With all love from

MAURICE.

My love to Bayard. Tell him that I miss him and that I *really love* him.

Thursday, p.m.

DEAREST MABEL,

A little while ago I sent off a letter I wrote this morning, but as I returned from lunch I found your two letters of yesterday, so I'd better answer at once. Thanks, darling, for your really deep anxiety to help me in every way you can. I am sorry to have made that remark about psychoanalysis. After all, we must judge a thing by results and if it really helps you, it must be a good thing for you. I also saw a decided change to the better in Leo, last time we were together—much less of the searchlight which I resented so much—a searchlight not to see, but rather to disclose blemishes. Instead a much warmer glow somewhere inside of him.

I am glad that I am not alone with those "theories" about the influence of some of your visitors. I felt that Bayard must feel the same way about it, though we have *never* discussed it. But *I don't* feel this about Bayard. I didn't feel it even at times when he must have undergone the most ghastly struggles. It is true we *have* irritated one another over the war. But my resentment was always a feeling of anger that so fine a fellow as he is, and a dear friend of whom I am so fond, should be so unjust to the Germans. We agree on everything else.

But enough, I must get to work. So do you think I shouldn't have any hopes that anything will come out of Mrs. Whitney's request? At present, I am working on a landscape—I could have done exactly the same at Croton—if I *could*.

Love from

MAURICE.

P.S. Please, darling, don't for a moment believe that I want you in any way to change your life. You must retain your complete liberty to ask anyone you please to come out to the Farm even when I am there. But only if it gives you real pleasure and you think it helps them. . . .

M.

Thursday, 5 p.m.

DEAREST MABEL,

I just came back from sketching out of doors until my hands and feet were frozen stiff and as the light is failing and I can't work any more today, I thought I'd write to you, sweetheart. Mabel, how long do you think your psychoanalysis will take? It just occurred to me that since most of the trouble between us began when you started the course, it would perhaps be advisable that I stay here until you are through with it.

You see, dear, I look upon a love relationship such as ours, as something very beautiful in its privacy, a source of beauty which should be for the *two* only. I have always thought it crude and vulgar when that which two feel at moments of deepest self-revelation and self-giving is revealed to a third. When I knew that what to me are wonderful mystic rites, you were laying bare on the psychoanalytical operating table, I felt outraged and insulted. I suppose the reasons you did it and the object in view should be considered, but I can't! This is the *true* cause of my jealousy of Dr. Jelliffe. I wasn't jealous of him in the ordinary sense. I felt that you were *giving* yourself spiritually to him, that his influence over you was growing daily, that potentially you wouldn't stop at anything if he convinced you of its pragmatic value. All this was painful, but still I believe I could bear it. The only thing I couldn't bear is the fear that you may lose that which differentiates you from all the women I have known—that which gives you your real strength and *beauty*—what I love in you more than anything else and which forges me firmer and firmer to you—your fundamental *honesty* and *truthfulness*.

Now I felt that the more you endeavored to dig out the deep buried truth from the remotest Past, the less reverence you would feel for the

450

truth of today. There is no gain without some loss. But this, Mabel, would be paying too dearly.

For God's sake, Mabel, even should you lose *everything* else, don't lose that.

I must tell you the dream I had the other night. I was driving your car. I don't remember who else was in it, only Albert, or rather his voice, for I don't remember seeing him. I went along smoothly and at high speed when suddenly I came to a place that looked like this: [drawing]—the street where I intended to go all torn up and excavated. Through the scaffolding one could see deep holes in the earth. I didn't know how to stop the car, in fact there seemed no way of stopping it. I realized that to go straight ahead would destroy me. I then decided to go straight for the protruding wall, but before the car could touch it, I shot out my legs and received the blow with my feet. Then the car bounced back a moment but didn't stop, but went for the wall again. This kept up a long time, I always by shooting out my legs and pulling up my knees saving the car from ruin.

Gradually the driving force of the car seemed to lessen and my strength was leaving me, but Albert's voice always encouraging me on. When I had the car stopped, a very important-looking man, big and fat, with a bundle of tools, came up saying he'd stop it. I remonstrated, feeling that I ought to get the credit, but he didn't mind me, got busy with his tools, and when I looked at the bottom of the car I found that he had made a deep round hole in it.

Strange dream, isn't it? I have interpreted it my own way. Shall I tell you? Your car: our relationship. I was driving full speed to destruction. The brick wall: Pottsville. I batter away at Pottsville and save our love. Then Dr. Jelliffe with his psychoanalytical technique, comes along and claims the credit for something I did myself.—But I don't like the hole in the bottom of the car.

You'll be thinking that I am getting foolish out here.

So long, sweetheart.

MAURICE.

Friday, 6 p.m.
Feb. 18th.

Darling Mabel, another wonderful awakening this morning. Your special delivery letter was brought to me in bed. Yes, sweetheart, I hate to telephone, it always upsets me and I always vow never to do it again— and of course I noticed the "distance" (I mean real distance) in your voice —but only for a moment did it upset me. Those things can't have a deep effect on me any longer—such things can't shake my confidence in you as my faith is my love. Did you send the night letter you mention or did the *capo stazione* scare you? I didn't receive it.

I thought a great deal last night over what could have been the causes of those resistances we felt against each other at the very time when in a way we loved one another passionately. And I came to the conclusion that our love was destroying *itself,* and today I got your letter in which you say that we can't go wrong in love without suffering for it. Isn't that what you meant, dearest? No, darling, I *still* believe that the man should be just as faithful as the woman though I still think that physiologically there *is* a fundamental difference. But spiritually there is none—and we must be true to the spirit and not only to the body. I won't deny that I am aware of the possibility of being attracted now and then to other women. What Hazel once told you is in a way true. I am attracted by beauty. I feel a certain tactile call from it. But that doesn't mean that I should follow my impulses. You see, darling, there is a great deal of the Eastern ascetic in me. I believe in renunciation, I value a thing according to the price I pay for it, according to the price I am willing to pay. Now in love we should be willing not only to make sacrifices for it, but should *make* them, and *through it the love should become enhanced.* With some it is otherwise, they develop a feeling of resentment and bitterness against the object which has evoked the sacrifice. But after all, sacrifice is the wrong word for it— we should renounce freely, buoyantly, we should place our love on an altar, worship it and keep the fire burning on it day and night. But I know you will disagree, for you believe that love should be strong enough to neutralize all feeling for others. But after all, we are all different. Each one ought to be true to the highest in him. I must be true to *my* ideals. And then there is another reason why you should trust me. I have inherited from my father a passionate love for justice. My father was nicknamed "Sterne the Just." Now don't you see, sweetheart, that it would be unjust to sublimate some of our love energy for creative expression, as we shall do, and then go and waste it elsewhere!—I couldn't do it, Mabel. It would make me feel guilty towards you, it would make me suffer and I want to be happy. But still, forgive me, darling, if I tell you that sometimes my old doubts of you come back! I must explain to you, sweetheart, what I mean. Sometime ago you spoke in one of your letters about your spontaneous libido, which flows out in its greatest possible intensity in the moment. Now, Mabel, this is your strength and at the same time your most serious weakness against which you must be continually on your guard. In Art this is responsible for much bad, though virile stuff and in life it is the cause of our gravest mistakes and regretful occurrences. The moment to

452

you, Mabel, becomes a detached all-important whole. You have often felt over things which should have been of minor significance, as a question of life and death. It is only later, when you get a retrospective view of the experience, that it becomes organically part of you. What you lack is a protective coherent appreciation of the moment in its true relation not only to the past but to the future. Whether your impatience is its cause or effect, I don't know, but I feel it is closely connected with it.

This, Mabel, is the danger which I have in mind when I feel doubtful of you. You have one thing which should help you to overcome it: intuition. But that is not enough, we must have more: intuitive perception.

I don't think that you should feel sad that through psychoanalysis some of those queer creepy ghostly things are slipping away from you. Those things are only impediments, atmospheric stratas which make self-realization difficult. But you must not allow it to influence your real spirituality. I mean your mysticism, your love for abstract religion. That is wonderful to me.

Yes, I also noticed that you are becoming more "normal." Don't! I love your independence, your disregard of the opinion of "society." Don't become social whatever you do!

I can hardly await the moment when we'll be together again, sweetheart! Two more days! I expect to take an afternoon train and reach Croton in the evening.

Give my regards to Hazel and Mrs. Bull. Don't be uneasy, darling, about Bayard. I feel he will come out of it all right. I wrote him a short letter yesterday—hope he received it. I caught cold this morning working at my open window and am worried for I want to feel fine when I go to you.

Arivederci, carissima!

MAURICE.

P.S. I just read over part of my letter and am afraid to send it. You may begin to try to perceive the true significance of the moment—and feeling that you have often erred, you may begin to err the other way—for you are extreme. But I am not afraid. If you can see the import of the moment you *will* realize how deeply, how truly, how permanently, how faithfully I love you!

M.

Now I'll prepare my supper. Gracious, I forgot to thank you for that box of wonderful things which came this afternoon from Charles! Enough to last me a life time! Does that mean that you want to make me stay away very long from Croton? But *please,* dearest, don't do it again. There are very fine shops here and you mustn't take all that trouble.

MAURICE.

And what do you mean by sending back my check! I owe you that money and you'll have to accept it!

Give my love to *John.*

I kept on trying my best to lure him to be analyzed, too, by Dr. Jelliffe, but he never would, although he began to watch his dreams and tell them to me, hoping, I think, that I would recount them to the analyst. His psyche dealt with him as though he were a child and presented him with the most kindergarten dreams that he could scarcely fail to understand. They warned him of an imminent catastrophe, when showing Dr. Jelliffe as a mechanic with a bag of tools! Still he refused, and we went on as before.

I am afraid I did not learn much about myself with Jelliffe, but I did get a very complete line on *him,* and on Bayard, and on Leo, and I enjoyed my outings in his office.

While Maurice was in Pottsville, I had a great many people out at Finney Farm that I had been neglecting for him, and I saw more of Elizabeth Duncan and her children than I had for a long time. Elizabeth had grown resigned to my lapses away from her when I was all preoccupied with Maurice. She just raised her eyebrows and giggled. But I scarcely ever left the farm to go to her, nor had the children there because of their irresistible attraction for him that, when they danced, burned up into a pure love of beauty, but when, dancing over, and they were again only lovely little girls in the room, made him furtive and shy and watchful for an occasion to lay his large, white hand upon them. He was one on Elizabeth's mental list of "men one had to look out for"; he and his friend Dr. Asch, and Dr. Genthe and Bourgeois were rather *suspecte.* Well, she was right about nearly all of them. Several of them got a little girl, finally; Bourgeois married Teresa. Maurice, some years later, modeled a head of Senta that is now, I believe, in the Metropolitan or the Brooklyn Museum—or else in the Lewisohn Collection. Then she ran away and was never heard of again.

Elizabeth's care of the children was very great, but it wasn't based on conventional reasons. It wasn't maternal as we are accustomed to gauge maternity. It was both aesthetic and practical. Well, she had her school to think of, of course. The care she took of them wasn't even worldly—it was not saving them for good marriages. No, it was more

like the care of an artist for his materials, and "the man" must not
come near them to lift them out of the realm of fancy and of dream
in which they dwelt, bringing fresh charm and fairy-like delights to
tired mortals in the Dances and the Exhibitions. Yet, insisted Elizabeth,
"I do not teach *dancing,* I teach a way to Live." Really it was a way
not to live, for it had nothing to do with pain, mortification, responsibility, or doubt. It was horizontal and not perpendicular. It was all
about the "long line" ("try to reach the hill, children, with your finger-
tips!") and the ("loose, loose, children") free, floating, flowing life.

How they loved it, too! I never have seen a child who did not love
to be in the Duncan School. For they were fed with fantasies that made
the slim fare of porridge and apples and potatoes seem enchanted.
Everything was made *attractive* around them, even if it was frugal
and uncomfortable. They, dressed for New York in their little blue
capes and caps, may have felt cold in the unkind streets, but they did
not suffer from it because they also all felt they were fairy prin-
cesses—as they were. (But, oh, dear! in the years to come, it must have
been hard for them to know what to do sometimes!)

Little Elizabeth Duncan was a sort of witch, there is no doubt about
it. She was a witch. No one who came under her influence ever got
completely away from it afterwards. I sometimes think that John,
under his Bond Street clothes, still wears the blue tunic of the Duncan
School that he wore for a season in perfect harmony and naturalness,
while he shot with the bow in his archery class, and listened to Elizabeth's reminiscences about Hymettus.

When Maurice came back from Pottsville to spend a week-end, he
found me changed, for I was free of him. He found a houseful of
friends of mine, not his, and conversation going on once more that
left him out. On Sunday night, however, in my bed against the window where we looked out upon the snowy hillside where the apple
trees were etched in black, he reclaimed me and I sank down, down,
beneath that weight of sensuous life that poured out of his body and
that was rich and somber and real, but heavy, oh, so heavy, weighing
one down, pulling one *down,* reaching a kind of bottom, basic, and
fundamental. There are levels, true all of them, and Maurice made me,
then, truest at the lowest, or perhaps most primitive. Jelliffe had taught
me to use that word: primitive. Later, Brill taught me another one:
archaic.

Maurice had not been away long enough for me to resume much of my real poise; only long enough to allow my great craving for love to grow stronger—fastening more securely upon him for its satisfaction. While he was away, I had felt love in me and supposed it was for him; love that had only occasionally reached the surface of my perceptions when we were together; and this love that I wrote to him about in exalted letters attracted and drew him back to Croton where, alas, his presence caused it to sink down in me again, leaving only the strain and the agony of wishing for a different and more adequate object for its fulfillment.

Dr. Jelliffe, I realized, had been trying to pry us apart, had been ready to accept, for me, anything that would take my attention off Maurice long enough for me to become independent and separate from him, for he felt that my subjective feeling for Maurice made me sick, and that I was mired in an unsuitable situation. Not that it was immoral or anything like that (although he did feel that the social unconventionality of my life was uncongenial to my particular make-up), but simply that Maurice and I were not essentially suited to each other. So when he saw me taking a greater interest in Bayard, with whom I was thrown a great deal more with Maurice away, he encouraged it. Bayard was beginning to be more alert where I was concerned, or rather I was growing more aware of him, perhaps, and I noted how he was flashing keen smiles from his northern blue eyes when he read his poems to me in the evenings by the fire. It was curious, I thought, how the atmosphere had changed in the white, fire-lighted room. So clear and thin and frosty that the red Amaryllis flower above the fireplace that Maurice had painted was like a dark blaze slowly congealing in that high air, losing its vibration, almost fading out. Seeing Jelliffe welcome Bayard's appearance in my dreams, I asked him slyly:

"Do you really think that flirtation is a form of sublimation—a suitable outlet?"

"Surely," he replied. "At times it may become the necessary and constructive tool that one requires."

"For an amputation, you mean?" I asked him quickly. For I had never admitted to him that Maurice *was* detrimental to me. I never admitted it. I was never really disloyal to the relationship that I clung to, I only wanted it *fixed up* so that we could be happy, and anyway, these new ideas faded away at home. He smiled at me:

"Come! Come!" he murmured, reassuringly. "I do not want anything for you that you do not want for yourself. This is *your* affair. You yourself have that in you which will decide what is best. Your judgment, not mine, will solve your problem."

That was the way he threw me back upon myself. When I looked within, I saw myself floundering, yet would not—yet—save myself. I continued to believe that somehow, someway, *I* could be fixed, or Maurice could be fixed, so that we would fit together like the covers of a book.

Dear Maurice, too, poor fellow, thought and thought about what should be done to make it all right. I often accused him of being still attached, spiritually, to B., I felt he was attached *some*where, for he didn't seem free to give himself completely to me and make me feel fulfilled by him; so it seemed to me B. must be the element that held him. If he were free to be mine, then he would not pull me down as he did, into those singular depths of sensuality where the body was appeased and the spirit left gasping for air. It seemed to me that if only there was love between us, it would somehow lift us.

He was full of good will—ready to do anything to make it right between us. He agreed with me that perhaps he should go through the act of breaking with B., that he should see her and tell her he loved someone else now. Perhaps that would cut a bond that still existed though he no longer felt conscious of it; and he spoke of going to Europe to see her. At that suggestion my fear of losing him completely flared up in me. I could not face losing my torturer!

I said, "I can't see why you don't *write* it to her! Why should you have to *go* all that distance just to *say* it? It is an excuse—you want to get away." And then the old reproaches of distrust began again.

"How can I *ever* be trustworthy, Mabel, if you won't trust me?" he implored in despair. He seemed to need my faith in order to be faithful. Faith in the face of unfaith, belief in spite of the fact, this was something I did not experience until later.

We struggled on and on through the winter, through the spring.

CHAPTER XVI

Struggling On

THE Torrences were spending a week-end with us once. His pale, blond type, his fair hair, his large, blue eyes and his somewhat impish American humor were in great contrast to Maurice and it made me feel dizzy. When Sunday evening came, and I left them all sitting before the fire: Bobby, Ridgely, Olivia, and Maurice, while I went upstairs to change my dress for supper, I found myself vaguely wondering why I did not prefer these familiar Americans who were so much easier to understand and get along with than the dark stranger who shared my life.

Changing meant going from one white silk dress to another, for I wore nothing but the soft, washable, two-piece gowns that I had copied from Elizabeth and her girls; a pleated skirt with a tunic over it made of white Chinese silk. I always wore these at home at Finney Farm. They looked fresh and attractive in the white room and they were suited to the scene.

I went up and brushed out my hair and wandered about for a few moments. The low sun shone in the upper windows from across the Hudson and it looked like Sunday evening, but it did not feel like it. There was instead a terrible nostalgia in the quiet house, sad—sad! Oh, why could I not come home to myself?

I felt nervous and irritable from an inharmonious afternoon. I just couldn't mix Maurice with my other friends. He showed up strange, I thought, against almost everyone. I was weary of the charitable efforts I thought people always seemed to be making to help along situations that I had brought about by taking Maurice into my environment. All the afternoon he had sat there—solid, imperturable, smoking his cigar, sure of his seat and ready to mingle or to retire into himself. I felt Bobby and Ridgely invisibly united against him, and I couldn't

458

join with either of them or with Maurice, but had to shuttle back and forth between them.

Sadly I wandered into Maurice's bedroom. There was little there to show his presence. A brush and comb upon the dressing table, a couple of cigars and a nail file. A large, flat pair of bedroom slippers sat under the bed with the look of Maurice's feet printed upon them. His black silk dressing-gown hung over the end of the bed. He had few belongings and traveled light. There was nothing in the room to show how deeply he had dug himself into the place. I thought of Reed and how he had come and gone in my life and had left so little mark.

As the fall deepened, I heard from one person and another the indignant things Boardman Robinson was saying about me. He told people how I had jilted Reed just when the boy was happiest over his return to America. How he had talked of me, the feeling he had for me, the house he would build for me in the Ramapo Hills. They had worked in prison together on the plans for that house. Robinson said it was the most heartless thing any woman had ever done. As he lived on the other side of Mt. Airy alongside Max Eastman and some of the other radicals who had cottages there, I often saw cold looks and disdainful faces turned in my direction when I went through the village. I didn't care much. I was too preoccupied with the present problem and the past seemed unreal compared to it.

Well, the weeks passed, and many people came and went in Finney Farm. The people Maurice brought there, I gradually perceived, were Germans or German sympathizers: Bourgeois, Coomaraswamy, Meier-Riefstahl. . . . Now, although I did not feel connected with the War in any way and had really no prejudice against the Germans (had I not adopted Elizabeth and the whole school of German children along with Merz?), still I was weary of being broadminded and Germans were unpopular. Bourgeois and he, always talking about the progress of the War with a scarcely concealed indignation against the Allies, made me nervous perhaps because they made me feel they were distinctly on another side, away from me and mine.

Hutch came out occasionally to spend the night with us. Determined to be sympathetic now that he finally realized Maurice and I were living together, which I had ended by confiding to him, he tried to make friends with him, and succeeded so well that I felt he had deserted me. I was always lonelier after he went away.

459

Hartley had stayed for a while in the drear north guest room. To soften the repellent light he hung scraps of chiffon here and there upon the walls. But I don't know—there was something solitary and unassimilable about Marsden and it hurt me more to have him there than to write him he must go! He replied:

Sunday.

DEAR MABEL:

Nina gave me your note on the train. I am glad to have it even though I feel always a chill in words on paper, for they make pictures too often. I needed, however, just that kind of clarity for I understand much more than I supposed would ever be necessary, which proves that one should never become that familiar with places or situations. I have had extremest moments of perplexity of late and now my horizon is clear of much that is alien to it. There is, I would say, no reason whatsoever for secrecy with people like ourselves who in the face of pain should be just and submissive to the higher degrees of delicacy. It is silly and idle to embarrass simple situations with all sorts of complexity. This much has been taught me in the terrible hours of shadow in which I have lived of late. I want you to know that now I am not misunderstanding anything half so much as understanding too well. I had been doubting myself a little, but that is over because I have returned to these things with which I can be less obtrusive, to which I am much less the spectacle, and one like myself should figure in nothing actually. There is a supremacy, a true dignity in that. I am "too far alike, too far dissimilar" ever to be quite that which is imagined or expected. I belong really to less specialized spaces, to commoner elements. I must never do more, at most, than walk in as graciously as possible, sit a little, and pass out again for there is always the quality of wonder in being really not quite anywhere at all times. That is my kind of activity I am thinking. In some instances I must have failed because the cloud is in my head and my eyes are filmed with mist. I have expected too much of expanse in truth, for the dust about my feet is not star-like and that is always disconcerting in amid the precariousness of these celestial ascensions.

For Bayard I am profoundly sorry. If there is a more tragic spectacle than a man's soul suffering, I do not know it. There is something wrong in it for men are born to greater trivialities. I wish for him the highest release and it is certain he will be achieving that. The suspense in waiting for the interval of delivery is the only quality of disaster.

I shall need to come once again to the hill to get my things together, to bring them and my pictures down and re-establish myself with a temporary sense of home. It is really much better. I will telephone and ask when this is agreeable. In the meantime believe me to be less wretched in my contact with the mediocrities and wiser, striding as it were another league toward the haven of my wish and will.

As always,

MARSDEN H.

The exhibition of "Portrait Drawings of Mabel Dodge" came on at the Bourgeois Gallery with success. Maurice was there most of the time, talking to women who also aspired to be drawn by him. He had a good time while that was going on, for the critics were flattering and many people attended the show. The sculpturesque quality of the work was commented upon, and I tried to draw Maurice nearer to my unfailing wish for him to model in clay, but he continued to put me off, although he was accomplishing nothing in paint.

I built a studio for him in the orchard, and got him to give up the New York room, and I used to go into New York and buy him fresh flowers to work on, hoping that if he must paint, that the contemplation of their color would help to lift him out of the greens and browns of his palette. He worked assiduously, but without delight, upon flowers and fruit, and they came out looking more like him than like themselves!

Once, early in our year there, I had brought him one beautiful amaryllis bloom. It was a great scarlet flower nearly eight inches long, with petals forming an unblemished pure shape. I put it in a vase for Maurice, and he exclaimed excitedly:

"But look! It is made in the Sign of David!" And I saw in the intertwined triangles made by the red fleshly petals.

He painted a portrait of it, face on, over life size, and it had a most singular intensity. To encourage him, and perhaps myself, too I framed it in an old, dark, Italian frame and hung it over the fireplace; and from there it dominated the white room, a portentous, smiling, red flower, bending its mysterious visage down upon the muslins and embroidered linens of that environment and overcoming it. It was like a violation of something. I thought I saw that it was Maurice himself I had set up there on high to lord it over our different kind of culture, and it made me squirm: but I left it there just the same.

I collected a number of large Chinese porcelain cocks and one hen, and placed them in a row along the chimney place. In the center of the row, the delicately colored hen sat brooding, on either side the

461

cocky roosters stood tense and proud, two in white with red combs and two in soft pastel colors. The flower was above them like a great crimson blood emblem, for Maurice had painted it so that the pigment looked sanguinary.

When Marion and Percy MacKaye came for a week-end, he wrote a little verse about our *ambiente*.

MABEL: A Sketch

What Mabel is she makes to be
The heart of hospitality:
A mute, unconscious artistry
  Of friendship, by which spell
The purring cat, the sweet house-bird,
The hearth-bred flower, the quiet word
Of the wood-fire, the stately, good
  Wise China cockerel—
Are spirits, whose taciturnities
Half hide, yet hint, what Mabel is.

                For Mabel Dodge
                from Percy MacKaye
                28 March.

One day Emily and Seward made their way out to Finney Farm to lunch. When Emily went into the living room, holding on to the white curtains in the wide doorway, she was transfixed when her eyes fell upon the sprightly birds at the end of the room where the fire burned cheerfully below them, and she murmured as though to herself:

"Her mother was queer and her father was queer, and now look at all those chickens!"

It seemed strange to me that she should ignore the Sign of David that appeared, at least to me, so much more dominating than anything else in the room; but to each one his own observations!

I ordered several hundred pounds of clay which I had mixed in a big box in Maurice's studio, and I set to work myself to build an armature for a heroic figure! There was no limit to what I was ready to do or try to do to make that man start to model! It seemed to me that the sight of the wet clay would prove irresistible to him. I slyly persuaded him to help me hammer the big armature together, believing there was magic in getting actually involved in an undertaking, that it drew one imperceptibly into itself. But it was a miscalculation. While I hung handfuls of the damp clay onto the skeleton, Maurice, his face distorted in an exasperated frown, continued to paint hyacinths and tulips and felt affronted at my interference.

My friends were surprised to find the large, sad figure of a clay woman in the studio after a short time. I kept her covered with a wet sheet at first, but when I realized that Maurice was indifferent to the chance to model and go me one better (as he could have done with his eyes shut), I could not continue with it. I was not at all interested in modeling for its own sake. So the moisture slowly dried into the clay, and the folds of the sheet stiffened upon the figure beneath it until there was left only the unmalleable effigy of an unfinished female thing, gradually turning into stone. Oh, Galatea!

Since he would not be a sculptor, then I would show him how, at least, to be a painter! So I laid in a stock of paper, paint and paintbrushes, and in the bright dining-room I, too, painted hyacinths and tulips! I worked very hard for short spurts of time. Curiously enough, the form of them came out very much like Maurice's! The delicate flowers did not breathe themselves into manifest reality as in their actual life. No, they were there as though they were hammered into being. I painted a blue Persian deer among the flowers, vases of iris, zinnias in blue bowls. All very clean and pure in color, I thought. The cleanest one of all was a geranium plant with a single flower, bright red and simple.

Now it didn't either interest or please Maurice to have me painting, so my "pure color" had no effect upon him. When he would come in after his own struggle and his eyes would light on mine, a peculiarly sick smile would be forced onto his face. Bravely, as though wishing to be a sportsman, he would say:

"R-r-really, dar-r-ling, that is very good! Perhaps—if you would study the Form a little closer. . . ."

I did not paint for long, either. There seemed to be no *reason* to do so. I continued to go to Dr. Jelliffe's, even though Maurice's distaste for this increased. He never stopped saying that he felt it was a violation of the spirit and particularly of our shared spiritual life. Since he would not go and be analyzed, then I made Bayard go now. He seemed to be very much interested and Dr. Jelliffe kept me *au courant* with his case, for he simply couldn't resist talking things over with someone who really took an intelligent interest, and his speculative mind flashed into the dark corners of life and lighted up many hidden places. It entertained him very much to find that Bayard had once raised three crops of alfalfa in one year on his fields in Athol, and had since that time completely lain back upon this achievement as though he would let the knowledge of it support him in idleness for the rest of his life! Those three crops were forever coming up in his analysis! They constituted his justification and his doom. Jelliffe's duty was to remove this fantasy of accomplishment so that some activity might flow in him once more. So he started to amputate it from poor Bayard. The end of the first month came and Jelliffe was still prying it out of him. Then Bayard decided it was too expensive to continue. Jelliffe shook his head sadly but with a humorous twinkle in his eyes.

"It is the resistance," he told me. "He does not want to give up his neurosis and I am a danger to it."

But Bayard did not return to be analyzed any further. He retired to the Green House again, with his memories, and sat musing by the hour, a glass in his hand, while the two macaws chewed at the framework around the window and he never noticed them.

CHAPTER XVII

Emma Curtis Hopkins

JOHN came to spend week-ends when he got leave from his school in Morristown, and there was that painful antagonism between him and Maurice, for the American ideal that the school was careful to develop in young Americans, found no satisfaction in the Oriental type. Maurice, sensitive to anything that concerned him, was acutely aware of John's criticism. John turned to Bayard with eager relief, for Bayard was such a Nordic little gentleman; this flattered Bayard, so the two of them developed together a kind of mob spirit that shut poor Maurice out in the cold. But there was in Maurice the patriarchal spirit that longed for the family to guide and protect. He could not resist assuming the parental attitude—and with his cigar between his fingers, smoothing his long, black hair with thoughtful deliberation, he would throw back his head and attempt, in a kind, serious voice, to question John about his school work, trying to win confidence and to inspire it. John would give him a long stare, refusing to respond, and would reply in the briefest terms, barely courteous, but not quite rude, for that would not be really American, of course.

They not only did not understand each other, perhaps they did not want to. They were jealous of each other, not so much on my account as on the account of each one's suffering ego.

Bayard, of course, was fond of John, as he was of Hutch's children, and undertook to interest himself in John's writing. For years I had insisted upon a "theme" being produced every day both at school and when he was at home. A theme on any subject he might choose, two or three pages long. I thought it would help him in at least two ways; that it would help any boy, not only John: It would develop a vocabulary less meager than that of most American men, and it would, by giving him the habit of expressing himself, help him to analyze and understand himself and the life he would pass through. He wrote some very vivid, free pages on all kinds of subjects. I would not let the schoolmaster criticize or correct them for anything but the grammar and punctuation—and this left him unrestricted and unselfconscious. As time went on I saw that from this daily exercise, he was forming the habit of understanding and defining things around him, and he would sum up a person or a situation with a quick, live word that just expressed what he saw. He did not hesitate to say what he thought of all of us. For instance:

MOTHER

I bet she could never get on well with a crowd that she had been always with and nobody else. She changes so. Sometimes she's a Christian Scientist and at other times she's sick in bed.

She hates to travel and yet she likes new places. She hates to have trouble with a cook and yet she likes different food. She hates parties and yet she likes to meet different kinds of people. She is impossible.

I should think she would quarrel with Mrs. Hapgood as I do with Boyce but she hasn't quarreled yet. They ought to live together but they can't because Boyce and I are alive.

She gets a nice house in Italy, fills it with everything, rebuilds a part of it, and then after six years of preparing she decides its too big to live in.

We haven't got the Finney Farm yet but when we get it she might decide its too quiet to live in, but "you never can tell!"

Gosh what a world of "somethings always wrong." But as I'm only 13 I should worry.

NAMES

I think that people should know people well before they call them by their Christian names. I think I have known Bayard long enough to call him that.

I dont know Mr. Sterne well enough to call him by his good name. He is still dark. I would like to but I cant.

To Mr. Jones I never will speak to by any other than Mr. Jones. Although he is nice and all that he is very mysterious. I have tried to call him Bobby but I cant make it fit him.

I cant call anybody by their names if I dont know them. By knowing them I mean *feel* towards them. I like all the crowd but I dont *feel* towards them all. I feel towards Bayard, I would like to feel towards Mr. Jones. and I nearly feel towards Mr. Sterne. I guess he will be next.

All three of these dissimilar beings wrote! Bayard distilling little scholarly poems, very neat and distinguished; John these untidy, expressive "themes," sometimes full of rage or impatience, formless and chaotic but unhampered in feeling, and Maurice, long letters to his friends that he would compose and then recopy. Letters from Maurice were compositions: he enjoyed producing fine, analytic phrases with a ring to them. His letters were full of ideas about Art and Life and he was able to define his ideas in good solid English. He had form in whatever he did. He loved to assume, with me, the fatherly tone when he was not creating himself as the wise but ardent lover, and then he gave one an irresistible impression of his dignity and weight.

He, after all, of the three of these, was the only one who was deeply self-critical and longing to "improve." I think the other two were quite self-satisfied, but Maurice was passionately anxious to be good, to be noble, to be right; and this, perhaps, was the "strain of pure gold" in him that he dimly felt and told me of, and that gave one a sense of the massive, solid character under the little idiosyncrasies of his behavior. One knew, somehow, that he was a serious person and worthy of respect. He had aspiration, and there is nothing more compelling in any human being. His strivings were Promethean, his attainments divine, considering his difficulties. He, too, was trying to overcome the handicaps of ignorance and stupidity with which life had conditioned him. Probably for love of the struggles which were breaking him, I could not give him up. We were, Maurice and I, both so terribly earnest!

But trying and trying without understanding is, apparently, useless. Jelliffe couldn't really help me to understanding, and when the amusing speculations had gone on for a few months, they finally ceased to amuse, and the old fatigue and depression came back. Then someone— was it Eve?—introduced me to Emma Curtis Hopkins, and she, for a while, soothed me into "the effortless way."

She sat in her little drawing room, in the Iroquois Hotel, clothed in an exquisite gown all soft black lace and silk, a large-brimmed lace hat on her soft white hair, and she smoothed and relaxed one so that at the end of one's hour one was renewed and reassured.

I sat before her in a comfortable armchair three times a week. The shades were lowered and fresh flowers filled the room. The traffic in that street in the Forties made a distant rumble like a sullen river far away, and her violet eyes held mine as she—really inspired quite often

—rambled on and on in an exhortation that fitted in very well with **my** old doctrine of "Let It decide!"

The effortless way—that was the way she counseled. Not to try, not to work, not to struggle. "Be still and know that I am God"—that sort of advice. An emphasis upon the power within that knows all and does all without the interception of the poor little "wandering, lunatic mind," or the powerless, stubborn will. Her teaching was based upon intuition and there was a great deal of truth in it. Her counsels were full of quaint turns of phrase and native spice, for Emma Curtis was an old-fashioned New Englander from Boston. She had made her debut with Mary Baker Eddy, who called her her star—but then had come one of those periodic upheavals when one star displaced another in the Eddy constellation, and Mrs. Hopkins had started to teach her own Doctrine. She had formulated it into Twelve Lessons in Mysticism, and each lesson consumed an hour to tell. One went away saturated, and the effect lasted until the next time. When they were all at an end, one was either made over or one began and took the whole course once more. Some people just took it all the year round, or at least when they were in New York. Bobby was one of these. He was practically supported in the upper ether by Emma Curtis Hopkins for years.

She stimulated and renewed one—causing the love and faith that life congealed to flow again. And she was so flattering! She loved us all, or seemed to, and she appreciated us. She called me her "child from Atlantis," and to the others she explained me away by telling them that I was an Atlantean and could only be understood by other Atlanteans. This explained me nicely to myself and lessened my feeling of doubt and conflict. I gradually impelled all my entourage to her quiet asylum. Bobby, Maurice, Nina, Elizabeth, Andrew, and others— they all followed me there. She looked at us in turn and saw only the undying spirit buried in us and she cared only for that. She would gaze at us during our hour with eyes of shining love and tenderness, enhancing in each of us our feeling of worth; and then at the end of the hour she would rise, go to the door, and, smiling a little coldly, grown remote, she would bow us out, appearing loath to shake the grateful hand or to continue the intimacy she had seemingly established, so we grew to understand that the love she felt for us did not really extend to the person—it was for the hidden self.

468

Maurice, she told me, was "a great soul, a giant among men." I liked to hear this, for it endorsed my suppositions about him and dignified our relation. Bobby she called a Genius, and she restored his confidence whenever it waned. She just suited Elizabeth, whose teaching coincided with hers. Elizabeth loved her admonitions to relax into "the Intense Inane," letting constraints lapse away, forgetting the worldly strife of men for little rewards. Here I was back again with what, all alone with myself, I had called Nature, that invisible power that was in me and gratified every need.

So for a while things went better for us all, since we did not *try* so hard. I used to remind the others, when they forgot the Teaching, of our mutual belief, quoting to them my new slogan: "The saddest words of voice or pen are, 'I'll try!'" So we all endeavored to live more like the lilies of the field, and sure enough all things came easier to us when we ceased to go after them, and even Maurice's work was, for a time, more free and flowing.

The spring deepened at Finney Farm. The trees were voluminous with green leaves and the flowers were almost tropical in their profusion. The heat grew heavy and moist and the sun on the river deepened the humidity which rose in bands of gray creeping up the hill. It was hard to do anything—and any effort wearied one. The most I could do was to drive into New York for my hour three times a week. In through the hot little towns and through the long stretches outside New York that were filling up with box-like apartment houses. Along the flat reaches of the Highway one automatically read the enormous colored billboards advertising new plays, cigarettes and automobiles. It was a dreary, uninspired drive after one left the suburban towns of Tarrytown, Hastings, and Dobbs Ferry. Nothing to feed the mind or the soul. The trains clanged past, the air smelled of hot asphalt, and the atmosphere was stale. But down Riverside Drive, where small yachts and large battleships loomed through the mist of the river, over to Fifth Avenue and then down to the little dreary hotel whose small lobby contained hard-faced men with straw hats on the backs of their heads, up to her door and inside—ah, then it was all right!

She sat in the dim room among her roses and lilies, her immaculate toilet forever fresh and charming—and what she gave one was worth all the dusty miles and the dismal journey through the inferno of America.

Bayard, however, was never persuaded to her side. He remained himself, cold and aloof, skeptical in his agony, perhaps more gallant than any of us in his endurance of things as they were.

Once I somehow induced Mrs. Hopkins to go with me to see Eva Thompson, who was very ill near Kingston on the other side of the Hudson. After my trustee, David Thompson, died, Eva bought a place out there in the country and, as many people thought very suitably, married the Reverend Mr. Royce, rector of the village church. Eva had been a great talker all her life. She talked and talked between her projecting teeth in an effervescence that no one had ever controlled. But the Reverend Royce was a talker, too, and soon after they were married, one saw the struggle that went on between them. After all, like all flesh is grass, all talk is air, and both of these people were constructed like hot-air pipes leading to furnaces. They *had* to talk—both of them. It was dangerous not to.

It was very painful to be with them, especially when confined to the dinner table. Eva would begin spluttering and laughing, the words bursting out in gusts between her teeth; and Royce would begin, too, at the same time, he blinking and winking his eyes rapidly and exclaiming: "Sito! Sito!" to her in an undertone to stop her and give him a chance, thinking no one understood he was telling her to shut up, since "sito" doesn't sound like "shut up," Italian being a more elegant language than English.

They would both go on at a great rate—his more ponderous style and heavy diction, though, interspersed with the occasional light "sito," finally weighing her down and corking her up, until she would sit looking at him with a face one did not know, since closed lips were all too unfamiliar there, especially with that desperate look in her eyes. And then she would grasp the knives or forks in one hand and nervously clink them together.

Sometimes I would motor out there for lunch with a group of my friends who did not always fit in very well. John succeeds in the following theme in giving an idea of one of these parties.

Have *you* ever run across a person who calls the set he or she has been born in, snobs, just because she or he cant keep up with that set?

The trip yesterday was rather boring because everybody seemed to find fault with everybody else. When we arrived the bunch were sitting on the porch. We sat down and pretty soon another car drove up. The lady of the house "looked at its contents, made a wry face, and received the con-sequences with a smile." In other words, she made some remark that was not very complimentary to them, and then received them with smiles. I could almost have sworn that she must have done the same when we drove up.

She was against England because they were snobs of no character. She is a cousin of Winston Churchill. The other people listened to her talk and laughed uproariously at all her jokes and in many other ways humored her.

The gentlemen who had driven up remarked to Mr. Fred Howe, "There is one thing that came from hell, is hell, and is going to hell; the d—— labor unions!" Poor Mr. Howe turned red and forced a laugh.

There was an oldish deaf lady there. She and Mr. Stein carried on a conversation at the table. Unfortunately, they were not seated together. The lady in between them had to put up with wires, batteries, etc., and had to hold the deaf lady's instrument.

Mr. Sterne looked very meek and scared all the time. And well he might. He was cornered by a young lady together with Mr. Howe. She remarked to me afterwards, "I am so glad I did it; it was my only chance."

I had gone there very rarely of late, being preoccupied with my own repressions. One day a letter came from little Eva, the adopted niece: "Aunt Eva is very, very ill. She wants to see you." I begged Mrs. Hop-kins to go—perhaps she could help, surely she could. Eva was such an old, old friend. I had known her ever since I was a child. I had been the only one of all the Cook grandchildren she had ever taken any interest in. She had always said that the whole family, except Aunt Georgia and I, were "country."

Mrs. Hopkins and I motored out there one hot afternoon. She beamed and blessed all through the indeterminate scenes of advertise-ment and flat tired country; across the river in the ferry boat she beamed and blessed, not seeing the dingy planks nor smelling the *fâde* odors of manure and gasoline. We reached the "Rectory" at the end of the day and the dusk remained heavy and sad and without relief.

The Reverend Royce met us in the hall. He looked across and he waggled his bushy gray eyebrows at Mrs. Hopkins, for instinctively he smelt heresy and competition in Divinity—although all I said to him was: "I have brought a friend, Mrs. Hopkins, to see Eva. I think she can *help* her." The words "help her" had caused an instantaneous an-tagonism to rise in the Reverend man. He distrusted all such phrases.

He would have kept us out if he dared; but Mrs. Hopkins was such an evident *lady,* so exquisite, so fashionable, and so smilingly sure of her welcome, that he turned to me with a look almost of despair and entreaty on his puzzled face. But I was determined, and my strong self was uppermost. I led the way with a ruthless smile on my face to Eva's room, drawing my Teacher with me. We went into the darkened room, and when our eyes grew accustomed, we observed a great barrel-shaped form under the bed-clothes. A faint, continuous babbling stream of sound came from it. We tiptoed to the bedside, he behind us.

"Eva, Eva!" I said, bending over. Her swollen face, sunk in the pillow, was yellow; her eyes—those gay, malicious eyes—were almost lost in the diseased flesh. Her body was swollen beyond belief. When she recognized me, she began piteously:

"Mabel, help me! He is *killing* me. He is killing me."

"Sito! Sito!" hissed the Reverend man uncontrollably, behind me.

"He has done it. He shuts me up. He won't let me say a word. . . ."

"Eva! *Sito!* She doesn't know what she is saying! I have had the best doctors. . . . It is water, you know!"

Condensed conversation! I looked at Mrs. Hopkins appealingly. What could she do? She was bending over poor Eva and smiling like an angel.

"You forget all those thoughts," she said. "None of that counts at all. Just remember, 'My Word is the Everlasting Life.' Say to yourself, 'My Word become flesh.' That is all you have to know. Now try to sleep. I am going to help you tonight."

Eva's unrecognizable eyes peered up from her distorted face: "Who are you?" she asked, like a child.

"Oh, I am a friend of our dear little Mabel. We came to see you this beautiful summer day, and you will feel more like yourself, I hope, presently. Now try to go to sleep."

I cannot describe the revolt that Dr. Royce felt for this unorthodox scene. He was one of those who feel that God and the Scriptures belong in Church and should *not* be introduced into social situations. He felt as embarrassed as though something indecent had taken place—and he remembered he had never approved of me anyway, for I wore such queer clothes. The dinner we sat through together was made possible by Mrs. Hopkins' serenity and by her apparent ignorance of his distaste for us both. She smiled and praised and enjoyed herself so much that he melted with the coffee and found himself giving her an account of his work in the parish.

She saw Eva once more in the morning before we left. That poor soul murmured: "Peaceful! Peaceful!" looking up into the gay old face above her.

"I know you are peaceful," she rallied. " 'He that believeth in *My* Word shall have Everlasting Life.' "

And then we left her there in that peacefulness among the fields of the little, unknown parish. I never saw her again, for she died in about three months.

CHAPTER XVIII

Change

SOMETIMES we went down to the Hapgoods' in Dobbs Ferry, and quite often John and Boyce went back and forth visiting each other. The two boys had a passion for everything "Western." They pored over Sears, Roebuck catalogues and when they could they ordered Stetson hats, chaps, quirts, and all kinds of cowboy paraphernalia from Chicago. They cultivated hard, ruthless expressions and thrust out their lower jaws. "The West" had become for them both the land beyond pain, beyond fathers and mothers and their appendages. John and Boyce spent long hours lying in the grass in the upper field comparing notes, voicing their miseries. For John, Maurice—that "guilty stranger" as he once called him—was the constant, galling presence that poisoned his home; and for Boyce, it was Hutch who criticized and kept after him the way fathers do until he was sealed up like a rocky cave. Perhaps Hutch was a little jealous of Boyce, as so many fathers have to be of their sons, for Neith undoubtedly loved him so much that he drew her out more than others did. He was not a wonder or a special kind of boy, he had no special gifts except his fine, well-developed harmonious body, he was never strange or worrisome or weird, or too intelligent, but maybe she was tired of intelligence, of paradox and epigram. Hutch's intensity and mental energy had worn her out a little. She loved Boyce for being a lovely boy. She rested in him.

Boyce had one inalterable intention and that was to get out West and be a cowboy, something entirely different from Hutch. He would dissociate himself from all that. He began by changing his name. He called himself "Harry" and made John call him that. Up in his room on the top floor of the square red brick house, Harry led his other life. There he kept his guns and his cowboy clothes in an immaculate and museum-like order. It looked like a room "out West," he thought. Perhaps later he learned how little resemblance there was when his "outfit" grew worn and soiled and his Stetson, stained with sweat, lay in a corner of the bunkhouse. John wrote:

PUBLICITY

Boyce says he would rather be well known as a sheriff who had captured 8 men alone than a writer who is made public by his works.

The sheriff captures 8 men physically, while the writer catches hundreds of men mentally. That is, he captures their minds and perhaps changes them to good while the sheriff gets the men and puts them in jail and turns them to criminals.

I would much rather be the author who enlightens hundreds, than the sheriff who darkens eight. An anarchistic author is in more danger than the sheriff both mentally and physically; he is against the law and against conservativeness.

The sheriff is weaker than the author. He is *with* the law and governs people while the author is *without* the law and governs more people.

The physician who has discovered a wonderful cure and the football champion are the same. One saves hundreds, while the other disables many, both seeking publicity, both getting it in their own way. But the one who works with his mind, for the good of mankind, always wins against the man who works physically for his own interest.

Summer grew older and more humid. We were all enervated and weary. In the later afternoon, I would turn on the hose and water the rich, thick, drooping flowers all around the house, and then turn it on myself. That was refreshing for a moment.

In the uncultivated corners of the farm, in low ditches where water trickled, there were monstrous plants with large, thick, porous leaves and queer blooms. It was lush. The vegetation was so riotous it seemed menacing—it threatened to bury us. I supposed it was like the tropics and decided I detested them. John wrote his theme and said:

APPROACHING NIGHT

Everything is tired. The leaves aren't strong enough to hold the drops of the recent shower, and every little puff of wind sends a little shower on the home-coming work-man.

A woodpecker runs madly up and down the trunk of his tree and goes to bed. A lonesome whippoorwill, whips. An apple falls. All is quiet.

A deep foghorn is bellowing on the river. The woodpecker sees a fly buzzing a few yards from his hole. He dashes out, scaring a care worn chipmunk, sitting on a branch below who runs blustering into his own hole. All is quiet again.

The sun has set and a belated crow flaps noisily through the woods. A gunshot is heard. The crow falls cawing to the ground. The woodpecker looks out of his hole and then goes back to bed. All is quiet again.

The lassitude that we all indulged was more enervating every day. Bayard sitting in the Green House in a daze, Maurice puttering around, John living his separate existence but showing his dumb criticism of us whenever he came near—it was all too exasperating. The damp heat made one grow white and puffy like some bloodless, porous vegetable. One day John brought some lines about the cats:

Animals are nice in lots of different ways. Some are rotten. Scuro, for example, is treacherous and he will scratch you when you don't expect it just to let off some steam. Everybody likes his looks but he has a poor character. Everybody handles him with great care. He is a regular witch cat.

Chiara is very pretty but she has a poor character, which is just the opposite of Scuro's. She is slovenly and lazy and tropical.

Mrs. Cat I like best. She has the nicest character and grace of them all. She is a little bit bored and tired at times. But who wouldn't be in her place? She is the queen of them all. Just think how courageous she has to be.

Pinkie is a very wise rat. He is very persevering and industrious. He got covered with coal one night and next morning he was clean. He is just a bit selfish.

Let us hope Augustus or Molly (the new parrot which will be named one of the two names according to her or his character) will be a brave fool or a sweet housewife.

We were growing more and more discouraged and irritable with each other and either maintaining a critical silence, or, as in John's case, writing his feelings out on paper as in the following:

Women change their minds too much. First you said to write when I wanted to and now you make me write when you want me to.

If grown-ups had to do it there wouldn't be a writer in the world.

I'll have enough school this winter instead of writing when I dont want to. If its going to be like this Im not going to be a writer.

poise without strain. He fixed his large, blue eyes upon objects slightly to one side of one, not avoiding one's gaze from any duplicity in himself so much as to protect himself from the emotions and the agonies of others. He felt life too keenly to take chances. But this single façade he had created was inadequate for any conversations that went beyond an impersonal exchange of ideas. It was perfect for dialectics, but no use when something happened. And something was certainly happening when I talked to him that July day!

I realized the upheaval that was taking place in him as he visualized the change before him. The return to the lonely farm, his incapacity for dealing with external life, with the horses and dogs with which he surrounded himself, and the enormous effort it required just to get himself fed and to have his clothes laundered. But no sign of agitation showed in his face. The Greek mask held.

"When do you want me to go?" he asked politely. I felt a rush of pity for him.

"Oh, it will be all right to stay awhile yet, Bayard. I don't want to hurry you. But you understand, don't you? It *hurts* me to see you like this. I like something going *on* around me! This is stagnation." There was an appeal for some sympathy for myself in my voice. Couldn't he *see* how hard all this had grown for me? He raised his eyebrows slightly and deepened the smile a trifle.

"I had thought it was very pleasant," he answered. He risked a flicker of a look directly at me and I saw despair in the blue of his brave eyes before he turned them. I felt as though I were getting away in a small boat and pushing him down into the depths, rapping his knuckles with an oar where his hands clung to the stern. But I couldn't help it. I myself was that small boat and difficult enough I was finding navigation, never having been trained for it. But I had to go. I had always, finally, had to go.

I enjoyed every moment of the trip, away from it all, and I think John did too. It was so strange how, the moment I got away from Maurice, I would snap back with elasticity into the *usualness* of life, and find I was able to participate in all the familiar, easy aspects of the American environment. When I was with him, he took me away from what I was used to. I was obliged to share his strong, confused and foreign perception of things. He held nearly all my attention, so that what portion I could wrest away from him for others was feeble and unable to fully seize the values that differed from his essence.

This divided me and split me up, making me perpetually *distraite*. Had I been able to accept him, as I had started out to do, choosing him freely from the variety life offered, I could have immolated myself and found a resting place. But this was not a free choice; it was one of those "fatal attachments." So he and I blamed "Destiny" for it all and stood it as well as we could, which wasn't very well, to be sure! There is nothing more unfortunate than to form an unsuitable relationship, for once grown together, who can detach the two victims?

John was feeling satisfied because I had allowed him to shoot Scuro before we left. Scuro really caught too many birds, and he finally got on my nerves always prowling around and licking his chops. I suppose John felt as though he had executed Maurice, so this was the height of achievement for him. I dared not tell poor Maurice before I left, for he had always loved the black devil, but he telegraphed me when he found it out:

CROTON-ON-HUDSON, N. Y.

JULY 24TH.

MABEL DODGE

CARE HAPGOOD PROVINCETOWN, MASS.

DID YOU GIVE JOHN PERMISSION TO SHOOT SCURO BEFORE LEAVING? PLEASE WIRE ANSWER.

MAURICE.

Now only Chiara—that blue-eyed angel—was cat at Finney Farm.

"Tante Rose" Clark came to stay there while I was away. It was a nice change for her from her sweltering studio apartment in Washington Square, where the uneven polished floor reflected the scraps of tattered embroidery and the old blue and white china. It was too hot in July for even such a lady-like paucity of furnishing, and the rear windows, open, to let in any faint breath of air, revealed another world too crude and violent to seem real to Tante Rose. She looked upon the shattering Italian existence beneath her with screwed-up eyelids, seeking only "tones" and lovely colors among those fluttering rags Reed had called "the short and simple flannels of the poor!"

She loved Finney Farm, though it was hard for her to assimilate Mr. Sterne along with it. He had hopes of using her studio in exchange. I think he longed for noise and agitation.

Even on the way to Provincetown, in the long hours as they unrolled, I realized how much I had been suffering at Finney Farm and I decided I was through with it. I re-lived my irritation with Bayard, with Jerry the farm hand, even with that old horse, Charley, who just stood out in the barn eating and never doing a lick of work. There wasn't any for him to do, because we didn't farm. We bought everything in the village. I had an excessive amount of irritation over these scapegoats because I refused to allow any of it to pass to Maurice, who was the source of it all. But I could not permit myself to be annoyed with him much. That would have been too devastating, since I was chained to him.

This expedient loyalty is not uncommon, for loyalty exists most strongly where it is most useful. This bastard loyalty is the mask of the displaced irritation in the world. One must land it somewhere! John, living always in my blood, so close to me, had in his short life been the target for successive accumulations of this kind, for all my loves had been unsuitable. As Mrs. Hopkins remarked sagely: "Mabel has been unlucky in men." *Conscious* selection had not come into existence for me before the War, so all love was chancy and most of it was sad.

But away alone with John, we both had a good time. It was too bad it so seldom happened. Since I had made plans to undo the Croton Cosmos before we reached Provincetown, once there all my taut nerves relaxed in the soft sea air. Nothing ever pleased me so much as that lovely salt breeze that bathed the little town night and day. "Untied are the knots of the heart!"

I fell into the Hapgoods' embrace. We had always liked each other and we always would. I loved to be once again in that entourage with Neith's quiet, aloof smile to warm me, and Hutch's booming voice rumbling through the board partitions! John and Boyce swarmed together and formed one undifferentiated boy-thing. We were both assuaged as soon as we arrived.

CHAPTER XIX

Deeper Change

BUT empty of my love for Maurice I was empty indeed! Soon an emptiness was all I experienced. It was sinking down to the old depressed nothingness, which was all I was without a man. Be he ever so unsuitable, a man was what gave me identity, I thought. Now I had no motive power. I stayed in bed a great deal of the time and read a thick book called *Mysticism* by Evelyn Underhill. Again I felt that I was passing through "the dark night of the soul" like the mystics and saints she told of, and I tried to find somewhere inside me that presence they had known about and reached to after various earthly trials. I wrote a plaintive letter to Bayard seeking a solution of the misery in me. He replied:

Royalston, Mass., 1 Aug.

DEAR MABEL:

I find it difficult to write as my nerves are in a bad way; and, besides, most of your questions are hard to answer. As to Maurice, I should say (to use the jargon) that he is suffering from an unsuccessful effort to sublimate, due to introversion. He tries sincerely to take a great attitude towards his art, but does not fully realize that a complete spiritual reconstruction must precede successful work. He is turned inward nearly all the time.

I think, by the way, that he may have gone to Field, for Bourgeois is in New York. A few hours before I left Croton, M. told me that he would go in town with me; but when I went away he was still undecided as to whether he would go to the Catskills or to Maine. . . . He spoke of the telegrams a good deal, but only as the incident pertained to John's cruelty. He did not seem much affected.

As to yourself—well, I think the problem is to make continuous those moments of self-transcendence which you so often show. With Maurice and myself, you were, to say the least, handicapped. I think you need, above all else, a purpose outside yourself—a purpose that is *not* connected with a person. The purpose connected with a person can exist also, but it

482

must be secondary. If you would (this will come strangely from me) accept the values of the world on their own rather rotten basis and then try to better them, you would find a just outlet for your superabundant energy. Your writings in New York sometime ago were an indication of the truth of what I say; but they were only a scattering of energy. . . . To be specific: you should be, not merely a medium and an instigator of work, but a worker yourself. I should like to see you the head of a school, with your own duties of supervision, etc. I don't think anyone of strong character can have a tranquil life without making very positive contributions to life.

Certainly we can't go on at Croton as we have. A repetition of last year would be infinitely terrible! . . .

I have not diagnosed myself in this letter because my present spiritual state is so elaborately unpleasant that a detailed account would make rather sorry reading. However, I get, each day, a clearer understanding; and I know the task before me. But I will add this: had I had a true idea of what reconstruction would cost, I should not have undertaken it.

BAYARD.

Of course I wrote to Maurice and tried to inject a little love into the pages. Also I summoned up the physical strength to write directions for those I had left behind me. By letter I dismissed Domenico, the Italian who had been with me in the New York apartment and who was caretaker there, and I ordered it closed up. I wrote Bayard that he must prepare to leave soon, for I was closing down the farm. I ordered old Charley shot to save him from some hard, unknown master, and then Maurice was left on my hands! I told him to come and live near by in Wellfleet where I would take some rooms for him and he could do that portrait which always hung in our minds' eye, waiting to be painted to justify to ourselves and to the world our painful liaison. This magnificent Mona Lisa, we both hoped, would make up for all.

I soon wanted to get a little house of my own, be it ever so small. The confused cheerfulness in the Hapgood family gradually got on my nerves, although it was so fond and friendly.

I wanted to get outside Provincetown where Reed lived with Louise Bryant a little way up the street in a white clapboarded cottage that had a geranium in the upstairs bedroom window. When I saw Reed on the street, he steeled himself against me. Though I wanted to be friends, he wouldn't. People said Louise was having an affair with

483

young 'Gene O'Neill, who lived in a shack across the street with Terry and I thought Reed would be glad to see me if things were like that between him and Louise—but he wasn't. Jig Cook was writing a play—or was it Susan's play? Anyway, Louise was going to be in it. Hutch came in one evening with Jig—who was large and kind and had a shiny face with unidentified brown eyes. They were both rather drunk and they were talking theater. Jig was saying sententiously:

"Louise has very kindly consented to appear nude in that scene where she has to be carried in. . . ."

All these people disheartened me. I didn't want to be a part of it. I preferred to stay in my own slump rather than to emerge with them. I wanted God to lift me up. If He wouldn't, then I would stay in my depths until He did.

'Gene was often drunk. Everyone drank a good deal, but it was of a very superior kind of excess that stimulated the kindliness of hearts and brought out all the pleasure of these people. 'Gene's unhappy young face had desperate dark eyes staring out of it and drink must have eased him. Terry of course was always drunk. A handsome skeleton, I thought. Jig Cook was often tippling along with genial Hutch. The women worked quite regularly, even when they, too, drank; and I envied them their ease and ran away from it.

I found a tiny wooden house on the bay a little way outside the town next to one the Colliers had that I could have in a short while. The three beautiful little Collier boys played all day on the empty beach stark naked. Lucy loved her children, a warm mother, always making lovely pictures with them about her, and I wanted to live near and see this sweet life often.

Ida Rauh lived in one of the tiny white clapboarded houses on the main street. She had Dan with her—a most noble-looking child—two or three years old, I think. Ida was separating herself from Max—or trying to accustom herself to the idea. She looked wonderfully smooth and relieved and had lost that frown which made her resemble the lions outside the Public Library on Fifth Avenue.

"Oh! I feel as big as the world!" she exclaimed one day, throwing her arms wide open. How well I knew what she meant! The world retrieved—when one returned after the painful absence. One seemed able lovingly to contain it all as it poured back into one, appearing so beautiful and so new! However, Dan got sick and Max had to be summoned to his bedside, and above him they flowed together again so it was all to do over.

While I waited for the little wooden shack upon the beach above the town, I withdrew continually into my big, mystical book; but when August came and I could move into it, I flung it aside for pots of blue paint. In an enveloping apron, I painted it all up, fresh and sweet. It was one of those rude little, crude places with rough, hand-made cupboards set in the wall and small, square windows that opened upon low, spreading branches of the sort of dwarfed tree that grows in sand. Wild sweet-peas straggled round the door and the laurel smelt very good. I made curtains of red and white checked gingham for the windows—and these were the first ones to be imported from the English cottage into the States, as, in the Sharkey Cottage in Croton, yellow sprigged calico had appeared for the first time.

While I paused in Provincetown during these first days, trying to collect myself, trying to fill the emptiness with God, I wrote rather cold letters to Maurice, for when feelings left me I could not remember how it had been when they filled me. So I could never deceive him. I know I encouraged him impersonally to get away from the enervating air of Croton and to come to live at a distance from me. But these signs of my independence of him aroused the old instinct of self-preservation and he who always appeared lacking in initiative when there was anyone to act for him, suddenly packed up and went to Ogunquit on the Maine Coast where his friend and great admirer, Hamilton Field, operated a little art colony.

I wrote to Bayard who had returned to Agdar Farm. I missed his cool, intelligent counsels when I was away from him, and I valued his opinions, though I could not take his advice even when I recognized it as good. We enjoyed talking things over together. He replied to me:

Royalston, Mass., August.

DEAR MABEL:

Had Hutch spoken facetiously, I should understand what he meant about Lippmann. The latter can explain (in rather a cocksure fashion) everything, because he leaves out everything essential. I like him, however, and consider him valuable to the country just as I consider reason valuable: both are correctors, reformers, not creators and formers, and it is not for us to condemn, though so many justly criticize his attitude and activities.

. . . The trouble with Hutch (on this point) is, that he tries to defend his imaginings on a reasonable basis, and when out-reasoned, he falls back on imagination and mere asseveration. . . .

Please do not write Lewisohn as yet, for I begin to see possibilities here for the near future, which I ought not to give up. Just now, I must be at the same time in myself and out of myself—a difficult proposition, which can be, I trust, managed—but it must be here for the present.

I hope you have as much cheerfulness as your letter conveyed; and I am more than glad that you have taken again 23 Fifth Ave. The country would do you worlds of good—if you lived in the city! Seriously, I think you need more in your environment than Croton can give. One doesn't escape chaos by avoiding it, but by helping to mold it. (That seems to sound like Jelliffe.)

I actually wrote some verse this morning; and yesterday I discovered a lot about beech trees. The trouble with our modern verse, by the way, is that our "poets" are writing with prose—energy for their emotions, but without the intellectual energy necessary for good prose. Hence their loose-kneed meanderings in queerly shaped lines. Their "originality" consists in avoiding the difficulties of both prose and verse.

The above was written about four days ago, and it will be sent to you if I can get through another night. No—on second thought—I shall send it only if the next few days show me positively that I have won—won, that is, for the time; for I begin to see that this thing will be a torment perpetual. The nights grow worse, and only momentarily do the days grow better.

Yours,

BAYARD.

P.S. I am writing again on my novel—not very much, to be sure, but of a quality to make me somewhat hopeful.

There was an unbridgeable gap between people like Hutch and Walter. Hutch thought him uninspired because he was so unimpeded and unhesitant. He thought Walter was one of the more unfortunate signs of the times. And Walter thought Hutch was irrational and of no consequence because he was obviously not very successful in this world. Walter had an active mind but it was active about action and active people; he didn't think about people like Hutch very often but Hutch thought about him and the very image of him rankled. Hutch had a contemplative mind and action seemed unimportant to him.

Of all my friends none irritated him more and he sometimes used

486

to think my liking for Walter was an added indication of the way things were going more and more in the wrong direction in the universe! Once he sent me this letter from Boston:

DEAR MABEL,   *Boston, 9 p.m.*

I have been thinking a good deal about you—and perhaps that's why this saloon reminds me of you. I looked for some time before I found a place with chairs in it. The Puritanism of Boston seems to consist largely in not having chairs in the saloons. Plenty of whiskey but no decent opportunity to enjoy it.

But why does a saloon with chairs in it remind me of you? It is not because you particularly like to sit down. You do sit down, but you do not intensely like to. But you *do* like good chairs—and then you contrast so with these men who are sitting down. In some way, they have got *something*—something *secure*.

At the same table with me there sits a man drinking whiskey *very* slowly. His face looks as if everything had happened to him—but his eyes are dull and superficially quiet. The man has misery in his look. He has evidently been trying to find how his Libido might find a worthy object. His emotional Center has been dynamited. Woman, Ambitions—these have shown to him the speck in the Peach. What is there left? How can he re-establish the Center, the Unity of feeling in which all the parts, the details, have beauty? The answer is very simple—and you will think false—the answer is whiskey—drunk slowly, very slowly—if possible alone.

Well, Mabel, let's try, you and I, not to be harmful. Let's try to quit being egotists. Isn't it better, really, to rot in a saloon than to be what you and I are? You are a little worse than I am, and therefore a little better. You use your will more than I do. But don't use it on me, because I believe in whiskey—and whiskey is better than anything I know except God. And that is why Bayard is right—negatively—and why you in spite of your will are right—because you helped Bayard—to go down—as he wants and should do. . . .

If you sometimes will go down to the Bowery and see the Booze victims, you will see another way in which God manifests himself. God doesn't manifest himself *at all* in Walter Lippmann.

Walter made me laugh so much—he appeared to me so much like the ultimate vaudevillian that I had to have another drink and could write no more. . . .

HUTCH.

Maurice had decided he wanted to paint rocks. His first letter was written with the exhilaration of change:

487

Friday Morning,
Ogunquit, Maine.

Dearest Sweetheart, you were right. There is something poisonous about the summer air at Croton. I left it on Wednesday full of resentment and suspicions of you—and awake here full of love and affection for you, darling. I got your telegram at the Somerset yesterday. Arrived here last night and the first impression was very discouraging. Field seems to have here a sort of combination boarding house and art school. The studio he had for me is already taken and when I asked him what about meals, he said that I should take them at his boarding house. I was quite staggered. I told him that I wouldn't think of eating or associating with a lot of youngsters. I impressed it on him that I must be alone and eat alone. He said it can be managed. I haven't discussed yet details with him. But the air is wonderful and my rheumatism is almost gone. I suppose you are surprised that I came to the Maine coast after I told you that I did not want to go to Cape Cod on account of my rheumatism. Bourgeois, who has chronic rheumatism, told me that there isn't a better place for it than Maine, not the coast, but more in the mountains, so I decided to come here first, expecting to hear from Hamilton Field, who has been living here for 20 years, about other possibilities. I just took an early morning walk along the cliffs. It is really sublime, or rather was when I went out, but wasn't quite that when I returned. You have no idea, darling, how wonderful in expression some of the rocks are: huge masses protruding from the sea, the expression on the land side grave and longing, on the side facing the sea full of horror and passion, as if the rocks were shrieking to the waves to give them a rest. And what wonderfully rhythmic spirals and curves in the reflections of the rocks in the water, so sensitive—shapes formed by the least change in the air. I want to study that. But after I sat there a while and decided to go back to my room to write to you, the place was quite different. From between the cliffs suddenly peeped out a girl's hat, or the top of an easel, or the squinting eye of a male painter. I really felt that I couldn't stand it. But I'll see and try it for a week or so. After all, one can be alone if one chooses. And Ogunquit I hear is much worse. This is about a mile away from there, a tiny fishing place with Field's, and a painter, Woodbury's houses the only palazzi.

I haven't received word from you since last Monday. I was frightfully upset Tuesday when I didn't get a letter from you—this together with my lumbago drove me away from Croton. I just telegraphed to Mrs. Cruger to forward letters here. Darling Mabel, don't let us do anything which could harm our relationship—will you try? There are only two things in life left for me: you and my work. Nothing else and no one else interests me. I am sure we could make something really big and worth-while if we want it.

I hear someone is going to the village so I must finish this. With more love than I have ever felt for you before—

M.

Address: Thurenscoe, Ogunquit, Me.

P.S. I forgot to tell you the main reason why, if I can only stick it out, I'd like to stay here: a splendid model, professional athlete—he could pose for me half a day. You have no idea how anxious I am to get back to the nude.

M.

I can imagine the flutter that started among the muslins and the wools of art students when Field announced at the communal supper-table: "Maurice Sterne is here with us!" The conspicuous figure of Maurice with his so dark hair and eyes in his so definite red and white face, his serious frown above the aquiline nose—rather disdainful, although with quick, nervous glances in all directions—must have startled the rather low-toned atmosphere of the nesting artists in the little cove.

And upon his second letter I was drawn back to cope with my problem. "How banal!" I thought. "Why does he relapse into that second-rate sort of thing?" And forthwith my energy ran out like quicksilver to find what he wanted, only it should be of the most superior quality, of the highest distinction available. If he had to have rocks, then they must be the rockiest rocks in Maine in the most distinguished setting I could find—rocks really aloof and undomesticated, something different indeed from the intimate and over-used coast of Ogunquit that I visualized from his letters, with the boarding house and the art school all mixed up together and easels stuck up all over the place. He wrote me that a girl's hat peeped out from behind every rock! Also that one of the first evenings he was there, a girl got at him almost in spite of himself, and he had her out on the beach in the dark.

Friday.

What is the matter, dearest? You say you have been quite sick the past few days. I also have been sort of out of sorts—an awful feeling of depression and loneliness. Today I was on the verge of telegraphing to you if you could have Albert meet me at Boston—but instead went out on the rocks and did the best study I have made here. I wonder if I can stick it out here this month. In spite of the crowd I am so terribly lonely. At first I mixed quite freely with the rest—in fact I have been told that contrary to all expectations, Sterne is quite human. But these past few days I have begun to dislike them for their bad art, small natures, narrow minds and now they probably say that I am quite inhuman after all. I have also left the large table and take my meals at a little table in a separate room all by myself—so I suppose I am a snob too! There is also some other thing that is very unpleasant—that girl. I feel uncomfortable whenever we meet. I wish to heavens that had never occurred—I would feel much more at ease. Mabel, darling, you ask me to search within myself whether my love is deep, inevitable, if I really need you. I don't know. I only know that you appeal to the deepest, biggest in me, that you inspire me with a passionate desire to go down to the rock bottom truth, that the earnestness with which I have all my life pursued my art, I also wish to apply to my life—to realize the essentials in nature has been my endeavor and now I am trying to realize this in my life also. But this at times scares me and makes me feel like breaking it up. I wonder if my work would not benefit from an undivided interest—if I should not rather play with life and look at it as a recreation, rather than an all-absorbing art.

Darling, how I have longed for you these past few days—in the day and in the night—for the light and warmth of your spirit and your body.

You ask me if there is anything I have not told you during our life together—nothing of any importance that I can think of. Only one thing— do you remember that day I had lunch with B. G. and we met later and went to the cina? I kissed her that day at the library and do you know why? I felt that you were unfaithful to me at the same time, somewhere, somehow. At times I get those damned low suspicions of you and then I am ready to do anything.

I have nothing else to confess, Mabel. Believe me. What a strange thing human nature is, dearest: you hold me when you let go of your hold on me. . . .

Today was perfect—the untiring attack of the waves against the rocks was really superb. I am anxious to do some color studies. How is your painting getting on? My wood carving is progressing nicely. Please, dearest, as soon as you get this, tell me how I can reach Bobby. I want him to get some things for me in Chinatown, some Chinese ink in round sticks. I am all out of it and can't get on without it and don't know anyone else in town who could procure it for me.

Give my love to John. I am gradually getting over my resentment over Scuro's murder. Also remember me to Leo, Hutch and Neith.

All love,
MAURICE.

This peculiarly abundant incontinence in Maurice made me absolutely furious. I could not understand it or condone it. All I knew was that I would not permit it. The only way to stem the uncontrolled flow was to be on hand and superintend it myself. Was this to be my life work? I regained a sense of significance from Maurice's lapse on the beach, for again he reappeared in my imagination as a *job*. I must personally direct and canalize this rich stream and see that it was metamorphosed into Art. That Portrait of me should take care of this.

Of late we had proceeded from the idea of it in paint to a head carved in wood, and Maurice had been experimenting with new materials, with fine, sharp tools and woods of varying degrees of resistance. The head was to be carved and then painted in polychrome, for Maurice could not be divorced all at once from his pigments. Gold leaf was to play a part, too.

CHAPTER XX

Monhegan Island

SOMEONE told me about Monhegan Island, describing its rugged
and remote position, its few summer houses among the native ones,
and its adequate *raison d'être*. It supported a great, lonely lighthouse
that protected ships from the long, jagged Maine coast. This, I thought,
sounds more dignified for him. So I had spent only a few days in peace
in my little cottage when I was impelled out to reconnoiter for that
man.

"Oh, well, 'It's a heartbreak to the wise that it's for a short space we
have the same things only,'" I quoted again to myself. I forget who
went with me in the motor, but I believe Neith went along to stop
and stay for a while in a farmhouse they had in New Hampshire
near Bayard.

I passed a night in rather a bleak neighborhood and Neith was
there, as I look back upon it. More particularly I recall making my
way one morning into a bare and desolate frame house where num-
berless dogs had, during the night, left pools of water upon the floors,
and where books strewed the dingy chairs. Bayard *chez lui!* He came
down the carpetless stairs to greet me, elegant and correct, his fabricated smile upon his Nordic face. I sighed with a feeling of nervousness for the way life hurt people. All the world seemed populated with
the wrecks of men. Outside that house, magnificent evergreens climbed
the hillsides, strong and virile and uncontaminated by the humanity
which was only so much debris beneath their boughs. I hastened away
from there. John was beside me in the car.

There were fascinating antique shops to explore in Maine. *En pas-
sant,* I bought two painted black beds, and one carved mahogany
four-poster, and also a fine, plain, unpainted and unstained desk with
a cupboard top.

Arriving in Ogunquit, I found Maurice looking quite festive. The sea had tanned him and the crisp wind blew his soft, black hair backwards off his brow. He wore his white shirt open at the neck and had acquired quite an easy, happy look. Why could I not leave him there in peace among the lesser lives of arty folks? He flourishes in the medium areas of life, I thought to myself, but I could not give him up to these. Telling him I would go on and find out what Monhegan Island was like, I forged ahead.

Monhegan! A black rock in the Atlantic Ocean with cruel cliffs against which the water, always of a nondescript color, angrily lurched and broke night and day. A small boat motored one out to that gaunt and repellent island, then turned around and hastily left. Near the boat-landing a few dwellings clung together, also the post-office, the store, a small hotel. But away across a kind of moor, covered with coarse grass, there were several wooden houses facing out to the open sea; built low to resist the wind, and weathered to a dark brown.

I was able to rent the largest of these seaside homes, for the owners were not coming to occupy it that year; and I determined to take it, for the whole place had a certain intensity that satisfied me. It had character. It reminded me of Charlotte Brontë, George Sand, and Brittany, only it was more austere, more tragic, than any of these. It was a suitable background for the turbulent artist and there were rocks piled all along the edge of the water below the cliffs—black rocks, terribly indented and carved by the intransigent sea.

The only neighbors were a couple called Lee. Gerald Stanley Lee was a tall, thin, hectic man who saw all idealistic life in terms of advertising. He sublimated advertising, and she was just a wife. They had the house in charge and rented it to me and it was called "Lodestar Cottage"! They were very cordial to John and me, hoping for company, I suppose. They instructed me about meals for since I could not cook, we had to carry them over from the hotel. I had sent for little Elizabeth from the Duncan School: she and John would be able to bring our food to us in baskets. We would live as simply as possible—the rocks were the principal consideration!

Somewhere near, the great lighthouse stood. I don't remember it very well—only at night, when the perpetual flash of light went through the dark house amidst the creakings of the dried timbers in the wind.

The sun, already northern in its pallor, had not the yellow warmth

I was accustomed to. Everything about Monhegan was ascetic and screwed up to the endurance of life, rather than to an enjoyment of it. Every outline was hard. There were no amenities. One had to get one's pleasure out of qualities of salubriousness, briskness and rugged strength. The queer blackness of the rocks made them seem volcanic, and I often wondered if perhaps we were not perched on the lateral remains of a sunken explosion.

The sunsets (and perhaps the sunrises, too—I did not know about the latter) were magnificent. They were not soothingly lyrical and sweet like those to which I had grown accustomed. No, vast conflagrations spread over the sky, crimsons and purples, shadowed by lurid blackish-greens, that made the night to follow seem like a dark, charred husk of after-life. Too intense. Everything, I shortly discovered, was really almost too intense on Monhegan. Windswept, bleak island in the gray Atlantic—what a challenge to little mortals like ourselves. However, Maurice rose to it, while I sank.

I had undertaken something that was really too much for me, for this was the first time I had ventured out into the world alone with Maurice. It was not, perhaps, so much that I was alone with *him* as with my irregular situation with him. There was no doubt about it, I was not an emancipated woman. I was so intensely conscious of *average opinion* that I must have shared it myself and perhaps this had been the cause of the careful camouflage the Green House had provided at the Farm; I had never lived anywhere with Maurice except at Finney Farm and in Provincetown where separate establishments had seemed necessary to me.

But here—here I was among strangers in a rented house—I, Mabel Dodge, with him, Maurice Sterne! I shuddered and quaked the moment he stepped off the launch, grinning his crescent smile, so sure of himself and so noticeable in the drear surroundings. I had not realized until that moment how I would shrink and suffer from the unconventional situation. True, I had brought John, and I had sent for little Elizabeth and they would neutralize as far as might be the sinful presence of Maurice by creating the semblance of a family but to my despair these children did not seem to counterbalance his conspicuous relationship with me.

He was apparently relieved of self-consciousness at the moment; I had assumed all there was in the air! It has always seemed to me there is just so much suffering surrounding one at any given time, and unless it is divided and shared, one may take it all.

He strode towards me and embraced me with a loud smack. I felt the eyes of everyone directed at us: the boatmen, the urchins at the little dock, the nondescript characters who lounged about—all these seemed to be gazing at us with undisguised interest, suspicion and disrespect. I tried to become invisible and immediately retired so deep into my shell that it took months to get me out again.

Our life at the Lodestar Cottage commenced, then, in a little agony that increased every day. Maurice was committed to the black rocks and they fascinated him. Every morning after our silent breakfast, he departed for the rocky shore, his portfolio under his arm. The two children disappeared—and what did I do? I haven't the faintest idea, for not the vestige of a recollection of my days there is registered anywhere in my memory—so I suppose I did nothing. Sat looking straight ahead, perhaps! These blank spaces, when one is neither coming or going, leave no pictures on the soul.

At noons, though, Maurice swims back into consciousness. I can see him, now, striding into the silent house, frowning prodigiously, his temper as black as the rocks among which he passed his days, identified with them, or rather with his vision of them. From the window I can see, now, the children struggling over the moor carrying the heavy basket between them: the dinner consisting of pallid soup, the stringy, island chicken or boiled mutton, and the mashed potato congealed by the journey into a stiff mound. Not all their care prevented the soup from encroaching upon the meat—or the peas upon the potatoes!

Maurice always stuck his morning's work out on a chair where he could look at it while he ate and see that it was good. These drawings really frightened me. Apparently in the stones and rocks of Monhegan he detected all the evil of the world. Monstrous forms and faces emerged in the blackest of charcoal mediums, distorted leering horrors that lurk at the bottom of the pit and are never allowed egress— Maurice was letting them all out now! These ghosts were gradually filling the living room as the days passed. They were pinned to all sides of the wooden walls.

Maurice ignored us all. He was deep in his subterranean world and my own darkness deepened day by day. I didn't leave the place and I

495

never went over to the other shore where the few inhabitants lived. The Lees tried, I think, to be neighborly and Mr. Lee came soon one evening to ask us to come over and see their place, but it was no good. We sat in the circle of light from the oil lamp on the table, and I was sealed in with my speculations regarding his opinion of us—not blaming him for the criticism I thought he concealed, but rejecting what must have been, I fancied, his charitable and broad-minded impulse in coming over to our unconventional establishment. I knew that what I was doing was not done. I tried to comfort myself with the thought that I was a pioneer in living openly and honestly with Maurice instead of clandestinely, as so many other people conducted their unmarried affairs. But it was no good. I was not interested in being a pioneer. It was no comfort at all.

Maurice, rendered independent of everything outside him by the luxurious experience of expression which the painting of flowers had never given him, sat there so cold and aloof that he repelled the friendly man who disappeared in no time. Maurice, then, went on smoking his dark cigar and gazing at the evil images that surrounded us.

The nights were no better than the days, for my awareness of what I believed Public Opinion to be regarding our sensual relation, froze my blood and prevented me from enjoying the sin for which I endured it. I had never suffered this way with Reed! Why did I imagine such things off here with Maurice? Was it because there was really something sinful in our conjunction that had been absent when Reed and I were together, or was it because this was the first time I was out alone in the cold, cold world, unprotected by the walls of my own environment, away from my friends and admirers? I had no admirers here—no legendary glamor to reinforce me. I had not even Maurice, for he absented himself more and more every day. I felt I ceased to exist and this negative sensation deepened as the weeks passed.

The autumn drew closer, while summer, always rather pinched in that northern state, disappeared imperceptibly. At night the wind howled over the house and penetrated the thin wooden walls. Doors banged suddenly in the darkness, and shutters slammed against windows. How long this period actually lasted, I do not know—probably not the eternity it seemed—for the acceleration of depression was so rapid.

One night I left my narrow bed and crept to Maurice, awakening him. "I feel so badly," I whimpered. "Everything seems terrible. I don't know what to do!"

Maurice had not a variety of sympathetic responses. He knew, however, the old, unfailing one. I forced my exhausted nerves to rise and meet him, but the dose was not the one required for my exigency. In the morning I felt so broken and distraught that at last I was frightened.

One of these sudden decisions that always arose to save me at the ultimate hour came to me now. I decided to leave Monhegan Island with the children—to leave him there with the rocks and the storms and to rush out of these depths back to Finney Farm.

Maurice was mildly surprised, but he did not try to stop me. He wanted those rocks more than anything else and he let us go. John went back to school in Morristown and started to write a book. Little Elizabeth returned to the Duncan School. John started out:

BEGINNING OF PREFACE

This book is not an autobiography. It is not a novel. It is a book of Facts and ideas about life. It is a book of ideas and things that I have every day. Some days are bad. I will write Bad. Some days are good. I will write better. But there will be only one best, that is the last. You cannot understand the last unless you read the rest. This book is not to be criticized. How can anybody criticize it when they don't know? If anybody criticizes it he shall write a better one. This book will be finished when I am fifteen. It will be my present to mother at Christmas to whom it is dedicated. This book is on love, skill, work, life and animals. I write on these because they are everything. Love and hate are one and the same. If there was no love there would be no hate. If there were no hate there would be no love. How could there be? I write on skill for the same reasons, and work, life, and animals *do*. By *do* I mean *are*. Animals and people are the same. Work and life are the same. Thus, People skillfully love, live and do. And animals hate, work and *are*. If you criticize that you are fools. If you dont, you understand it. Now lets see you criticize it.

P.S. That poem about you is the dedication. I wont write any more on this until I come home after thanksgiving. Why should I go to college?"

I was alone: I had to have help and I thought of Dr. Brill. He had helped Andrew and Grace Johnson and others I knew of, and I could not go back to Jelliffe, for I didn't want to *talk*, now, I wanted to live.

When I went to see Brill, he was taking his vacation and only coming to his office once a week. He saw me and told me he could not take me until later in the fall; but I told him I was badly in need of something, I didn't know what. I was frightened, for I felt I could not endure my terrible burden of melancholy. He said, oh, yes, I could, and he turned me away. I found he was right.

I could bear it and I did bear it, for away from Maurice the old force, dormant at the bottom of me, began to rise once more. I opened Finney Farm and lived looking forward to the analysis with the new doctor: this time it would be Freudian, instead of with Jung's method which Dr. Jelliffe purported to practice.

Then Maurice wrote me with his mind at rest:

Monhegan,
Sunday night.

DEAREST MABEL,

Thank you for your telegram which reached me only today. I met someone on the rocks who told me that someone somewhere had a telegram for me. After a high and low hunt for it, I at last located it. It was really reassuring and I am happy to hear that you have reached Croton safely and that you like the farm. Are you enjoying the food!—and how about the flowers? Anything blooming now? I am very lonely here, but not lonesome. I have no need for people. I suppose if I wanted to I could see Lee, and Mrs. Lee sent word that she would be very pleased if I would call some eve, but if I can't be with you, dearest, I'd rather be alone. My life is getting smoothened out somehow—formerly there were so many possibilities, now it has come down to two only—either a life with you or a life all alone!—Both have a great fascination for me, but the worst of it is that when I have the one I want the other!

I worked very well today. I made five color sketches! This is the first day that I really worked well (since you left). Yesterday and the day before we were again shrouded in a thick fog and the horn blew until it drove me almost crazy. But even if I haven't much to show, I've worked all the time. You see my loathing for palettes and tubes and brushes is getting stronger every day, and I am trying to devise some scheme of painting without that paraphernalia. I am making only tentative experiments. This will be my last chance—either I'll devise something or throw all my paints and brushes in the sea and take to sculpture! Of course I will take to sculpture anyway, but I don't wish to be conquered by the foolish paints! Did you have a typical Finney Sunday? with all the Sunday paper sprawling all over the place, with some friends surrounding you whilst "the center" is stretched in the hammock with her knees drawn up?

With all my love—

MAURICE.

Lodestar Cottage
Burnt Head
Monhegan, Maine

Oct. 9th,
Monday night.

DEAREST MABEL,

This is like Bali. Since Saturday no boat has arrived, or will leave until tomorrow. A few more days and I shall be leaving, too. You tell me to stay as long as I feel that I am working well here, but I feel that I'll be able to work just as well at Croton and everything pulls me back there. I want to get right to work on your head. We have had a couple of very cold days. I froze, especially at night, but today was warmer again. I am tired of dish-washing! and I am lonely without you. As long as I had the *Possessed* I didn't mind it, and when I finished that I went back to the *Dead Souls*. I don't know any book aside from Dostoyevski's that I enjoyed so much. I finished it yesterday. You see I read here five hours every night from 7 to 12. But I don't believe anyone but a Russian can really appreciate that work. Wonderful, wonderful character studies, each an essential expression of an existing type—a stupendous work, every variety of the Russian portrayed sympathetically and complete. Unlike Dostoyevski who created types composed of all human potentialities.

I wonder if you will find something to occupy you this winter. Strange that you should look for outside things when within you is locked up a really significant writer. Why not take up a "big task." If I could write I would write a book on Moses. Why shouldn't you tackle it. Get your material from the Bible, create a *new* Moses, not the Biblical Michael Angelesque—a meek, modest, *nervous* little Jew, a stammering fanatic, an emaciated body, but the spirit aflame. There are four versions of the New Testament, and still that didn't prevent Renan from writing a really significant Life of Jesus—and now you tell me that Moore also did an excellent job. If you don't do it, I'll try to get Hutch. Don't laugh—what you all need is a task.

With all my might, my body, my heart, my head, my nerves, my blood, my soul, I mean to plunge into sculpture this winter. If I can't manage it at Croton, I'll take a place in N. Y., but I feel that I can't abstain from it any longer. The sculptor in me demands a release. If I don't draw the cork, the bottle will burst and it will all go to hell!

I see it is 11:30—Good night, dearest.

With all my love and devotion,

MAURICE.

So he was gradually turning more and more to the idea of sculpture at last!

As my psychological tension lessened I began to have pains of a physical nature in my side. When these increased I consulted Brill again and he sent me to his family doctor, who decided I needed an operation.

This doctor, whose name I have forgotten, was an excellent surgeon; and though he seemed very practical and cold-minded, he was in reality extremely understanding. I went to the Woman's Hospital and was given a charming room with chintz curtains and attractive furniture. The morning before he operated, the doctor stood over me smiling a little quizzically:

"I have to be careful with these nurses and assistants," he murmured. "They think I am crazy. But I am going to tell you something now and I will try to repeat it to you when you are going to sleep. *You will go off to sleep so sweetly and when you wake up you will have a feeling of bien-être and of ease—you won't have a bit of discomfort. You are going to enjoy this operation.*"

I smiled and believed him. On the operating table, I lay relaxed and comfortable while the nurses, anonymous in their white starch, bustled around the chill instruments. When all was ready, my doctor entered. I hardly knew him in his disguise. He too was all in white and there was a kind of mask over his pointed gray beard. I could see a smile, though, in his eyes. He made a sign at one of the nurses. She lowered the ether cone over my face, and then I felt him take my hand and I heard him saying in a very low voice: "You will wake up happy and at ease—no discomfort, no pain—" . . . then I was gone.

Really I did come to myself with the most delicious feeling of happiness and relief. I lay in my nice room basking in the first contentment I had known for a long, long time. And all through that convalescence I sailed along as though upon a quiet sea—mending harmoniously.

Sometimes a letter came from Maurice, showing him to be still preoccupied with our mysterious troubles:

Wednesday night,
September 28th,
Monhegan.

DEAREST MABEL,

Your Monday letter didn't sound very cheerful—all of them, the whole group, seem to be "possessed" and the worst of it is that we are not just an isolated group but I believe it expresses all the stratas of life. I think that the mischief lies in the so-called evolution, but what I call degeneration of mankind. We are getting out of the *artisan* phase, the happy state when men put spirit into matter and expressed abstractions with a material body. The trouble with all our "group" is that it really is not in the clutch of expression—it wants to live, live, experience, but hasn't the vital need of recording the experiences. You are a good example, but you at least sometimes have the need to record your experience. But I wonder if you are really driven to express it by an inner irresistible force? It flows so naturally from you that I almost believe it. But why can you only just portray an experience, why not try to create characters with inevitable events and consequences.

Your "Parting" is good, only it hurts.

I wonder if you have taken the house on 10th St.? You are wondering what the winter has in store for you, so do I. We don't want to repeat the last winter—we were both on the edge of a nervous collapse. What *is* the secret of this tie between us? It seems to persist, in spite of us. When it abates in one sense, it grows stronger in another. How often you have asked me, "Do you love me?" Whenever you have asked me this, I was at once conscious of a searching look in your eyes and I became self-conscious. Do you think love can flow easily, unimpaired, when the beloved has the look of a district attorney?

To revert to your "Parting" you thought it strange that at the time when you suffered most I could stroll into an amusement park. Because you couldn't have done it, you can't understand how I could. It is because there is a strong, self-preservative instinct in me (perhaps racial). When in despair, anguish, I seek to escape from it. I have to—and when necessary I can even create delusions about the unknown to serve that purpose; for instance, if you told me that you have decided to break it up, I should feel more terrible than you imagine—but I really don't think that which I wrote you in my last letter, that it is either you or a solitary life, is really true. I would probably force myself into a new relationship simply as a means to mitigate the pain. No one, of course, could replace you, but I am childishly naïve about the unknown, and I should probably go from one to another in order to escape from the gap in my life made by you.

But if I should merely shut myself up and brood over my loss, I would just make an end of it all.

Darling, I am lonely without you. If you were here now, I should pour out my love and passion and affection and friendship to you, for you. It is getting late (I must look at the time)—11 o'clock! And as I get up at 6:30 I'd better turn in. Last night it was freezing cold and I longed for your heat. I couldn't escape the Lees. Yesterday they sent word that they were leaving on Saturday and wanted me to have supper with them. I did! Mrs. Lee is quite a naïve visionary. She hopes for a great art, greater than Michael Angelo, Leonardo, etc., to come out of democracy! Out of the Crowds! When will all these people realize that art is an expression of aristocracy, individualism, and not an expression of the masses!

Lovingly,
MAURICE.

Why don't you sign your letters Mabel any longer, not just M. D. I don't like it!

But I was free from thoughts of love.

Soon the doctor told me I was a good patient, "Considering what you went through," he said.

"I *like* operations," I confided to him. "Do your patients *all* have a good time like this?" I enquired.

"When I can tell them to. But I have to look out for those damned nurses, and the other doctors. They wouldn't stand for it! They'd call it malpractice or something!"

"But you can do *wonders!* Maybe you wouldn't have to cut people if you can reach them by *talking,*" I exclaimed, eagerly. "Maybe you could just tell even a cancer to *stop* and it would!" I was excited by these possibilities.

"We know too little." He shook his head. "We know *nothing* yet. Until we learn how to address the conscious intelligence of the cell, we must use the knife."

I have never forgotten these words.

Finally the time came for Maurice to leave the cold island and he wrote:

Wednesday morning.

Hello. Just had a delicious breakfast (toast and tea). That is the only meal I enjoy, for I take it in the dining room. I place my chair right in the path of sunlight and put the tray in front of me. Then comes my cigar and just now I reread your Saturday letter. Really, Mabel, I fear if you will hear much more praise about both your achievements and potentialities, you'll get conceited,—conceit in a man is bad, but in a woman it is abominable. This is my last day here, I fear, as far as work is concerned. I must allow at least two full days for packing and cleaning house as I can't reckon on Saturday morning—the boat now leaves at 8 A.M. sharp. Then I shall start on a new phase. I wonder if that which is to come is really not only preordained but if it really already exists. I fear many of us have now the tendency to conceive life as a cinematograph that is as if an infinite film roll for each individual is placed somehow, somewhere, and only needs time to unfold it. But as Leo would say, I am afraid it isn't as simple as that. I had a weird dream last night. An English friend of mine, a painter, was led into my room by another; then I saw that he was blind. With a look I questioned his guide, with a look he responded, and I knew that he lost his sight in the war. Then the blind man said, "Why don't you question me? Don't think I am sensitive about my infirmity. I love to speak of it. I am proud and happy—never have been so happy before." I think we waste too much sympathy upon the war cripples. The spiritual illusion of having made a sacrifice of one's legs or eyes for a great cause, not only mitigates it, but does more: it has given them an ideal which they lived up to. The fact that the sacrifice was not voluntary, that it was forced upon them, will, I fear and hope, occur to few only. And besides, vanity being the main reason for living (said the preacher) you will see that cripples who heretofore have shunned the outside world, will suddenly develop a passion for outdoor exercise. But the blind one is to be pitied most; now and then he will recall with a pang the movies!

No, Mabel, I am not cynical about it. I fear that I understand humanity well, at least its weaknesses.

Lovingly, your

MAURICE.

Give my love to Mary and Hutch.

Will you please send the enclosed letter to Mr. Dubernet? I don't know the address; you can look it up in the telephone book.

When he came, Bourgeois was amazed at his pile of drawings and very admiring; he promised him an exhibition during the winter. Meanwhile he took Maurice to Chicago for a show at the Art Institute; and this left me free to recuperate in peace. I relaxed and began to be quietly gay and able to think of impersonal things.

Woman's Hospital
New York

Saturday.

Up again in a chair, dearest. Just had a very measly note from you dated Thursday—postmarked Wednesday. You were running out to look for a hotel. Don't fail to go and get my letters already sent to Blackstone. I don't see why you stay there if you don't like it. Is it a death struggle? Are you and the other artists in a deadly combat to sell? I don't like all this much. You know best, though, for yourself.

Here's an amusing letter from Walter. I wrote him that I had lost my identity here as well as what he calls my "authority," that the doctor treats me like a dear little woman who is anxious to get back to her teas and must be handled with a playful but at the same time a strong, firm will— and that I pass the time discussing crochet stitches with the nurses!

He, as all others I have seen, does not see peace in Germany's proposal. This morning Russia refuses to negotiate! Fierce old Russia!

Andrew is out at Croton. He sent word if it was all the same to me, he would like to go out and work there for a bit—and in return help me with my chicken-pigeon problem. I was glad. Someone must help me get the hang of it. I *should* have fresh eggs—and chickens and squabs for eating with all the stock I have and the feed bills. As it is, I have to *buy* eggs and squabs! . . .

CHAPTER XXI

Dr. Brill

THE "analysis" with Dr. Brill was very different from what I was accustomed to! When I sat down before him with his flat, mahogany desk-table between us, I started right off to initiate him about myself.

"I have a very bad Oedipus complex . . ." I began, but he interrupted me.

"Never mind about that," he said. "I want your dreams. I want you to organize your life so that you have plenty of occupation and I want you to bring me in at least one dream every time you come."

"But I hardly ever dream," I protested.

"Well, you will."

"How do you mean, 'organize' my life?" I went on, somewhat impatiently.

"Make a program for yourself and stick to it. How do you occupy yourself at home?"

How *did* I?

"Do you attend to your household? Do you like to paint or write? My impression is you are out of place in the country. I think you should be working with a number of people. I may be wrong, but I believe *people* constitute your best medium."

"That's because you saw me first at one of my evenings here in New York. Oh! I got tired of all that! I hate the city!"

"That doesn't make any difference. Perhaps you belong in it just the same. Why do you hate it?"

"Oh, the noise and the smells—the hurrying around after nothing! I can't stand it. . . ."

"It is the *norm*—the usual environment of the period you are living in. If you can't stand it, you are maladjusted. That's why you are here this morning. We're going to see about that." He smiled a kind of owlish grin.

"Do you mean to say you're going to adjust me to the wild, crude noises of city streets, barbarous horns and yells, and the stinking smells of gasoline, hot asphalt and all the others that most people are too insensitive to notice?"

"They may be insensitive—but they are able to *stand* them."

"Why *should* they? Why *should* one accept a perfectly uncivilized environment? I don't *want* to. I can imagine *altering* an environment, but I can't imagine meekly accepting it if I don't like it. That's subnormal. I'm interested in the super-normal, myself."

"Oh, but you should at least *be able* to accept it. And you say you are not able. Well, my job is with the norm. I'm not interested in the super-normal. *The normal* average life—that is quite an achievement, you know. Do not call it subnormal until you can live it."

Thus began our unending argument. . . . Brill was all for action, whereas Jelliffe was speculative and considered the play of the psyche and the mind a good outlet in itself. Brill believed in externalizing things. Apparently nothing counted unless it was painted, written down, or formulated into some life-pattern composed of persons and their movements. Of course, my previous existence at 23 Fifth Avenue, with its Movements, Leagues, Unions, its Evenings and all, evidently had, to his mind, constituted the perfect adjustment for me. Something in me had risen to spoil it. We must find out the destructive agent within and analyze it away. He did not seem to attach much importance to Maurice, but looked upon him more or less as a mere element in a composite arrangement that I had carefully but mistakenly built up to defeat my own best interests.

I liked Brill immensely from the very first. One could have confidence in him, for his integrity was apparent at once, but it took me quite a while to learn that I could not continue my interesting speculations with him. I would begin hopefully:

"Do you believe a manic-depressive can cure herself? Jelliffe—"

"That's enough," he would interrupt. "You are not here for conversation."

Then he refused to accept my belief that one could drive one's energy from the lower to the higher centers and so increase power. But I thought, later, he did have much the same idea when he talked of repression and sublimation, only he apparently considered that repressions were involuntary and that only sublimations could be directed. He seemed to consider that neurotics were the only people who accomplished anything in this world. I asked him if, from his standpoint, sublimations of sex in painting, writing, inventing and so on were not to be considered merely by-products and their chief function not to create beauty and a more abundant life, but to keep people out of insane asylums.

What would happen, I asked, when sublimations were exhausted, used up and no longer sublime? Perhaps the world was already overfull of these productions, of pictures, books, music, inventions!

"Is civilization just an effort not to go crazy?"

He told me not to try to be clever but to tell him a dream!

Brill was certain from the first that I had no use for the country, that I was wasting my life in Croton. He had an idea, I think, that I would be more at home in some skyscraper with telephones, pushbuttons, and alert secretaries to carry out my plans, than among the sweet williams and the pheasants of Finney Farm!

I fought this notion with all my heart, for I did not want to go back to New York. I had tried to make a new pattern in Croton by asking Hazel to come and spend the winter, for I felt the comfort of having another woman to talk to would overcome my anxiety at Maurice's inevitable attack upon her, but she had not been able to arrange it. I don't know who I had after all. My attention was less and less upon the place. I remember more vividly than anything else sitting in my bed and writing short articles for the *New York Journal*. For more than any other reason, I began to write to appease Brill, and get him off that idea of my return to town! So I had asked Arthur Brisbane for work on the *Journal,* and since he had been insisting for fifteen years that I was a *writer* (perhaps because he himself was one!) he could not very well refuse me a chance to be one.

Arthur gave me an order for two or three little *feuilletons* a week upon any subject I cared to write about, and paid me thirty dollars apiece for them! I think the first one I wrote was called "Strange Mary MacLane." Arthur was anxious to have them start right and wrote instructions to this effect to the city editor of the *Journal,* and to me he wrote:

The Washington Times
Washington, D. C.

July 15th.

MY DEAR MABEL:

As you were leaving today you suggested, speaking of Mary MacLane, a very good article—short and to the point. In your sentence, "She wants to find a master," I think you could write on: "Why every woman wants to find a master, why it is that women long to be bossed." Of course it dates back to the days when they were knocked senseless and dragged into the cave by some gentleman who had previously killed the other gentleman. That is shown in Patagonia where the marriage ceremony consists in standing the woman up against a tree, and knocking out her two upper front teeth.

Of course in real life things are different. Every woman thinks that she wants to find a master. And every man imagines that he wants to find a slave. And when the dust settles, the woman is nearly always the master and the man nearly always the slave. You might write this.

Yours sincerely,
A. BRISBANE.

The Washington Times
Washington, D. C.

August 3rd.

DEAR MABEL:

Your article on Mary MacLane will be published next Monday. I enclose copy of letter that I have written to Mr. Hastings giving the order. Don't you think it would be a good idea to print one of your photographs as we do Elizabeth Jordan's? If you like your old photographs better than the present ones—I do not—you can use the old ones. The picture that we use of Elizabeth Jordan was taken when I first knew her—twenty years ago. She has changed a little which, needless to say, you have not. You might print one of these photographs of yourself and write a few lines under it, saying, "I could remember distinctly when this was me. When you look like this you can't know anything," or words to that effect. This might be an article of advice to women, not to mourn over their childish youth. A new hatched chicken, all yellow, with no real feathers, unable to scratch, bite or lay eggs, would be foolish if it wanted to stay that way always.

Anyhow your articles are started, and I hope your genius will find vent and go on growing.

I am sorry you have delayed so long.

Yours sincerely,
A. BRISBANE.

P.S. In your article "The Growth of Love" I have changed the word "pervert" to dreadful failures. The word "pervert" by the crowd is understood in one vile way, and represents a thought which I do not want to put into the minds of millions of people even for the sake of the truth. It doesn't hurt your article, however. Anything worth printing can be told in the kind of language that you would use talking to a girl twelve years ago.

The sub captions in this article set in typewritten capital letters are all right, but they should have in a ring below them the letters fflc with a ring around as an indication to the printer. Tell your typewriter, this will save me doing it in each case.

I am going to read your articles myself for a while; then when you settle down to a good safe gallop, I'll let the editors read them in the usual way. It is pretty hard for me to look after individual writing, with the other things I have on hand.

A. B.

He was always patient with me and nursed me along, writing occasional instructions:

New York Evening Journal
Office of A. Brisbane

MY DEAR MABEL:

Be careful not to let the pleasure of writing make you forget that you are writing not primarily but SOLELY to interest others. If you seem to have some success, and I know that you will, do not let it divert you from the task of interesting others, to the more pleasant task of EXPRESSING YOURSELF.

Samuel Johnson said approximately, "Do not believe that any man ever wrote well except for pay." You are at a disadvantage in the fact that you do not need to earn money. Your danger will be writing as YOU please, instead of writing as the public pleases.

I am going to read your articles for a little while, but of course I cannot undertake to read them indefinitely. It is not possible for me to attend to MSS., even for my friends.

I shall look at the present copy, change it or reject it—after that it will go through the regular channel that the products of the other writers go through, and it will stand or fall on the impression that it makes upon those that handle the general copy.

You can do this work well; if you choose to make yourself do it, as THE MILLIONS OF READERS WANT IT.

Don't think of your own little group of people when you write, but think of the woman making up the beds in the hotel, or the woman working in the store, or the mother raising a family of children.

All this sounds very dull, I know, but it is just as important as it is dull.

Yours sincerely,
A. BRISBANE.

509

P.S. In your article "The In Between Times" which is quite good, although perhaps a little bit too philosophical for the start, you start off nicely with sub-heads FFLC. After one or two you forget to put them in and you forget to write fflc with a ring around it, after each of these sub-heads.

I should probably write you praising your articles much more earnestly than I do. But I am afraid to make you satisfied—if I do that, you are ended. You must be absolutely dissatisfied with everything. And you must remember that if I had not happened to know you, I probably should not have taken the articles at all—which in my opinion would have been a mistake.

You have had an easy start on the best page of the paper with the biggest circulation in the United States, and have not had to go through the dry experience of your friend the acorn. Don't let it keep you from doing your best work.

A. B.

I remembered Hutch's job on the *Globe* and tried to copy him! These little *feuilletons* of mine took me an hour or so to write and they amused me very much. I held my public in my mind, the shop-girls and young clerks who, Arthur said, read the *New York Journal,* and I wrote down for them all I learned about psychoanalysis and about myself, and anything else that came along. The editors immediately boomed them and advertised them in black letters two inches high: "Mabel Dodge Writes About Mother Love!" "Mabel Dodge Asks Do You *Work* for a *Living?*" The city editor's captions were always embarrassing! They were syndicated in every Hearst paper in the United States and "Mabel Dodge" entered the circle of Dorothy Dix and suchlike.

But this was not *work* at all. It was just to enable me to live at Finney Farm where, in spite of Brill, I thought I wanted to live; and indeed it seemed to pacify him. He seemed contented if my name appeared in large black type and if I brought him my dreams. Once I confessed to him that I had made up a dream when I hadn't really had any real one to bring, and he had nodded and said, "Just as good. Any one you make up will be as revealing as any you could dream!"

He never let my mind wander, though. He had no use at all for wonderings. He accepted the dream when I presented it, and then he enquired: "And what does that suggest to you?"

These words usually created a blank in my mind. "Absolutely nothing," I would reply, stubbornly.

"Well, relax—and tell me what comes into your mind." I would relax, but I could not tell him what I thought, because it would be something like:

"You old fool! Don't you know you're losing a most interesting chance to hear some really amusing ideas if you wouldn't hold me down like this?"

No, I had to be careful and not hurt him, I thought. I liked him very much, for he was so real and substantial. At times one could see his eyes alter in expression while he sat peering at one behind his specs. Something swam and fused and glowed in his gray pupils, and one was able to observe the action of ratiocination. It was as fascinating to watch as the action of any heat on any substance, and seemed more creative than most. After a moment of this fireless cooking, he would generally announce something devastating but intense that would make one jump—although he tried *not* to bring himself and his opinions too much into this affair. He wished to leave it all to the one before him. He figured that his job was to bring the horse to water. All the real effort must be mine.

By this time I did not know exactly what I was working *for,* since my depression had ceased and I was enjoying perfect health, so I only continued to write to keep him quiet. But it kept me quiet too! As John wrote one day: "Themes are good safety valves. You can let off a lot of steam through them. I haven't any steam in me at present. . . ." I was feeling very contented but when I tentatively attempted to say I thought I might stop coming to him since I felt so much better, he sternly replied, with an angry gleam in his glasses:

"Don't be ridiculous! You have scarcely begun your analysis yet!" So I did not dare to discontinue my visits.

I continued to see Mrs. Hopkins now about once a week but I had to keep this dark as best I could, for Brill called all my mysticism a fantasy life and frowned upon it severely. He became arbitrary and dogmatic. Anything "religious" was anathema to him. He consistently tried to remove every vestige of my belief in an inner power, and when I haltingly endeavored to convince him of something that counseled me and impelled me from my depths, he said scathing things about a Jehovah complex! It was only later that I realized I should have referred to God and Nature as "the Unconscious"—and then they would have gotten by!

Gradually coming under his influence, I altered my convictions and lost a good deal of color out of my life along with the surplus of tension. It took me some time to recover my indisputable realization of the Force that may be directed, but that, directed or not, rules all life. All the analysts, I thought, become dogmatic at some point, and each one feels he must fit one into his own pattern.

He did not like me to have interests outside of his own tastes, or at least I drew that conclusion. For instance, he had not much use for my radical friends and he considered that their beliefs were generally only rationalized prejudices, and that their prejudices were due to their conditioned early years and that when they got together they bolstered up each other's complexes.

And of course I had to conceal him from Mrs. Hopkins as well! She would not have approved at all. My life has always been divided into compartments like that, where I would flit in and out, not letting my right hand know what my left hand was doing! In and out of all the different worlds, partaking of each.

Maurice did not feel the antagonism for Dr. Brill that he had felt for Jelliffe, and after a time he actually began to go and be analyzed himself. We were united at last in a common undertaking and our life, while it continued, was "all smoothened out"!

Dr. Brill did not seem to try to remove me from Maurice; the most he did was to insist that my feeling for him was aesthetic and not sexual, and that in that sense it was not real and direct. However, he did not press this point, for he trusted to the analytic method itself to bring a final clarification and readjustment in my ideas and feelings.

CHAPTER XXII

Dr. Bernard

THERE were other new and more active elements in my life that winter. With Bayard gone and Maurice and myself so occupied, more natural relationships seemed to grow up between the outside world and myself. Now Nina was coming and going. Nina had also taken a house on the Hudson. She, though, lived across the river at Nyack and there she had made friends with Sister Beatrix! Lovely Sister Bee!

She had belonged to a group of lay sisters who had a girl's school farther up the river somewhere—Sisters of the High Episcopalian Church. She had grown restless and left there—and had now her own little school at Nyack. She had a sweet face, professionally serene, with hazel eyes and rosy cheeks; she was rather plump, and had she not worn her hair Madonna-wise, so smooth and resigned, her beauty would have appeared quite sensuous. She had turned her warmth all into maternalism. Margaret Budd, who was a rich pupil, had accompanied her on her departure down the river; "Buddy" and Sister Bee had an affectionate friendship and "Buddy" helped to pay for Sister's school project.

Sister wanted a becoming "habit." She felt the little black bonnet and veil over her black cashmere dress was too severe. "The children don't like it, I am sure," she said. "I should have something more *attractive.*"

I summoned Bobby, who adored costuming people. He looked Sister up and down and began to make water-color sketches. In a trice there was Sister in a lovely dress of heliotrope *crêpe de Chine* made with a full skirt reaching to the ground and lightened with turned over collar and cuffs of tucked batiste; on her head a long veil of the same stuff that flowed down her back. It looked as though she merely bound it in pleats around her head and pinned it back and let it fall, but it was cunningly made on a crinoline form that fitted her head. She was

513

adorable in these clothes, for she was really a beautiful woman.

Nina lived in her white house in Nyack with her little boy Harry, a child of ten, and Eve Schroer. Her two girls were in Sister's school almost next door, and down the road quite near by, the strange son of Nina's ex-husband's second wife, Johnny Turner, lived, married to Evelyn Sears, Nina's niece. Johnny's mother had been Harry Bull's stenographer and I believe he married her because she was feminine and softly housewifely, different from Nina, who was always searching for some solution to life, a frown between her brows and two deep lines running down her cheeks.

I think I gave Nina an impression of successful living. I know this was quite a usual assumption among my friends. All they saw was an effect of rich and varied life. Something like a cornucopia full of prizes showering down around me: luxury, intelligence, movement! Men! Always plenty of men, and real men at that. Men who did things, or else were handsome—never banal ones like the average *husband*. Nina seemed to admire my existence, and I supposed that others, too, envied my high-handed way of managing my life. I thought they never knew the agonies and the doubts that were the almost continuous accompaniment of what may have looked like a triumphal progress. Only Jelliffe and Brill knew those and even they would never know the whole of it.

Well, Johnny Turner was a strange, slim youth with very large, blue eyes and transparent ears. The pupils of his eyes were not clear, but changeable and opaque—the kind that always denotes a mixed nature. Nina idealized him, for she said he had a mysterious power in him.

Johnny did not mind being deified. He took advantage of Nina's opinion of him to borrow money from her, but he was not a rascal. He himself felt some mysterious force within him that convinced him Nina was right about his Power. It made him do strange things, and occasionally seemed to lift him above the little conventions and laws of other men who did not have it.

Of Nina's two little girls, one resembled her father. The other was delicate-looking and old for her age. She had a quaintness about her that made her seem like the heroine of almost any of the nineteenth-century English novels. Nina loved this child Katherine more than anyone else in the world. Maybe she hoped that Katherine would be a happy child as she herself had never been, and that she would carry out all her own defeated hopes of a vivid life of carefree accomplishment. The little girl wrote poems derived from the books Nina constantly read out loud to her—Whitman, Carpenter, and Tagore—and Nina kept them all in a notebook.

So the two little girls lived and slept in Sister's school near by, which had once been a summer hotel. Sister was wise about children. She wanted to give Katherine a more childlike atmosphere, to take her away from the serious surroundings that Nina created; and she had persuaded Nina to let her put them both with the other boarding school pupils. They slept in a white dormitory in company with a little crowd of more or less normal American children, and Katherine began to lose her over-sensitive, unchildlike, solemn look.

"Buddy" wasn't particularly interested in the school. That was Sister Bee's, she considered. "Buddy" was an attractive, fresh-skinned girl with blue eyes. She had a passion for cleanliness and was always going into New York to the Gym, or to take a Turkish bath.

Shortly after I met this couple, I found out it had been "Buddy's" house we had lived in on Monhegan Island! Lodestar Cottage! Of course Sister had named it! They had heard of Maurice and me from the Lees, who had described us in a way that made us seem perfectly fascinating. Maurice had seemed to the Lees like the hero of a Russian novel, and I had been "dark and aloof, but very interesting-looking." They had conjectured that I "wrote." "Probably something along mystical lines." I had given them an impression of austerity. Ah, me!

Just when everything was completed in this little group at Nyack, with Sister's cottage, where she and "Buddy" lived close to the school, all home-like and sweet with chintz and white paint, the garden growing, the school running smoothly, Nina walking bare-footed contentedly in her garden, while perhaps she dreamed of Katherine's future and occasionally drove around with Johnny—just when all this pattern was achieved, "Buddy" met someone who took her to see Dr. Bernard in New York.

He had a sort of "cult" up on Riverside Drive. A Yankee from somewhere out west, he was a mixture of a Medicine Man in a country circus, and an East Indian Yogi. I went to see him once to find out for myself what he was like. Tall and lean, but with a curious resilience in his body like a tiger, he had thin lips and shrewd, handsome eyes. He stared at me somberly, trying to read my thoughts, while he smoked a long, black cigar. He had lived for years in India and studied with Himalayan priests, and mind-reading, hypnotism, muscle control —all these things were elementary studies there, he told me in the course of our talk.

Dr. Bernard was one of the shrewdest opportunists I ever met. He had thought things out and had settled himself in New York to exploit one of our national weaknesses: constipation! He determined that the constipation of American women should win him a fortune. Of course Jelliffe had taught me the close connection between excrement and gold in the symbolism of the psyche, and I had observed the relationship between our money-making fixation and the great signs advertising all kinds of laxatives that decorated the billboards of our country and the back pages of magazines. No other nation bought and sold physic like Americans, that was obvious.

Well, Dr. Bernard fixed attention more firmly than ever upon elimination. Under his guidance, the rectum assumed the *beau rôle* that was ordinarily held by the simple sex center. It was all carried out in the most dignified manner with a well-planned arrangement of spotless cubicles and nurses in uniforms, as well as young assistant doctors. All the personnel of the place had wonderful schoolgirl complexions and sparkling eyes, as the advertisements promised.

When I went to see him, Dr. Bernard himself initiated me into the first steps of his course, for I had not let him read my thoughts. I pretended to be convinced. He rang a bell on his desk, and a white linen form appeared at the door whom he told to bring the first something-or-other, I did not catch the words. She returned with a small, beautifully made mahogany box that he opened, which contained three glass objects in increasing sizes lying in a row on a purple velvet background.

"Twenty dollars," he murmured, and then continued: "These are to dilate the rectum. The rectum of the average American is abnormally small and has in many cases lost its elasticity. The intestines cannot evacuate through the American rectum. Now we begin with these and gradually increase the size until the rectal muscles become readjusted. At the same time we stimulate them with various douches and applications so they will regain their vitality. Elimination, after one of our courses, becomes the natural and pleasurable activity it is with primi-

tive people and children, instead of the anxious, nerve-racking performance it has grown into in civilized times."

"Do these *hurt?*" I asked him timidly, examining the phallic glass
objects that were constructed quite simply on the lemon-squeezer plan,
only that they were longish, instead of cone-shaped.

"Indeed not!" he rejoined with animation. "After the first and initial
experience of the Dilator, you will look forward to the treatment. The
nerves lining the rectal cavity are very sensitive," he went on, shifting
his cigar and staring up at the ceiling. He suddenly threw up his legs
and planted his feet against the top of his desk. He looked more than
ever a Yankee vendor at the fair. "Very sensitive! You will shortly
realize that evacuation as I induce it is a pleasure with which none
other can compare! *None* other," he repeated, and banged the top of
the table.

"Is this all?" I asked him. I had heard of strange doings; that, as
time went on and the patient proved worthy of it, she was let into
other mysteries. There were "advanced" courses. Not everyone got as
far as these, and some took the simple Dilation Treatment and departed, never even knowing that there were higher branches to the
cult, esoteric and concealed. Dr. Bernard was canny. He knew whom
to include and whom to send on their way merely "rectum conscious"
and relieved of tension.

"Not *quite* all," he answered my question thoughtfully. "You will be
instructed in the art of reversion."

"*Reversion?*" I asked, hopefully. This began to sound interesting,
though it scared me a little.

"Yes. You will learn to stand on your head. Not once, but many
times a day. You will reverse your circulation, the position of every one
of your internal organs, and completely alter your metabolism. Everything inside the ordinary person is the victim of this damned perpendicular habit of ours! We are the only living animals who never
alter their muscular posture."

"When we're asleep?" I ventured, weakly.

"*No.* That's not *muscular* activity. That's the very opposite. *No!*
Only by consciously reversing the stress of the muscles, turning the
organs upside down, creating a new set of tensions within, can we
bring new life to the tired, old tissues that have been stagnating for
so long in one position. You will be given a Pad and, in the Bernard

Bloomers, you will be assisted, at first, into the new posture. When you have developed sufficiently to take the pose by yourself, you may buy a Pad and exercise at home. For it is the frequency, the rapidity and the frequency of the change in position that produces the great benefit. Soon it becomes as natural to one as standing upright. Without thinking, at any hour of the day, you will find yourself practicing Reversion and enjoying the refreshment it brings. Like this," he added, standing up and stepping aside from his desk. With no effort, graceful as a cat, he flung his heels into the air and rested on the top of his head supported lightly by the fingers of each hand. He continued to smoke his cigar the while, and to talk at the same time.

"Just a moment or two—and you resume the usual pose with every cell in your body washed clean by the changed direction of the blood stream!" He was on his feet by my side, not a hair displaced, though a faint flush had appeared on his cheek-bones. To tell the truth, he made me long to practice Reversion! I bought a box of Dilators and took them home with me and promised to return to take the Course. But I never did. I was, perhaps, as canny as he!

Inside a month, Margaret Budd had introduced the Bernard system into the Nyack School for Girls. In Bernard Bloomers, Sister Beatrix, Nina, "Buddy" and all the little girls stood on their heads upon Bernard Pads. Sister Bee herself was one of the most enthusiastic Reversionists. I cannot describe the curious effect she produced with her sweet Madonna face seen upside down, her plump legs in the air. The contrast between her violet robes, her dignified demeanor and this unfamiliar aspect, made one think of Alice in Wonderland or some outlandish dream. I do not think they brought the Dilators into the Home or the School, but they all went to the Institute and used them. It is true that complexions improved and the course certainly sweetened dispositions. "The Bernard Bath of Blood," as he so euphoniously described it, must indeed have cheered the tired intestines and enlivened the internal secretions.

It was not long after that the police raided the Institute one afternoon and arrested Dr. Bernard. "Buddy" had fallen in love with one of the young assistants, and she married him. Later, when Bernard was released, there was a shifting and a reorganizing that resulted in the end of Sister's school, with Dr. Bernard now installed in that building in Nyack that had been once a hotel, and later a children's school!

"Buddy" had become an instructor along with her young husband, and Sister dwelt alone in her chintzy cottage. The Institute throve under a new name, and many fashionable New York women came out and stayed there for weeks at a time, taking courses and learning to Reverse! There were Vanderbilts and Astors and what-not, all changing the direction of their blood streams.

Some time that year when little Katherine died, it seemed to me one of the saddest things that ever happened. I couldn't bear thinking of Nina climbing up Bear Mountain alone and scattering the few little ashes. Later, she had Katherine's poems published in a "slender vol." and gave them to her friends.

CHAPTER XXIII

Sister Beatrix's Advice

SISTER BEE sometimes looked anxious but generally she smiled. Although she had beautiful hazel eyes and a lovely skin, her features had the plebeian cast of many American women. It comes, I suppose, from the material of their thoughts and the lack of tension in their culture. There is strain in the life of American women, but no aspiration, not much nobility, and no great art. All other races have really suffered and been molded by suffering in the past, but Americans have only been nervous. No culture results from nerves, and no real faces. Our faces are blurred, they lack edge and modeling and are without the pride and endurance that give distinction.

Sister came across the river for lunch one day and I noticed she had a purposeful look. When we were alone in the living room by the window where the afternoon sun came through the ruffled white muslin curtains, she suddenly leaned forward impulsively and seized both my hands. Her soft draperies fell into Biblical folds. She might have been Martha on a visit to Mary.

"I want to say something very frank to you, dear. May I?"

"Surely, Sister. What?"

"It is about you and Mr. Sterne. You are in such a false position here! People who *know* you admire and respect you, of course. But those who *don't* know you are bound to misunderstand."

"Well, I have to accept that, don't I? I can't live to suit everybody. If my friends don't mind, that is all I can hope for."

"They may not tell *you* they mind—but I'm sure *every*body would rather see you living differently. Mr. Sterne is such a fine person—just as you are yourself. Surely you have a responsibility towards the public . . . as an example, I mean. You are neither of you insignificant or obscure people; everything you do is observed. Come! Think it over. I know you will decide to take a step. . . ."

520

A step! Would we—could we take that step? It had been alluring and repelling us for so long! I decided it was foolish to let any legal act assume so much importance one way or the other, when one remembered the inception of every one of our laws. They had all been created for convenience—they should be used for convenience. Well— some day, perhaps: my thoughts ran on rapidly while I looked out of the window. There was a strange leaden sinking in my heart whenever I considered marrying Maurice that was quite out of proportion to my considered opinion of marriage!

"Oh, Sister Bee! How boring! Why does one always have to *do* or *not* do or *un*do!"

"Well, child, I suppose that's what life is!"

She was not so very much older than I, but her uniform gave her that ageless feeling and she was always maternal. She was really dear, and had a heart; only it was not a thinking heart, nor an intuitive heart. It was just a loving heart, the kind that makes the most trouble of all. Her words sank in and added themselves to others I had heard: but I did not act upon them.

The winter was wearing along. Both Maurice and I continued to go regularly to Brill, and Maurice felt he was really going to "smoothen" him out! Andrew was, by this time, almost a graduate of the psychoanalytic course and only went to consult him once in a while. He had come a long way from the days when there had been attraction and resistance between us. Now we had an easy, pleasant friendship that we wished to make into something creative, to make up for the destructive impulses between us in the past. With Brill's approval, he asked me to let him come and farm the place at Croton so that it would pay for itself and really function instead of being a farm in name only! I was glad to have him. I had always wanted the place to be *real,* and it had turned into something far different from my first hopes. A retreat, an escape—anything but a live center.

Andrew came out, then, and threw himself into the new activity. Farming was congenial to him. He limped around in a pair of corduroys and an old sweater; his bright pink cheeks glowed with energy and his rough blond hair stood up on end. By the time spring came, all our fields were in crops and the table fairly groaned with our own supplies—milk and poultry, butter and eggs. Not having much practical experience, however, we were almost buried under an enormous crop of Swiss chard that rioted in front of the house and down along the driveway. We were positively embarrassed by Swiss chard that summer, and finally had to feed it to the stock! However, this was a minor grief and a mistake in bountifulness rather than one of lack, from which we had suffered before the fields were planted. I loved to see the burgeoning greens and feel the activity going on outside.

The only drawback was the German atmosphere of our evenings! Andrew and Maurice discussed the war with enthusiasm and undisguised sympathy for the German side. I took no interest in it at all, paid no attention to the newspapers, and just tried to forget it. It all seemed so idiotic and greedy and far apart. But these men brought it into the house, into our living and thinking life. Not only that, but being on what seemed to me to be the most *stupid* side of all, they made me mad. I really didn't think the "Allies," so called, amounted to much, but the Germans did seem to be cruder and more blatant. There did not seem to be much more to choose between them than between Republicans and Democrats, I thought. I complained to Brill and tried to talk it out and be relieved of my irritation; but alas! he himself was of German origin and he did not help at all. Or was he simply more objective and fair than I?

However, I was not vitally injured by the pro-German influences— not even, really, influenced by them. I was writing and painting and I was comparatively free of my anguish over Maurice. Occasionally I had to go to see different people and interview them for my little *feuilletons,* and this amused me. Such dissimilar characters as Sarah Bernhardt, Clarence Darrow, or "Uncle Joe" Cannon provided the most diverting and varied diet in personalities!

Once Elizabeth and Bobby and I motored to Washington to call upon "Uncle Joe." In floating veils, attended by the pale young man with a beard, Elizabeth and I sailed into the restaurant of the Corcoran Hotel, giggling and gay. Arthur Brisbane was lunching near by with some politicians and he looked over at me quizzically. I suppose we were a queer sight. He joined us for coffee and afterwards wrote me:

The Washington Times
Washington, D. C.

My dear Mabel:

I find your note here at the office after dinner. I am quite certain you will make a real success of the writing. As I told you, I could not have encouraged you in it if I had not thought so. Get to work on the Clark thing. Be very careful about it. Write and rewrite. You can afford the time and you have the energy. Read your copy—get somebody else to read it. Then have it read out loud to you. We shall publish anything in our newspapers that goes into the hands of two millions of people. In other words, it means that you are having two million separate conversations. It is worth while to prepare and revise such conversations. . . .

I was very glad to meet your friends. Mr. Jones I like, an interesting man. And I guess Miss Duncan did a great deal to make her sister. The sister has longer legs—I mean the dancing sister. But the sister I met has a longer head.

Yours sincerely,

A. BRISBANE.

"Uncle Joe," the Speaker of the House, turned out to be an old man of benevolent habit, a mere kindly automaton in a somewhat stained waistcoat. He treated me paternally and handed me some phrases—and we motored back to Croton through country roads full of scents and bird-songs.

Bobby was getting along very well and that was a comfort to me. During this spring these notices were sent out:

MRS. HAPGOOD Presents

The First Colored Dramatic Company to Appear on Broadway in
THREE ONE-ACT PLAYS by Ridgely Torrence
under the direction of Robert Edmond Jones
at the Garden Theatre, Thursday, April 5th.

I had just enough activity in my life then; enough coming and going; with most of the nights spent in my peaceful bed beside the silent orchard. Maurice lessened in significance and became only one of the parts of my life, instead of the whole of it, as I had wanted him to be. I forgot to try to make a sculptor of him.

I wrote Hutch a long letter and tried to describe to him how "activity" had finally helped "to smoothen out my life." Activity after our fierce rejection of it when we believed we were contemplatives! He replied:

Provincetown, Mass.,
November 5th.

DEAREST MABEL,

Yours is an extraordinary letter. You couldn't have written it a few years ago. What struck me is the *form* of your thought and feeling now, firmly

523

modeled, accepted and digested. What you said about me and Neith, about Reed and you, is of the greatest interest, as showing your own attitude about life, love, and all the rest. I feel indeed like congratulating you. And what you say might apply to many concrete cases.

It does not, however, apply with any exactness to my particular case. You state exactly some of my tendencies and closely picture what has happened. But you forget that, although you and I have the passing or impersonal *theory* in common, yet we have greatly different temperaments. Our philosophy, our *strain,* is the same—but it is only my mind and imagination that is impersonal. I am not *temperamentally* impersonal. You are impersonal temperamentally as well as mentally and imaginatively. You see, you *cannot* be held, for that reason, and for that reason I *must* be held.

Everything you wrote is true, but much of it doesn't apply. What you wrote about Neith's condition is true only as an element, an element that probably is easily overbalanced by her love, her children, her experience. But I am not expressive just now—so I shall not try to say all I mean. But your letter makes me all the more eager to talk to you. Some time this fall or winter I shall have to go to New York and I shall then stay with you, if convenient for you, and I want to make it a *long* visit. I believe we'll find more than ever to talk about in a rich way. I feel that you are getting stronger and surer all the time. I either misjudged you radically that first winter or else you have greatly developed.

With real love for you,

Hutch.

One night in August, on the seventeenth, to be exact, Alice Thursby brought Agnes Pelton out to stay for a couple of days. Agnes, whom I did not know very well, awakened some of the old, strained feeling about "my situation." The need to pretend, to say good night in a somewhat obvious and conscious way to Maurice when he and Andrew withdrew to the Green House.

Then something flared up in me. The need to be done with all that once and for all—to demonstrate its lack of importance by being casual about it! When Maurice came over to breakfast, I called him up to my room.

"Let's go and get married!" I said, raising one eyebrow.

"But, dearest! Why this morning? Are you sure you want to?" A flush broke over his face and a look of pleasure.

"Yes, I want to. We'll have Alice and Agnes for witnesses! We can go up to Peekskill and get a Notary Public or something!"

"Oh, darling! I hope we are doing the right thing!"

"Well, we're doing it, anyway," I replied succinctly, getting out of bed.

When I descended to the dining room the others were still at breakfast. I saw Maurice had broken the news!

"What's this we hear!" began Alice, looking nervous and blinking her long lashes.

"Oh, we thought it such a nice day we would go and get married," I answered, casually. I *would* keep it casual, because it was casual. It just didn't amount to anything.

We motored along the river in the sunny morning hours and Maurice bought a ring (a hideous, heavy gold band) and we found the right person to perform the ceremony—if that was what it was.

I made the responses in a cold, tight voice, wishing it were over; but Maurice's voice shook and sounded solemn. When it was finished, I was surprised to see tears in his eyes! We went and had luncheon in a dismal hotel, and when Alice got me alone, she said:

"You didn't care at all, but Mr. Sterne really felt what he was saying."

Mr. Sterne! This man I had married would always be that to my friends!

"I'd like to go away on a little trip," said Maurice that evening. The others had gone back to New York with, actually, a feeling that it was our wedding night. I felt terribly alone when they left me, and now we were out on the porch, I in the hammock and Maurice in the big rocking-chair. Even Andrew had gone to town. Deep in summer, with stars shining and the heavy trees motionless before the house—abandoned, abandoned. Maurice was smoking one of those long cigars of his, and I felt all contracted and contrary.

"Shouldn't we have a little honeymoon, darling?" he continued. He gave a gusty, involuntary laugh, half-nervous, half-tender.

"Oh, Maurice! *You* go. I'd rather stay here and go on with what I'm doing. Where do you want to go?"

"Bourgeois wants me to go out West with him on his vacation. Somewhere near John's camp, I think. I might look in on John while I am out there and see what kind of place the Rumseys have." I couldn't see Maurice in Cody at Bob Rumsey's very well, but I said nothing. "I am very fond of John, you know, Mabel," Maurice went on seriously. "I want to have him like me, and come to me if he needs anything. I have wondered sometimes if he was not a little jealous. But now everything will be smoothened out—won't it?"

Would it?

"Well, Maurice dear, you go on a little honeymoon with Bourgeois and I will stay here. You know my lease on the apartment at 23 is up the first of September. They are going to tear down the old Sickles house. Too bad. . . . Maybe I'll look around for another place. I have to put the furniture *somewhere*. Shall we stay in town this winter for a change?"

"Well, darling, you know *I* always like the city. It is you who get so nervous about me. . . ."

The evening waned imperceptibly away. Why did life always die on one when Maurice and I were alone? After a while I said in a strangled voice:

"Well, I guess I'll go to bed."

We moved into the hall—and the house seemed filled with death, so silent and empty and motionless it was. I looked at Maurice unsmilingly.

"Well, good night, darling," he said, blushing a trifle and holding out his hand with embarrassment.

"Good night," I replied and turned and went upstairs.

The next morning the *New York Herald's* caption was:

Mrs. Mabel Dodge secretly married to Russian Artist. . . . "No romance," says Maurice Sterne, "we just decided to wed."

I was still alone upstairs that morning when Marie Howe, that great suffragist, came up to see me from her house below on the Highway. She was waiting for me down in the living room. When I came in, she came up to me and took my hands in hers and gave me a long, grave look.

"I suppose I should congratulate you," she said. "Probably everyone else will. But I cannot help feeling a little sad."

"Why?" I asked politely, seeing her pause for it.

"You have *counted* so much for Women!" she exclaimed. "Your Example has stood for courage and strength! I wonder if you realize that hundreds of women and girls have been heartened and fortified by the position you took?"

"Which one?" I asked.

"Why! By your life here! The fact that you had the nerve to live your own life openly and frankly—to take a lover if you wished, without hiding under the law. You have shown women they had the *right* to live as they chose to live and that they do not lose respect by assuming that right. But *now!* When I think of the *disappointment* in the whole woman's world today!" Her beautiful dark eyes were filled with tears. I sighed. Everything seemed very tiresome and difficult. She kissed me and moved to the door. "I *had* to come and tell you," she murmured, and went away.

Maurice went to town and I sent the car to fetch Elizabeth over to lunch. She was living, now, in a medieval castle on a hill in Tarrytown. She came up the steps, her soft Greek skirts hiked up above her knees, and she looked particularly like an Irish guttersnipe that morning: impudent and humorous, her nose well up in the air.

"Well! well! well!" she giggled in a high falsetto. "Whatever did you do *that* for? Of course it's none of *my* business, but I never thought much of marriage myself. Isadora always called it 'that dirty trick'!"

"Oh, Elizabeth! I'm not Isadora. And it's more *convenient* to be married. . . ."

"*Is* it? I shouldn't have thought it would be. And to Mr. Sterne, too! He's not *my* idea of a marrying man!"

"Well, he's married now, and that's the end of it," I said, hoping the subject would soon be exhausted.

"Yes, I should imagine it would be," she giggled impertinently. "Of course Mr. Sterne is a Mensch—he is Something. He is like Herr V. said when he saw you: '*Das ist Eine* . . .' But a husband—oh, my!!" and she laughed fit to split her sides.

That evening Bobby came out to Finney Farm. He brought a bunch of hot-house flowers with him and he looked as though he'd come to a funeral. He congratulated Maurice politely and said a few nervous words to me. He was never so remote with me before. It was as though I had crossed a great gulf and left him on the other side. The evening passed, somehow, but was different from all other evenings in that house.

Again that night I mounted the stairs alone, preventing Maurice, by something forbidding I threw into my manner, from accompanying me as he evidently hoped to do. Not so much, I felt, from any desire to be with me, as from a wish to do the right thing and to assert his new prerogatives in the presence of Bobby and Andrew. But never since I had been with him was I so separate from him in will and inclination. Instead of being unimportant, marriage had acquired the enormous significance of a barrier.

When I motored down to my appointment with Dr. Brill, the next morning, I was very much on the defensive. I entered his office ready to fight, for I expected him to attack me. Instead, he looked at me sadly and without animosity.

"Couldn't you have waited?" he asked.

"Waited for *what?*" I asked in a hard voice.

"To finish your analysis," he answered. "Then you would never have taken this step."

"Oh, I don't know. . . ." I began.

"Well, we will not argue about it. The thing is done. We will continue our work. Have you any dreams to tell me?"

There wasn't a single happy word given to me over the affair. Wherever I went, whoever I saw, disapproved of the match. My conventional friends hated it and my unconventional ones did too!

"So you have prostituted yourself in marriage!" exclaimed the redoubtable Madame Strindberg.

Maurice seemed to have acquired a new feeling of Security. He grew less nervous day by day and more and more proprietary in his thoughts, even though I prevented him from getting them into action. I hurried him away on his wedding trip as fast as I could. He went to Wyoming and, sure enough, on to Cody to that Rumsey environment where John took refuge with other one-hundred-percent American boys.

John was away on a hunting trip when Maurice arrived, and I heard afterwards of the flurry Maurice gave Mrs. Rumsey's motherly heart. She ran to meet John when he came back "to break the news" to him; and, as John told me long afterwards: "That was really pretty bad!"

After he left I had a few letters of congratulation from my friends. Hutch wrote:

R. D. No. 2,
Athol, Mass., Sept. 1.

DEAR MABEL,

I got back from an interesting trip in the West a day or two ago, and was told about your marriage to Maurice.

Maurice told me once that the essence of your nature is impatience—and his remark seemed to me curiously truthful.

But this marriage seems to me the great exception, if not the proof of the untruthfulness of the remark. You have tested the relation with patient persistence and ought to reap the reward in security and permanence. I hope it will solve all your problems—and not make Maurice's more difficult.

To him my regards and affectionate hopes. To you my love and interest.

HUTCH.

P.S. I wish you would write me about John and his life and work on the ranch. I am trying to find an Agricultural school for Boyce, where he can see the larger and more distinct meaning of his ranching interests.

And Leo, somewhat cryptically:

Nantucket, Mass.

DEAR MABEL,

It's well disposed, for it has looked for some time as though it had to be. May happiness in full measure attend the consummation, for now as teacher to the great public you must with the plain people look upon happiness and the well contented day as a real good. However, I suppose that really you always did, for there was underlying you at all times that implicit insistence on the plain man's virtues and rewards.

Remember me to Maurice when you write.

Yours ever,

LEO.

And Brill wrote me when he read the news:

DEAR MABEL,

Your letter was interesting but not surprising. For some time I anticipated the good news and I will confess that a few weeks ago I was sure that you were married. Now please accept my most cordial wishes and congratulations. You did not have to ask me to wish you luck; you realize, I hope, that both you and Maurice are very near my heart and that my objections were purely academic. I never said that I disapproved but I counseled waiting a bit longer. I have no doubt that you will be very happy as Maurice is a very fine fellow and as far as I know has always tried his very best to please you. I wish you to convey my best wishes to him and would like to see you soon.

As ever,

A. A. BRILL.

529

New York Evening Journal
Office of A. Brisbane

MY DEAR MABEL,

This is addressed in the old way, because the postman might not get the new name so soon. I congratulate you, for I know that if you are married, it is because you want to be, and know just what you are doing. I congratulate your husband about a thousand times as much. And if my stenographer did not have much to do, I would mention each of the thousand reasons.

I suppose you will go on with your writing, and not let marriage make any difference. I need hardly say that I was surprised by Alice's announcement when I arrived from Washington yesterday evening.

Yours sincerely,
A. BRISBANE.

P.S. If you continue writing, you will of course not change the signature to your articles.

A little later Arthur wrote again:

The Washington Times
Washington, D. C.

September 15th.

MY DEAR MABEL:

Thanks for your letter which is interesting. Write one like it and print it. Tell why women like to be married—pulling against the stake, like a little goat tied with a string.

Of course what women want, and everybody else wants, is what they haven't got. This keeps them struggling and striving, which is Nature's intention.

I do not think it was a very good idea for you to get married. But if you want me to think it was a good idea, I am perfectly willing. We strive to please, as Abraham said when he prepared to sacrifice his son.

I haven't met your husband, so of course it is all theory. I am glad that your mother has taken the wise view. I knew that she would do so.

Yours sincerely,
A. BRISBANE.

CHAPTER XXIV

The End of That

WHILE Maurice was away, I went all over town looking for a new apartment; and the most likely one was the top floor of a beautiful house on North Washington Square that Ralph Adams Cram had done over. It, too, was number twenty-three. If not a lucky number, at least a familiar one, I thought, and wondered if destiny had designed it, for I still thought in terms of Fate, in spite of Brill!

I was interested and busy with a new house again, and I did not think about Maurice very much. He wrote from Cody:

Blackwater Camp
Cody, Wyoming

September 3rd.

DEAREST MABEL:

Tomorrow two weeks since I left you and not a word from you! I am sure you must have written, but where your letters are, God only knows. I have informed the Postmaster and the Mayo ranch of my present address and if I don't get a letter from you shortly I'll do something desperate. It is wonderfully quiet here now and I have never in my life been so serene. I think of you all day, and at night I dream of you. In my dreams you, dearest, are radiant with beauty—you have such a wonderful expression it warms and thrills me.

Today for the first time I got from this place what I hoped to get. There is a beautiful woods here similar to the Cathedral woods at Monhegan, only infinitely grander and bigger, surrounded by giant mountains and a lively creek tumbling over the rocks in a thousand cataracts. The earth covered with a thick carpet of pine needles and littered with the skeletons of old fir trees, ashy gray.

There I went today with the Bible in my pocket. I never before understood the Demon on the mountain as I understand it today. I always thought it an ideal—but now I grasp it as a reality, as something to live and practice—not merely aspire to!

531

Was the place symbolic? the vivacious stream, my new faith, energy flowing unchecked over obstacles—the gray skeletons of my past crumbling
away?

Good night to you, my *dear dear* little wife!

MAURICE.

When he returned, I was settled in the apartment. I had been absent
from him long enough to create images in my mind of a domestic
existence, with evenings of ease before the big fireplace, with em-
broidery and books and flowers and friends. A pattern that had always
returned at intervals to allure me, but one I had never achieved.
Something was always missing—generally the ease.

Well, he returned. The first night we went out to dinner at an
Italian restaurant below the Square, and before we had finished our
spaghetti Maurice was fixing his eyes over my shoulder upon someone
behind me. The unmistakable magnetism of his dark gaze flowed past
me like a stream of lava. He had relapsed!

I rose, instantly. Standing there and looking down on him, I announced from a great distance: "I didn't marry you for this, Maurice.
It's not good enough." And I walked out of the place. On the way, I
saw the amused and interested smile of the woman who had caught
his attention. Quite an ordinary, nice-looking girl, with the casual
manners of Greenwich Village.

He finished his meal and followed me home, where I sat smoking
endless cigarettes before the fireless chimney place.

"Really, darling, you embarrass me," he began, as he hurried in and
laid his hat and stick on a chair. I interrupted him.

"It's no use, Maurice. We can't make a go of it here. One of us
must leave. And *I* want to stay here. I'm going to send you out to
the Southwest. I've heard there are wonderful things to paint. Indians.
Maybe you can do something of the same kind as your Bali pictures. . . ."

It was as clear to me as that. I just gave it all up and began to plan
something different and Maurice took to the idea at once. He always
liked to go to new places. I procured letters for him to people in Santa
Fe and to the Hubbells in New Mexico, and before long he was gone.

Then I fell ill. A mysterious aching and swelling in the left side of
my throat, in the thyroid gland. My dreams ceased to come to me and
Dr. Brill said to discontinue the analysis until I felt better. The only

one who helped me was a little woman Mrs. Hopkins sent to me, not a nurse exactly, but a soothing person. When she rubbed my throat gently, she seemed to pass a delicate, infinitesimal vibration from her finger-tips into the nerves of that sensitive place, and it sang the pain to sleep.

The weeks passed without incident in the kind of hinterland one goes to when one is not physically well. Maurice wrote enthusiastic letters about New Mexico and he seemed to like Santa Fe very much. He had a little house and friends across the street from him. He even began to encourage me to come out and join him, but oh, no! I had no heart for that.

In his absence, though, I gradually grew better and felt like myself once more; but I did not resume my analysis. I was off that. It seemed to me I had gone as far as I could with Brill, and away from him I began to resent his interference with my fancies about the unseen powers and influences that appear to guide us and that are not *all,* as he would have me believe, the promptings of our own unconscious wishes. No. I reverted to my earlier beliefs.

One day a mere acquaintance, a woman I had met at Adele Lewisohn's, came to lunch and told me about a curious medium she had heard of over in Brooklyn: "Someone told me she is marvelous," she said. "Goes into trances and tells you things!"

"Let's go and call on her, just for fun," I cried. I was feeling more like my carefree, easily amused self than I had for ages.

We motored for miles over to the dingy frame house, and the woman saw us at once. An insignificant, sad little thing, she was, without the energy to be either curious or interested in her visitors or in life, apparently. She was listless. When we each gave her five dollars, she sat down and took my hand and began to shake all over. Her eyelids remained open, but her eyes rolled up so that only the whites showed.

"Not yet—not yet," she murmured. "Later. Then you are surrounded by many people—they are pressing up around you . . . dark people . . . dark faces—they are Indians, I guess. You are to help them—you are for them. All alone. Yes. . . . Now I see an older man. He is standing behind your chair and you are writing—writing. He is your master. Your guide. This is much later. This is your life. First all those people, then the old man. Ah, the pain . . . it hurts."

Gradually she struggled up out of the invisible maze in the ether.

533

"Well!" exclaimed Mrs. Struthers, "that's what I call a future!"

I laughed, but I was impressed. I wondered about it—especially about the Indians out there where Maurice was living.

Elizabeth sometimes came to spend a night and slept beside me in the other bed in my room. We were having, again, something like the fun and companionship I had known with her two or three years before. Though I was not well yet, I was much stronger every day. But I still felt delicate—fragile—as though the malady from which I suffered in the gland created an alteration in the psyche.

Once I awakened in the middle of the night. I passed from unconsciousness into a state of super-consciousness without transition. I lay staring into the darkness, when before my eyes I saw a large image of Maurice's head. Just his face, there before me, with its handsome features and its alien Oriental expression. It frightened me and I shuddered. Then, as I gazed his began to fade and another face replaced it, with green leaves twinkling and glistening all around it—a dark face with wide-apart eyes that stared at me with a strong look, intense and calm. This was an Indian face and it affected me like a medicine after the one that had been before it. I sighed and let it take me and cleanse me. . . . A movement in Elizabeth's bed and she sat up. So did I, and when I turned on the bedside light and looked at her, she giggled nervously:

"Oh! I thought you were dead! I woke up and looked over, and right along the whole length of your body there was another form, like a light. I thought it was your spirit outside you! Oh, dear! You *are* a queer one!"

"I've had a queer dream or something," I said, rubbing my forehead. "I saw an Indian face in some green leaves."

Then Maurice wrote me from Santa Fe:

Santa Fe, Nov. 30th.

DEAREST GIRL—

Do you want an object in life? Save the Indians, their art-culture—reveal it to the world! I hear astonishing things here about the insensitiveness of our Indian office—through ignorance, solely, for they mean well—the stupidity and the pathetic crimes committed by its agents through a sense of superiority of the white color and white civilization (including, I suppose, the "Great White Way"—Broadway at night, over anything which has *color*).

That which Emilie Hapgood and others are doing for the Negroes, you could, if you wanted to, do for the Indians, for you have energy and are the most sensitive little girl in the world—and, above all, there is somehow a strange relationship between yourself and the Indians. You'll say it is different with the Negroes—they are scattered all over the U. S. A.—so that it is easier to bring them before the public. This isn't at all an advantage, for we have become too familiar with them, and our antagonism towards them was deep-rooted, whereas, as far as the public is concerned, no prejudice exists against the Indians, only a patronizing attitude which to my mind is worse as far as the Indian is concerned.

And it would be the easiest thing in the world to get a number of Indians from different parts of the country to perform at N. Y. and above all at Washington, to make the American people realize that there are such things as other forms of civilization besides ours.

I spoke to some people about it here, and they told me that they were doubtful—for several years ago a number of very fine dancers were taken to Coney Island by an enterprising Yankee, but hardly anyone went to see them: the people preferred to shoot the chutes. This signifies nothing—so would an exhibition of Sung paintings fare at Coney Island. . . .

It is to be done on a *great* scale—beautifully.

I saw a wonderful dance yesterday. . . .

With all my love,

MAURICE.

Index